COBBETT STEINBERG

REEL
FACTS

THE MOVIE BOOK
OF RECORDS

VINTAGE BOOKS
A Division of Random House New York

A VINTAGE ORIGINAL April 1978

First Edition

Copyright © 1978 by Cobbett Steinberg

*Grateful acknowledgment is made to the following for
permission to reprint the following material:*
Film Culture Magazine: Independent Film Awards.
Film Heritage: Film Heritage's "Women in Film Pick the Ten Best
Films About Women" (on page 300).
Motion Picture Association of America, Inc.: The Production
Code; the Advertising Code; the Code of Self-Regulation.
Newspaper Enterprise Association: chart of Motion Picture
Company Profits 1952–1972 (on page 392), from *The
Economist,* dated 7/7/73.
The New York Times: The *New York Times* Annual 10 Best Films
Lists 1924–1976 (on page 309). © 1924–1976.
Time, The Weekly Newsmagazine: *Time* Best Movies Lists
1945–76 (on page 319). Copyright Time Inc. 1945–76.
Variety Inc.: Top 200 on the All Time Box Office Champs list
(on page 326); Top 20 films on the annual Box Office Champs
of the Year, 1947–1976 (on page 343); Most Popular Films on
Television—top 50 films (on page 355).

Library of Congress Cataloging in Publication Data

Steinberg, Cobbett.
    Reel facts.

    1. Moving-pictures—Handbooks, manuals, etc.
I. Title.
PN1998.S73   1978   791.43'029   77–76560
ISBN 0–394–72416–X

ACKNOWLEDGMENTS

I should like to thank the Library of the Academy of Motion Picture Arts and Sciences and the Theater Arts Library of the University of California at Los Angeles. Without their facilities and the efficiency of their staffs, this book would have been difficult to compile. I should also like to extend my gratitude to Syd Silverman of *Variety* for his generosity and to the Hollywood Foreign Press Association for their friendly help. Both the Motion Picture Association of America and the *Harvard Lampoon* supplied information that would otherwise have been difficult to locate, and I thank them for their time. Albert J. LaValley of Rutgers University helped to conceive this book, and Gail Winston of Random House gave me numerous helpful suggestions throughout its gestation. I should also like to thank my sister Barbara for her early enthusiasm, and most of all, Larry Fields for his patience.

CONTENTS

Introduction xi

I. THE AWARDS

II. THE "TEN BEST" LISTS

III. THE MARKETPLACE

IV. THE STUDIOS

V. THE STARS

VI. THE FESTIVALS

VII. THE CODES AND REGULATIONS

INTRODUCTION:
"THE WHOLE EQUATION"

> "You can take Hollywood for granted like I did, or you can dismiss it with the contempt we reserve for what we don't understand. It can be understood too, but only dimly and in flashes. Not half a dozen men have ever been able to keep the whole equation of pictures in their heads."
> —F. Scott Fitzgerald,
> The Last Tycoon

In the March 22, 1973, issue of *The New York Review of Books*, the well-known screenwriter and novelist Joan Didion published an essay that aroused the furor of American film critics. In her essay—prefaced by the above quotation from *The Last Tycoon*—Didion argued that film reviewers never keep "the whole equation" of pictures in their heads. Completely ignorant of the Byzantine economics of the film industry, American film critics, according to Didion, approach the truth about films only occasionally, accidentally. They refuse to acknowledge the economic reality of movies, they forget the importance of production accidents and compromises, they don't understand that a deal memo can determine a movie's success as much as the script itself, and they ignore the fact that a film can be more influenced by the clauses of its financing than by any director's "vision." Film reviewers, Didion implied, simply forget that film is first and foremost an industry, not an art.

Critics, understandably incensed by Didion's contempt, were quick to answer, claiming a reviewer should indeed work with the art *on* the screen and not with the wheeling and dealing *behind* it. After all, they argued, isn't the film itself the real magic? Regardless of the compromises, accidents and deals, movies are an art, and what is there on the screen can be "described, analyzed, and evaluated just as work in the other arts is," as one critic angrily contended with Didion.

The controversy over whether film is an art or an industry did not, of course, begin with Joan Didion. Throughout film's history, moviegoers have argued just how important or unimportant the business aspects of films really are. In one of his first columns for *The Nation,* James Agee, for example—often considered one of America's most perceptive film critics—believed it advantageous to forget the insider's preoccupation with the box office. Rather than become involved in the analysis of an industry, it was better, Agee said, simply to describe "what my eyes tell me as I watch any given screen." In the National Society's first anthology Richard Schickel, on the other hand, argued that since commerce had a way of intruding upon experiences that should ideally be free of crass consideration, responsible film criticism demanded "an alertness to factors that customarily lie beyond the purview of critics in the other arts."

There have even been swings of fashion in the controversy. During the late fifties and throughout the sixties, when film studies were becoming a part of American academia, it was popular to see films in terms of their directors' "artistic visions." In the seventies, when the national economy has often been shaky and when Marxist criticism has gained popularity, it is common to stress a film's "economic profile." Paul Schrader, for example, one of Hollywood's most praised young writers, believes that most people today are interested in statistics: "You go to a film campus and eight out of ten questions will be about business."

Even as early as 1915 the controversy over whether film

was merely an industry or an art form was important enough to be brought before the Supreme Court. In the famous *Mutual Film Corporation* v. *Ohio* case, the Court unanimously ruled that movies were only an item of commerce, not subject to the protection of the free-speech clauses in state constitutions. "The exhibition of moving pictures," the Court declared, "is a business pure and simple, originated and conducted for profit . . ."

In was not until 1952, in fact, that the Supreme Court reversed its position and ruled that movies were indeed a medium of public opinion subject to similar protection as books and newspapers. In this celebrated *Burstyn* v. *Wilson* decision concerning Rossellini's *The Miracle,* the Court unanimously declared that it could not be doubted that "motion pictures are a significant medium for the communication of ideas. They may affect public attitudes and behavior in a variety of ways, ranging from direct espousal of a political or social doctrine to the subtle shaping of thought which characterizes all artistic expression."

The Court's belief in the artistic expression of films, however far-reaching its consequences, hardly settled the question of film's schizy nature. People both within and outside the industry still like to give their own very definite opinions on the issue. Charlie Chaplin, for example, amused reporters after receiving an honorary Academy Award in 1972 by stating that though he appreciated the honor, he had to confess that "I went into the business for money and the art grew out of it. If people are disillusioned by that remark, I can't help it. It's the truth."

It would be easy to dismiss the controversy by saying the obvious: movies are both an art *and* an industry. But the obvious would not take into account the intricacy with which the art and the business are intertwined. If there is something like a "whole equation" of motion pictures as Fitzgerald suggested, it is certainly nothing as simple as: film = ½ art + ½ industry. Surely our familiarity with what occurs off the screen has heightened our fascination with what happens on it. The industry's fast money, big deals and rags-to-riches anecdotes are as representative of American life as the stories on the screen. The very facts of filmmaking have fed our fantasies.

Reel Facts is a compendium of statistics, lists and surveys that suggests just how complicated that "whole equation" is. Some of the entries, like the Academy's technical awards, stress the practical side of filmmaking. Other entries, like the studios' incomes, emphasize the financial. Still other sections, like the New York Film Festival programs, remind us of the personal and creative elements. And still other selections, like the annual box-office champs, record the social and popular appeal films exert. Many entries reveal how all the different elements are intertwined.

The mixture is intentional. When critics dwell on sophisticated issues like the "semiotics" of cinema, it is tonic to remember just how often the art of film has depended on such practical matters as the discovery of a new electric cable, of a spotlight or even of a new type of artificial snow. And when movie moguls go on and on about percentages, points and "bankability," it is good to be reminded just how many dazzling directors have been showcased at international film festivals. *Reel Facts* is an eclectic book about an eclectic art. In collecting a wide range of information about what happens both on and off the screen, it serves a modest but, I hope, useful function: to urge us to keep "the whole equation" of pictures in our heads.

—C.S.

I. THE AWARDS

1. THE ACADEMY AWARDS

From their very beginnings at the turn of the century down to the present day, movies have frequently been attacked for corrupting American morals and ideals. Rather than face government regulations or further public criticism that could be financially disastrous, the film industry has invariably handled such attacks by trying to take matters into its own hands: internal control has always been preferred to external intervention.

In 1909, for example, when more and more outside groups were calling for film censorship, key figures in the movie industry established the National Board of Censorship (later renamed the National Board of Review) to preview films and to provide guidelines for possible necessary changes. In 1922, during the Fatty Arbuckle scandal and continued calls for censorship, Hollywood moguls formed the Motion Picture Producers and Distributors Association to placate their critics: Will H. Hays, a conservative former member of Harding's Cabinet, was the organization's first president.

And in 1927, when Hollywood's reputation was once again suffering, the industry founded the Academy of Motion Picture Arts and Sciences to raise the "cultural, educational, and scientific standards" of film. Even the association's name was calculated to enhance the industry's status: an "academy" suggested refined activity, and "arts and sciences" were hardly conducive to immorality. The new organization's title conveniently contained no suggestion of the two things for which Hollywood was best known: mass entertainment and big business.

There were thirty-six charter members of the Academy; Douglas Fairbanks was its first president; and one of the Academy's first functions was to give annual achievement awards. Thus, the Academy Awards were born. To be eligible for an award, a film must be shown in a commercial theater in the Los Angeles area for at least a week during the previous year. For the first six annual presentations, the awards were based on seasonal, not calendar years; that is, on the period from August 1 of one year to July 31 of the next year. Since 1934, however, the calendar year has been used.

Only a handful of Academy members determined the awards for 1927/28 and 1928/29. But in 1929/30 the entire Academy was allowed to vote for the nominees and the winners. For the 1937 prizes, the final voting was further expanded to include some 15,000 people in the movie industry, although the nominations had been limited to Academy members only. Later the procedure was reversed and the film industry at large selected the nominations, but only the Academy decided the winners. For the 1957 awards, voting policies changed once again, so that all voting was—and is—confined to the Academy.

The Academy is divided into several branches, such as the acting branch, the editing branch, the writing branch, the directing branch, etc. All branches determine the five nominees for Best Picture but the nominations for all other regular categories are selected by each specific branch. For example, the nominations for writing awards are made by the Academy Writers Branch, for directing awards by the Academy Directors Branch. All Academy members are then allowed to vote for the final winners.

The honorary and special awards, such as the Thalberg Memorial Award and the Jean Hersholt Humanitarian Award, are chosen by the Academy's Board of Governors. The scientific or technical awards are voted by the Board of Governors based on recommendations made by the Scientific or Technical Awards Committee. These scientific and technical awards are given in three classes: Class I winners receive a statuette, Class II a plaque, and Class III a certificate. (From 1930/31 to 1937, the technical or scientific awards were conferred on a slightly different basis: Class I winners received an Academy statuette and plaque, Class II winners a certificate of honorable mention, and Class III an honorable mention in the report of the Board of Judges.) The nominations in the documentary categories are voted by the Documentary Awards Committee, but the Academy at large decides the winner.

Prior to 1956, the Best Foreign-Language Film was an honorary award voted by the Board of Governors. But beginning in 1956, the vote was opened to the entire Academy membership. The five nominations in this category are selected by a special Foreign-Language Film Awards Committee. Every country is invited to submit films to this committee, but only one film from any one nation can be nominated in any particular year. Unlike the awards in most of the Academy's other categories, a movie does not have to be released commercially in Los Angeles to be eligible for the Best Foreign-Language Film. This special eligibility explains why a film may be nominated for Best Foreign-Language Film one year, while its cast and crew may be nominated in other categories the following year. In 1973, for example, *Day for Night* won the Best Foreign-Language Film Award before it had been commercially released in the Los Angeles area, but in 1974, after its commercial showing, both its director (Francois Truffaut) and supporting actress (Valentina Cortese) were nominated in those respective categories. For the 1976 Best Foreign-Language Film, an Academy member had to have seen all five nominated movies before voting. Many people said this particular requirement was responsible for the little-known film *Black-and-White in Color* winning the award over the more popular movies *Cousin, Cousine* and *Seven Beauties*.

Originally the awards were presented at small banquets held in one of Hollywood's hotels, like the Ambassador or the Biltmore. Due to increasing attention, the presentations moved in 1944 to the large Grauman's Chinese Theatre, and in 1947 to the even larger Shrine Auditorium, where the public was allowed to attend. When the major studios refused to continue to pay for the presentations in 1949, the awards were held at the Academy's own small theater. The RKO Pantages Theatre in Hollywood was the site of the presentations from 1950 to 1959. In 1961 the vast Santa Monica Civic Auditorium was needed to house the event. In 1969 they moved once again, this time to the present home of the awards presentation, the Dorothy Chandler Pavilion of the Los Angeles Music Center.

The winners of the first awards in 1927/28 had been known some three months before the night of the banquet. During the next several years, prizes were announced a week prior to their presentation; later the names of the winners were released on the morning of the presentation. In 1941 the policy of sealed envelopes was initiated, and it remains in effect today.

The Oscar statuette has a bronze interior with a gold exterior and costs more than $100 to make. (During World War II the figure was made of plaster.) There is still some uncertainty over the origin of its name. Some say that when Academy librarian Margaret Herrick first saw the statuette, she exclaimed, "Why, it looks just like my Uncle Oscar." Supposedly a reporter overheard the remark, printed the story, and the name stuck. Others claim that Bette Davis nicknamed the figure after her first husband, Harmon Oscar Nelson, Jr.

The 1928/29 awards were carried live by a local Los Angeles radio station. In 1945, national radio broadcast the event. Television coverage began in 1953; the first color broadcast was in 1966.

Arthur Freed, former Academy president, once said that the Oscars "honor artistic achievement, with little regard for popularity, box-office success or other yardsticks applied by critics or the general public." But the awards have been repeatedly criticized for having virtually no connection whatsoever to artistic achievement. Even as early as the 1928/29 awards, when Mary Pickford was selected Best Actress for her role in *Coquette,* people began complaining that the prizes were given on a political or social rather than artistic basis. Since then, the Academy's "poor" judgments have become legendary: almost everyone has his favorite example of the Academy's strange choices. Many people, for example, like to point out that *Citizen Kane,* one of the most important films ever made, won only a single Oscar in 1941—for Best Original Screenplay.

The Academy's popular and sentimental standards of selection do work, I think, to the Academy's advantage in the long run. The Academy's habit of awarding sentimental favorites, for example, might give Hollywood the image of being emotional, human, kind-hearted, even soft-headed, but such an image advantageously counteracts Hollywood's other image of being a cold, calculating, and cynically ruthless town. And the Academy's predilection for selecting the most popular and not necessarily the "best" film each year reinforces one of Hollywood's most cherished beliefs: that the average filmgoer who makes those films popular *does* have good taste, and that the people and not the critics *do* know what's best.

Thus, the Academy's selections may be questionable at best, ridiculous at worst, but even so, such inadequacies can work for and not against Hollywood. The Oscars give Hollywood a sense of community, a sense that Hollywood "takes care of its own kind"—a sentiment most Americans understand. On Oscar night, Hollywood has the intimacy of a community, the importance of international attention— and the combination is hard to beat. Hollywood As Global Village is almost impossible to resist.

Besides Douglas Fairbanks, the presidents of the Academy have been William C. DeMille, M. C. Levee, Conrad Nagel, J. Theodore Reed, Frank Lloyd, Frank Capra, Walter Wanger, Bette Davis, Jean Hersholt, Charles Brackett, George Seaton, George Stevens, B. B. Kahane, Valentine Davies, Arthur Freed, Gregory Peck, Daniel Taradash and Walter Mirisch.

Both nominees and winners are given below in the categories of directing, acting, writing, cinematography, Best Picture and Best Foreign-Language Picture. In all other categories, only the winners are listed. In the listings of the Special Effects category given below, the photography technicians (mentioned first) are separated from the sound technicians by a semicolon whenever the Academy made such a distinction. Similarly, in the listings for Interior Decoration, the art designers (cited first) are separated from the set designers by a semicolon whenever that distinction was made by the Academy. (Until 1955, art designers were given Oscars; the set designers were awarded plaques.) In the Best Song category, the composer is listed first, followed by the lyricist.

1927 / 28

BEST PICTURE

- *Wings* (Paramount)
  The Last Command (Paramount)
  The Racket (Paramount)
  Seventh Heaven (Fox)
  The Way of All Flesh (Paramount)

BEST DIRECTOR

- Frank Borzage, *Seventh Heaven*
  Herbert Brenon, *Sorrell and Son*
  King Vidor, *The Crowd*

BEST COMEDY DIRECTOR

- Lewis Milestone, *Two Arabian Knights*
  Ted Wilde, *Speedy*
  Charles Chaplin, *The Circus*

BEST ACTOR

- Emil Jannings, *The Last Command; The Way of All Flesh*
  Richard Barthelmess, *The Noose*
  Richard Barthelmess, *The Patent Leather Kid*
  Charles Chaplin, *The Circus*

BEST ACTRESS

- Janet Gaynor, *Seventh Heaven; Street Angel; Sunrise*
  Gloria Swanson, *Sadie Thompson*
  Louise Dresser, *A Ship Comes In*

WRITING (ADAPTATION)

- Benjamin Glazer, *Seventh Heaven*
  Anthony Coldeway, *Glorious Betsy*
  Alfred Cohn, *The Jazz Singer*

WRITING (ORIGINAL STORY)

- Ben Hecht, *Underworld*
  Lajos Biro, *The Last Command*
  Rupert Hughes, *The Patent Leather Kid*

CINEMATOGRAPHY

- Charles Rosher, Karl Struss, *Sunrise*
  George Barnes, *Devil Dancer*
  Karl Struss, *Drums of Love*
  George Barnes, *Magic Flame*
  Charles Rosher, *My Best Girl*
  George Barnes, *Sadie Thompson*
  Charles Rosher, *The Tempest*

OTHER AWARDS:

TITLE WRITING

- Joseph Farnham, *The Fair Co-Ed*
- Joseph Farnham, *Laugh, Clown, Laugh*
- Joseph Farnham, *Telling the World*

ENGINEERING EFFECTS

- Roy Pomeroy, *Wings*

ARTISTIC QUALITY OF PRODUCTION

- Fox, *Sunrise*

■ Indicates winner

INTERIOR DECORATION

- William Cameron Menzies, *The Dove*
- William Cameron Menzies, *The Tempest*

SPECIAL AWARDS

- Warner Bros., *The Jazz Singer*, the pioneer talking picture, which has revolutionized the industry
- Charles Chaplin, *The Circus*, for versatility and genius in writing, acting, directing and producing

---

1928 / 29

BEST PICTURE

- *The Broadway Melody* (MGM)
  Alibi (United Artists)
  Hollywood Revue (MGM)
  In Old Arizona (Fox)
  The Patriot (Paramount)

BEST DIRECTOR

- Frank Lloyd, *The Divine Lady*
  Lionel Barrymore, *Madame X*
  Harry Beaumont, *Broadway Melody*
  Irving Cummings, *In Old Arizona*
  Frank Lloyd, *Weary River*
  Frank Lloyd, *Drag*
  Ernst Lubitsch, *The Patriot*

BEST ACTOR

- Warner Baxter, *In Old Arizona*
  Chester Morris, *Alibi*
  Paul Muni, *The Valiant*
  George Bancroft, *Thunderbolt*
  Lewis Stone, *The Patriot*

BEST ACTRESS

- Mary Pickford, *Coquette*
  Ruth Chatterton, *Madam X*
  Betty Compson, *The Barker*
  Jeanne Eagles, *The Letter*
  Bessie Love, *Broadway Melody*

WRITING

- Hans Kraly, *The Patriot*
  Tom Barry, *In Old Arizona*
  Elliott Clawson, *The Leatherneck*
  Josephine Lovett, *Our Dancing Daughters*
  Tom Barry, *The Valiant*
  Bess Meredyth, *Wonder of Women*

CINEMATOGRAPHY

- Clyde De Vinna, *White Shadows in the South Seas*
  John Seitz, *The Divine Lady*
  Ernest Palmer, *Four Devils*
  Arthur Edeson, *In Old Arizona*
  George Barnes, *Our Dancing Daughters*
  Ernest Palmer, *Street Angel*

OTHER AWARDS:

INTERIOR DECORATION

- Cedric Gibbons, *The Bridge of San Luis Rey*

1929 / 30

BEST PICTURE

- *All Quiet on the Western Front* (Universal)
  The Big House (MGM)
  Disraeli (Warner Bros.)
  The Divorcee (MGM)
  The Love Parade (Paramount)

BEST DIRECTOR

- Lewis Milestone, *All Quiet on the Western Front*
  Clarence Brown, *Anna Christie*
  Clarence Brown, *Romance*
  Robert Leonard, *The Divorcee*
  Ernst Lubitsch, *The Love Parade*
  King Vidor, *Hallelujah*

BEST ACTOR

- George Arliss, *Disraeli*
  George Arliss, *The Green Goddess*
  Wallace Beery, *The Big House*
  Maurice Chevalier, *The Love Parade*
  Maurice Chevalier, *The Big Pond*
  Ronald Colman, *Bulldog Drummond*
  Ronald Colman, *Condemned*
  Lawrence Tibbett, *The Rogue Song*

BEST ACTRESS

- Norma Shearer, *The Divorcee*
  Nancy Carroll, *The Devil's Holiday*
  Ruth Chatterton, *Sarah and Son*
  Greta Garbo, *Anna Christie*
  Greta Garbo, *Romance*
  Norma Shearer, *Their Own Desire*
  Gloria Swanson, *The Trespasser*

WRITING

- Francis Marion, *The Big House*
  Julian Josephson, *Disraeli*
  John Meehan, *The Divorcee*
  Howard Estabrook, *Street of Chance*
  George Abbott, Maxwell Anderson, Dell Andrews, *All Quiet on the Western Front*

CINEMATOGRAPHY

- Joseph T. Rucker, William Van Der Veer, *With Byrd at the South Pole*
  Arthur Edeson, *All Quiet on the Western Front*
  William Daniels, *Anna Christie*
  Gaetano Gaudio, Harry Perry, *Hell's Angels*
  Victor Milner, *The Love Parade*

OTHER AWARDS:

INTERIOR DECORATION

- Herman Rosse, *King of Jazz*

SOUND RECORDING

- Douglas Shearer, *The Big House*

1930 / 31

BEST PICTURE

- *Cimarron* (RKO Radio)
  East Lynne (Fox)
  The Front Page (United Artists)
  Skippy (Paramount)
  Trader Horn (MGM)

BEST DIRECTOR

- Norman Taurog, *Skippy*
  Clarence Brown, *A Free Soul*
  Lewis Milestone, *The Front Page*
  Wesley Ruggles, *Cimarron*
  Josef von Sternberg, *Morocco*

BEST ACTOR

- Lionel Barrymore, *A Free Soul*
  Jackie Cooper, *Skippy*
  Richard Dix, *Cimarron*
  Fredric March, *The Royal Family of Broadway*
  Adolphe Menjou, *The Front Page*

BEST ACTRESS

- Marie Dressler, *Min and Bill*
  Marlene Dietrich, *Morocco*
  Irene Dunne, *Cimarron*
  Ann Harding, *Holiday*
  Norma Shearer, *A Free Soul*

WRITING (ADAPTATION)

- Howard Estabrook, *Cimarron*
  Seton Miller, Fred Niblo Jr., *Criminal Code*
  Horace Jackson, *Holiday*
  Francis Faragoh, Robert N. Lee, *Little Caesar*
  Joseph Mankiewicz, Sam Mintz, *Skippy*

WRITING (ORIGINAL STORY)

- John Monk Saunders, *The Dawn Patrol*
  Rowland Brown, *Doorway to Hell*
  Harry d'Abbadie d'Arrast, Douglas Doty, Donald Ogden Stewart, *Laughter*
  John Bright, Kubec Glasmon, *Public Enemy*
  Lucien Hubbard, Joseph Jackson, *Smart Money*

CINEMATOGRAPHY

- Floyd Crosby, *Tabu*
  Edward Cronjager, *Cimarron*
  Lee Garmes, *Morocco*
  Charles Lang, *The Right to Love*
  Barney McGill, *Svengali*

OTHER AWARDS:

INTERIOR DECORATION

- Max Ree, *Cimarron*

SOUND RECORDING

- Paramount Studio Sound Dept.

SCIENTIFIC OR TECHNICAL AWARDS

Class I:

- Electrical Research Products, Inc., RCA and RKO Radio Pictures, Inc., for noise-reduction recording equipment
- Du Pont Film Manufacturing Corporation and Eastman Kodak, for super-sensitive panchromatic film

Class II:
- Fox Film Corp., for effective use of synchro-projection composite photography

Class III:
- Electrical Research Products, for moving coil microphone transmitters
- RKO, for reflex type microphone concentrators
- RCA, for ribbon microphone transmitters

1931 / 32

BEST PICTURE

- *Grand Hotel* (MGM)
  Arrowsmith (Goldwyn-UA)
  Bad Girl (Fox)
  The Champ (MGM)
  Five Star Final (First National)
  One Hour with You (Paramount)
  Shanghai Express (Paramount)
  Smiling Lieutenant (Paramount)

DIRECTING

- Frank Borzage, *Bad Girl*
  King Vidor, *The Champ*
  Joseph von Sternberg, *Shanghai Express*

BEST ACTOR

- Wallace Beery, *The Champ*
- Fredric March, *Dr. Jekyll and Mr. Hyde*
  Alfred Lunt, *The Guardsman*

BEST ACTRESS

- Helen Hayes, *The Sin of Madelon Claudet*
  Marie Dressler, *Emma*
  Lynn Fontanne, *The Guardsman*

WRITING (ADAPTATION)

- Edwin Burke, *Bad Girl*
  Sidney Howard, *Arrowsmith*
  Percy Heath, Samuel Hoffenstein, *Dr. Jekyll and Mr. Hyde*

WRITING (ORIGINAL STORY)

- Frances Marion, *The Champ*
  Grover Jones, William Slavens McNutt, *Lady and Gent*
  Lucien Hubbard, *Star Witness*
  Adela Rogers St. John, *What Price Hollywood*

CINEMATOGRAPHY

- Lee Garmes, *Shanghai Express*
  Ray June, *Arrowsmith*
  Karl Struss, *Dr. Jekyll and Mr. Hyde*

OTHER AWARDS:

INTERIOR DECORATION

- Gordon Wiles, *Transatlantic*

SOUND RECORDING

- Paramount Studio

SHORT SUBJECTS

Cartoons:
- Walt Disney (UA), *Flowers and Trees*

Comedy:
- Hal Roach (MGM), *The Music Box*

Novelty:
- Mack Sennett (Educational), *Wrestling Swordfish*

SPECIAL AWARD
- Walt Disney, for creation of Mickey Mouse

SCIENTIFIC OR TECHNICAL AWARDS

Class II:
- Technicolor M.P. Corp., for color cartoon process

Class III:
- Eastman Kodak, for the type Two-B sensitometer

1932 / 33

BEST PICTURE
- *Cavalcade* (Fox)
  A Farewell to Arms (Paramount)
  Forty-Second Street (Warner Bros.)
  I Am a Fugitive from a Chain Gang (Warner Bros.)
  Lady for a Day (Columbia)
  Little Women (RKO Radio)
  The Private Life of Henry VIII (UA)
  She Done Him Wrong (Paramount)
  Smilin' Through (MGM)
  State Fair (Fox)

DIRECTING
- Frank Lloyd, *Cavalcade*
  Frank Capra, *Lady for a Day*
  George Cukor, *Little Women*

BEST ACTOR
- Charles Laughton, *Private Life of Henry VIII*
  Leslie Howard, *Berkeley Square*
  Paul Muni, *I Am a Fugitive from a Chain Gang*

BEST ACTRESS
- Katharine Hepburn, *Morning Glory*

May Robson, *Lady for a Day*
Diana Wynward, *Cavalcade*

WRITING (ADAPTATION)
- Victor Heerman, Sarah Y. Mason, *Little Women*
  Robert Riskin, *Lady for a Day*
  Paul Green, Sonya Levien, *State Fair*

WRITING (ORIGINAL STORY)
- Robert Lord, *One Way Passage*
  Francis Marion, *The Prizefighter and the Lady*
  Charles MacArthur, *Rasputin and the Empress*

CINEMATOGRAPHY
- Charles Bryant Lang, Jr., *A Farewell to Arms*
  George J. Folsey, Jr., *Reunion in Vienna*
  Karl Struss, *The Sign of the Cross*

OTHER AWARDS:

INTERIOR DECORATION
- William S. Darling, *Cavalcade*

SOUND RECORDING
- Harold C. Lewis, *A Farewell to Arms*

SHORT SUBJECTS

Cartoons:
- Walt Disney (UA), *Three Little Pigs*

Comedy:
- RKO Radio, *So This Is Harris*

Novelty:
- Educational, *Krakatoa*

ASSISTANT DIRECTOR

- Charles Barton (Paramount)
- Scott Beal (Universal)
- Charles Dorian (MGM)
- Fred Fox (UA)
- Gordon Hollingshead (Warner Bros.)
- Dewey Starkey (RKO Radio)
- William Tummel (Fox)

SCIENTIFIC OR TECHNICAL AWARDS

Class II:
- Electrical Research Products, for wide range recording/reproducing system
- RCA, for high-fidelity recording/reproducing system

Class III:
- Fox Film Corp., Fred Jackman, and Warner Bros. Pictures, and Sidney Sanders of RKO, for development and effective use of translucent cellulose screen in composite photography

1934

BEST PICTURE

- *It Happened One Night* (Columbia)
- *The Barretts of Wimpole Street* (MGM)
- *Cleopatra* (Paramount)
- *Flirtation Walk* (First National)
- *The Gay Divorcee* (RKO Radio)
- *Here Comes the Navy* (Warner Bros.)
- *The House of Rothschild* (20th Century–UA)
- *Imitation of Life* (Universal)
- *One Night of Love* (Columbia)
- *The Thin Man* (MGM)
- *Viva Villa* (MGM)
- *The White Parade* (Fox)

BEST DIRECTOR

- Frank Capra, *It Happened One Night*
- Victor Schertzinger, *One Night of Love*
- W. S. Van Dyke, *The Thin Man*

BEST ACTOR

- Clark Gable, *It Happened One Night*
- Frank Morgan, *Affairs of Cellini*
- William Powell, *The Thin Man*

BEST ACTRESS

- Claudette Colbert, *It Happened One Night*
- Grace Moore, *One Night of Love*
- Norma Shearer, *The Barretts of Wimpole Street*

WRITING (ADAPTATION)

- Robert Riskin, *It Happened One Night*

Frances Goodrich, Albert Hackett, *The Thin Man*
Ben Hecht, *Viva Villa*

WRITING (ORIGINAL STORY)

- Arthur Caesar, *Manhattan Melodrama*
  Mauri Grashin, *Hide-Out*
  Norman Krasna, *Richest Girl In the World*

CINEMATOGRAPHY

- Victor Milner, *Cleopatra*
  Charles Rosher, *Affairs of Cellini*
  George Folsey, *Operator 13*

OTHER AWARDS:

INTERIOR DECORATION

- Cedric Gibbons, Frederic Hope, *The Merry Widow*

SOUND RECORDING

- Paul Neal, *One Night of Love*

SHORT SUBJECTS

Cartoons:
- Walt Disney, *The Tortoise and the Hare*
Comedy:
- RKO Radio, *La Cucaracha*
Novelty:
- Educational, *City of Wax*

MUSIC

Best Song:
- Con Conrad, Herb Magidson, "Continental" *(The Gay Divorcee)*
Best Score:
- Louis Silvers, *One Night of Love*

FILM EDITING

- Conrad Nervig, *Eskimo*

ASSISTANT DIRECTOR

- John Waters, *Viva Villa*

SPECIAL AWARD

- Shirley Temple, in grateful recognition of her outstanding contribution to screen entertainment during the year 1934

SCIENTIFIC OR TECHNICAL AWARDS

Class II:
- Electrical Research Products, Inc., for development of the vertical cut disc method of recording sound (hill and dale recording)
Class III:
- Columbia Pictures Corp., for their application of the vertical cut disc method to actual studio production, with their recording of the sound on *One Night of Love*
- Bell & Howell Co., for development of the Bell & Howell fully automatic sound and picture printer

1935

BEST PICTURE

- *Mutiny on the Bounty* (MGM)
  Alice Adams (RKO Radio)
  Broadway Melody of 1936 (MGM)
  Captain Blood (Cosmopolitan-Warner Bros.)
  David Copperfield (MGM)
  The Informer (RKO Radio)
  Les Misérables (20th Century–UA)
  The Lives of a Bengal Lancer (Paramount)
  A Midsummer Night's Dream (Warner Bros.)
  Naughty Marietta (MGM)
  Ruggles of Red Gap (Paramount)
  Top Hat (RKO Radio)

BEST DIRECTOR

- John Ford, *The Informer*
  Henry Hathaway, *The Lives of a Bengal Lancer*
  Frank Lloyd, *Mutiny on the Bounty*

BEST ACTOR

- Victor McLaglen, *The Informer*
  Clark Gable, *Mutiny on the Bounty*
  Charles Laughton, *Mutiny on the Bounty*
  Franchot Tone, *Mutiny on the Bounty*

BEST ACTRESS

- Bette Davis, *Dangerous*
  Elisabeth Bergner, *Escape Me Never*
  Claudette Colbert, *Private Worlds*
  Katharine Hepburn, *Alice Adams*
  Miriam Hopkins, *Becky Sharp*
  Merle Oberon, *The Dark Angel*

WRITING (ORIGINAL STORY)

- Ben Hecht, Charles MacArthur, *The Scoundrel*
  Moss Hart, *Broadway Melody of 1936*
  Don Hartman, Stephen Avery, *The Gay Deception*

WRITING (SCREENPLAY)

- Dudley Nichols, *The Informer*
  Achmed Abdullah, John L. Balderston, Grover Jones, William Slavens McNutt, Waldemar Young, *The Lives of a Bengal Lancer*
  Jules Furthman, Talbot Jennings, Carey Wilson, *Mutiny on the Bounty*

CINEMATOGRAPHY

- Hal Mohr, *A Midsummer Night's Dream*
  Ray June, *Barbary Coast*
  Victor Milner, *The Crusades*
  Gregg Toland, *Les Misérables*

OTHER AWARDS:

INTERIOR DECORATION

- Richard Day, *The Dark Angel*

SOUND RECORDING

- Douglas Shearer, *Naughty Marietta*

SHORT SUBJECTS

Cartoons:
- Walt Disney (UA), *Three Orphan Kittens*

Comedy:
- MGM, *How to Sleep*

Novelty:
- Educational, *Wings Over Mt. Everest*

FILM EDITING
- Ralph Dawson, *A Midsummer Night's Dream*

MUSIC
Best Song:
- Harry Warren, Al Dubin, "Lullaby of Broadway" *(Gold Diggers of 1935)*

Best Score:
- Max Steiner, *The Informer*

ASSISTANT DIRECTOR
- Clem Beauchamp, *The Lives of a Bengal Lancer*
- Paul Wing, *The Lives of a Bengal Lancer*

DANCE DIRECTION
- Dave Gould, "I've Got a Feeling You're Fooling" *(Broadway Melody)* and "Straw Hat" *(Folies Bergère)*

SPECIAL AWARD
- D. W. Griffith, for his distinguished achievements as director and producer and his invaluable initiative and lasting contributions to the progress of the motion picture arts

SCIENTIFIC OR TECHNICAL AWARDS
Class II:
- AGFA Ansco Corp., for development of the Agfa infra-red film
- Eastman Kodak Co., for development of Eastman Pola-Screen

Class III:
- MGM Studio, for development of anti-directional negative and positive development by means of jet turbulation, and the application of the method to all negative and print processing of the entire product of a major producing company
- William A. Mueller of Warner Bros.–First National Studio Sound Dept., for his method of dubbing, in which the level of the dialogue automatically controls the level of the accompanying music and sound effects
- Mole-Richardson Co., for development of the "Solar-spot" spot lamps
- Douglas Shearer and MGM Studio Sound Dept., for their automatic control system for cameras and sound-recording machines and auxiliary stage equipment
- Electrical Research Products, Inc., for their study and development of equipment to analyze and measure flutter resulting from the travel of film through the mechanisms used in the recording and reproduction of sound
- Paramount Productions, Inc., for the design and construction of the Paramount transparency air turbine developing machine
- Nathan Levinson, director of Sound Recording for Warner Bros.–First National Studio, for the method of intercutting variable density and variable area sound tracks to secure an increase in the effective volume range of sound recorded for motion pictures

1936

BEST PICTURE

■ *The Great Ziegfeld* (MGM)
  Anthony Adverse (Warner Bros.)
  Dodsworth (Goldwyn-UA)
  Libeled Lady (MGM)
  Mr. Deeds Goes to Town (Columbia)
  Romeo and Juliet (MGM)
  San Francisco (MGM)
  The Story of Louis Pasteur (Warner Bros.)
  A Tale of Two Cities (MGM)
  Three Smart Girls (Universal)

BEST DIRECTOR

■ Frank Capra, *Mr. Deeds Goes to Town*
  Gregory La Cava, *My Man Godfrey*
  Robert Z. Leonard, *The Great Ziegfeld*
  W. S. Van Dyke, *San Francisco*
  William Wyler, *Dodsworth*

BEST ACTOR

■ Paul Muni, *The Story of Louis Pasteur*
  Gary Cooper, *Mr. Deeds Goes to Town*
  William Powell, *My Man Godfrey*
  Walter Huston, *Dodsworth*
  Spencer Tracy, *San Francisco*

BEST ACTRESS

■ Luise Rainer, *The Great Ziegfeld*
  Irene Dunne, *Theodora Goes Wild*
  Gladys George, *Valiant Is the Word for Carrie*
  Carole Lombard, *My Man Godfrey*
  Norma Shearer, *Romeo and Juliet*

BEST SUPPORTING ACTOR

■ Walter Brennan, *Come and Get It*
  Mischa Auer, *My Man Godfrey*
  Stuart Erwin, *Pigskin Parade*
  Basil Rathbone, *Romeo and Juliet*
  Akim Tamiroff, *The General Died at Dawn*

BEST SUPPORTING ACTRESS

■ Gale Sondergaard, *Anthony Adverse*
  Beulah Bondi, *The Gorgeous Hussy*
  Alice Brady, *My Man Godfrey*
  Bonita Granville, *These Three*
  Maria Ouspenskaya, *Dodsworth*

WRITING (ORIGINAL STORY)

■ Pierre Collings, Sheridan Gibney, *The Story of Louis Pasteur*
  Norman Krasna, *Fury*
  William Anthony McGuire, *The Great Ziegfeld*
  Robert Hopkins, *San Francisco*
  Adele Commandini, *Three Smart Girls*

WRITING (SCREENPLAY)

■ Pierre Collings, Sheridan Gibney, *The Story of Louis Pasteur*
  Frances Goodrich, Albert Hackett, *After the Thin Man*

Sidney Howard, *Dodsworth*
Robert Riskin, *Mr. Deeds Goes to Town*
Eric Hatch, Morris Ryskind, *My Man Godfrey*

CINEMATOGRAPHY

■ Gaetano Gaudio, *Anthony Adverse*
Victor Milner, *The General Died at Dawn*
George Folsey, *The Gorgeous Hussy*

OTHER AWARDS:

INTERIOR DECORATION

■ Richard Day, *Dodsworth*

SOUND RECORDING

■ Douglas Shearer, *San Francisco*

SHORT SUBJECTS

Cartoons:
■ Walt Disney (UA), *Country Cousin*
One-Reel:
■ Hal Roach (MGM), *Bored of Education*
Two-Reel:
■ MGM, *The Public Pays*
Color:
■ Warner Bros., *Give Me Liberty*

MUSIC

Best Song:
■ Jerome Kern, Dorothy Fields, "The Way You Look Tonight" *(Swing Time)*
Best Score:
■ Leo Forbstein, *Anthony Adverse*

FILM EDITING

■ Ralph Dawson, *Anthony Adverse*

ASSISTANT DIRECTOR

■ Jack Sullivan, *The Charge of the Light Brigade*

DANCE DIRECTION

■ Seymour Felix, "A Pretty Girl Is Like a Melody" *(The Great Ziegfeld)*

SPECIAL AWARDS

■ The March of Time, for its significance to motion pictures and for having revolutionized one of the most important branches of the industry—the newsreel
■ W. Howard Greene and Harold Rosson, for the color cinematography of *The Garden of Allah* (Selznick Intern.)

SCIENTIFIC OR TECHNICAL AWARDS

Class I:
■ Douglas Shearer and MGM Studio Sound Dept., for development of a practical two-way horn system, and a biased Class A push-pull recording system
Class II:
■ E. C. Wente and Bell Telephone Laboratories, for multicellular high-frequency horn and receiver
■ RCA Manufacturing Co., Inc., for their rotary stabilizer sound head
Class III:
■ RCA Manufacturing Co., Inc., for development of a method of recording and printing sound records utilizing a restricted spectrum (known as ultraviolet light recording)
■ Electrical Research Products,

Inc., for the ERPI "Type Q" portable recording channel
- RCA Manufacturing Co., Inc., for furnishing a practical design and specifications for a nonslip printer
- United Artists Studio Corp., for development of a practical, efficient and quiet wind machine

1937

BEST PICTURE

- *The Life of Emile Zola* (Warner Bros.)
  The Awful Truth (Columbia)
  Captains Courageous (MGM)
  Dead End (Goldwyn-UA)
  The Good Earth (MGM)
  In Old Chicago (20th Century-Fox)
  Lost Horizon (Columbia)
  100 Men and a Girl (Universal)
  Stage Door (RKO Radio)
  A Star Is Born (Selznick-UA)

BEST DIRECTOR

- Leo McCarey, *The Awful Truth*
  Sidney Franklin, *The Good Earth*
  William Dieterle, *The Life of Emile Zola*
  Gregory La Cava, *Stage Door*
  William Wellman, *A Star Is Born*

BEST ACTOR

- Spencer Tracy, *Captains Courageous*
  Charles Boyer, *Conquest*
  Fredric March, *A Star Is Born*
  Robert Montgomery, *Night Must Fall*
  Paul Muni, *The Life of Emile Zola*

BEST ACTRESS

- Luise Rainer, *The Good Earth*
  Irene Dunne, *The Awful Truth*
  Greta Garbo, *Camille*
  Janet Gaynor, *A Star Is Born*
  Barbara Stanwyck, *Stella Dallas*

BEST SUPPORTING ACTOR

- Joseph Schildkraut, *The Life of Emile Zola*
  Ralph Bellamy, *The Awful Truth*
  Thomas Mitchell, *Hurricane*
  H. B. Warner, *Lost Horizon*
  Roland Young, *Topper*

BEST SUPPORTING ACTRESS

- Alice Brady, *In Old Chicago*
  Andrea Leeds, *Stage Door*
  Anne Shirley, *Stella Dallas*
  Claire Trevor, *Dead End*
  Dame May Whitty, *Night Must Fall*

WRITING (ORIGINAL STORY)

- William A. Wellman, Robert Carson, *A Star Is Born*
  Robert Lord, *Black Legion*
  Niven Busch, *In Old Chicago*
  Heinz Herald, Geza Herczeg, *The Life of Emile Zola*
  Hans Kraly, *100 Men and a Girl*

WRITING (SCREENPLAY)

■ Heinz Herald, Geza Herczeg, Norman Reilly Raine, *The Life of Emile Zola*
Vina Delmar, *The Awful Truth*
Marc Connolly, John Lee Mahin, Dale Van Every, *Captains Courageous*
Morris Ryskind, Anthony Veiller, *Stage Door*
Alan Campbell, Robert Carson, Dorothy Parker, *A Star Is Born*

CINEMATOGRAPHY

■ Karl Freund, *The Good Earth*
Gregg Toland, *Dead End*
Joseph Valentine, *Wings Over Honolulu*

OTHER AWARDS:

INTERIOR DECORATION

■ Stephen Goosson, *Lost Horizon*

SOUND RECORDING

■ Thomas Moulton, *The Hurricane*

SHORT SUBJECTS

Cartoons:
■ Walt Disney (RKO), *The Old Mill*
One-Reel:
■ Educational, *Private Life of the Gannets*
Two-Reel:
■ MGM, *Torture Money*
Color:
■ Pete Smith (MGM), *Penny Wisdom*

MUSIC

Best Song:
■ Harry Owens, "Sweet Leilani" (*Waikiki Wedding*)
Best Score:
■ Charles Previn, *100 Men and a Girl*

FILM EDITING

■ Gene Havlick, Gene Milford, *Lost Horizon*

ASSISTANT DIRECTOR

■ Robert Webb, *In Old Chicago*

DANCE DIRECTION

■ Hermes Pan, "Fun House" (*Damsel in Distress*)

SPECIAL AWARDS

■ Mack Sennett, for his lasting contribution to the comedy technique of the screen, the basic principles of which are as important today as when they were first put into practice, the Academy presents a Special Award to that master of fun, discoverer of stars, sympathetic, kindly, understanding comedy genius
■ Edgar Bergen for his outstanding comedy creation, Charlie McCarthy
■ The Museum of Modern Art Film Library for its significant work in collecting films dating from 1895 to the present and for the first time making available to the public the means of studying the historical and aesthetic development of the motion picture as one of the major arts
■ W. Howard Greene for the color photography of *A Star Is Born*. (This Award was recommended by a committee of leading cinematographers after viewing all the color pictures made during the year.)

IRVING G. THALBERG MEMORIAL AWARD

- Darryl F. Zanuck

SCIENTIFIC OR TECHNICAL AWARDS

Class I:
- AGFA Ansco Corp., for Agfa Supreme and Agfa Ultra Speed pan motion picture negatives

Class II:
- Walt Disney Prods. Ltd., for design and application to production of the Multi-Plane Camera
- Eastman Kodak Co., for two fine-grain duplicating film stocks
- Farciot Edourat and Paramount Pictures, Inc., for development of the Paramount dual screen transparency camera setup
- Douglas Shearer and MGM Studio Sound Dept., for a method of varying the scanning width of variable density sound tracks (squeeze tracks) for the purpose of obtaining an increased amount of noise reduction

Class III:
- John Arnold and MGM Studio Camera Dept., for their improvement of the semi-automatic follow focus device and its application to all of the cameras used by MGM Studio
- John Livadary, director of Sound Recording for Columbia Pictures Corp., for the application of the bi-planar light valve to motion picture sound recording
- Thomas T. Moulton and the United Artists Studio Sound Dept., for the application to motion picture sound recording of volume indicators which have peak-reading response and linear decibel scales
- RCA Manufacturing Co., Inc., for introduction of the modulated high-frequency method of determining optimum photographic processing conditions for variable width sound tracks
- Joseph E. Robbins and Paramount Pictures, Inc., for an exceptional application of acoustic principles to the sound proofing of gasoline generator and water pumps
- Douglas Shearer and MGM Studio Sound Dept., for the design of the film mechanism incorporated in the ERPI 1010 reproducer

1938

BEST PICTURE

- *You Can't Take It with You* (Columbia)
  The Adventures of Robin Hood (Warner Bros.)
  Alexander's Ragtime Band (20th Century-Fox)
  Boys Town (MGM)
  The Citadel (MGM)
  Four Daughters (Warners-First National)
  Grand Illusion (R.A.C.-World Pictures)
  Jezebel (Warner Bros.)
  Pygmalion (MGM)
  Test Pilot (MGM)

BEST DIRECTOR

- Frank Capra, *You Can't Take It with You*
  Michael Curtiz, *Angels with Dirty Faces*
  Michael Curtiz, *Four Daughters*
  Norman Taurog, *Boys Town*
  King Vidor, *The Citadel*

BEST ACTOR

- Spencer Tracy, *Boys Town*
  Charles Boyer, *Algiers*
  James Cagney, *Angels with Dirty Faces*
  Robert Donat, *The Citadel*
  Leslie Howard, *Pygmalion*

BEST ACTRESS

- Bette Davis, *Jezebel*
  Fay Bainter, *White Banners*
  Wendy Hiller, *Pygmalion*
  Norma Shearer, *Marie Antoinette*
  Margaret Sullavan, *Three Comrades*

BEST SUPPORTING ACTOR

- Walter Brennan, *Kentucky*
  John Garfield, *Four Daughters*
  Gene Lockhart, *Algiers*
  Robert Morely, *Marie Antoinette*
  Basil Rathbone, *If I Were King*

BEST SUPPORTING ACTRESS

- Fay Bainter, *Jezebel*
  Beulah Bondi, *Of Human Hearts*
  Billie Burke, *Merrily We Live*
  Spring Byington, *You Can't Take It with You*
  Miliza Korjus, *The Great Waltz*

WRITING (ADAPTATION)

- Ian Dalrymple, Cecil Lewis, W. P. Lipscomb, *Pygmalion* (Only nomination)

WRITING (ORIGINAL STORY)

- Eleanore Griffin, Dore Schary, *Boys Town*
  Irving Berlin, *Alexander's Ragtime Band*
  Rowland Brown, *Angels with Dirty Faces*
  John Howard Lawson, *Blockade*
  Marcella Burke, Frederick Kohner, *Mad About Music*
  Frank Wead, *Test Pilot*

WRITING (SCREENPLAY)

- George Bernard Shaw, *Pygmalion*
  John Meehan, Dore Schary, *Boys Town*
  Ian Dalrymple, Elizabeth Hill, Frank Wead, *The Citadel*
  Lenore Coffee, Julius J. Epstein, *Four Daughters*

Robert Riskin, *You Can't Take It with You*

CINEMATOGRAPHY

- Joseph Ruttenberg, *The Great Waltz*
  James Wong Howe, *Algiers*
  Ernest Miller, Harry Wild, *Army Girl*
  Victor Milner, *The Buccaneer*
  Ernest Haller, *Jezebel*
  Joseph Valentine, *Mad About Music*
  Norbert Brodine, *Merrily We Live*
  Peverell Marley, *Suez*
  Robert de Grasse, *Vivacious Lady*
  Joseph Walker, *You Can't Take It with You*
  Leon Shamroy, *The Young at Heart*

OTHER AWARDS:

INTERIOR DECORATION

- Carl J. Weyl, *The Adventures of Robin Hood*

SOUND RECORDING

- Thomas Moulton, *The Cowboy and the Lady*

SHORT SUBJECTS

Cartoons:
- Walt Disney (RKO), *Ferdinand the Bull*
One-Reel:
- MGM, *That Mothers Might Live*
Two-Reel:
- Warner Bros., *Declaration of Independence*

MUSIC

Best Song:
- Ralph Rainger, Leo Robin, "Thanks for the Memory," *The Big Broadcast of 1938*

Best Score:
- Alfred Newman, *Alexander's Ragtime Band*
Original Score:
- Erich Wolfgang Korngold, *The Adventures of Robin Hood*

FILM EDITING

- Ralph Dawson, *The Adventures of Robin Hood*

SPECIAL AWARDS

- Deanna Durbin and Mickey Rooney for their significant contribution in bringing to the screen the spirit and personification of youth, and as juvenile players setting a high standard of ability and achievement
- Harry M. Warner in recognition of patriotic service in the production of historical short subjects presenting significant episodes in the early struggle of the American people for liberty
- Walt Disney for *Snow White and the Seven Dwarfs*, recognized as a significant screen innovation which has charmed millions and pioneered a great new entertainment field for the motion picture cartoon
- Oliver Marsh and Allen Davey for the color cinematography of the MGM production, *Sweethearts*
- For outstanding achievement in creating Special Photographic and Sound Effects in the Paramount production, *Spawn of the North*. Special effects by Gordon Jennings, assisted by Jan Domela, Dev Jennings, Irmin Roberts and Art Smith. Transparencies by Farciot

Edouart, assisted by Loyal Griggs. Sound Effects by Loren Ryder, assisted by Harry Mills, Louis H. Mesenkop and Walter Oberst
- J. Arthur Ball for his outstanding contributions to the advancement of color in picture motion photography

IRVING G. THALBERG MEMORIAL AWARD
- Hal B. Wallis

SCIENTIFIC OR TECHNICAL AWARDS
Class III:
- John Aalberg and RKO Studio Sound Dept., for application of compression to variable area recording in motion picture production
- Byron Haskin and Special Effects Dept. of Warner Bros. Studio, for pioneering the development and the first practical application to motion picture production of the triple head background projector

1939

BEST PICTURE
- *Gone With the Wind* (MGM)
  Dark Victory (Warner Bros.)
  Goodbye, Mr. Chips (MGM)
  Love Affair (RKO Radio)
  Mr. Smith Goes to Washington (Columbia)
  Ninotchka (MGM)
  Of Mice and Men (Ral Roach–UA)
  Stagecoach (Walter Wanger–UA)
  The Wizard of Oz (MGM)
  Wuthering Heights (Goldwyn–UA)

BEST DIRECTOR
- Victor Fleming, *Gone With the Wind*
  Frank Capra, *Mr. Smith Goes to Washington*
  John Ford, *Stagecoach*
  Sam Wood, *Goodbye, Mr. Chips*

William Wyler, *Wuthering Heights*

BEST ACTOR
- Robert Donat, *Goodbye, Mr. Chips*
  Clark Gable, *Gone With the Wind*
  Laurence Olivier, *Wuthering Heights*
  Mickey Rooney, *Babes in Arms*
  James Stewart, *Mr. Smith Goes to Washington*

BEST ACTRESS
- Vivien Leigh, *Gone With the Wind*
  Bette Davis, *Dark Victory*
  Irene Dunne, *Love Affair*
  Greta Garbo, *Ninotchka*
  Greer Garson, *Goodbye, Mr. Chips*

BEST SUPPORTING ACTOR

■ Thomas Mitchell, *Stagecoach*
Brian Aherne, *Juarez*
Harry Carey, *Mr. Smith Goes to Washington*
Brian Donlevy, *Beau Geste*
Claude Rains, *Mr. Smith Goes to Washington*

BEST SUPPORTING ACTRESS

■ Hattie McDaniel, *Gone With the Wind*
Olivia de Havilland, *Gone With the Wind*
Geraldine Fitzgerald, *Wuthering Heights*
Edna May Oliver, *Drums Along the Mohawk*
Maria Ouspenskaya, *Love Affair*

WRITING (ORIGINAL STORY)

■ Lewis R. Foster, *Mr. Smith Goes to Washington*
Felix Jackson, *Bachelor Mother*
Mildred Cram, Leo McCarey, *Love Affair*
Melchior Lengyel, *Ninotchka*
Lamar Trotti, *Young Mr. Lincoln*

WRITING (SCREENPLAY)

■ Sidney Howard, *Gone With the Wind*
Eric Maschwitz, R. C. Sheriff, Claudine West, *Goodbye, Mr. Chips*
Sidney Buchman, *Mr. Smith Goes to Washington*
Charles Brackett, Walter Reisch, Billy Wilder, *Ninotchka*
Ben Hecht, Charles Mac-Arthur, *Wuthering Heights*

CINEMATOGRAPHY (BLACK-AND-WHITE)

■ Gregg Toland, *Wuthering Heights*
Bert Glennon, *Stagecoach*

CINEMATOGRAPHY (COLOR)

■ Ernest Haller, Ray Rennahan, *Gone With the Wind*
Sol Polito, W. Howard Greene, *The Private Lives of Elizabeth and Essex*

OTHER AWARDS:

INTERIOR DECORATION

■ Lyle Wheeler, *Gone With the Wind*

SOUND RECORDING

■ Bernard B. Brown, *When Tomorrow Comes*

SHORT SUBJECTS

Cartoons:
■ Walt Disney (RKO Radio), *The Ugly Duckling*
One-Reel:
■ Paramount, *Busy Little Bears*
Two-Reel:
■ Warner Bros., *Sons of Liberty*

MUSIC

Best Song:
■ Harold Arlen, E. Y. Harburg, "Over the Rainbow," *The Wizard of Oz*
Best Score:
■ Richard Hageman, Franke Harling, John Leipold, Leo Shuken, *Stagecoach*
Original Score:
■ Herbert Stothart, *The Wizard of Oz*

FILM EDITING

■ Hal C. Kern, James E. Newcom, *Gone With the Wind*

SPECIAL EFFECTS

- E. H. Hansen, Fred Sersen, *The Rains Came*

SPECIAL AWARDS

- Douglas Fairbanks (Commemorative Award). Recognizing the unique and outstanding contribution of Douglas Fairbanks, first President of the Academy, to the international development of the motion picture
- The Motion Picture Relief Fund, acknowledging the outstanding services to the industry during the past year of the Motion Picture Relief Fund and its progressive leadership. Presented to Jean Hersholt, President; Ralph Morgan, Chairman of the Executive Committee; Ralph Block, First Vice-President; Conrad Nagle
- Technicolor Company, for its contributions in successfully bringing three-color feature production to the screen
- Judy Garland, for her outstanding performance as a screen juvenile during the past year
- William Cameron Menzies, for outstanding achievement in the use of color for the enhancement of dramatic mood in the production, *Gone With the Wind*

SCIENTIFIC OR TECHNICAL AWARDS

Class III:
- George Anderson of Warner Bros. Studio, for an improved positive head for sun arcs

- John Arnold of MGM Studio, for the MGM mobile camera crane
- Thomas T. Moulton, Fred Albin and Sound Dept. of the Samuel Goldwyn Studio, for the origination and application of the Delta db test to sound recording in motion pictures
- Farciot Edouart, Joseph E. Robbins, William Rudolph and Paramount Pictures, Inc., for the design and construction of a quiet portable treadmill
- Emery Huse and Ralph B. Atkinson of Eastman Kodak Co., for their specifications for chemical analysis of photographic developers and fixing baths
- Harold Nye of Warner Bros. Studio, for a miniature incandescent spot lamp
- A. J. Tondreau of Warner Bros. Studio, for the design and manufacture of an improved sound track printer

Multiple Award for important contributions in cooperative development of new improved Process Projection Equipment:

- F. R. Abbott, Haller Belt, Alan Cook and Bausch & Lomb Optical Co., for faster projection lens
- Mitchell Camera Co., for a new type process projection head
- Mole-Richardson Co., for a new type automatically controlled projection arc lamp
- Charles Handley, David Joy and National Carbon Co., for improved and more stable high-intensity carbons
- Winton Hoch and Technicolor Motion Picture Corp., for an auxiliary optical system

■ Don Musgrave and Selznick International Pictures, Inc., for pioneering in the use of coordinated equipment in the production *Gone With the Wind*

1940

BEST PICTURE

■ *Rebecca* (Selznick–UA)
All This, and Heaven Too (Warner Bros.)
Foreign Correspondent (Wanger–UA)
The Grapes of Wrath (20th Century-Fox)
The Great Dictator (Chaplin–UA)
Kitty Foyle (RKO Radio)
The Letter (Warner Bros.)
The Long Voyage Home (Wanger–UA)
Our Town (Lesser–UA)
The Philadelphia Story (MGM)

BEST DIRECTOR

■ John Ford, *The Grapes of Wrath*
George Cukor, *The Philadelphia Story*
Alfred Hitchcock, *Rebecca*
Sam Wood, *Kitty Foyle*
William Wyler, *The Letter*

BEST ACTOR

■ James Stewart, *The Philadelphia Story*
Charles Chaplin, *The Great Dictator*
Henry Fonda, *The Grapes of Wrath*
Raymond Massey, *Abe Lincoln in Illinois*
Laurence Olivier, *Rebecca*

BEST ACTRESS

■ Ginger Rogers, *Kitty Foyle*
Bette Davis, *The Letter*
Joan Fontaine, *Rebecca*
Katharine Hepburn, *The Philadelphia Story*
Martha Scott, *Our Town*

BEST SUPPORTING ACTOR

■ Walter Brennan, *The Westerner*
Albert Basserman, *Foreign Correspondent*
William Gargan, *They Knew What They Wanted*
Jack Oakie, *The Great Dictator*
James Stephenson, *The Letter*

BEST SUPPORTING ACTRESS

■ Jane Darwell, *The Grapes of Wrath*
Judith Anderson, *Rebecca*
Ruth Hussey, *The Philadelphia Story*
Barbara O'Neil, *All This, and Heaven Too*
Marjorie Rambeau, *Primrose Path*

WRITING (ORIGINAL STORY)

■ Benjamin Glazer, John S. Toldy, *Arise, My Love*
Walter Reisch, *Comrade X*
Hugo Butler, Dory Schary, *Edison the Man*
Leo McCarey, Bella Spewack, Samuel Spewack, *My Favorite Wife*
Stuart N. Lake, *The Westerner*

WRITING (ORIGINAL SCREENPLAY)

- Preston Sturges, *The Great McGinty*

  Ben Hecht, *Angels Over Broadway*

  Norman Burnside, Heinz Herald, John Huston, *Dr. Ehrlich's Magic Bullet*

  Charles Bennett, Joan Harrison, *Foreign Correspondent*

  Charles Chaplin, *The Great Dictator*

WRITING (SCREENPLAY)

- Donald Ogden Stewart, *The Philadelphia Story*

  Nunnally Johnson, *The Grapes of Wrath*

  Dalton Trumbo, *Kitty Foyle*

  Dudley Nichols, *The Long Voyage Home*

  Robert E. Sherwood, Joan Harrison, *Rebecca*

CINEMATOGRAPHY (BLACK-AND-WHITE)

- George Barnes, *Rebecca*

  James Wong Howe, *Abe Lincoln in Illinois*

  Ernest Haller, *All This, and Heaven Too*

  Charles B. Lang, Jr., *Arise, My Love*

  Harold Rosson, *Boom Town*

  Rudolph Mate, *Foreign Correspondent*

  Gaetano Gaudio, *The Letter*

  Gregg Toland, *The Long Voyage Home*

  Joseph Valentine, *Spring Parade*

  Joseph Ruttenberg, *Waterloo Bridge*

CINEMATOGRAPHY (COLOR)

- George Perinal, *The Thief of Bagdad*

Oliver T. Marsh, Allen Davey, *Bitter Sweet*

Arthur Miller, Ray Rennahan, *The Blue Bird*

Leon Shamroy, Ray Rennehan, *Down Argentine Way*

Victor Milner, W. Howard Greene, *North West Mounted Police*

Sidney Wagner, William V. Skall, *Northwest Passage*

OTHER AWARDS:

INTERIOR DECORATION

Black-and-White:
- Paul Groesse, Cedric Gibbons, *Pride and Prejudice*

Color:
- Vincent Korda, *The Thief of Bagdad*

SOUND RECORDING

- Douglas Shearer, *Strike Up the Band*

SHORT SUBJECTS

Cartoons:
- MGM, *Milky Way*

One-Reel:
- Pete Smith (MGM), *Quicker 'n a Wink*

Two-Reel:
- Warner Bros., *Teddy, The Rough Rider*

MUSIC

Best Song:
- Leigh Harline, Ned Washington, "When You Wish Upon a Star," *Pinocchio*

Best Score:
- Alfred Newman, *Tin Pan Alley*

Original Score:
- Leigh Harline, Paul J. Smith, Ned Washington, *Pinocchio*

FILM EDITING

- Anne Bauchens, *North West Mounted Police*

SPECIAL EFFECTS

- Lawrence Butler, *Jack Whitney*, *The Thief of Bagdad*

SPECIAL AWARDS

- Bob Hope, in recognition of his unselfish services to the motion picture industry
- Colonel Nathan Levinson, for his outstanding service to the industry and the Army during the past nine years, which has made possible the present efficient mobilization of the motion picture industry facilities for the production of Army Training Films

SCIENTIFIC OR TECHNICAL AWARDS

Class I:

- 20th Century-Fox Film Corp., for the design and construction of the 20th Century Silenced Camera, developed by Daniel Clark, Grover Laube, Charles Miller, and Robert W. Stevens

Class III:

- Warner Bros. Studio Art Dept. and Anton Grot, for the design and perfection of the Warner Bros. water ripple and wave illusion machine

---

1941

BEST PICTURE

- *How Green Was My Valley* (20th Century-Fox)
  Blossoms in the Dust (MGM)
  Citizen Kane (Mercury-RKO Radio)
  Here Comes Mr. Jordan (Columbia)
  Hold Back the Dawn (Paramount)
  The Little Foxes (Goldwyn-RKO Radio)
  The Maltese Falcon (Warner Bros.)
  One Foot In Heaven (Warner Bros.)
  Sergeant York (Warner Bros.)
  Suspicion (RKO Radio)

BEST DIRECTOR

- John Ford, *How Green Was My Valley*
  Alexander Hall, *Here Comes Mr. Jordan*
  Howard Hawks, *Sergeant York*
  Orson Welles, *Citizen Kane*
  William Wyler, *The Little Foxes*

BEST ACTOR

- Gary Cooper, *Sergeant York*
  Cary Grant, *Penny Serenade*
  Walter Huston, *All That Money Can Buy*
  Robert Montgomery, *Here Comes Mr. Jordan*
  Orson Welles, *Citizen Kane*

BEST ACTRESS

- Joan Fontaine, *Suspicion*
  Bette Davis, *The Little Foxes*
  Greer Garson, *Blossoms in the Dust*

Olivia de Havilland, *Hold Back the Dawn*

Barbara Stanwyck, *Ball of Fire*

BEST SUPPORTING ACTOR

- Donald Crisp, *How Green Was My Valley*

Walter Brennan, *Sergeant York*

Charles Coburn, *The Devil and Miss Jones*

James Gleason, *Here Comes Mr. Jordan*

Sydney Greenstreet, *The Maltese Falcon*

BEST SUPPORTING ACTRESS

- Mary Astor, *The Great Lie*

Sara Allgood, *How Green Was My Valley*

Patricia Collinge, *The Little Foxes*

Teresa Wright, *The Little Foxes*

Margaret Wycherly, *Sergeant York*

WRITING (ORIGINAL STORY)

- Harry Segall, *Here Comes Mr. Jordan*

Thomas Monroe, Billy Wilder, *Ball of Fire*

Monckton Hoffe, *The Lady Eve*

Richard Connell, Robert Presnell, *Meet John Doe*

Gordon Wellesley, *Night Train*

WRITING (ORIGINAL SCREENPLAY)

- Herman J. Mankiewicz, Orson Welles, *Citizen Kane*

Norman Krasna, *The Devil and Miss Jones*

Harry Chandlee, Abem Finkel, John Huston, Howard Koch, *Sergeant York*

Karl Tunberg, Darrell Ware, *Tall, Dark, and Handsome*

Paul Jarrico, *Tom, Dick and Harry*

WRITING (SCREENPLAY)

- Sidney Buchman, Seton I. Miller, *Here Comes Mr. Jordan*

Charles Brackett, Billy Wilder, *Hold Back the Dawn*

Philip Dunne, *How Green Was My Valley*

Lillian Hellman, *The Little Foxes*

John Huston, *The Maltese Falcon*

CINEMATOGRAPHY (BLACK-AND-WHITE)

- Arthur Miller, *How Green Was My Valley*

Karl Freund, *The Chocolate Soldier*

Gregg Toland, *Citizen Kane*

Joseph Ruttenberg, *Dr. Jekyll and Mr. Hyde*

Leo Tover, *Hold Back the Dawn*

Sol Polito, *Sergeant York*

Edward Cronjager, *Sun Valley Serenade*

Charles Lang, *Sundown*

Rudolph Mate, *That Hamilton Woman*

Joseph Walker, *Here Comes Mr. Jordan*

CINEMATOGRAPHY (COLOR)

- Ernest Palmer, Ray Rennahan, *Blood and Sand*

Wildred M. Cline, Karl Struss, William Snyder, *Aloma of the South Seas*

William V. Skall, Leonard Smith, *Billy the Kid*

Karl Freund, W. Howard Greene, *Blossoms in the Dust*

Bert Glennon, *Dive Bomber*

Harry Hallenberger, Ray

Rennahan, *Louisiana Purchase*

OTHER AWARDS:
INTERIOR DECORATION

Black-and-White:
- Richard Day, Nathan Juran; Thomas Little, *How Green Was My Valley*

Color:
- Cedric Gibbons, Urie McCleary; Edwin B. Willis, *Blossoms in the Dust*

SOUND RECORDING

- Jack Whitney (General Service), *That Hamilton Woman*

SHORT SUBJECTS

Cartoons:
- Walt Disney (RKO), *Lend a Paw*

One-Reel:
- MGM, *Of Pups and Puzzles*

Two-Reel:
- MGM, *Main Street on the March*

DOCUMENTARY

- UA, *Churchill's Island*

MUSIC

Best Song:
- Jerome Kern, Oscar Hammerstein II, "The Last Time I Saw Paris," *Lady Be Good*

Scoring of a Dramatic Picture:
- Bernard Herrmann, *All That Money Can Buy*

Scoring of a Musical Picture:
- Frank Churchill, Oliver Wallace, *Dumbo*

FILM EDITING

- William Holmes, *Sergeant York*

SPECIAL EFFECTS

- Farciot Edouart, Gordon Jennings; Louis Mesenkop, *I Wanted Wings*

SPECIAL AWARDS

- *Churchill's Island,* Canadian National Film Board. Citation for distinctive achievement in short subjects Documentary production
- Rey Scott, for his extraordinary achievement in producing *Kuhan,* the film record of China's struggle, including its photography with a 16mm camera under the most difficult and dangerous conditions
- The British Ministry of Information, for its vivid and dramatic presentation of the heroism of the R.A.F. in the documentary film, *Target for Tonight*
- Walt Disney, William Garity, John N. A. Hawkins and RCA, for their outstanding contribution to the advancement of the use of sound in motion pictures through the production of *Fantasia*
- Leopold Stokowski and his associates, for their unique achievement in the creation of a new form of visualized music in Walt Disney's production *Fantasia,* thereby widening the scope of the motion picture as entertainment and as an art form

IRVING G. THALBERG MEMORIAL AWARD

- Walt Disney

SCIENTIFIC OR TECHNICAL AWARDS

Class II:
- Electrical Research Products Division of Western Electric

Co., Inc., for the development of the precision integrating sphere densitometer
- RCA Manufacturing Co., for the design and development of the MI-3043 Unidirectional microphone

Class III:
- Ray Wilkinson and the Paramount Studio Laboratory, for pioneering in the use of and for the first application to release printing of fine grain positive stock
- Charles Lootens and the Republic Studio Sound Dept., for pioneering the use of and the first practical application to motion picture production of Class B push-pull variable area recording
- Wilbur Silvertooth and Paramount Studio Engineering Dept., for the design and computation of a relay condenser system applicable to transparency process projection, delivering considerably more usable light
- Paramount Pictures, Inc., and 20th Century-Fox Film Corp., for the development and first practical application to motion picture production of an automatic scene slating device
- Douglas Shearer and MGM Studio Sound Dept. and Loren Ryder and the Paramount Studio Sound Dept., for pioneering the development of fine grain emulsions for variable density original sound recording in studio production

---

1942

BEST PICTURE
- *Mrs. Miniver* (MGM)
  The Invaders (Columbia)
  The Magnificent Ambersons (Mercury-RKO)
  The Pied Piper (20th Century-Fox)
  Pride of the Yankees (Goldwyn-RKO)
  Random Harvest (MGM)
  Talk of the Town (Columbia)
  Wake Island (Paramount)
  Yankee Doodle Dandy (Warner Bros.)
  Kings Row (Warner Bros.)

BEST DIRECTOR
- William Wyler, *Mrs. Miniver*
  Michael Curtiz, *Yankee Doodle Dandy*
  John Farrow, *Wake Island*
  Mervyn LeRoy, *Random Harvest*
  Sam Wood, *Kings Row*

BEST ACTOR
- James Cagney, *Yankee Doodle Dandy*
  Ronald Colman, *Random Harvest*
  Gary Cooper, *Pride of the Yankees*
  Walter Pidgeon, *Mrs. Miniver*
  Monty Woolley, *The Pied Piper*

BEST ACTRESS

- Greer Garson, *Mrs. Miniver*
  Bette Davis, *Now, Voyager*
  Katharine Hepburn, *Woman of the Year*
  Rosalind Russell, *My Sister Eileen*
  Teresa Wright, *Pride of the Yankees*

BEST SUPPORTING ACTOR

- Van Heflin, *Johnny Eager*
  William Bendix, *Wake Island*
  Walter Huston, *Yankee Doodle Dandy*
  Frank Morgan, *Tortilla Flat*
  Henry Travers, *Mrs. Miniver*

BEST SUPPORTING ACTRESS

- Teresa Wright, *Mrs. Miniver*
  Gladys Cooper, *Now, Voyager*
  Agnes Moorehead, *The Magnificent Ambersons*
  Susan Peters, *Random Harvest*
  Dame May Whitty, *Mrs. Miniver*

WRITING (ORIGINAL STORY)

- Emeric Pressburger, *The Invaders*
  Irving Berlin, *Holiday Inn*
  Paul Gallico, *Pride of the Yankees*
  Sidney Harmon, *Talk of the Town*
  Robert Buckner, *Yankee Doodle Dandy*

WRITING (ORIGINAL SCREENPLAY)

- Michael Kanin, Ring Lardner, Jr., *Woman of the Year*
  Michael Powell, Emeric Pressburger, *One of Our Aircraft Is Missing*
  Frank Butler, Don Hartman, *Road to Morocco*
  W. R. Burnett, Frank Butler, *Wake Island*

George Oppenheimer, *The War Against Mrs. Hadley*

WRITING (SCREENPLAY)

- George Froeschel, James Hilton, Claudine West, Arthur Wimperis, *Mrs. Miniver*
  Rodney Ackland, Emeric Pressburger, *The Invaders*
  Herman J. Mankiewicz, Jo Swerling, *Pride of the Yankees*
  George Froeschel, Claudine West, Arthur Wimperis, *Random Harvest*
  Sidney Buchman, Irwin Shaw, *Talk of the Town*

CINEMATOGRAPHY (BLACK-AND-WHITE)

- Joseph Ruttenberg, *Mrs. Miniver*
  James Wong Howe, *Kings Row*
  Stanley Cortez, *The Magnificent Ambersons*
  Charles Clarke, *Moontide*
  Edward Cronjager, *The Pied Piper*
  Rudolph Mate, *Pride of the Yankees*
  John Mescall, *Take a Letter, Darling*
  Ted Tetzlaff, *Talk of the Town*
  Leon Shamroy, *Ten Gentlemen from West Point*
  Arthur Miller, *This Above All*

CINEMATOGRAPHY (COLOR)

- Leon Shamroy, *The Black Swan*
  Milton Krasner, William V. Skall, W. Howard Greene, *Arabian Nights*
  Sol Polito, *Captains of the Clouds*
  W. Howard Greene, *Jungle Book*
  Victor Milner, William V. Skall, *Reap the Wild Wind*

Edward Cronjager, William V. Skall, *To the Shores of Tripoli*

OTHER AWARDS:

INTERIOR DECORATION

Black-and-White:
- Richard Day, Joseph Wright; Thomas Little, *This Above All*

Color:
- Richard Day, Joseph Wright; Thomas Little, *My Gal Sal*

SOUND RECORDING
- Nathan Levinson, *Yankee Doodle Dandy*

SHORT SUBJECTS

Cartoons:
- Walt Disney-RKO, *Der Fuehrer's Face*

One-Reel:
- Paramount, *Speaking of Animals and Their Families*

Two-Reel:
- Warner Bros., *Beyond the Line of Duty*

DOCUMENTARY
- 20th Century-Fox, *Battle of Midway*

MUSIC

Best Song:
- Irving Berlin, "White Christmas," *Holiday Inn*

Best Score of a Dramatic or Comedy Picture:
- Max Steiner, *Now, Voyager*

Best Score of a Musical Picture:
- Ray Heindorf, Heinz Roemheld, *Yankee Doodle Dandy*

FILM EDITING
- Daniel Mandell, *Pride of the Yankees*

SPECIAL EFFECTS
- Farciot Edouart, Gordon Jannings, William L. Pereira; Louis Mesenkop, *Reap the Wild Wind*

SPECIAL AWARDS
- Charles Boyer, for his progressive cultural achievement in establishing the French Research Foundation in Los Angeles as a source of reference for the Hollywood Motion Picture Industry
- Noël Coward, for his outstanding production achievement, *In Which We Serve*
- MGM Studio, for its achievement in representing the American Way of Life in the production of the "Andy Hardy" series of films

IRVING G. THALBERG MEMORIAL AWARD
- Sidney Franklin

SCIENTIFIC OR TECHNICAL AWARDS

Class II:
- Carroll Clark, F. Thomas Thompson and RKO Radio Studio Art and Miniature Depts., for the design and construction of a moving cloud and horizon machine
- Daniel B. Clark and 20th Century-Fox Film Corp., for the development of a lens calibration system and the application of this system to exposure control in cinematography

Class III:
- Robert Henderson and Paramount Studio Engineering and Transparency Depts., for the design and construction

of adjustable light bridges and frames for transparency process photography
■ Daniel J. Bloomberg and Republic Studio Sound Dept., for the design and application to motion picture production of a device for marking action negative for pre-selection purposes

1943

BEST PICTURE

■ *Casablanca* (Warner Bros.)
For Whom the Bell Tolls (Paramount)
Heaven Can Wait (20th Century-Fox)
The Human Comedy (MGM)
In Which We Serve (United Artists)
Madame Curie (MGM)
The More the Merrier (Columbia)
The Ox-Bow Incident (20th Century-Fox)
The Song of Bernadette (20th Century-Fox)
Watch on the Rhine (Warner Bros.)

BEST DIRECTOR

■ Michael Curtiz, *Casablanca*
Clarence Brown, *The Human Comedy*
Henry King, *The Song of Bernadette*
Ernst Lubitsch, *Heaven Can Wait*
George Stevens, *The More the Merrier*

BEST ACTOR

■ Paul Lukas, *Watch on the Rhine*
Humphrey Bogart, *Casablanca*
Gary Cooper, *For Whom the Bell Tolls*
Walter Pidgeon, *Madame Curie*
Mickey Rooney, *The Human Comedy*

BEST ACTRESS

■ Jennifer Jones, *The Song of Bernadette*
Jean Arthur, *The More the Merrier*
Ingrid Bergman, *For Whom the Bell Tolls*
Joan Fontaine, *The Constant Nymph*
Greer Garson, *Madame Curie*

BEST SUPPORTING ACTOR

■ Charles Coburn, *The More the Merrier*
Charles Bickford, *The Song of Bernadette*
J. Carroll Naish, *Sahara*
Claude Rains, *Casablanca*
Akim Tamiroff, *For Whom the Bell Tolls*

BEST SUPPORTING ACTRESS

■ Katina Paxinou, *For Whom the Bell Tolls*
Gladys Cooper, *The Song of Bernadette*
Paulette Goddard, *So Proudly We Hail*
Anne Revere, *The Song of Bernadette*

Lucile Watson, *Watch on the Rhine*

WRITING (ORIGINAL STORY)

■ William Saroyan, *The Human Comedy*
  Guy Gilpatric, *Action in the North Atlantic*
  Steve Fisher, *Destination Tokyo*
  Frank Ross, Robert Russell, *The More the Merrier*
  Gordon McDonell, *The Shadow of a Doubt*

WRITING (ORIGINAL SCREENPLAY)

■ Norman Krasna, *Princess O'Rourke*
  Dudley Nichols, *Air Force*
  Noël Coward, *In Which We Serve*
  Allan Scott, *So Proudly We Hail*
  Lillian Hellman, *The North Star*

WRITING (SCREENPLAY)

■ Julius J. Epstein, Philip G. Epstein, Howard Koch, *Casablanca*
  Nunnally Johnson, *Holy Matrimony*
  Richard Flournoy, Lewis R. Foster, Frank Ross, Robert Russell, *The More the Merrier*
  George Seaton, *The Song of Bernadette*
  Dashiell Hammett, *Watch on the Rhine*

CINEMATOGRAPHY (BLACK-AND-WHITE)

■ Arthur Miller, *The Song of Bernadette*
  James Wong Howe, Elmer Dyer, Charles Marshall, *Air Force*
  Arthur Edeson, *Casablanca*

Tony Gaudio, *Corvette K-225*
John Seitz, *Five Graves to Cairo*
Harry Stradling, *The Human Comedy*
Joseph Ruttenberg, *Madame Curie*
James Wong Howe, *The North Star*
Rudolph Mate, *Sahara*
Charles Lang, *So Proudly We Hail*

CINEMATOGRAPHY (COLOR)

■ Hal Mohr, W. Howard Greene, *The Phantom of the Opera*
  Ray Rennahan, *For Whom the Bell Tolls*
  Edward Cronjager, *Heaven Can Wait*
  Charles G. Clarke, Allen Davey, *Hello, Frisco, Hello*
  Leonard Smith, *Lassie Come Home*
  George Folsey, *Thousands Cheer*

OTHER AWARDS:

INTERIOR DECORATION

Black-and-White:
■ James Basevi, William Darling; Thomas Little, *The Song of Bernadette*
Color:
■ Alexander Golitzen, John B. Goodman; Russell A. Gausman, Ira S. Webb, *The Phantom of the Opera*

SOUND RECORDING

■ Stephen Dunn, *This Land Is Mine*

SHORT SUBJECTS

Cartoons:
■ MGM, *Yankee Doodle Mouse*
One-Reel:
■ Paramount, *Amphibious Fighters*

Two-Reel:
- MGM, *Heavenly Music*

DOCUMENTARY

Short Subjects:
- U.S. Navy, *December 7th*

Features:
- British Ministry of Information, *Desert Victory*

MUSIC

Best Song:
- Harry Warren, Mack Gordon, "You'll Never Know," *Hello, Frisco, Hello*

Best Score of a Dramatic or Comedy Picture:
- Alfred Newman, *The Song of Bernadette*

Best Score of a Musical Picture:
- Ray Heindorf, *This Is the Army*

FILM EDITING

- George Amy, *Air Force*

SPECIAL EFFECTS

- Fred Sersen; Roger Heman, *Crash Dive*

SPECIAL AWARDS

- George Pal, for the development of novel methods and techniques in the production of short subjects known as Puppetoons

IRVING G. THALBERG MEMORIAL AWARD

- Hal B. Wallis

SCIENTIFIC OR TEHNICAL AWARDS

Class II:
- Farciot Edouart, Earle Morgan, Barton Thompson and Paramount Studio Engineering and Transparency Depts., for the development and practical application to motion picture production of a method of duplicating and enlarging natural color photographs, transferring the image emulsions to glass plates and projecting these slides by especially designed stereopticon equipment
- Photo Products Dept., E.I. du Pont de Nemours and Co., Inc., for the development of fine-grain motion picture films

Class III:
- Daniel J. Bloomberg and Republic Studio Sound Dept., for the design and development of an inexpensive method of converting Movieolas to Class B push-pull reproduction
- Charles Galloway Clarke and 20th Century-Fox Studio Camera Dept., for the development and practical application of a device for composing artificial clouds into motion picture scenes during production photography
- Farciot Edouart and Paramount Studio Transparency Dept., for an automatic electric transparency cueing timer
- Willard H. Turner and RKO Studio Sound Dept., for design and construction of the phono-cue starter

1944

BEST PICTURE

- *Going My Way* (Paramount)
  Double Indemnity (Paramount)
  Gaslight (MGM)
  Since You Went Away
  (Selznick–UA)
  Wilson (20th Century-Fox)

BEST DIRECTOR

- Leo McCarey, *Going My Way*
  Alfred Hitchcock, *Lifeboat*
  Henry King, *Wilson*
  Otto Preminger, *Laura*
  Billy Wilder, *Double Indemnity*

BEST ACTOR

- Bing Crosby, *Going My Way*
  Charles Boyer, *Gaslight*
  Barry Fitzgerald, *Going My Way*
  Cary Grant, *None But the Lonely Heart*
  Alexander Knox, *Wilson*

BEST ACTRESS

- Ingrid Bergman, *Gaslight*
  Claudette Colbert, *Since You Went Away*
  Bette Davis, *Mr. Skeffington*
  Greer Garson, *Mrs. Parkington*
  Barbara Stanwyck, *Double Indemnity*

BEST SUPPORTING ACTOR

- Barry Fitzgerald, *Going My Way*
  Hume Cronyn, *The Seventh Cross*
  Claude Rains, *Mr. Skeffington*
  Clifton Webb, *Laura*
  Monty Woolley, *Since You Went Away*

BEST SUPPORTING ACTRESS

- Ethel Barrymore, *None But the Lonely Heart*
  Jennifer Jones, *Since You Went Away*
  Angela Lansbury, *Gaslight*
  Aline MacMahon, *Dragon Seed*
  Agnes Moorehead, *Mrs. Parkington*

WRITING (ORIGINAL STORY)

- Leo McCarey, *Going My Way*
  David Boehm, Chandler Sprague, *A Guy Named Joe*
  John Steinbeck, *Lifeboat*
  Alfred Neumann, Joseph Than, *None Shall Escape*
  Edward Doherty, Jules Schermer, *The Sullivans*

WRITING (ORIGINAL SCREENPLAY)

- Lamar Trotti, *Wilson*
  Preston Sturges, *Hail the Conquering Hero*
  Richard Connell, Gladys Lehman, *Two Girls and a Sailor*
  Jerome Cady, *Wing and a Prayer*
  Preston Sturges, *The Miracle of Morgan's Creek*

CINEMATOGRAPHY (BLACK-AND-WHITE)

- Joseph LaShelle, *Laura*
  John Seitz, *Double Indemnity*
  Sidney Wagner, *Dragon Seed*
  Joseph Ruttenberg, *Gaslight*
  Lionel Lindon, *Going My Way*
  Glen MacWilliams, *Lifeboat*
  Stanley Cortez, Lee Garmes, *Since You Went Away*
  Robert Surtees, Harold

Rosson, *Thirty Seconds Over Tokyo*
Charles Lang, *The Uninvited*
George Folsey, *The White Cliffs of Dover*

CINEMATOGRAPHY (COLOR)

- Leon Shamroy, *Wilson*
  Rudy Mate, Allen M. Davey, *Cover Girl*
  Edward Cronjager, *Home in Indiana*
  Charles Rosher, *Kismet*
  Ray Rennahan, *Lady in the Dark*
  George Folsey, *Meet Me in St. Louis*

OTHER AWARDS:

INTERIOR DECORATION

Black-and-White:
- Cedric Gibbons, William Ferrari; Edwin B. Willis, Paul Huldschinsky, *Gaslight*
Color:
- Wiard Ihnen; Thomas Little, *Wilson*

SOUND RECORDING

- E. H. Hansen, *Wilson*

SHORT SUBJECTS

Cartoons:
- MGM, *Mouse Trouble*
One-Reel:
- Paramount, *Who's Who in Animal Land*
Two-Reel:
- Warner Bros., *I Won't Play*

DOCUMENTARY

Short Subjects:
- U.S. Marine Corps, *With the Marines at Tarawa*
Features:
- 20th Century-Fox, U.S. Navy, *The Fighting Lady*

MUSIC

Best Song:
- James Van Heusen, Johnny Burke, "Swinging on a Star," *Going My Way*
Best Score of a Dramatic or Comedy Picture:
- Max Steiner, *Since You Went Away*
Best Score of a Musical Picture:
- Carmen Dragon, Morris Stoloff, *Cover Girl*

FILM EDITING

- Barbara McLean, *Wilson*

SPECIAL EFFECTS

- A. Arnold Gillespie, Donald Jahraus, Warren Newcombe; Douglas Shearer, *Thirty Seconds Over Tokyo*

SPECIAL AWARDS

- Margaret O'Brien, for outstanding child actress of 1944
- Bob Hope, for his many services to the Academy

IRVING G. THALBERG MEMORIAL AWARD

- Darryl F. Zanuck

SCIENTIFIC OR TECHNICAL AWARDS

Class II:
- Stephen Dunn and RKO Studio Sound Dept. and RCA, for the design and development of the electronic compressor-limiter
Class III:
- Linwood Dunn, Cecil Love and Acme Tool Manufacturing Co., for the design and construction of the Acme-Dunn Optical Printer

- Grover Laube and 20th Century-Fox Studio Camera Dept., for the development of a continuous loop projection device
- Western Electric Co., for the design and construction of the 1126A Limiting Amplifier for variable density sound recording
- Russell Brown, Ray Hinsdale and Joseph E. Robbins, for the development and production use of the Paramount floating hydraulic boat rocker
- Gordon Jennings, for the design and construction of the Paramount nodal point tripod
- RCA and the RKO Radio Studio Sound Dept., for the design and construction of the RKO reverberation chamber

- Daniel J. Bloomberg and the Republic Studio Sound Dept., for the design and development of a multi-interlock selector switch
- Bernard B. Brown and John P. Livadary, for the design and engineering of a separate soloist and chorus recording room
- Paul Zeff, S. J. Twining and George Seid of the Columbia Studio Laboratory, for the formula and application to production of a simplified variable area sound negative developer
- Paul Lerpae, for the design and construction of the Paramount traveling matte projection and photographing device

1945

BEST PICTURE

- *The Lost Weekend* (Paramount)
  Anchors Aweigh (MGM)
  The Bells of St. Mary's (Rainbow-RKO)
  Mildred Pierce (Warner Bros.)
  Spellbound (Selznick–UA)

BEST DIRECTOR

- Billy Wilder, *The Lost Weekend*
  Clarence Brown, *National Velvet*
  Alfred Hitchcock, *Spellbound*
  Leo McCarey, *The Bells of St. Mary's*
  Jean Renoir, *The Southerner*

BEST ACTOR

- Ray Milland, *The Lost Weekend*
  Bing Crosby, *The Bells of St. Mary's*
  Gene Kelly, *Anchors Aweigh*
  Gregory Peck, *The Keys of the Kingdom*
  Cornel Wilde, *A Song to Remember*

BEST ACTRESS

- Joan Crawford, *Mildred Pierce*
  Ingrid Bergman, *The Bells of St. Mary's*
  Greer Garson, *The Valley of Decision*
  Jennifer Jones, *Love Letters*

Gene Tierney, *Leave Her to Heaven*

BEST SUPPORTING ACTOR

■ James Dunn, *A Tree Grows In Brooklyn*
Michael Chekhov, *Spellbound*
John Dall, *The Corn Is Green*
Robert Mitchum, *G.I. Joe*
J. Carroll Naish, *A Medal for Benny*

BEST SUPPORTING ACTRESS

■ Anne Revere, *National Velvet*
Eve Arden, *Mildred Pierce*
Ann Blyth, *Mildred Pierce*
Angela Lansbury, *The Picture of Dorian Gray*
Joan Lorring, *The Corn Is Green*

WRITING (ORIGINAL STORY)

■ Charles G. Booth, *The House on 92nd Street*
Laszlo Gorog, Thomas Monroe, *The Affairs of Susan*
John Steinbeck, Jack Wagner, *A Medal for Benny*
Alvah Bessie, *Objective— Burma*
Ernst Marischka, *A Song to Remember*

WRITING (ORIGINAL SCREENPLAY)

■ Richard Schweizer, *Marie Louise*
Philip Yordan, *Dillinger*
Myles Connolly, *Music for Millions*
Milton Holmes, *Salty O'Rourke*
Harry Kurnitz, *What Next, Corporal Hargrove?*

WRITING (SCREENPLAY)

■ Charles Brackett, Billy Wilder, *The Lost Weekend*
Leopold Atlas, Guy Endore, Philip Stevenson, *G.I. Joe*

Ranald MacDougall, *Mildred Pierce*
Albert Maltz, *Pride of the Marines*
Frank Davis, Tess Slesinger, *A Tree Grows in Brooklyn*

CINEMATOGRAPHY (BLACK-AND-WHITE)

■ Harry Stradling, *The Picture of Dorian Gray*
Arthur Miller, *The Keys of the Kingdom*
John F. Seitz, *The Lost Weekend*
Ernest Haller, *Mildred Pierce*
George Barnes, *Spellbound*

CINEMATOGRAPHY (COLOR)

■ Leon Shamroy, *Leave Her to Heaven*
Robert Planck, Charles Boyle, *Anchors Aweigh*
Leonard Smith, *National Velvet*
Tony Gaudio, Allen M. Davey, *A Song to Remember*
George Barnes, *The Spanish Main*

OTHER AWARDS:

INTERIOR DECORATION

Black-and-White:
■ Wiard Ihnen; A. Roland Fields, *Blood on the Sun*
Color:
■ Hans Dreier, Ernest Fegte; Sam Comer, *Frenchman's Creek*

SOUND RECORDING

■ Stephen Dunn, *The Bells of St. Mary's*

SHORT SUBJECTS

Cartoons:
■ MGM, *Quiet Please*
One-Reel:
■ MGM, *Stairway to Light*

Two-Reel:
- Warner Bros., *Star In the Night*

DOCUMENTARY

Short Subjects:
- Warner Bros., *Hitler Lives*

Features:
- England and the U.S., *The True Glory*

MUSIC

Best Song:
- Richard Rodgers, Oscar Hammerstein II, "It Might As Well Be Spring," *State Fair*

Best Score of a Dramatic or Comedy Picture:
- Miklos Rozsa, *Spellbound*

Best Score of a Musical Picture:
- Georgie Stoll, *Anchors Aweigh*

FILM EDITING
- Robert J. Kern, *National Velvet*

SPECIAL EFFECTS
- John Fulton; A. W. Johns, *Wonder Man*

SPECIAL AWARDS
- Walter Wanger, for his six years' service as president of the Academy
- Peggy Ann Garner, outstanding child actress of 1945
- *The House I Live In*, tolerance short subject; produced by Frank Ross and Mervyn LeRoy; directed by Mervyn LeRoy; screenplay by Albert Maltz; song "The House I Live In," music by Earl Robinson, lyrics by Lewis Allen; starring Frank Sinatra; released by RKO Radio
- Republic Studios, Daniel J. Bloomberg and the Republic Studio Sound Dept., for the building of an outstanding musical scoring auditorium which provides optimum recording conditions and combines all elements of acoustic and engineering design

SCIENTIFIC OR TECHNICAL AWARDS

Class III:
- Loren L. Ryder, Charles R. Daily and the Paramount Studio Sound Dept., for the design, construction and use of the first dial-controlled step-by-step sound channel line-up and test circuit
- Michael S. Leshing, Benjamin C. Robinson, Arthur B. Chatelain and Robert C. Stevens of 20th Century-Fox Studio, and John G. Capstaff of Eastman Kodak Co., for the 20th Century-Fox film processing machine

---

1946

BEST PICTURE
- *The Best Years of Our Lives* (Samuel Goldwyn–RKO)

Henry V (United Artists)

It's a Wonderful Life (Liberty-RKO)

The Razor's Edge (20th Century-Fox)

The Yearling (MGM)

BEST DIRECTOR

- William Wyler, *The Best Years of Our Lives*
  Clarence Brown, *The Yearling*
  Frank Capra, *It's a Wonderful Life*
  David Lean, *Brief Encounter*
  Robert Siodmak, *The Killers*

BEST ACTOR

- Fredric March, *The Best Years of Our Lives*
  Laurence Olivier, *Henry V*
  Larry Parks, *The Jolson Story*
  Gregory Peck, *The Yearling*
  James Stewart, *It's a Wonderful Life*

BEST ACTRESS

- Olivia de Havilland, *To Each His Own*
  Celia Johnson, *Brief Encounter*
  Jennifer Jones, *Duel in the Sun*
  Rosalind Russell, *Sister Kenny*
  Jane Wyman, *The Yearling*

BEST SUPPORTING ACTOR

- Harold Russell, *The Best Years of Our Lives*
  Charles Coburn, *The Green Years*
  William Demarest, *The Jolson Story*
  Claude Rains, *Notorious*
  Clifton Webb, *The Razor's Edge*

BEST SUPPORTING ACTRESS

- Anne Baxter, *The Razor's Edge*
  Ethel Barrymore, *The Spiral Staircase*
  Lillian Gish, *Duel in the Sun*
  Flora Robson, *Saratoga Trunk*
  Gale Sondergaard, *Anna and the King of Siam*

WRITING (ORIGINAL STORY)

- Clemence Dane, *Vacation from Marriage*
  Vladimir Pozner, *The Dark Mirror*
  Jack Patrick, *The Strange Love of Martha Ivers*
  Victor Trivas, *The Stranger*
  Charles Brackett, *To Each His Own*

WRITING (ORIGINAL SCREENPLAY)

- Muriel Box, Sydney Box, *The Seventh Veil*
  Raymond Chandler, *The Blue Dahlia*
  Jacques Prevert, *Children of Paradise*
  Ben Hecht, *Notorious*
  Norman Panama, Melvin Frank, *The Road to Utopia*

WRITING (SCREENPLAY)

- Robert E. Sherwood, *The Best Years of Our Lives*
  Sally Benson, Talbot Jennings, *Anna and the King of Siam*
  Anthony Havelock-Allan, David Lean, Ronald Neame, *Brief Encounter*
  Anthony Veiller, *The Killers*
  Sergio Amidei, Federico Fellini, *Open City*

CINEMATOGRAPHY (BLACK-AND-WHITE)

- Arthur Miller, *Anna and the King of Siam*
  George Folsey, *The Green Years*

CINEMATOGRAPHY (COLOR)

- Charles Rosher, Leonard Smith, Arthur Arling, *The Yearling*
  Joseph Walker, *The Jolson Story*

OTHER AWARDS:

INTERIOR DECORATION

Black-and-White:
- Lyle Wheeler, William Darling; Thomas Little, Frank E. Hughes, *Anna and the King of Siam*

Color:
- Cedric Gibbons, Paul Groesse; Edwin B. Willis, *The Yearling*

SOUND RECORDING
- John Livadary, *The Jolson Story*

SHORT SUBJECTS

Cartoons:
- MGM, *The Cat Concerto*

One-Reel:
- Warner Bros., *Facing Your Danger*

Two-Reel:
- Warner Bros., *A Boy and His Dog*

DOCUMENTARY

Short Subjects:
- U.S. War Dept., *Seeds of Destiny*

Features:
  (none nominated this year)

MUSIC

Best Song:
- Harry Warren, Johnny Mercer, "On the Atchison, Topeka and the Santa Fe," *The Harvey Girls*

Best Score of a Dramatic or Comedy Picture:
- Hugo Friedhofer, *The Best Years of Our Lives*

Best Score of a Musical Picture:
- Morris Stoloff, *The Jolson Story*

FILM EDITING
- Daniel Mandell, *The Best Years of Our Lives*

SPECIAL EFFECTS
- Thomas Howard, *Blithe Spirit*

SPECIAL AWARDS
- Laurence Olivier, for his outstanding achievement as actor, producer and director in bringing *Henry V* to the screen
- Harold Russell, for bringing hope and courage to his fellow veterans through his appearance in *The Best Years of Our Lives*
- Ernst Lubitsch, for his distinguished contributions to the art of the motion picture
- Claude Jarman Jr., outstanding child actor of 1946

IRVING G. THALBERG MEMORIAL AWARD
- Samuel Goldwyn

SCIENTIFIC OR TECHNICAL AWARDS

Class III:
- Harlan L. Baumbach and Paramount West Coast Laboratory, for an improved method for the quantitative determination of hydroquinone and metol in photographic developing baths
- Herbert E. Britt for the development and application of formulas and equipment for producing cloud and smoke effects
- Burton F. Miller and the Warner Bros. Studio Sound and Electrical Depts., for the design and construction of a motion picture arc lighting generator filter

- Carl Faulkner of the 20th Century-Fox Studio Sound Dept., for the reversed bias method, including a double bias method for light valve and galvanometer density recording
- Mole-Richardson Co., for the Type 450 super high intensity carbon arc lamp
- Arthur F. Blinn, Robert O. Cook, C. O. Slyfield and Walt Disney Studio Sound Dept., for the design and development of an audio finder and track viewer for checking and locating noise in sound tracks
- Burton F. Miller and Warner Bros. Studio Sound Dept., for the design and application of an equalizer to eliminate relative spectral energy distortion in electronic compressors
- Marty Martin and Hal Adkins of RKO Radio Studio Miniature Dept., for the design and construction of equipment providing visual bullet effects
- Harold Nye and Warner Bros. Electrical Dept., for development of the electronically controlled fire and gaslight effect

1947

BEST PICTURE

- *Gentleman's Agreement* (20th Century-Fox)
  The Bishop's Wife (Goldwyn-RKO)
  Crossfire (RKO)
  Great Expectations (Universal-International)
  Miracle on 34th Street (20th Century-Fox)

BEST DIRECTOR

- Elia Kazan, *Gentleman's Agreement*
  George Cukor, *A Double Life*
  Edward Dmytryk, *Crossfire*
  Henry Koster, *The Bishop's Wife*
  David Lean, *Great Expectations*

BEST ACTOR

- Ronald Colman, *A Double Life*
  John Garfield, *Body and Soul*
  Gregory Peck, *Gentleman's Agreement*
  William Powell, *Life with Father*
  Michael Redgrave, *Mourning Becomes Electra*

BEST ACTRESS

- Loretta Young, *The Farmer's Daughter*
  Joan Crawford, *Possessed*
  Susan Hayward, *Smash Up—The Story of a Woman*
  Dorothy McGuire, *Gentleman's Agreement*
  Rosalind Russell, *Mourning Becomes Electra*

BEST SUPPORTING ACTOR

- Edmund Gwenn, *Miracle on 34th Street*
  Charles Bickford, *The Farmer's Daughter*
  Thomas Gomez, *Ride the Pink Horse*
  Robert Ryan, *Crossfire*
  Richard Widmark, *Kiss of Death*

BEST SUPPORTING ACTRESS

- Celeste Holm, *Gentleman's Agreement*
  Ethel Barrymore, *The Paradine Case*
  Gloria Grahame, *Crossfire*
  Marjorie Main, *The Egg and I*
  Anne Revere, *Gentleman's Agreement*

WRITING (ORIGINAL STORY)

- Valentine Davies, *Miracle on 34th Street*
  Georges Chaperot, Rene Wheeler, *A Cage of Nightingales*
  Herbert Clyde Lewis, Frederick Stephani, *It Happened on Fifth Avenue*
  Eleazar Lipsky, *Kiss of Death*
  Dorothy Parker, Frank Cavett, *Smash Up—The Story of a Woman*

WRITING (ORIGINAL SCREENPLAY)

- Sidney Sheldon, *The Bachelor and the Bobbysoxer*
  Abraham Polonsky, *Body and Soul*
  Ruth Gordon, Garson Kanin, *A Double Life*
  Charles Chaplin, *Monsieur Verdoux*
  Sergio Amidel, Adolfo Franci, C. G. Viola, Cesare Zavattini, *Shoeshine*

WRITING (SCREENPLAY)

- George Seaton, *Miracle on 34th Street*
  Richard Murphy, *Boomerang*
  John Paxton, *Crossfire*
  Moss Hart, *Gentleman's Agreement*
  David Lean, Ronald Neame, Anthony Havelock-Allan, *Great Expectations*

CINEMATOGRAPHY (BLACK-AND-WHITE)

- Guy Green, *Great Expectations*
  Charles Lang, Jr., *The Ghost and Mrs. Muir*
  George Folsey, *Green Dolphin Street*

CINEMATOGRAPHY (COLOR)

- Jack Cardiff, *Black Narcissus*
  Peverell Marley, William J. Skall, *Life with Father*
  Harry Jackson, *Mother Wore Tights*

OTHER AWARDS:

ART DIRECTION / SET DECORATION

Black-and-White:
- John Bryan; Wilfred Shingleton, *Great Expectations*
Color:
- Alfred Junge, *Black Narcissus*

SOUND RECORDING

- Goldwyn Sound Dept., *The Bishop's Wife*

SHORT SUBJECTS

Cartoons:
- Warner Bros., *Tweetie Pie*
One-Reel:
- MGM, *Goodbye Miss Turlock*
Two-Reel:
- Monogram, *Climbing the Matterhorn*

DOCUMENTARY

Short Subjects:

- U.N. Films and Visual Education, *First Steps*

Features:

- RKO, *Design for Death*

MUSIC

Best Song:

- Allie Wrubel, Ray Gilbert, "Zip-a-dee-doo-dah," *Song of the South*

Best Score of a Dramatic or Comedy Picture:

- Miklos Rozsa, *A Double Life*

Best Score of a Musical Picture:

- Alfred Newman, *Mother Wore Tights*

FILM EDITING

- Francis Lyon, Robert Parrish, *Body and Soul*

SPECIAL EFFECTS

- A. Arnold Gillespie, Warren Newcombe; Douglas Shearer, Michael Steinore, *Green Dolphin Street*

SPECIAL AWARDS

- James Baskette, for his characterization of Uncle Remus in *Song of the South*
- *Bill and Coo*, for a novel and entertaining use of the motion picture
- *Shoeshine*, an Italian production of superlative quality made under adverse circumstances
- Colonel William N. Selig, Albert E. Smith, Thomas Armat and George K. Spoor, as pioneers whose belief in a new medium blazed the trail along which the motion picture has progressed

SCIENTIFIC OR TECHNICAL AWARDS

Class II:

- C. C. Davis and Electrical Research Products, Division of Western Electric Co., for the development and application of an improved film drive filter mechanism
- C. R. Daily and Paramount Studio Film Laboratory, Still and Engineering Depts., for the development and first practical application to motion picture and still photography of a method of increasing film speed as first suggested to the industry by E. I. du Pont de Nemours & Co.

Class III:

- Nathan Levinson and Warner Bros. Studio Sound Dept., for the design and construction of a constant-speed sound editing machine
- Farciot Edouart, C. R. Daily, Hal Corl, H. G. Cartwright and the Paramount Studio Transparency and Engineering Depts., for the first application of a special anti-solarizing glass to high intensity background and spot arc projectors
- Fred Ponedel of Warner Bros. Studio, for pioneering the fabrication and practical application to motion picture color photography of large translucent photographic backgrounds
- Kurt Singer and RCA-Victor Division of RCA, for the design and development of a continuously variable band elimination filter

■ James Gibbons of Warner Bros. Studio, for development and production of large dyed plastic filters for motion picture photography

---

1948

BEST PICTURE

■ *Hamlet* (Universal-International)
Johnny Belinda (Warner Bros.)
The Red Shoes (Eagle Lion)
The Snake Pit (20th Century-Fox)
Treasure of Sierra Madre (Warner Bros.)

BEST DIRECTOR

■ John Huston, *Treasure of Sierra Madre*
Anatole Litvak, *The Snake Pit*
Jean Negulesco, *Johnny Belinda*
Laurence Olivier, *Hamlet*
Fred Zinnemann, *The Search*

BEST ACTOR

■ Lawrence Olivier, *Hamlet*
Lew Ayres, *Johnny Belinda*
Montgomery Clift, *The Search*
Dan Dailey, *When My Baby Smiles at Me*
Clifton Webb, *Sitting Pretty*

BEST ACTRESS

■ Jane Wyman, *Johnny Belinda*
Ingrid Bergman, *Joan of Arc*
Olivia de Havilland, *The Snake Pit*
Irene Dunne, *I Remember Mama*
Barbara Stanwyck, *Sorry, Wrong Number*

BEST SUPPORTING ACTOR

■ Walter Huston, *Treasure of Sierra Madre*
Charles Bickford, *Johnny Belinda*
José Ferrer, *Joan of Arc*
Oscar Homolka, *I Remember Mama*
Cecil Kellaway, *The Luck of the Irish*

BEST SUPPORTING ACTRESS

■ Claire Trevor, *Key Largo*
Barbara Bel Geddes, *I Remember Mama*
Ellen Corby, *I Remember Mama*
Agnes Moorehead, *Johnny Belinda*
Jean Simmons, *Hamlet*

WRITING (MOTION PICTURE STORY)

■ Richard Schweizer, David Wechsler, *The Search*
Frances Flaherty, Robert Flaherty, *The Louisiana Story*
Malvin Wald, *The Naked City*
Borden Chase, *Red River*
Emeric Pressburger, *The Red Shoes*

WRITING (SCREENPLAY)

■ John Huston, *Treasure of Sierra Madre*
Charles Brackett, Billy Wilder, Richard L. Breen, *A Foreign Affair*

Irmgard Von Cube, Allen Vincent, *Johnny Belinda*
Richard Schweizer, David Wechsler, *The Search*
Frank Partos, Millen Brand, *The Snake Pit*

CINEMATOGRAPHY (BLACK-AND-WHITE)

■ William Daniels, *The Naked City*
Charles B. Lang, Jr., *A Foreign Affair*
Nicholas Musuraca, *I Remember Mama*
Ted McCord, *Johnny Belinda*
Joseph August, *Portrait of Jennie*

CINEMATOGRAPHY (COLOR)

■ Joseph Valentine, William V. Skall, Winton Hoch, *Joan of Arc*
Charles G. Clarke, *Green Grass of Wyoming*
William Snyder, *The Loves of Carmen*
Robert Planck, *The Three Musketeers*

OTHER AWARDS:

ART DIRECTION / SET DIRECTION

Black-and-White:
■ Roger K. Furse; Carmen Dillon, *Hamlet*
Color:
■ Hein Heckroth; Arthur Lawson, *The Red Shoes*

SOUND RECORDING

■ 20th Century-Fox Sound Dept., *The Snake Pit*

DOCUMENTARY

Short Subjects:
■ U.S. Army, *Toward Independence*

Features:
■ U.S. Navy, MGM, *The Secret Land*

SHORT SUBJECTS

Cartoons:
■ MGM, *The Little Orphan*
One-Reel:
■ 20th Century-Fox, *Symphony of a City*
Two-Reel:
■ Walt Disney-RKO, *Seal Island*

MUSIC

Best Song:
■ Jay Livingston, Ray Evans, "Buttons and Bows," *Paleface*
Best Score of a Dramatic or Comedy Picture:
■ Brian Easdale, *The Red Shoes*
Best Score of a Musical Picture:
■ Johnny Green, Roger Edens, *Eastern Parade*

FILM EDITING

■ Paul Weatherwax, *The Naked City*

SPECIAL EFFECTS

■ Paul Eagler, J. McMillan Johnson, Russell Shearman, Clarence Slifer; Charles Freeman, James G. Stewart, *Portrait of Jennie*

COSTUME DESIGN

Black-and-White:
■ Roger K. Furse, *Hamlet*
Color:
■ Dorothy Jeakins, Karinska, *Joan of Arc*

SPECIAL AWARDS

■ *Monsieur Vincent*, as the most outstanding foreign film of 1948
■ Ivan Jandl, for outstanding

juvenile performance in *The Search*
- Sid Grauman, who raised the standard of motion picture exhibition
- Adolph Zukor, for services over forty years to the industry
- Walter Wanger, for distinguished service to the industry in adding to its moral stature in the world community by his production of *Joan of Arc*

IRVING G. THALBERG AWARD
- Jerry Wald

SCIENTIFIC OR TECHNICAL AWARDS

Class II:
- Victor Caccialanza, Maurice Ayers and Paramount Studio Set Construction Dept., for the development and application of "Paralite," a new lightweight plaster process for set construction
- Nick Kalten, Louis J. Witti and 20th Century-Fox Studio Mechanical Effects Dept., for a process of preserving and flame-proofing foliage

Class III:
- Marty Martin, Jack Lannon, Russell Shearman and RKO Radio Studio Special Effects Dept., for development of a new method of simulating falling snow on motion picture sets
- A. J. Moran and Warner Bros. Studio Electrical Dept., for a method of remote control for shutters on motion picture arc lighting equipment

1949

BEST PICTURE
- *All the King's Men* (Columbia)
  Battleground (MGM)
  The Heiress (Paramount)
  A Letter to Three Wives (20th Century-Fox)
  Twelve O'Clock High (20th Century-Fox)

BEST DIRECTOR
- Joseph L. Mankiewicz, *A Letter to Three Wives*
  Carol Reed, *The Fallen Idol*
  Robert Rossen, *All the King's Men*
  William A. Wellman, *Battleground*
  William Wyler, *The Heiress*

BEST ACTOR
- Broderick Crawford, *All the King's Men*
  Kirk Douglas, *Champion*
  Gregory Peck, *Twelve O'Clock High*
  Richard Todd, *The Hasty Heart*
  John Wayne, *Sands of Iwo Jima*

BEST ACTRESS

- Olivia de Havilland, *The Heiress*
  Jeanne Crain, *Pinky*
  Susan Hayward, *My Foolish Heart*
  Deborah Kerr, *Edward My Son*
  Loretta Young, *Come to the Stable*

BEST SUPPORTING ACTOR

- Dean Jagger, *Twelve O'Clock High*
  John Ireland, *All the King's Men*
  Arthur Kennedy, *Champion*
  Ralph Richardson, *The Heiress*
  James Whitmore, *Battleground*

BEST SUPPORTING ACTRESS

- Mercedes McCambridge, *All the King's Men*
  Ethel Barrymore, *Pinky*
  Celest Holm, *Come to the Stable*
  Elsa Lanchester, *Come to the Stable*
  Ethel Waters, *Pinky*

WRITING (MOTION PICTURE STORY)

- Douglas Morrow, *The Stratton Story*
  Clare Boothe Luce, *Come to the Stable*
  Shirley W. Smith, Valentine Davies, *It Happens Every Spring*
  Harry Brown, *Sands of Iwo Jima*
  Virginia Kellogg, *White Heat*

WRITING (SCREENPLAY)

- Joseph L. Mankiewicz, *A Letter to Three Wives*
  Robert Rossen, *All the King's Men*

Cesare Zavattini, *The Bicycle Thief*
Carl Foreman, *Champion*
Graham Greene, *The Fallen Idol*

WRITING (STORY AND SCREENPLAY)

- Robert Pirosh, *Battleground*
  Sidney Buchman, *Jolson Sings Again*
  Alfred Hayes, Federico Fellini, Sergio Amidei, Marcello Pagliero, Roberto Rossellini, *Paisan*
  T. E. B. Clarke, *Passport to Pimlico*
  Helen Levitt, Janice Loeb, Sidney Meyers, *The Quiet One*

CINEMATOGRAPHY (BLACK-AND-WHITE)

- Paul C. Vogel, *Battleground*
  Frank Planer, *Champion*
  Joseph LaShelle, *Come to the Stable*
  Leo Tover, *The Heiress*
  Leon Shamroy, *Prince of Foxes*

CINEMATOGRAPHY (COLOR)

- Winton Hoch, *She Wore a Yellow Ribbon*
  Harry Stradling, *The Barkleys of Broadway*
  William Snyder, *Jolson Sings Again*
  Robert Planck, Charles Schoenbaum, *Little Women*
  Charles G. Clarke, *Sand*

OTHER AWARDS:

ART DIRECTION / SET DIRECTION

Black-and-White:

- John Meehan, Harry Horner; Emile Kuri, *The Heiress*

Color:
- Cedric Gibbons, Paul Groesse; Edwin B. Willis, Jack D. Moore, *Little Women*

SOUND RECORDING
- 20th Century-Fox Sound Dept., *Twelve O'Clock High*

SHORT SUBJECTS
Cartoons:
- Warner Bros., *For Scent-Imental Reasons*

One-Reel:
- Paramount, *Aquatic House-Party*

Two-Reel:
- Canton-Weiner, *Van Gogh*

DOCUMENTARY
Short Subjects:
- 20th Century-Fox, *A Chance to Live*

Features:
- British Information Services, *Daybreak in Udi*

MUSIC
Best Song:
- Frank Loesser, "Baby, It's Cold Outside," *Neptune's Daughter*

Best Scoring of a Dramatic or Comedy Picture:
- Aaron Copland, *The Heiress*

Best Scoring of a Musical Picture:
- Roger Edens, Lennie Hayton, *On the Town*

FILM EDITING
- Harry Gerstad, *Champion*

SPECIAL EFFECTS
- RKO-Radio, *Mighty Joe Young*

COSTUME DESIGN
Black-and-White:
- Edith Head, Gile Steele, *The Heiress*

Color:
- Leah Rhodes, Travilla, Marjorie Best, *Adventures of Don Juan*

SPECIAL AWARDS
- *The Bicycle Thief*, as most outstanding foreign film
- Bobby Driscoll, as outstanding juvenile actor of 1949
- Fred Astaire, for his contributions to the technique of musical pictures and unique artistry
- Jean Hersholt, for distinguished service to the industry
- Cecil B. DeMille, distinguished motion picture pioneer, for 37 years of brilliant showmanship

SCIENTIFIC OR TECHNICAL AWARDS
Class I:
- Eastman Kodak Co., for development and introduction of an improved safety base motion picture film

Class III:
- Loren L. Ryder, Bruce H. Denney, Robert Carr and Paramount Studio Sound Dept., for the development and application of the supersonic playback and public address system
- M. B. Paul for the first successful large-area seamless translucent backgrounds
- Herbert Britt, for development and application of formulas and equipment producing

artificial snow and ice for
dressing motion picture sets
- André Coutant and Jacques
Mathot, for the design of
the Eclair Camerette
- Charles R. Daily, Steve Csillag
and Paramount Studio
Engineering, Editorial and
Music Depts., for a new
precision method of com-
puting variable tempo-click
tracks
- International Projector Corp.,
for a simplified and self-
adjusting take-up device for
projection machines
- Alexander Velcoff, for the
application to production of
the infra-red photographic
evaluator

1950

BEST PICTURE

- *All About Eve* (20th Century-Fox)
Born Yesterday (Columbia)
Father of the Bride (MGM)
King Solomon's Mines (MGM)
Sunset Boulevard (Paramount)

BEST DIRECTOR

- Joseph L. Mankiewicz, *All About Eve*
George Cukor, *Born Yesterday*
John Huston, *Asphalt Jungle*
Carol Reed, *The Third Man*
Billy Wilder, *Sunset Boulevard*

BEST ACTOR

- José Ferrer, *Cyrano de Bergerac*
Louis Calhern, *The Magnificent Yankee*
William Holden, *Sunset Boulevard*
James Stewart, *Harvey*
Spencer Tracy, *Father of the Bride*

BEST ACTRESS

- Judy Holliday, *Born Yesterday*
Anne Baxter, *All Aboue Eve*
Bette Davis, *All About Eve*
Eleanor Parker, *Caged*
Gloria Swanson, *Sunset Boulevard*

BEST SUPPORTING ACTOR

- George Sanders, *All About Eve*
Jeff Chandler, *Broken Arrow*
Edmund Gwenn, *Mister 880*
Sam Jaffee, *The Asphalt Jungle*
Eric von Stroheim, *Sunset Boulevard*

BEST SUPPORTING ACTRESS

- Josephine Hull, *Harvey*
Hope Emerson, *Caged*
Celeste Holm, *All About Eve*
Nancy Olson, *Sunset Boulevard*
Thelma Ritter, *All About Eve*

WRITING (MOTION PICTURE STORY)

- Edna Anhalt, Edward Anhalt, *Panic in the Streets*
Guiseppe De Santis, Carlo Lizzani, *Bitter Rice*
Leonard Spigelgass, *Mystery Street*
William Bowers, André de Toth, *The Gunfighter*
Sy Gomberg, *When Willie Comes Marching Home*

WRITING (SCREENPLAY)

- Joseph L. Mankiewicz, *All About Eve*
  Ben Maddow, John Huston, *The Asphalt Jungle*
  Albert Mannheimer, *Born Yesterday*
  Michael Blankfort, *Broken Arrow*
  Frances Goodrich, Albert Hackett, *Father of the Bride*

WRITING (STORY AND SCREENPLAY)

- Charles Brackett, Billy Wilder, D. M. Marshman, Jr., *Sunset Boulevard*
  Ruth Gordon, Garson Kanin, *Adam's Rib*
  Virginia Kellogg, Bernard C. Schoenfeld, *Caged*
  Carl Foreman, *The Men*
  Joseph L. Mankiewicz, Lesser Samuels, *No Way Out*

CINEMATOGRAPHY (BLACK-AND-WHITE)

- Robert Krasker, *The Third Man*
  Milton Krasner, *All About Eve*
  Harold Rosson, *The Asphalt Jungle*
  Victor Milner, *The Furies*
  John F. Seitz, *Sunset Boulevard*

CINEMATOGRAPHY (COLOR)

- Robert Surtees, *King Solomon's Mines*
  Charles Rosher, *Annie Get Your Gun*
  Ernest Palmer, *Broken Arrow*
  Ernest Haller, *The Flame and the Arrow*
  George Barnes, *Samson and Delilah*

OTHER AWARDS:

ART DIRECTION / SET DIRECTION

Black-and-White:
- Hans Dreier, John Meehan; Sam Comer, Ray Moyer, *Sunset Boulevard*

Color:
- Hans Dreier, Walter Tyler; Sam Comer, Ray Moyer, *Samson and Delilah*

SOUND RECORDING

- 20th Century-Fox Sound Dept., *All About Eve*

SHORT SUBJECTS

Cartoons:
- UPA-Columbia, *Gerald McBoing-Boing*

One-Reel:
- Warner Bros., *Grandad of Races*

Two-Reel:
- Walt Disney, RKO, *In Beaver Valley*

DOCUMENTARY

Short Subjects:
- 20th Century-Fox, *Why Korea?*

Features:
- Classics Pictures, *The Titan: Story of Michelangelo*

MUSIC

Best Song:
- Jay Livingston, Ray Evans, "Mona Lisa," *Captain Carey, USA*

Best Score of a Dramatic or Comedy Picture:
- Franz Waxman, *Sunset Boulevard*

Best Score of a Musical Picture:
- Adolph Deutsch, Roger Edens, *Annie Get Your Gun*

FILM EDITING

- Ralph E. Winters, Conrad A. Nervig, *King Solomon's Mines*

SPECIAL EFFECTS

- Eagle-Lion, *Destination Moon*

COSTUME DESIGN

Black-and-White:
- Edith Head, Charles LeMaire, *All About Eve*

Color:
- Edith Head, Dorothy Jeakins, Eloise Jenssen, Gile Steele, Gwen Wakeling, *Samson and Delilah*

HONORARY AND OTHER AWARDS

- George Murphy, for services in interpreting the industry to the country at large
- Louis B. Mayer, for distinguished service to the industry
- *The Walls of Malapaga* (Franco-Italian), voted by the Board of Governors as the most outstanding foreign-language film released in the United States in 1950

IRVING G. THALBERG MEMORIAL AWARD

- Darryl F. Zanuck

SCIENTIFIC OR TECHNICAL AWARDS

Class II:
- James B. Gordon and 20th Century-Fox Studio Camera Dept., for the design and development of a multiple-image film viewer
- John Paul Livadary, Floyd Campbell, L. W. Russell and Columbia Studio Sound Dept., for the development of a multi-track magnetic re-recording system
- Loren L. Ryder and Paramount Studio Sound Dept., for the first studio-wide application of magnetic sound recording to motion picture production

1951

BEST PICTURE

- *An American in Paris* (MGM)
  Decision Before Dawn (20th Century-Fox)
  A Place in the Sun (Paramount)
  Quo Vadis (MGM)
  A Streetcar Named Desire (Feldman-Warner Bros.)

BEST DIRECTOR

- George Stevens, *A Place in the Sun*
  John Huston, *The African Queen*
  Elia Kazan, *A Streetcar Named Desire*
  Vincente Minnelli, *An American in Paris*
  William Wyler, *Detective Story*

BEST ACTOR

■ Humphrey Bogart, *The African Queen*
Marlon Brando, *A Streetcar Named Desire*
Montgomery Clift, *A Place in the Sun*
Arthur Kennedy, *Bright Victory*
Fredric March, *Death of a Salesman*

BEST ACTRESS

■ Vivien Leigh, *A Streetcar Named Desire*
Katharine Hepburn, *The African Queen*
Eleanor Parker, *Detective Story*
Shelley Winters, *A Place in the Sun*
Jane Wyman, *The Blue Veil*

BEST SUPPORTING ACTOR

■ Karl Malden, *A Streetcar Named Desire*
Leo Genn, *Quo Vadis*
Kevin McCarthy, *Death of a Salesman*
Peter Ustinov, *Quo Vadis*
Gig Young, *Come Fill the Cup*

BEST SUPPORTING ACTRESS

■ Kim Hunter, *A Streetcar Named Desire*
Joan Blondell, *The Blue Veil*
Mildred Dunnock, *Death of a Salesman*
Lee Grant, *Detective Story*
Thelma Ritter, *The Mating Season*

WRITING (MOTION PICTURE STORY)

■ Paul Dehn, James Bernard, *Seven Days to Noon*
Budd Boetticher, Ray Nazarro, *The Bullfighter and the Lady*
Oscar Millard, *The Frogmen*

Robert Riskin, Liam O'Brien, *Here Comes the Groom*
Alfred Hayes, Stewart Stern, *Teresa*

WRITING (SCREENPLAY)

■ Michael Wilson, Harry Brown, *A Place in the Sun*
James Agee, John Huston, *The African Queen*
Philip Yordan, Robert Wyler, *Detective Story*
Jacques Natanson, Max Ophuls, *La Ronde*
Tennessee Williams, *A Streetcar Named Desire*

WRITING (STORY AND SCREENPLAY)

■ Alan Jay Lerner, *An American in Paris*
Billy Wilder, Lesser Samuels, Walter Newman, *The Big Carnival*
Philip Dunne, *David and Bathsheba*
Robert Pirosh, *Go For Broke*
Clarence Greene, Russell Rouse, *The Well*

CINEMATOGRAPHY (BLACK-AND-WHITE)

■ William C. Mellor, *A Place in the Sun*
Frank Planer, *Death of a Salesman*
Norbert Brodine, *The Frogmen*
Robert Burks, *Strangers on a Train*
Harry Stradling, *A Streetcar Named Desire*

CINEMATOGRAPHY (COLOR)

■ Alfred Gilks, John Alton, *An American in Paris*
Leon Shamroy, *David and Bathsheba*
Robert Surtees, William V. Skall, *Quo Vadis*

Charles Rosher, *Show Boat*
John F. Seitz, W. Howard Greene, *When Worlds Collide*

OTHER AWARDS:

ART DIRECTION / SET DIRECTION

Black-and-White:
- Richard Day; George James Hopkins, *A Streetcar Named Desire*

Color:
- Cedric Gibbons, Preston Ames; Edwin B. Willis, Keogh Gleason, *An American in Paris*

SOUND RECORDING
- Douglas Shearer, *The Great Caruso*

SHORT SUBJECTS

Cartoons:
- MGM, *Two Mouseketeers*

One-Reel:
- Warner Bros., *World of Kids*

Two-Reel:
- Walt Disney, RKO, *Nature's Half Acre*

DOCUMENTARY

Short Subjects:
- Fred Zinnemann, *Benjy*

Features:
- RKO Radio, *Kon-Tiki*

MUSIC

Best Song:
- Hoagy Carmichael, Johnny Mercer, "In the Cool, Cool, Cool of the Evening," *Here Comes the Groom*

Best Score of a Dramatic or Comedy Picture:
- Franz Waxman, *A Place in the Sun*

Best Score of a Musical Picture:
- Johnny Green, Saul Chaplin, *An American in Paris*

FILM EDITING
- William Hornbeck, *A Place in the Sun*

SPECIAL EFFECTS

(1951 through 1953 classified as an "other" award; thus no nominations)
- Paramount, *When Worlds Collide*

COSTUME DESIGN

Black-and-White:
- Edith Head, *A Place in the Sun*

Color:
- Orry-Kelly, Walter Plunkett, Irene Sharaff, *An American in Paris*

HONORARY AND OTHER AWARDS
- Gene Kelly, in appreciation of his versatility as actor, singer, director and dancer, and specifically for his brilliant achievements in the art of choreography on film
- *Rashomon* (Japanese), voted by the Board of Governors as the most outstanding foreign-language film released in the United States during 1951

IRVING G. THALBERG MEMORIAL AWARD
- Arthur Freed

SCIENTIFIC OR TECHNICAL AWARDS

Class II:
- Gordon Jennings, S. L. Stancliffe and Paramount Studio

Special Photographic and Engineering Depts: for the design, construction and application of a servo-operated recording and repeating device
■ Olin L. Dupy of MGM Studio, for the design, construction and application of a motion picture reproducing system
■ RCA, Victor Division, for pioneering direct positive recording with anticipatory noise reduction

Class III:
■ Richard N. Haff, Frank P. Herrnfeld, Garland C. Misener and the Ansco Film Division of General Aniline and Film Corp., for the development of the Ansco color scene tester

■ Fred Ponedel, Ralph Ayres and George Brown of Warner Bros. Studio, for an air-driven water motor to provide flow, wake, and white water for marine sequences in motion pictures
■ Glen Robinson and MGM Studio Construction Dept., for the development of a new music wire and cable cutter
■ Jack Gaylord and MGM Studio Construction Dept., for development of balsa falling snow
■ Carlos Rivas of MGM Studio, for the development of an automatic magnetic film splicer

1952

BEST PICTURE

■ *The Greatest Show on Earth* (DeMille–Paramount)
High Noon (Kramer–UA)
Ivanhoe (MGM)
Moulin Rouge (Romulus–UA)
The Quiet Man (Argosy–Republic)

BEST DIRECTOR

■ John Ford, *The Quiet Man*
Cecil B. DeMille, *The Greatest Show on Earth*
John Huston, *Moulin Rouge*
Joseph L. Mankiewicz, *Five Fingers*
Fred Zinnemann, *High Noon*

BEST ACTOR

■ Gary Cooper, *High Noon*
Marlon Brando, *Viva Zapata!*
Kirk Douglas, *The Bad and the Beautiful*
José Ferrer, *Moulin Rouge*
Alec Guinness, *The Lavender Hill Mob*

BEST ACTRESS

■ Shirley Booth, *Come Back, Little Sheba*
Joan Crawford, *Sudden Fear*
Bette Davis, *The Star*
Julie Harris, *The Member of the Wedding*
Susan Hayward, *With a Song in My Heart*

BEST SUPPORTING ACTOR

- Anthony Quinn, *Viva Zapata!*
  Richard Burton, *My Cousin Rachel*
  Arthur Hunnicutt, *The Big Sky*
  Victor McLaglen, *The Quiet Man*
  Jack Palance, *Sudden Fear*

BEST SUPPORTING ACTRESS

- Gloria Grahame, *The Bad and the Beautiful*
  Jean Hagen, *Singin' in the Rain*
  Colette Marchand, *Moulin Rouge*
  Terry Moore, *Come Back, Little Sheba*
  Thelma Ritter, *With a Song in My Heart*

WRITING (MOTION PICTURE STORY)

- Frederic M. Frank, Theodore St. John, Frank Cavett, *The Greatest Show on Earth*
  Leo McCarey, *My Son John*
  Martin Goldsmith, Jack Leonard, *The Narrow Margin*
  Guy Trosper, *The Pride of St. Louis*
  Edna Anhalt, Edward Anhalt, *The Sniper*

WRITING (SCREENPLAY)

- Charles Schnee, *The Bad and the Beautiful*
  Michael Wilson, *Five Fingers*
  Carl Foreman, *High Noon*
  Roger MacDougall, John Dighton, Alexander Mackendrick, *The Man in the White Suit*
  Frank S. Nugent, *The Quiet Man*

WRITING (STORY AND SCREENPLAY)

- T. E. B. Clarke, *The Lavender Hill Mob*
  Sydney Boehm, *The Atomic City*
  Terence Rattigan, *Breaking the Sound Barrier*
  Ruth Gordon, Garson Kanin, *Pat and Mike*
  John Steinbeck, *Viva Zapata!*

CINEMATOGRAPHY (BLACK-AND-WHITE)

- Robert Surtees, *The Bad and the Beautiful*
  Russell Harlan, *The Big Sky*
  Joseph LaShelle, *My Cousin Rachel*
  Virgil E. Miller, *Navajo*
  Charles B. Lang, Jr., *Sudden Fear*

CINEMATOGRAPHY (COLOR)

- Winton C. Hoch, Archie Stout, *The Quiet Man*
  Harry Stradling, *Hans Christian Andersen*
  F. A. Young, *Ivanhoe*
  George J. Folsey, *Million Dollar Mermaid*
  Leon Shamroy, *The Snows of Kilimanjaro*

OTHER AWARDS:

ART DIRECTION / SET DIRECTION

Black-and-White:
- Cedric Gibbons, Edward Carfagno; Edwin B. Willis, Keogh Gleason, *The Bad and the Beautiful*

Color:
- Paul Sheriff; Marcel Vertes, *Moulin Rouge*

SOUND RECORDING

- London Film Sound Dept., *Breaking the Sound Barrier*

SHORT SUBJECTS

Cartoons:
- MGM, *Johann Mouse*

One-Reel:
- 20th Century-Fox, *Light in the Window*

Two-Reel:
- Walt Disney, RKO, *Water Birds*

DOCUMENTARY

Short Subjects:
- National Film Board of Canada, *Neighbours*

Features:
- RKO Radio, *The Sea Around Us*

MUSIC

Best Song:
- Dimitri Tiomkin, Ned Washington, "High Noon," *High Noon*

Best Scoring of a Dramatic or Comedy Picture:
- Dimitri Tiomkin, *High Noon*

Best Scoring of a Musical Picture:
- Alfred Newman, *With a Song in My Heart*

FILM EDITING

- Elmo Williams, Harry Gerstad, *High Noon*

SPECIAL EFFECTS

(1951–1953 classified as an "other" award; hence no nominations)
- MGM, *Plymouth Adventure*

COSTUME DESIGN

Black-and-White:
- Helen Rose, *The Bad and the Beautiful*

Color:
- Marcel Vertes, *Moulin Rouge*

HONORARY AND OTHER AWARDS

- George Alfred Mitchell, for design/development of the camera which bears his name and for his continued and dominant presence in the field of cinematography
- Joseph M. Schenck, for long and distinguished service to motion picture industry
- Merian C. Cooper, for his many innovations and contributions to the art of motion pictures
- Harold Lloyd, master comedian and good citizen
- Bob Hope, for his contribution to laughter, his service to the industry; and his devotion to the American premise
- *Forbidden Games* (France), for best foreign-language film, first released in the United States during 1952

IRVING G. THALBERG MEMORIAL AWARD

- Cecil B. DeMille

SCIENTIFIC OR TECHNICAL AWARDS

Class I:
- Eastman Kodak Co., for the introduction of Eastman color negative and Eastman color print film
- Ansco Division, General Aniline and Film Corp., for introduction of Ansco color negative and Ansco color print film

Class II:
- Technicolor Motion Picture Corp., for an improved

method of color motion picture photography under incandescent light

Class III:

- Projection, Still Photographic and Development Engineering Depts. of MGM Studio, for an improved method of projecting photographic backgrounds
- John G. Frayne and R. R. Scoville and Westrex Corp., for a method of measuring distortion in sound reproduction
- Photo Research Corp., for creating the Spectra color temperature meter
- Gustav Jirouch, for the design of the Robot automatic film splicer
- Carlos Rivas of MGM Studio, for the development of a sound reproducer for magnetic film

1953

BEST PICTURE

- *From Here to Eternity* (Columbia)
  Julius Caesar (MGM)
  The Robe (20th Century-Fox)
  Roman Holiday (Paramount)
  Shane (Paramount)

BEST DIRECTOR

- Fred Zinnemann, *From Here to Eternity*
  George Stevens, *Shane*
  Charles Walters, *Lili*
  Billy Wilder, *Stalag 17*
  William Wyler, *Roman Holiday*

BEST ACTOR

- William Holden, *Stalag 17*
  Marlon Brando, *Julius Caesar*
  Richard Burton, *The Robe*
  Montgomery Clift, *From Here to Eternity*
  Burt Lancaster, *From Here to Eternity*

BEST ACTRESS

- Audrey Hepburn, *Roman Holiday*
  Leslie Caron, *Lili*
  Ava Gardner, *Mogambo*
  Deborah Kerr, *From Here to Eternity*
  Maggie McNamara, *The Moon Is Blue*

BEST SUPPORTING ACTOR

- Frank Sinatra, *From Here to Eternity*
  Eddie Albert, *Roman Holiday*
  Brandon De Wilde, *Shane*
  Jack Palance, *Shane*
  Robert Strauss, *Stalag 17*

BEST SUPPORTING ACTRESS

- Donna Reed, *From Here to Eternity*
  Grace Kelly, *Mogambo*
  Geraldine Page, *Hondo*
  Marjorie Rambeau, *Torch Song*
  Thelma Ritter, *Pickup on South Street*

WRITING (MOTION PICTURE STORY)

- Ian McLellan Hunter, *Roman Holiday*

Beirne Lay, Jr., *Above and Beyond*

Alec Coppel, *The Captain's Paradise*

Joseph Burstyn, Ray Ashley, Morris Engel, Ruth Orkin, *The Little Fugitive*

Hondo (writer not eligible under Academy laws, since story was not an original)

WRITING (SCREENPLAY)

■ Daniel Taradash, *From Here to Eternity*

Eric Ambler, *The Cruel Sea*

Helen Deutsch, *Lili*

Ian McLellan Hunter, John Dighton, *Roman Holiday*

A. B. Guthrie, Jr., *Shane*

WRITING (STORY AND SCREENPLAY

■ Charles Brackett, Walter Reisch, Richard Breen, *Titanic*

Betty Comden, Adolph Green, *The Band Wagon*

Richard Murphy, *The Desert Rats*

Sam Rolfe, Harold Jack Bloom, *The Naked Spur*

Millard Kaufman, *Take the High Ground*

CINEMATOGRAPHY (BLACK-AND-WHITE)

■ Burnett Guffey, *From Here to Eternity*

Hal Mohr, *The Four Poster*

Joseph Ruttenberg, *Julius Caesar*

Joseph C. Brun, *Martin Luther*

Frank Planer, Henry Alekan, *Roman Holiday*

CINEMATOGRAPHY (COLOR)

■ Loyal Griggs, *Shane*

George Folsey, *All the Brothers Were Valiant*

Edward Cronjager, *Beneath the Twelve-Mile Reef*

Robert Planck, *Lili*

Leon Shamroy, *The Robe*

OTHER AWARDS:

ART DIRECTION / SET DIRECTION

Black-and-White:

■ Cedric Gibbons, Edward Carfagno; Edwin B. Willis, Hugh Hunt, *Julius Caesar*

Color:

■ Lyle Wheeler, George W. Davis; Walter M. Scott, Paul S. Fox, *The Robe*

SOUND RECORDING

■ Columbia Sound Dept., *From Here to Eternity*

SHORT SUBJECTS

Cartoons:

■ Walt Disney, Buena Vista, *Toot, Whistle, Plunk and Boom*

One-Reel:

■ MGM, *The Merry Wives of Windsor Overture*

Two-Reel:

■ Walt Disney, RKO, *Bear Country*

DOCUMENTARY

Short Subjects:

■ Walt Disney, RKO, *The Alaskan Eskimo*

Features:

■ Walt Disney, Buena Vista, *The Living Desert*

MUSIC

Best Song:

■ Sammy Fain, Paul Francis Webster, "Secret Love," *Calamity Jane*

Best Scoring of a Dramatic or Comedy Picture:

■ Bronislau Kaper, *Lili*

Best Scoring of a Musical Picture:
- Alfred Newman, *Call Me Madam*

FILM EDITING
- William Lyon, *From Here to Eternity*

SPECIAL EFFECTS

(from 1951–1953 given as an "other" award; hence no nominations)
- Paramount, *The War of the Worlds*

COSTUME DESIGN

Black-and-White:
- Edith Head, *Roman Holiday*

Color:
- Charles LeMaire, Emile Santiago, *The Robe*

HONORARY AND OTHER AWARDS
- Pete Smith, for his witty and pungent observations on the American scene in "Pete Smith Specialties"
- 20th Century-Fox Corp., in recognition of their imagination, showmanship and foresight in introducing CinemaScope
- Joseph I. Breen, for his conscientious, open-minded and dignified management of the Motion Picture Production Code

- Bell & Howell Co., for their pioneering achievements in advancing the motion picture industry

IRVING G. THALBERG MEMORIAL AWARD
- George Stevens

SCIENTIFIC OR TECHNICAL AWARDS

Class I:
- Professor Henri Chretien and Earl Sponable, Sol Halprin, Lorin Grignon, Herbert Bragg and Carl Faulkner of 20th Century-Fox Studios, for creating, developing, and engineering the equipment, processes and techniques known as CinemaScope
- Fred Waller, for designing and developing the multiple photographic and projection systems which culminated in Cinerama

Class II:
- Reeves Soundcraft Corp., for their development of a process of applying stripes of magnetic oxide to motion picture film for sound recording and reproduction

Class III:
- Westrex Corp., for the design and construction of a new film-editing machine

1954

BEST PICTURE

■ *On the Waterfront* (Columbia)
The Caine Mutiny (Kramer-Columbia)
The Country Girl (Paramount)
Seven Brides for Seven Brothers (MGM)
Three Coins in the Fountain (20th Century-Fox)

BEST DIRECTOR

■ Elia Kazan, *On the Waterfront*
Alfred Hitchcock, *Rear Window*
George Seaton, *The Country Girl*
William Wellman, *The High and the Mighty*
Billy Wilder, *Sabrina*

BEST ACTOR

■ Marlon Brando, *On the Waterfront*
Humphrey Bogart, *The Caine Mutiny*
Bing Crosby, *The Country Girl*
James Mason, *A Star Is Born*
Dan O'Herlihy, *Adventures of Robinson Crusoe*

BEST ACTRESS

■ Grace Kelly, *The Country Girl*
Dorothy Dandridge, *Carmen Jones*
Judy Garland, *A Star Is Born*
Audrey Hepburn, *Sabrina*
Jane Wyman, *Magnificent Obsession*

BEST SUPPORTING ACTOR

■ Edmond O'Brien, *The Barefoot Contessa*
Lee J. Cobb, *On the Waterfront*
Karl Malden, *On the Waterfront*
Rod Steiger, *On the Waterfront*
Tom Tully, *The Caine Mutiny*

BEST SUPPORTING ACTRESS

■ Eva Marie Saint, *On the Waterfront*
Nina Foch, *Executive Suite*
Katy Jurado, *Broken Lance*
Jan Sterling, *The High and the Mighty*
Claire Trevor, *The High and the Mighty*

WRITING (MOTION PICTURE STORY)

■ Philip Yordan, *Broken Lance*
Ettore Margadonna, *Bread, Love, and Dreams*
François Boyer, *Forbidden Games*
Jed Harris, Tom Reed, *Night People*
Lamar Trotti, *There's No Business Like Show Business*

WRITING (SCREENPLAY)

■ George Seaton, *The Country Girl*
Stanley Roberts, *The Caine Mutiny*
John Michael Hayes, *Rear Window*
Billy Wilder, Samuel Taylor, Ernest Lehman, *Sabrina*
Albert Hackett, Frances Goodrich, Dorothy Kingsley, *Seven Brides for Seven Brothers*

WRITING (STORY AND SCREENPLAY)

- Budd Schulberg, *On the Waterfront*

Joseph L. Mankiewicz, *The Barefoot Contessa*

William Rose, *Genevieve*

Valentine Davies, Oscar Brodney, *The Glenn Miller Story*

Norman Panama, Melvin Frank, *Knock on Wood*

CINEMATOGRAPHY (BLACK-AND-WHITE)

- Boris Kaufman, *On the Waterfront*

George Folsey, *Executive Suite*

John F. Warren, *The Country Girl*

John Seitz, *Rogue Cop*

Charles Lang, Jr., *Sabrina*

CINEMATOGRAPHY (COLOR)

- Milton Krasner, *Three Coins in the Fountain*

Leon Shamroy, *The Egyptian*

Robert Burks, *Rear Window*

George Folsey, *Seven Brides for Seven Brothers*

William V. Skall, *The Silver Chalice*

OTHER AWARDS:

ART DIRECTION / SET DIRECTION

Black-and-White:
- Richard Day, *On the Waterfront*

Color:
- John Meehan; Emile Kuri, *20,000 Leagues under the Sea*

SOUND RECORDING

- Leslie I. Carey, *The Glenn Miller Story*

SHORT SUBJECTS

Cartoons:
- UPA, Columbia, *When Magoo Flew*

One-Reel:
- Warner Bros., *This Mechanical Age*

Two-Reel:
- Carnival Productions, *A Time Out of War*

DOCUMENTARY

Short Subjects:
- British Information Services, *Thursday's Children*

Features:
- Walt Disney, Buena Vista, *The Vanishing Prairie*

MUSIC

Best Song:
- Jule Styne, Sammy Cahn, "Three Coins in the Fountain," *Three Coins in the Fountain*

Best Scoring of a Dramatic or Comedy Picture:
- Dimitri Tiomkin, *The High and the Mighty*

Best Scoring of a Musical Picture:
- Adolph Deutsch, Saul Chaplin, *Seven Brides for Seven Brothers*

FILM EDITING

- Gene Milford, *On the Waterfront*

SPECIAL EFFECTS

- Walt Disney, *20,000 Leagues under the Sea*

COSTUME DESIGN

Black-and-White:
- Edith Head, *Sabrina*

Color:
- Sanzo Wada, *Gate of Hell*

HONORARY AND OTHER AWARDS

- Bausch & Lomb Optical Co., for their contributions to the advancement of the motion picture industry
- Kemp R. Niver, for development of Renovare Process, which has made possible restoration of Library of Congress Paper Film Collection
- Greta Garbo, for her unforgettable screen performances
- Danny Kaye, for his unique talents, service to the Academy, the industry, and the American people
- Jon Whitely, for his outstanding juvenile performance in *The Little Kidnappers*
- Vincent Winter, for his outstanding juvenile performance in *The Little Kidnappers*
- *Gate of Hell* (Japan), for best foreign film released in the United States during 1954

SCIENTIFIC OR TECHNICAL AWARDS

Class I:

- Paramount Pictures, Inc., Loren L. Ryder, John R. Bishop, and all the members of the technical and engineering staff, for developing a method of producing and exhibiting motion pictures known as VistaVision

Class III:

- David S. Horsley and the Universal-International Studio Special Photographic Dept., for a portable remote-control device for process projectors
- Karl Freund and Frank Crandell of Photo Research Corp., for the design and development of a direct reading brightness meter
- Wesley C. Miller, J. W. Stafford, K. M. Frierson and MGM Studio Sound Dept., for an electronic sound-printing comparison device
- John P. Livadary, Lloyd Russell and the Columbia Studio Sound Dept., for an improved limiting amplifier as applied to sound level comparison devices
- Roland Miller and Max Goeppiger of Magnascope Corp., for the design and development of a cathode ray magnetic soundtrack viewer
- Carlos Rivas, G. M. Sprague and MGM Studio Sound Dept., for the design of a magntic sound editing machine
- Fred Wilson of the Samuel Goldwyn Studio Sound Dept., the design of a variable multiple-band equalizer
- P. C. Young of the MGM Studio Production Dept., for the practical application of a variable focal length attachment of motion picture projection lenses
- Fred Knoth and Orien Ernest of the Universal-International Studio Technical Dept., for the development of a hand-portable, electric, dry oil-fog machine

1955

BEST PICTURE

- *Marty* (Hecht-Lancaster, UA)
  *Love Is a Many-Splendored
  Thing* (20th Century-Fox)
  Mister Roberts (Warner Bros.)
  Picnic (Columbia)
  The Rose Tattoo (Wallis,
  Paramount)

BEST DIRECTOR

- Delbert Mann, *Marty*
  Elia Kazan, *East of Eden*
  David Lean, *Summertime*
  Joshua Logan, *Picnic*
  John Sturges, *Bad Day at Black
  Rock*

BEST ACTOR

- Ernest Borgnine, *Marty*
  James Cagney, *Love Me or
  Leave Me*
  James Dean, *East of Eden*
  Frank Sinatra, *The Man with
  the Golden Arm*
  Spencer Tracy, *Bad Day at
  Black Rock*

BEST ACTRESS

- Anna Magnani, *The Rose
  Tattoo*
  Susan Hayward, *I'll Cry
  Tomorrow*
  Katharine Hepburn, *Summer-
  time*
  Jennifer Jones, *Love Is a
  Many-Splendored Thing*
  Eleanor Parker, *Interrupted
  Melody*

BEST SUPPORTING ACTOR

- Jack Lemmon, *Mister Roberts*
  Arthur Kennedy, *Trial*
  Joe Mantell, *Marty*

Sal Mineo, *Rebel Without a
Cause*
Arthur O'Connell, *Picnic*

BEST SUPPORTING ACTRESS

- Jo Van Fleet, *East of Eden*
  Betsy Blair, *Marty*
  Peggy Lee, *Pete Kelly's Blues*
  Marisa Pavan, *The Rose Tattoo*
  Natalie Wood, *Rebel Without a
  Cause*

WRITING (MOTION PICTURE STORY)

- Daniel Fuchs, *Love Me or
  Leave Me*
  Joe Connelly, Bob Mosher,
  *The Private War of Major
  Benson*
  Nicholas Ray, *Rebel Without a
  Cause*
  Jean Marsan, Henry Troyat,
  Jacques Perrett, Henri
  Verneuil, Raoul Ploquin, *The
  Sheep Has Five Legs*
  Beirne Lay, Jr., *Strategic Air
  Command*

WRITING (SCREENPLAY)

- Paddy Chayefsky, *Marty*
  Millard Kaufman, *Bad Day at
  Black Rock*
  Richard Brooks, *The Black-
  board Jungle*
  Paul Osborn, *East of Eden*
  Daniel Fuchs, Isobel Lennart,
  Love Me or Leave Me

WRITING (STORY AND SCREENPLAY)

- William Ludwig, Sonya Levien,
  Interrupted Melody
  Milton Sperling, Emmet

Lavery, *The Court Martial of Billy Mitchell*

Betty Comden, Adolph Green, *It's Always Fair Weather*

Jacques Tati, Henri Marquet, *Mr. Hulot's Holiday*

Melville Shavelson, Jack Rose, *The Seven Little Foys*

CINEMATOGRAPHY (BLACK-AND-WHITE)

- James Wong Howe, *The Rose Tattoo*

  Russell Harlan, *Blackboard Jungle*

  Arthur E. Arling, *I'll Cry Tomorrow*

  Joseph LaShelle, *Marty*

  Charles Lang, *Queen Bee*

CINEMATOGRAPHY (COLOR)

- Robert Burks, *To Catch a Thief*

  Harry Stradling, *Guys and Dolls*

  Leon Shamroy, *Love Is a Many-Splendored Thing*

  Harold Lipstein, *A Man Called Peter*

  Robert Surtees, *Oklahoma!*

OTHER AWARDS:

ART DIRECTION / SET DIRECTION

Black-and-White:
- Hal Pereira, Tambi Larsen; Sam Comer, Arthur Krams, *The Rose Tattoo*

Color:
- William Flannery, Joe Mielziner; Robert Priestley, *Picnic*

SOUND RECORDING

- Todd-AO Sound Dept., *Oklahoma!*

SHORT SUBJECTS

Cartoons:
- Warner Bros., *Speedy Gonzales*

One-Reel:
- 20th Century-Fox, *Survival City*

Two-Reel:
- University of Southern California, *The Face of Lincoln*

DOCUMENTARY

Short Subjects:
- Walt Disney, Buena Vista, *Men Against the Arctic*

Features:
- Nancy Hamilton, *Helen Keller in Her Story*

MUSIC

Best Song:
- Sammy Fain, Paul Francis Webster, "Love Is a Many-Splendored Thing," *Love Is a Many-Splendored Thing*

Best Scoring of a Dramatic or Comedy Picture:
- Alfred Newman, *Love Is a Many-Splendored Thing*

Best Scoring of a Musical Picture:
- Robert Russell Bennett, Jay Blackton, Adolph Deutsch, *Oklahoma!*

FILM EDITING

- Charles Nelson, William A. Lyon, *Picnic*

SPECIAL EFFECTS

- Paramount, *The Bridges at Toko-Ri*

COSTUME DESIGN

Black-and-White:
- Helen Rose, *I'll Cry Tomorrow*

Color:
- Charles LeMaire, *Love Is a Many-Splendored Thing*

HONORARY AND OTHER AWARDS

- *Samurai* (Japan), for best foreign-language film, first released in the United States during 1955

SCIENTIFIC OR TECHNICAL AWARDS

Class I:
- National Carbon Co., for the development and production of a high-efficiency yellow flame carbon for motion picture color photography

Class II:
- Eastman Kodak Co., for Eastman Tri-X panchromatic negative film
- Farciot Edouart, Hal Corl and Paramount Studio Transparency Dept., for the engineering and development of a double-frame, triple-head background projector

Class III:
- 20th Century-Fox Studio and Bausch & Lomb Co., for the new combination lenses for CinemaScope photography

- Walter Jolley, Maurice Larson, and R. H. Spies of 20th Century-Fox Studio, for a spraying process which creates simulated metallic surfaces
- Steve Krilanovich, for an improved camera dolly incorporating multidirectional steering
- David Anderson of 20th Century Studio, for an improved spotlight capable of maintaining a fixed circle of light at constant intensity over varied distances
- Loren L. Ryder, Charles West, Henry Fracker and Paramount Studio, for a projection film index to establish proper framing for various aspect ratios
- Farciot Edouart, Hal Corl and Paramount Studio Transparency Dept., for an improved dual stereopticon background projector

1956

BEST PICTURE
- *Around the World in 80 Days* (Todd-UA)
  Friendly Persuasion (Allied Artists)
  Giant (Warner Bros.)
  The King and I (20th Century-Fox)
  The Ten Commandments (DeMille-Paramount)

BEST DIRECTOR
- George Stevens, *Giant*
  Michael Anderson, *Around the World in 80 Days*
  Walter Lang, *The King and I*
  King Vidor, *War and Peace*
  William Wyler, *Friendly Persuasion*

BEST ACTOR
- Yul Brynner, *The King and I*
  James Dean, *Giant*
  Kirk Douglas, *Lust for Life*

Rock Hudson, *Giant*
Sir Laurence Olivier, *Richard III*

BEST ACTRESS

- Ingrid Bergman, *Anastasia*
Carroll Baker, *Baby Doll*
Katharine Hepburn, *The Rainmaker*
Nancy Kelly, *The Bad Seed*
Deborah Kerr, *The King and I*

BEST SUPPORTING ACTOR

- Anthony Quinn, *Lust for Life*
Don Murray, *Bus Stop*
Anthony Perkins, *Friendly Persuasion*
Mickey Rooney, *The Bold and the Brave*
Robert Stack, *Written on the Wind*

BEST SUPPORTING ACTRESS

- Dorothy Malone, *Written on the Wind*
Mildred Dunnock, *Baby Doll*
Eileen Heckart, *The Bad Seed*
Mercedes McCambridge, *Giant*
Patty McCormack, *The Bad Seed*

WRITING (MOTION PICTURE STORY)

- *The Brave One* (At the time of the award, writer credit had not been established. The story was attributed to "Robert Rich," pseudonym for Dalton Trumbo, one of the blacklisted Hollywood Ten. In May 1975 Trumbo at last received the award.)
Leo Katcher, *The Eddy Duchin Story*
Edward Bernds, Elwood Ullman (withdrawn from final ballot), *High Society*

Jean-Paul Sartre, *The Proud and the Beautiful*
Cesare Zavattini, *Umberto D.*

WRITING (BEST SCREENPLAY) ADAPTED)

- James Poe, John Farrow, S. J. Perelman, *Around the World in 80 Days*
Tennessee Williams, *Baby Doll*
Fred Guiol, Ivan Moffat, *Giant*
Norman Corwin, *Lust for Life*
Friendly Persuasion (Writer ineligible for nomination under Academy bylaws which forbid any person who is a professed Communist or who refuses to deny such to receive an Academy Award. This bylaw was in effect from February 1957 to January 1959.)

WRITING (BEST SCREENPLAY) ORIGINAL)

- Albert Lamorisse, *The Red Balloon*
Robert Lewin, *The Bold and the Brave*
Federico Fellini, Tullio Pinelli, *La Strada*
William Rose, *The Lady Killers*
Andrew L. Stone, *Julie*

CINEMATOGRAPHY (BLACK-AND-WHITE)

- Joseph Ruttenberg, *Somebody Up There Likes Me*
Boris Kaufman, *Baby Doll*
Hal Rosson, *The Bad Seed*
Burnett Guffey, *The Harder They Fall*
Walter Strenge, *Stagecoach to Fury*

CINEMATOGRAPHY (COLOR)

- Lionel Lindon, *Around the World in 80 Days*

Harry Stradling, *The Eddy Duchin Story*
Leon Shamroy, *The King and I*
Loyal Griggs, *The Ten Commandments*
Jack Cardiff, *War and Peace*

FOREIGN-LANGUAGE FILM

(first year of nomination)

- *La Strada* (Italy)
  The Captain of Koepenick (Germany)
  Gervaise (France)
  Harp of Burma (Japan)
  Qivitoq (Denmark)

OTHER AWARDS:

ART DIRECTION / SET DIRECTION

Black-and-White:
- Cedric Gibbons, Malcolm F. Brown; Edwin B. Willis, F. Keogh Gleason, *Somebody Up There Likes Me*

Color:
- Lyle R. Wheeler, John DeCuir; Walter M. Scott, Paul S. Fox, *The King and I*

SOUND RECORDING

- 20th Century-Fox Sound Dept., *The King and I*

SHORT SUBJECTS

Cartoons:
- UPA, Columbia, *Mister Magoo's Puddle Jumper*

One-Reel:
- Warner Bros., *Crashing the Water Barrier*

Two-Reel:
- George K. Arthur, *The Bespoke Overcoat*

DOCUMENTARY

Short Subjects:
- Camera Eye Pictures, *The True Story of the Civil War*

Features:
- Cousteau-Columbia, *The Silent World*

MUSIC

Best Song:
- Jay Livingston, Ray Evans, "Whatever Will Be, Will Be," *The Man Who Knew Too Much*

Best Scoring of a Dramatic or Comedy Picture:
- Victor Young, *Around the World in 80 Days*

Best Scoring of a Musical Picture:
- Alfred Newman, Ken Darby, *The King and I*

FILM EDITING

- Gene Ruggiero, Paul Weatherwax, *Around the World in 80 Days*

SPECIAL EFFECTS

- John Fulton, *The Ten Commandments*

COSTUME DESIGN

Black-and-White:
- Jean Louis, *The Solid Gold Cadillac*

Color:
- Irene Sharaff, *The King and I*

HONORARY AND OTHER AWARDS

- Eddie Cantor, for distinguished service to the film industry

IRVING G. THALBERG MEMORIAL AWARD

- Buddy Adler

JEAN HERSHOLT HUMANITARIAN AWARD

- Y. Frank Freeman

SCIENTIFIC OR TECHNICAL AWARDS

Class III:

- Richard H. Ranger of Ranger-tone, Inc., for the development of a synchronous recording and reproducing system for quarter-inch magnetic tape
- Ted Hirsch, Carl Hauge and Edward Reichard of Consolidated Film Industries, for an automatic scene counter for laboratory projection rooms
- Technical Depts. of Paramount Pictures Corp., for the engineering and development of the Paramount lightweight horizontal-movement Vista-Vision camera
- Roy C. Stewart and Sons of Stewart-Trans Lux Corp., Dr. C. R. Daily and the Transparency Dept. of Paramount Pictures Corp., for the engineering and development of the HiTrans and Para-HiTrans rear projection screens
- Construction Dept. of MGM Studio, for a new hand-portable fog machine
- Daniel J. Bloomberg, John Pond, William Wade and the Engineering and Camera Depts. of Republic Studio, for the Naturama adaptation to the Mitchell camera

---

1957

BEST PICTURE

- *The Bridge on the River Kwai* (Columbia)

  Peyton Place (20th Century-Fox)

  Sayonara (Warner Bros.)

  Twelve Angry Men (UA)

  Witness for the Prosecution (UA)

BEST DIRECTOR

- David Lean, *The Bridge on the River Kwai*

  Joshua Logan, *Sayonara*

  Sidney Lumet, *Twelve Angry Men*

  Mark Robson, *Peyton Place*

  Billy Wilder, *Witness for the Prosecution*

BEST ACTOR

- Alec Guinness, *The Bridge on the River Kwai*

  Marlon Brando, *Sayonara*

  Anthony Franciosa, *A Hatful of Rain*

  Charles Laughton, *Witness for the Prosecution*

  Anthony Quinn, *Wild Is the Wind*

BEST ACTRESS

- Joanne Woodward, *The Three Faces of Eve*

  Deborah Kerr, *Heaven Knows, Mr. Allison*

  Anna Magnani, *Wild Is the Wind*

  Elizabeth Taylor, *Raintree County*

  Lana Turner, *Peyton Place*

BEST SUPPORTING ACTOR

- Red Buttons, *Sayonara*
  Vittorio De Sica, *A Farewell to Arms*
  Sessue Hayakawa, *The Bridge on the River Kwai*
  Arthur Kennedy, *Peyton Place*
  Russ Tamblyn, *Peyton Place*

BEST SUPPORTING ACTRESS

- Miyoshi Umeki, *Sayonara*
  Carolyn Jones, *The Bachelor Party*
  Elsa Lanchester, *Witness for the Prosecution*
  Hope Lange, *Peyton Place*
  Diane Varsi, *Peyton Place*

BEST SCREENPLAY (BASED ON MATERIAL FROM ANOTHER MEDIUM)

- Pierre Boulle, *The Bridge on the River Kwai*
  John Lee Mahin, John Huston, *Heaven Knows, Mr. Allison*
  John Michael Hayes, *Peyton Place*
  Paul Osborn, *Sayonara*
  Reginald Rose, *Twelve Angry Men*

BEST STORY AND SCREENPLAY (WRITTEN DIRECTLY FOR THE SCREEN)

- George Wells, *Designing Woman*
  Leonard Gershe, *Funny Face*
  Ralph Wheelwright, R. Right Campbell, Ivan Goff, Ben Roberts, *Man of a Thousand Faces*
  Barney Slater, Joel Kane, Dudley Nichols, *The Tin Star*
  Federico Fellini, Ennio Flajano, Tullio Pinelli, *I Vitelloni*

CINEMATOGRAPHY

(not separated this year into black-and-white and color)

- Jack Hildyard, *The Bridge on the River Kwai*
  Milton Krasner, *An Affair to Remember*
  Ray June, *Funny Face*
  William Mellor, *Peyton Place*
  Ellsworth Fredericks, *Sayonara*

FOREIGN-LANGUAGE FILM

- *The Nights of Cabiria* (Italy)
  The Devil Came at Night (Germany)
  Gates of Paris (France)
  Mother India (India)
  Nine Lives (Norway)

OTHER AWARDS:

ART DIRECTION / SET DIRECTION

(awards not separated this year into black-and-white and color)

- Ted Haworth; Robert Priestley, *Sayonara*

SOUND RECORDING

- Warner Bros. Sound Dept., *Sayonara*

SHORT SUBJECTS

(rules changed this year to two awards instead of three)

Cartoons:
- Warner Bros., *Birds Anonymous*

Live Action Subjects:
- Walt Disney, Buena Vista, *The Wetback Hound*

DOCUMENTARY

(no short subject voted this year)

Features:

- Hill and Anderson, Louis de Rochemont, *Albert Schweitzer*

MUSIC

Best Song:

- James Van Heusen, Sammy Cahn, "All the Way," *The Joker Is Wild*

Best Score:

(awards not divided this year into "dramatic or comedy" and "musical" categories)

- Malcolm Arnold, *The Bridge on the River Kwai*

FILM EDITING

- Peter Taylor, *The Bridge on the River Kwai*

SPECIAL EFFECTS

- Walter Rossi, *The Enemy Below*

COSTUME DESIGN

(one award given this year instead of the previous two)

- Orry-Kelly, *Les Girls*

HONORARY AND OTHER AWARDS

- Charles Brackett, for outstanding service to the Academy
- B. B. Kahane, for distinguished service to the motion picture industry
- Gilbert M. ("Broncho Billy") Anderson, for his contributions to development of movies as entertainment
- Society of Motion Picture and Television Engineers, for their contributions to the advancement of the industry

JEAN HERSHOLT HUMANITARIAN AWARD

- Samuel Goldwyn

SCIENTIFIC OR TECHNICAL AWARDS

Class I:

- Todd-AO Corp. and Westrex Corp., for developing a method of producing and exhibiting wide-film motion pictures known as the Todd-AO System
- Motion Picture Research Council, for the design and development of a high-efficiency projection screen for drive-in theaters

Class II:

- The Société d'Optique et de Mécanique de Haute Précision, for the development of a high-speed vari-focal photographic lens
- Harlan L. Baumbach, Lorand Wargo, Howard M. Little and the Unicorn Engineering Corp., for the development of an automatic printer light selector

Class III:

- Charles E. Sutter, William B. Smith, Paramount Pictures Corp. and General Cable Corp., for the engineering and application to studio use of aluminum lightweight electrical cable and connectors

1958

BEST PICTURE

- *Gigi* (MGM)
  Auntie Mame (Warner Bros.)
  Cat on a Hot Tin Roof (MGM)
  The Defiant Ones (Kramer–UA)
  Separate Tables (Hecht-Hill-Lancaster–UA)

BEST DIRECTOR

- Vincente Minnelli, *Gigi*
  Richard Brooks, *Cat on a Hot Tin Roof*
  Stanley Kramer, *The Defiant Ones*
  Mark Robson, *The Inn of the Sixth Happiness*
  Robert Wise, *I Want to Live!*

BEST ACTOR

- David Niven, *Separate Tables*
  Tony Curtis, *The Defiant Ones*
  Paul Newman, *Cat on a Hot Tin Roof*
  Sidney Poitier, *The Defiant Ones*
  Spencer Tracy, *The Old Man and the Sea*

BEST ACTRESS

- Susan Hayward, *I Want to Live!*
  Deborah Kerr, *Separate Tables*
  Shirley MacLaine, *Some Came Running*
  Rosalind Russell, *Auntie Mame*
  Elizabeth Taylor, *Cat on a Hot Tin Roof*

BEST SUPPORTING ACTOR

- Burl Ives, *The Big Country*
  Theodore Bikel, *The Defiant Ones*
  Lee J. Cobb, *The Brothers Karamazov*
  Arthur Kennedy, *Some Came Running*
  Gig Young, *Teacher's Pet*

BEST SUPPORTING ACTRESS

- Wendy Hiller, *Separate Tables*
  Peggy Cass, *Auntie Mame*
  Martha Hyer, *Some Came Running*
  Maureen Stapleton, *Lonelyhearts*
  Cara Williams, *The Defiant Ones*

BEST SCREENPLAY (BASED ON MATERIAL FROM ANOTHER MEDIUM)

- Alan Jay Lerner, *Gigi*
  Richard Brooks, James Poe, *Cat on a Hot Tin Roof*
  Alec Guinness, *The Horse's Mouth*
  Nelson Gidding, Don Mankiewicz, *I Want to Live!*
  Terence Rattigan, John Gay, *Separate Tables*

BEST STORY AND SCREENPLAY (WRITING DIRECTLY FOR THE SCREEN)

- Nathan E. Douglas, Harold Jacob Smith, *The Defiant Ones*
  Paddy Chayefsky, *The Goddess*
  Melville Shavelson, Jack Rose, *Houseboat*
  James Edward Grant (story); William Bowers and James Edward Grant (screenplay), *The Sheepmen*
  Fay and Michael Kanin, *Teacher's Pet*

CINEMATOGRAPHY (BLACK-AND-WHITE)

- Sam Leavitt, *The Defiant Ones*
  Daniel L. Fapp, *Desire Under the Elms*
  Lionel Lindon, *I Want to Live!*
  Charles Lang, Jr., *Separate Tables*
  Joe MacDonald, *The Young Lions*

CINEMATOGRAPHY (COLOR)

- Joseph Ruttenberg, *Gigi*
  Harry Stradling, *Auntie Mame*
  William Daniels, *Cat on a Hot Tin Roof*
  James Wong Howe, *The Old Man and the Sea*
  Leon Shamroy, *South Pacific*

FOREIGN-LANGUAGE FILM

- *My Uncle* (France)
  Arms and the Man (Germany)
  La Venganza (Spain)
  The Road a Year Long (Yugoslavia)
  The Usual Unidentified Thieves (Italy)

OTHER AWARDS:

ART DIRECTION / SET DIRECTION

- William A. Horning, Preston Ames; Henry Grace, Keogh Gleason, *Gigi*

SOUND

- Todd-AO Sound Dept., *South Pacific*

SHORT SUBJECTS

Cartoons:
- Warner Bros., *Knighty Knight Bugs*

Live Action Subjects:
- Walt Disney, Buena Vista, *Grand Canyon*

DOCUMENTARY

Short Subjects:
- Walt Disney, Buena Vista, *Ama Girls*

Features:
- Walt Disney, Buena Vista, *White Wilderness*

MUSIC

Best Song:
- Frederick Loewe, Alan Jay Lerner, "Gigi," *Gigi*

Best Scoring of a Dramatic or Comedy Picture:
- Dimitri Tiomkin, *The Old Man and the Sea*

Best Scoring of a Musical Picture:
- André Previn, *Gigi*

FILM EDITING

- Adrienne Fazan, *Gigi*

SPECIAL EFFECTS

- Tom Howard, *tom thumb*

COSTUME DESIGN

Black-and-White or Color:
- Cecil Beaton, *Gigi*

HONORARY AND OTHER AWARDS

- Maurice Chevalier, for his contributions to world of entertainment for more than half a century

IRVING G. THALBERG MEMORIAL AWARD

- Jack L. Warner

SCIENTIFIC OR TECHNICAL AWARDS

Class II:
- Don W. Prideaux, LeRoy G. Leighton and the Lamp Division of General Electric Co., for the development

and production of an improved 10-kilowatt lamp for motion picture set lighting

- Panavision, Inc., for the design and development of the Auto Panatar anamorphic photographic lens for 35mm CinemaScope photography

Class III:

- Willy Borberg of the General Precision Laboratory, Inc.,

for the development of a high-speed intermittent movement for 35mm motion picture theater projection equipment

- Fred Ponedel, George Brown and Conrad Boye of the Warner Bros. Special Effects Dept., for the design and fabrication of a new rapid-fire marble gun

---

1959

BEST PICTURE

- *Ben-Hur* (MGM)
  Anatomy of a Murder (Preminger-Columbia)
  The Diary of Anne Frank (Stevens–20th Century-Fox)
  The Nun's Story (Zinnemann–Warner Bros.)
  Room at the Top (Continental)

BEST DIRECTOR

- William Wyler, *Ben-Hur*
  Jack Clayton, *Room at the Top*
  George Stevens, *The Diary of Anne Frank*
  Billy Wilder, *Some Like It Hot*
  Fred Zinnemann, *The Nun's Story*

BEST ACTOR

- Charlton Heston, *Ben-Hur*
  Laurence Harvey, *Room at the Top*
  Jack Lemmon, *Some Like It Hot*
  Paul Muni, *The Last Angry Man*
  James Stewart, *Anatomy of a Murder*

BEST ACTRESS

- Simone Signoret, *Room at the Top*
  Doris Day, *Pillow Talk*
  Audrey Hepburn, *The Nun's Story*
  Katharine Hepburn, *Suddenly, Last Summer*
  Elizabeth Taylor. *Suddenly, Last Summer*

BEST SUPPORTING ACTOR

- Hugh Griffith, *Ben-Hur*
  Arthur O'Connell, *Anatomy of a Murder*
  George C. Scott, *Anatomy of a Murder*
  Robert Vaughn, *The Young Philadelphians*
  Ed Wynn, *The Diary of Anne Frank*

BEST SUPPORTING ACTRESS

- Shelley Winters, *The Diary of Anne Frank*
  Hermione Baddeley, *Room at the Top*
  Juanita Moore, *Imitation of Life*

Susan Kohner, *Imitation of Life*
Thelma Ritter, *Pillow Talk*

BEST SCREENPLAY (BASED ON MATERIAL FROM ANOTHER MEDIUM)

- Neil Paterson, *Room at the Top*
  Wendell Mayes, *Anatomy of a Murder*
  Karl Tunberg, *Ben-Hur*
  Robert Anderson, *The Nun's Story*
  Billy Wilder, I. A. L. Diamond, *Some Like It Hot*

BEST STORY AND SCREENPLAY (WRITTEN DIRECTLY FOR THE SCREEN)

- Russell Rouse, Clarence Greene (story); Stanley Shapiro, Maurice Richlin (screenplay), *Pillow Talk*
  François Truffaut, Marcel Moussy, *The 400 Blows*
  Ernest Lehman, *North by Northwest*
  Paul King, Joseph Stone (story); Stanley Shapiro, Maurice Richlin (screenplay), *Operation Petticoat*
  Ingmar Bergman, *Wild Strawberries*

CINEMATOGRAPHY (BLACK-AND-WHITE)

- William C. Mellor, *The Diary of Anne Frank*
  Sam Leavitt, *Anatomy of a Murder*
  Joseph LaShelle, *Career*
  Charles Lang, Jr., *Some Like It Hot*
  Harry Stradling, *The Young Philadelphians*

CINEMATOGRAPHY (COLOR)

- Robert L. Surtees, *Ben-Hur*
  Lee Garmes, *The Big Fisherman*

Daniel L. Fapp, *The Five Pennies*
Franz Planer, *The Nun's Story*
Leon Shamroy, *Porgy and Bess*

FOREIGN-LANGUAGE FILM

- *Black Orpheus* (France)
  The Bridge (Germany)
  The Great War (Italy)
  Paw (Denmark)
  The Village on the River (The Netherlands)

OTHER AWARDS:

ART DIRECTION / SET DIRECTION

Black-and-White:
- Lyle R. Wheeler, George W. Davis; Walter M. Scott, Stuart A. Reiss, *The Diary of Anne Frank*

Color:
- William A. Horning, Edward Carfagno; Hugh Hunt, *Ben-Hur*

SOUND

- MGM Sound Dept., *Ben-Hur*

SHORT SUBJECTS

Cartoons:
- Storybook, Inc., *Moonbird*

Live Action Subjects:
- Jacques-Yves Cousteau, *The Golden Fish*

DOCUMENTARY

Short Subjects:
- George K. Arthur, Netherlands govn., *Glass*

Features:
- Okapia-Film Prod., Transocean-Film, *Serengeti Shall Not Die*

MUSIC

Best Song:
- James Van Heusen, Sammy

Cahn, "High Hopes," *A Hole in the Head*

Best Scoring of a Dramatic or Comedy Picture:

- Miklos Rozsa, *Ben-Hur*

Best Scoring of a Musical Picture:

- André Previn, Ken Darby, *Porgy and Bess*

FILM EDITING

- Ralph E. Winters, John D. Dunning, *Ben-Hur*

SPECIAL EFFECTS

- A. Arnold Gillespie, Robert MacDonald, Milo Lory, *Ben-Hur*

COSTUME DESIGN

Black-and-White:

- Orry-Kelly, *Some Like It Hot*

Color:

- Elizabeth Haffenden, *Ben-Hur*

HONORARY AND OTHER AWARDS

- Lee De Forest, for his pioneering inventions which brought sound to the motion picture
- Buster Keaton, for his unique talents which brought immortal comedies to the screen

JEAN HERSHOLT HUMANITARIAN AWARD

- Bob Hope

SCIENTIFIC OR TECHNICAL AWARDS

Class II:

- Douglas G. Shearer of MGM, Inc., and Robert E. Gottschalk and John R. Moore of Panavision Inc., for the development of a system of producing and exhibiting wide-film motion pictures known as Camera 65
- Wadsworth E. Pohl, William Evans, Werner Hopf, S. E. Howse, Thomas P. Dixon, Stanford Research Institute and Technicolor Corp., for the design and development of the Technicolor electronic printing timer
- Wadsworth E. Pohl, Jack Alford, Henry Imus, Joseph Schmit, Paul Fassnacht, Al Lofquist and Technicolor Corp., for the development and practical application of equipment for wet printing
- Dr. Howard S. Coleman, Dr. A. Francis Turner, Harold H. Schroeder, James R. Benford and Harold E. Rosenberger of the Bausch & Lomb Optical Co., for the design and development of the Balcold projection mirror
- Robert P. Gutterman of General Kinetics, Inc., and Lipsner-Smith Corp., for the design and development of the CF-2 Ultra-sonic Film Cleaner

Class III:

- Ub Iwerks of Walt Disney Prods., for the design of an improved optical printer for special effects and matte shots
- E. L. Stones, Glen Robinson, Winfield Hubbard and Luther Newman of MGM Studio Construction Dept., for the design of a multiple-cable remote-controlled winch

1960

BEST PICTURE

■ *The Apartment* (Mirisch–
   UA)
The Alamo (UA)
Elmer Gantry (UA)
Sons and Lovers (Wald–20th
   Century-Fox)
The Sundowners (Warner
   Bros.)

BEST DIRECTOR

■ Billy Wilder, *The Apartment*
Jack Cardiff, *Sons and Lovers*
Jules Dassin, *Never on Sunday*
Alfred Hitchcock, *Psycho*
Fred Zinnemann, *The Sun-
   downers*

BEST ACTOR

■ Burt Lancaster, *Elmer Gantry*
Trevor Howard, *Sons and
   Lovers*
Jack Lemmon, *The Apartment*
Laurence Olivier, *The
   Entertainer*
Spencer Tracy, *Inherit the
   Wind*

BEST ACTRESS

■ Elizabeth Taylor, *Butterfield 8*
Greer Garson, *Sunrise at
   Campobello*
Deborah Kerr, *The Sundowners*
Shirley MacLaine, *The
   Apartment*
Melina Mercouri, *Never on
   Sunday*

BEST SUPPORTING ACTOR

■ Peter Ustinov, *Spartacus*
Peter Falk, *Murder, Inc.*
Jack Kruschen, *The Apartment*

Sal Mineo, *Exodus*
Chill Wills, *The Alamo*

BEST SUPPORTING ACTRESS

■ Shirley Jones, *Elmer Gantry*
Glynis Johns, *The Sundowners*
Shirley Knight, *The Dark at the
   Top of the Stairs*
Janet Leigh, *Psycho*
Mary Ure, *Sons and Lovers*

BEST SCREENPLAY (BASED ON MATERIAL FROM ANOTHER MEDIUM)

■ Richard Brooks, *Elmer Gantry*
Nathan E. Douglas, Harold
   Jacob Smith, *Inherit the
   Wind*
Gavin Lambert, T. E. B. Clarke,
   Sons and Lovers
Isobel Lennart, *The Sun-
   downers*
James Kennaway, *Tunes of
   Glory*

BEST STORY AND SCREENPLAY (WRITTEN DIRECTLY FOR THE SCREEN)

■ Billy Wilder, I. A. L. Diamond,
   The Apartment
Richard Gregson, Michael
   Craig, Bryan Forbes, *The
   Angry Silence*
Norman Panama, Melvin Frank,
   The Facts of Life
Marguerite Duras, *Hiroshima,
   Mon Amour*
Jules Dassin, *Never on Sunday*

CINEMATOGRAPHY (BLACK-AND-WHITE)

■ Freddie Francis, *Sons and
   Lovers*

Joseph LaShelle, *The Apartment*
Charles B. Lang, Jr., *The Facts of Life*
Ernest Laszlo, *Inherit the Wind*
John L. Russell, *Psycho*

CINEMATOGRAPHY (COLOR)

- Russell Metty, *Spartacus*
  William H. Clothier, *The Alamo*
  Joseph Ruttenberg, Charles Harten, *Butterfield 8*
  Sam Leavitt, *Exodus*
  Joe MacDonald, *Pepe*

FOREIGN-LANGUAGE FILM

- *The Virgin Spring* (Sweden)
  Kapo (Italy)
  La Vérité (France)
  Macario (Mexico)
  The Ninth Circle (Yugoslavia)

OTHER AWARDS:

ART DIRECTION / SET DIRECTION

Black-and-White:
- Alexander Trauner; Edward G. Boyle, *The Apartment*

Color:
- Alexander Golitzen, Eric Orbom; Russell A. Gausman, Julia Heron, *Spartacus*

SOUND

- Samuel Goldwyn Studio Sound Dept. and Todd-AO Sound Dept., *The Alamo*

SHORT SUBJECTS

Cartoons:
- Rembrandt Films, Film Representations, Inc., *Munro*

Live Action Subjects:
- Kingsley–Union Films, *Day of the Painter*

DOCUMENTARY

Short Subjects:
- James Hill Prod., Lester A.

Schoenfeld Films, *Giuseppina*

Features:
- Walt Disney, Buena Vista, *The Horse with the Flying Tail*

MUSIC

Best Song:
- Manos Hadjidakis, "Never on Sunday," *Never on Sunday*

Best Scoring of a Dramatic or Comedy Picture:
- Ernest Gold, *Exodus*

Best Scoring of a Musical Picture:
- Morris Stoloff, Harry Sukman, *Song Without End*

FILM EDITING

- Daniel Mandell, *The Apartment*

SPECIAL EFFECTS

- Gene Warren, Tim Baar, *The Time Machine*

COSTUME DESIGN

Black-and-White:
- Edith Head, Edward Stevenson, *The Facts of Life*

Color:
- Valles, Bill Thomas, *Spartacus*

HONORARY AND OTHER AWARDS

- Gary Cooper, for his many memorable performances and the international recognition he, as an individual, has gained for the industry
- Stan Laurel, for his creative pioneering in the field of cinema comedy
- Hayley Mills, for *Pollyanna*, the most outstanding juvenile performance during 1960

JEAN HERSHOLT HUMANITARIAN AWARD

- Sol Lesser

SCIENTIFIC OR TECHNICAL AWARDS

Class II:

- Ampex Professional Products Co., for the production of a well-engineered multipurpose sound system combining high standards of quality with convenience of control, dependable operation and simplified emergency provisions

Class III:

- Arthur Holcomb, Petro Vlahos and Columbia Studio Camera Dept., for a camera flicker indicating device
- Anthony Paglia and 20th Century-Fox Studio Mechanical Effects Dept., for the design and construction of a miniature flak gun and ammunition
- Carl Hauge, Robert Grubel and Edward Reichard of Consolidated Film Industries, for the development of an automatic developer replenisher system

1961

BEST PICTURE

- *West Side Story* (Mirisch–UA)
  Fanny (Logan–Warner Bros.)
  The Guns of Navarone (Foreman-Columbia)
  The Hustler (Rossen–20th Century-Fox)
  Judgment at Nuremberg (Kramer–UA)

BEST DIRECTOR

- Robert Wise, Jerome Robbins, *West Side Story*
  Federico Fellini, *La Dolce Vita*
  Stanley Kramer, *Judgment at Nuremberg*
  Robert Rossen, *The Hustler*
  J. Lee Thompson, *The Guns of Navarone*

BEST ACTOR

- Maximilian Schell, *Judgment at Nuremberg*
  Charles Boyer, *Fanny*
  Paul Newman, *The Hustler*
  Spencer Tracy, *Judgment at Nuremberg*
  Stuart Whitman, *The Mark*

BEST ACTRESS

- Sophia Loren, *Two Women*
  Audrey Hepburn, *Breakfast at Tiffany's*
  Piper Laurie, *The Hustler*
  Geraldine Page, *Summer and Smoke*
  Natalie Wood, *Splendor in the Grass*

BEST SUPPORTING ACTOR

- George Chakiris, *West Side Story*
  Montgomery Clift, *Judgment at Nuremberg*
  Peter Falk, *Pocketful of Miracles*
  Jackie Gleason, *The Hustler*

George C. Scott, *The Hustler*
(nomination refused)

BEST SUPPORTING ACTRESS

- Rita Moreno, *West Side Story*
Fay Bainter, *The Children's Hour*
Judy Garland, *Judgment at Nuremberg*
Lotte Lenya, *The Roman Spring of Mrs. Stone*
Una Merkel, *Summer and Smoke*

BEST SCREENPLAY (BASED ON MATERIAL FROM ANOTHER MEDIUM)

- Abby Mann, *Judgment at Nuremberg*
George Axelrod, *Breakfast at Tiffany's*
Carl Foreman, *The Guns of Navarone*
Sidney Carroll, Robert Rossen, *The Hustler*
Ernest Lehman, *West Side Story*

BEST STORY AND SCREENPLAY (WRITTEN DIRECTLY FOR THE SCREEN)

- William Inge, *Splendor in the Grass*
Valentin Yoshov, Grigori Chukhrai, *Ballad of a Soldier*
Sergio Amidei, Diego Fabbri, Indro Montanelli, *General della Rovere*
Federico Fellini, Tullio Pinelli, Ennio Flaiano, Brunello Rondi, *La Dolce Vita*
Stanley Shapiro, Paul Henning, *Lover Come Back*

CINEMATOGRAPHY (BLACK-AND-WHITE)

- Eugen Shuftan, *The Hustler*
Edward Colman, *The Absent-Minded Professor*

Franz F. Planer, *The Children's Hour*
Ernest Laszlo, *Judgment at Nuremberg*
Daniel L. Fapp, *One, Two, Three*

CINEMATOGRAPHY (COLOR)

- Daniel L. Fapp, *West Side Story*
Jack Cardiff, *Fanny*
Russell Metty, *Flower Drum Song*
Harry Stradling, *A Majority of One*
Charles Lang, Jr., *One-Eyed Jacks*

FOREIGN-LANGUAGE FILM

- *Through a Glass Darkly* (Sweden)
Harry and the Butler (Denmark)
Immortal Love (Japan)
The Important Man (Mexico)
Placido (Spain)

OTHER AWARDS:

ART DIRECTION / SET DIRECTION

Black-and-White:
- Harry Horner; Gene Callahan, *The Hustler*
Color:
- Boris Leven; Victor Gangelin, *West Side Story*

SOUND

- Todd-AO Sound Dept. and Samuel Goldwyn Sound Dept., *West Side Story*

SHORT SUBJECTS

Cartoons:
- Zagreb Film, *Erstaz*
Live Action Subjects:
- Templar Film Studios, *Seawards the Great Ships*

DOCUMENTARY

Short Subjects:
- Klaeger Film, *Project Hope*

Features:
- Ardennes Films and Michael Arthur Films Prods., Rank Film Distributors, *Le Ciel et la Boue* (The Sky Above and the Mud Below)

MUSIC

Best Song:
- Henry Mancini, Johnny Mercer, "Moon River," *Breakfast at Tiffany's*

Best Scoring of a Dramatic or Comedy Picture:
- Henry Mancini, *Breakfast at Tiffany's*

Best Scoring of a Musical Picture:
- Saul Chaplin, Johnny Green, Sid Ramin, Irwin Kostal, *West Side Story*

FILM EDITING

- Thomas Stanford, *West Side Story*

SPECIAL EFFECTS

- Bill Warrington, Vivian C. Greeham, *The Guns of Navarone*

COSTUME DESIGN

Black-and-White:
- Piero Gherardi, *La Dolce Vita*

Color:
- Irene Sharaff, *West Side Story*

HONORARY AND OTHER AWARDS

- William L. Hendricks, for his outstanding patriotic service in the Marine Corps Film *A Force in Readiness* which has brought honor to the Academy and the industry

- Fred L. Metzler, for his dedication and outstanding service to the Academy
- Jerome Robbins, for his brilliant achievements in film choreography

IRVING G. THALBERG MEMORIAL AWARD

- Stanley Kramer

JEAN HERSHOLT HUMANITARIAN AWARD

- George Seaton

SCIENTIFIC OR TECHNICAL AWARDS

Class II:
- Sylvania Electric Products, Inc., for the development of a hand-held high-power photographic lighting unit known as the Sun Gun Professional
- James Dale, S. Wilson, H. E. Rice, John Rude, Laurie Atkin, Wadsworth E. Pohl, H. Peasgood and Technicolor Corp., for a process of automatic selective printing
- 20th Century-Fox Research Dept., under the direction of E. I. Sponable and Herbert E. Bragg, DeLuxe Laboratories, Inc., with the assistance of F. D. Leslie, R. D. Whitmore, A. A. Alden, Endel Pool and James B. Gordon, for a system of decompressing and recomposing CinemaScope pictures for conventional aspect ratios

Class III:
- Hurletron, Inc., Electric Eye Equipment Division, for an automatic light changing system for motion picture printers

■ Wadsworth E. Pohl and Technicolor Corp., for an integrated sound and picture transfer process

1962

BEST PICTURE

■ *Lawrence of Arabia* (Horizon-Columbia)
The Longest Day (Zanuck–20th Century-Fox)
The Music Man (Warner Bros.)
Mutiny on the Bounty (MGM)
To Kill a Mockingbird (Universal-International)

BEST DIRECTOR

■ David Lean, *Lawrence of Arabia*
Pietro Germi, *Divorce—Italian Style*
Robert Mulligan, *To Kill a Mockingbird*
Arthur Penn, *The Miracle Worker*
Frank Perry, *David and Lisa*

BEST ACTOR

■ Gregory Peck, *To Kill a Mockingbird*
Burt Lancaster, *Birdman of Alcatraz*
Jack Lemmon, *Days of Wine and Roses*
Marcello Mastroianni, *Divorce—Italian Style*
Peter O'Toole, *Lawrence of Arabia*

BEST ACTRESS

■ Anne Bancroft, *The Miracle Worker*
Bette Davis, *What Ever Happened to Baby Jane?*
Katharine Hepburn, *Long Day's Journey Into Night*
Geraldine Page, *Sweet Bird of Youth*
Lee Remick, *Days of Wine and Roses*

BEST SUPPORTING ACTOR

■ Ed Begley, *Sweet Bird of Youth*
Victor Buono, *What Ever Happened to Baby Jane?*
Telly Savalas, *Birdman of Alcatraz*
Omar Sharif, *Lawrence of Arabia*
Terence Stamp, *Billy Budd*

BEST SUPPORTING ACTRESS

■ Patty Duke, *The Miracle Worker*
Mary Badham, *To Kill a Mockingbird*
Shirley Knight, *Sweet Bird of Youth*
Angela Lansbury, *The Manchurian Candidate*
Thelma Ritter, *Birdman of Alcatraz*

BEST SCREENPLAY (BASED ON MATERIAL FROM ANOTHER MEDIUM)

■ Horton Foote, *To Kill a Mockingbird*
Eleanor Perry, *David and Lisa*
Robert Bolt, *Lawrence of Arabia*
Vladimir Nabokov, *Lolita*
William Gibson, *The Miracle Worker*

BEST STORY AND SCREENPLAY (WRITTEN DIRECTLY FOR THE SCREEN)

- Ennio de Concini, Alfredo Giannetti, Pietro Germi, *Divorce—Italian Style*

  Charles Kaufman, Wolfgang Reinhardt, *Freud*

  Alain Robbe-Grillet, *Last Year at Marienbad*

  Stanley Shapiro, Nate Monaster, *That Touch of Mink*

  Ingmar Bergman, *Through a Glass Darkly*

CINEMATOGRAPHY (BLACK-AND-WHITE)

- Jean Bourgoin, Henri Persin, Walter Wottitz, *The Longest Day*

  Burnett Guffey, *Birdman of Alcatraz*

  Russell Harlan, *To Kill a Mockingbird*

  Ted McCord, *Two for the Seesaw*

  Ernest Haller, *What Ever Happened to Baby Jane?*

CINEMATOGRAPHY (COLOR)

- Fred A. Young, *Lawrence of Arabia*

  Harry Stradling, *Gypsy*

  Robert L. Surtees, *Mutiny on the Bounty*

  Russell Harlan, *Hatari!*

  Paul C. Vogel, *The Wonderful World of the Brothers Grimm*

FOREIGN-LANGUAGE FILM

- *Sundays and Cybele* (France)

  Electra (Greece)

  Four Days of Naples (Italy)

  Keeper of Promises (The Given Word) (Brazil)

  Tlayucan (Mexico)

OTHER AWARDS:

ART DIRECTION / SET DIRECTION

Black-and-White:
- Alexander Golitzen, Henry Bumstead; Oliver Emert, *To Kill a Mockingbird*

Color:
- John Box, John Stroll; Dario Simoni, *Lawrence of Arabia*

SOUND

- Shepperton Studio Sound Dept., *Lawrence of Arabia*

SHORT SUBJECTS

Cartoons:
- Brandon Films, *The Hole*

Live Action Subjects:
- CAPAC Prods., Atlantic Pictures Corp., TWW Ltd., Janus Films, *Heureux Anniversaire*

DOCUMENTARY

Short Subjects:
- (Welsh) *Dylan Thomas*

Features:
- Astor Pictures, *Black Fox*

MUSIC

Best Song:
- Henry Mancini, Johnny Mercer, "Days of Wine and Roses," *Days of Wine and Roses*

Best Music Score— Substantially Original: *(new classification this year)*
- Maurice Jarre, *Lawrence of Arabia*

Best Music Score—Adaptation or Treatment: *(new classification this year)*
- Ray Heindorf, *The Music Man*

FILM EDITING

- Anne Coates, *Lawrence of Arabia*

SPECIAL EFFECTS

- Robert MacDonald; Jacques Maumont, *The Longest Day*

COSTUME DESIGN

Black-and-White:
- Norman Koch, *What Ever Happened to Baby Jane?*

Color:
- Mary Wills, *The Wonderful World of the Brothers Grimm*

JEAN HERSHOLT HUMANITARIAN AWARD

- Steve Broidy

SCIENTIFIC OR TECHNICAL AWARDS

Class II:
- Ralph Chapman, for the design and development of an advanced motion picture camera crane

- Albert S. Pratt, James L. Wassell and Hans C. Wohlrab of the Professional Division, Bell & Howell Co., for the design and development of a new and improved automatic motion picture additive color printer
- North American Philips Co., Inc., for the design and engineering of the Norelco Universal 70/35mm motion picture projector
- Charles E. Sutter, William Bryson Smith and Louis C. Kennell of Paramount Pictures Corp., for the engineering and application to motion picture production of a new system of electric power distribution

Class III:
- Electro-Voice, Inc., for a highly directional dynamic line microphone
- Louis G. MacKenzie, for a selective sound effects repeater

1963

BEST PICTURE

- *Tom Jones* (Lopert–UA)
  America America (Kazan–Warner Bros.)
  Cleopatra (20th Century-Fox)
  How the West Was Won (MGM, Cinerama)
  Lilies of the Field (UA)

BEST DIRECTOR

- Tony Richardson, *Tom Jones*
  Federico Fellini, *8½*
  Elia Kazan, *America America*
  Otto Preminger, *The Cardinal*
  Martin Ritt, *Hud*

BEST ACTOR

- Sidney Poitier, *Lilies of the Field*
  Albert Finney, *Tom Jones*
  Richard Harris, *This Sporting Life*
  Rex Harrison, *Cleopatra*
  Paul Newman, *Hud*

BEST ACTRESS

- Patricia Neal, *Hud*
  Leslie Caron, *The L-Shaped Room*
  Shirley MacLaine, *Irma La Douce*
  Rachael Roberts, *This Sporting Life*
  Natalie Wood, *Love with the Proper Stranger*

BEST SUPPORTING ACTOR

- Melvyn Douglas, *Hud*
  Nick Adams, *Twilight of Honor*
  Bobby Darin, *Captain Newman, M.D.*
  Hugh Griffith, *Tom Jones*
  John Huston, *The Cardinal*

BEST SUPPORTING ACTRESS

- Margaret Rutherford, *The V.I.P.s*
  Diane Cilento, *Tom Jones*
  Edith Evans, *Tom Jones*
  Joyce Redman, *Tom Jones*
  Lilia Skala, *Lilies of the Field*

BEST SCREENPLAY (BASED ON MATERIAL FROM ANOTHER MEDIUM)

- John Osborne, *Tom Jones*
  Richard L. Breen, Phoebe and Henry Ephron, *Captain Newman, M.D.*
  Irving Ravetch, Harriet Frank Jr., *Hud*
  James Poe, *Lilies of the Field*
  Serge Bourguignon, Antonio Tudal, *Sundays and Cybele*

BEST STORY AND SCREENPLAY (WRITTEN DIRECTLY FOR THE SCREEN)

- James R. Webb, *How the West Was Won*
  Elia Kazan, *America America*
  Federico Fellini, Tullio Pinelli, Ennio Flaiano, Brunello Rondi, *8½*
  Pasquale Festa Campanile, Massimo Franciosa, Nanni Loy, Vasco Pratolini, Carlo Bernari, *Four Days of Naples*
  Arnold Schulman, *Love with the Proper Stranger*

CINEMATOGRAPHY (BLACK-AND-WHITE)

- James Wong Howe, *Hud*
  George Folsey, *The Balcony*
  Lucien Ballard, *The Caretakers*
  Ernest Haller, *Lilies of the Field*
  Milton Krasner, *Love with the Proper Stranger*

CINEMATOGRAPHY (COLOR)

- Leon Shamroy, *Cleopatra*
  Leon Shamroy, *The Cardinal*
  William H. Daniels, Milton Krasner, Charles Lang, Jr., Joseph LaShelle, *How the West Was Won*
  Joseph LaShelle, *Irma La Douce*
  Ernest Laszlo, *It's a Mad, Mad, Mad, Mad World*

FOREIGN-LANGUAGE FILM

- *8½* (Italy)
  Knife in the Water (Poland)
  Los Tarantos (Spain)
  The Red Lanterns (Greece)
  Twin Sisters of Kyoto (Japan)

OTHER AWARDS:

ART DIRECTION / SET DIRECTION

Black-and-White:
- Gene Callahan, *America America*

Color:
- John DeCuir, Jack Martin Smith, Hilyard Brown, Herman Blumenthal, Elven Webb, Maurice Pelling, Boris Juraga; Walter M. Scott,

Paul S. Fox, Ray Moyer, *Cleopatra*

SOUND

- MGM Sound Dept., *How the West Was Won*

SHORT SUBJECTS

Cartoons:
- Columbia, *The Critic*

Live Action Subjects:
- Janus Films, *An Occurrence at Owl Creek Bridge*

DOCUMENTARY

Short Subjects:
- Auerbach-Flag Films, *Chagall*

Features:
- WGBH Educational Foundation, *Robert Frost: A Lover's Quarrel with the World*

MUSIC

Best Song:
- James Van Heusen, Sammy Cahn, "Call Me Irresponsible," *Papa's Delicate Condition*

Best Musical Score— Substantially Original:
- John Addison, *Tom Jones*

Best Musical Score— Adaptation or Treatment:
- André Previn, *Irma La Douce*

FILM EDITING

- Harold F. Kress, *How the West Was Won*

SPECIAL EFFECTS

- Emile Kosa, Jr., *Cleopatra*

SOUND EFFECTS
(new category this year)

- Walter G. Elliott, *It's a Mad, Mad, Mad, Mad World*

COSTUME DESIGN

Black-and-White:
- Piero Gherardi, *8½*

Color:
- Irene Sharaff, Vittorio Nino Novarese, Renie, *Cleopatra*

IRVING G. THALBERG MEMORIAL AWARD

- Sam Spiegel

SCIENTIFIC OR TECHNICAL AWARDS

Class III:
- Douglas A. Shearer and A. Arnold Gillespie of MGM Studios, for the engineering of an improved Background Process Projection System

---

1964

BEST PICTURE

- *My Fair Lady* (Warner Bros.)
  Becket (Wallis-Paramount)
  Dr. Strangelove (Kubrick-Columbia)
  Mary Poppins (Disney-Buena Vista)
  Zorba the Greek (Intern'l Classics–20th Century-Fox)

BEST DIRECTOR

- George Cukor, *My Fair Lady*
  Michael Cacoyannis, *Zorba the Greek*
  Peter Glenville, *Becket*

Stanley Kubrick, *Dr. Strangelove*
Robert Stevenson, *Mary Poppins*

BEST ACTOR

■ Rex Harrison, *My Fair Lady*
Richard Burton, *Becket*
Peter O'Toole, *Becket*
Anthony Quinn, *Zorba the Greek*
Peter Sellers, *Dr. Strangelove*

BEST ACTRESS

■ Julie Andrews, *Mary Poppins*
Anne Bancroft, *The Pumpkin Eater*
Sophia Loren, *Marriage Italian Style*
Debbie Reynolds, *The Unsinkable Molly Brown*
Kim Stanley, *Séance on a Wet Afternoon*

BEST SUPPORTING ACTOR

■ Peter Ustinov, *Topkapi*
John Gielgud, *Becket*
Stanley Holloway, *My Fair Lady*
Edmond O'Brien, *Seven Days in May*
Lee Tracy, *The Best Man*

BEST SUPPORTING ACTRESS

■ Lila Kedrova, *Zorba the Greek*
Gladys Cooper, *My Fair Lady*
Edith Evans, *The Chalk Garden*
Grayson Hall, *The Night of the Iguana*
Agnes Moorehead, *Hush . . . Hush, Sweet Charlotte*

BEST SCREENPLAY (BASED ON MATERIAL FROM ANOTHER MEDIUM)

■ Edward Anhalt, *Becket*
Stanley Kubrick, Peter George, Terry Southern, *Dr. Strangelove*

Bill Walsh, Don DaGradi, *Mary Poppins*
Alan Jay Lerner, *My Fair Lady*
Michael Cacoyannis, *Zorba the Greek*

BEST STORY AND SCREENPLAY (WRITTEN DIRECTLY FOR THE SCREEN)

■ S. H. Barnett (story); Peter Stone, Frank Tarloff (screenplay), *Father Goose*
Alun Owen, *A Hard Day's Night*
Orville H. Hampton, Raphael Hayes, *One Potato, Two Potato*
Age (a.k.a. "Agenore Incrocci"), Scarpelli (a.k.a. "Furio Scarpelli"), Mario Monicelli, *The Organizer*
J. P. Rapeneau, Ariane Mnouchkine, Daniel Boulanger, Philippe De Broca, *That Man from Rio*

CINEMATOGRAPHY (BLACK-AND-WHITE)

■ Walter Lassally, *Zorba the Greek*
Philip H. Lathrop, *The Americanization of Emily*
Milton Krasner, *Fate Is the Hunter*
Joseph Biroc, *Hush . . . Hush, Sweet Charlotte*
Gabriel Figueroa, *The Night of the Iguana*

CINEMATOGRAPHY (COLOR)

■ Harry Stradling, *My Fair Lady*
Geoffrey Unsworth, *Becket*
William Clothier, *Cheyenne Autumn*
Edward Colman, *Mary Poppins*
Daniel L. Fapp, *The Unsinkable Molly Brown*

FOREIGN-LANGUAGE FILM

- *Yesterday, Today, and Tomorrow* (Italy)

  Raven's End (Sweden)

  Sallah (Israel)

  The Umbrellas of Cherbourg (France)

  Woman in the Dunes (Japan)

OTHER AWARDS:

ART DIRECTION / SET DIRECTION

Black-and-White:
- Vassilis Photopoulos, *Zorba the Greek*

Color:
- Gene Allen, Cecil Beaton; George James Hopkins, *My Fair Lady*

SOUND

- Warner Bros. Sound Dept., *My Fair Lady*

SHORT SUBJECTS

Cartoons:
- Mirisch–United Artists, *The Pink Phink*

Live Action Subjects:
- Thalia-Beckman Corp., *Casals Conducts: 1964*

DOCUMENTARY

Short Subjects:
- Guggenheim Productions, *Nine from Little Rock*

Features:
- Columbia, *Jacques-Yves Cousteau's World Without Sun*

MUSIC

Best Song:
- Richard M. Sherman, Robert B. Sherman, "Chim-Chim Cher-ee," *Mary Poppins*

Best Musical Scoring— Substantially Original Music:
- Richard M. Sherman, Robert B. Sherman, *Mary Poppins*

Best Musical Scoring— Adaptation or Treatment:
- André Previn, *My Fair Lady*

FILM EDITING

- Cotton Warburton, *Mary Poppins*

SOUND EFFECTS

- Norman Wanstall, *Goldfinger*

VISUAL EFFECTS

(new classification)
- Peter Ellenshaw, *Mary Poppins*

COSTUME DESIGN

Black-and-White:
- Dorothy Jeakins, *The Night of the Iguana*

Color:
- Cecil Beaton, *My Fair Lady*

HONORARY AND OTHER AWARDS

- William Tuttle, for his outstanding make-up achievement for *The Seven Faces of Dr. Lao*

SCIENTIFIC OR TECHNICAL AWARDS

Class I:
- Petro Vlahos, Wadsworth E. Pohl and Ub Iwerks, for the conception and perfection of techniques for Color Traveling Matte Composite Cinematography

Class II:
- Sidney P. Solow, Edward H. Reichard, Carl W. Hauge and Job Sanderson of Consolidated Film Industries, for the design and development

of a versatile Automatic 35mm Composite Color Printer

■ Pierre Angenieux, for the development of a ten-to-one Zoom Lens for cinematography

Class III:

■ Milton Forman, Richard B. Glickman and Daniel J. Pearlman of Color Tran Industries, for advancements in the design and application to motion picture photography of lighting units using quartz iodine lamps

■ Stewart Filmscreen Corporation, for a seamless translucent Blue Screen for Traveling Matte Color Cinematography

■ Anthony Paglia and the 20th Century-Fox Studio Mechanical Effects Dept., for an Improved method of producing Explosion Flash Effects for motion pictures

■ Edward H. Reichard and Carl W. Hauge of Consolidated Film Industries, for the design of a Proximity Cue Detector and its application to motion picture printers

■ Edward H. Reichard, Leonard L. Sokolow and Carl W. Hauge of Consolidated Film Industries, for the design and application to motion picture laboratory practice of a Stroboscopic Scene Tester for color and black-and-white film

■ Nelson Tyler, for the design and construction of an improved Helicopter Camera System

1965

BEST PICTURE

■ *The Sound of Music* (20th Century-Fox)
Darling (Embassy)
Doctor Zhivago (Ponti-MGM)
Ship of Fools (Kramer-Columbia)
A Thousand Clowns (UA)

BEST DIRECTOR

■ Robert Wise, *The Sound of Music*
David Lean, *Doctor Zhivago*
Hiroshi Teshigahara, *Woman In the Dunes*
John Schlesinger, *Darling*
William Wyler, *The Collector*

BEST ACTOR

■ Lee Marvin, *Cat Ballou*
Richard Burton, *The Spy Who Came In from the Cold*
Laurence Olivier, *Othello*
Rod Steiger, *The Pawnbroker*
Oskar Werner, *Ship of Fools*

BEST ACTRESS

■ Julie Christie, *Darling*
Julie Andrews, *The Sound of Music*
Samantha Eggar, *The Collector*
Elizabeth Hartman, *A Patch of Blue*
Simone Signoret, *Ship of Fools*

BEST SUPPORTING ACTOR

■ Martin Balsam, *A Thousand Clowns*
Ian Bannen, *The Flight of the Phoenix*
Tom Courtenay, *Doctor Zhivago*
Michael Dunn, *Ship of Fools*
Frank Finlay, *Othello*

BEST SUPPORTING ACTRESS

■ Shelley Winters, *A Patch of Blue*
Ruth Gordon, *Inside Daisy Clover*
Joyce Redman, *Othello*
Maggie Smith, *Othello*
Peggy Wood, *The Sound of Music*

BEST SCREENPLAY (BASED ON MATERIAL FROM ANOTHER MEDIUM)

■ Robert Bolt, *Doctor Zhivago*
Walter Newman, Frank R. Pierson, *Cat Ballou*
Stanley Mann, John Kohn, *The Collector*
Abby Mann, *Ship of Fools*
Herb Gardner, *A Thousand Clowns*

BEST STORY AND SCREENPLAY (WRITTEN DIRECTLY FOR THE SCREEN)

■ Frederick Raphael, *Darling*
Age (a.k.a. "Agenore Incrocci"), Scarpelli (a.k.a. "Furio Scarpelli"), Mario Monicelli, Tonino Guerra, Giorgio Salvioni, Suso Cecchi D'Amico, *Casanova '70*
Jack Davies, Ken Annakin, *Those Magnificent Men in Their Flying Machines*
Franklin Coen, Frank Davis, *The Train*

Jacques Demy, *The Umbrellas of Cherbourg*

CINEMATOGRAPHY (BLACK-AND-WHITE)

■ Ernest Laszlo, *Ship of Fools*
Loyal Griggs, *In Harm's Way*
Burnett Guffey, *King Rat*
Robert Burks, *A Patch of Blue*
Conrad Hall, *Morituri*

CINEMATOGRAPHY (COLOR)

■ Freddie Young, *Doctor Zhivago*
Leon Shamroy, *The Agony and the Ecstasy*
Russell Harlan, *The Great Race*
William C. Mellor, Loyal Griggs, *The Greatest Story Ever Told*
Ted McCord, *The Sound of Music*

FOREIGN-LANGUAGE FILM

■ *The Shop on Main Street* (Czechoslovakia)
Blood on the Land (Greece)
Dear John (Sweden)
Kwaidan (Japan)
Marriage Italian Style (Italy)

OTHER AWARDS:

ART DIRECTION / SET DIRECTION

Black-and-White:
■ Robert Clatworthy; Joseph Kish, *Ship of Fools*
Color:
■ John Box, Terry March; Dario Simoni, *Doctor Zhivago*

SOUND

■ 20th Century-Fox Sound Dept., *The Sound of Music*

SHORT SUBJECTS

Cartoons:
■ MGM, *The Dot and the Line*

Live Action Subjects:
- Renn-Pathé Contemporary, *The Chicken* (Le Poulet)

DOCUMENTARY

Short Subjects:
- Johnson's Wax, *To Be Alive!*

Features:
- Glazier–American International, *The Eleanor Roosevelt Story*

MUSIC

Best Song:
- Johnny Mandel, Paul Francis Webster, "The Shadow of Your Smile," *The Sandpiper*

Best Musical Scoring— Substantially Original:
- Maurice Jarre, *Doctor Zhivago*

Best Musical Scoring— Adaptation or Treatment:
- Irwin Kostal, *The Sound of Music*

FILM EDITING

- William Reynolds, *The Sound of Music*

SOUND EFFECTS

- Tregoweth Brown, *The Great Race*

VISUAL EFFECTS

- John Stears, *Thunderball*

COSTUME DESIGN

Black-and-White:
- Julie Harris, *Darling*

Color:
- Phyllis Dalton, *Doctor Zhivago*

HONORARY AND OTHER AWARDS

- Bob Hope, for unique and distinguished service to the Industry and the Academy

IRVING G. THALBERG MEMORIAL AWARD

- William Wyler

JEAN HERSHOLT HUMANITARIAN AWARD

- Edmond L. DePatie

SCIENTIFIC OR TECHNICAL AWARDS

Class II:
- Arthur J. Hatch of the Strong Electric Corp., subsidiary of General Precision Equipment Corp., for the design and development of an Air Blown Carbon Arc Projection Lamp
- Stefan Kudelski, for the design and development of the Nagra portable quarter-inch tape-recording system for motion picture sound recording

1966

BEST PICTURE

- *A Man for All Seasons* (Columbia)
Alfie (Paramount)
The Russians Are Coming, The Russians Are Coming (UA)
The Sand Pebbles (20th Century-Fox)
Who's Afraid of Virginia Woolf? (Warner Bros.)

BEST DIRECTOR

- Fred Zinnemann, *A Man for All Seasons*
- Michelangelo Antonioni, *Blow-Up*
- Richard Brooks, *The Professionals*
- Claude Lelouch, *A Man and a Woman*
- Mike Nichols, *Who's Afraid of Virginia Woolf?*

BEST ACTOR

- Paul Scofield, *A Man for All Seasons*
- Alan Arkin, *The Russians Are Coming, The Russians Are Coming*
- Richard Burton, *Who's Afraid of Virginia Woolf?*
- Michael Caine, *Alfie*
- Steve McQueen, *The Sand Pebbles*

BEST ACTRESS

- Elizabeth Taylor, *Who's Afraid of Virginia Woolf?*
- Anouk Aimée, *A Man and a Woman*
- Ida Kaminska, *The Shop on Main Street*
- Lynn Redgrave, *Georgy Girl*
- Vanessa Redgrave, *Morgan!*

BEST SUPPORTING ACTOR

- Walter Matthau, *The Fortune Cookie*
- Mako, *The Sand Pebbles*
- James Mason, *Georgy Girl*
- George Segal, *Who's Afraid of Virginia Woolf?*
- Robert Shaw, *A Man for All Seasons*

BEST SUPPORTING ACTRESS

- Sandy Dennis, *Who's Afraid of Virginia Woolf?*
- Wendy Hiller, *A Man for All Seasons*
- Jocelyn Lagarde, *Hawaii*
- Vivien Merchant, *Alfie*
- Geraldine Page, *You're a Big Boy Now*

BEST SCREENPLAY (BASED ON MATERIAL FROM ANOTHER MEDIUM)

- Robert Bolt, *A Man for All Seasons*
- Richard Brooks, *The Professionals*
- William Rose, *The Russians Are Coming, The Russians Are Coming*
- Ernest Lehman, *Who's Afraid of Virginia Woolf?*
- Bill Naughton, *Alfie*

BEST STORY AND SCREENPLAY (WRITTEN DIRECTLY FOR THE SCREEN)

- Claude Lelouch (story); Pierre Uytterhoeven and Claude Lelouch (screenplay), *A Man and a Woman*
- Michelangelo Antonioni, Tonino Guerra, Edward Bond, *Blow-Up*
- Billy Wilder, I. A. L. Diamond, *The Fortune Cookie*
- Clint Johnston, Don Peters, *The Naked Prey*
- Robert Ardrey, *Khartoum*

CINEMATOGRAPHY (BLACK-AND-WHITE)

- Haskell Wexler, *Who's Afraid of Virginia Woolf?*
- Joseph LaShelle, *The Fortune Cookie*
- Ken Higgings, *Georgy Girl*
- Marcel Grignon, *Is Paris Burning*
- James Wong Howe, *Seconds*

CINEMATOGRAPHY (COLOR)

- Ted Moore, *A Man for All Seasons*

Ernest Laszlo, *Fantastic Voyage*
Russell Harlan, *Hawaii*
Conrad Hall, *The Professionals*
Joseph MacDonald, *The Sand Pebbles*

FOREIGN-LANGUAGE FILM

■ *A Man and a Woman* (France)
The Battle of Algiers (Italy)
Loves of a Blonde (Czechoslovakia)
Pharaoh (Poland)
Three (Yugoslavia)

OTHER AWARDS:

ART DIRECTION / SET DIRECTION

Black-and-White:
■ Richard Sylbert; George James Hopkins, *Who's Afraid of Virginia Woolf?*
Color:
■ Jack Martin Smith, Dale Hennesy; Walter M. Scott, Stuart A. Reiss, *Fantastic Voyage*

SOUND

■ MGM Sound Dept., *Grand Prix*

SHORT SUBJECTS

Cartoons:
■ Hubley-Paramount, *Herb Alpert and the Tijuana Brass Double Feature*
Live Action Subjects:
■ British Transport Films, Manson Distributing, *Wild Wings*

DOCUMENTARY

Short Subjects:
■ Office of Economic Opportunity, *A Year Toward Tomorrow*
Features:
■ Pathé Contemporary Films, *The War Game*

MUSIC

Best Song:
■ John Barry, Don Black, "Born Free," *Born Free*
Best Original Score:
(for which only the composer shall be eligible)
■ John Barry, *Born Free*
Best Scoring—Adaptation or Treatment:
■ Ken Thorne, *A Funny Thing Happened on the Way to the Forum*

FILM EDITING

■ Fredric Steinkamp, Henry Berman, Stewart Linder, Frank Santillo, *Grand Prix*

SOUND EFFECTS

■ Gordon Daniel, *Grand Prix*

SPECIAL VISUAL EFFECTS

■ Art Cruickshank, *Fantastic Voyage*

COSTUME DESIGN

Black-and-White:
■ Irene Sharaff, *Who's Afraid of Virginia Woolf?*
Color:
■ Elizabeth Haffenden, Joan Bridge, *A Man for All Seasons*

HONORARY AND OTHER AWARDS

■ Y. Frank Freeman, for unusual and outstanding service to the Academy during his 30 years in Hollywood
■ Yakima Canutt, for pioneering film stunt work

IRVING G. THALBERG MEMORIAL AWARD

■ Robert Wise

JEAN HERSHOLT HUMANITARIAN AWARD

- George Bagnall

SCIENTIFIC OR TECHNICAL AWARDS

Class II:

- Mitchell Camera Corporation, for the design and development of the Mitchell Mark II 35mm Portable Motion Picture Reflex Camera
- Arnold & Richter KG, for the design and development of the Arriflex 35mm Portable Motion Picture Reflex Camera

Class III:

- Panavision, Inc., for the design of the Panatron Power Inverter and its application to motion picture camera operation
- Carroll Knudson for the production of a Composers Manual for Motion Picture Music Synchronization
- Ruby Raksin, for the production of a Composers Manual for Motion Picture Music Synchronization

1967

BEST PICTURE

- *In the Heat of the Night* (Mirisch-UA)
  Bonnie and Clyde (Warner Bros.–Seven Arts)
  Doctor Dolittle (20th Century-Fox)
  The Graduate (Embassy)
  Guess Who's Coming to Dinner (Kramer-Columbia)

BEST DIRECTOR

- Mike Nichols, *The Graduate*
  Richard Brooks, *In Cold Blood*
  Norman Jewison, *In the Heat of the Night*
  Stanley Kramer, *Guess Who's Coming to Dinner*
  Arthur Penn, *Bonnie and Clyde*

BEST ACTOR

- Rod Steiger, *In the Heat of the Night*
  Warren Beatty, *Bonnie and Clyde*

  Dustin Hoffman, *The Graduate*
  Paul Newman, *Cool Hand Luke*
  Spencer Tracy, *Guess Who's Coming to Dinner*

BEST ACTRESS

- Katharine Hepburn, *Guess Who's Coming to Dinner*
  Anne Bancroft, *The Graduate*
  Faye Dunaway, *Bonnie and Clyde*
  Dame Edith Evans, *The Whisperers*
  Audrey Hepburn, *Wait Until Dark*

BEST SUPPORTING ACTOR

- George Kennedy, *Cool Hand Luke*
  John Cassavetes, *The Dirty Dozen*
  Gene Hackman, *Bonnie and Clyde*
  Cecil Kellaway, *Guess Who's Coming to Dinner*

Michael J. Pollard, *Bonnie and Clyde*

BEST SUPPORTING ACTRESS

■ Estelle Parsons, *Bonnie and Clyde*
Carol Channing, *Thoroughly Modern Millie*
Mildred Natwick, *Barefoot in the Park*
Beah Richards, *Guess Who's Coming to Dinner*
Katharine Ross, *The Graduate*

BEST SCREENPLAY (BASED ON MATERIAL FROM ANOTHER MEDIUM)

■ Stirling Silliphant, *In the Heat of the Night*
Don Pearce, Frank R. Pierson, *Cool Hand Luke*
Calder Willingham, Buck Henry, *The Graduate*
Richard Brooks, *In Cold Blood*
Joseph Strick, Fred Haines, *Ulysses*

BEST STORY AND SCREENPLAY (WRITTEN DIRECTLY FOR THE SCREEN)

■ William Rose, *Guess Who's Coming to Dinner*
David Newman, Robert Benton, *Bonnie and Clyde*
Robert Kaufman, Norman Lear, *Divorce American Style*
Jorge Semprun, *La Guerre Est Finie*
Frederick Raphael, *Two for the Road*

CINEMATOGRAPHY

(rules changed to one award; no longer separate awards for black-and-white and color)

■ Burnett Guffey, *Bonnie and Clyde*

Richard H. Kline, *Camelot*
Robert Surtees, *Doctor Dolittle*
Robert Surtees, *The Graduate*
Conrad Hall, *In Cold Blood*

FOREIGN-LANGUAGE FILM

■ *Closely Watched Trains* (Czechoslovakia)
El Amor Brujo (Spain)
I Ever Met Happy Gypsies (Yugoslavia)
Live for Life (France)
Portrait of Chieko (Japan)

OTHER AWARDS:

ART DIRECTION / SET DIRECTION

(rules changed to only one award; no longer separate color and black-and-white awards)

■ John Truscott, Edward Carrere; John W. Brown, *Camelot*

SOUND

■ Samuel Goldwyn Studio Sound Dept., *In the Heat of the Night*

SHORT SUBJECTS

Cartoons:
■ Murakami Wolf–Brandon, *The Box*
Live Action Subjects:
■ A.T.D.F.-Columbia, *A Place to Stand*

DOCUMENTARY

Short Subjects:
■ King Screen Productions, *The Redwoods*
Features:
■ French Broadcasting System, *The Anderson Platoon*

MUSIC

Best Song:
- Leslie Bricusse, "Talk to the Animals," *Doctor Dolittle*

Best Original Score:
(for which only the composer shall be eligible)
- Elmer Bernstein, *Thoroughly Modern Millie*

Best Scoring of Music— Adaptation or Treatment:
(for which only the adapter and/or music director shall be eligible)
- Alfred Newman, Ken Darby, *Camelot*

FILM EDITING
- Hal Ashby, *In the Heat of the Night*

SOUND EFFECTS
- John Poyner, *The Dirty Dozen*

SPECIAL VISUAL EFFECTS
- L. B. Abbott, *Doctor Dolittle*

COSTUME DESIGN
(rules changed this year to only one award; no longer separate categories)
- John Truscott, *Camelot*

HONORARY AND OTHER AWARDS
- Arthur Freed, for distinguished service to the Academy and the production of six top-rated Awards telecasts

IRVING G. THALBERG MEMORIAL AWARD
- Alfred Hitchcock

JEAN HERSHOLT HUMANITARIAN AWARD
- Gregory Peck

SCIENTIFIC OR TECHNICAL AWARDS

Class III:
- Electro-Optical Division of the Kollmorgen Corp., for the design and development of a series of Motion Picture Projection Lenses
- Panavision, Inc., for a Variable Speed Motor for Motion Picture Cameras
- Fred R. Wilson of the Samuel Goldwyn Studio Sound Dept., for an Audio Level Clamper
- Waldon O. Watson and the Universal City Studio Sound Dept., for new concepts in the design of a Music Scoring Stage

---

1968

BEST PICTURE
- *Oliver!* (Romulus-Columbia)
  Funny Girl (Rastar-Columbia)
  The Lion in Winter (Avco-Embassy)
  Rachel, Rachel (Warner Bros.–Seven Arts)
  Romeo and Juliet (Zeffirelli-Paramount)

BEST DIRECTOR

- Carol Reed, *Oliver!*
  Anthony Harvey, *The Lion in Winter*
  Stanley Kubrick, *2001: A Space Odyssey*
  Gillo Pontecorvo, *The Battle of Algiers*
  Franco Zeffirelli, *Romeo and Juliet*

BEST ACTOR

- Cliff Robertson, *Charly*
  Alan Arkin, *The Heart Is a Lonely Hunter*
  Alan Bates, *The Fixer*
  Ron Moody, *Oliver!*
  Peter O'Toole, *The Lion in Winter*

BEST ACTRESS

- Katharine Hepburn, *The Lion in Winter*
- Barbra Streisand, *Funny Girl*
  Patricia Neal, *The Subject Was Roses*
  Vanessa Redgrave, *Isadora*
  Joanne Woodward, *Rachel, Rachel*

BEST SUPPORTING ACTOR

- Jack Albertson, *The Subject Was Roses*
  Seymour Cassel, *Faces*
  Daniel Massey, *Star!*
  Jack Wild, *Oliver!*
  Gene Wilder, *The Producers*

BEST SUPPORTING ACTRESS

- Ruth Gordon, *Rosemary's Baby*
  Lynn Carlin, *Faces*
  Sondra Locke, *The Heart Is a Lonely Hunter*
  Kay Medford, *Funny Girl*
  Estelle Parsons, *Rachel, Rachel*

BEST SCREENPLAY (BASED ON MATERIAL FROM ANOTHER MEDIUM)

- James Goldman, *The Lion in Winter*
  Neil Simon, *The Odd Couple*
  Vernon Harris, *Oliver!*
  Stewart Stern, *Rachel, Rachel*
  Roman Polanski, *Rosemary's Baby*

BEST STORY AND SCREENPLAY (WRITTEN DIRECTLY FOR THE SCREEN)

- Mel Brooks, *The Producers*
  Franco Solinas, Gillo Pontecorvo, *The Battle of Algiers*
  John Cassavetes, *Faces*
  Ira Wallach, Peter Ustinov, *Hot Millions*
  Stanley Kubrick, Arthur C. Clarke, *2001: A Space Odyssey*

CINEMATOGRAPHY

- Pasqualino De Santis, *Romeo and Juliet*
  Harry Stradling, *Funny Girl*
  Daniel L. Fapp, *Ice Station Zebra*
  Oswald Morris, *Oliver!*
  Ernest Laszlo, *Star!*

FOREIGN-LANGUAGE FILM

- *War and Peace* (Russia)
  The Boys of Paul Street (Hungary)
  The Fireman's Ball (Czechslovakia)
  The Girl with the Pistol (Italy)
  Stolen Kisses (France)

OTHER AWARDS:

ART DIRECTION / SET DIRECTION

- John Box, Terence Marsh; Vernon Dixon, Ken Muggleston, *Oliver!*

SOUND
- Shepperton Studio Sound Dept., *Oliver!*

SHORT SUBJECTS

Cartoons:
- Walt Disney, *Winnie the Pooh and the Blustery Day*

Live Action Subjects:
- Guggenheim–National General, *Robert Kennedy Remembered*

DOCUMENTARY

Short Subjects:
- Saul Bass, *Why Man Creates*

Features:
- Western Behavioral Sciences Institute, *Journey Into Self (Columbia's Young Americans was originally voted the award but on May 7, 1969, declared ineligible when it was learned that the film had been shown in 1967 and hence was ineligible for a 1968 award.)*

MUSIC

Best Song:
- Michel Legrand, Alan and Marilyn Bergman, "The Windmills of Your Mind," *The Thomas Crown Affair*

Best Original Score for a Non-Musical Picture:
(for which only the composer shall be eligible)
- John Barry, *The Lion in Winter*

Best Score of a Musical Picture, Original or Adaptation:
(for which the composer, lyricist and the adapter shall be eligible if the music score was written directly for the screen, but only the adapter if the score was adapted from another medium)
- John Green, *Oliver!*

FILM EDITING
- Frank P. Keller, *Bullitt*

SPECIAL VISUAL EFFECTS
- Stanley Kubrick, *2001: A Space Odyssey*

COSTUME DESIGN
- Danilo Donati, *Romeo and Juliet*

HONORARY AND OTHER AWARDS
- Onna White, for her outstanding choreography of *Oliver!*
- John Chambers, for his make-up design for *Planet of the Apes*

JEAN HERSHOLT HUMANITARIAN AWARD
- Martha Raye

SCIENTIFIC OR TECHNICAL AWARDS

Class I:
- Philip V. Palmquist of Minnesota Mining and Manufacturing Co.; Dr. Herbert Meyer of the Motion Picture and Television Research Center; and Charles D. Staffell of the Rank Organisation, for the development of a successful embodiment of the reflex background projection system for composite cinematography
- Eastman Kodak Company, for the development and introduction of a color reversal intermediate film for motion pictures.

Class II:
- Donald W. Norwood, for the design and development of

the Norwood Photographic Exposure Meters
- Eastman Kodak Company and Producers Service Company, for the development of a new high-speed stereoptical reduction printer
- Edmund M. DiGiulio, Niels G. Petersen and Norman S. Hughes of the Cinema Product Development Company, for the design and application of a conversion which makes available the reflex viewing system for motion picture cameras
- Optical Coating Laboratory, Inc., for the development of an improved antireflection coating for photographic and projection lens systems
- Eastman Kodak Company, for the introduction of a new high-speed motion picture color negative film

- Panavision, Inc., for the conception, design and introduction of a 65mm hand-held motion picture camera
- Todd-AO Company and the Mitchell Camera Company, for the design and engineering of the Todd-AO hand-held motion picture camera

Class III:
- Carl W. Hauge and Edward H. Reichard of Consolidated Film Industries and E. Michael Meahl and Roy J. Ridenour of Ramtronics, for engineering an automatic exposure control for printing-machine lamps
- Eastman Kodak Company, for a new direct positive film, and Consolidated Film Industries, for the application of this film to the making of post-production work prints

1969

BEST PICTURE
- *Midnight Cowboy* (UA)
  Anne of the Thousand Days (Wallis-Universal)
  Butch Cassidy and the Sundance Kid (20th Century-Fox)
  Hello, Dolly! (Chenault–20th Century-Fox)
  Z (Cinema V)

BEST DIRECTOR
- John Schlesinger, *Midnight Cowboy*
  Costa-Gavras, *Z*

Arthur Penn, *Alice's Restaurant*
Sydney Pollack, *They Shoot Horses, Don't They?*
George Roy Hill, *Butch Cassidy and the Sundance Kid*

BEST ACTOR
- John Wayne, *True Grit*
  Richard Burton, *Anne of the Thousand Days*
  Dustin Hoffman, *Midnight Cowboy*
  Peter O'Toole, *Goodbye, Mr. Chips*
  Jon Voight, *Midnight Cowboy*

BEST ACTRESS

■ Maggie Smith, *The Prime of Miss Jean Brodie*
Genevieve Bujold, *Anne of the Thousand Days*
Jane Fonda, *They Shoot Horses, Don't They?*
Liza Minnelli, *The Sterile Cuckoo*
Jean Simmons, *The Happy Ending*

BEST SUPPORTING ACTOR

■ Gig Young, *They Shoot Horses, Don't They?*
Rupert Crosse, *The Reivers*
Elliott Gould, *Bob & Carol & Ted & Alice*
Jack Nicholson, *Easy Rider*
Anthony Quayle, *Anne of the Thousand Days*

BEST SUPPORTING ACTRESS

■ Goldie Hawn, *Cactus Flower*
Catherine Burns, *Last Summer*
Dyan Cannon, *Bob & Carol & Ted & Alice*
Sylvia Miles, *Midnight Cowboy*
Susannah York, *They Shoot Horses, Don't They?*

BEST SCREENPLAY (BASED ON MATERIAL FROM ANOTHER MEDIUM)

■ Waldo Salt, *Midnight Cowboy*
John Hale, Bridget Boland, Richard Sokolove, *Anne of the Thousand Days*
Arnold Schulman, *Goodbye, Columbus*
James Poe, Robert E. Thompson, *They Shoot Horses, Don't They?*
Jorge Semprun, Costa-Gavras, *Z*

BEST STORY AND SCREENPLAY (BASED ON MATERIAL NOT PREVIOUSLY PUBLISHED OR PRODUCED)

■ William Goldman, *Butch Cassidy and the Sundance Kid*
Paul Mazursky, Larry Tucker, *Bob & Carol & Ted & Alice*
Nicola Badalucco, Enrico Medioli, Luchino Visconti, *The Damned*
Peter Fonda, Dennis Hopper, Terry Southern, *Easy Rider*
Walon Green, Roy N. Sickner, Sam Peckinpah, *The Wild Bunch*

CINEMATOGRAPHY

■ Conrad Hall, *Butch Cassidy and the Sundance Kid*
Arthur Ibbetson, *Anne of the Thousand Days*
Charres B. Lang, *Bob & Carol & Ted & Alice*
Harry Stradling, *Hello, Dolly!*
Daniel Fapp, *Marooned*

FOREIGN-LANGUAGE FILM

■ *Z* (Algeria)
Ådalen '31 (Sweden)
The Battle of Neretva (Yugoslavia)
The Brothers Karamazov (USSR)
My Night at Maud's (France)

OTHER AWARDS:

ART DIRESTION / SET DIRECTION

■ John DeCuir, Jack Martin Smith, Herman Blumenthal; Walter M. Scott, George Hopkins, Raphael Bretton, *Hello, Dolly!*

SOUND

- Jack Solomon, Murray Spivack, *Hello, Dolly!*

SHORT SUBJECTS

Cartoons:
- Walt Disney, Buena Vista, *It's Tough to Be a Bird*

Live Action Subjects:
- Fly-by-Night Productions—Manson, *The Magic Machines*

DOCUMENTARY

Short Subjects:
- Sanders-Fresco-USIA, *Czechoslovakia 1968*

Features:
- Midem Production, *Artur Rubinstein—The Love of Life*

MUSIC

Best Song:
- Burt Bacharach, Hal David, "Raindrops Keep Fallin' on My Head," *Butch Cassidy and the Sundance Kid*

Best Original Score of a Nonmusical Picture:
(for which only the composer shall be eligible)
- Burt Bacharach, *Butch Cassidy and the Sundance Kid*

Best Scoring of a Musical Picture—Original or Adaptation:
(for which the composer, lyricist, and adapter shall be eligible if the music was written directly for the screen, but only adapter shall be eligible if score is an adaptation)
- Lennie Hayton, Lionel Newman, *Hello, Dolly!*

FILM EDITING

- Francoise Bonnot, *Z*

SPECIAL VISUAL EFFECTS

- Robbie Robertson, *Marooned*

COSTUME DESIGN

- Margaret Furse, *Anne of the Thousand Days*

HONORARY AND OTHER AWARDS

- Cary Grant, for his unique mastery of the art of screen acting, with the respect and affection of his colleagues

JEAN HERSHOLT HUMANITARIAN AWARD

- George Jessel

SCIENTIFIC OR TECHNICAL AWARDS

Class II:
- Hazeltine Corporation, for the design and development of the Hazeltine Color Film Analyzer
- Fouad Said, for the design and introduction of the Cinemobile series of equipment trucks for location motion picture production
- Juan De La Cierva and Dynasciences Corporation, for the design and development of the Dynalens optical image motion compensator

Class III:
- Otto Popelka of Magna-Tech Electronic Co., Inc., for the development of an Electronically Controlled Looping System
- Fenton Hamilton of MGM Studios, for the concept and engineering of a mobile battery power unit for location lighting
- Panavision, Inc., for the design and development of the

Panaspeed Motion Picture Camera Motor
- Robert M. Flynn and Russell of Universal City Studios, Inc.,

for a machine-gun modification for motion picture photography

---

1970

BEST PICTURE

- *Patton* (20th Century-Fox)
  Airport (Hunter-Universal)
  Five Easy Pieces (BBS-Columbia)
  Love Story (Paramount)
  M*A*S*H (20th Century-Fox)

BEST DIRECTOR

- Franklin J. Schaffner, *Patton*
  Robert Altman, *M*A*S*H*
  Federico Fellini, *Satyricon*
  Arthur Hiller, *Love Story*
  Ken Russell, *Women in Love*

BEST ACTOR

- George C. Scott, *Patton* (award declined)
  Melvyn Douglas, *I Never Sang for My Father*
  James Earl Jones, *The Great White Hope*
  Jack Nicholson, *Five Easy Pieces*
  Ryan O'Neal, *Love Story*

BEST ACTRESS

- Glenda Jackson, *Women in Love*
  Carrie Snodgress, *Diary of a Mad Housewife*
  Jane Alexander, *The Great White Hope*
  Ali MacGraw, *Love Story*
  Sarah Miles, *Ryan's Daughter*

BEST SUPPORTING ACTOR

- John Mills, *Ryan's Daughter*
  Richard Castellano, *Lovers and Other Strangers*
  Chief Dan George, *Little Big Man*
  Gene Hackman, *I Never Sang for My Father*
  John Marley, *Love Story*

BEST SUPPORTING ACTRESS

- Helen Hayes, *Airport*
  Karen Black, *Five Easy Pieces*
  Lee Grant, *The Landlord*
  Sally Kellerman, *M*A*S*H*
  Maureen Stapleton, *Airport*

BEST SCREENPLAY (BASED ON MATERIAL FROM ANOTHER MEDIUM)

- Ring Lardner, Jr., *M*A*S*H*
  George Seaton, *Airport*
  Robert Anderson, *I Never Sang for My Father*
  Renée Taylor, Joseph Bologna, David Zelag Goodman, *Lovers and Other Strangers*
  Larry Kramer, *Women in Love*

BEST STORY AND SCREENPLAY (BASED ON FACTUAL MATERIAL OR MATERIAL NOT PREVIOUSLY PUBLISHED)

- Francis Ford Coppola, Edmund H. North, *Patton*
  Bob Rafelson, Adrien Joyce, *Five Easy Pieces*

Norman Wexler, *Joe*
Erich Segal, *Love Story*
Eric Rohmer, *My Night at Maud's*

CINEMATOGRAPHY

■ Freddie Young, *Ryan's Daughter*
Ernest Laszlo, *Airport*
Fred Koenekamp, *Patton*
Charles F. Wheeler, Osami Furuya, Sinsaku Himeda, Masamichi Satoh, *Tora! Tora! Tora!*
Billy Williams, *Women in Love*

FOREIGN-LANGUAGE FILM

■ *Investigation of a Citizen Above Suspicion* (Italy)
First Love (Switzerland)
Hoa-Binh (France)
Paix sur les champs (Belgium)
Tristana (Spain)

OTHER AWARDS:

ART DIRECTION / SET DIRECTION

■ Urie McClearly, Gil Parrondo; Antonio Mateos, Pierre-Louis Thevenet, *Patton*

SOUND

■ Douglas Williams, Don Bassman, *Patton*

SHORT SUBJECTS

Cartoons:
■ Stephen Bosustow Prod., Schoenfeld Films, *Is It Always Right to be Right?*
Live Action Subjects:
■ USC Dept. of Cinema, Universal, *The Resurrection of Broncho Billy*

DOCUMENTARY

Short Subjects:
■ Laser Film Corp., *Interviews with My Lai Veterans*

Features:
■ Wadleigh-Maurice, Warner Bros., *Woodstock*

MUSIC

Best Song:
■ Fred Karlin, Robb Wilson, Arthur James, "For All We Know," *Lovers and Other Strangers*
Best Original Score:
for which the composer and collaborator, if any, shall be eligible)
■ Francis Lai, *Love Story*
Best Original Song Score:
(for which the song writer or writers and adapter, if any, shall be eligible)
■ The Beatles, *Let It Be*

FILM EDITING

■ Hugh S. Fowler, *Patton*

SPECIAL VISUAL EFFECTS

■ A. D. Flowers, L. B. Abbott, *Tora! Tora! Tora!*

COSTUME DESIGN

■ Nino Novarese, *Cromwell*

HONORARY AND OTHER AWARDS

■ Lillian Gish, for superlative artistry and for distinguished contribution to the progress of motion pictures
■ Orson Welles, for superlative artistry and versatility in the creation of motion pictures

IRVING G. THALBERG MEMORIAL AWARD

■ Ingmar Bergman

JEAN HERSHOLT HUMANITARIAN AWARD

■ Frank Sinatra

SCIENTIFIC OR TECHNICAL AWARDS

Class II:

- Leonard Sokolow and Edward H. Reichard of Consolidated Film Industries, for the concept and engineering of the Color Proofing Printer for motion pictures

Class III:

- Sylvania Electric Product, Inc., for the development and introduction of a series of compact tungsten halogen lamps for motion picture production

- B. J. Losmandy, for the concept, design and application of micro-miniature solid-state amplifier modules used in motion picture recording equipment
- Eastman Kodak Company and Photo Electronics Corp., for the design and engineering of an improved video color analyzer for motion picture laboratories
- Electro Sound Inc., for the design and introduction of the Series 8000 Sound System for motion picture theaters

---

1971

BEST PICTURE

- *The French Connection* (20th Century-Fox)
  A Clockwork Orange (Warner Bros.)
  Fiddler on the Roof (Mirisch-UA)
  The Last Picture Show (BBS-Columbia)
  Nicholas and Alexandra (Horizon-Columbia)

BEST DIRECTOR

- William Friedkin, *The French Connection*
  Peter Bogdanovich, *The Last Picture Show*
  Norman Jewison, *Fiddler on the Roof*
  Stanley Kubrick, *A Clockwork Orange*
  John Schlesinger, *Sunday Bloody Sunday*

BEST ACTOR

- Gene Hackman, *The French Connection*
  Peter Finch, *Sunday Bloody Sunday*
  Walter Matthau, *Kotch*
  George C. Scott, *The Hospital*
  Topol, *Fiddler on the Roof*

BEST ACTRESS

- Jane Fonda, *Klute*
  Julie Christie, *McCabe & Mrs. Miller*
  Glenda Jackson, *Sunday Bloody Sunday*
  Vanessa Redgrave, *Mary, Queen of Scots*
  Janet Suzman, *Nicholas and Alexandra*

BEST SUPPORTING ACTOR

- Ben Johnson, *The Last Picture Show*

Jeff Bridges, *The Last Picture Show*

Leonard Frey, *Fiddler on the Roof*

Richard Jaeckel, *Sometimes a Great Notion*

Roy Scheider, *The French Connection*

BEST SUPPORTING ACTRESS

■ Cloris Leachman, *The Last Picture Show*

Ellen Burstyn, *The Last Picture Show*

Barbara Harris, *Who Is Harry Kellerman and Why Is He Saying All Those Terrible Things About Me?*

Margaret Leighton, *The Go-Between*

Ann-Margret, *Carnal Knowledge*

BEST SCREENPLAY (BASED ON MATERIAL FROM ANOTHER MEDIUM)

■ Ernest Tidyman, *The French Connection*

Stanley Kubrick, *A Clockwork Orange*

Bernardo Bertolucci, *The Conformist*

Ugo Pirro, Vittorio Bonicelli, *The Garden of the Finzi-Continis*

Larry McMurtry, Peter Bogdanovich, *The Last Picture Show*

BEST STORY AND SCREENPLAY (BASED ON FACTUAL MATERIAL OR MATERIAL NOT PREVIOUSLY PUBLISHED)

■ Paddy Chayefsky, *The Hospital*

Elio Petri, Ugo Pirro, *Investigation of a Citizen Above Suspicion*

Andy and Dave Lewis, *Klute*

Herman Raucher, *Summer of '42*

Penelope Gilliatt, *Sunday Bloody Sunday*

CINEMATOGRAPHY

■ Oswald Morris, *Fiddler on the Roof*

Owen Roizman, *The French Connection*

Robert Surtees, *The Last Picture Show*

Freddie Young, *Nicholas and Alexandra*

Robert Surtees, *Summer of '42*

FOREIGN-LANGUAGE FILM

■ *The Garden of the Finzi-Continis* (Italy)

Dodes 'Ka-Den (Japan)

The Emigrants (Sweden)

The Policeman (Israel)

Tchaikovsky (USSR)

OTHER AWARDS:

ART DIRECTION / SET DIRECTION

■ John Box, Ernest Archer, Jack Maxsted, Gil Parrondo; Vernon Dixon, *Nicholas and Alexandra*

SOUND

■ Gordon K. McCallum, David Hildyard, *Fiddler on the Roof*

SHORT SUBJECTS

Cartoons:

■ Maxwell-Petok Prod., Regency Films, *The Crunch Bird*

Live Action Subjects:

■ Producciones Concord, Paramount, *Sentinels of Silence*

DOCUMENTARY

Short Subjects:

■ Producciones Concord, Paramount, *Sentinels of Silence*

Features:

- David Wolper–Cinema 5, *Hellstrom Chronicle*

MUSIC

Best Song:

- Isaac Hayes, "Theme from Shaft," *Shaft*

Best Original Score:
(for which only the composer shall be eligible)

- Michel Legrand, *Summer of '42*

Best Scoring: Adaptation and Original Song Score:
(for which the composer, lyricist and adapter shall be eligible if the material was written for or first used in an eligible motion picture, but only the adapter shall be eligible if the material is an adaptation or has been previously used)

- John Williams, *Fiddler on the Roof*

FILM EDITING

- Jerry Greenberg, *The French Connection*

SPECIAL VISUAL EFFECTS

- Danny Lee, Eustace Lycett, Alan Maley, *Bedknobs and Broomsticks*

COSTUME DESIGN

- Yvonne Blake, Antonio Castillo, *Nicholas and Alexandra*

HONORARY AND OTHER AWARDS

- Charles Chaplin, for the incalculable effect he has had in making motion pictures the art form of this country

SCIENTIFIC OR TECHNICAL AWARDS

Class II:

- John N. Wilkinson of Optical Radiation Corp., for the development and engineering of a system of xenon arc lamphouses for motion picture projection

Class III:

- Thomas Jefferson Hutchinson, James R. Rochester and Fenton Hamilton, for the development and introduction of the Sunbrute system of xenon arc lamps for location lighting in motion picture projection
- Photo Research, a division of Kollmorgen Corp., for the development and introduction of the film-lens balanced Three Color Meter
- Robert D. August and Cinema Products Company, for the development and introduction of a new crystal-controlled lightweight motor for the Arriflex 35mm motion picture camera
- Producers Service Corp. and Consolidated Film Industries, and Cinema Research Corp. and Research Products, Inc., for the engineering and implementation of fully automated blowup motion picture printing systems
- Cinema Products Company, for a control motor to actuate zoom lenses on motion picture cameras

1972

BEST PICTURE

- *The Godfather* (Paramount)
  Cabaret (ABC Pictures, Allied Artists)
  Deliverance (Warner Bros.)
  The Emigrants (Warner Bros.)
  Sounder (Radnitz, Mattel, 20th Century-Fox)

BEST DIRECTOR

- Bob Fosse, *Cabaret*
  John Boorman, *Deliverance*
  Francis Ford Coppola, *The Godfather*
  Joseph L. Mankiewicz, *Sleuth*
  Jan Troell, *The Emigrants*

BEST ACTOR

- Marlon Brando, *The Godfather* (award declined)
  Michael Caine, *Sleuth*
  Laurence Olivier, *Sleuth*
  Peter O'Toole, *The Ruling Class*
  Paul Winfield, *Sounder*

BEST ACTRESS

- Liza Minnelli, *Cabaret*
  Diana Ross, *Lady Sings the Blues*
  Maggie Smith, *Travels with My Aunt*
  Cicely Tyson, *Sounder*
  Liv Ullmann, *The Emigrants*

BEST SUPPORTING ACTOR

- Joel Grey, *Cabaret*
  Eddie Albert, *The Heartbreak Kid*
  James Caan, *The Godfather*
  Robert Duvall, *The Godfather*
  Al Pacino, *The Godfather*

BEST SUPPORTING ACTRESS

- Eileen Heckart, *Butterflies Are Free*
  Jeannie Berlin, *The Heartbreak Kid*
  Geraldine Page, *Pete 'n' Tillie*
  Susan Tyrrell, *Fat City*
  Shelley Winters, *The Poseidon Adventure*

BEST SCREENPLAY (BASED ON MATERIAL FROM ANOTHER MEDIUM)

- Mario Puzo, Francis Ford Coppola, *The Godfather*
  Jan Troell, Bengt Forslund, *The Emigrants*
  Jay Allen, *Cabaret*
  Julius J. Epstein, *Pete 'n' Tillie*
  Lonne Elder III, *Sounder*

BEST STORY AND SCREENPLAY (BASED ON FACTUAL MATERIAL OR MATERIAL NOT PREVIOUSLY PUBLISHED)

- Jeremy Larner, *The Candidate*
  Luis Buñuel, *The Discreet Charm of the Bourgeoisie*
  Terence McCloy, Chris Clark, Suzanne de Passe, *Lady Sings the Blues*
  Louis Malle, *Murmur of the Heart*
  Carl Foreman, *Young Winston*

CINEMATOGRAPHY

- Geoffrey Unsworth, *Cabaret*
  Charles B. Lang, *Butterflies Are Free*
  Harold E. Stine, *The Poseidon Adventure*

Harry Stradling, Jr., *1776*
Douglas Slocombe, *Travels with My Aunt*

FOREIGN-LANGUAGE FILM

▪ *The Discreet Charm of the Bourgeoisie* (France)
The Dawns Here Are Quiet (USSR)
I Love You Rosa (Israel)
My Dearest Señorita (Spain)
The New Land (Sweden)

OTHER AWARDS:

ART DIRECTION / SET DIRECTION

▪ Rolf Zehetbauer, Jurgen Kiebach; Herbert Strabl, *Cabaret*

SOUND

▪ Robert Knudson, David Hildyard, *Cabaret*

SHORT SUBJECTS
Cartoons:

▪ Richard Williams (ABC), *A Christmas Carol*
Live Action Subjects:
▪ Concepts Unlimited Production–United Artists, *Norman Rockwell's World ... An American Dream*

DOCUMENTARY
Short Subjects:

▪ Charles Huguenot van der Linden Productions, *This Tiny World*
Features:
▪ Cinema X, Cinema 5, Ltd., *Marjoe*

MUSIC

Best Song:

▪ Al Kasha, Joel Hirschhorn, "The Morning After," *The Poseidon Adventure*

Best Original Dramatic Score:
(for which only the composer shall be eligible)*
▪ Charles Chaplin, Raymond Rasch, Larry Russell, *Limelight*
Best Scoring:
(for which the composer, the lyricist and the adapter shall be eligible if the score was written or first used for an eligible picture, but only the adapter shall be eligible if the material is an adaptation)
▪ Ralph Burns, *Cabaret*

FILM EDITING

▪ David Bretherton, *Cabaret*

COSTUME DESIGN

▪ Anthony Powell, *Travels with My Aunt*

HONORARY AND OTHER AWARDS

▪ Edward G. Robinson, who achieved greatness as a player, a patron of the arts and a dedicated citizen ... in sum, a Renaissance man
▪ Charles Boren, leader for 38 years of the industry's enlightened labor relations and architect of its policy of non-discrimination
▪ L. B. Abbott and A. D. Flowers for their special visual effects in *The Poseidon Adventure*

---

* *The Godfather* score, composed by Nino Rota, was originally announced as one of the five nominees, but was later declared ineligible when it was discovered that portions of the composition had been used in Rota's score for a 1958 Italian film, *Fortunella*.

JEAN HERSHOLT HUMANITARIAN AWARD
- Rosalind Russell

SCIENTIFIC OR TECHNICAL AWARDS
Class II:
- Joseph E. Bluth, for research and development in the field of electronic photography and transfer of video tape to motion picture film
- Edward H. Reichard and Howard T. Lazare of Consolidated Film Industries, and Edward Efron of IBM, for the engineering of a computerized light valve monitoring system for motion picture printing
- Panavision, Inc., for the development and engineering of a Panaflex motion picture camera
Class III:
- Photo Research, a division of Kollmorgen Corp., and Producers Service for the Spectra Film Gate Photometer, for motion picture printers

- Carter Equipment Company and Ramtronics, for the Ramtronics light-valve photometer for motion picture printers
- David Degenkolb, Harry Larson, Manfred Michelson and Fred Scobey of DeLuxe General, for the development of a computerized motion picture printer and process control system
- Jiro Mukai and Ryusho Hirose of Canon, Inc., and Wilton R. Holm of the AMPTP Motion Picture and Television Research Center, for development of the Canon Macro Zoom Lens for motion picture photography
- Philip V. Palmquist and Leonard I. Olson of the 3M Company and Frank P. Clark of the AMPTP Research Center, for development of the Nextel simulated blood for motion picture color photography
- E. H. Geissler and G. M. Berggren of Wil-Kin, Inc., for engineering of the Ultra-Vision Motion Picture Theater Projection System

---

1973

BEST PICTURE
- *The Sting* (Zanuck-Brown–Universal)
  American Graffiti (Universal)
  Cries and Whispers (New World)
  The Exorcist (Warner Bros.)
  A Touch of Class (Brut–Avco Embassy)

BEST DIRECTOR
- George Roy Hill, *The Sting*
  Ingmar Bergman, *Cries and Whispers*
  Bernardo Bertolucci, *Last Tango in Paris*
  William Friedkin, *The Exorcist*
  George Lucas, *American Graffiti*

BEST ACTOR

- Jack Lemmon, *Save the Tiger*
  Marlon Brando, *Last Tango in Paris*
  Jack Nicholson, *The Last Detail*
  Al Pacino, *Serpico*
  Robert Redford, *The Sting*

BEST ACTRESS

- Glenda Jackson, *A Touch of Class*
  Ellen Burstyn, *The Exorcist*
  Marsha Mason, *Cinderella Liberty*
  Barbra Streisand, *The Way We Were*
  Joanne Woodward, *Summer Wishes, Winter Dreams*

BEST SUPPORTING ACTOR

- John Houseman, *The Paper Chase*
  Vincent Gardenia, *Bang the Drum Slowly*
  Jack Gilford, *Save the Tiger*
  Jason Miller, *The Exorcist*
  Randy Quaid, *The Last Detail*

BEST SUPPORTING ACTRESS

- Tatum O'Neal, *Paper Moon*
  Linda Blair, *The Exorcist*
  Candy Clark, *American Graffiti*
  Madeline Kahn, *Paper Moon*
  Sylvia Sidney, *Summer Wishes, Winter Dreams*

BEST SCREENPLAY (BASED ON MATERIAL FROM ANOTHER MEDIUM)

- William Peter Blatty, *The Exorcist*
  Robert Towne, *The Last Detail*
  James Bridges, *The Paper Chase*
  Alvin Sargent, *Paper Moon*
  Waldo Salt, Norman Wexler, *Serpico*

BEST STORY AND SCREENPLAY (BASED ON FACTUAL MATERIAL OR MATERIAL NOT PREVIOUSLY PUBLISHED)

- David S. Ward, *The Sting*
  George Lucas, Gloria Katz, Willard Huyck, *American Graffiti*
  Ingmar Bergman, *Cries and Whispers*
  Steve Shagan, *Save the Tiger*
  Melvin Frank, Jack Rose, *A Touch of Class*

CINEMATOGRAPHY

- Sven Nykvist, *Cries and Whispers*
  Owen Roizman, *The Exorcist*
  Jack Couffer, *Jonathan Livingston Seagull*
  Robert Surtees, *The Sting*
  Harry Stradling, Jr., *The Way We Were*

FOREIGN-LANGUAGE FILM

- *Day for Night* (France)
  The House on Chelouche Street (Israel)
  L'Invitation (Switzerland)
  The Pedestrian (West Germany)
  Turkish Delight (The Netherlands)

OTHER AWARDS:

ART DIRECTION / SET DIRECTION

- Henry Bumstead; James Payne, *The Sting*

MUSIC

Best Song:

- Marvin Hamlisch, Alan and Marilyn Bergman, "The Way We Were," *The Way We Were*

Best Original Dramatic Score:
- Marvin Hamlisch, *The Way We Were*

Best Scoring—Original Song Score and Adaptation; or Best Scoring—Adaptation:
- Marvin Hamlisch, *The Sting*

SOUND
- Robert Knudson, Chris Newman, *The Exorcist*

SHORT SUBJECTS
Cartoons:
- Frank Mouris Production, *Frank Film*

Live Action Subjects:
- Allan Miller Production, *The Bolero*

DOCUMENTARY
Short Subjects:
- Krainin-Sage Productions, *Princeton: A Search for Answers*

Features:
- Kieth Merrill, Rodeo Films, *The Great American Cowboy*

FILM EDITING
- William Reynolds, *The Sting*

COSTUME DESIGN
- Edith Head, *The Sting*

HONORARY AND OTHER AWARDS
- Groucho Marx, for his brilliant creativity and unequaled achievements of the Marx Brothers in the art of motion picture comedy
- Henri Langlois, for his untiring devotion to the art of film, for his massive contributions toward preserving its historical past and his unswerving faith in its future

IRVING G. THALBERG MEMORIAL AWARD
- Lawrence Weingarten

JEAN HERSHOLT HUMANITARIAN AWARD
- Lew Wasserman

SCIENTIFIC OR TECHNICAL AWARDS
Class II:
- Joachim Gerb and Erich Kastner of the Arnold and Richter Company, for the development and engineering of the Arriflex 35BL motion picture camera
- Magna-Tech Electronic Company, for the engineering and development of a high-speed re-recording system for motion picture production
- William W. Vallant of PSC Technology, Inc., Howard F. Ott of Eastman Kodak Company and Gerry Diebold of the Richmark Camera Service, Inc., for the development of a liquid-gate system for motion picture printers
- Harold A. Scheib, Clifford H. Ellis and Roger W. Banks of Research Products, Incorporated, for the concept and engineering of the model 2101 optical printer for motion picture optical effects

Class III:
- Rosco Laboratories, Inc., for the technical advances and development of a complete system of light-control materials for motion picture photography

■ Richard H. Vetter of the Todd-AO Corporation, for the design of an improved anamorphic focusing system for motion picture photography

1974

BEST PICTURE

■ *The Godfather Part II* (Paramount)
Chinatown (Paramount)
The Conversation (Paramount)
Lenny (UA)
The Towering Inferno (20th Century-Fox–Warner Bros.)

BEST DIRECTOR

■ Francis Ford Coppola, *The Godfather Part II*
John Cassavetes, *A Woman Under the Influence*
Bob Fosse, *Lenny*
Roman Polanski, *Chinatown*
François Truffaut, *Day for Night*

BEST ACTOR

■ Art Carney, *Harry and Tonto*
Albert Finney, *Murder on the Orient Express*
Dustin Hoffman, *Lenny*
Jack Nicholson, *Chinatown*
Al Pacino, *The Godfather Part II*

BEST ACTRESS

■ Ellen Burstyn, *Alice Doesn't Live Here Anymore*
Diahann Carroll, *Claudine*
Faye Dunaway, *Chinatown*
Valerie Perrine, *Lenny*
Gena Rowlands, *A Woman Under the Influence*

BEST SUPPORTING ACTOR

■ Robert De Niro, *The Godfather Part II*
Fred Astaire, *The Towering Inferno*
Jeff Bridges, *Thunderbolt and Lightfoot*
Michael V. Gazzo, *The Godfather Part II*
Lee Strasberg, *The Godfather Part II*

BEST SUPPORTING ACTRESS

■ Ingrid Bergman, *Murder on the Orient Express*
Valentina Cortese, *Day for Night*
Madeline Kahn, *Blazing Saddles*
Diane Ladd, *Alice Doesn't Live Here Anymore*
Talia Shire, *The Godfather Part II*

BEST SCREENPLAY (ADAPTED FROM OTHER MATERIAL)

■ Francis Ford Coppola, Mario Puzo, *The Godfather Part II*
Mordecai Richler, Lionel Chetwynd, *The Apprenticeship of Duddy Kravitz*
Julian Barry, *Lenny*
Paul Dehn, *Murder on the Orient Express*
Gene Wilder, Mel Brooks, *Young Frankenstein*

BEST ORIGINAL SCREENPLAY

- Robert Towne, *Chinatown*
  Robert Getchell, *Alice Doesn't Live Here Anymore*
  Francis Ford Coppola, *The Conversation*
  François Truffaut, Jean-Louis Richard, Suzanne Schiffman, *Day for Night*
  Paul Mazursky, Josh Greenfeld, *Harry and Tonto*

CINEMATOGRAPHY

- Fred Koenekamp, Joseph Biroc, *The Towering Inferno*
  John A. Alonzo, *Chinatown*
  Philip Lathrop, *Earthquake*
  Bruce Surtees, *Lenny*
  Geoffrey Unsworth, *Murder on the Orient Express*

FOREIGN-LANGUAGE FILM

- *Amarcord* (Italy)
  Catsplay (Hungary)
  The Deluge (Poland)
  Lacombe, Lucien (France)
  The Truce (Argentina)

OTHER AWARDS:

ART DIRECTION / SET DIRECTION

- Dean Tavoularis, Angelo Graham; George R. Nelson, *The Godfather Part II*

SOUND

- Ronald Pierce, Melvin Metcalfe, Sr., *Earthquake*

SHORT SUBJECTS
Cartoons:

- Lighthouse Productions, *Closed Mondays*
  Live Action:
- C.A.P.A.C. (Paris), *One-Eyed Men Are Kings*

DOCUMENTARY
Short Subjects:

- R. A. Films, *Don't*
  Features:
- BBS-Rainbow Pictures, *Hearts and Minds*

MUSIC
Best Song:

- Al Kasha, Joel Hirschhorn, "We May Never Love Like This Again," *The Towering Inferno*
  Best Original Dramatic Score:
- Nino Rota, Carmine Coppola, *The Godfather Part II*
  Best Scoring: Original Song Score and / or Adaptation:
- Nelson Riddle, *The Great Gatsby*

FILM EDITING

- Harold F. Kress, Carl Kress, *The Towering Inferno*

COSTUME DESIGN

- Theoni V. Aldredge, *The Great Gatsby*

HONORARY AND OTHER AWARDS

- Howard Hawks, as a giant of the American cinema whose pictures, taken as a whole, represent one of the most consistent, vivid and varied bodies of work in world cinema
- Jean Renoir, as a filmmaker who has worked with grace, responsibility and enviable competence through silent film, sound film, feature, documentary and television
- *Earthquake*, a special achievement award for visual effects to Frank Brendel,

Albert Whitlock, and Glen Robinson

JEAN HERSHOLT HUMANITARIAN AWARD
- Arthur Krim

SCIENTIFIC OR TECHNICAL AWARDS
Class II:
- Joseph D. Kelley of Glen Glenn Sound, for designing new audio control consoles for film sound recording and re-recording
- Quad-Eight Sound Corp., for engineering and constructing new audio control consoles designed by Burbank Studios Sound and Goldwyn Sound Dept.
- Waldon O. Watson, Richard J. Stumpf, Robert J. Leonard and the Universal Studios Sound Dept., for their development and engineering of the "Sensurround" system
- Burbank Studios Sound Dept., for the design of new audio control consoles engineered and constructed by Quad-Eight Sound Corp.
- Samuel Goldwyn Studios Sound Dept., for the design of new audio control consoles engineered and constructed by Quad-Eight Sound Corp.

Class III:
- Elemack Company, for the introduction of the Spyder camera dolly
- Louis Ami of Universal Studios, for designing and constructing a reciprocating camera platform used for filming special visual effects

1975

BEST PICTURE
- *One Flew Over the Cuckoo's Nest* (Fantasy-UA)
  Barry Lyndon (Warner Bros.)
  Dog Day Afternoon (Warner Bros.)
  Jaws (Universal)
  Nashville (ABC–Paramount)

BEST DIRECTOR
- Milos Forman, *One Flew Over the Cuckoo's Nest*
  Robert Altman, *Nashville*
  Federico Fellini, *Amarcord*
  Stanley Kubrick, *Barry Lyndon*
  Sidney Lumet, *Dog Day Afternoon*

BEST ACTOR
- Jack Nicholson, *One Flew Over the Cuckoo's Nest*
  Walter Matthau, *The Sunshine Boys*
  Al Pacino, *Dog Day Afternoon*
  Maximilian Schell, *The Man in the Glass Booth*
  James Whitmore, *Give 'em Hell, Harry!*

BEST ACTRESS
- Louise Fletcher, *One Flew Over the Cuckoo's Nest*
  Isabelle Adjani, *The Story of Adele H.*
  Ann-Margret, *Tommy*

Glenda Jackson, *Hedda*

Carol Kane, *Hester Street*

BEST SUPPORTING ACTOR

- George Burns, *The Sunshine Boys*

  Brad Dourif, *One Flew Over the Cuckoo's Nest*

  Burgess Meredith, *The Day of the Locust*

  Chris Sarandon, *Dog Day Afternoon*

  Jack Warden, *Shampoo*

BEST SUPPORTING ACTRESS

- Lee Grant, *Shampoo*

  Ronee Blakley, *Nashville*

  Sylvia Miles, *Farewell, My Lovely*

  Lily Tomlin, *Nashville*

  Brenda Vaccaro, *Once Is Not Enough*

BEST SCREENPLAY (ADAPTED FROM ANOTHER MEDIUM)

- Lawrence Hauben, Bo Goldman, *One Flew Over the Cuckoo's Nest*

  Stanley Kubrick, *Barry Lyndon*

  John Huston, Gladys Hill, *The Man Who Would Be King*

  Ruggero Maccari, Dino Risi, *Scent of a Woman*

  Neil Simon, *The Sunshine Boys*

BEST ORIGINAL SCREENPLAY

- Frank Pierson, *Dog Day Afternoon*

  Federico Fellini, Tonino Guerra, *Amarcord*

  Claude Lelouch, Pierre Uytterhoeven, *And Now My Love*

  Ted Allan, *Lies My Father Told Me*

  Robert Towne, Warren Beatty, *Shampoo*

CINEMATOGRAPHY

- John Alcott, *Barry Lyndon*

  Conrad Hall, *The Day of the Locust*

  James Wong Howe, *Funny Lady*

  Robert Surtees, *The Hindenburg*

  Haskell Wexler, Bill Butler, *One Flew Over the Cuckoo's Nest*

FOREIGN-LANGUAGE FILM

- *Dersu Uzala* (USSR)

  Land of Promise (Poland)

  Letters from Marusia (Mexico)

  Sandakan No. 8 (Japan)

  Scent of a Woman (Italy)

OTHER AWARDS:

ART DIRECTION / SET DIRECTION

- Ken Adam, Roy Walker; Vernon Dixon, *Barry Lyndon*

SOUND

- Robert L. Hoyt, Roger Heman, Earl Madery, John Carter, *Jaws*

SHORT SUBJECTS

Cartoons:
- Granstern Ltd./British Lion, *Great*

Live Action:
- Bert Salzman Productions, *Angel and Big Joe*

DOCUMENTARY

Short Subjects:
- Opus Films, Ltd., *The End of the Game*

Features:
- Crawley Films, *The Man Who Skied Down Everest*

MUSIC

Best Song:
- Keith Carradine, "I'm Easy," *Nashville*

Best Original Score:
- John Williams, *Jaws*

Best Original Song Score and Adaptation; or Best Scoring, Adaptation only:
Leonard Rosenman, *Barry Lyndon*

FILM EDITING

- Verna Fields, *Jaws*

COSTUME DESIGN

- Ulla-Britt Soderlund, Milena Canonero, *Barry Lyndon*

HONORARY AND OTHER AWARDS

- Mary Pickford, in recognition of her unique contributions to the industry and the development of film as an artistic medium
- *The Hindenburg,* for its visual effects by Albert Whitlock and Glen Robinson and its sound effects by Peter Berkos

IRVING G. THALBERG MEMORIAL AWARD

- Mervin LeRoy

JEAN HERSHOLT HUMANITARIAN AWARD

- Jules Stein

SCIENTIFIC OR TECHNICAL AWARDS

Class II:
- Chadwell O'Connor of the O'Connor Engineering Laboratories, for the concept and engineering of a fluid-damped camera-head for motion picture photography
- William F. Miner of Universal City Studios, for the development and engineering of a solid-state, 500-kilowatt, direct-current static rectifier for motion picture lighting

Class III:
- Lawrence W. Butler and Roger Banks, for the concept of applying low inertia and stepping electric motors to film transport systems and optical printers for motion picture production
- David J. Degenkolb and Fred Scobey of DeLuxe General, Incorporated, and John C. Dolan and Richard DuBois of the Akwaklame Company, for the development of a technique for silver recovery from photographic wash-waters by ion exchange
- Joseph Westheimer, for the development of a device to obtain shadowed titles on motion picture film
- The Carter Equipment Co., Inc., and Ramtronics, for the engineering and manufacture of a computerized tape punching system for programming laboratory printing machines
- Bell & Howell, for the engineering and manufacture of a computerized tape punching system for programming laboratory printing machines
- Fredrik Schlyter, for the engineering and manufacture of a computerized tape punching system for programming laboratory printing machines
- Hollywood Film Co., for the engineering and manufac-

ture of a computerized tape punching system for pro-

gramming laboratory printing machines

1976

BEST PICTURE

■ *Rocky* (Chartoff–Winkler-UA)
All the President's Men (Wildwood-Warner)
Bound for Glory (UA)
Network (MGM-UA)
Taxi Driver (Columbia)

BEST DIRECTOR

■ John G. Avildsen, *Rocky*
Alan J. Pakula, *All the President's Men*
Ingmar Bergman, *Face to Face*
Sidney Lumet, *Network*
Lina Wertmüller, *Seven Beauties*

BEST ACTOR

■ Peter Finch, *Network*
Robert De Niro, *Taxi Driver*
Giancarlo Giannini, *Seven Beauties*
William Holden, *Network*
Sylvester Stallone, *Rocky*

BEST ACTRESS

■ Faye Dunaway, *Network*
Marie-Christine Barrault, *Cousin, Cousine*
Talia Shire, *Rocky*
Sissy Spacek, *Carrie*
Liv Ullmann, *Face to Face*

BEST SUPPORTING ACTOR

■ Jason Robards, *All the President's Men*
Ned Beatty, *Network*
Burgess Meredith, *Rocky*

Laurence Olivier, *Marathon Man*
Burt Young, *Rocky*

BEST SUPPORTING ACTRESS

■ Beatrice Straight, *Network*
Jane Alexander, *All the President's Men*
Jodie Foster, *Taxi Driver*
Lee Grant, *Voyage of the Damned*
Piper Laurie, *Carrie*

BEST SCREENPLAY ADAPTATION

■ William Goldman, *All the President's Men*
Robert Getchell, *Bound for Glory*
Federico Fellini, Bernardino Zapponi, *Casanova*
Nicholas Meyer, *The Seven-Per-Cent Solution*
Steve Shagan, David Butler, *Voyage of the Damned*

BEST ORIGINAL SCREENPLAY

■ Paddy Chayefsky, *Network*
Jean-Charles Tacchella, Daniele Thompson, *Cousin, Cousine*
Walter Bernstein, *The Front*
Sylvester Stallone, *Rocky*
Lina Wertmüller, *Seven Beauties*

CINEMATOGRAPHY

■ Haskell Wexler, *Bound for Glory*

Richard H. Kline, *King Kong*
Ernest Laszlo, *Logan's Run*
Owen Roizman, *Network*
Robert Surtees, *A Star Is Born*

FOREIGN-LANGUAGE FILM

- *Black and White in Color* (Ivory Coast)
  Cousin, Cousine (France)
  Jacob, the Liar (German Democratic Republic)
  Nights and Days (Poland)
  Seven Beauties (Italy)

OTHER AWARDS:

ART DIRECTION / SET DIRECTION

- George Jenkins; George Gaines, *All the President's Men*

SOUND

- Arthur Piantadosi, Les Fresholtz, Dick Alexander, Jim Webb, *All the President's Men*

SHORT SUBJECTS

Cartoons:
- Suzanne Baker, Film Australian Prod., *Leisure*

Live Action:
- André Guttfreund Production, *In the Region of Ice*

DOCUMENTARY

Short Subjects:
- Community Television of Southern California, *Number Our Days*

Features:
- Cabin Creek Films, producer, *Harlan County U.S.A.*

MUSIC

Best Song:
- Paul Williams, Barbra Streisand, "Evergreen," *A Star Is Born*

Best Original Score:
- Jerry Goldsmith, *The Omen*

Best Original Song Score:
- Leonard Rosenman, *Bound for Glory*

FILM EDITING

- Richard Halsey, Scott Conrad, *Rocky*

COSTUME DESIGN

- Danilo Donati, *Fellini's Casanova*

IRVING G. THALBERG MEMORIAL AWARD

- Pandro S. Berman

HONORARY AND OTHER AWARDS

- Carlo Rambaldi, Glen Robinson and Frank Van Der Veer, for the visual effects of *King Kong*
- L. B. Abbott, Glen Robinson and Matthew Yuricich, for visual effects of *Logan's Run*

SCIENTIFIC OR TECHNICAL AWARDS

Class II:
- Consolidated Film Industries and the Barnebey-Cheney Co., for the development of a system for the recovery of film-cleaning solvent vapors in a motion picture laboratory
- William L. Graham, Manfred G. Michelson, Geoffrey F. Norman and Siegfried Seiber of Technicolor, for the development and engineering of a Continuous, High-Speed, Color Motion Picture Printing System

Class III:

- Fred Bartscher of the Kollmorgen Corp. and Glenn Berggren of the Schneider Corp., for the design and development of a single-lens magnifier for motion picture projection lenses
- Panavision, Inc., for the design and development of super-speed lenses for motion picture photography
- Hiroshi Suzukawa of Canon and Wilton R. Holm of the AMPTP Motion Picture and Television Research Center, for the design and development of super-speed lenses for motion picture photography
- Carl Zeiss Company, for the design and development of super-speed lenses for motion picture photography
- Photo Research Division of the Kollmorgen Corp., for the engineering and manufacture of the Spectra TriColor Meter

2. THE NATIONAL SOCIETY OF FILM CRITICS AWARDS

When the National Society of Film Critics was founded in late 1966, its pronounced function was fourfold: first, to give annual recognition to the best work in films of the preceding year without distinction of nationality; second, to promote throughout the year films the Society deemed worthy of support; third, to register protest against any practice in film production, distribution or exhibition that the Society thought injurious to films or the public interest; and fourth, to serve fraternal purposes among filmmakers and film critics, American and foreign.

During its first years the National Society stressed that although its members held widely divergent views and practiced considerably different critical methods, all its members took films seriously and deemed them worthy of the highest standards of criticism. The seriousness of the Society's standards was obvious in its first awards: whereas older organizations like the New York Film Critics Circle, the National Board of Review and the Academy selected *A Man for All Seasons* as the Best Picture of 1966, the newly formed National Society chose the much more interesting and much more complicated *Blow-Up*. And in

1967, while those older groups honored films like *In the Heat of the Night* and *Far from the Madding Crowd,* the National Society gave its accolade to *Persona.* Whether the National Society was being eccentric or avant-garde, more perceptive or more obscurantist, remained—as John Simon said in his introduction to the 1967 awards—a question for each viewer to answer.

Although the Society claimed its purpose was not to combat any previously existing series of awards, many critics believed that it was founded to counter the "middle-brow" propensities of such groups as the New York Film Critics Circle, which had for some time demonstrated the same tastes as the Academy. (Later the New York Film Critics Circle changed its membership, voting procedures and award categories to come closer to those of the National Society.)

In 1966 the National Society consisted of eleven voting members. Most of these members—despite the "National" in the Society's name—lived in New York. In 1972 the Society became a more truly national group, as the membership grew to twenty-four with the addition of several critics from Los Angeles, San Francisco and Chicago. These additions, however, caused John Simon to withdraw from the group as many of the newly elected fell "far below the minimal requirements of critical competence." Stanley Kauffmann also left the Society that year. The Society has continued to elect new members.

The voting procedures for the Society are simple and reasonable: each critic is asked to vote for three candidates in each category. The first choice is worth three points, the second two, and the third one. A simple plurality establishes the winner. The votes are not secret: for seven years the complete tabulations were published in the Society's annual anthologies, *Film 67/68, Film 68/69,* etc.

Besides Simon *(New Leader),* the original members were Hollis Alpert *(Saturday Review);* Brad Darrach *(Time);* Brendan Gill *(The New Yorker);* Philip T. Hartung *(Commonweal);* Pauline Kael (then for *New Republic,* soon to write for *The New Yorker);* Stanley Kauffmann (then for Channel 13, soon to write for *New Republic);* Arthur

Knight (Saturday Review); Joseph Morgenstern (Newsweek); Andrew Sarris (Village Voice); Richard Schickel (Life).

1966

Best Picture:
Blow Up
Best Director:
Michelangelo Antonioni
Best Actor:
Michael Caine, Alfie
Best Actress:
Sylvie, The Shameless Old Lady

1967

Best Picture:
Persona
Best Director:
Ingmar Bergman, Persona
Best Actor:
Rod Steiger, In the Heat of the Night
Best Actress:
Bibi Andersson, Persona
Best Supporting Actor:
Gene Hackman, Bonnie and Clyde
Best Supporting Actress:
Marjorie Rhodes, The Family Way
Best Screenplay:
David Newman and Robert Benton, Bonnie and Clyde
Best Cinematography:
Haskell Wexler, In the Heat of the Night

1968

Best Picture:
Shame
Best Director:
Ingmar Bergman, Shame; Hour of the Wolf
Best Actor:
Per Oscarsson, Hunger
Best Actress:
Liv Ullmann, Shame
Best Supporting Actor:
Seymour Cassel, Faces
Best Supporting Actress:
Billie Whitelaw, Charlie Bubbles
Best Cinematography:
William A. Fraker, Bullitt
Best Screenplay:
John Cassavetes, Faces
Special Awards:
Allan King's Warrendale and Eugene S. Jones's A Face of War for feature-length documentary
Yellow Submarine for feature-length animation

1969

Best Picture:
Z
Best Director:
François Truffaut, Stolen Kisses
Best Actor:
Jon Voight, Midnight Cowboy
Best Actress:
Vanessa Redgrave, The Loves of Isadora

Best Supporting Actor:
Jack Nicholson, *Easy Rider*
Best Supporting Actress:
Sian Phillips, *Goodbye, Mr. Chips*
Best Screenplay:
Paul Mazursky and Larry Tucker, *Bob & Carol & Ted & Alice*
Best Cinematography:
Lucien Ballard, *The Wild Bunch*
Special Awards:
Ivan Passer, for *Intimate Lighting,* a first film of great originality
Dennis Hopper, for *Easy Rider* as director, co-writer and co-star

1970

Best Picture:
*M*A*S*H*
Best Director:
Ingmar Bergman, *The Passion of Anna*
Best Actor:
George C. Scott, *Patton*
Best Actress:
Glenda Jackson, *Women in Love*
Best Supporting Actor:
Chief Dan George, *Little Big Man*
Best Supporting Actress:
Lois Smith, *Five Easy Pieces*
Best Screenplay:
Eric Rohmer, *My Night at Maud's*
Best Cinematography:
Nestor Almendros, *The Wild Child* and *My Night at Maud's*
Special Awards:
Donald Richie and the Film Dept. of the Museum of Modern Art, for the three-month retrospective of Japanese films
Daniel Talbot of the New Yorker Theatre, for the contribution he has made to the cinema by showing films that otherwise might not have been available to the public

1971

Best Picture:
Claire's Knee
Best Director:
Bernardo Bertolucci, *The Conformist*
Best Actor:
Peter Finch, *Sunday Bloody Sunday*
Best Actress:
Jane Fonda, *Klute*
Best Supporting Actor:
Bruce Dern, *Drive, He Said*
Best Supporting Actress:
Ellen Burstyn, *The Last Picture Show*
Best Screenplay:
Penelope Gilliatt, *Sunday Bloody Sunday*
Best Cinematography:
Vittorio Storaro, *The Conformist*
Special Award:
The Sorrow and the Pity, directed by Marcel Ophuls, a film of extraordinary public interest and distinction

1972

Best Picture:
The Discreet Charm of the Bourgeoisie
Best Director:
Luis Buñuel, *The Discreet Charm . . .*

Best Actor:
Al Pacino, *The Godfather*
Best Actress:
Cicely Tyson, *Sounder*
Best Supporting Actor:
Joel Grey, *Cabaret*
Eddie Albert, *The Heartbreak Kid*
Best Supporting Actress:
Jeannie Berlin, *The Heartbreak Kid*
Best Screenplay:
Ingmar Bergman, *Cries and Whispers*
Best Cinematography:
Sven Nykvist, *Cries and Whispers*
Richard and Hinda Rosenthal Foundation Awards:
My Uncle Antoine, directed by Claude Jutra (for a film which, although not sufficiently recognized by public attendance, has nevertheless been an outstanding cinematic achievement)
Ivan Passer, director of *Intimate Lighting*, and Robert Kaylor, director of *Derby* (for a person working in cinema whose contribution to film art has not yet received due public recognition)

1973

Best Picture:
Day for Night
Best Director:
François Truffaut, *Day for Night*
Best Actor:
Marlon Brando, *Last Tango in Paris*
Best Actress:
Liv Ullmann, *The New Land*

Best Supporting Actor:
Robert De Niro, *Mean Streets*
Best Supporting Actress:
Valentina Cortese, *Day for Night*
Best Screenplay:
George Lucas, Gloria Katz and Willard Huyck, *American Graffiti*
Best Cinematography:
Vilmos Zsigmond, *The Long Goodbye*
Richard and Hinda Rosenthal Foundation Awards:
Memories of Underdevelopment, directed by Tomás Gutiérrez Alea (for a film which, although not sufficiently recognized by public attendance has nevertheless been an outstanding cinematic achievement)
Daryl Duke, director of *Payday* (to a person working in cinema whose contribution to film art has not yet received due public recognition)
Special Award:
Robert Ryan (awarded posthumously), for his performance in *The Iceman Cometh*

1974

Best Picture:
Scenes from a Marriage
Best Director:
Francis Ford Coppola, *The Conversation* and *The Godfather Part II*
Best Actor:
Jack Nicholson, *The Last Detail* and *Chinatown*
Best Actress:
Liv Ullmann, *Scenes from a Marriage*

Best Supporting Actor:
Holger Lowenadler, *Lacombe, Lucien*

Best Supporting Actress:
Bibi Andersson, *Scenes from a Marriage*

Best Screenplay:
Ingmar Bergman, *Scenes from a Marriage*

Best Cinematography:
Gordon Willis, *The Godfather Part II* and *The Parallax View*

Special Award:
Jean Renoir

1975

Best Picture:
Nashville

Best Director:
Robert Altman, *Nashville*

Best Actor:
Jack Nicholson, *One Flew Over the Cuckoo's Nest*

Best Actress:
Isabelle Adjani, *The Story of Adele H.*

Best Supporting Actor:
Henry Gibson, *Nashville*

Best Supporting Actress:
Lily Tomlin, *Nashville*

Best Screenplay:
Robert Towne, Warren Beatty, *Shampoo*

Best Cinematography:
John Alcott, *Barry Lyndon*

Special Award:
Ingmar Bergman's *The Magic Flute*, for demonstrating how pleasurable opera can be on film

1976

Best Picture:
All the President's Men

Best Director:
Martin Scorsese, *Taxi Driver*

Best Actor:
Robert De Niro, *Taxi Driver*

Best Actress:
Sissy Spacek, *Carrie*

Best Supporting Actor:
Jason Robards, *All the President's Men*

Best Supporting Actress:
Jodie Foster, *Taxi Driver*

Best Screenplay:
Alain Tanner, John Berger; *Jonah, Who Will Be 25 in the Year 2000*

Best Cinematography:
Haskell Wexler, *Bound for Glory*

1977

Best Picture:
Annie Hall

Best Director:
Luis Buñuel, *That Obscure Object of Desire*

Best Actor:
Art Carney, *The Late Show*

Best Actress:
Diane Keaton, *Annie Hall*

Best Supporting Actor:
Edward Fox, *A Bridge Too Far*

Best Supporting Actress:
Ann Wedgeworth, *Handle With Care*

Best Screenplay:
Woody Allen and Marshall Brickman, *Annie Hall*

Best Cinematography:
Thomas Mauch, *Aguirre, The Wrath of God*

3. THE NEW YORK FILM CRITICS AWARDS

The New York Film Critics was founded in 1935 to recognize the finest achievements in motion pictures and to maintain the importance of film criticism. A few years after it was established, the organization came under the strong influence of Bosley Crowther, the first-string film critic of the *New York Times* who for nearly three decades was the most powerful movie reviewer in America. Crowther supported films that dealt with "significant" social issues, films like *The Lost Weekend* and *Gentleman's Agreement* that espoused general liberal causes. And unlike many of today's critics, Crowther favored Hollywood's BIG BIG products adapted from other media, films like *Ben Hur, Gigi,* and *West Side Story.*

Crowther's taste for serious humanism and faithful adaptation was certainly reflected in the New York Film Critics annual prizes: *Going My Way, The Best Years of Our Lives, All the King's Men, Marty* and *On the Waterfront* all won Best Picture awards during his tenure at the *Times.* Hollywood, which liked to think of itself as an active force in the betterment of America, shared Crowther's penchant for honoring its more "serious" movies: eighteen of the Best Picture choices during Crowther's twenty-eight-year membership in the New York Film Critics also won the Academy vote.

In 1969, one year after Crowther left the *Times,* the New York Film Critics underwent radical changes: it invited several new critics to join (including some from the recently established National Society of Film Critics); it employed new voting procedures; it dropped the foreign-versus-domestic distinction that had hitherto been used in the Best Picture voting; and it added some new categories. These changes have made the New York Film Critics awards more similar to those of the National Society, and less like those of the Academy—since 1969 the Academy and the New York Film Critics have not agreed once on their respective choices for Best Picture.

The original voting procedure was this: each member voted for one nominee in each category. If on the first ballot no nominee had received two thirds of the votes of the members present or those represented by proxy, another ballot was cast. After the first two ballots, only nominees who had received two or more votes were retained for following ballots. If no nominee had received the required two-thirds majority by the sixth ballot, the winner was established by a plurality of votes. The voting was by secret ballot—only the totals given the various nominees were officially announced.

In 1969 the procedure changed to that employed by the National Society: each member is asked to vote for three candidates in each category. The first choice is worth three points, the second two, and the third one. A simple plurality establishes the winner.

1935

Best Motion Picture:
The Informer
Best Actor:
Charles Laughton, Mutiny on the Bounty; Ruggles of Red Gap
Best Actress:
Greta Garbo, Anna Karenina
Best Direction:
John Ford, The Informer

1936

Best Motion Picture:
Mr. Deeds Goes to Town
Best Actor:
Walter Huston, Dodsworth
Best Actress:
Luise Rainer, The Great Ziegfeld

Best Direction:
Rouben Mamoulian, The Gay Desperado
Best Foreign Flim:
La Kermesse Héroïque (France)

1937

Best Motion Picture:
The Life of Emile Zola
Best Actor:
Paul Muni, The Life of Emile Zola
Best Actress:
Greta Garbo, Camille
Best Direction:
Gregory La Cava, Stage Door
Best Foreign Film:
Mayerling (France)

1938

Best Motion Picture:
The Citadel
Best Actor:
James Cagney, *Angels with
    Dirty Faces*
Best Actress:
Margaret Sullavan, *Three
    Comrades*
Best Direction:
Alfred Hitchcock, *The Lady
    Vanishes*
Best Foreign Film:
La Grande Illusion (France)
Special Award:
*Snow White and the Seven
    Dwarfs*

1939

Best Motion Picture:
Wuthering Heights
Best Actor:
James Stewart, *Mr. Smith
    Goes to Washington*
Best Actress:
Vivien Leigh, *Gone With the
    Wind*
Best Direction:
John Ford, *Stagecoach*
Best Foreign Film:
Harvest (France)

1940

Best Motion Picture:
The Grapes of Wrath
Best Actor:
Charles Chaplin, *The Great
    Dictator* (award refused)
Best Actress:
Katharine Hepburn, *The
    Philadelphia Story*

Best Direction:
John Ford, *The Grapes of
    Wrath; The Long Voyage
    Home*
Best Foreign Film:
The Baker's Wife (France)
Special Award:
Walt Disney, *Fantasia*

1941

Best Picture:
Citizen Kane
Best Actor:
Gary Cooper, *Sergeant York*
Best Actress:
Joan Fontaine, *Suspicion*
Best Direction:
John Ford, *How Green Was My
    Valley*

1942

Best Motion Picture:
In Which We Serve
Best Actor:
James Cagney, *Yankee Doodle
    Dandy*
Best Actress:
Agnes Moorehead, *The Mag-
    nificent Ambersons*
Best Direction:
John Farrow, *Wake Island*

1943

Best Motion Picture:
Watch on the Rhine
Best Actor:
Paul Lukas, *Watch on the
    Rhine*
Best Actress:
Ida Lupino, *The Hard Way*

Best Direction:
George Stevens, *The More the Merrier*

1944

Best Motion Picture:
Going My Way
Best Actor:
Barry Fitzgerald, *Going My Way*
Best Actress:
Tallulah Bankhead, *Lifeboat*
Best Direction:
Leo McCarey, *Going My Way*

1945

Best Motion Pitcure:
The Lost Weekend
Best Actor:
Ray Milland, *The Lost Weekend*
Best Actress:
Ingrid Bergman, *Spellbound; The Bells of St. Mary's*
Best Direction:
Billy Wilder, *The Lost Weekend*
Special Awards:
The True Glory; The Fighting Lady (U.S. documentaries)

1946

Best Motion Picture:
The Best Years of Our Lives
Best Actor:
Laurence Olivier, *Henry V*
Best Actress:
Celia Johnson, *Brief Encounter*
Best Direction:
William Wyler, *The Best Years of Our Lives*
Best Foreign Film:
Open City (Italy)

1947

Best Motion Picture:
Gentleman's Agreement
Best Actor:
William Powell, *Life with Father; The Senator Was Indiscreet*
Best Actress:
Deborah Kerr, *Black Narcissus; The Adventuress*
Best Direction:
Elia Kazan, *Gentleman's Agreement; Boomerang*
Best Foreign Film:
To Live in Peace (Italy)

1948

Best Motion Picture:
Treasure of Sierra Madre
Best Actor:
Laurence Olivier, *Hamlet*
Best Actress:
Olivia de Havilland, *The Snake Pit*
Best Direction:
John Huston, *Treasure of Sierra Madre*
Best Foreign Film:
Paisan (Italy)

1949

Best Motion Picture:
All the King's Men
Best Actor:
Broderick Crawford, *All the King's Men*
Best Actress:
Olivia de Havilland, *The Heiress*
Best Direction:
Carol Reed, *The Fallen Idol*

Best Foreign Film:
The Bicycle Thief (Italy)

1950

Best Motion Picture:
All About Eve
Best Actor:
Gregory Peck, *Twelve O'Clock High*
Best Actress:
Bette Davis, *All About Eve*
Best Direction:
Joseph L. Mankiewicz, *All About Eve*
Best Foreign Film:
Ways of Love (Italy/France)

1951

Best Motion Picture:
A Streetcar Named Desire
Best Actor:
Arthur Kennedy, *Bright Victory*
Best Actress:
Vivien Leigh, *A Streetcar Named Desire*
Best Direction:
Elia Kazan, *A Streetcar Named Desire*
Best Foreign Film:
Miracle in Milan (Italy)

1952

Best Motion Picture:
High Noon
Best Actor:
Ralph Richardson, *Breaking the Sound Barrier*
Best Actress:
Shirley Booth, *Come Back, Little Sheba*
Best Direction:
Fred Zinnemann, *High Noon*

Best Foreign Film:
Forbidden Games (France)

1953

Best Motion Picture:
From Here to Eternity
Best Actor:
Burt Lancaster, *From Here to Eternity*
Best Actress:
Audrey Hepburn, *Roman Holiday*
Best Direction:
Fred Zinnemann, *From Here to Eternity*
Best Foreign Film:
Justice Is Done (France)

1954

Best Motion Picture:
On the Waterfront
Best Actor:
Marlon Brando, *On the Waterfront*
Best Actress:
Grace Kelley, *The Country Girl; Rear Window; Dial M for Murder*
Best Direction:
Elia Kazan, *On the Waterfront*
Best Foreign Film:
Gate of Hell (Japan)

1955

Best Motion Picture:
Marty
Best Actor:
Ernest Borgnine, *Marty*
Best Actress:
Anna Magnani, *The Rose Tattoo*

Best Direction:
David Lean, *Summertime*
Best Foreign Film:
a tie between *Umberto D.*
(Italy) and *Diabolique*
(France)

1956

Best Motion Picture:
Around the World in 80 Days
Best Actor:
Kirk Douglas, *Lust for Life*
Best Actress:
Ingrid Bergman, *Anastasia*
Best Direction:
John Huston, *Moby Dick*
Best Foreign Film:
La Strada (Italy)
Best Writing:
S. J. Perelman, *Around the
World in 80 Days*

1957

Best Motion Picture:
The Bridge on the River Kwai
Best Actor:
Alec Guinness, *The Bridge on
the River Kwai*
Best Actress:
Deborah Kerr, *Heaven Knows,
Mr. Allison*
Best Direction:
David Lean, *The Bridge on the
River Kwai*
Best Foreign Film:
Gervaise (France)

1958

Best Motion Picture:
The Defiant Ones
Best Actor:
David Niven, *Separate Tables*

Best Actress:
Susan Hayward, *I Want to Live!*
Best Direction:
Stanley Kramer, *The Defiant
Ones*
Best Foreign Film:
My Uncle (France)
Best Writing:
Nathan E. Douglas, Harold
Jacob Smith, *The Defiant
Ones*

1959

Best Motion Picture:
Ben-Hur
Best Actor:
James Stewart, *Anatomy of a
Murder*
Best Actress:
Audrey Hepburn, *The Nun's
Story*
Best Direction:
Fred Zinnemann, *The Nun's
Story*
Best Foreign Film:
The 400 Blows (France)
Best Writing:
Wendell Mayes, *Anatomy of a
Murder*

1960

Best Motion Picture:
a tie between *The Apartment*
and *Sons and Lovers*
Best Actor:
Burt Lancaster, *Elmer Gantry*
Best Actress:
Deborah Kerr, *The Sundowners*
Best Direction:
a tie between Billy Wilder *(The
Apartment)* and Jack Cardiff
(Sons and Lovers)

Best Foreign Film:
Hiroshima, Mon Amour
 (France/Japan)
Best Writing:
Billy Wilder, I. A. l. Diamond,
 The Apartment

1961

Best Motion Picture:
West Side Story
Best Actor:
Maximilian Schell, *Judgment at
 Nuremberg*
Best Actress:
Sophia Loren, *Two Women*
Best Direction:
Robert Rossen, *The Hustler*
Best Foreign Film:
La Dolce Vita (Italy)

1962

(None)

1963

Best Motion Picture:
Tom Jones
Best Actor:
Albert Finney, *Tom Jones*
Best Actress:
Patricia Neal, *Hud*
Best Direction:
Tony Richardson, *Tom Jones*
Best Foreign Film:
8½ (Italy)

1964

Best Motion Picture:
My Fair Lady

Best Actor:
Rex Harrison, *My Fair Lady*
Best Actress:
Kim Stanley, *Séance on a Wet
 Afternoon*
Best Direction:
Stanley Kubrick, *Dr.
 Strangelove*
Best Foreign Film:
That Man from Rio (France)
Best Screenwriting:
Harold Pinter, *The Servant*
Special Citation:
To Be Alive! (Johnson's Wax)

1965

Best Motion Picture:
Darling
Best Actor:
Oskar Werner, *Ship of Fools*
Best Actress:
Julie Christie, *Darling*
Best Direction:
John Schlesinger, *Darling*
Best Foreign Film:
Juliet of the Spirits (Italy)

1966

Best Motion Picture:
A Man for All Seasons
Best Actor:
Paul Scofield, *A Man for All
 Seasons*
Best Actress:
a tie between Elizabeth Taylor
 (*Who's Afraid of Virginia
 Woolf?*) and Lynn Redgrave
 (*Georgy Girl*)
Best Direction:
Fred Zinnemann, *A Man for All
 Seasons*
Best Foreign Film:
The Shop on Main Street
 (Czechoslovakia)

Best Screenwriting:
Robert Bolt, *A Man for All Seasons*

1967

Best Motion Picture:
In the Heat of the Night
Best Actor:
Rod Steiger, *In the Heat of the Night*
Best Actress:
Edith Evans, *The Whisperers*
Best Direction:
Mike Nichols, *The Graduate*
Best Foreign Film:
La Guerre Est Finie (France)
Best Screenwriting:
David Newman, Robert Benton, *Bonnie and Clyde*
Special Award:
Bosley Crowther

1968

Best Motion Picture:
The Lion in Winter
Best Actor:
Alan Arkin, *The Heart Is a Lonely Hunter*
Best Actress:
Joanne Woodward, *Rachel, Rachel*
Best Direction:
Paul Newman, *Rachel, Rachel*
Best Foreign Film:
War and Peace (Russia)
Best Screenwriting:
Lorenzo Semple, Jr., *Pretty Poison*

1969

Best Motion Picture:
Z

Best Actor:
Jon Voight, *Midnight Cowboy*
Best Actress:
Jane Fonda, *They Shoot Horses, Don't They?*
Best Supporting Actor:
Jack Nicholson, *Easy Rider*
Best Supporting Actress:
Dyan Cannon, *Bob & Carol & Ted & Alice*
Best Direction:
Costa-Gavras, *Z*
Best Screenwriting:
Bob & Carol & Ted & Alice (as film, not to the individual writers)

1970

Best Motion Picture:
Five Easy Pieces
Best Actor:
George C. Scott, *Patton*
Best Actress:
Glenda Jackson, *Women in Love*
Best Supporting Actor:
Chief Dan George, *Little Big Man*
Best Supporting Actress:
Karen Black, *Five Easy Pieces*
Best Direction:
Bob Rafelson, *Five Easy Pieces*
Best Screenwriting:
Eric Rohmer, *My Night at Maud's*

1971

Best Motion Picture:
A Clockwork Orange
Best Actor:
Gene Hackman, *The French Connection*
Best Actress:
Jane Fonda, *Klute*

Best Supporting Actor:
Ben Johnson, *The Last Picture Show*

Best Supporting Actress:
Ellen Burstyn, *The Last Picture Show*

Best Direction:
Stanley Kubrick, *A Clockwork Orange*

Best Screenwriting:
a tie between Peter Bogdanovich and Larry McMurtry for *The Last Picture Show;* and Penelope Gilliatt for *Sunday Bloody Sunday*

1972

Best Motion Picture:
Cries and Whispers

Best Actor:
Laurence Olivier, *Sleuth*

Best Actress:
Liv Ullmann, *Cries and Whispers; The Emigrants*

Best Supporting Actor:
Robert Duvall, *The Godfather*

Best Supporting Actress:
Jeannie Berlin, *The Heartbreak Kid*

Best Direction:
Ingmar Bergman, *Cries and Whispers*

Best Screenwriting:
Ingmar Bergman, *Cries and Whispers*

Special Citation:
The Sorrow and the Pity, as the years's best documentary

1973

Best Motion Picture:
Day for Night

Best Direction:
Francois Truffaut, *Day for Night*

Best Actor:
Marlon Brando, *Last Tango in Paris*

Best Actress:
Joanne Woodward, *Summer Wishes, Winter Dreams*

Best Supporting Actor:
Robert De Niro, *Bang the Drum Slowly*

Best Supporting Actress:
Valentina Cortese, *Day for Night*

Best Screenwriting:
George Lucas, Gloria Katz, Willard Huyck, *American Graffiti*

1974

Best Motion Picture:
Amarcord

Best Direction:
Federico Fellini, *Amarcord*

Best Actor:
Jack Nicholson, *Chinatown* and *The Last Detail*

Best Actress:
Liv Ullmann, *Scenes from a Marriage*

Best Supporting Actor:
Charles Boyer, *Stavisky*

Best Supporting Actress:
Valerie Perrine, *Lenny*

Best Screenwriting:
Ingmar Bergman, *Scenes from a Marriage*

Special Award:
Fabiano Canosa, for his innovative programs at the First Ave. Screening Room

1975

Best Motion Picture:
Nashville
Best Direction:
Robert Altman, *Nashville*
Best Actor:
Jack Nicholson, *One Flew Over the Cuckoo's Nest*
Best Actress:
Isabelle Adjani, *The Story of Adele H.*
Best Supporting Actor:
Alan Arkin, *Hearts of the West*
Best Supporting Actress:
Lily Tomlin, *Nashville*
Best Screenwriting:
François Truffaut, Jean Gruault and Suzanne Schiffman, *The Story of Adele H.*

1976

Best Motion Picture:
All the President's Men
Best Direction:
Alan Pakula, *All the President's Men*

Best Actor:
Robert De Niro, *Taxi Driver*
Best Actress:
Liv Ullmann, *Face to Face*
Best Supporting Actor:
Jason Robards, *All the President's Men*
Best Supporting Actress:
Talia Shire, *Rocky*
Best Screenwriting:
Paddy Chayefsky, *Network*

1977

Best Motion Picture:
Annie Hall
Best Director:
Woody Allen, *Annie Hall*
Best Actor:
John Gielgud, *Providence*
Best Actress:
Diane Keaton, *Annie Hall*
Best Supporting Actor:
Maximilian Schell, *Julia*
Best Supporting Actress:
Sissy Spacek, *Three Women*
Best Screenplay:
Woody Allen and Marshall Brickman, *Annie Hall*

4. THE NATIONAL BOARD OF REVIEW AWARDS

Almost from their beginnings, movies were attacked for their purported immorality. Religious and reform groups, quick to realize the seductive powers of cinema, strongly criticized the motion picture's influence on American morals and ideals. The film industry, understandably fearful of government regulations, often chose voluntary regulation rather than federal intervention. In 1908, for example, representatives of the industry asked Dr. Charles Sprague Smith (the head of a social research bureau) to establish a citizens' committee to preview films before they were exhibited in theaters. Smith's committee was founded in March 1909 and was initially named the National Board of Censorship of Motion Pictures.

Through the work of a large number of volunteers in various parts of the country, the National Board examined new films and gave its opinions, suggesting possible changes whenever it thought changes necessary. Because the Board could not legally censor but merely suggest and advise, its official title was changed in 1915 to the National Board of Review of Motion Pictures.

Although the National Board was praised at first as a valuable method of avoiding official censorship through a voluntary public committee, it soon came under attack, most particularly for the fact that it was financially dependent upon the film industry itself. (A fee was required to review each film and this fee was paid by the film's producer.) In order to counter such criticism, the Board expanded its attempts to improve the artistic, moral and educational values of film patrons and producers alike.

Among these attempts was the creation in 1916 of the National Committee for Better Films, whose function was "to both liberate and formulate thought regarding motion pictures, their uses and possibilities, and the best way to achieve a free screen of the most desirable kind." The Committee issued lists of approved movies—"Pictures Boys Want and Grown-Ups Endorse," "Monthly List of Selected Pictures," "Motion Picture Aids to Sermons," etc. —in order to improve the public's taste. (Many scholars later criticized the National Board for trying to influence the public's taste instead of the studios'.) These lists were both widely distributed and used.

Although the power of the National Board was considerably diminished in 1922 when the film industry established its own self-regulatory board under the leadership of Will H. Hays (the Motion Picture Producers and Distributors of America, Inc., now called the Motion Picture Association of America), the National Board continued its work.

In 1920 it had started to award Best Film prizes in order

"to increase public awareness of the meritorious aspects of movies." Later its annual awards were expanded to include lists of best American films and of best foreign movies. The Board has continued to award these prizes to the present day and is now considered the oldest of the "best picture" polls.

The awards are voted by the Board's Committee on Exceptional Films and are usually the first of the many movie prizes to be selected each year, the winners being announced in late December or early January. In 1930 and 1931 the committee listed its choices for the ten best films alphabetically. From 1932 to 1935 it selected one Best Film of the year and announced its nine other choices alphabetically. The following year the Board began citing the films according to the number of votes each film received.

The awards were expanded in 1937 to include acting awards, in 1943 to include directing citations, and in 1948 to include writing prizes. (Screenplay awards were later dropped.) From 1945 to 1949 the Board did not use separate categories for American and foreign films, and it has often changed its policy regarding American versus English-language movies. (These distinctions are given in the listings below.)

The Academy and the National Board have seldom seen eye to eye. Since 1934, when the Academy began using the calendar year, the Academy and the National Board have only agreed nine times on their choice for Best Film.

In addition to the selections made by the Committee on Exceptional Films, the National Board has announced many other annual awards. The Board's Review Committee, for example, selects a list of Ten Most Popular Films each year which, unlike the Best Films lists, are chosen only with regard to popular appeal and entertainment value. These lists of popular movies, however, have often overlapped the lists based on artistic merit and are not listed below because of limited space.

1930

Best American Films:
All Quiet on the Western Front
Holiday
Laughter
The Man from Blankely's
Men Without Women
Morocco
Outward Bound
Romance
The Street of Chance
Tol'able David
Best Foreign Films:
High Treason
Old and New
Soil
Storm Over Asia
Zwei Herzen im 3/4 Takt

1931

Best American Films:
Cimarron
City Lights
City Streets
Dishonored
The Front Page
The Guardsman
Quick Millions
Rango
Surrender
Tabu
Best Foreign Films:
Die Dreigroschenoper
Das Lied vom Leben
Le Million
Sous les Toits de Paris
Vier von der Infanterie

1932

Best American Films:
I Am a Fugitive from a Chain Gang
As You Desire Me
A Bill of Divorcement
A Farewell to Arms
Madame Racketeer
Payment Deferred
Scarface
Tarzan the Ape Man
Trouble in Paradise
Two Seconds
Best Foreign Films:
A Nous la Liberté
Der Andere
The Battle of Gallipoli
Golden Mountains
Kameradschaft
Mädchen in Uniform
Der Raub der Mona Lisa
Reserved for Ladies
Road to Life
Zwei Menschen

1933

Best American Films:
Topaze
Berkeley Square
Cavalcade
Little Women
Mama Loves Papa
The Pied Piper
She Done Him Wrong
State Fair
Three-Cornered Moon
Zoo in Budapest
Best Foreign Films:
Hertha's Erwachen
Ivan
M
Morgenroth
Niemandsland

Poil de Carotte
The Private Life of Henry VIII
Quatorze Juillet
Rome Express
Le Sang d'un Poète

La Maternelle
The New Gulliver
Peasants
Thunder in the East
The Youth of Maxim

1934

Best American Films:
It Happened One Night
The Count of Monte Cristo
Crime Without Passion
Eskimo
The First World War
The Lost Patrol
Lot in Sodom (a short)
No Greater Glory
The Thin Man
Viva Villa!
Best Foreign Films:
Man of Aran
The Blue Light
Catherine the Great
The Constant Nymph
Madame Bovary

1935

Best American Films:
The Informer
Alice Adams
Anna Karenina
David Copperfield
The Gilded Lily
Les Misérables
The Lives of a Bengal Lancer
Mutiny on the Bounty
Ruggles of Red Gap
Who Killed Cock Robin?
Best Foreign Films:
Chapayev
Crime and Punishment
Le Dernier Milliardaire
The Man Who Knew Too Much
Marie Chapdelaine

1936

Best American Films:
Mr. Deeds Goes to Town
The Story of Louis Pasteur
Modern Times
Fury
Winterset
The Devil Is a Sissy
Ceiling Zero
Romeo and Juliet
The Prisoner of Shark Island
Green Pastures
Best Foreign Films:
Carnival in Flanders
    (La Kermesse Héroïque)
The New Earth
Rembrandt
The Ghost Goes West
Nine Days a Queen
We are from Kronstadt
Son of Mongolia
The Yellow Cruise
Les Misérables
The Secret Agent

1937

Best American Films:
Night Must Fall
The Life of Emile Zola
Black Legion
Camille
Make Way for Tomorrow
The Good Earth
They Won't Forget
Captains Courageous
A Star Is Born
Stage Door

Best Foreign Films:
The Eternal Mask
The Lower Depths
Baltic Deputy
Mayerling
The Spanish Earth
Golgotha
Elephant Boy
Rembrandt
Janosik
The Wedding of Palo
Best Acting:
(listed alphabetically)
Harry Baur, *The Golem*
Humphrey Bogart, *Black Legion*
Charles Boyer, *Conquest*
Nikolai Cherkassov, *Baltic Deputy*
Danielle Darrieux, *Mayerling*
Greta Garbo, *Camille*
Robert Montgomery, *Night Must Fall*
Maria Ouspenskaya, *Conquest*
Luise Rainer, *The Good Earth*
Joseph Schildkraut, *The Life of Emile Zola*
Mathias Wieman, *The Eternal Mask*
Dame May Whitty, *Night Must Fall*

Un Carnet de Bal
Generals Without Buttons
Peter the First
Best Acting:
(alphabetically)
Lew Ayres, *Holiday*
Pierre Blanchar, Harry Baur, Louis Jouvet and Raimu, *Un Carnet de Bal*
James Cagney, *Angels with Dirty Faces*
Joseph Calleia, *Algiers*
Chico, *The Adventures of Chico*
Robert Donat, *The Citadel*
Will Fyffe, *To the Victor*
Pierre Fresnay, Jean Gabin, Dita Parlo and Erich von Stroheim, *La Grande Illusion*
John Garfield, *Four Daughters*
Wendy Hiller, *Pygmalion*
Charles Laughton and Elsa Lanchester, *The Beachcomber*
Robert Morley, *Marie Antoinette*
Ralph Richardson, *South Riding* and *The Citadel*
Margaret Sullavan, *Three Comrades*
Spencer Tracy, *Boys Town*

1938

Best English-Language Films:
The Citadel
Snow White and the Seven Dwarfs
The Beachcomber
To the Victor
Sing You Sinners
The Edge of the World
Of Human Hearts
Jezebel
South Riding
Three Comrades
Best Foreign Films:
La Grande Illusion
Ballerina

1939

Best English-Language Films:
Confessions of a Nazi Spy
Wuthering Heights
Stagecoach
Ninotchka
Young Mr. Lincoln
Crisis
Goodbye, Mr. Chips
Mr. Smith Goes to Washington
The Roaring Twenties
U-Boat 29
Best Foreign Films:
Port of Shadows
Harvest

Alexander Nevsky
The End of a Day
Robert Koch
Best Acting:
(alphabetically)
James Cagney, The Roaring
Twenties
Bette Davis, Dark Victory and
The Old Maid
Geraldine Fitzgerald, Dark
Victory and Wuthering
Heights
Henry Fonda, Young Mr.
Lincoln
Jean Gabin, Port of Shadows
Greta Garbo, Ninotchka
Francis Lederer and Paul
Lukas, Confessions of a Nazi
Spy
Thomas Mitchell, Stagecoach
Laurence Olivier, Wuthering
Heights
Flora Robson, We Are Not
Alone
Michel Simon, Port of Shadows
and The End of a Day

Jane Darwell, The Grapes of
Wrath
Betty Field, Of Mice and Men
Henry Fonda, The Grapes of
Wrath and Return of Frank
James
Joan Fontaine, Rebecca
Greer Garson, Pride and
Prejudice
William Holden, Our Town
Vivien Leigh, Gone With the
Wind and Waterloo Bridge
Thomas Mitchell, The Long
Voyage Home
Raimu, The Baker's Wife
Ralph Richardson, The Fugitive
Ginger Rogers, The Primrose
Path
George Sanders, Rebecca
Martha Scott, Our Town
James Stewart, The Shop
Around the Corner
Conrad Veidt, Escape
Best Documentary:
The Fight for Life

1940

Best American Films:
The Grapes of Wrath
The Great Dictator
Of Mice and Men
Our Town
Fantasia
The Long Voyage Home
Foreign Correspondent
The Biscuit Eater
Gone With the Wind
Rebecca
Best Foreign Film:
The Baker's Wife
Best Acting:
(alphabetically)
Jane Bryan, We Are Not Alone
Charles Chaplin, The Great
Dictator

1941

Best American Films:
Citizen Kane
How Green Was My Valley
The Little Foxes
The Stars Look Down
Dumbo
High Sierra
Here Comes Mr. Jordan
Tom, Dick and Harry
The Road to Zanzibar
The Lady Eve
Best Foreign Film:
Pépé le Moko
Best Documentaries:
Target for Tonight
The Forgotten Village
Ku Kan
The Land

Best Acting:
(alphabetically)
Sara Allgood, *How Green Was My Valley*
Mary Astor, *The Great Lie* and *The Maltese Falcon*
Ingrid Bergman, *Rage in Heaven*
Humphrey Bogart, *High Sierra* and *The Maltese Falcon*
Gary Cooper, *Sergeant York*
Donald Crisp, *How Green Was My Valley*
Bing Crosby, *The Road to Zanzibar* and *Birth of the Blues*
George Coulouris, *Citizen Kane*
Patricia Collinge and Bette Davis, *The Little Foxes*
Isobel Elsom, *Ladies in Retirement*
Joan Fontaine, *Suspicion*
Greta Garbo, *Two-Faced Woman*
James Gleason, *Meet John Doe* and *Here Comes Mr. Jordan*
Walter Huston, *All That Money Can Buy*
Ida Lupino, *High Sierra* and *Ladies in Retirement*
Roddy McDowall, *How Green Was My Valley*
Robert Montgomery, *Rage in Heaven* and *Here Comes Mr. Jordan*
Ginger Rogers, *Kitty Foyle* and *Tom, Dick and Harry*
James Stephenson, *The Letter* and *Shining Victory*
Orson Welles, *Citizen Kane*

1942

Best English-Language Films:
In Which We Serve
One of Our Aircraft Is Missing
Mrs. Miniver
Journey for Margaret
Wake Island
The Male Animal
The Major and the Minor
Sullivan's Travels
The Moon and Sixpence
The Pied Piper

Best Foreign Films:
(none cited this year)

Best Documentary:
Moscow Strikes Back

Best Acting:
(alphabetically)
Ernest Anderson, *In This Our Life*
Florence Bates, *The Moon and Sixpence*
James Cagney, *Yankee Doodle Dandy*
Jack Carson, *The Male Animal*
Charles Coburn, *H. M. Pulham, Esq.; In This Our Life;* and *Kings Row*
Greer Garson, *Mrs. Miniver* and *Random Harvest*
Sidney Greenstreet, *Across the Pacific*
William Holden, *The Remarkable Andrew*
Tim Holt, *The Magnificent Ambersons*
Glynis Johns, *The Invaders*
Gene Kelly, *For Me and My Gal*
Diana Lynn, *The Major and the Minor*
Ida Lupino, *Moontide*
Bernard Miles and John Mills, *In Which We Serve*
Agnes Moorehead, *The Magnificent Ambersons*
Hattie McDaniel, *In This Our Life*
Thomas Mitchell, *Moontide*
Margaret O'Brien, *Journey for Margaret*
Susan Peters, *Random Harvest*

Edward G. Robinson, *Tales of Manhattan*

Ginger Rogers, *Roxie Hart* and *The Major and the Minor*

George Sanders, *The Moon and Sixpence*

Ann Sheridan, *Kings Row*

William Severn, *Journey for Margaret*

Rudy Vallee, *The Palm Beach Story*

Anton Walbrook, *The Invaders*

Googie Withers, *One of Our Aircraft Is Missing*

Monty Woolley, *The Pied Piper*

Teresa Wright, *Mrs. Miniver*

Robert Young, *H. M. Pulham, Esq.; Joe Smith; American;* and *Journey for Margaret*

1943

Best English-Language Films:
The Ox-Bow Incident
Watch on the Rhine
Air Force
Holy Matrimony
The Hard Way
Casablanca
Lassie Come Home
Bataan
The Moon Is Down
The Next of Kin
Best Foreign Films:
(none cited this year)
Best Documentaries:
Desert Victory
Battle of Russia
Prelude to War
Saludos Amigos
The Silent Village
Best Director:
William A. Wellman, *The Ox-Bow Incident*
Tay Garnett, *Bataan* and *The Cross of Lorraine*

Michael Curtiz, *Casablanca* and *This is the Army*

Best Actresses:
Gracie Fields, *Holy Matrimony*
Katina Paxinou, *For Whom the Bell Tolls*
Teresa Wright, *Shadow of a Doubt*

Best Actors:
Paul Lukas, *Watch on the Rhine*
Henry Morgan, *The Ox-Bow Incident* and *Happy Land*
Cedric Hardwicke, *The Moon Is Down* and *The Cross of Lorraine*

1944

Best English-Language Films:
None But the Lonely Heart
Going My Way
The Miracle of Morgan's Creek
Hail the Conquering Hero
The Song of Bernadette
Wilson
Meet Me in St. Louis
Thirty Seconds Over Tokyo
Thunder Rock
Lifeboat
Best Foreign Films:
(none cited this year)
Best Documentaries:
The Memphis Belle
Attack! The Battle for New Britain
With the Marines at Tarawa
Battle for the Marianas
Tunisian Victory
Best Acting:
(alphabetically)
Ethel Barrymore, *None But the Lonely Heart*
Ingrid Bergman, *Gaslight*
Eddie Bracken, *Hail the Conquering Hero*

Humphrey Bogart, *To Have and Have Not*
Bing Crosby, *Going My Way*
June Duprez, *None But the Lonely Heart*
Barry Fitzgerald, *Going My Way*
Betty Hutton, *The Miracle of Morgan's Creek*
Margaret O'Brien, *Meet Me in St. Louis*
Franklin Pangborn, *Hail the Conquering Hero*

1945

Best Film:
The True Glory
Best Director:
Jean Renoir, *The Southerner*
Best Actress:
Joan Crawford, *Mildred Pierce*
Best Actor:
Ray Milland, *The Lost Weekend*
Best Foreign Films:
(none cited)
Ten Best Films:
(including documentaries as well as English-language features)
The True Glory
The Lost Weekend
The Southerner
The Story of G.I. Joe
The Last Chance
Colonel Blimp
A Tree Grows in Brooklyn
The Fighting Lady
The Way Ahead
The Clock

1946

Best Picture:
Henry V

Best Director:
William Wyler, *The Best Years of Our Lives*
Best Actress:
Anna Magnani, *Open City*
Best Actor:
Laurence Olivier, *Henry V*
Ten Best Films:
(including foreign)
Henry V
Open City (also voted Best Foreign-Language Film)
The Best Years of Our Lives
Brief Encounter
A Walk in the Sun
It Happened at the Inn
My Darling Clementine
The Diary of a Chambermaid
The Killers
Anna and the King of Siam

1947

Best Picture:
Monsieur Verdoux
Best Director:
Elia Kazan, *Boomerang* and *Gentleman's Agreement*
Best Actress:
Celia Johnson, *This Happy Breed*
Best Actor:
Michael Redgrave, *Mourning Becomes Electra*
Ten Best Films:
(including foreign)
Monsieur Verdoux
Great Expectations
Shoeshine
Crossfire
Boomerang
Odd Man Out
Gentleman's Agreement
To Live in Peace
It's a Wonderful Life
The Overlanders

1948

Best Picture:
Paisan
Best Director:
Roberto Rossellini, *Paisan*
Best Actress:
Olivia de Havilland, *The Snake Pit*
Best Actor:
Walter Huston, *Treasure of Sierra Madre*
Best Script:
John Huston, *Treasure of Sierra Madre*
Ten Best Films:
(including foreign)
Paisan
Day of Wrath
The Search
Treasure of Sierra Madre.
Louisiana Story
Hamlet
The Snake Pit
Johnny Belinda
Joan of Arc
The Red Shoes

1949

Best Picture:
The Bicycle Thief
Best Director:
Vittorio De Sica, *The Bicycle Thief*
Best Actress:
(none cited this year)
Best Actor:
Ralph Richardson, *The Heiress* and *The Fallen Idol*
Best Script:
Graham Greene, *The Fallen Idol*

Ten Best Films:
(including foreign)
The Bicycle Thief
The Quiet One
Intruder in the Dust
The Heiress
Devil in the Flesh
Quartet
Germany
Year Zero
Home of the Brave
Letter to Three Wives
The Fallen Idol

1950

Best American Film:
Sunset Boulevard
Best Foreign Film:
The Titan
Best Director:
John Huston, *The Asphalt Jungle*
Best Actress:
Gloria Swanson, *Sunset Boulevard*
Best Actor:
Alec Guinness, *Kind Hearts and Coronets*
Best American Films:
Sunset Boulevard
All About Eve
The Asphalt Jungle
The Men
Edge of Doom
Twelve O'Clock High
Panic in the Streets
Cyrano de Bergerac
No Way Out
Stage Fright
Best Foreign Films:
The Titan
Tight Little Island
The Third Man
Kind Heart and Coronets
Paris 1900

1951

Best American Film:
A Place in the Sun
Best Foreign Film:
Rashomon
Best Director:
Akira Kurosawa, *Rashomon*
Best Actress:
Jan Sterling, *The Big Carnival*
Best Actor:
Richard Basehart, *Fourteen Hours*
Best Script:
T. E. B. Clarke, *The Lavender Hill Mob*
Best American Films:
A Place in the Sun
Red Badge of Courage
An American in Paris
Death of a Salesman
Detective Story
A Streetcar Named Desire
Decision Before Dawn
Strangers on a Train
Quo Vadis
Fourteen Hours
Best Foreign Films:
Rashomon
The River
Miracle in Milan
Kon-Tiki
The Browning Version

1952

Best American Film:
The Quiet Man
Best Foreign Film:
Breaking the Sound Barrier
Best Director:
David Lean, *Breaking the Sound Barrier*
Best Actress:
Shirley Booth, *Come Back, Little Sheba*

Best Actor:
Ralph Richardson, *Breaking the Sound Barrier*
Best American Films:
The Quiet Man
High Noon
Limelight
Five Fingers
The Snows of Kilimanjaro
The Thief
The Bad and the Beautiful
Singin' in the Rain
Above and Beyond
My Son John
Best Foreign Films:
Breaking the Sound Barrier
The Man in the White Suit
Forbidden Games
Beauty and the Devil
Ivory Hunter

1953

Best American Picture:
Julius Caesar
Best Foreign Picture:
A Queen Is Crowned
Best Director:
George Stevens, *Shane*
Best Actress:
Jean Simmons, *Young Bess; The Robe;* and *The Actress*
Best Actor:
James Mason, *Face to Face; The Desert Rats; The Man Between;* and *Julius Caesar*
Best American Films:
Julius Caesar
Shane
From Here to Eternity
Martin Luther
Lili
Roman Holiday
Stalag 17
Little Fugitive
Mogambo
The Robe

Best Foreign Films:
A Queen Is Crowned
Moulin Rouge
The Little World of Don
   Camillo
Strange Deception
Conquest of Everest

1954

Best American Picture:
On the Waterfront
Best Foreign Picture:
Romeo and Juliet
Best Director:
Renato Castellani, Romeo and
   Juliet
Best Actress:
Grace Kelly, The Country Girl;
   Dial M for Murder; and Rear
   Window
Best Actor:
Bing Crosby, The Country Girl
Best Supporting Actress:
Nina Foch, Executive Suite
Best Supporting Actor:
John Williams, Sabrina and
   Dial M for Murder
Special Citations:
For the choreography of
   Michael Kidd in Seven
   Brides for Seven Brothers
For the modernization of
   traditional Japanese acting
   by Machiko Kyo in Gate of
   Hell and Ugetsu
For the new methods of mov-
   ing puppets in Hansel and
   Gretel
Best American Films:
On the Waterfront
Seven Brides for Seven
   Brothers
The Country Girl
A Star Is Born
Executive Suite
The Vanishing Prince
Sabrina

20,000 Leagues Under the Sea
The Unconquered
Beat the Devil
Best Foreign Films:
Romeo and Juliet
The Heart of the Matter
Gate of Hell
Diary of a Country Priest
The Little Kidnappers
Genevieve
Beauties of the Night
Mr. Hulot's Holiday
The Detective
Bread, Love and Dreams

1955

Best American Picture:
Marty
Best Foreign Picture:
The Prisoner
Best Director:
William Wyler, The Desperate
   Hours
Best Actress:
Anna Magnani, The Rose
   Tattoo
Best Actor:
Ernest Borgnine, Marty
Best Supporting Actress:
Marjorie Rambeau, A Man
   Called Peter and The View
   from Pompey's Head
Best Supporting Actor:
Charles Bickford, Not as a
   Stranger
Special Citation:
For aerial photography in
   Strategic Air Command
Best American Films:
Marty
East of Eden
Mister Roberts
Bad Day at Black Rock
Summertime
The Rose Tattoo
A Man Called Peter
Not as a Stranger

Picnic
The African Lion
Best Foreign Films:
The Prisoner
The Great Adventure
The Divided Heart
Diabolique
The End of the Affair

1956

Best American Picture:
Around the World in 80 Days
Best Foreign Picture:
The Silent World
Best Director:
John Huston, *Moby Dick*
Best Actress:
Dorothy McGuire, *Friendly Persuasion*
Best Actor:
Yul Brynner, *The King and I; Anastasia;* and *The Ten Commandments*
Best Supporting Actress:
Debbie Reynolds, *The Catered Affair*
Best Supporting Actor:
Richard Basehart, *Moby Dick*
Best American Films:
Around the World in 80 Days
Moby Dick
The King and I
Lust for Life
Friendly Persuasion
Somebody Up There Likes Me
The Catered Affair
Anastasia
The Man Who Never Was
Bus Stop
Best Foreign Films:
The Silent World
War and Peace
Richard III
La Strada
Rififi

1957

Best American Picture:
The Bridge on the River Kwai
Best Foreign Picture:
Ordet
Best Director:
David Lean, *The Bridge on the River Kwai*
Best Actress:
Joanne Woodward, *The Three Faces of Eve* and *No Down Payment*
Best Actor:
Alec Guinness, *The Bridge on The River Kwai*
Best Supporting Actress:
Dame Sybil Thorndike, *The Prince and the Showgirl*
Best Supporting Actor:
Sessue Hayakawa, *The Bridge on the River Kwai*
Special Citation:
For the photographic innovations in *Funny Face*
Best American Films:
The Bridge on the River Kwai
Twelve Angry Men
The Spirit of St. Louis
The Rising of the Moon
Albert Schweitzer
Funny Face
The Bachelor Party
Enemy Below
A Hatful of Rain
A Farewell to Arms
Best Foreign Films:
Ordet
Gervaise
Torero!
The Red Balloon
A Man Escaped

1958

Best American Picture:
The Old Man and the Sea
Best Foreign Picture:
Pather Panchali
Best Director:
John Ford, The Last Hurrah
Best Actress:
Ingrid Bergman, The Inn of the
Sixth Happiness
Best Actor:
Spencer Tracy, The Old Man
and the Sea and The Last
Hurrah
Best Supporting Actress:
Kay Walsh, The Horse's Mouth
Best Supporting Actor:
Albert Salmi, The Brothers
Karamazov and The Bravados
Special Citation:
For the valor of Robert Donat's
last performance in The Inn
of the Sixth Happiness
Best American Films:
The Old Man and the Sea
Separate Tables
The Last Hurrah
The Long Hot Summer
Windjammer
Cat on a Hot Tin Roof
The Goddess
The Brothers Karamazov
Me and the Colonel
Gigi
Best Foreign Films:
Pather Panchali
Rouge et Noir
The Horse's Mouth
My Uncle
A Night to Remember

1959

Best American Picture:
The Nun's Story
Best Foreign Picture:
Wild Strawberries
Best Director:
Fred Zinnemann, The Nun's
Story
Best Actress:
Simone Signoret, Room at the
Top
Best Actor:
Victor Seastrom, Wild
Strawberries
Best Supporting Actress:
Dame Edith Evans, The Nun's
Story
Best Supporting Actor:
Hugh Griffith, Ben-Hur
Special Citations:
To Ingmar Bergman for the
body of his work
To Andrew Marton and Yakima
Canutt for their direction of
the chariot race in Ben-Hur
Best American Films:
The Nun's Story
Ben-Hur
Anatomy of a Murder
The Diary of Anne Frank
Middle of the Night
The Man Who Understood
Women
Some Like It Hot
Suddenly, Last Summer
On the Beach
North by Northwest
Best Foreign Films:
Wild Strawberries
Room at the Top
Aparajito
The Roof
Look Back in Anger

1960

Best American Picture:
Sons and Lovers
Best Foreign Picture:
The World of Apu

Best Director:
Jack Cardiff, *Sons and Lovers*
Best Actress:
Greer Garson, *Sunrise at Campobello*
Best Actor:
Robert Mitchum, *Home from the Hill* and *The Sundowners*
Best Supporting Actress:
Shirley Jones, *Elmer Gantry*
Best Supporting Actor:
George Peppard, *Home from the Hill*
Best American Films:
Sons and Lovers
The Alamo
The Sundowners
Inherit the Wind
Sunrise at Campobello
Elmer Gantry
Home from the Hill
The Apartment
Wild River
The Dark at the Top of the Stairs
Best Foreign Films:
The World of Apu
General della Rovere
The Angry Silence
I'm All Right, Jack
Hiroshima, Mon Amour

1961

Best American Picture:
Question 7
Best Foreign Picture:
The Bridge
Best Director:
Jack Clayton, *The Innocents*
Best Actress:
Geraldine Page, *Summer and Smoke*
Best Actor:
Albert Finney, *Saturday Night and Sunday Morning*
Best Supporting Actress:
Ruby Dee, *A Raisin in the Sun*

Best Supporting Actor:
Jackie Gleason, *The Hustler*
Best American Films:
Question 7
The Hustler
West Side Story
The Innocents
The Hoodlum Priest
Summer and Smoke
The Young Doctors
Judgment at Nuremberg
One, Two, Three
Fanny
Best Foreign Films:
The Bridge
La Dolce Vita
Two Women
Saturday Night and Sunday Morning
A Summer to Remember

1962

Best English-Language Picture:
The Longest Day
Best Foreign-Language Picture:
Sundays and Cybele
Best Director:
David Lean, *Lawrence of Arabia*
Best Actress:
Anne Bancroft, *The Miracle Worker*
Best Actor:
Jason Robards, *Long Day's Journey into Night* and *Tender Is the Night*
Best Supporting Actress:
Angela Lansbury, *The Manchurian Candidate* and *All Fall Down*
Best Supporting Actor:
Burgess Meredith, *Advise and Consent*
Best English-Language Films:
The Longest Day
Billy Budd
The Miracle Worker

Lawrence of Arabia
Long Day's Journey Into Night
Whistle Down the Wind
Requiem for a Heavyweight
A Taste of Honey
Birdman of Alcatraz
War Hunt
Best Foreign-Language Films:
Sundays and Cybele
Barabbas
Divorce—Italian Style
The Island
Through a Glass Darkly

1963

Best English-Language Picture:
Tom Jones
Best Foreign-Language Picture:
8½
Best Director:
Tony Richardson, *Tom Jones*
Best Actress:
Patricia Neal, *Hud*
Best Actor:
Rex Harrison, *Cleopatra*
Best Supporting Actress:
Margaret Rutherford, *The
   V.I.P.s*
Best Supporting Actor:
Melvyn Douglas, *Hud*
Best English-Language Films:
Tom Jones
Lilies of the Field
All the Way Home
Hud
This Sporting Life
Lord of the Flies
The L-Shaped Room
The Great Escape
How the West Was Won
The Cardinal
Best Foreign-Language Films:
8½
The Four Days of Naples
Winter Light
The Leopard
Any Number Can Win

1964

Best English-Language Picture:
Becket
Best Foreign-Language Picture:
World Without Sun
Best Director:
Desmond Davis, *The Girl with
   Green Eyes*
Best Actress:
Kim Stanley, *Séance on a Wet
   Afternoon*
Best Actor:
Anthony Quinn, *Zorba the
   Greek*
Best Supporting Actress:
Edith Evans, *The Chalk Garden*
Best Supporting Actor:
Martin Balsam, *The Carpet-
   baggers*
Best English-Language Films:
Becket
My Fair Lady
The Girl with Green Eyes
The World of Henry Orient
Zorba the Greek
Topkapi
The Chalk Garden
The Finest Hours
Four Days in November
Séance on a Wet Afternoon
Best Foreign-Language Films:
World Without Sun
The Organizer
Anatomy of a Marriage
Seduced and Abandoned
*Yesterday, Today and
   Tomorrow*

1965

Best English-Language Picture:
The Eleanor Roosevelt Story
Best Foreign-Language Story:
Juliet of the Spirits

Best Director:
John Schlesinger, *Darling*
Best Actress:
Julie Christie, Darling and
   Doctor Zhivago
Best Actor:
Lee Marvin, *Cat Ballou* and
   Ship of Fools
Best Supporting Actress:
Joan Blondell, *The Cincinnati
   Kid*
Best Supporting Actor:
Harry Andrews, *The Agony and
   the Ecstasy* and *The Hill*
Best English-Language Films:
The Eleanor Roosevelt Story
The Agony and the Ecstasy
Doctor Zhivago
Ship of Fools
The Spy Who Came In from
   the Cold
Darling
The Greatest Story Ever Told
A Thousand Clowns
The Train
The Sound of Music
Best Foreign-Language Films:
Juliet of the Spirits
The Overcoat
La Bohème
La Tia Tula
Gertrud

1966

Best English-Language Picture:
A Man for All Seasons
Best Foreign-Language Picture:
The Sleeping Car Murders
Best Director:
Fred Zinnemann, *A Man for All
   Seasons*
Best Actress:
Elizabeth Taylor, *Who's Afraid
   of Virginia Woolf?*
Best Actor:
Paul Scofield, *A Man for All
   Seasons*

Best Supporting Actress:
Vivien Merchant, *Alfie*
Best Supporting Actor:
Robert Shaw, *A Man for All
   Seasons*
Best English-Language Films:
A Man for All Seasons
Born Free
Alfie
*Who's Afraid of Virginia
   Woolf?*
The Bible
Georgy Girl
*Years of Lightning, Day of
   Drums*
It Happened Here
*The Russians Are Coming, The
   Russians Are Coming*
Shakespeare Wallah
Best Foreign-Language Films:
The Sleeping Car Murders
*The Gospel According to St.
   Matthew*
The Shameless Old Lady
A Man and a Woman
Hamlet

1967

Best English-Language Picture:
Far from the Madding Crowd
Best Foreign-Language Picture:
Elvira Madigan
Best Director:
Richard Brooks, *In Cold Blood*
Best Actress:
Edith Evans, *The Whisperers*
Best Actor:
Peter Finch, *Far from the
   Madding Crowd*
Best Supporting Actress:
Marjorie Rhodes, *The Family
   Way*
Best Supporting Actor:
Paul Ford, *The Comedians*
Best English-Language Films:
Far from the Madding Crowd
The Whisperers

Ulysses
In Cold Blood
The Family Way
The Taming of the Shrew
Doctor Dolittle
The Graduate
The Comedians
Accident
Best Foreign-Language Films:
Elvira Madigan
The Hunt
Africa Addio
Persona
The Great British Train
   Robbery

1968

Best English-Language Picture:
The Shoes of the Fisherman
Best Foreign-Language Picture:
War and Peace
Best Director:
Franco Zeffirelli, Romeo and
   Juliet
Best Actress:
Liv Ullmann, Hour of the Wolf
   and Shame
Best Actor:
Cliff Robertson, Charly
Best Supporting Actress:
Virginia Maskell, Interlude
Best Supporting Actor:
Leo McKern, The Shoes of the
   Fisherman
Best English-Language Films:
The Shoes of the Fisherman
Romeo and Juliet
Yellow Submarine
Charly
Rachel, Rachel
The Subject Was Roses
The Lion in Winter
Planet of the Apes
Oliver
2001: A Space Odyssey
Best Foreign-Language Films:
War and Peace

Hagbard and Signo
Hunger
The Two of Us
The Bride Wore Black

1969

Best English-Language Picture:
They Shoot Horses, Don't
   They?
Best Foreign-Language Picture:
Shame
Best Director:
Alfred Hitchcock, Topaz
Best Actress:
Geraldine Page, Trilogy
Best Actor:
Peter O'Toole, Goodbye, Mr.
   Chips
Best Supporting Actress:
Pamela Franklin, The Prime of
   Miss Jean Brodie
Best Supporting Actor:
Philippe Noiret, Topaz
Best English-Language Films:
They Shoot Horses, Don't
   They?
Ring of Bright Water
Topaz
Goodbye, Mr. Chips
Battle of Britain
The Loves of Isadora
The Prime of Miss Jean Brodie
Support Your Local Sheriff
True Grit
Midnight Cowboy
Best Foreign-Language Films:
Shame
Stolen Kisses
The Damned
La Femme Infidèle
Adalen '31

1970

Best English-Language Picture:
Patton
Best Foreign-Language Picture:
The Wild Child
Best Director:
François Truffaut, *The Wild Child*
Best Actress:
Glenda Jackson, *Women In Love*
Best Actor:
George C. Scott, *Patton*
Best Supporting Actress:
Karen Black, *Five Easy Pieces*
Best Supporting Actor:
Frank Langella, *Diary of a Mad Housewife* and *The Twelve Chairs*
Best English-Language Films:
Patton
Kes
Women In Love
Five Easy Pieces
Ryan's Daughter
I Never Sang for My Father
Diary of a Mad Housewife
Love Story
The Virgin and the Gypsy
Tora! Tora! Tora!
Best Foreign-Language Films:
The Wild Child
My Night at Maud's
The Passion of Anna
The Confession
This Man Must Die

1971

Best English-Language Picture:
Macbeth
Best Foreign-Language Picture:
Claire's Knee

Best Director:
Ken Russell, *The Devils* and *The Boy Friend*
Best Actress:
Irene Papas, *The Trojan Women*
Best Actor:
Gene Hackman, *The French Connection*
Best Supporting Actress:
Cloris Leachman, *The Last Picture Show*
Best Supporting Actor:
Ben Johnson, *The Last Picture Show*
Best English-Language Films:
Macbeth
The Boy Friend
One Day in the Life of Ivan Denisovich
The French Connection
The Last Picture Show
Nicholas and Alexandra
The Go-Between
King Lear
Peter Rabbit and Tales of Beatrix Potter
Death in Venice
Best Foreign-Language Films:
Claire's Knee
Bed and Board
The Clowns
The Garden of the Finzi-Continis
The Conformist

1972

Best English-Language Picture:
Cabaret
Best Foreign-Language Picture:
The Sorrow and the Pity
Best Director:
Bob Fosse, *Cabaret*
Best Actress:
Cicely Tyson, *Sounder*

Best Actor:
Peter O'Toole, *The Ruling Class* and *Man of La Mancha*
Best Supporting Actress:
Marisa Berenson, *Cabaret*
Best Supporting Actor:
Joel Grey, *Cabaret*
Al Pacino, *The Godfather*
Best English-Language Films:
Cabaret
Man of La Mancha
The Godfather
Sounder
1776
The Effect of Gamma Rays on Man-in-the-Moon Marigolds
Deliverance
The Ruling Class
The Candidate
Frenzy
Best Foreign-Language Films:
The Sorrow and the Pity
The Emigrants
The Discreet Charm of the Bourgeoisie
Chloë in the Afternoon
Uncle Vanya

1973

Best English-Language Picture:
The Sting
Best Foreign-Language Picture:
Cries and Whispers
Best Director:
Ingmar Bergman, *Cries and Whispers*
Best Actress:
Liv Ullmann, *The New Land*
Best Actor:
Al Pacino, *Serpico*
Robert Ryan, *The Iceman Cometh*
Best Supporting Actress:
Sylvia Sidney, *Summer Wishes, Winter Dreams*

Best Supporting Actor:
John Houseman, *The Paper Chase*
Special Citations:
American Film Theatre and Ely Landau
Woody Allen for his script *Sleeper*
Walt Disney Productions for *Robin Hood*
Paramount for *Charlotte's Web*
Best English-Language Films:
The Sting
Paper Moon
The Homecoming
Bang the Drum Slowly
Serpico
O Lucky Man
The Last American Hero
The Hireling
The Day of the Dolphin
The Way We Were
Best Foreign-Language Films:
Cries and Whispers
Day for Night
The New Land
The Tall Blond Man with One Black Shoe
Alfredo, Alfredo
Traffic

1974

Best English-Language Picture:
The Conversation
Best Foreign-Language Picture:
Amarcord
Best Director:
Francis Ford Coppola, *The Conversation*
Best Actress:
Gena Rowlands, *A Woman Under the Influence*
Best Actor:
Gene Hackman, *The Conversation*
Best Supporting Actress:
Valerie Perrine, *Lenny*

Best Supporting Actor:
Holger Lowenadler, *Lacombe, Lucien*
Best English-Language Films:
The Conversation
Murder on the Orient Express
Chinatown
The Last Detail
Harry and Tonto
A Woman Under the Influence
Thieves Like Us
Lenny
Daisy Miller
The Three Musketeers
Best Foreign-Language Films:
Amarcord
Lacombe, Lucien
Scenes from a Marriage
The Phantom of Liberté
The Pedestrian
Special Citations:
Special effects in *The Golden Voyage of Sinbad; Earthquake;* and *Towering Inferno*
The film industry for increasing care in subsidiary casting of many films
Robert G. Youngson for his twenty-five-year work with tasteful and intelligent compilation of films

Best Supporting Actress:
Ronee Blakley, *Nashville*
Best Supporting Actor:
Charles Durning, *Dog Day Afternoon*
Special Citation:
Ingmar Bergman's *The Magic Flute,* outstanding in its translation of opera to screen
Best English-Language Films:
Barry Lyndon/Nashville
Conduct Unbecoming
One Flew Over the Cuckoo's Nest
Lies My Father Told Me
Dog Day Afternoon
Day of the Locust
The Passenger
Hearts of the West
Farewell, My Lovely
Alice Doesn't Live Here Anymore
Best Foreign-Language Films:
The Story of Adele H.
A Brief Vacation
Special Section
Stavisky
Swept Away . . .

1975

Best English-Language Picture:
Nashville
Barry Lyndon
Best Foreign-Language Picture:
The Story of Adele H.
Best Director:
Robert Altman, *Nashville*
Stanley Kubrick, *Barry Lyndon*
Best Actress:
Isabelle Adjani, *The Story of Adele H.*
Best Actor:
Jack Nicholson, *One Flew Over the Cuckoo's Nest*

1976

Best English-Language Picture:
All the President's Men
Best Foreign-Language Picture:
The Marquise of O
Best Director:
Alan Pakula, *All the President's Men*
Best Actress:
Liv Ullmann, *Face to Face*
Best Actor:
David Carradine, *Bound for Glory*
Best Supporting Actress:
Talia Shire, *Rocky*

Best Supporting Actor:
Jason Robards, *All the President's Men*
Best English-Language Films
All the President's Men
Network
Rocky
The Last Tycoon
The Seven-Per-Cent Solution
The Front
The Shootist
Family Plot
Silent Movie
Obsession
Best Foreign-Language Films
The Marquise of O
Face to Face
Small Change
Cousin, Cousine
The Clockmaker

1977

Best English-Language Picture:
The Turning Point
Best Foreign-Language Picture:
That Obscure Object of Desire
Best Director:
Luis Buñuel, *That Obscure Object of Desire*
Best Actress:
Anne Bancroft, *The Turning Point*

Best Actor:
John Travolta, *Saturday Night Fever*
Best Supporting Actress:
Diane Keaton, *Annie Hall*
Best Supporting Actor:
Tom Skerritt, *The Turning Point*
Best English-Language Films:
The Turning Point
Annie Hall
Julia
Star Wars
Close Encounters of the Third Kind
The Late Show
Saturday Night Fever
Equus
The Picture Show Man
Harlan County, U.S.A.
Best Foreign-Language Films:
That Obscure Object of Desire
The Man Who Loved Women
A Special Day
Cría
The American Friend
Special Awards:
Walt Disney Studios for restoring and upgrading animation in *The Rescuers*
Columbia Pictures for special effects in *Close Encounters of the Third Kind*

---

5. THE GOLDEN GLOBE AWARDS

The Hollywood Foreign Press Association, established in 1940, is an association of foreign journalists who cover the entertainment industries in Los Angeles. In 1944 the association presented its first Golden Globe Awards, honoring film achievements of 1943, and the awards have been presented annually ever since.

There are now more than 80 active members in the

association, representing some 100 million readers in over 50 countries. All members vote both for the nominees and winners in the various categories.

Although modeled on the Academy Awards, the Golden Globe categories do differ in several respects. For one thing, the Best Film and Best Actor/Actress categories are subdivided into one award for Drama and another for Comedy/Musical. (Many feel this is a legitimate distinction and have urged the Academy to make a similar division.) Secondly, film Golden Globes are given in several popular categories for which there are no corresponding prizes in the Oscars: starting with the 1949 awards, for example, promising newcomers have been honored; and since the 1950 prizes, World Film Favorites have been selected. And thirdly, since 1955 the Golden Globes have honored achievements in television as well as those in cinema. (Television Golden Globes are not listed here. For a few years the Association announced awards for achievements in the recording industry. Like the TV prizes, these are not listed below.)

The Golden Globes and the Academy Awards have coincided regularly in their selections. In its choice for Best Film, for example, the Golden Globes in thirty-four years of awards have only disagreed eight times with the Oscars. For Best Actor, the Golden Globes and the Oscars have concurred on twenty-six occasions; for Best Actress, on nineteen. (These statistics take into account the Golden Globes' subdivided categories.)

The Golden Globes are usually announced in late January-early February. They are now nationally televised.

1943

Best Motion Picture—Drama:
The Song of Bernadette
Best Actress:
Jennifer Jones, The Song of Bernadette

Best Actor:
Paul Lukas, Watch on the Rhine

1944

Best Motion Picture—Drama:
Going My Way

Best Actress:
Ingrid Bergman, *The Bells of St. Mary*
Best Actor:
Alexander Knox, *President Wilson*

1945

Best Motion Picture—Drama:
The Lost Weekend
Best Actress:
Ingrid Bergman, *Gaslight*
Best Actor:
Ray Milland, *The Lost Weekend*
Best Supporting Actress:
Angela Lansberry, *Gaslight*
Best Supporting Actor:
J. Carrol Naish, *Gaslight*

1946

Best Motion Picture—Drama:
The Best Years of Our Lives
Best Director:
Frank Capra, *It's a Wonderful Life*
Best Actress:
Rosalind Russell, *Sister Kenny*
Best Actor:
Gregory Peck, *The Yearling*
Best Supporting Actress:
Anne Baxter, *The Razor's Edge*
Best Supporting Actor:
Clifton Webb, *The Razor's Edge*
Best Film Promoting International Understanding:
The Last Chance (Switzerland)
Award for Best Nonprofessional Acting:
Harold Russell, *The Best Years of Our Lives*

1947

Best Motion Picture—Drama:
Gentleman's Agreement
Best Director:
Elia Kazan, *Gentleman's Agreement*
Best Actress:
Rosalind Russell, *Mourning Becomes Electra*
Best Actor:
Ronald Colman, *A Double Life*
Best Supporting Actress:
Celeste Holm, *Gentleman's Agreement*
Best Supporting Actor:
Edmund Gwenn, *Miracle on 34th Street*
Most Promising Female Newcomer:
Lois Maxwell, *That Hagen Girl*
Most Promising Male Newcomer:
Richard Widmark, *Kiss of Death*
Best Screenplay:
George Seaton, *Miracle on 34th Street*
Best Score:
Max Steiner, *Life with Father*
Best Cinematography:
Jack Cardiff, *Black Narcissus*
Special Award to Best Juvenile Actor:
Dean Stockwell, *Gentleman's Agreement*
Special Award for Furthering the Influence of the Screen:
Walt Disney, *Bambi* (the Hindustani version)

1948

Best Motion Picture—Drama:
Treasure of Sierra Madre
Johnny Belinda

Best Motion Picture—Foreign:
Hamlet (England)
Best Director:
John Huston, *Treasure of
Sierra Madre*
Best Actress:
Jane Wyman, *Johnny Belinda*
Best Actor:
Laurence Olivier, *Hamlet*
Best Supporting Actress
Ellen Corby, I Remember Mama
Best Supporting Actor:
Walter Huston, *Treasure of
Sierra Madre*
Best Screenplay:
Richard Schweizer, *The Search*
Best Score:
Brian Easdale, *The Red Shoes*
Best Cinematography:
Gabriel Figueroa, *The Pearl*
**Best Film Promoting
International Understanding:**
The Search
**Special Award to Best
Juvenile Actor:**
Ivan Yandl, *The Search*

1949

Best Motion Picture—Drama:
All the King's Men
Best Foreign Film:
The Bicycle Thief (Italy)
Best Director:
Robert Rossen, *All the King's
Men*
Best Actress:
Olivia de Havilland, *The
Heiress*
Best Actor:
Broderick Crawford, *All the
King's Men*
Best Supporting Actress:
Mercedes McCambridge, *All
the King's Men*
Best Supporting Actor:
James Whitmore, *Battleground*

**Most Promising Female
Newcomer:**
Mercedes McCambridge, *All
the King's Men*
**Most Promising Male
Newcomer:**
Richard Todd, *The Hasty Heart*
Best Screenplay:
Robert Pirosh, *Battleground*
Best Score:
Johnny Green, *The Inspector
General*
**Best Cinematography—
Black-and-White:**
Frank Planer, *Champion*
Best Cinematography—Color:
Walt Disney Studios, *Ichabod
& Mr. Toad*
**Best Film Promoting
International Understanding:**
The Hasty Heart

1950

Best Motion Picture—Drama:
Sunset Boulevard
Best Director:
Billy Wilder, *Sunset Boulevard*
Best Actress—Drama:
Gloria Swanson, *Sunset
Boulevard*
Best Actor—Drama:
José Ferrer, *Cyrano de
Bergerac*
**Best Actress—
Musical / Comedy:**
Judy Holliday, *Born Yesterday*
Best Actor—Musical / Comedy:
Fred Astaire, *Three Little
Words*
Best Supporting Actress:
Josephine Hull, *Harvey*
Best Supporting Actor:
Edmund Gwenn, *Mister 880*
Most Promising Newcomer:
Gene Nelson, *Tea for Two*

Best Screenplay:
Joseph Mankiewicz, *All About Eve*
Best Score:
Franz Waxman, *Sunset Boulevard*
Best Cinematography—Black-and-White:
Frank Planer, *Cyrano de Bergerac*
Best Cinematography—Color:
Robert Surtees, *King Solomon's Mines*
Best Film Promoting International Understanding:
Broken Arrow
World Film Favorite—Female:
Jane Wyman
World Film Favorite—Male:
Gregory Peck

Most Promising Newcomers:
Pier Angeli, *Teresa*
Kevin McCarthy, *Death of a Salesman*
Best Screenplay:
Robert Buckner, *Bright Victory*
Best Score:
Victor Young, *September Affair*
Best Cinematography—Black-and-White:
Frank Planer, *Death of a Salesman*
Best Cinematography—Color:
Robert Surtees, William V. Skall, *Quo Vadis*
Best Film Promoting International Understanding:
The Day the Earth Stood Still
Cecil B. DeMille Award:
Cecil B. DeMille

1951

Best Motion Picture—Drama:
A Place in the Sun
Best Motion Picture—Musical / Comedy:
An American in Paris
Best Director:
Laslo Benedek, *Death of a Salesman*
Best Actress—Drama:
Jane Wyman, *The Blue Veil*
Best Actor—Drama:
Fredric March, *Death of a Salesman*
Best Actress—Musical / Comedy:
June Allyson, *Too Young to Kiss*
Best Actor—Musical / Comedy:
Danny Kaye, *On the Riviera*
Best Supporting Actress:
Kim Hunter, *A Streetcar Named Desire*
Best Supporting Actor:
Peter Ustinov, *Quo Vadis*

1952

Best Motion Picture—Drama:
The Greatest Show on Earth
Best Motion Picture—Musical / Comedy:
With a Song in My Heart
Best Director:
Cecil B. DeMille, *The Greatest Show on Earth*
Best Actress—Drama:
Shirley Booth, *Come Back, Little Sheba*
Best Actor—Drama:
Gary Cooper, *High Noon*
Best Actress—Musical / Comedy:
Susan Hayward, *With a Song in My Heart*
Best Actor—Musical / Comedy:
Donald O'Connor, *Singin' in the Rain*
Best Supporting Actress:
Katy Jurado, *High Noon*
Best Supporting Actor:
Millard Mitchell, *My Six Convicts*

Most Promising Newcomers:
Colette Marchand, *Moulin Rouge*
Richard Burton, *My Cousin Rachel*
Best Screenplay:
Michael Wilson, *Five Fingers*
Best Score:
Dimitri Tiomkin, *High Noon*
Best Cinematography—Black-and-White:
Floyd Crosby, *High Noon*
Best Cinematography—Color:
George Barnes, J. Peverell Marley, *The Greatest Show on Earth*
Best Film Promoting International Understanding:
Anything Can Happen
Cecil B. DeMille Award:
Walt Disney
World Film Favorite—Female:
Susan Hayward
World Film Favorite—Male:
John Wayne
Special Award for Best Juvenile Actor:
Brandon DeWilde, *Member of the Wedding*
Francis Kee Teller, *Navajo*

1953

Best Motion Picture—Drama:
The Robe
Best Director:
Fred Zinnemann, *From Here to Eternity*
Best Actress—Drama
Audrey Hepburn, *Roman Holiday*
Best Actor—Drama:
Spencer Tracy, *The Actress*
Best Actress—Musical / Comedy:
Ethel Merman, *Call Me Madam*

Best Actor—Musical / Comedy:
David Niven, *The Moon Is Blue*
Best Supporting Actress:
Grace Kelly, *Mogambo*
Best Supporting Actor:
Frank Sinatra, *From Here to Eternity*
Most Promising Newcomers—Female:
Pat Crowley, Bella Darvi, Barbara Rush
Most Promising Newcomers—Male:
Hugh O'Brian, Steve Forrest, Richard Egan
Best Screenplay:
Helen Deutsch, *Lili*
Best Film Promoting International Understanding:
Little Boy Lost
Cecil B. DeMille Award:
Darryl Zanuck
World Film Favorite—Female:
Marilyn Monroe
World Film Favorite—Male:
Robert Taylor
Alan Ladd
Best Documentary of Historical Interest:
A Queen Is Crowned
Best Western Star:
Guy Madison
Special Award:
Walt Disney, *The Living Desert*
Honor Award:
Jack Cummings (producer for thirty years at MGM)

1954

Best Motion Picture—Drama:
On the Waterfront
Best Motion Picture—Musical / Comedy:
Carmen Jones
Best Foreign Films:
Genevieve (England), *No Way Back* (Germany), *Twenty-*

four Eyes (Japan), *La Mujer de las Camelias* (Argentina)

Best Director:
Elia Kazan, *On the Waterfront*

Best Actress—Drama:
Grace Kelly, *The Country Girl*

Best Actor—Drama:
Marlon Brando, *On the Waterfront*

Best Actress—Musical / Comedy:
Judy Garland, *A Star Is Born*

Best Actor—Musical / Comedy:
James Mason, *A Star Is Born*

Best Supporting Actress:
Jan Sterling, *The High and the Mighty*

Best Supporting Actor:
Edmond O'Brien, *The Barefoot Contessa*

Most Promising Newcomers—Female:
Shirley MacLaine, Kim Novak, Karen Sharpe

Most Promising Newcomers—Male:
Joe Adams, George Nader, Jeff Richards

Best Screenplay:
Billy Wilder, Samuel Taylor, Ernest Lehman, *Sabrina*

Best Cinematography—Black-and-White:
Boris Kaufman, *On the Waterfront*

Best Cinematography—Color:
Joseph Ruttenberg, *Brigadoon*

Best Film Promoting International Understanding:
Broken Lance

Cecil B. DeMille Award:
Jean Hersholt

World Film Favorite—Female:
Audrey Hepburn

World Film Favorite—Male:
Gregory Peck

Pioneer Award:
John Ford

Pioneer Award for Color:
Dr. Herbert Kalmus

Special Award for Creative Musical Contribution:
Dimitri Tiomkin

Special Award for Experimental Film:
Anywhere in Our Time (Germany)

1955

Best Motion Picture—Drama:
East of Eden

Best Motion Picture—Musical / Comedy:
Guys and Dolls

Best Foreign Films:
Ordet (Denmark), *Stella* (Greece), *Eyes of Children* (Japan), *Sons, Mothers, and a General* (Germany), *Dangerous Curves* (Brazil)

Best Outdoor Drama:
Wichita

Best Director:
Joshua Logan, *Picnic*

Best Actress—Drama:
Anna Magnani, *The Rose Tattoo*

Best Actor—Drama:
Ernest Borgnine, *Marty*

Best Actress—Musical / Comedy:
Jean Simmons, *Guys and Dolls*

Best Actor/Musical / Comedy:
Tow Ewell, *The Seven-Year Itch*

Best Support Actress:
Marisa Pavan, *The Rose Tattoo*

Best Supporting Actor:
Arthur Kennedy, *The Trial*

Most Promising Newcomers—Female:
Anita Ekberg, Virginia Shaw, Dana Wynter

Most Promising Newcomers—Male:
Ray Danton, Russ Tamblyn

Best Film Promoting International Understanding:
Love Is a Many-Splendored Thing

Cecil B. DeMille Award:
Jack Warner

World Film Favorite—Female:
Grace Kelly

World Film Favorite—Male:
Marlon Brando

Hollywood Citizenship Award:
Esther Williams

Posthumous Award for Best Dramatic Actor:
James Dean

1956

Best Motion Picture—Drama:
Around the World in 80 Days

Best Motion Picture—Musical / Comedy:
The King and I

Best English-Language Foreign Film:
Richard III

Best Foreign-Language Foreign Film:
The White Reindeer (Finland), *Before Sundown* (Germany), *The Girls in Black* (Greece), *Rose on the Arm* (Japan), *War and Peace* (Italy)

Best Director:
Elia Kazan, *Baby Doll*

Best Actress—Drama:
Ingrid Bergman, *Anastasia*

Best Actor—Drama:
Kirk Douglas, *Lust for Life*

Best Actress—Musical / Comedy:
Deborah Kerr, *The King and I*

Best Actor—Musical / Comedy:
Cantinflas, *Around the World in 80 Days*

Best Supporting Actress:
Eileen Heckart, *The Bad Seed*

Best Supporting Actor:
Earl Holliman, *The Rainmaker*

Most Promising Newcomers—Female:
Carroll Baker, Jayne Mansfield, Natalie Wood

Most Promising Newcomers—Male:
John Kerr, Paul Newman, Tony Perkins

Foreign Newcomer Award—Female:
Taina Elg (Finland)

Foreign Newcomer Award—Male:
Jacques Bergerac (France)

Best Film Promoting International Understanding:
Battle Hymn

Recognition Award for Music:
Dimitri Tiomkin

Cecil B. DeMille Award:
Mervyn LeRoy

World Film Favorite—Female:
Kim Novak

World Film Favorite—Male:
James Dean

Special Award for Advancing Film Industry:
Edwin Schallert

Hollywood Citizenship Award:
Ronald Reagan

Special Award for Consistent Performance:
Elizabeth Taylor

1957

Best Motion Picture—Drama:
The Bridge on the River Kwai

Best Motion Picture—Musical / Comedy:
Les Girls

Best English-Language Foreign Film:
Woman in a Dressing Gown

**Best Foreign-Language
Foreign Film:**
The Confessions of Felix Krull
(Germany), *Yellow Crow*
(Japan), *Tizok* (Mexico)
Best Director:
David Lean, *The Bridge on the
River Kwai*
Best Actress—Drama:
Joanne Woodward, *Three
Faces of Eve*
Best Actor—Drama:
Alec Guinness, *The Bridge on
the River Kwai*
**Best Actress—
Musical / Comedy:**
Kay Kendall, *Les Girls*
Best Actor—Musical / Comedy:
Frank Sinatra, *Pal Joey*
Best Supporting Actress:
Elsa Lanchester, *Witness for
the Prosecution*
Best Supporting Actor:
Red Buttons, *Sayonara*
**Most Promising Newcomers—
Female:**
Sandra Dee, Carolyn Jones,
Diana Varsi
**Most Promising Newcomers—
Male:**
James Garner, John Saxon,
Pat Wayne
**Best Film Promoting
International Understanding:**
The Happy Road
**Special Award for Bettering
the Standard of Motion
Picture Music:**
Hugo Friedhofer
Cecil B. DeMille Award:
Buddy Adler
World Film Favorite—Female:
Doris Day
World Film Favorite—Male:
Tony Curtis
Best Film Choreography:
Le Roy Prinz

**Best World Entertainment
through Musical Films:**
George Sidney
Most Versatile Actress:
Jean Simmons
Most Glamorous Actress:
Zsa Zsa Gabor
Ambassador of Good Will:
Bob Hope

1958

Best Motion Picture—Drama:
The Defiant Ones
Best Motion Picture—Comedy:
Auntie Mame
Best Motion Picture—Musical:
Gigi
**Best English-Language
Foreign Film:**
A Night to Remember
**Best Foreign-Language
Foreign Film:**
The Road a Year Long
(Yugoslavia), *The Girl and
the River* (France), *The Girl
Rose Marie* (Germany)
Best Director:
Vincente Minnelli, *Gigi*
Best Actress—Drama:
Susan Hayward, *I Want to Live!*
Best Actor—Drama:
David Niven, *Separate Tables*
**Best Actress—
Comedy / Musical:**
Rosalind Russell, *Auntie Mame*
Best Actor—Comedy / Musical:
Danny Kaye, *Me and the
Colonel*
Best Supporting Actress:
Hermione Gingold, *Gigi*
Best Supporting Actor:
Burl Ives, *The Big Country*
**Most Promising Newcomers—
Female:**
Linda Cristal, Susan Kohner,
Tina Louise

Most Promising Newcomers—Male:
Bradford Dillman, John Gavin, Efrem Zimbalist, Jr.
Samuel Goldwyn Award:
Two Eyes, Twelve Hands (Italy)
Cecil B. DeMille Award:
Maurice Chevalier
World Film Favorite—Female:
Deborah Kerr
World Film Favorite—Male:
Rock Hudson
Best Film Promoting International Understanding:
The Inn of the Sixth Happiness
Special Award to Best Juvenile:
David Ladd
Special Award to Most Versatile Actress:
Shirley MacLaine

1959

Best Motion Picture—Drama:
Ben-Hur
Best Motion Picture—Comedy:
Some Like It Hot
Best Motion Picture—Musical:
Porgy and Bess
Best Foreign Films:
Black Orpheus (France), *Odd Obsession* (Japan), *The Bridge* (Germany), *Wild Strawberries* (Sweden), *Aren't We Wonderful?* (Germany)
Best Director:
William Wyler, *Ben-Hur*
Best Actress—Drama:
Elizabeth Taylor, *Suddenly, Last Summer*
Best Actor—Drama:
Anthony Franciosa, *Career*
Best Actress—Musical / Comedy:
Marilyn Monroe, *Some Like It Hot*

Best Actor—Musical / Comedy:
Jack Lemmon, *Some Like It Hot*
Best Supporting Actress:
Susan Kohner, *Imitation of Life*
Best Supporting Actor:
Stephen Boyd, *Ben-Hur*
Most Promising Newcomers—Female:
Tuesday Weld, Angie Dickenson, Janet Munro, Stella Stevens
Most Promising Newcomers—Male:
James Shigata, Barry Coe, Troy Donahue, George Hamilton
Special Award for Directing the Chariot Race in Ben-Hur:
Andrew Morton
Best Score:
Ernest Gold, *On the Beach*
Best Film Promoting International Understanding:
The Diary of Anne Frank
Cecil B. DeMille Award:
Bing Crosby
Samuel Goldwyn Award:
Room at the Top
World Film Favorite—Female:
Doris Day
World Film Favorite—Male:
Rock Hudson
Outstanding Merit:
The Nun's Story
Journalistic Merit Awards:
Hedda Hopper, Louella Parsons
Special Awards to Famous Silent-Film Stars:
Francis X. Bushman, Ramon Navarro

1960

Best Motion Picture—Drama:
Spartacus
Best Motion Picture—Comedy:
The Apartment

Best Motion Picture—Musical:
Song Without End
Best English-Language Foreign Film:
The Man with the Green Carnation
Best Foreign-Language Foreign Film:
La Vérité (France), *The Virgin Spring* (Sweden)
Best Director:
Jack Cardiff, *Sons and Lovers*
Best Actress—Drama:
Greer Garson, *Sunrise at Campobello*
Best Actor—Drama:
Burt Lancaster, *Elmer Gantry*
Best Actress— Musical / Comedy:
Shirley MacLaine, *The Apartment*
Best Actor—Musical / Comedy:
Jack Lemmon, *The Apartment*
Best Supporting Actress:
Janet Leigh, *Psycho*
Best Supporting Actor:
Sal Mineo, *Exodus*
Most Promising Newcomers— Female:
Ina Balin, Nancy Kwan, Hayley Mills
Most Promising Newcomers— Male:
Michael Callan, Mark Kamon, Brett Halsey
Best Score:
Dimitri Tiomkin, *Alamo*
Samuel Goldwyn Award:
Never on Sunday (Greece)
Cecile B. DeMille Award:
Fred Astaire
Best Film Promoting International Understanding:
Hand in Hand
World Film Favorite—Female:
Gina Lollobrigida
World Film Favorite—Male:
Rock Hudson, Tony Curtis

Special Award for Comedy:
Cantinflas
Special Award for Artistic Integrity:
Stanley Kramer
Merit Award:
The Sundowners

1961

Best Motion Picture—Drama:
The Guns of Navarone
Best Motion Picture—Comedy:
A Majority of One
Best Motion Picture—Musical:
West Side Story
Best Foreign-Language Foreign Film:
Two Women (Italy)
Silver Globes: *Animas Trujano* (Mexico)
The Good Soldier Schweik (Germany)
Best Director:
Stanley Kramer, *Judgment at Nuremberg*
Best Actress—Drama:
Geraldine Page, *Summer and Smoke*
Best Actor—Drama:
Maximilian Schell, *Judgment at Nuremberg*
Best Actress— Musical / Comedy:
Rosalind Russell, *A Majority of One*
Best Actor—Musical / Comedy:
Glenn Ford, *Pocketful of Miracles*
Best Supporting Actress:
Rita Moreno, *West Side Story*
Best Supporting Actor:
George Chakiris, *West Side Story*

Most Promising Newcomers—Female:
Christine Kaufmann, Ann-Margret, Jane Fonda

Most Promising Newcomers—Male:
Richard Beymer, Bobby Darin, Warren Beatty

Best Song:
Dimitri Tiomkin, Ned Washington, "Town Without Pity," *Town Without Pity*

Best Score:
Dimitri Tiomkin, *The Guns of Navarone*

Samuel Goldwyn Award for Best English Film:
The Mark

Cecil B. DeMille Award:
Judy Garland

World Film Favorite—Female:
Marilyn Monroe

World Film Favorite—Male:
Charlton Heston

Best Film Promoting International Understanding:
A Majority of One

Special Merit Award:
Samuel Bronston, *El Cid*

Special Journalistic Merit Awards:
Army Archerd *(Daily Variety)*
Mike Connolly *(Hollywood Reporter)*

1962

Best Motion Picture—Drama:
Lawrence of Arabia

Best Motion Picture—Comedy:
That Touch of Mink

Best Motion Picture—Musical:
The Music Man

Best Foreign-Language Foreign Film:
Divorce—Italian Style (Italy), *Best of Enemies* (Italy)

Best Director:
David Lean, *Lawrence of Arabia*

Best Actress—Drama:
Geraldine Page, *Sweet Bird of Youth*

Best Actor—Drama:
Gregory Peck, *To Kill a Mockingbird*

Best Actress—Musical / Comedy:
Rosalind Russell, *Gypsy*

Best Actor—Musical / Comedy:
Marcello Mastroianni, *Divorce —Italian Style*

Best Supporting Actress:
Angela Lansbury, *The Manchurian Candidate*

Best Supporting Actor:
Omar Sharif, *Lawrence of Arabia*

Most Promising Newcomers—Female:
Patty Duke, Sue Lyon, Rita Tushingham

Most Promising Newcomers—Male:
Keir Dullea, Omar Sharif, Terence Stamp

Best Original Score:
Elmer Bernstein, *To Kill a Mockingbird*

Best Film Promoting International Understanding:
To Kill a Mockingbird

Cecil B. DeMille Award:
Bob Hope

World Film Favorite—Female:
Doris Day

World Film Favorite—Male:
Rock Hudson

Samuel Goldwyn Award:
Sundays and Cybele (France)

Best Cinematography—Black-and-White:
Henri Persin, Walter Wottitz, Jean Bourgoin, *The Longest Day*

Best Cinematography—Color:
F. A. Young, *Lawrence of Arabia*

1963

Best Motion Picture—Drama:
The Cardinal
Best Motion Picture—Musical / Comedy:
Tom Jones
Best English-Language Foreign Film:
Tom Jones
Best Foreign-Language Foreign Film:
Any Number Can Win (France)
Best Director:
Elia Kazan, *America, America*
Best Actress—Drama:
Leslie Caron, *The L-Shaped Room*
Best Actor—Drama:
Sidney Poitier, *Lilies of the Field*
Best Actress—Musical / Comedy:
Shirley MacLaine, *Irma La Douce*
Best Actor—Musical / Comedy:
Alberto Sordi, *To Bed or Not to Bed*
Best Supporting Actress:
Margaret Rutherford, *The V.I.P.s*
Best Supporting Actor:
John Huston, *The Cardinal*
Most Promising Newcomers—Female:
Ursula Andress, Tippi Hedren, Elke Sommers
Most Promising Newcomers—Male:
Albert Finney, Robert Walker, Stathis Giallelis
Best Motion Picture Promoting International Understanding:
Lilies of the Field

Samuel Goldwyn International Award:
Yesterday, Today and Tomorrow
Cecil B. DeMille Award:
Joseph E. Levine
World Film Favorite—Female:
Sophia Loren
World Film Favorite—Male:
Paul Newman

1964

Best Motion Picture—Drama:
Becket
Best Motion Picture—Musical / Comedy:
My Fair Lady
Best English-Language Film:
The Girl with Green Eyes
Best Foreign-Language Foreign Film:
Marriage Italian Style (Italy), *Sallah* (Israel)
Best Director:
George Cukor, *My Fair Lady*
Best Actress—Drama:
Anne Bancroft, *The Pumpkin Eater*
Best Actor—Drama:
Peter O'Toole, *Becket*
Best Actress—Musical / Comedy:
Julie Andrews, *Mary Poppins*
Best Actor—Musical / Comedy:
Rex Harrison, *My Fair Lady*
Best Supporting Actress:
Agnes Moorehead, *Hush . . . Hush, Sweet Charlotte*
Best Supporting Actor:
Edmond O'Brien, *Seven Days in May*
Most Promising Newcomers—Female:
Mia Farrow, Celia Kaye, Mary Ann Mobley

Most Promising Newcomers—Male:
Harv Presnell, George Segal, Chaim Topol

Best Original Score:
Dimitri Tiomkin, *The Fall of the Roman Empire*

Best Song:
Dimitri Tiomkin, Ned Washington, "Circus World," *Circus World*

Cecil B. DeMille Award:
James Stewart

World Film Favorite—Female:
Sophia Loren

World Film Favorite—Male:
Marcello Mastrioanni

1965

Best Motion Picture—Drama:
Doctor Zhivago

Best Motion Picture—Musical / Comedy:
The Sound of Music

Best English-Language Foreign Film:
Darling

Best Foreign-Language Foreign Film:
Juliet of the Spirits (Italy)

Best Director:
David Lean, *Doctor Zhivago*

Best Actress—Drama:
Samantha Eggar, *The Collector*

Best Actor—Drama:
Omar Sharif, *Doctor Zhivago*

Best Actress—Musical / Comedy:
Julie Andrews, *The Sound of Music*

Best Actor—Musical / Comedy:
Lee Marvin, *Cat Ballou*

Best Supporting Actress:
Ruth Gordon, *Inside Daisy Clover*

Best Supporting Actor:
Oskar Werner, *The Spy Who Came In from the Cold*

Most Promising Newcomer—Female:
Elizabeth Hartman, *A Patch of Blue*

Most Promising Newcomer—Male:
Robert Redford, *Inside Daisy Clover*

Best Screenplay:
Robert Bolt, *Doctor Zhivago*

Best Original Score:
Maurice Jarre, *Doctor Zhivago*

Best Original Song:
"Forget Domani," *The Yellow Rolls Royce*

Cecil B. DeMille Award:
John Wayne

World Film Favorite—Female:
Natalie Wood

World Film Favorite—Male:
Paul Newman

1966

Best Motion Picture—Drama:
A Man for All Seasons

Best Motion Picture—Musical / Comedy:
The Russians Are Coming, The Russians Are Coming

Best English-Language Foreign Film:
Alfie

Best Foreign-Language Foreign Film:
A Man and a Woman (France)

Best Director:
Fred Zinnemann, *A Man for All Seasons*

Best Actress—Drama:
Anouk Aimée, *A Man and a Woman*

Best Actor—Drama:
Paul Scofield, *A Man for All Seasons*

Best Actress—Musical / Comedy:
Lynn Redgrave, *Georgy Girl*
Best Actor—Musical / Comedy:
Alan Arkin, *The Russians Are Coming, The Russians Are Coming*
Best Supporting Actress:
Jocelyn La Garde, *Hawaii*
Best Supporting Actor:
Richard Attenborough, *The Sand Pebbles*
Most Promising Newcomer—Female:
Camilla Sparv, *Dead on a Merry Go Round*
Most Promising Newcomer—Male:
James Farentino, *The Pad*
Best Screenplay:
Robert Bolt, *A Man for All Seasons*
Best Original Score:
Elmer Bernstein, *Hawaii*
Best Original Song:
"Strangers in the Night," *A Man Could Get Killed*
Cecil B. DeMille Award:
Charlton Heston
World Film Favorite—Female:
Julie Andrews
World Film Favorite—Male:
Steve McQueen

1967

Best Motion Picture—Drama:
In the Heat of the Night
Best Motion Picture—Musical / Comedy:
The Graduate
Best English-Language Foreign Film:
The Fox (Canada)
Best Foreign-Language Foreign Film:
Live for Life (France)
Best Director:
Mike Nichols, *The Graduate*
Best Actress—Drama:
Dame Edith Evans, *The Whisperers*
Best Actor—Drama:
Rod Steiger, *In the Heat of the Night*
Best Actress—Musical / Comedy:
Anne Bancroft, *The Graduate*
Best Actor—Musical / Comedy:
Richard Harris, *Camelot*
Best Supporting Actress:
Carol Channing, *Thoroughly Modern Millie*
Best Supporting Actor:
Richard Attenborough, *Doctor Dolittle*
Most Promising Newcomer—Female:
Katharine Ross, *The Graduate*
Most Promising Newcomer—Male:
Dustin Hoffman, *The Graduate*
Best Screenplay:
Stirling Silliphant, *In the Heat of the Night*
Best Original Score:
Frederick Loewe, *Camelot*
Best Original Song:
"If Ever I Should Leave You," *Camelot*
Cecil B. DeMille Award:
Kirk Douglas
World Film Favorite—Female:
Julie Andrews
World Film Favorite—Male:
Paul Newman

1968

Best Motion Picture—Drama:
The Lion in Winter
Best Motion Picture—Musical / Comedy:
Oliver!

**Best English-Language
Foreign Film:**
Romeo and Juliet
**Best Foreign-Language
Foreign Film:**
War and Peace (Russia)
Best Director:
Paul Newman, *Rachel, Rachel*
Best Actress—Drama:
Joanne Woodward, *Rachel,
Rachel*
Best Actor—Drama:
Peter O'Toole, *The Lion in
Winter*
**Best Actress—
Musical / Comedy:**
Barbra Streisand, *Funny Girl*
Best Actor—Musical / Comedy:
Ron Moody, *Oliver!*
Best Supporting Actress:
Ruth Gordon, *Rosemary's Baby*
Best Supporting Actor:
Daniel Massey, *Star!*
**Most Promising Newcomer—
Female:**
Olivia Hussey, *Romeo and
Juliet*
**Most Promising Newcomer—
Male:**
Leonard Whiting, *Romeo and
Juliet*
Best Screenplay:
Stirling Silliphant, *Charly*
Best Original Score:
Alex North, *The Shoes of the
Fisherman*
Best Original Song:
Michel Legrand, Alan and
Marilyn Bergman, "The
Windmills of Your Mind,"
The Thomas Crown Affair
Cecil B. DeMille Award:
Gregory Peck
World Film Favorite—Female:
Sophia Loren
World Film Favorite—Male:
Sidney Poitier

1969

Best Motion Picture—Drama:
Anne of the Thousand Days
**Best Motion Picture—
Musical / Comedy:**
The Secret of Santa Vittoria
**Best English-Language
Foreign Film:**
Oh, What a Lovely War!
**Best Foreign-Language
Foreign Film:**
Z (Algeria)
Best Director:
Charles Jarrott, *Anne of the
Thousand Days*
Best Actress—Drama:
Genevieve Bujold, *Anne of the
Thousand Days*
Best Actor—Drama:
John Wayne, *True Grit*
**Best Actress—
Musical / Comedy:**
Patty Duke, *Me, Natalie*
Best Actor—Musical / Comedy:
Peter O'Toole, *Goodbye, Mr.
Chips*
Best Supporting Actress:
Goldie Hawn, *Cactus Flower*
Best Supporting Actor:
Gig Young, *They Shoot Horses,
Don't They?*
**Most Promising Newcomer—
Female:**
Ali MacGraw, *Goodbye,
Columbus*
**Most Promising Newcomer—
Male:**
Jon Voight, *Midnight Cowboy*
Best Screenplay:
John Hale, Bridget Boland,
Richard Sokolove, *Anne of
the Thousand Days*
Best Original Score:
Burt Bacharach, *Butch Cassidy
and the Sundance Kid*

Best Original Song:
Rod McKuen, "Jean," *The Prime of Miss Jean Brodie*
Cecil B. DeMille Award:
Joan Crawford
World Film Favorite—Female:
Barbra Streisand
World Film Favorite—Male:
Steve McQueen

1970

Best Motion Picture—Drama:
Love Story
Best Motion Picture—Musical / Comedy:
M*A*S*H
Best English-Language Foreign Film:
Women in Love
Best Foreign-Language Foreign Film:
Rider on the Rain (France)
Best Director:
Arthur Hiller, *Love Story*
Best Actress—Drama:
Ali MacGraw, *Love Story*
Best Actor—Drama:
George C. Scott, *Patton*
Best Actress—Musical / Comedy:
Carrie Snodgress, *Diary of a Mad Housewife*
Best Actor—Musical / Comedy:
Albert Finney, *Scrooge*
Best Supporting Actress:
Karen Black, *Five Easy Pieces*
Maureen Stapleton, *Airport*
Best Supporting Actor:
John Mills, *Ryan's Daughter*
Most Promising Newcomer—Female:
Carrie Snodgress, *Diary of a Mad Housewife*
Most Promising Newcomer—Male:
James Earl Jones, *The Great White Hope*

Best Screenplay:
Erich Segal, *Love Story*
Best Original Score:
Francis Lai, *Love Story*
Best Original Song:
Henry Mancini, Johnny Mercer, "Whistling Away the Dark," *Darling Lili*
Cecil B: DeMille Award:
Frank Sinatra
World Film Favorite—Female:
Barbra Streisand
World Film Favorite—Male:
Clint Eastwood

1971

Best Motion Picture—Drama:
The French Connection
Best Motion Picture—Musical / Comedy:
Fiddler on the Roof
Best English-Language Foreign Film:
Sunday Bloody Sunday
Best Foreign-Language Foreign Film:
The Policeman (Israel)
Best Director:
William Friedkin, *The French Connection*
Best Actress—Drama:
Jane Fonda, *Klute*
Best Actor—Drama:
Gene Hackman, *The French Connection*
Best Actress—Musical / Comedy:
Twiggy, *The Boy Friend*
Best Actor—Musical / Comedy:
Topol, *Fiddler on the Roof*
Best Supporting Actress:
Ann-Margret, *Carnal Knowledge*
Best Supporting Actor:
Ben Johnson, *The Last Picture Show*

Most Promising Newcomer—Female:
Twiggy, *The Boy Friend*

Most Promising Newcomer—Male:
Desi Arnaz, Jr., *Red Sky at Morning*

Best Screenplay:
Paddy Chayefsky, *The Hospital*

Best Original Score:
Isaac Hayes, *Shaft*

Best Original Song:
Marvin Hamlisch, Johnny Mercer, "Life Is What You Make It," *Kotch*

Cecil B. DeMille Award:
Alfred Hitchcock

World Film Favorite—Female:
Ali MacGraw

World Film Favorites—Male:
Charles Bronson
Sean Connery

1972

Best Motion Picture—Drama:
The Godfather

Best Motion Picture—Musical / Comedy:
Cabaret

Best English-Language Foreign Films:
Young Winston

Best Foreign-Language Foreign Films:
The Emigrants (Sweden)
The New Land (Sweden)

Best Director:
Francis Ford Coppola, *The Godfather*

Best Actress—Drama:
Liv Ullmann, *The Emigrants*

Best Actor—Drama:
Marlon Brando, *The Godfather*

Best Actress—Musical / Comedy:
Liza Minnelli, *Cabaret*

Best Actor—Musical / Comedy:
Jack Lemmon, *Avanti*

Best Supporting Actress:
Shelley Winters, *The Poseidon Adventure*

Best Supporting Actor:
Joel Grey, *Cabaret*

Most Promising Newcomer—Female:
Diana Ross, *Lady Sings the Blues*

Most Promising Newcomer—Male:
Edward Albert, *Butterflies Are Free*

Best Screenplay:
Francis Ford Coppola, Mario Puzo, *The Godfather*

Best Original Score:
Nino Rota, *The Godfather*

Best Original Song:
Walter Scharf, Don Black, "Ben," *Ben*

Best Documentary Films:
Elvis on Tour
Walls of Fire

Cecil B. DeMille Award:
Samuel Goldwyn

World Film Favorite—Female:
Jane Fonda

World Film Favorite—Male:
Marlon Brando

1973

Best Motion Picture—Drama:
The Exorcist

Best Motion Picture—Musical / Comedy:
American Graffiti

Best Foreign-Language Foreign Film:
The Pedestrian (West Germany)

Best Director:
William Friedkin, *The Exorcist*

Best Actress—Drama:
Marsha Mason, *Cinderella Liberty*
Best Actor—Drama:
Al Pacino, *Serpico*
Best Actress— Musical / Comedy:
Glenda Jackson, *A Touch of Class*
Best Actor—Musical / Comedy:
George Segal, *A Touch of Class*
Best Supporting Actress:
Linda Blair, *The Exorcist*
Best Supporting Actor:
John Houseman, *The Paper Chase*
Most Promising Newcomer— Female:
Tatum O'Neal, *Paper Moon*
Most Promising Newcomer— Male:
Paul Le Mat, *American Graffiti*
Best Screenplay:
William Peter Blatty, *The Exorcist*
Best Original Score:
Neil Diamond, *Jonathan Livingstone Seagull*
Best Original Song:
Marvin Hamlisch, Alan and Marilyn Bergman, "The Way We Were," *The Way We Were*
Best Documentary Film:
Visions of Eight
Cecil B. DeMille Award:
Bette Davis
World Film Favorite—Female:
Elizabeth Taylor
World Film Favorite—Male:
Marlon Brando

1974

Best Motion Picture—Drama:
Chinatown

Best Motion Picture— Musical / Comedy:
The Longest Yard
Best Foreign Film:
Scenes from a Marriage (Sweden)
Best Director:
Roman Polanski, *Chinatown*
Best Actress—Drama:
Gena Rowlands, *A Woman Under the Influence*
Best Actor—Drama:
Jack Nicholson, *Chinatown*
Best Actress— Musical / Comedy:
Raquel Welch, *The Three Musketeers*
Best Actor—Musical / Comedy:
Art Carney, *Harry and Tonto*
Best Supporting Actress:
Karen Black, *The Great Gatsby*
Best Supporting Actor:
Fred Astaire, *The Towering Inferno*
Most Promising Newcomer— Female:
Susan Flannery, *The Towering Inferno*
Most Promising Newcomer— Male:
Joseph Bottoms, *The Dove*
Best Screenplay:
Robert Towne, *Chinatown*
Best Original Score:
Alan Jay Lerner, Frederick Loewe, *The Little Prince*
Best Original Song:
Euel and Betty Box, "I Feel Love," *Benji*
Best Documentary Film:
Beautiful People
Cecil B. DeMille Award:
Hal B. Wallis
World Film Favorite—Female:
Barbra Streisand
World Film Favorite—Male:
Robert Redford

1975

Best Motion Picture—Drama:
One Flew Over the Cuckoo's Nest
Best Motion Picture—Musical / Comedy:
The Sunshine Boys
Best Foreign Film:
Lies My Father Told Me (Canada)
Best Director:
Milos Forman, *One Flew Over the Cuckoo's Nest*
Best Actress—Drama:
Louise Fletcher, *One Flew Over the Cuckoo's Nest*
Best Actor—Drama:
Jack Nicholson, *One Flew Over the Cuckoo's Nest*
Best Actress—Musical / Comedy:
Ann-Margret, *Tommy*
Best Actor—Musical / Comedy:
Walter Matthau, *The Sunshine Boys*
Best Supporting Actress:
Brenda Vaccaro, *Once Is Not Enough*
Best Supporting Actor:
Richard Benjamin, *The Sunshine Boys*
Best Acting Debut—Female:
Marilyn Hassett, *The Other Side of the Mountain*
Best Acting Debut—Male:
Brad Dourif, *One Flew Over the Cuckoo's Nest*
Best Screenplay:
Laurence Hauben, Bo Goldman, *One Flew Over the Cuckoo's Nest*
Best Original Score:
John Williams, *Jaws*
Best Original Song:
Keith Carradine, "I'm Easy," *Nashville*
Best Documentary Film:
Youthquake

1976

Best Motion Picture—Drama:
Rocky
Best Motion Picture—Musical / Comedy:
A Star Is Born
Best Foreign Film:
Face to Face (Sweden)
Best Director:
Sidney Lumet, *Network*
Best Actress—Drama:
Faye Dunaway, *Network*
Best Actor—Drama:
Peter Finch, *Network*
Best Actress—Musical / Comedy:
Barbra Streisand, *A Star Is Born*
Best Actor—Musical / Comedy:
Kris Kristofferson, *A Star Is Born*
Best Supporting Actress:
Katharine Ross, *Voyage of the Damned*
Best Supporting Actor:
Laurence Olivier, *Marathon Man*
Best Acting Debut—Female:
Jessica Lange, *King Kong*
Best Acting Debut—Male:
Arnold Schwarzenegger, *Stay Hungry*
Best Screenplay:
Paddy Chayefsky, *Network*
Best Original Score:
Paul Williams, Kenny Ascher, *A Star Is Born*
Best Original Song:
Paul Williams, Barbra Streisand, "Evergreen," *A Star Is Born*

Best Documentary Film:
Altars of the World
Cecil B. DeMille Award:
Walter Mirisch

World Film Favorite—Female:
Sophia Loren
World Film Favorite—Male:
Robert Redford

6. THE WRITERS GUILD OF AMERICA AWARDS

The Hollywood writer has probably suffered more abuse and enjoyed less recognition than any other member of the filmmaking team. According to the Eastern literary establishment, the Hollywood writer betrays his talent and belittles his art if he stays in Hollywood too long. (Edmund Wilson, for example, once claimed that the failures of F. Scott Fitzgerald and Nathanael West to get the best out of their best years "may certainly be laid partly to Hollywood with its already appalling record of talent depraved and wasted.") According to the industry, the Hollywood writer is more of a commodity than an artist. (An efficiency expert at RKO during the 1930s once angrily announced, "I've been through the whole Writers Building, every office, twenty-eight writers—and you know how many of them were writing? Three!") And according to the film scholar, the Hollywood writer hardly has anything to do with a film's success. (The influential *auteur* theory, argues that it's the director and not the writer who is the author of a film.)

Recently the Hollywood writer's reputation has been rehabilitated and he is at long last beginning to receive due recognition. Tom Dardis' *Some Time in the Sun,* for example, maintains that the famous novelists who went to Hollywood actually learned, not suffered from their Hollywood careers. Pauline Kael's *Raising Kane* claims that the importance of *Citizen Kane* is due as much to screenwriter Herman J. Mankiewicz as to director Orson Welles. And most important, Richard Corliss' *Talking Pictures: Screenwriters in the American Cinema* and his anthology, *The Hollywood Screenwriters,* radically revise our ideas about the screenwriter's importance.

D. W. Griffith, himself a director of overwhelming importance, once claimed that the director could only play "Paderewski to the screenwriter's Beethoven," that movies could not be a great art form without great screenwriters. Perhaps we are not approaching the day when Griffith's largely forgotten sentiments will be shared by the film community.

The Screen Writers Guild of America was founded in the 1920s and underwent extensive reorganization in 1933. In its attempt to protect the screenwriter's rights, the Guild met considerable opposition in the 1930s from the producers. In 1933, when the Guild prohibited its members from signing long-term contracts, Louis B. Mayer threatened to fire all Guild members who were under contract with his studio. Only after years of bitter conflict did the Guild win the right to be the collective-bargaining agent for writers.

Throughout the years, one of the principal activities of the Guild has been credit arbitration. Because Hollywood screenplays are so often written by a string of writers, it is frequently difficult to decide who rightfully deserves screen credit and the Guild has worked tirelessly in the field of credit jurisdiction. The Guild, then, is a divided creature: at once a labor union occupied with economics and an art guild concerned with the freedom of creativity.

In 1949 the Guild presented its first awards for writing achievements and has continued to honor excellence in screenwriting down to the present day. The awards have filled an important gap, for although the Academy has honored screenwriting achievements since its first awards, film writing has been neglected by many other organizations. There are, for example, no Pulitzer Prizes for screenwriters, no Nobels. More than twenty years passed before the New York Film Critics included writing among their prizes, and the National Board of Review still does not confer annual awards for film scripts.

In 1954 the Screen Writers Guild merged with the Radio Writers Guild and the Television Writers Guild to form the

Writers Guild of America, East and West. Motion-picture writers belong to the Screen Branch of the Writers Guild of America, West. In addition to film awards, the Writers Guild also confers prizes in the fields of television and radio. These awards, however, are not listed here.

The following is a list of special film prizes conferred by the Guild:

The Robert Meltzer Award "given for the screenplay dealing most ably with problems of the American scene" (presented 1948–1951).

The Laurel Award for Achievement "given annually to that member of the Guild who, in the opinion of the current Executive Board of the Screen Branch, has advanced the literature of the motion picture through the years, and who has made outstanding contributions to the profession of the Screen Writer" (first presented 1953).

The Valentine Davies Award. "In memory of Valentine Davies, whose contribution to the motion picture community brought dignity and honor to writers everywhere" (first presented 1962).

Founders Award (first presented 1966).

The Morgan Cox Award "presented to that member or group of members whose vital ideas, continuing efforts and personal sacrifices best exemplify the ideal of service to the Guild which the life of Morgan Cox so fully represented" (first presented 1969).

Medallion Award (first presented 1971).

1948

Best-Written American Comedy:
F. Hugh Herbert, *Sitting Pretty*

Best-Written American Drama:
Frank Partos, Millen Brand, *The Snake Pit*

Best-Written American Western:
John Huston, *Treasure of Sierra Madre*

Best-Written American Musical:
Sidney Sheldon, Frances Goodrich, Albert Hackett (screenplay); Frances Goodrich, Albert Hackett (story), *Easter Parade*

Screenplay Dealing Most Ably with Problems of the American Scene (Robert Meltzer Award):
Frank Partos, Millen Brand, *The Snake Pit*

1949

Best-Written American Comedy:
Joseph L. Mankiewicz, *A Letter to Three Wives*
Best-Written American Drama:
Robert Rossen, *All the King's Men*
Best-Written American Western:
Lamar Trotti (screenplay); W. R. Burnett (story), *Yellow Sky*
Best-Written American Musical:
Betty Comden, Adolph Green, *On the Town* (based on an idea by Jerome Robbins)
Screenplay Dealing Most Ably with Problems of the American Scene (Robert Meltzer Award):
Robert Rossen, *All the King's Men*

1950

Best-Written American Comedy:
Joseph L. Mankiewicz, *All About Eve* (also entered as Drama)
Best-Written American Drama:
Charles Brackett, Billy Wilder, D. M. Marshman, Jr., *Sunset Boulevard*
Best-Written American Western:
Michael Blankfort, *Broken Arrow*

Best-Written American Musical:
Sidney Sheldon, *Annie Get Your Gun*
Screenplay Dealing Most Ably with Problems of the American Scene (Robert Meltzer Award):
Carl Foreman, *The Men*

1951

Best-Written American Comedy:
Frances Goodrich, Albert Hackett, *Father's Little Dividend*
Best-Written American Drama:
Michael Wilson, Harry Brown, *A Place in the Sun*
Best-Written American Low-Budget Film:
Samuel Fuller, *The Steel Helmet*
Best-Written American Musical:
Alan Jay Lerner, *An American in Paris*
Screenplay Dealing Most Ably with Problems of the American Scene (Robert Meltzer Award):
Robert Buckner, *Bright Victory*

1952

Best-Written American Comedy:
Frank S. Nugent, *The Quiet Man*
Best-Written American Drama:
Carl Foreman, *High Noon*
Best-Written American Musical:
Betty Comden, Adolph Green, *Singin' In the Rain*

Laurel Award for Achievement:
Sonya Levien

1953

Best-Written American Comedy:
Ian McLellan Hunter, John Dighton (screenplay); Ian McLellan Hunter (story), *Roman Holiday*
Best-Written American Drama:
Daniel Taradash, *From Here to Eternity*
Best-Written American Musical:
Helen Deutsch, *Lili*
Laurel Award for Achievement:
Dudley Nichols

1954

Best-Written American Comedy:
Billy Wilder, Samuel Taylor, Ernest Lehman, *Sabrina*
Best-Written American Drama:
Budd Schulberg, *On the Waterfront*
Best-Written American Musical:
Albert Hackett, Frances Goodrich, Dorothy Kingsley, *Seven Brides for Seven Brothers*
Laurel Award for Achievement:
Robert Riskin

1955

Best-Written American Comedy:
Frank Nugent, Joshua Logan, *Mister Roberts*
Best-Written American Drama:
Paddy Chayefsky, *Marty*
Best-Written American Musical:
Daniel Fuchs, Isobel Lennart (screenplay); Daniel Fuchs (story), *Love Me or Leave Me*
Laurel Award for Achievement:
Frances Goodrich, Albert Hackett, Julius J. and Philip G. Epstein

1956

Best-Written American Comedy:
James Poe, John Farrow, S. J. Perelman, *Around the World In 80 Days*
Best-Written American Drama:
Michael Wilson, *Friendly Persuasion*
Best-American Musical:
Ernest Lehman, *The King and I*
Laurel Award for Achievement:
Charles Brackett and Billy Wilder

1957

Best-Written American Comedy:
Billy Wilder, I.A.L. Diamond, *Love in the Afternoon*

Best-Written American Drama:
Reginald Rose, *Twelve Angry Men*

Best-Written American Musical:
John Patrick (screenplay); Vera Caspary (story), *Les Girls*

Laurel Award for Achievement:
John Lee Mahin

1958

Best-Written American Comedy:
S. N. Behrman, George Froeschel, *Me and the Colonel*

Best-Written American Drama:
Harold Jacob Smith, Nathan E. Douglas, *The Defiant Ones*

Best-Written American Musical:
Alan Jay Lerner, *Gigi*

Laurel Award for Achievement:
Nunnally Johnson

1959

Best-Written American Comedy:
Billy Wilder, I. A. L. Diamond, *Some Like It Hot*

Best-Written American Drama:
Frances Goodrich, Albert Hackett, *The Diary of Anne Frank*

Best-Written American Musical:
Melville Shavelson, Jack Rose (screenplay), Robert Smith (story), *Five Pennies*

Laurel Award for Achievement:
Norman Krasna

1960

Best-Written American Comedy:
Billy Wilder, I. A. L. Diamond, *The Apartment*

Best-Written America Drama:
Richard Brooks, *Elmer Gantry*

Best-Written American Musical:
Betty Comden, Adolph Green, *The Bells Are Ringing*

Laurel Award for Achievement:
George Seaton

1961

Best-Written American Comedy:
George Axelrod, *Breakfast at Tiffany's*

Best-Written American Drama:
Sidney Carroll, Robert Rossen, *The Hustler*

Best-Written American Musical:
Ernest Lehman, *West Side Story*

Laurel Award for Achievement:
Philip Dunne

Valentine Davies Award for bringing dignity and honor to writers everywhere:
Mary C. McCall, Jr.

1962

Best-Written American Comedy:
Stanley Shapiro, Nate Monaster, *That Touch of Mink*
Best-Written American Drama:
Horton Foote, *To Kill a Mockingbird*
Best-Written American Musical:
Marion Hargrove, *The Music Man*
Laurel Award for Achievement:
Joseph L. Mankiewicz
Valentine Davies Award:
Allen Rivkin

1963

Best-Written American Comedy:
James Poe, *Lilies of the Field*
Best-Written American Drama:
Harriet Frank, Jr., Irving Ravetch, *Hud*
Best-Written American Musical:
(no award presented this year)
Laurel Award for Achievement:
John Huston
Valentine Davies Award:
Morgan Cox

1964

Best-Written American Comedy:
Stanley Kubrick, Peter George, Terry Southern (screen-play); Peter George (story), *Dr. Strangelove*
Best-Written American Drama:
Edward Anhalt, *Becket*
Best-Written American Musical:
Bill Walsh, Don Da Gradi, *Mary Poppins*
Laurel Award for Achievement:
Sidney Buchman
Valentine Davies Award:
James R. Webb

1965

Best-Written American Comedy:
Herb Gardner, *A Thousand Clowns*
Best-Written American Drama:
Morton Fine, David Friedkin, *The Pawnbroker*
Best-Written American Musical:
Ernest Lehman, *The Sound of Music* (no other nominations this year in this category)
Laurel Award for Achievement:
Isobel Lennart
Valentine Davies Award:
Leonard Spigelgass

1966

Best-Written American Comedy:
William Rose, *The Russians Are Coming, The Russians Are Coming*
Best-Written American Drama:
Ernest Lehman, *Who's Afraid of Virginia Woolf?*

Best-Written American Musical:
(no award presented this year)
Laurel Award for Achievement:
Richard Brooks
Valentine Davies Award:
Edmund L. North
Founders Award:
Charles Brackett and Richard Breen

1967

Best-Written American Comedy:
Calder Willingham, Buck Henry, *The Graduate*
Best-Written American Drama:
David Newman, Robert Benton, *Bonnie and Clyde*
Best-Written American Musical:
Richard Morris, *Thoroughly Modern Millie*
Best-Written Original Screenplay:
David Newman, Robert Benton, *Bonnie and Clyde*
Laurel Award for Achievement:
Casey Robinson
Valentine Davies Award:
George Seaton

1968

Best-Written American Comedy:
Neil Simon, *The Odd Couple*
Best-Written American Drama:
James Goldman, *The Lion in Winter*
Best-Written American Musical:
Isobel Lennart, *Funny Girl*

Best-Written Original Screenplay:
Mel Brooks, *The Producers*
Laurel Award for Achievement:
Carl Foreman
Valentine Davies Award:
Dore Schary

1969

Best-Written American Comedy Written Directly for the Screen:
Paul Mazursky, Larry Tucker, *Bob & Carol & Ted & Alice*
Best-Written American Comedy Adapted from Another Medium:
Arnold Schulman, *Goodbye, Columbus*
Best-Written American Drama Written Directly for the Screen:
William Goldman, *Butch Cassidy and the Sundance Kid*
Best-Written Drama Adapted from Another Medium:
Waldo Salt, *Midnight Cowboy*
Laurel Award for Achievement:
Dalton Trumbo
Valentine Davies Award:
Richard Murphy
Morgan Cox Award:
Barry Trivers

1970

Best-Written American Comedy Written Directly for the Screen:
Neil Simon, *The Out-of-Towners*

Best-Written American Comedy Adapted from Another Medium:
Ring Lardner, Jr., *M*A*S*H*

Best-Written American Drama Written Directly for the Screen:
Francis Ford Coppola, Edmund H. North, *Patton*

Best-Written Drama Adapted from Another Medium:
Robert Anderson, *I Never Sang for My Father*

Laurel Award for Achievement:
James Poe

Morgan Cox Award:
Leonard Spigelgass

Founders Award:
Lamar Trotti

Valentine Davies Award:
Daniel Taradash

1971

Best-Written Comedy Written Directly for the Screen:
Paddy Chayefsky, *The Hospital*

Best-Written Comedy Adapted from Another Medium:
John Paxton, *Kotch*

Best-Written Drama Written Directly for the Screen:
Penelope Gilliatt, *Sunday Bloody Sunday*

Best-Written Drama Adapted from Another Medium:
Ernest Tidyman, *The French Connection*

Laurel Award for Achievement:
Ernest Lehman

Valentine Davies Award:
Michael Blankfort, Norman Corin

Morgan Cox Award:
Allen Rivkin

Medallion Award:
(first time presented)
Charles Chaplin

1972

Best-Written Comedy Written Directly for the Screen:
Buck Henry, David Newman, Robert Benton, *What's Up, Doc?*

Best-Written Comedy Adapted from Another Medium:
Jay Presson Allen, *Cabaret*

Best-Written Drama Written Directly for the Screen:
Jeremy Larmer, *The Candidate*

Best-Written Drama Adapted from Another Medium:
Mario Puzo, Francis Ford Coppola, *The Godfather*

Laurel Award for Achievement:
William Rose

Valentine Davies Award:
William Ludwig

Morgan Cox Award:
David Harmon

1973

Best-Written Comedy Written Directly for the Screen:
Melvin Frank, Jack Rose, *A Touch of Class*

Best-Written Comedy Adapted from Another Medium:
Alvin Sargent, *Paper Moon*

Best-Written Drama Written Directly for the Screen:
Steve Shagan, *Save the Tiger*

Best-Written Drama Adapted from Another Medium:
Waldo Salt, Norman Wexler, *Serpico*

Laurel Award for Achievement:
Paddy Chayefsky
Valentine Davies Award:
Ray Bradbury, Philip Dunne
Morgan Cox Award:
James R. Webb

1974

Best-Written Comedy Written Directly for the Screen:
Mel Brooks, Norman Steinberg, Andrew Bergman, Richard Pryor, Alan Uger, *Blazing Saddles*
Best-Written Adapted Comedy:
Mordecai Richler, Lionel Chetwynd, *The Apprenticeship of Duddy Kravitz*
Best-Written Drama Written Directly for the Screen:
Robert Towne, *Chinatown*
Best-Written Drama Adapted from Another Medium:
Francis Ford Coppola, Mario Puzo, *The Godfather Part II*
Laurel Award for Achievement:
Preston Sturges (posthumously)
Valentine Davies Award:
Fay Kanin
Morgan Cox Award:
Edmund North

1975

Best-Written Comedy Written Directly for the Screen:
Robert Towne, Warren Beatty, *Shampoo*
Best-Written Comedy Adapted from Another Medium:
Neil Simon, *The Sunshine Boys*

Best-Written Drama Written Directly for the Screen:
Frank Pierson, *Dog Day Afternoon*
Best-Written Drama Adapted from Another Medium:
Laurence Hauben, Bo Goldman, *One Flew Over the Cuckoo's Nest*
Laurel Award for Achievement:
Michael Wilson
Valentine Davies Award:
Winston Miller
Morgan Cox Award:
William Ludwig

1976

Best-Written Comedy Written Directly for the Screen:
Bill Lancaster, *The Bad News Bears*
Best-Written Comedy Adapted from Another Medium:
Frank Waldman, Blake Edwards, *The Pink Panther Strikes Again*
Best-Written Drama Written Directly for the Screen:
Paddy Chayefsky, *Network*
Best-Written Drama Adapted from Another Medium:
William Goldman, *All the President's Men*
Laurel Award for Achievement:
Samson Raphaelson
Valentine Davies Award:
Carl Foreman
Morgan Cox Award:
Herbert Baker
Medallion Award:
Cesare Zavattini

7. THE DIRECTORS GUILD OF AMERICA AWARDS

The functions and status of the film director have undergone a series of radical changes over the years. During the earliest years of filmmaking, the director really did not have much to do. Because each scene in the first movies was filmed in one long take with no cutting and little or no camera movement, the director's influence was severely limited: he merely made sure that the story had continuity and that the actors' best performances were recorded by the camera.

When film technique advanced with the well-known discoveries of Edwin S. Porter and D. W. Griffith, the director's responsibility grew and his opportunities to inform a film with his own personal style similarly expanded. The placement, angle and movement of the camera, as well as such important matters as casting, costumes, sets and acting, could all be influenced or determined by the director. Despite this influence, for most of cinema's history the director—particularly the Hollywood director—has been considered only one of many members in the filmmaking crew: he was thought to be subordinate to the producer; he often had no say whatsoever in editing the film; and his name was rarely known by the public, who selected films according to their stars. (There were, of course, obvious exceptions; Griffith, DeMille and Hitchcock were attractions in their own right.)

The director's status was greatly enhanced during the 1950s, when a group of French critics writing for *Cahiers du Cinéma* (among them Truffaut, Godard, Chabrol and Rohmer) postulated that the director was in fact the *auteur,* or author, of a film, that he was in the most favorable position to inform a film with artistic qualities. As a result of this influential "theory," attention became focused on directors' themes and styles, and many earlier American directors were favorably reassessed.

Although the *auteur* theory has come under attack in recent years, no longer being considered a complete enough approach to the complex art of film, people still think and talk about a film largely in terms of its director. Movies are often advertised by their director's name, as in Robert Altman's *Nashville* or Martin Scorsese's *Taxi Driver.* And most international film festivals list their entries by title, director and country, again suggesting that the director holds first place among the filmmaking team.

The Directors Guild, founded in 1936, presented its first awards for the seasonal year 1948/49. The calendar year became the basis for the awards in 1951, resulting in some overlapping prizes that year.

Because it announces its awards prior to the Academy Awards presentation, the Guild is often used to predict who will win the Academy's choice for Best Director. Over the past twenty-six years since it has given awards based on the calendar year, the Guild has only disagreed twice with the Academy for its choice of Best Director: in 1968, when the Guild selected Anthony Harvey *(The Lion in Winter),* while the Academy chose Carol Reed *(Oliver!);* and in 1972, when the Academy honored Bob Fosse *(Cabaret),* while the Guild awarded Francis Ford Coppola *(The Godfather).*

The Guild also confers prizes for best direction in the field of television. These awards have not been listed here.

1948 / 49

Quarterly Awards:
Fred Zinnemann, *The Search*
Howard Hawks, *Red River*
Anatole Litvak, *The Snake Pit*
Joseph L. Mankiewicz, *A Letter to Three Wives*
Annual Award:
Joseph L. Mankiewicz

1949 / 50

Quarterly Awards:
Mark Robson, *The Champion*
Alfred L. Werker, *Lost Boundaries*
Robert Rossen, *All the King's Men*
Carol Reed, *The Third Man*
Annual Award:
Robert Rossen

1950 / 51

Quarterly Awards:
Billy Wilder, *Sunset Boulevard*
John Huston, *The Asphalt Jungle*
Joseph L. Mankiewicz, *All About Eve*
Vincente Minnelli, *Father's Little Dividend*
Annual Award:
Joseph L. Mankiewicz, *All About Eve*

1951

Quarterly Awards:
Alfred Hitchcock, *Strangers on a Train*
George Stevens, *A Place in the Sun*
Vincente Minnelli, *An American in Paris*
Annual Award:
George Stevens, *A Place in the Sun*

1952

Quarterly Awards:
Charles Crichton, *The Lavender Hill Mob*
Joseph L. Mankiewicz, *Five Fingers*
Fred Zinnemann, *High Noon*
John Ford, *The Quiet Man*
Annual Award:
John Ford

1953

Most Outstanding Directorial Achievement:
Fred Zinnemann, *From Here to Eternity*
Outstanding Directorial Achievement:
Charles Walters, *Lili*
William Wyler, *Roman Holiday*
George Stevens, *Shane*
Billy Wilder, *Stalag 17*
Critic Award:
Bosley Crowther, *New York Times*

1954

Most Outstanding Directorial Achievement:
Elia Kazan, *On the Waterfront*
Outstanding Directorial Achievement:
George Seaton, *The Country Girl*
Alfred Hitchcock, *Rear Window*
Billy Wilder, *Sabrina*
William Wellman, *The High and the Mighty*
Critic Award:
Harold V. Cohen, *Pittsburgh Post-Gazette*

1955

Most Outstanding Directorial Achievement:
Delbert Mann, *Marty*
Outstanding Directorial Achievement:
John Sturges, *Bad Day at Black Rock*

John Ford and Mervyn LeRoy,
  Mister Roberts
Elia Kazan, *East of Eden*
Joshua Logan, *Picnic*
Critic Award:
John Rosenfield, Dallas
  Morning-Evening Star

1956

**Most Outstanding Directorial
Achievement:**
George Stevens, *Giant*
**Outstanding Directorial
Achievement:**
Michael Anderson, *Around the
  World in 80 Days*
William Wyler, *Friendly
  Persuasion*
King Vidor, *War and Peace*
Walter Lang, *The King and I*
Critic Award:
Francis J. Carmody, *Washington News*
D. W. Griffith Award:
King Vidor

1957

**Most Outstanding Directorial
Achievement:**
David Lean, *The Bridge on the
  River Kwai*
**Outstanding Directorial
Achievement:**
Joshua Logan, *Sayonara*
Sidney Lumet, *Twelve Angry
  Men*
Mark Robson, *Peyton Place*
Billy Wilder, *Witness for the
  Prosecution*
Critic Award:
Hollis Alpert and Arthur
  Knight, *Saturday Review*

1958

Grand Award for Direction:
Vincente Minnelli, *Gigi*
D. W. Griffith Award:
Frank Capra
Critic Award:
Philip K. Scheuer, Los Angeles
  Times
Special Award:
Louella Parsons
**Best Directed Non-English
Film:**
René Clair, *Gates of Paris*

1959

Grand Award for Direction:
William Wyler, *Ben-Hur*
Critic Award:
John E. Fitzgerald, *Our Sunday
  Visitor*

1960

Grand Award for Direction:
Billy Wilder, *The Apartment*
Critic Award:
Paul Beckley, New York *Herald
  Tribune*
**Special Award of Honorary
Membership:**
Y. Frank Freeman

1961

Director Award:
Robert Wise, Jerome Robbins,
  West Side Story
Critic Award:
John Beaufort, *Christian
  Science Monitor*

1962

Director Award:
David Lean, *Lawrence of Arabia*

1963

Director Award:
Tony Richardson, *Tom Jones*
Critic Award:
Paine Knickerbocker, San Francisco *Chronicle*

1964

Director Award:
George Cukor, *My Fair Lady*
Critic Award:
James Meade, San Diego *Union*

1965

Director Award:
Robert Wise, *The Sound of Music*
Critic Award:
Sam Lesner, Chicago *Daily News*
D. W. Griffith Award:
William Wyler

1966

Director Award:
Fred Zinnemann, *A Man for All Seasons*

1967

Director Award:
Mike Nichols, *The Graduate*

1968

Director Award:
Anthony Harvey, *The Lion in Winter*
D. W. Griffith Award:
Alfred Hitchcock

1969

Director Award:
John Schlesinger, *Midnight Cowboy*
D. W. Griffith Award:
Fred Zinnemann

1970

Director Award:
Franklin Schaffner, *Patton*

1971

Director Award:
William Friedkin, *The French Connection*

1972

Director Award:
Francis Ford Coppola, *The Godfather*

1973

Director Award:
George Roy Hill, *The Sting*

1974

Director Award:
Francis Ford Coppola, *The Godfather II*

1975

Director Award:
Milos Forman, *One Flew Over the Cuckoo's Nest*

1976

Director Award:
John G. Avildsen, *Rocky*

8. DIRECTORS OF THE YEAR AWARDS

The *International Film Guide,* the annual compendium of world film information, each year honors five directors with a profile of each director's life, a critique of his work, and a thorough filmography. Although a director may be selected for his overall contribution to film rather than for any single work, each honored director must be both still living (so a great director like Eisenstein has never been cited) and must have produced *recent* major work (so great directors like Renoir and Hawks have been omitted). The awards are nonrecurrent: once a director is honored, he is ineligible for future selection.

Peter Cowie, editor of the *Guide,* realizes that authorship in cinema is not a clear issue, that screenwriters, producers, stars, cinematographers and editors can certainly exert a major influence over a movie. But despite these other contributors, it is the director who most clearly can impose his signature on the film, according to Cowie. Years before the *auteur* theory ever originated in France, cinema, Cowie says, was almost exclusively appreciated in terms of directors. And he wishes to maintain that appreciation: the goal of the *International Film Guide,* Cowie says, is "to place an uncompromising emphasis on the role of the director."

In selecting the Directors of the Year, Cowie claims not

to make any arbitrary distinctions between commercial Hollywood movies and the European "art" film; rather, his criterion is "quality within any given genre or style." A popular Hollywood movie can of course merit our attention, Cowie says, as much as an experimental film: what counts in the director's personal vision.

The Directors of the Year awards from the first ten volumes of the *International Film Guide* have been collected in book form. Above quotations are taken from this collection, entitled *50 Major Film-Makers*.

1964
Visconti
Welles
Truffaut
Wajda
Hitchcock

1965
Fellini
Ray
  (Satyajit)
Buñuel
Malle
Kubrick

1966
Kurosawa
Rosi
Demy
Brooks
Haanstra

1967
Franju
Losey
Polanski
Frankenheimer
Torre Nilsson

1968
Widerberg
Ivens
Lumet

Nemec
Antonioni

1969
Bondarchuk
Forman
Jancso
Penn
Tati

1970
Anderson
Chabrol
Ichikawa
Pasolini
Skolimowski

1970
Donskoi
Kazan
Melville
Oshima
Schorm

1972
Bertolucci
Donner
Kozintsev
Rohmer
Troell

1973
Bergman
Bresson

Makavejev
Resnais
Schlesinger

1974
Boorman
Gaal
Godard
Huston
Ivory

1975
Altman
Ferreri
Has
Lester
Sjoman

1976
Cacoyannis
Cassavetes
Coppola
Fassbinder
Zanussi

1977
Allen
  (Woody)
Cukor
Kobayashi
Sautet
Wertmüller

9. THE INDEPENDENT FILM AWARDS

Experimental artists have often encountered problems in this country, but experimental filmmakers have a particularly difficult time here. Whereas an avant-garde poet or painter can at least practice his art (even if he can't always get published or exhibited), the expense of filmmaking severely limits the frequency with which an avant-garde filmmaker can even work in his medium. Despite the increasing availability of inexpensive 16mm stock and equipment, filmmaking is still much more costly than poetry or painting. Thus, experimental films look radically different from Hollywood productions not only by design but by necessity as well: without the financial resources of a major studio, the independent filmmaker has had to rely on his own ingenuity to make films.

Experimental filmmakers have also suffered neglect by most of our major newspapers and magazines. Even today, many of our most highly respected film critics confine their attention largely to more "conventional" narrative movies. In order to rectify this situation, Jonas Mekas started to publish *Film Culture* in 1955, the first American journal to take the avant-garde cinema seriously. Calling for the "thorough revision of the prevalent attitude to the function of cinema," *Film Culture* has often been compared to the French journal *Cahiers du Cinéma,* which has also been a voice for innovative filmmakers.

The first issues of *Film Culture* focused on European films, although some attention—mostly negative—was given to the embryonic experimental cinema in America. Plagued by financial difficulties from its beginnings, in 1958 the magazine collapsed as a monthly and started publishing on an irregular basis. At that time, *Film Culture* reversed its position and began to give attention to the experimental cinema of which it had been so critical. The magazine also turned its eyes from European to American filmmakers, and Andrew Sarris—usually credited with introducing the *auteur* theory to America—began publishing his now famous series of essays on Hollywood directors in *Film Culture*.

With its nineteenth issue, in 1959, *Film Culture* established the Independent Film Award to "point out original and unique American contributors to the cinema." During the late fifties and early sixties, Mekas' concept of the independent film was broader than it has become under the policies of such editors of P. Adams Sitney. The first years the awards went to narrative films like *Shadows* and *Primary,* which many current experimental filmmakers would no longer consider quite so experimental now that conceptualism and minimalism are so strongly favored.

The American underground cinema is still a matter of controversy. When the Museum of Modern Art screened a seven-evening series of "The History of the American Avant-Garde Cinema" in the spring of 1976, it aroused numerous debates. Andrew Sarris wrote a long review in the *Village Voice,* claiming that experimental cinema simply wasn't as important, diverse, interesting or even as truly experimental as commercial cinema. And Amos Vogel published an article in *Film Comment* arguing that the seven programs did not represent the *real* American avant-garde cinema.

It is, of course, the nature of the avant-garde to be controversial. But whatever one thinks of American Independent Cinema, one can't deny its achievements and the necessity of diverse film forms.

The Independent Film Awards listed below are accompanied by texts written by *Film Culture*'s editors. For Michael Snow's prize, however, no text was printed at the time of the award's announcement, since in the same issue as the prize, several pieces about and by Snow were published. The editors of *Film Culture* have asked that brief excerpts from those articles be included here to serve as an accompanying text.

FIRST INDEPENDENT FILM AWARD (for 1959) to:
John Cassavetes for *Shadows*

Since John Cassavetes's film *Shadows*, independently produced by Maurice McEndree and Seymour Cassel, more than any other recent American film, presents contemporary reality in a fresh and unconventional manner, it rightly deserves the first Independent Film Award.

Cassavetes in *Shadows* was able to break out of conventional molds and traps, and retain original freshness. The improvisation, spontaneity, and free inspiration that are almost entirely lost in most films from an excess of professionalism are fully used in this film. The situations and atmosphere of New York night life are vividly, cinematically, and truly caught in *Shadows*. It breathes an immediacy that the cinema of today vitally needs if it is to be a living and contemporary art.

SECOND INDEPENDENT FILM AWARD (for 1960) to:
Robert Frank and Alfred Leslie's *Pull My Daisy*

Looking back through our last year's film production, we have found a sad and infested landscape, with our official cinema still perpetuating long-dead styles and long-dead subjects. Our official cinema is completely out of tune with the times. We however believe that no art in modern times has any value if it is not modern. Only modern art can be creative, and only modern can be moral, since it does not place obstacles of clichés of life and art between man and the immediacy of life.

Pull My Daisy has all these qualities. Its modernity and its honesty, its sincerity and its humility, its imagination and its humor, its youth, its freshness, and its truth is without comparison in our last year's pompous cinematic production. In its camera work, it effectively breaks with the accepted and 1,000-years-old official rules of slick polished Alton Y Co. cinematographic schmaltz. It breathes an immediacy that the cinema of today vitally needs if it is to be a living and contemporary art.

THIRD INDEPENDENT FILM AWARD (for 1961) to:
Ricky Leacock, Don Pennebaker, Robert Drew, Al Maysles for the film *Primary*

Looking back through our last year's film production, we have found that *Primary*, more than any other film, reveals new cinematic techniques of recording life on film. Whereas the usual fiction film is drowned in heavy theatrics, and the usual theatrical and television documentary has become a pallid and dehumanized illustration of literary texts, in *Primary*, as well as in their film *Cuba Si, Yankee No*, Ricky Leacock, Don Pennebaker, Robert Drew, and Al Maysles have caught scenes of real life with unprecedented authenticity, immediacy, and truth. They have done so by daringly and spontaneously renouncing old controlled techniques; by letting themselves be guided by the happening scene itself; by concentrating themselves only on man himself, without imposing on him any preconceived "form" or "idea" or "importance." We see *Primary* as a revolutionary step and a breaking point in the recording of reality in cinema. We further believe that the fiction film too, could intelligently profit from *Primary*'s techniques.

Shadows and *Pull My Daisy* have indicated new cinematic approaches stylistically and formally. *Primary* goes one step further: By exploring new camera, sound, and lighting methods, it enables the film-maker to pierce deeper into the area of new content as well. The main handicap of cinema has been its expensiveness and its need for teamwork. Since most of human creation is a private personal action, the most sensitive artists have avoided cinema. The techniques of *Primary* indicate that we are entering a long-awaited era, when the budget of a sound film is the same as that of a book of poems, and when a film-maker can shoot his film with sound, alone and by himself and unobtrusively, almost the same way as a poet observing a scene. Thus, heralded by *Primary*, we see another turning point in cinema.

There is a feeling in the air that cinema is only just beginning.

FOURTH INDEPENDENT FILM AWARD (for 1962) to:
Stan Brakhage for his films *The Dead* and *Prelude*

Looking back through last year's film production, we have found that Stan Brakhage's films, *The Dead* and *Prelude*, stand out as works of exquisite beauty; they point to the unexplored possibilities of the poetic cinema.

Singlemindedly and persistently, during the last ten years, Stan Brakhage has been pursuing his own personal vision. He has developed a style and a filmic language that is able to express with utmost subtlety the unpredictable movements of his inner eye. He has mastered silence as no other film-maker has done, he has made it an integral part of his films. He has eliminated from his work all literary elements, making it a unique and pure cinematic experience.

Whereas the bulk of the independent film-making in America

and elsewhere follows the dramatic and the documentary film traditions, Brakhage has chosen poetry for his artistic self-expression. He has directed his eye inwards, into man's subconscious, wherefrom he draws snatches of the beauty and the meaning of man and the world. He has kept away from the obvious, the explainable, the banal, giving the cinema an intelligence and a subtlety that is usually the province of the older arts, and he has done this with fanatical consistency, upholding—and setting an example for others—the absolute independence of the film artist.

FIFTH INDEPENDENT FILM AWARD (for 1963) to:
Jack Smith for his film *Flaming Creatures*

In *Flaming Creatures,* Smith has graced the anarchic liberation of new American cinema with graphic and rhythmic power worthy of the best of formal cinema. He has attained for the first time in motion pictures a high level of art that is absolutely lacking in decorum; and a treatment of sex that makes us aware of the restraint of all previous film-makers.

He has shown more clearly than anyone before how the poet's license includes all things, not only of spirit, but also of flesh; not only of dreams and of symbol, but also of solid reality. In no other art but the movies could this have so fully been done, and their capacity was realized by Smith.

He has borne us a terrible beauty in *Flaming Creatures,* at a time when terror and beauty are growing more and more apart, indeed are more and more denied. He has shocked us with the sting of mortal beauty. He has struck us with not the mere pity or curiosity of the perverse, but the glory, the pageantry of Transylvania and the magic of Fairyland. He has lit up a part of life, although it is a part which most men scorn.

No higher single praise can be given an artist than this, that he has expressed a fresh vision of life. We cannot wish more for Jack Smith that this: that he continues to expand that vision, and make it visible to us in flickering light and shadow, and in flame.

SIXTH INDEPENDENT FILM AWARD (for 1964) to:
Andy Warhol for his films *Sleep, Haircut, Eat, Kiss* and *Empire*

Andy Warhol is taking cinema back to its origins, to the days of Lumière, for a rejuvenation and a cleansing. In his work, he has abandoned all the "cinematic" form and subject adornments that cinema had gathered around itself until now. He has focused his lens on the plainest images possible in the plainest manner possible. With his artist's intuition as his only guide, he records, almost obsessively, man's daily activities, the things he sees around him.

A strange thing occurs. The world becomes transposed, intensified, electrified. We see it sharper than before. Not in dramatic, rearranged contexts and meanings, not in the service of something else (even Cinéma Vérité did not escape this subjection of the objective reality to ideas) but as pure as it is in itself: eating as eating, sleeping as sleeping, haircut as haircut.

We watch a Warhol movie with no hurry. The first thing he does is that he stops us from running. His camera rarely moves. It stays fixed on the subject like there was nothing more meaningful and nothing more important than that subject. It stays there longer than we are used to. Long enough for us to begin to free ourselves from all that we thought about haircutting or eating or the Empire State Building; or, for that matter, about cinema. We begin to realize that we have never, really, seen haircutting or eating. We have cut our hair, we have eaten, but we have never really seen those actions. The whole reality around become *differently* interesting, and we feel like we have to begin filming everything anew. A new way of looking at things and the screen is given through the personal vision of Andy Warhol; a new angle, a new insight—a shift necessitated, no doubt, by the inner changes that are taking place in man.

As a result of Andy Warhol's work, we are going to see soon these simple phenomena, like Eating, or Trees, or Sunrise filmed by a number of different artists, each time differently, each time a new Tree, a new Eating, a new Sunrise. Some of them will be bad, some good, some mediocre, like any other movie—and somebody will make a masterpiece. In any case, it will be a new adventure; the world seen through a consciousness that is not running after big dramatic events but is focused on more subtle changes and nuances. Andy Warhol's cinema is a mediation on the objective world; in a sense, it is a cinema of happiness.

**SEVENTH INDEPENDENT FILM AWARD (for 1965) to:
Harry Smith**

Harry Smith's creative work reaches across two important fields of film:

His abstract works, both in color and black and white are among the most complex and rich, among the most beautiful, yet to come out of cinema. The modulations of color and form are so certain and subtle, delicate and bold, that these films rank among the very few where attempt is absolutely realized in attainment.

As an animator, Harry Smith is remarkable in perfection of

technique, and in intensity of vision, unique. To the decorative wasteland of contemporary animation, he has brought fantastic opulent growth and orgiastic opiate undergrowth, the purest ritual, the most direct uncompromising magic—whether viewed as enchantment, beguilement, invocation; or as Boschian document of possibilities of Earth, Heaven, and Hell in our world and time.

For a generation, Harry Smith has been creating unquestionable masterworks. Now his films have come to light, and we are delighted to give them and their maker this recognition so long and well deserved.

EIGHTH INDEPENDENT FILM AWARD (for 1966) to: Gregory Markopoulos

It is now almost twenty years that Gregory Markopoulos has been perfecting that quality so unlikely in the avant-garde, in the independent film—an imagistic elegance, a measured eloquence of editing, a delicate balance of all elements of plot, character, theme—a harmony as classic as the Greek myths of his major works.

At the same time, he has constantly been at the forefront among innovators, developing techniques of rapid cutting and subjective treatments of narrative time that were more than experimental, that were and remain truly new.

Such is the achievement of Gregory Markopoulos, from *Psyche* and *Swain* through *Twice a Man* and his latest completed work *Galaxie,* an achievement in which the traditions of classic and romantic are fused with the most modern art in the roundedness and lucidity of crystal.

NINTH INDEPENDENT FILM AWARD (for 1967) to: Michael Snow for his film *Wavelength*

Wavelength is a "definitive statement of pure Film space and time, a balancing of 'illusion' and 'fact,' all about seeing." A continuous zoom which takes 45 minutes to go from its widest field to its smallest and final field, *Wavelength* is a work "whose PROCESS is so profoundly simple, tragic and inevitable, that it offers no human consolation, no compromise . . . In terms of the relationship of the viewer and the work, Michael Snow is pushing into new areas." And *Wavelength* is a summation of everything he has thought about, his nervous system, his religious inklings, his aesthetic ideas, everything.

TENTH INDEPENDENT FILM AWARD (for 1969) to:
Kenneth Anger

for his film *Invocation of My Demon Brother* specifically, and for his entire creative work in general; for his unique fusion of magick, symbolism, myth, mystery, and vision with the most modern sensibilities, techniques, and rhythms of being; for revealing it all in a refreshed light, persistently, constantly and with a growing complexity of means and content; at the same time, for doing it with an amazing clarity, directness and sureness; for giving to our eye and our senses some of the most sensuous and mysterious images cinema has created; for being the Keeper of the Art of Cinema as well as the Keeper of the Eternal Magick Directions.

ELEVENTH INDEPENDENT FILM AWARD (for 1972) to:
Robert Breer

for his film work of the last twenty years. Since 1952 he has continued to produce a cinema of the highest quality, fusing the best of the earliest abstract cinema with the dynamics of the American Avantgarde Film. The liveliness of his films has restored the root meaning to "animation" at a time when most animated films invoked deadly tradition. For his unique contribution to the language of cinema in the exploration of the thresholds of rapid montage; for his pioneering work in the collage film; for his enrichment of the formal cinema with works that are visually, rhythmically, and intellectually exciting, enduring, new and clear, this award is presented.

TWELTH INDEPENDENT FILM AWARD (for 1975) to:
James Broughton

We here celebrate this mystery that for thirty years James Broughton has sustained the vitality and freshness of vision that make him—one suddenly sees—the grand classic master of Independent Cinema. He is, as well, the old master of comedy among all directors anywhere now and—that most incongruous phenomenon—an avantgarde film-maker not merely with humor but dedicated to primal panic sacraments, the ancient sudden gusto, breath of absolute release, very spirit of the laugh.

This comic career now culminates in the autopsychographical *Testament,* surely Broughton's most moving picture; a ritual mask with sardonic bite which opens to giddy depths and let out the roar of good old animal spirits.

And over all these years, constant formal innovation too, an exaltation of essential image over the conveniences and conveyances of narrative; a concentration of time and purification of action which serve the revel, revelation of, not just absurdities or even enormities, but the largeness of life which necessarily naturally evokes that most manifestly gut reaction—laughter.

10. LIFE ACHIEVEMENT AWARDS

The American Film Institute (AFI) established the Life Achievement Award in 1973 to honor the total career contributions of a filmmaker—regardless of place of birth—whose "talent has fundamentally advanced the art of American film or television, whose accomplishments have been acknowledged by scholars, critics, professional peers, and the general public, and whose work has withstood the test of time." The award, based on the collective judgment of AFI's Board of Trustees, is also accompanied by: a televised salute featuring film clips from the winner's career; scholarships in the winner's name to deserving students at the Institute's Center for Advanced Film Studies; a retrospective in the AFI Washington theater; an attempt to preserve all the films of the awards' recipient; and (since 1976) a special tribute in *American Film,* the official publication of AFI and now one of the most widely circulated film and television publications in the world.

The American Film Institute is an independent nonprofit organization established in 1967 by the National Endowment for the Arts to advance the art of film and television in the United States. The Institute preserves films, operates an advanced conservatory for filmmakers, gives assistance to new American filmmakers through grants and internships, provides guidance to film teachers and educators, publishes film books, periodicals and reference works, supports basic research and operates a national film repertory exhibition program. One of AFI's admirable archival efforts, for example, is cataloguing the entire output of American cinema since 1893. So far, two decades of the Institute Catalog of Feature Films have been published—1921-30 and 1961-70—and work on the volume covering 1911-20 is under way. The Directing Workshop for Women, now in its third year assisting women already involved in film to develop their skills as directors, is another example of AFI's valuable activities. Each workshop student selects her own script and assembles, with the help of AFI, a volunteer crew and cast to shoot and edit her own project with complete artistic control. Past graduates of the workshop include such notable actresses as Lee Grant, Ellen Burstyn and Dyan Cannon, and the students for the 1977-78 program include Joanne Woodward and Cicely Tyson.

George Stevens, Jr., is the director of AFI, a post he has held since the inception of the Institute. Its Board of Trustees (now chaired by Charlton Heston) includes the presidents of both the Motion Picture Association of America and the Academy of Motion Picture Arts and Sciences, as well as representatives from the fields of acting, writing, directing, producing and scholarly research. Although it is impossible to deny AFI's achievements—it has already preserved more than 14,000 films from the early years of American filmmaking—the Institute does have its critics. Some complain that *American Film,* despite its claims to cover film and television without fear or favor, is rather a safe and cautious magazine, decidedly middle-brow. Others have argued that AFI is more interested in its image than in its activities. Paul Schrader, the celebrated writer of *Taxi Driver* and one of the first of the 2,000 Fellows selected by AFI for its Center for Advanced Film Study at Greystone Mansion in Beverly Hills, has argued that AFI wastes its money on luxuries. The definitive mistake in AFI's history, Schrader says, is the lavish Greystone Mansion itself, which mistakenly equates filmmaking with wealth and which offers students the rewards of being successful without demanding the successful products.

The AFI Independent Filmmaker Program, which awards grants to finance projects ranging from experimental and animated films to documentary and narrative productions and which, funded by the National Endowment for the Arts, is the nation's major competition for independent filmmakers, has also come under attack. So far, $1.7 million has been funded to 230 filmmakers, but some say that too many well-known and established filmmakers have been among the recipients.

America at the Movies, the AFI-produced feature formed from nearly a hundred scenes from American films to celebrate the Bicentennial, has similarly been the target of controversy. New York critics faulted the film for its biased coverage and questioned AFI's sense of the film history, many reviewers complaining that the feature contained an excess number of clips from films directed by George Stevens, Sr., the father of AFI's director.

The history of the American Film Institute, in short, mirrors those of many other film organizations. Like the Academy of Motion Picture Arts and Sciences or like the National Board of Review, AFI began as an organization to advance the art of film, but which in doing so has itself become the target of criticism. Hollywood, always being attacked, has protected itself with agencies, institutes and academies that themselves have increased rather than decreased the industry's supposed flaws. At times the history of Hollywood resembles a series of attacks that arouses defenses that arouse renewed attacks.

Few people, however, have criticized the Life Achievement Awards; the qualifications of its recipients are unquestionable. The only complaint heard is that at the rate of only one award a year, AFI cannot pay tribute to the dozens of people who also deserve its honors.

1973	1975	1977
John Ford	Orson Welles	Bette Davis
1974	1976	
James Cagney	William Wyler	

11. "MOVIE WORSTS" AWARDS

In 1940 the *Harvard Lampoon* announced its first "Movie Worsts" awards for those films released in 1939. The Academy Awards were then little more than a decade old, the New York Film Critics Awards had been presented for only five years, and the Golden Globes has not even been established yet. But already the *Lampoon* realized that film awards were a great subject for parody: film awards could be as inane as they were becoming numerous. "Every time you buy a bag of peanuts in this town," a character says in *Citizen Kane*, "they give you an award." The *Lampoon* could hardly agree more. So almost every year since 1940, the *Lampoon*—with cruelty, acerbity and great wit—has presented its "Movie Worsts."

In its preface to the 1963 awards, the *Lampoon*—in a rare moment of seriousness—said the "Movie Worsts" had four functions: (1) to express rage and disappointment over the failure of Hollywood either to entertain or to educate; (2) to rectify this failure through criticism; (3) to supply a tonic to cure the ballyhoo and inanity of the Academy Awards; and (4) to infuriate people over trivialities.

Although the target of the *Lampoon*'s criticism has varied over the years, the "Movie Worsts" have most frequently attacked Hollywood's sentimentality and pretentiousness. Religious epics, overdone literary adaptations and silly spectaculars have consistently been lambasted for their "extravagance and blundering ineffectiveness," to quote the citation from one of the *Lampoon*'s funniest prizes, "The Please-Don't-Put-Us-Through-DeMille-Again Award." And children and animals —over which Americans can be infinitely sentimental— have similarly aroused the *Lampoon*'s wrath.

The "Movie Worsts" awards have often been received with great hostility. Lawsuits have been threatened, and many fans have attacked the magazine for its awards. According to *The Harvard Lampoon Centennial Celebration*, more people were enraged about the choice of Dean Martin and Jerry Lewis in 1952 than about any other single award. But starting in the sixties, more and more people received the awards in the humor with which they were given. In 1961 one staff member of Walt Disney Productions even nominated Annette Funicello for Worst Actress even before the film she was then working on was finished. And in 1966 Natalie Wood surprised everyone by showing up to receive her Worst Actress award, and thereby started a tradition. (Instead of the Academy's gold-plated Oscar, Natalie Wood received a living 220-pound man dressed in gold lamé.) Since then, such people as Judith Crist and George Peppard have written the *Lampoon* letters thanking the magazine for awarding them "Movie Worsts" prizes, and even Elizabeth Taylor has appeared at Harvard to pick up her Worst Actress awards.

In recent years—ever since American academics granted film studies legitimacy—it has been popular to find the art beneath the surface of Hollywood films. Although it would be impossible to deny that in many of our films there is indeed gold where we once thought there was only dross, the *Lampoon*'s "Movie Worsts" remind us that in all too many movies the dross is indeed only dross.

1939

Ten Worst Pictures:
The Rains Came
Hollywood Cavalcade
Winter Carnival
St. Louis Blues
Five Little Peppers
Bad Little Angel
The Fighting 69th
Idiot's Delight
20,000 Men a Year
The Man in the Iron Mask
Worst Actor:
Tyrone Power, *The Rains Came*
Worst Actress:
Norma Shearer, *Idiot's Delight*

Most Consistently Bad Performances:
Dorothy Lamour
Don Ameche
Most Colossal Flop:
The Wizard of Oz

1940

Ten Worst Pictures:
The Howards of Virginia
Swanee River
The Great Victor Herbert
1,000,000 B.C.
I Take This Woman
My Son, My Son
Green Hell
Lillian Russell

Typhoon
Boom Town

1941

Ten Worst Pictures:
Hudson's Bay
Wild Geese Calling
Belle Starr
Navy Blues
Honky Tonk
You Belong to Me
This Woman Is Mine
Lady Be Good
Aloma of the South Seas
Smilin' Through
Worst Performer:
Betty Grable
Worst Script:
Feminine Touch
Worst Discovery:
Veronica Lake
Most Unattractive Actress:
Jeanette MacDonald
Fastest-on-the-Downward-Pass Award:
Alice Faye and Nelson Eddy
Greatest Disappointment:
Sundown

1942

(Awards not presented this year)

1943

(Awards not presented this year)

1944

Ten Worst Pictures:
Kismet
A Song to Remember
Frenchman's Creek
Tonight and Every Night
Mr. Skeffington
Hollywood Canteen
Follow the Boys
Till We Meet Again
Thousands Cheer
Winged Victory
Worst Discovery:
Maria Montez in anything
Frank Sinatra and/or Van Johnson
Worst Script:
A Song to Remember
Most in Need of Retirement:
Paul Muni
Worst Scene:
The ketchup on the keys in *A Song to Remember*
Fastest-on-the-Downward-Pass Award:
Don Ameche
Most Unattractive:
Andrews Sisters in anything but a total blackout

1945

Ten Worst Pictures:
Weekend at the Waldorf
Music for Millions
This Love of Ours
The Enchanted Cottage
Where Do We Go from Here
Spellbound
Anchors Aweigh
Guest Wife
She Wouldn't Say Yes
Uncle Harry

Worst Single Performance—Female:
June Allyson, *Her Highness and the Bellboy*

Worst Single Performance—Male:
Van Johnson, *Thrill of a Romance*

Most Consistently Bovine Performances:
Alexis Smith

Oldest Actress of the Year:
Joan Crawford (honorable mention to Joan Bennett)

1946

Ten Worst Pictures:
(12 listed)
Night and Day
I've Always Loved You
Leave Her to Heaven
Margie
Adventure
Make Mine Music
The Searching Wind
No Leave, No Love
Road to Utopia
Of Human Bondage
Scarlet Street
The Harvey Girls

Worst Single Performance—Female:
Alexis Smith, *Night and Day*

Worst Single Performance—Male:
Orson Welles, *The Stranger*

Worst Supporting Performance—Female:
Linda Darnell, *Anna and the King of Siam*

Worst Supporting Performance—Male:
Andy Devine, *Canyon Passage*

Most Miscast—Female:
Ginny Simms as Ethel Merman, *Night and Day*

Most Miscast—Male:
Paul Henreid as Somerset Maugham in *Of Human Bondage*

Most Outrageous Misrepresentation of Fact:
Cornel Wilde as a former *Lampoon* editor in *Leave Her to Heaven*

Worst Juvenile Performance:
Jane Powell, *Holiday in Mexico*

Actress With Most Toes in the Graves:
Joan Crawford

Most Welcome Retirements:
Errol Flynn and Faye Emerson

Least Talented New Finds:
Glenn Ford and Catherine MacLeod

Worst Movie Couple:
Merle Oberon and Turhan Bey, *Night in Paradise*

Worst Script:
Three Strangers

Most Confusing Plot:
The Big Sleep

Worst Dialogue:
Adventure

Biggest Disappointment:
Song of the South

Least Stimulating Scene:
Nose-rubbing scene in *Notorious*

Most Ludicrous Scene:
Mickey Rooney dancing with a 6'6" chorus girl in *Love Laughs at Andy Hardy*

Series Most in Need of Discontinuation:
Claudia and Co.

Most Tiresome Movie Device:
Twin-sisters routine as exemplified in *A Stolen Life* (Bette Davises) and *The Dark Mirror* (Olivia de Havillands)

Most Frankly Cribbed Plot:
Angel on My Shoulder

1947

(Awards not presented this year)

1948

Ten Worst Movies:
Winter Meeting
Homecoming
The Emperor Waltz
The Miracle of the Bells
Beyond Glory
On an Island with You
The Paradine Case
The Three Musketeers
Arch of Triumph
Sorry, Wrong Number
Worst Performances:
Lana Turner, *The Three Musketeers*
Burt Lancaster, *I Walk Alone*
Shirley Temple, *Fort Apache*
Worst Fraud:
Eleanor Parker as Margaret Sullavan as Sally Middleton, *The Voice of the Turtle*
Worst Scene:
Ida Lupino sticking out her tongue at Errol Flynn in *Escape Me Never*
Worst Duo:
Dennis Morgan and Jack Carson, alone, together, or in any combination
Worst Deception:
Joan Fontaine as a sixteen-year-old girl in *Letter from an Unknown Woman*
Worst Reincarnation:
Jeannette MacDonald, *Three Daring Daughters*
Worst Title:
That Wonderful Urge

Due for a Pension:
Deanna Durbin
Career up in Smoke:
Robert Mitchum
Most Stonefaced:
Lizabeth Scott
**Best of this Year
(OR ANY YEAR):**
Four Feathers
Actress Most Likely to Drag Down Her Husband's Dubious Rep. as an Actor:
Mrs. Agar
All-Time Worst Hoyden:
Mrs. Agar
Most Nauseating Screen Voice:
Mrs. Agar

1949

Ten Worst Pictures of the Year:

Special Award:
Worst Picture of the Century:
Joan of Arc

The Other Nine:
The Great Gatsby
The Night Has a Thousand Eyes
Flamingo Road
Look for the Silver Lining
Top o' the Morning
The Fountainhead
The Fan
That Midnight Kiss
A Connecticut Yankee In King Arthur's Court
Worst Moment:
Ginger Rogers, in *The Barkeleys of Broadway* singing the "Marseillaise" to the "bravos" and "encores" of the Académie Française, in French, thank God

Worst Performance—Female:
Shirley Temple, *Mr. Belvedere Goes to College*
Worst Performance—Male:
Gregory Peck, *The Great Sinner*
Runner-up:
Gregory Peck in practically anything
Most Implausible:
Paulette Goddard as Lucrezia Borgia, *Bride of Vengeance*
Most Sickening Combination:
Claude Jarman, Jr., and Lassie
Most Consistently Unamusing:
Co-holders; Abbott and Costello
Least Likely to Warm Cockles of Heart:
Barry Fitzgerald
Least Likely to Warm Anything:
Barry Fitzgerald
Least Deserving but Most Due for a Pension:
Barry Fitzgerald
Also Overdue for Retirement:
Margaret O'Brien
Most Ridiculous Import:
Louis Jourdan
Worst Deceit:
Larry Parks as *Al Jolson*
Most Expressionless:
Alan Ladd
Least Frightening:
Mighty Joe Young
Most Frightening:
Tom Drake singing "Words and Music"
Finest Example for Clean-Cut American Youth:
Mrs. Aly Khan
Runner-up:
Shirley Temple
Best-known Wife of Race-Horse Owner:
Mrs. Aly Khan
Meatball:
Aly Khan

1950

Ten Worst Pictures:
Our Very Own
Sampson and Delilah
Three Came Home
The Next Voice You Hear
An American Guerilla in the Philippines
Cheaper by the Dozen
Stromboli
The Flame and the Arrow
The Conspirators
The Duchess of Idaho
Worst Performances of the Year:
Clifton Webb, *Cheaper by the Dozen*
Elizabeth Taylor, *The Conspirators*
Worst Supporting Performances:
Cornell Wilde, *Two Flags West*
Celeste Holm, *All About Eve*
Most Depressing Discovery:
Faith Domergue
Least Likely to Succeed:
Cecile Aubrey
Worst Duo:
Esther Williams and Van Johnson, alone, together, or in any combination
Most Objectionable Movie Children:
Dean Stockwell
Elizabeth Taylor
Most Objectionable Ingénue:
Elizabeth Taylor
Most Unnecessary Contribution to the American Way of Life:
Bing Crosby, in anything
Most Miscast:
Burt Lancaster, as a sturdy Lombard peasant in *The Flame and the Arrow*

Greatest Travesty of the Holy Year:
Samson and Delilah

Worst Comedy:
Fancy Pants

Dullest:
Never a Dull Moment

Happiest Event of the Year:
Shirley Temple's announced retirement

Arrested Development:
William "Hopalong" Boyd

Worst Scene:
Micheline Presle huskily singing an old French Christmas carol between clinches with Tyrone Power in *An American Guerilla in the Philippines*

Worst Insult to the American Fighting Man:
John Wayne

Worst Assistant Producer:
Robert Goelet, Jr., for *Rapture*

Worst Title:
Oh, You Beautiful Doll

The Roscoe Award:
Elizabeth Taylor for so gallantly persisting in her career despite a total inability to act

---

1951

Ten Worst:
Tales of Hoffman
Valentino
Alice in Wonderland
That's My Boy
Texas Carnival
Take Care of My Little Girl
The Flame of Araby
Here Comes the Groom
David and Bathsheba
I Want You

Worst Performances of the Year:
Robert Taylor, *Quo Vadis*
Corinne Calvet, *On the Riviera*

Worst Supporting Performances:
Peter Lawford, *Royal Wedding*
Ava Gardner, *Showboat*

Worst Musical:
Painting the Clouds with Sunshine

Worst Double-bill:
Hard, Fast, and Beautiful
Rich, Young, and Pretty

Biggest Argument for Stricter Immigration Laws:
Mario Lanza

Finest Example of Idyllic Young Love:
Ava Gardner and Frank Sinatra

Most Unexpected Revival:
The Ape-man of Kawaloa, starring Barbara Peyton

Most Miscast:
Franchot Tone as a Boston Brahmin in *Here Comes the Groom*

Most Noteworthy Examples of Physical Fitness:
Franchot Tone kicking Miss Florabella Muir
Humphrey Bogart felling unidentified girl in *El Morocco*

Great Travesty of the Year:
Walt Disney's *Alice in Wonderland*

Should Have Stayed Home:
Ezio Pinza, principal victim of *Mr. Imperium* and *Strictly Dishonorable*

Most Unattractive Connotations:
The Model and the Marriage Broker

Worst Dialogue:
St. Peter interviewing God in *Quo Vadis*

Worst Comic Duo:
Martin and Lewis in anything

1952

Ten Worst Pictures:
Jumping Jacks
Snows of Kilimanjaro
Quo Vadis
Son of Paleface
Million Dollar Mermaid
Bloodhounds of Broadway
Niagara
Because You're Mine
Affair in Trinidad
The Merry Widow
Worst Male Performance:
Jerry Lewis, *Sailor Beware,
    Jumping Jacks,* etc.
**Worst Supporting Male
Performance:**
Dean Martin, *Sailor Beware,
    Jumping Jacks,* etc.
Worst Female Performance:
Marilyn Monroe, *Niagara*
**Strongest Indictment of
Academic Freedom:**
Bonzo Goes to College
Most Ill-advised Refilming:
The Merry Widow
Worst Foreign Importation:
Brandy for the Parson
**Most Unattractive
Connotations:**
*She's Working Her Way
    Through College*
**Most Inspiring Example of
American Virility:**
Jerry Lewis
**Most Embarrassing Infatuation
with One's Own Folksiness:**
Barry Fitzgerald
Edmund Gwenn
Most Brutally Exploited:
Ernest Hemingway
Sir Walter Scott
Hans Christian Andersen

Most Miscast:
Entire personnel of *Plymouth
    Adventure* as New England
    Puritans
Worst Moment:
Mtizi Gaynor mouthing "In the
    Sweet By and By" over her
    grandpappy's grave in
    Bloodhounds of Broadway
**Most Noteworthy Pre-Pubic
Flop:**
Tab "Sigh-Guy" Hunter
Shrewdest Business Move:
MGM's suspension of Mario
    Lanza
**Strongest Argument for Laxer
Divorce Laws:**
Marge and Gower Champion
    in *Everything I Have Is Yours*
Most Sophisticated Dialogue:
The Thief
The Roscoe Award:
Jerry Lewis, who, by dint of
    incessant struggle, has
    unquestionably established
    himself as The Worst
    Commedian of All Time

1953

Ten Worst Movies:
The Robe
Salome
Beneath the Twelve-Mile Reef
Hondo
Torch Song
Call Me Madam
How to Marry a Millionaire
Easy to Love
I, the Jury
Gentlemen Prefer Blondes
Worst Performances:
Terry Moore, *Beneath the
    Twelve-Mile Reef*
Victor Mature, *The Robe*

Worst Supporting Performances:
Brandon De Wilde, *Shane*
Zsa Zsa Gabor, *Moulin Rouge*

Greatest Setback to Christianity Since Nero:
The Robe

Most Depressing Dotage:
Charles Laughton slavering over Rita Hayworth's abdominal dancing in *Salome*

Unsung Hero:
Musician who blew the bugle for Montgomery Clift in *From Here to Eternity*

Most Miscast:
Louis Calhern as a doddering Caesar in *Julius Caesar*
Silvana Mangano as a nun in *Anna*

Best Argument for a Stronger Navy:
Paratroopers

Greatest Travesty:
Tony Curtis' systematic destruction of a legend in *Houdini*

Most Unattractive Connotations:
Call Me Madam
Girls in the Night

Most Degrading Moment:
Charles Laughton being hit over the head with a shovel by Lou Costello in *Abbott and Costello Meet Captain Kidd*

Most Unconvincing Dialogue:
Biff Elliot mouthing "It was easy" to a fading blonde in *I, the Jury*

Grossest Exploitation of Old Material:
Refilming *King Solomon's Mines* backwards to achieve *Mogambo*

The Roscoe Award:
Miss Terry Moore, the worst ingénue of 1953

1954

Ten Worst Movies:
Haaji Baba
No Business Like Show Business
The Egyptian
The High and the Mighty
Magnificent Obsession
Beau Brummel
The Student Prince
Knights of the Round Table
Demetrius and the Gladiators
White Christmas

Not Worth the Price of Admission:
Three Coins in the Fountain

Most Unconvincing Death Scene in Recent Years:
Stewart Granger in *Beau Brummel*

Most Fortuitous Drownings:
James Mason in *A Star Is Born* and *20,000 Leagues under the Sea*

Most Freudian Title:
River of No Return

Best Reasons for Healthy Paganism:
Demetrius and the Gladiators
The Silver Chalice

The Greatest Detriment to Anglo-Arabian Relations:
Haaji Baba

Most Thoughtful Deed of 1954:
The director of *The Student Prince* refusing to allow Mario Lanza to sing before the cameras

Most Convincing Nominee for Brood Mare of 1954:
Barbara Stanwyck, *Cattle Queen of Montana*

Greatest Mayhem Committed on a Myth:
White Christmas

Best Excuse for Another Thugee Rebellion in India:
The Bengal Brigade

Most Ingenuous Statement of the Year:
Gina Lollabridgida (quote in *Look*): "I am an actress . . . not a body."

Great Waste of Gas:
The Long, Long Trailer

Best Argument Against N.R.O.T.C.:
The Caine Mutiny

Saddest Evidence of Rapid Aging:
Jimmy Stewart impassively receiving a massage in *Rear Window*

The Roscoe Award:
Tony Curtis, whose marcelled and Mobilgreased locks have titillated scores of bobbysoxers, and Grace Kelly, who easily earns the title "Ironclad Virgin of 1954"

1955

Ten Worst Movies:
Not as a Stranger
Ulysses
The Prodigal
Hit the Deck
The Tall Men
The Rains of Ranchipur
Battle Cry
The Last Time I Saw Paris
The Long Grey Line
Underwater

Worst Actor:
Kirk Douglas, *Ulysses; Indian Fighter*

Worst Actress:
Debbie Reynolds, *Hit the Deck; Susan Slept Here*

Worst Supporting Actor:
Vic Damone, *Kismet*

Worst Supporting Actress:
Gloria Grahame, *Not as a Stranger*

First Annual Award for Crude Symbolism:
The fireworks in mounting crescendo as a backdrop for Grace Kelly and Cary Grant in their big scene in *To Catch a Thief*

Title With Most Interesting Alternatives:
Love Me or Leave Me

Most Pathetic Remnant of a Vanishing Race:
Victor Mature as Chief Crazy Horse in the movie of the same title

Most Mature Nature Movie:
The Seven-Year Itch

Most Unpropitious Return:
To Hell and Back

Greatest Threat to the Church Since Luther:
Johnny Ray becoming a priest in *No Business Like Show Business*

Most Heartening Decease:
Elizabeth Taylor, with Van Johnson at her deathbed, in *The Last Time I Saw Paris*

Greatest Gift to the Animal World Since Noah:
Walt Disney

Title With the Most Unattractive Connotations:
You're Never Too Young

Most Cretinous Performance:
Robert Mitchum, *Not as a Stranger*

Best Reason for Closing the Open Door:
Love Is a Many-Splendored Thing

Title With the Most Futile Advice:
Bring Your Smile Along

Most Monolithic Sleuth:
Jack Webb, *Pete Kelly's Blues*

Most Embarrassing Interlude:
Jennifer Jones, in *Love Is a Many-Splendored Thing*, standing disconsolately on the proverbial high and windy hill, waiting for the show to end, to the tune of a stirring chant from an archangel chorus: "When your fingers touched my silent heart and taught it how to sing"

Bosco:
(in recognition of the advances recently made in the science of geriatrics)
June Allyson, who with eternally girlish hominess, an aura of fresh-baked deep-dish apple pie like Mother used to make, and an endless supply of tears, bravely but vainly attempts to resist the onslaught of the advancing years

The Roscoe Award:
Sheree North *[This award was followed by a parody of a Sheree North questionnaire, which is too long to be reprinted here.]*

1956

Ten Worst Movies:
The Ten Commandments
Alexander the Great
Trapeze
The Benny Goodman Story
Gaby
Serenade
Bwohani Junction
Miracle in the Rain
The Vagabond King
The Proud and the Profane

Worst Actor:
Gregory Peck, *Moby Dick*

Worst Actress:
Jennifer Jones, *The Man in the Grey Flannel Suit*

Worst Supporting Actor:
Elvis Presley, *Love Me Tender*

Worst Supporting Actress:
Anne Baxter, *The Ten Commandments*

Life-Begins-at-Fifty Award:
A passionate Joan Crawford in throes of senilescence culminating her *Autumn Leaves* love affair by tossing about in the waves with Cliff Robertson

Best Alternative to the Ten Commandments:
All That Heaven Allows; Somebody Up There Likes Me; You Can't Run Away from It

Most Imaginative Locale:
Between Heaven and Hell

Greatest Argument for Birth Control:
Bundle of Joy

Most Thoroughly Unsatisfying Ending:
Rock Hudson's recovery in *All That Heaven Allows*

Publicity Agent of the Year:
Cardinal Spellman

The Mario Lanza Award for Most Oily Demise:
Oreste

Most Degrading Bow to American Morality Cults:
Tea and Sympathy's closing rebuttal of its own themes

Title With Most Unappealing Implications:
The Lieutenant Wore Tights

Hypocrisy-of-the-Year Award (Big-as-Texas Variety):
The five million dollars spent on the theme of anti-materialism in *Giant*

The Roscoe Award:
Anita Ekberg, who has breasted the tide of criticism in regard to her triumphant inability to act by spreading herself, in film after film, over CinemaScope screen like a great fleshy smörgåsbord, proving once and for all that delicacy can be as un-Swedish as it is un-American

1957

Ten Worst Movies:
Raintree County
The Pride and the Passion
Peyton Place
Island in the Sun
Jeanne Eagels
Funny Face
The Hunchback of Notre Dame
The Sun Also Rises
Pal Joey
April Love

Worst Actor:
Rock Hudson, *A Farewell to Arms*

Worst Actress:
Kim Novak, *Jeanne Eagels; Pal Joey*

Worst Supporting Actor:
MacGeorge Bundy, *To the Age That Is Waiting*

Worst Supporting Actress:
Joan Collins, *Island in the Sun*

The Janos Kadar Award:
Tyrone Power for his superlatively impotent performance in *The Sun Also Rises*

Better-Things-for-Better-Living-Through-Chemistry: A Commendation:
To the producers of *A Hatful of Rain* for giving the movie industry a long overdue shot in the arm

The Wayward Bus Award:
To Jayne Mansfield for her outstanding

The "Any Connection?" Prize:
Given jointly to Rita Hayworth, *Fire Down Below*, and Bing Crosby, *Man on Fire*

The Most Deceptive Title:
Something of Value

The Elsa Maxwell Kudo:
Given for the first time in thirty-seven years to *The Bachelor Party* as the most unattractive social event of the season

The Suzy Parker Award:
For the most inauspicious male debut: Pat Boone, *Bernadine*

The Pat Boone Award:
For the most inauspicious female debut: Suzy Parker, *Kiss Them for Me*

Most Outrageous Case of On-Screen Discrimination Toward a Minority:
Walt Disney's ruthless suppression of the Weasels and Martens in *Perri*

The Gloria Swanson Award for the Most Unexpected Comeback:
James Dean, *The James Dean Story*

What the Bachelor Party Needed Most:
Les Girls

Special Commendation:
Kay Kendall for rescuing *Les Girls* from the dismal mediocrity which only Gene Kelly can add to a picture

Most Telling Argument for Birth Control:
Full of Life

Most Appalling Example of the Inadequacy of Our Present Social Security Program:
Fred Astaire, forced once more out of retirement to don his high-heeled tap shoes and pursue Audrey Hepburn before an ill-focused camera lens in *Funny Face*

The Marquis De Sade Award:
Operation Madball

"Oh Yeah?" Department:
The Girl Can't Help It

The Emilio Boscoe Award:
Mrs. Natalie Wood Wagner, whose saccharine, whining caricatures of American girlhood have, in film after tedious film, raised her above the obstacles of talented competition, first-draft scripts, pubescent co-stars, and sleepy directors to the top of the Hollywood heap

The Roscoe Award:
Miss Jean Seberg, who, having allowed her ambition to out-strip her inability, has risen from student to starlet in little over a year, and demon-strated that she can be both soporific as a saint and insipid as a sinner

The Worst-Film-of-the-Century Award:
This award, given once every hundred years, is presented for the century 1857–1957 to Otto Preminger's *Saint Joan*

1958

Worst Ten Movies:
South Pacific
The Vikings
Roots of Heaven
The Last Hurrah
Marjorie Morningstar
The Buccaneers
Big Country
The Old Man and the Sea
A Certain Smile
Windjammer

Worst Actor:
Kirk Douglas, *The Vikings* (the trophy will be retired, since Mr. Douglas has won it for the third time)

Worst Actress:
Rita Hayworth, *Separate Tables*

Worst Supporting Actor:
Errol Flynn, *Roots of Heaven*

Worst Supporting Actress:
Christine Carrere, *A Certain Smile*

The "Any Connection?" Prize:
The Reluctant Debutante and *Home Before Dark*

The Venus De Milo Award:
A Farewell to Arms

The To-Say-the-Least Award:
Ingrid Bergman in *Indiscreet*

Tne Wilde Oscar:
(presented to that actor who is willing to flaunt conven-tion and reputation in the pursuit of artistic fulfill-ment)
Jerry Lewis in *The Geisha Boy*

Most Shocking Film of the Year:
Some Came Running

Most Unreasonable Request:
Susan Hayward in *I Wanna Live*

Special Award:
(to those actors and actresses who, despite the lack of entertaining scripts, still manage extemporaneously to entertain the nation)
Divided this year between Eddie Fisher, Debbie Reynolds, and Liz Taylor

The Fauntleroy Behest:
(a stipend set up in the will of the late Lord Fauntleroy to send a young lad to acting school)
Awarded to James (A Light in the Forest) MacArthur, with all dispatch

The Thank-God Award:
Marilyn Monroe, who in a sweeping public service has made no movies this year

The Roscoe Award:
Kim Novak, who, not satisfied with a performance in Vertigo that would have assured her of the Worst Actress of the Year Award, spurred herself to even greater heights in Bell, Book and Candle, immortalizing herself and her directors

---

1959

Ten Worst Movies:
The Best of Everything
The Miracle
Career
Never So Few
Solomon and Sheba
The Tempest
A Summer Place
They Came to Cordura
Say One for Me
Hercules
One Too Many

Worst Actor:
Sal Mineo, Tonka
Worst Actress:
Lana Turner, Imitation of Life
Worst Supporting Actress:
Sandra Dee, A Summer Place
Worst Supporting Actor:
Dick Nixon, The Best of Benson

The Bratwurst Award:
(to the worst child actor of the year, presented by the Delicatessen Owners' Assn.)
Eddie Hodges, A Hole in the Head

The Ghandi Grant:
(for the year's most attractive ribs)
May Britt, The Blue Angel

The Wish-It-Were-True Award:
Bing Crosby as a celibate priest in Say One for Me

The Miss Nomer Award:
The Best of Everything

The Not-Worth-It Award:
Five Pennies

The "Any Connection?" Prize:
(presented annually to those films which would best appear as double features)
The Girl with an Itch and The Tingler
Happy Is the Bride and Middle of the Night
The Nun's Story and Ask Any Girl
Arson for Hire and Some Like It Hot
Libel and Say One for Me
Thirty-Foot Bride of Candy Rock and Cast a Long Shadow
Room 43 and Grand Canyon Suite

The "It Was Funny the First Time" Award:
The Man Who Died Twice

The Eva Marie Saint Award:
  *(to the movie title most
  conducive to uninhibited
  speechmaking)*
Say One for Me
The Varsi Vase:
  *(awarded to the most dra-
  matic walkout in the field of
  entertainment)*
Jack Parr
The Luce Laurel:
Shirley MacLaine for gracing,
  if not monopolizing, the
  pages of *Life* magazine

1960

Ten Worst Movies:
Butterfield 8
Strangers When We Meet
The Gazebo
Ice Palace
Exodus
It Started in Naples
Pepe
Pollyanna
Because They're Young
High Time
Worst Actor:
Frank Sinatra, *Can-Can*
Worst Actress:
Eva Marie Saint, *Exodus*
Worst Supporting Actor:
Eddie Fisher, *Butterfield 8*
  (with honorable mention to
  Cameron Mitchell for failing
  to meet his alimony
  payments)
Worst Supporting Actress:
Annette Funicello, *The Horse
  Masters*
The Uncrossed Heart:
  *(awarded to the least prom-
  ising young actor of the
  year)*
Fabian, *North to Alaska*

The Merino Award:
  *(to that motion picture per-
  sonality who, in the opinion
  of the officers, editors, and
  staff of the Harvard Lampoon, has, during the past
  year, done the most to
  enhance the fame and glory
  of the merino)*
Maureen O'Hara
The Bratwurst Award:
  *(to the most obnoxious child
  star of the year)*
David Ladd, *Dog of Flanders*
**The But-Not-For-Us-Either
Award:**
But Not for Me
**The Mirror-On-The-Wall
Oblation:**
  *(to the movie whose title
  reflects the action of the
  audience rather than that of
  its characters)*
The Angry Silence
The-Off-Color Investiture
The Green Carnation
The Bad-Taste Citation:
Broth of a Boy
The Wilde Oscar:
  *(presented to that actor who
  is willing to flaunt conven-
  tion and reputation in the
  pursuit of artistic fulfill-
  ment)*
Jerry Lewis, *Cinderfella*
**The The-World-in-the-Future-
if-Karl-Marx's-Basic-Political-
Precepts-Are-Proved-Correct-
but-His-Hypothesis-That-the-
People-Will-Not-Be-
Disgruntled-Is-Sorely-in-Error
Award:**
The Angry Red Planet
The Along-the-Mohawk Grant:
  *(to that film with the most
  drummed-up publicity
  campaign)*
The Alamo

The Roscoe Award:
Robert Mitchum

1961

Ten Worst Movies:
King of Kings and *Parrish*
(tied)
By Love Possessed
The Devil at 4 O'Clock
The Last Sunset
The Young Doctors
Ada
Flower Drum Song
Babes in Toyland
Sergeants Three
The Kirk Douglas Award to the Worst Actor:
Richard Beymer, *West Side Story*
Worst Actress:
Susan Hayward, *Ada; Back Street*
Worst Supporting Actor:
Robert Ryan as John the Baptist, *King of Kings*
Worst Supporting Actress:
Sandra Dee, *Romanoff and Juliet; Come September*
The Uncrossed Heart:
(to the least promising young actor of the year)
Richard Beymer, *West Side Story*
The Worst All-Around Performance By a Cast in Toto:
Awarded this year to two movies:
King of Kings, with special mention to Jeffrey Hunter, Siobhan McKenna, Robert Ryan, and Frank Thring
The Last Sunset, with special mention to Kirk Douglas, Rock Hudson, Dorothy Malone, and Carol Lynley

The Best Argument for Vivisection:
Lad a Dog
The Worst Duos of the Year:
Troy Donahue and Connie Stevens
Natalie Wood and (1) Warren Beatty, (2) Richard Beymer, (3) Anyone
The Greatest Setback to Christianity Since *The Robe*:
King of Kings
The Hon. "W. W." Corrigan Memorial Palm:
(to the worst director)
Elia Kazan, *Splendor in the Grass*
The Tin Pan:
(to the most nauseating movie song of the year)
"Pocketful of Miracles"
The Merino Award:
Rita Moreno, for saving *West Side Story* from Richard Beymer and Natalie Wood
The Once-Was-Enough Award:
The Second Time Around
The Wilde Oscar:
(to that actor willing to flout convention and reputation in the pursuit of artistic fulfillment)
Mickey Rooney as Mr. Yunioshi, *Breakfast at Tiffany's*
The Great Ceremonial Hot Dog:
(for the worst scenes of the cinema season)
Kirk Douglas fighting a mad dog, *The Last Sunset*
Salome's Dance in *King of Kings'*
Richard Beymer singing "Maria" in *West Side Story*
The Along-the-Mohawk Grant:
(for the most drummed-up publicity campaign of the year)

Jayne Mansfield, her husband, and her publicity agent for the heroism they displayed during and after their near-tragic boating accident

The Arrested-Development Oblation:
(to that adult actor who displays the lowest level of maturity)
Jerry Lewis, *Errand Boy*

The Cellophane Figleaf:
This trophy, awarded annually for false modesty, is this year given to Warren Beatty, most of whose publicity has been based on his constant statements that he wants no publicity from the fact that he is Shirley MacLaine's younger brother

The Vanity Fair Citation:
(to that actress who most tirelessly champions the cause of womanhood)
Sophia Loren for carrying to court her fight to be billed above Charlton Heston for her performance in *El Cid*

The Off-Color Investiture:
The Green Mare

The Ok-Doc-Break-the-Arm-Again Award:
This citation, awarded annually for the most flagrant example of miscasting, goes this year to the producers of *A Majority of One* for putting Alec Guinness in the role of a Japanese businessman and Rosalind Russell in the role of a Jewish housewife

The Luce Laurel:
Awarded in 1960 to Shirley MacLaine for gracing, if not monopolizing, the pages of *Life* magazine, this year goes to . . .

Shirley MacLaine, for gracing, if not monopolizing, the pages of *Life* magazine

The "Any Connection?" Prize:
(awarded annually to those films which would best appear as double features)
The Unstoppable Man and *The Explosive Generation*
Anatomy of a Psycho and *The Man Who Wagged His Tail*
Capture That Capsule and *You Have to Run Fast*
The Sergeant Was a Lady and *Marines, Let's Go*
Deadly Campions and *Snow White and the Three Stooges*

Thank You:
To Victor Mature for not making a picture this year

The Roscoe Award:
To Natalie Wood for so gallantly persisting in her career despite a total inability to act.

1962

Ten Worst Movies:
The Chapman Report
If a Man Answers
Adventures of a Young Man
Diamond Head
The Wonderful World of the Brothers Grimm
White Slave Ship
Mutiny on the Bounty
Taras Bulba
Barabbas
The Mongols or *The Tartars* or *The Huns*

Worst Actress:
Jane Fonda, *The Chapman Report*

The Kirk Douglas Award to the Worst Actor:

Charlton Heston, *Diamond Head; The Pigeon That Took Rome*

Worst Supporting Actress:

Pier Angeli, *Sodom and Gomorrah*

Worst Supporting Actor:

William Frawley, *Safe at Home*

The Uncrossed Heart:

(to the least promising young performer)

Ann-Margret

The Tin Pan:

(to the most obnoxious movie song)

"Lolita, Yah-Yah"

The Wilde Oscar:

(to that performer who has been willing to flout convention and risk worldly reputation in order to pursue artistic fulfillment)

Pier Angeli, for her part as the Pillar of Salt in *Sodom and Gomorrah*

The Merino Award:

In 1960 to Maureen O'Hara; in 1961 to Rita Moreno; this year to Maureen O'Sullivan

The Diamond-in-the-Rough Award:

To Rosalind Russell for making *Gypsy* palatable despite Natalie Wood, Karl Malden, etc.

The Cellophane Figleaf:

(for false modesty)

Sue Lyon, who played the part of Lolita, and thereafter drummed up most of her publicity by insisting that she is not a Lolita in real life

The Bratwurst Award:

(to the most obnoxious child star)

A tie between Kevin Corcoran in *In Search of the Castaways* and the entire Vienna Boys Choir in *Almost Angels*

The Hon. "W.W." Corrigan Memorial Palm:

(for the worst direction of a film)

Otto Preminger for *Lolita*

The Timothy Cratchit Memorial Crutch:

To that Hollywood personality who offers the lamest justification for unsavory behavior: to Tony Curtis for calling a press conference to insist that there was nothing immoral about his living with Christine Kaufmann, since she had her parents' permission

The Arrested-Development Oblation:

(to that adult actor who has displayed the lowest level of maturity)

Jerry Lewis, *It's Only Money*

The Worst All-Around Peformance by a Cast in Toto:

To *The Longest Day*

The Please-Don't-Put-Us-Through-DeMille-Again Award:

Presented to that religious movie of the past year which best embodies the pretentious extravagance and blundering ineffectiveness of the traditional Christian Screen Spectacular:

Awarded this year to two equally poor movies: *Barabbas* and *Sodom and Gomorrah*

The Great Ceremonial Hot Dog:

(for the worst scenes of the past cinema season)

The Naming of the Fairy Tale Characters in *The Wonderful*

*World of the Brothers
Grimm* and The Polish Army
Hurtling over the Cliff in
Taras Bulba /

The Roscoe Award:
To Natalie Wood, for her
unquestionably atrocious
performance in *Gypsy,*
which she did her utmost to
ruin

1963

Ten Worst Movies:
*Cleopatra
The V.I.P.s
The Prize
It's a Mad, Mad, Mad, Mad
World
How the West Was Won
Heavens Above
55 Days at Peking
Act One
The Birds* and *Bye-Bye Birdie*
(tied)
Gidget Goes to Rome and
Tammy and the Doctor (tied)
Worst Film of the Century:
For the century 1863–1963 to
Cleopatra
*(This award was last pre-
sented in 1958 for the cen-
tury ending in that year)*
**The Kirk Douglas Award to the
Worst Actor:**
Burt Lancaster, *The Leopard;
Seven Days in May*
The Worst Actress:
Debbie Reynolds, *How the
West Was Won; Mary, Mary*
The Worst Supporting Actor:
Roy Cohn, *Point of Order*
The Worst Supporting Actress:
Carol Burnett, *Who's Been
Sleeping in My Bed?*

**The Timothy Cratchit Memorial
Crutch:**
*(to that Hollywood person-
ality who offers the lamest
justification for unsavory
behavior)*
Elizabeth Taylor for divorcing
Eddie Fisher on the grounds
of abandonment
The Tin Pan:
*(to the most obnoxious
movie song)*
"Love with a Proper Stranger"
**The Great Ceremonial Hot
Dog:**
*(for the worst scenes of the
cinema season)*
The five ax murders in
Straitjacket
The four murders in *Charade*
The delivery of a baby in the
back seat of a Rolls Royce
(with Doris Day as midwife)
in *The Thrill of It All!*
Cliff Richards twisting his way
across Europe in an open-
mesh T-shirt in *Summer
Holiday*
The Wilde Oscar:
*(to that performer who has
been willing to flout convention and risk worldly repu-
tation to pursue artistic
fulfillment)*
To the producers of *Becket* and
Night of the Iguana for
casting Richard Burton in
clerical roles
**The Ok-Doc-Break-the-Arm-
Again Award:**
*(for the most flagrant exam-
ple of miscasting)*
To the producers of *Take Her,
She's Mine* for placing
Sandra Dee in the role of a
Wellesley College student

The Drums-Along-the-Mohawk Grant:
(for the most drummed-up publicity campaign)
Frank Sinatra, Frank Sinatra, Jr., and the three kidnappers of the latter

The Bratwurst Award:
(to the most obnoxious child star of the year)
The entire cast of *The Lord of the Flies*

Worst Performance by a Cast in Toto:
It's A Mad, Mad, Mad, Mad World

The Hon. Wrong-Way Corrigan Memorial Palm:
(for the worst direction of a film)
Stanley Kramer, *It's a Mad, Mad, Mad, Mad World*

The Uncrossed Heart:
(to the least promising young performer)
Annette Funicello, *Beach Party; The Misadventures of Merlin Jones*

Thank You Again:
Victor Mature for not making a film this year

The-Please-Don't-Put-Us-Through-DeMille-Again Award:
(to that film which best embodies the pretentious extravagance and blundering ineffectiveness of the traditional Screen Spectacular)
Cleopatra

The Arrested-Development Oblation:
(to that adult actor who has displayed the lowest level of maturity)
Always given to Jerry Lewis

The Aerosol Bomb:
The Lord of the Flies

The Gilded Cage:
The Birds and *A Gathering of Eagles* with mention of *The Cardinal*

The Merino Award:
In 1960 to Maureen O'Hara; in 1961 to Rita Moreno; in 1962 to Maureen O'Sullivan; this year to the Marine standing sentry duty outside the American Embassy in Paris in *Charade*

Best Argument for Stricter Immigration Laws:
America America

The Gold Star-on-the-Wayne Laurel:
To *Donovan's Reef* and *McClintock*

The That-Was-the-Week-that-Was Trophy:
Seven Days in May

We-Heard-You-The-First-Time Award:
It's a Mad, Mad, Mad, Mad World; America America and *Twice Told Tales*

Best Argument for Vivisection:
Miracle of the White Stallions

The Marquis De Sade Memorial Whip:
A New Kind of Love

The Cellophane Figleaf:
(for false modesty)
Ann-Margret for insisting that she is not oversexed

The Vanity Fair Citation:
To Rex Harrison for carrying to court his fight to be portrayed on the *Cleopatra* poster

The Ayn Rand Award:
(to that writer whose bad books made worse movies)
Irving Wallace, author of *The Chapman Report* and *The Prize*

The Roscoe Award:
Doris Day, who has gotten
  away with it once too often

1964

Ten Worst Movies:
*The Greatest Story Ever Told,
  The Carpetbaggers, Sylvia,
  Cheyenne Autumn, Station
  Six Sahara, Kiss Me Stupid,*
  (tied)
*The Outrage
The Fall of the Roman Empire
One Potato, Two Potato
Youngblood Hawke
Kisses for My President
Good-bye Charlie
The Unsinkable Molly Brown
Muscle Beach Party*
**The Kirk Douglas Award to the
Worst Actor:**
James Franciscus, *Youngblood
  Hawke*
Worst Actress:
Carroll Baker in *The Greatest
  Story Ever Told; Sylvia;
  Cheyenne Autumn; The
  Carpetbaggers; Station Six
  Sahara*
Worst Supporting Actor:
Laurence Harvey, *The Outrage*
Worst Supporting Actress:
Honor Blackman as Pussy
  Galore in *Goldfinger*
The Merino Award:
In 1960 to Maureen O'Hara; in
  1961 to Rita Moreno; in 1962
  to Maureen O'Sullivan; in
  1963 to the Marine standing
  sentry duty outside the
  American Embassy in Paris
  in *Charade;* this year to
  marinophile Jacques
  Cousteau for his underwater
  documentary *World Without
  Sun*

The Uncrossed Heart:
  *(to the least promising
  young performer)*
For the second year in a row:
  Annette Funicello
The Tin Pan:
  *(to the most obnoxious
  movie song)*
"Sex and the Single Girl"
**The Arrested-Development
Oblation:**
  *(to that adult actor who has
  displayed the lowest level
  of maturity)*
Always given to Jerry Lewis
**The Hon. Wrong-Way Corrigan
Memorial Palm:**
  (to the worst direction)
Billy Wilder, *Kiss Me Stupid*
**The Diamond-in-the-Rough
Award:**
Ann Southern, *Sylvia*
The Cellophane Figleaf:
  (for false modesty)
Elke Sommer who, when
  accused of making nude
  movie scenes, said, "Those
  pictures were of me in flesh-
  tight leotards—and photog-
  raphers had the nerve to
  retouch them!"
The Bratwurst Award:
  *(to the most obnoxious
  child star)*
Hayley Mills, *The Chalk Garden*
**Worst Performance By a Cast
in Toto:**
The entire population of
  Western Europe for its performance in *The Fall of the
  Roman Empire*
**The Timothy Cratchit Memorial
Crutch:**
  *(to that Hollywood person-
  ality who offers the lamest
  justification for unsavory
  behavior)*
Ann-Margret, for hitting her
  director in the head with an

ashtray, inflicting a 19-stitch wound, and then excusing herself as having a passionate absorption in her craft

The Wilde Oscar:
(to that performer who has been willing to flout convention and risk worldly reputation in order to pursue artistic fulfillment)
Carroll Baker, for spending two weeks with a prostitute in Tijuana to help her adjust to her public image

The Please-Don't-Put-Us-Through-DeMille-Again Award:
(to that movie of the past year which best embodies the pretentions, extravagance and blundering ineffectiveness of the traditional Screen Spectacular)
The Greatest Story Ever Told

Best Argument for Stricter Immigration Laws:
Tosh-Togo for his performance as Odd-Job in *Goldfinger*

Thank You Again:
Victor Mature for not making a film this year

The Great Ceremonial Hot Dog:
(for the worst scenes)
The on-screen rape in *The New Interns*
The entire first reel of *The Silence*

The Ok-Doc-Break-the-Arm-Again Award:
(for the most flagrant example of miscasting)
Sex and the Single Girl, with Natalie Wood in the role of a psychiatrist, and to *None But the Brave*, featuring Frank Sinatra as an Irish medic

The Geritol Award:
Anthony Quinn, *Zorba the Greek*

Th Gold Star-on-the-Wayne Laurel:
To John Wayne, for "licking the Big C"

Best Argument for Vivisection:
Flipper's New Adventure and *Father Goose*

The Curse-of-the-Living-Corpse:
Bette Davis

The Marquis De Sade Memorial Whip:
Ann-Margret for her performance in *Kitten with a Whip* and the entire cast of *Advance to the Rear*

The Ayn Rand Award:
(to that author whose bad books made worse movies)
Matthew, Mark, Luke and John for *The Greatest Story Ever Told*

The Roscoe Award:
Carroll Baker, who is the first performer ever to win the Movie Worst Triple Crown

---

1965

Ten Worst Movies:
The Sandpiper
The Hallelujah Trail
Lord Jim
What's New, Pussycat?
The Agony and the Ecstasy
Shenandoah
Gengis Khan
Thunderball
The Great Race
The Yellow Rolls Royce

1966

Ten Worst Movies:
Is Paris Burning?
Hurry Sundown
The Oscar
The Fortune Cookie
The Bible
A Countess from Hong Kong
The Blue Max
Fantastic Voyage
Torn Curtain
Penelope

Kirk Douglas Award to Worst Actor:
George Peppard, *The Blue Max*

Natalie Wood Award to Worst Actress:
Ursula Andress, *Casino Royale*

Worst Supporting Actor:
John Huston, *The Bible*

Worst Supporting Actress:
Leslie Caron, *Is Paris Burning?*

The Ok-Doc-Break-the-Arm-Again Award:
(to that most flagrant example of miscasting
John Huston as the voice of God in *The Bible*

Der Otto:
Awarded annually to Otto Preminger for his yearly excursions in to the tawdry, the sordid and the silly. This year for his direction of *Hurry Sundown*

The Hon. Wrong-Way Corrigan Memorial Palm:
(for worst direction)
Charles Chaplin, *A Countess from Hong Kong*

The Cellophane Figleaf:
(for false modesty)
Jane Fonda for suing *Playboy* magazine for having printed nude snapshots of her on set with husband-director Roger Vadim. "Nasty voyeurs," she said

The Please-Don't-Put-Us-Through-DeMille-Again Award:
(to the film which best embodies the pretentions, extravagance and blundering ineffectiveness of the traditional Screen Spectacular)
The Bible

The Piltdown Mandible:
Presented annually for the lamest explanation of scientifically improbable phenomena: this year to the producers of *Fantastic Voyage* for assuming that the molecules which made up the submarine would not re-expand to normal size simply because said submarine had been devoured by a white corpuscle; and to the lone cow in *The Bible* who supplied an estimated nine hundred seventy-four thousand gallons of milk to all the animals on the Ark for forty days and forty nights

The Uncrossed Heart:
(to the least promising young performer)
Andrea Dromm, *The Russians Are Coming*

The Bratwurst Award:
(to the most obnoxious child star)
John Mark as the demented child in *Hurry Sundown*

The Best Argument for Vivisection:
To *Born Free* and the entire Ark in *The Bible*

The Ayn Rand Award:
(to that writer whose bad books make worse movies)

Norman Mailer, *The American Dream*

Worst Performance By a Cast in Toto:
The Chaplin family in *A Countess from Hong Kong*

The Arrested-Development Oblation:
(to that adult actor who has displayed the lowest level of maturity)
Always given to Jerry Lewis

The Elsa Maxwell Kudo:
(to the most unattractive social event)
Sodom goat seduction in *The Bible*

The Great Ceremonial Hot Dog:
(for the worst scenes of the cinema season)
The birth scene in *Hawaii* and Jane Fonda's mouthing of a saxophone in *Hurry Sundown*

The Tin Pan:
(to the most obnoxious movie song)
"Alfie" and "Born Free"

The Diamond-in-the-Rough Award:
(to that performer whose genuine talent has shown through the drivel and dross that is so characteristic of modern cinema)
Margaret Rutherford, *A Countess from Hong Kong*

The Timothy Crachit Memorial Crutch:
(to that Hollywood personality who offers the lamest justification for unsavory behavior)
Raquel Welch, for marrying her manager in order to be seen in her flesh-colored mini-wedding gown

Best Argument for Stricter Immigration Laws:
Milos Forman, *Loves of a Blonde*

The Tower of Babel Citation:
(to that foreign-language film which has the worst subtitles)
A Man and a Woman

The Bennett:
(to the worst suffering movie)
The Endless Summer

The Merino Award:
In 1960 to Maureen O'Hara; in 1961 to Rita Moreno; in 1962 to Maureen O'Sullivan; in 1963 to the Marine standing sentry duty outside the American Embassy in Paris in *Charade*; in 1964 to marinophile Jacques Cousteau for his underwater documentary *World Without Sun*; in 1965 to Merina Mercouli; this year to the two merinos on the Ark in *The Bible*

The Roscoe Award:
Stephen Boyd for his starring roles in *The Oscar* and *Fantastic Voyage*, and his brief but significant appearance as Nimrod in *The Bible*

1967

Ten Worst Movies:
Guess Who's Coming to Dinner
Valley of the Dolls
Up the Down Staircase
One Million Years B.C.
The Comedians
Reflections in a Golden Eye
Thoroughly Modern Millie
Doctor Dolittle
The Fox
Carmen Baby

Kirk Douglas Award for Worst Actor:
Richard Burton for his disheartening performances in *Doctor Faustus; The Comedians*

Natalie Wood Award for Worst Actress:
Raquel Welch, *One Million Years B.C.; The Biggest Bundle of Them All; Bedazzled*

Worst Supporting Actor:
Whatsisname, *Valley of the Dolls*

Worst Supporting Actress:
Jean Shrimpton, *Privilege*

The Ok-Doc-Break-the-Arm-Again Award:
(to the most flagrant example of miscasting)
The Comedians for the waste of Peter Ustinov and Alec Guinness in roles as dull as they were uninteresting; and to Charlton Heston for portraying a human being in *Planet of the Apes*

The Hey-Jack-Which-Way-to-Mecca Award:
(for worst direction)
Claude Lelouche, *Live for Life*

The Please-Don't-Put-Us-Through-DeMille-Again Award:
(to that film which best embodies the pretentions, extravagances and blundering ineffectiveness of the traditional Screen Spectacular
Camelot

The Piltdown Mandible:
(to the most obviously and unabashedly spurious scientific phenomena)
One Million Years B.C., for the contemporaneous existence of Raquel Welch and a passel of dinosaurs; an unscientific juxtaposition redounding entirely to the credit of the dinosaurs

The Uncrossed Heart:
(to the least promising young performer)
Katharine Hepburn's niece Katharine Houghton, *Guess Who's Coming to Dinner*

The Mobius Strip:
(to the most boring and unnecessary undressing scene)
Barbara Parkins preparing to meet the Fate Worse Than Death in *Valley of the Dolls*

The Beast of Buchenwald Award:
To those actors who most thoroughly degrade themselves in order to pull in the paycheck, this handsomely tooled lampshade goes to the extras who played the apes in the beginning of *2001: A Space Odyssey*

The Ayn Rand Award:
(to that writer whose bad books made worse movies)
Graham Green, an otherwise fine author, for *The Comedians*

The Dance of the Seven Scott Tissues Award:
(to the most lewd and competely unwarranted dancing scene)
Raquel Welch, *Bedazzled*

Worst Performance By a Cast in Toto:
The Mills family, *The Family Way*

The Arrested-Development Oblation:
(to the adult actor who has displayed the lowest level of maturity)
Always given to Jerry Lewis

The Elsa Maxwell Kudo:
*(to the most unattractive
social event)*
To the "show" in *Titicut
Follies*

**The Great Ceremonial Hot
Dog:**
*(for the worst scenes of the
cinema season)*
Patty Duke's withdrawal fit in
Valley of the Dolls

**The Tedium Is the Medium
Citation:**
(to the worst student film)
Tim Hunter's *Desire Is the Fire*

The Exhausted Udder:
Presented by the Dairy
Farmers Assn. in recognition
of the attempts to milk
every penny possible from a
marketable idea, such as film
versions of obviously unfilm-
able musicals, plays, best
sellers, etc.; this year, the
handsome prize in withered
polyurethane goes to the
producers of *The Fox*

The Tin Pan:
*(to the most obnoxious
movie song)*
Leslie Bricusse's "Let's Talk to
the Animals" in *Doctor
Dolittle,* for blood-curdling
anthropomorphism

**The Best Argument for
Reactivating Ellis Island:**
(to the worst foreign film)
Poor Cow

The Sentimental Mushmelon:
*(to the film that best
reminds us of that true
Poignancy, that bitter
Sweetness, which we know
as Life)*
Elvira Madigan

**The Cheap-at-Half-the-Price
Award:**
For the worst bargain in a film
from the last year, to *Half a
Sixpence*

**The Guess-Who's-Stepping-
Out-to-Tommy's-Lunch Award**
*Guess Who's Coming to
Dinner*

**The Timothy Cratchit Memorial
Crutch:**
*(to that Hollywood person-
ality who offers the lamest
justification for unsavory
behavior)*
Mia Farrow, who followed the
Maharishi all the way to
India just to be able to
cream an Indian reporter
with her handbag

The H. J. Heinz Laurel Wreath:
*(to that film that makes
most extensive use of the
company's various vegetable
derivatives)*
Bonnie and Clyde

The Bratwurst Award:
*(to the most obnoxious child
star)*
Lulu, as the warbling adolescent in *To Sir, With Love*

**The Best Argument for
Vivisection:**
*Doctor Dolittle, The Jungle
Book* and *The Fox,* an
unusual spate of bad senti-
mentalism and worse
symbolism

The Bennett:
(to the worst surfing movie)
Surfari

**The On-a-Clear-Day-You-Can-
See-Fall-River Citation:**
*(for the most stereotyped
New England scenery)*
Valley of the Dolls for the
eternally snow-blanketed
shots of "Lawrenceville,

N.H." which was really
Bedford, N.Y.

The Merino Award:
To the Pushme-Pullyou in
Doctor Dolittle, who is, as
we take it, a distant cousin
to merinos, and at any rate
leads just as tenuous an
existence

The Roscoe Award:
Sandy Dennis, *Up the Down
Staircase, The Fox*

1968

Ten Worst Movies:
*The Lion In Winter
Ice Station Zebra
Rosemary's Baby
Star!
The Boston Strangler
Candy
Barbarella
You Are What You Eat
The Seagull
Boom*

**Kirk Douglas Award for Worst
Actor:**
Sidney Poitier, *For Love of Ivy*

**Natalie Wood Award for
Worst Actress:**
Barbra Streisand, *Funny Girl*

Worst Supporting Actress:
Ewa Aulin, *Candy*

Worst Supporting Actor:
Rod Steiger, *No Way to Treat
a Lady*

The Roscoe Award:
*(to that performer who dis-
plays a certain unskilled,
clumsy quality)*
Tony Curtis, *The Boston
Strangler*

1969

Ten Worst Movies:
*Easy Rider
Medium Cool
Putney Swope
Bob & Carol & Ted & Alice
Topaz
The Maltese Bippy
True Grit
John and Mary
Hello, Dolly!
Last Summer*

**Kirk Douglas Award for Worst
Actor:**
Peter Fonda, *Easy Rider*

**Natalie Wood Award for
Worst Actress:**
Jane Fonda, *Spirits of the
Dead,* and for marrying
Roger Vadim

Worst Supporting Actor:
Dennis Hopper, *Easy Rider*

Worst Supporting Actress:
Mia Farrow, *Secret Ceremony*

**The Ok-Doc-Break-the-Arm-
Again Award:**
*(to the most flagrant exam-
ple of miscasting)*
Omar Sharif for his west-of-
center title role in *Che!*

**The Hey-Jack-Which-Way-to-
Mecca Award:**
(for the worst direction)
Jean-Luc Godard, *Sympathy
for the Devil*

The Uncrossed Heart:
*(to the least promising
young performer)*
Goldie Hawn, *Cactus Flower*

**The Please-Don't-Put-Us-
Through-DeMille-Again
Award:**
*(to that movie which best
embodies the pretentions,
extravagances and blundering ineffectiveness of the*

traditional Screen Spectacular)

Hello, Dolly!

The Piltdown Mandible:
(to the most obviously and unabashedly spurious scientific phenomena)

Krakatoa, East of Java, since Krakatoa, by all recent accounts, is a good two hundred miles west of Java

The Sentimental Mushmelon:
(to the film that most reminds us of that true Poignancy, that bitter Sweetness, which we know as Life)

The Reivers, a sledgehammer-on-a-marshmallow rendition of a squishy Faulkner novel

The Cheap-at-Half-the-Price Award:

Woody Allen's Take the Money and Run

The OhGodohGod, the Lights, the Shapes, the Colors Award:
(to that movie which makes us glad we have lungs to inhale with)

The revival of Walt Disney's Fantasia

The Timothy Cratchit Memorial Crutch:
(to that personality who offers the lamest justification for unsavory behavior)

President Richard Nixon, who screened the film Marooned, an epic of three spacemen lost in the great beyond, for apprehensive astronauts Armstrong, Collins and Young at a White House Kultur-fest

The Beast of Buchenwald Award:
(to those actors who most thoroughly degrade themselves in order to pull in the paycheck, this handsomely tooled lampshade is awarded)

The entire cast of Visconti's horror show, The Damned

The Great Ceremonial Hot Dog:
(for the worst scene of the cinema season)

Peter Fonda's I-love-you-I-hate-you acid trip in a New Orleans cemetery in Easy Rider

The Arrested-Development Oblation:
(to that adult actor who has displayed the lowest level of maturity)

Always given to Jerry Lewis, who, in spite of making no films this year, has managed to perpetuate the infantile tradition by his inimitable Cerebral Palsy telethons

The Ayn Rand Award:
(to that writer whose bad books make worse movies)

Petronius, who should have known better, for Satyricon

The Exhausted Udder:
(presented by the Dairy Farmers Assn. in recognition of attempts to milk every penny possible from a marketable idea)

Anyone who had anything to do with what we hope is the last James Bond film ever, On Her Majesty's Secret Service

The Tin Pan:
(to the most obnoxious movie song)

Rod McKuen's "Jean" from The Prime of Miss Jean Brodie

The Marquis De Sade Memorial Whip:

Raquel Welch in The Magic Christian, for a leather-and-

chains performance which
rivals Attila the Hun

**The Dance to the Seven Scott
Tissues Award:**
 *(to the most lewd and
 completely unwarranted
 dancing scene)*
To the fag ball in Andy
 Warhol's *Lonesome
 Cowboys*

**The Most Unnecessary
Contribution to the American
Way of Life:**
To the hippest people we
 know, the cool and groovy
 stars of *Bob & Carol & Ted &
 Alice*

**The Guess-Who's-Stepping-
Out-to-Tommy's-Lunch Award:**
 *(presented to that scene in
 a movie which makes us
 guess we'll step out to
 Tommy's lunch)*
The blow job in the movie
 balcony of *Midnight Cowboy*

**The Do-You-Know-the-Way-to-
San-Jose Award:**
 *(to that film which took the
 wrong turn on the Los
 Angeles freeway while
 shooting on the studio lot
 and ended up in the least
 likely location)*
*Butch Cassidy and the
 Sundance Kid* for its
 Bolivian sequences

**The Strongest Argument for
Laxer Divorce Laws:**
Paul Newman and Joanne
 Woodward for *Winning*, a
 loser

**The Dr. Christiaan Barnard
Award:**
 *(to that movie which shows
 the worst job of cutting)*
Rowan and Martin's *The
 Maltese Bippy*

The Bratwurst Award:
 *(to the most obnoxious child
 star)*
The entire cast of *Goodbye,
 Mr. Chips,* a movie which
 made us wish we were back
 at St. Paul's

The Elsa Maxwell Kudo:
 *(to the most unattractive
 social event)*
To the singles bar scenes in
 John and Mary

**The Best Argument for
Reactivating Ellis Island:**
To the entire country of
 Sweden, for bringing us such
 screaming turkeys as
 *Without a Stitch; Woman Is
 a Female Animal* and *I, a
 Man*

The Twenty-Cent Token:
 *(to that film which does the
 most fashionable injustice
 to a minority class)*
Putney Swope

**The Thanks-for-Nothing
Award:**
 *(given to that Hollywood
 performer who has blessedly
 not made a motion picture
 this year)*
Doris Day, who has saved us
 from guessing once again
 how it is that she will
 remain a post-menopausal
 virgin

The Wilde Oscar:
 *(to that performer who has
 been willing to flout convention and risk worldly reputation in order to pursue
 artistic fulfillment)*
Dustin Hoffman for playing a
 consumptive Italian hunchback in *Midnight Cowboy*

The H. J. Heinz Laurel Wreath:
 *(to that film that makes
 most extensive use of the*

company's various vegetable
derivatives)

The Battle of Britain

**The Wrong-Way Corrigan
Memorial Flight Jacket:**
(to the one line a film which
does more to distort the
course of history than
Lyndon Johnson's interviews
with Walter Cronkite)

Given, with apologies to the
American Barbers Assn., to
the Virgin Mary in Buñuel's
The Milky Way for her line,
"Jesus, don't cut off your
beard; you look handsome
with it."

**The Harvard Independent
Award:**
(to that film noted for its
ignominious failure as both
art and politics)

Medium Cool

**The Curse-of-the-Living-Corpse
Award:**
A fully-paid burial insurance
policy presented by the
American Morticians Assn.
as inducement to a speedy
interment, the award this
year goes to Mae West, who
is going to do it again in
Myra Breckenridge

**The It-Can't-Happen-Here
Award:**
(presented to that film that
shot a sequence which is
geographically closest to
The Lampoon Castle)

Goodbye, Columbus for a
scene in which Ali MacGraw,
an unconvincing "Cliffie,"
ambles down the steps of
romantic Widener Library

The Babar Boo-Boo:
(to those movies which do
most for the cause of
bestiality)

Futz! and *The End of the Road*,
two movies which were
especially illuminating on
the possibilities of doing it
with pigs and chickens

**The Hey-Boswell-Did-You-Get-
That-One-Down Award:**
(to that film whose dialogue
was, when not monosyllabic,
subhuman)

Easy Rider, for doing its own
thing in its own time

**The Charles Manson Memorial
Scalpel:**
Awarded without comment to
the gallant army doctors in
*M*A*S*H*

The Bosley:
(to that film critic who has
done most to perpetuate the
cult of kitsch)

Judith Crist, whose taste buds
died in 1952

**The Black-and-White-and-Red-
All-Over Award:**
(to that movie which has
done the most to eliminate
shades of grey)

The entire cast of *Z*

**The Best Argument for Stricter
Immigration Laws:**
Ingrid Bergman, who changed
the course of her career by
her prickly performance in
Cactus Flower

The Brass Brassiere:
(given to that man who, in
the tradition of Hugh Hefner
and Harold Robbins, has
done most to advance the
cause of male chauvinism)

Allen Funt for his epic of
women's lib, *What Do You
Say to a Naked Lady?*

**The Best Argument for
Keeping R.O.T.C. on Campus:**
Awarded with much apprehen-
sion to this year's most

courageous war movie,
Patton

The Doctor-Down Award:
*(to that movie which would
most likely cause a bummer
trip)*
*They Shoot Horses, Don't
They?*

**The Best Argument for
Vivisection:**
The Wild Bunch, which was as
graphic as it was unappe-
tizing

**The On-a-Clear-Day-You-Can-
See-Fall-River Citation:**
*(for the most stereotyped
New England scenery)*
Alice's Restaurant, whose
Stockbridge, Massachusetts,
was just like *Life* magazine
said it would be

The Merino Award:
In 1961 this one-quarter scale
Corfam mounted sheep went
to Maureen O'Hara; in 1962
to Rita Moreno; in 1963 to
Maureen O'Sullivan; in 1964
to Italian director Dario
Moreno; in 1965 to marinophile Jacques-Yves
Cousteau; in 1966 to Merino
Mercouli; in 1967 to the two
merinos on board the Ark in
The Bible; in 1968 to the
Pushme-Pullyou in *Doctor
Dolittle,* a distant cousin to
merinos; in 1969 to the cast
of *The Green Berets,* which
included only one black
Marine; and in 1970, to the
accompaniment of dull thuds
produced by beating a dead
sheep, the Merino Award
goes to Andy Warhol's *Blue
Movie,* which was filmed
entirely in lurid aqua-merino

The Ros(s)coe Award:
Katharine Ross, for her forget-
table performances in *Tell*

Them Willie Boy Is Here
and *Butch Cassidy and the
Sundance Kid*

1970

Ten Worst Movies:
Love Story
Airport
Patton
Joe
Soldier Blue
Getting Straight
The Strawberry Statement
Little Fauss and Big Halsy
Julius Caesar
The Statue

**Kirk Douglas Award for Worst
Actor:**
Elliott Gould, for *Getting
Straight* and for dumping
Barbra Streisand

**Natalie Wood Award for
Worst Actress:**
Ali MacGraw, *Love Story*

Worst Supporting Actor:
Jon Voight, *Catch-22*

Worst Supporting Actress:
Ruth Gordon, *Where's Poppa?*

**The Where-is-Erik-Erikson-Now-
That-We're-All-Going-Bananas
Award:**
The *Lampoon* is proud to
present a set of gold-plated
thumbscrews and a spicy
meatball to Jack Nicholson,
who, in *Five Easy Pieces,*
showed that it's never too
late to have an identity crisis

The Tin Pan:
*(to the most lethal movie
song)*
"Suicide Is Painless," from
M*A*S*H, written by
Michael Altman, the fifteen-
year old son of the director,
Robert Altman

**The Marquis De Sade
Memorial Whip:**
Richard Harris, for being a
brave brave in *A Man Called
Horse*

**The Hey-Boswell-Did-You-Get-
That-One-Down Award:**
(to that film whose dialogue
was, when not monosyllabic,
subhuman)
*The Sidelong Glances of a
Pigeon Kicker*

The Senuous Eunuch:
(to that man and / or woman
who has done the most to
advance the cause of male
chauvinism)
The Christine Jorgensen Story

**The Ok-Doc-Break-the-Arm-
Again Award:**
(to the most flagrant example of miscasting)
Dean Martin, who soberly
piloted a 707 to a belly-
landing in *Airport*

**The Guess-Who's-Stepping-
Out-to-Tommy's-Lunch Award:**
To the shooting-up scene in
Trash

**The Strongest Argument for
Laxer Divorce Laws:**
Bob Evans, president of Para-
mount Pictures, and Ali
MacGraw, for obvious
reasons

**The Dr. Christiaan Barnard
Award:**
(to that movie which shows
the worst job of cutting)
Claude Chabrol's *Le Boucher*

**The Please-Don't-Put-Us-
Through-DeMille-Again
Award:**
(to that movie which best
embodies the pretensions,
extravagances and blundering ineffectiveness of the

traditional Screen
Spectacular)
Woodstock

**The Beast of Buchenwald
Award:**
(to those actors who most
thoroughly degrade them-
selves in order to pull in the
paycheck, a handsomely
tooled lampshade)
The entire cast of *Fellini's
Satyricon*

**The What's-a-Nice-Boy-from-
Shaker-Heights-Doing-etc.
Award:**
(given to the most unneces-
sary contribution to the
American way of life)
Paul Newman, who proved that
he is no Merle Haggard in
WUSA

The Julia Child Cleft Palate:
Ryan O'Neil, for calling the
Hasty Pudding Club "boring"

**The Cheap-at-Half-the-Price
Award:**
(for the worst bargain in a
film)
Stewardesses in 3D, which in
addition to its $3.00 admis-
sion price charges 25¢ for a
sliver of twisted plastic. The
eyeshades transform the
colorful two-dimensional
slurry into a steamy three-
dimensional cesspool

**The Timothy Cratchit Memorial
Crutch:**
(to that personality who
offers the lamest justification for unsavory behavior)
For the second year in a row,
to President Nixon, who
gave *Patton* a careful screening the night before he
announced the Cambodian
invasion.

The Bratwurst Award:
(to the most endearing child star)
The entire cast of *Groupies*

The Dance of the Seven Scott Tissues Award:
(to the most lewd and completely unwarranted dancing scene)
Mick Jagger, who trips the light psychedelic in *Performance*

The Bare-assed in the Park Award:
This award, along with the traditional cellophane figleaf, is presented to Joey Heatherton, for marrying Lance Rentzel, whose let-it-all-hang-out performance in a Dallas park was the year's best argument for sex education in the locker room

The Piltdown Mandible:
(to the most obviously and unabashedly spurious scientific phenomenon)
On a Clear Day You Can See Forever, in which Yves Montand hypnotizes Barbra Streisand from twentieth-century Brooklyn into nineteenth-century England

The Sentimental Mushmelon:
(to that film which most reminds us of that true Poignancy, that bitter Sweetness, which we know as Life)
The squishy rendition of Robert Anderson's seedy play, *I Never Sang for My Father*

The Great Ceremonial Hot Dog:
(for the worst scene of the cinema season)
To Holly Woodlawn, for making it with a beer bottle in *Trash*

The Exhausted Udder:
(presented by the Dairy Farmers Assn. in recognition of attempts to milk every penny possible from a marketable idea)
Anyone who had anything to do with *Beyond the Valley of the Dolls* or *Beneath the Planet of the Apes*

The Hey-Jack-Which-Way-to-Mecca Award:
(for the worst direction)
Michelangelo Antonioni's *Zabriskie Point*

The Uncrossed Heart:
(to the least promising young performer)
Presented in a serious vain to *Trash*'s mainliner, Joe Dallesandro

The Within-You-But-Not-Without-Me Award:
Kama Sutra, for getting it together

Best Argument for Pay-TV:
Loving, in which George Segal and Eva Marie Saint make it in a playpen before a closed-circuit TV camera for the benefit of party guests next door

The Bosley:
(to that film critic whose writing consistently explores the farthest limits of bad taste)
This year uncontested: it goes with a hip flask of bile and a mortal dose of henbane, to John Simon, for his muddle-headed, obfuscatory, artless, splenetic and interminable . . . self

The Women-and-Children-First-Lt.-Calley Award:
A Fanner Fifty and a roll of Greenie Stickum Caps to John Wayne, for surprising

us with two new westerns,
Chisum and *Rio Lobo*

The Charles Manson Memorial Scalpel:

Awarded without comment to the side-splitting scene in *Catch-22*

The It-Can't-Happen-Here Award:

(presented to the film that shot a sequence which is geographically closest to The Lampoon Castle)

Love Story for showing the American public that the nicest things about Harvard are Cambridge winters, low-rent housing, Winthrop House and leukemia

The Merino Award:

In 1960 this one-quarter scale neoprene mounted sheep went to Maureen O'Hara; in 1961 to Rita Moreno; in 1962 to Maureen O'Sullivan; in 1963 to Italian director Dario Moreno; in 1964 to marinophile Jacques-Yves Cousteau; in 1965 to Merino Mercouli; in 1966 to the two merinos on board the Ark in *The Bible;* in 1967 to the Pushme-Pullyou in *Doctor Dolittle*, a distant cousin to merinos, leading as tenuous an existence; in 1968 to the cast of *The Green Berets*, which included only one black Marine; in 1969 with a dull thud to Andy Warhol's *Blue Movie*, filmed entirely in lurid aqua-merino; and in 1970 to the frumpy house-wife from a frumpy movie, *Airport*, Maureen O. Stapleton

The Wrong-Way Corrigan Memorial Flight Jacket:

(for the worst direction)

Ken Hughes, *Cromwell*

The Harvard Independent:

(to that film noted for its ignominious failure as both art and politics)

Strawberry Statement

The-Curse-of-the-Living-Corpse Award:

Helen Hayes, *Airport*

The Wilde Oscar:

(for that performer who has been willing to flout con-vention and risk worldly damnation in the pursuit of artistic fulfillment)

Liza Minnelli, *Tell Me You Love Me Junie Moon*

The H. J. Heinz Laurel Clot:

(to the film that makes most extensive use of the com-pany's various vegetable derivatives)

Soldier Blue

The Roscoe Award:

(to that performer who has most memorably displayed that certain unskilled clumsy quality that has marked the products of Hollywood since the early days)

Katharine Ross, *Fools*

The Elsa Maxwell Kudo:

(to the most unattractive social event of the year)

The party in *Boys in the Band*

The Best Argument for Activating Ellis Island:

Sexual Freedom in Denmark

The Twenty-Cent Token:

(to that film which does the most fashionable injustice to a minority class)

Little Big Man

Thanks for Nothing:

(to that Hollywood per-former who has blessedly

not made a motion picture this year)

Jane Fonda, for immigrating to the Third World

The Martha Mitchell Mug:

Peter Boyle for *Joe*

Prease Get off Tojo Award:

Darryl Zanuck for *Tora! Tora! Tora!*

Mary Martin Light-and-Lively Award:

(for worst musical)

Gimme Shelter

If Only Films Were Bio-degradable Award:

To those who recycled *My Fair Lady, Lawrence of Arabia, Dr. Zhivago,* and *Mutiny on the Bounty*

The Ayn Rand Award:

(to that writer whose bad books made worse movies)

Harold Robbins, *The Adventurers*

1971

Ten Worst Movies:

Clockwork Orange
Carnal Knowledge
Summer of '42
Fiddler on the Roof
The Last Movie
T. R. Baskin
Kotch
Willard
The Music Lovers
Dealing

Kirk Douglas Award for Worst Actor:

Jack Nicholson, *Carnal Knowledge*

Natalie Wood Award for Worst Actress:

Candice Bergen, *T. R. Baskin*

Worst Supporting Actor:

The real-life cop in *French Connection*

Worst Supporting Actress:

Lana Wood, *Diamonds Are Forever*

H. J. Heinz Laurel Clot:

(to the film that makes most extensive use of the company's various vegetable derivatives)

Dirty Harry

The Mary Martin Light-and-Lively Award:

(for worst musical)

200 Motels

The Twenty-Cent Token:

(to that film which does the most fashionable injustice to a minority class)

McCabe & Mrs. Miller for its gratuitous Negro espousals

The W-W Corrigan Memorial Flight Jacket:

(to the worst directed film)

Nicholas and Alexandra

The Best Argument for Reactivating Ellis Island:

The Godfather

The Elsa Maxwell Kudo:

To Buck Henry for losing the strip poker game in *Taking Off*

The Roscoe Award:

(to that performer who has most memorably displayed that certain unskilled clumsy quality)

Art Garfunkel, *Carnal Knowledge*

The Thanks-for-Nothing Award:

(to that Hollywood performer who has blessedly not made a motion picture this year)

Katharine Ross

The Harvard Independent:
 (to that film noted for its ignominious failure as both art and politics)
Sacco and Vanzetti

The Hey-Which-Way-Is-Mecca? Award:
 (for worst direction)
Dennis Hopper, *The Last Movie*

The Hey-Boswell-Did-You-Get-That-One-Down Award:
 (to the film with the worst dialogue)
To Steve McQueen for his exhaust-laden sweet nothings in *LeMans*

The Where-Is-Erik-Erikson-Now-That-We're-All-Going-Bananas Award:
Woody Allen, *Bananas*

The Wilde Oscar:
 (to that performer most willing to flout convention and risk worldly damnation in the pursuit of artistic fulfillment)
John Wayne for making two more saddle movies and standing behind our boys in Vietnam

The Sensuous Eunuch Award:
Jack Nicholson

The Ok-Doc-Break-the-Arm-Again Award:
 (to the most flagrant example of miscasting)
To Ingmar Bergman for letting Elliott Gould turn *The Touch* into a karate chop

The If-He-Gets-Through-This-One-We'll-Name-Him-Houdini Award:
The cretin pharmacist in *Summer of '42*

The Within-You-But-Not-Without-Me Award:
Ecstasy '72

The Bosley:
 (to the film critic whose writing has most consistently explored the limits of bad taste)
The entire Society of New York Film Critics for naming *Clockwork Orange* best film of the year

The Exhausted Udder:
 (in recognition of attempts to milk every penny possible from a marketable idea)
Diamonds Are Forever

The Uncrossed Heart:
 (to the least promising young performer)
Twiggy, the girl friend in *The Boy Friend*

The Ceremonial Hot Dog:
 (to the worst movie scene)
The morning-after scene in *Macbeth*

The Piltdown Mandible:
 (to the most obviously and unabashedly spurious scientific phenomenon)
The Andromeda Strain

The Cheap-at-Half-the-Price Award:
 (for the worst movie bargain)
Experience (the Harvard promotional flick)

The Women-and-Children-First-Lt.-Calley Award:
 (to the film whose violence was above and beyond the call of duty)
John Wayne, *Big Jake*

Ayn Rand Award:
 (to that writer whose bad books made even worse movies)
Michael Crichton, *Andromeda Strain*

The If-Only-Films-Were-Bio-degradable Award:
The recycling of Charlie Chaplin films

The Dance of the Seven Scott Tissues Award:
(to the most lewd and completely unwarranted dancing scene)
Malcolm MacDowell, *Clockwork Orange*

The Charles Manson Memorial Scalpel:
(to that film with the clumsiest job of cutting)
The Go Between for its time jumps

The Please-Don't-Put-Us-Through-DeMille-Again Award:
(to that film which best embodies the pretensions, extravagances, and blundering ineffectiveness of the traditional Screen Spectacular)
Waterloo

The Strongest Argument for Laxer Divorce Laws:
Renee Taylor and Joseph Bologna for *Made for Each Other*

The Guess-Who's-Stepping-Out-to-Tommy's-Lunch Award:
To the nuns who blew their wafers in *The Devils*

The Tar Baby:
(in recognition of Hollywood's continued exploitation of the black market)
To MGM for giving us *Shaft*

The Bratwurst Award:
(to the worst child actor)
The entire cast of *Bless the Beasts and Children*

The Cellophane Figleaf:
(to the most outstanding display of anemic false modesty)

Cybill Shepherd, *The Last Picture Show*

The Beast of Buchenwald Award:
(to that performer who most thoroughly degrades himself in order to pull in the paycheck, a handsomely tooled lampshade)
Ernest Borgnine, *Willard*

The Merino Award:
(to that figure who has done the most to enhance the fame and glory of the merino)
Murino eye drops for making Malcolm MacDowell see the light in *Clockwork Orange*

1972

Ten Worst Movies:
Last Tango in Paris
The Candidate
The Getaway
Sounder
Deliverance
Play It As It Lays
The Emigrants
What's Up, Doc?
Man of La Mancha
The Man

Kirk Douglas Award for Worst Actor:
Robert Redford, *The Candidate*

Natalie Wood Award for Worst Actress:
Ali MacGraw, *Getaway*

Worst Supporting Actor:
Burgess Meredith, *The Man*

Worst Supporting Actress:
Shelley Winters, *The Poseidon Adventure*

The We-Heard-You-the-First-Time Award:
Georgia, Georgia

The Charles Manson Memorial Scalpel:
(to the clumsiest job of cutting)
Play It As It Lays

The Jerry Van Dyke Clip-on Medallion:
(to the most consistently innocuous personality)
Fred MacMurray

The Please-Don't-Put-Us-Through-DeMille Award:
(to that movie which best embodies the pretensions, extravagances, and blundering ineffectiveness of the Screen Spectacular)
Lost Horizon

The Elsa Maxwell Kudo:
(to the most unattractive social event of the year)
The New Year's Eve splash party in *The Poseidon Adventure*

The Kill-It-Before-It-Spreads Citation:
(designed to cripple the career of a fledgling actor or actress)
Jeannie Berlin, *The Heartbreak Kid*

The Sentimental Mushmelon:
(to the film that most reminds us of that true Poignancy, that Bitter Sweetness, which we know as Life)
Butterflies Are Free

The Wrong-Way Corrigan Memorial Flight Jacket:
(for the worst direction)
Sam Peckinpah, *The Getaway; Junior Bonner*

The Uncrossed Heart:
(to the least promising young performer)
Cybill Shepherd, who has now gone two major films without once opening her eyes

The Twenty-Cent Token:
(to that film which does the most fashionable injustice to a minority class)
Sounder

The Women-and-Children-First-Lt.-Calley Award:
(designed to honor acts above and beyond the call of duty)
Sam Peckinpah, *The Getaway, Junior Bonner*

The Best Argument for Vivisection:
Fritz the Cat

The Tar Baby:
(in recognition of Hollywood's continued exploitation of the black market)
Blacula

The Brass Brassiere:
(to those who have done the most to advance the cause of male chauvinism)
Gene Hackman and Lee Marvin, *Prime Cut*

The Great Ceremonial Hot Dog:
(to the worst scene)
Carol Burnett, for her stunning impersonation of Charlie the Horse doing *Medea* in the bereavement scene of *Pete 'n' Tillie*

The Handlin Oscar:
(to the film which has most distorted the course of history)
Young Winston

The Yawns-of-Death Citation:
(to the most unremittingly depressing film)
The King of Marvin Gardens

The Tin Pan:
(to the most thoroughly obnoxious movie song)
"Cabaret," *Cabaret*

The Hey-Boswell-Did-You-Get-That-One-Down Award:
(to that film whose dialogue was, when not monosyllabic, subhuman)

Charles Bronson, *Da Valachi Papers; Da Mechanic*

The Dark Fedora:
(this citation names the villain you might have waited to discover with bated breath or stifled yawns at the end of a three-hour movie)

Sleuth, now that you know Michael Caine is Inspector Doppler

The Best Argumont for Reactivating Ellis Island:
The Emigrants, for showing us that even Swedes can act like Polacks

The Ok-Doc-Break-the-Arm-Again Award:
(to the most flagrant example of miscasting)

Sam Peckinpah for hiring Ali MacGraw to do a woman's job in *The Getaway*

The Caploe:
(to the actor or actress in a porno film)

Linda Lovelace, *Deep Throat*

The Worst Film of the Century Award:
The Poseidon Adventure

The Cheap-at-Half-the-Price Award:
(to the worst bargain in a film)

Deep Throat

The Timothy Cratchit Memorial Crutch:
(to that personality who offers the lamest excuse for unsavory behavior)

Ms. Sacheen Littlefeather, Marlon Brando's Oscar-night stand-in, who later parlayed her status as a representative of the American Indian cause into a three-page nude photo spread in *Playboy*

The Dance of the Seven Scott Tissues Award:
(to the most lewd and completely unwarranted dancing scene)

Marlon Brando, *Last Tango*

Worst Performance by a Cast in Toto:
The Poseidon Adventure

The Life-of-the-Party Award:
(to that actor who most thoroughly degrades himself in order to pull in the paycheck)

Richard Burton in *Bluebeard,* for methodically murdering six wives whose lips are out of sync

The Roscoe:
(to that performer who has displayed that certain unskilled clumsy quality)

Jon Voight, *Deliverance*

The Cellophane Figleaf:
(for the most outstanding display of anemic false modesty)

Valerie Perrine, *Slaughterhouse Five*

The Wilde Oscar:
(to that performer who has been willing to flout convention in the pursuit of artistic fulfillment)

Linda Lovelace

The Bosley:
(to that critic whose writing explores the farthest limits of bad taste)

Pauline Kael, whose hysterical encomium loosed Bertolucci's *Last Tango* upon an all-too-trusting world

The Guess-Who's-Stepping-Out-to-Tommy's-Lunch Award:

To the Mothers and Fathers of Italian Ancestry for a castration in *The Valachi Papers,* which finally proves that sopranos are made, not born

The Ayn Rand Award:
(to that writer whose bad books made worse movies)

John Knowles, *A Separate Peace*

The Strongest Argument for Laxer Divorce Laws:

Paul Newman, who should learn to control his wife, for *The Effects of Gamma Rays . . .*

The Well-It-Sure-Is-Different Award:
(to the most chicly incomprehensible film)

Fellini, *Roma*

The Curse-of-the-Living-Corpse Award:

Ernest Borgnine

The Arrested-Development Oblation:
(presented to that adult actor who has displayed the lowest level of maturity)

Jerry Lewis as always

The-Black-Symbolizes-Death, See? Award:
(to the worst student film)

Jean Pigozzi, *Hamburger*

The Victor Mature Memorial Award:
(to the most embarrassing line of dialogue since Richard Burton was asked at the foot of the cross, in The Robe, "Is this your first crucifixion?")

Nicholas and Alexandra, for a young Trotsky's angry reproach to the Father of Modern Communism: "Lenin, you've been avoiding me!"

The Piltdown Mandible:
(to the most unabashedly spurious scientific phenomenon)

Deep Throat, for the tired, hackneyed misplaced-clitoris routine

The Marquis de Sade Memorial Whip:

Ken Russell, *Savage Messiah*

The Harvard Independent Award:
(to that film noted for its ignominious failure as both art and politics)

The Candidate

The Not-Tonight-I-Have-a-Headache Award:
(to that movie which gave us the best excuse to turn in early)

Marcel Ophuls, *The Sorrow and the Pity*

The Stanislavsky Avardsk:
(to that performer who has undergone the greatest physical torment in the furtherance of Art)

Raquel Welch, who learned to roller-skate in *Kansas City Bomber*

The Exhausted Udder:
(in recognition of attempts to milk every penny from a marketable idea)

Conquest of the Planet of the Apes

The H. J. Heinz Award:
(to that film which makes most extensive use of the company's various vegetable derivatives)

The Valachi Papers

The Bratwurst Award:
(to the most endearing child stars)

The entire cast of *A Separate Peace*

The Thanks-for-Nothing Award:
> *(to that performer who has . blessedly not made a film this year)*

Stephen Boyd, whose career seems to have gone steadily downhill since his disembowelment in *Ben-Hur*

The Merino Award:
In 1960 to Maureen O'Hara; in 1961 to Rita Moreno; in 1962 to Maureen O'Sullivan; in 1963 to Italian director Dario Moreno; in 1964 to marinophile Jacques-Yves Cousteau; in 1965 to Merino Mercouli; in 1966 to the two merinos on board the Ark in *The Bible*; in 1967 to the Pushme-Pullyou in *Doctor Doolittle*, a distint cousin to the merino; in 1968 to the cast of *The Green Berets*, which included only one black marine; in 1969 to Andy Warhol's *Blue Movie*, filmed entirely in liquid aqua-merino; in 1970 to Maureen O. Stapleton; in 1971 to Murino eye drops, for making Malcolm MacDonald see the light in *A Clockwork Orange*; and for 1972 to Marino Schneider in *Last Tango*

1973

Ten Worst Movies:
The Great Gatsby
Day of the Dolphin
Jonathan Livingston Seagull
The Seven-Ups
A Touch of Class
Blume in Love
The Way We Were .
The Exorcist
Save the Tiger
American Graffiti

The Kirk Douglas Award for Worst Actor:
Jack Lemmon, *Save the Tiger*

The Natalie Wood Award for Worst Actress:
Barbra Streisand, *The Way We Were*

Worst Supporting Actor:
Dustin Hoffman, *Papillon*

Worst Supporting Actress:
Dyan Cannon, *Shamus; The Last of Sheila*

The Ok-Doc-Break-the-Arm-Again Award:
> *(to the most flagrant example of miscasting)*

The Great Gatsby, which cast Mia Farrow as Daisy Buchanan

The Wrong-Way Corrigan Memorial Flight Jacket:
> *(for worst direction)*

Mich Nichols, *Day of the Dolphin*

The Women-and-Children-First-Lt.-Calley Award:
> *(for acts of violence above and beyond the call of duty)*

Philip D'Antoni for the chase scene in *The Seven-Ups*

The Jerry Van Dyke Clip-on Medallion:
> *(for the most innocuous personality)*

Fred MacMurray

The Please-Don't-Put-Us-Through-DeMille-Again Award:
> *(to the film which best embodies the pretensions, extravagances, and blundering ineffectiveness of the Screen Spectacular)*

Papillon

The Handlin Oscar:
(to the film which most distorts history)
Hitler: The Last Ten Days

The Worst Performance by a Cast in Toto Award:
Bang the Drum Slowly, with Least Valuable Players citations going to Michael Moriarty and Robert DeNiro

The Great Ceremonial Hot Dog:
(to the worst scene)
Neil Young, *Journey Through the Past*, for assault with a flimsy weapon

The We-Heard-You-the-First-Time Award:
Money, Money, Money

The H. J. Heinz Laurel Clot:
(to that film which makes most extensive use of the company's vegetable derivatives)
Magnum Force

The Marquis de Sade Memorial Whip:
Clint Eastwood, *Magnum Force*

The Remember-You-Saw-It-Here-First Award:
Roberta Flack, who should kill us softly with her songs the first time we see her in the upcoming film biography of Bessie Smith

The Curse-of-the-Living-Corpse Award:
Lucille Ball, *Mame,* in which her actual age was cleverly concealed by a paper towel taped over the camera lens; someone should saw this lady in half and count the rings

The Elsa Maxwell Kudo:
(to the most unattractive social event)

The Grande Bouffe, for dishing up Death as a dessert at a banquet

The Wilde Oscar:
(to the performer who has been willing to flout convention in the pursuit of artistic fulfillment)
John Wayne, for giving up that plot on Boot Hill in exchange for a modest shrine in Forest Lawn

The Roscoe Award:
(to that performer who has most memorably displayed that certain unskilled clumsy quality)
Ann-Margret, who showed a distinct falling off in her Las Vegas act, if not deliberate slipshodness, in *The Train Robbers*

The Tin Pan:
(to the most obnoxious movie song)
Paul McCartney, *Live and Let Die*

The Best Argument for Reactivating Ellis Island:
The New Land

The Sentimental Mushmelon:
(to that film that most reminds us of that true poignancy, that bitter Sweetness which we know as Life)
Bang the Drum Slowly

The Guess-Who's-Stepping-Out-to-Tommy's-Lunch Award:
The probing scene in *The Exorcist*

The Harvard Independent Award:
(to the film most notable for its ignominious failure as both art and politics)
State of Siege, which escaped the criticism it so richly deserved because nobody criticized it for its failure as

art (since it never occurred
to anybody that is was art)
and because nobody criti-
cized it for its failure as
journalism (since it never
occurred to anybody that it
was journalism)

The Cosmic Blender:
Black Caesar, who brought the
mob to Harlem

The Twenty-Cent Token:
*(to that film which does the
most fashionable injustice
to a minority class)*
Cleopatra Jones

**The Timothy Cratchit
Memorial Crutch:**
*(to that personality who
offers the lamest justification for unsavory behavior)*
Colleen Dewhurst, who ap-
peared in *McQ* because, she
said, "I needed the money."

The Yawns-of-Death Citation:
*(to the most unremittingly
depressing film)*
The Way We Were

The Ayn Rand Award:
*(to that writer whose bad
books made worse movies)*
Hermann Hesse, who should
have been old enough to
know better than to write
Siddhartha

The Stanislavsky Avardsk:
*(to that performer who has
undergone the greatest
physical torment in the
furtherance of Art)*
Mercedes McCambridge, who,
well, sounded like hell in
The Exorcist

The Bratwurst Award:
*(to the most endearing
child star)*
Johnny "either Buffy or Jody"
Whitaker, *Tom Sawyer*

**The Strongest Argument for
Laxer Divorce Laws:**
To Mrs. Ryan O'Neal, who
should have fought harder
for custody of daughter
Tatum

**The Charles Manson Memorial
Scalpel:**
*(for the clumsiest job of
cutting)*
O Lucky Man, whose shooting
script was first published as
a deck of flash-cards by
Educational Playthings

The Brass Brassiere:
*(to that personality who has
done the most to advance
the cause of male chauvinism)*
Henry Fonda, for whom
Elizabeth Taylor had her face
lifted in *Ash Wednesday*

The Nippon-in-the-Bud Award:
To the current rash of Hong
Kong Flu films

**The Dance of the Seven Scott
Tissues Award:**
*(to the most lewd and com-
pletely unwarranted dancing
scene)*
Rudolph Nureyev for his unexceptional Royal Canadian
Air Force exercises in *I Am
a Dancer*

**The Cheap-at-Half-the-Price
Award:**
*(to the worst bargain in a
film)*
The Exorcist, in which the devil
gets far more than his due

The Exhausted Udder:
*(in recognition of attempts
to milk every penny possible
from a marketable idea)*
Anthony Quinn, *The Don Is
Dead*

The Hey-Boswell-Did-You-Get-That-One-Down Award:
(to that film whose dialogue was, when not monosyllabic, subhuman)
Bluce Ree, *Enter the Dragon*

The Dark Fedora:
(this citation reveals the tricky conclusion)
The Sting, which you will enjoy even less now that you know that Redford doesn't really double-cross Newman, that they don't really shoot each other, and of course, that they do "get away with it"

The Piltdown Mandible:
(to the most obviously and unabashedly spurious scientific phenomenon)
Chariots of the Gods (Could this film possibly be the remnant of a civilization vastly inferior to our own?)

The Uncrossed Heart:
(to the least promising young performer)
Linda Blair, *The Exorcist,* who turned a few heads around

The Life-of-the-Party Award:
(to that performer who most thoroughly degrades himself in order to pull in the paycheck)
The entire cast of *The Grande Bouffe,* who proved that what goes down must come up

The Bosley:
(to that critic who consistently explores the farthest limits of bad taste)
Penelope Gilliatt, who might have at least flipped a coin to decide whether or not she liked *The Great Gatsby,* if she saw *The Great Gatsby,* before she wrote about it—if she was writing about it—in *The New Yorker*

The Kill-It-Before-It-Spreads Citation:
(designed to cripple the career of a fledgling performer)
Keith Carradine and Shelley Duval, *Thieves Like Us*

The Thanks-for-Nothing Award:
(to that Hollywood performer who has blessedly not made a film this year)
To two-time Worst Actress Ali MacGraw, who was busy this year two-timing somewhere else

The Cellophane Figleaf:
(for the most outstanding display of anemic false modesty)
Julie Christie, *Don't Look Now,* who couldn't see to brazen her buff charms until this blockbuster came along

The Merino Award:
(to that figure who has done the most to enhance the fame and glory of the merino)
To that Merican actor and performer *ordinaire* Mario Moreno, who has announced plans to reappear as Cantinflas on same screen in the near future

Best Argument for Vivisection:
Jonathan Livingston Seagull

1974

Ten Worst Movies:
Lenny
S*P*Y*S
Harry and Tonto
Airport 1975
Blazing Saddles

The Night Porter
The Trial of Billy Jack
Murder on the Orient Express
Daisy Miller
The Front Page

Kirk Douglas Award for Worst Actor:
Burt Reynolds, *The Longest Yard*

Natalie Wood Award for Worst Actress:
Julie Andrews, *The Tamarind Seed*

Worst Supporting Actor:
Gene Wilder, *The Little Prince*

Worst Supporting Actress:
Carol Burnett, *The Front Page*

Worst Performance by a Cast in Toto:
Murder on the Orient Express

The Exhausted Udder Award:
(in recognition of attempts to milk every penny possible from a marketable idea)
To the producers of *Our Time*; *Macon County Line*; *The Lords of Flatbush*; and *Buster and Billie* for trying to eke piquancy from an era as colorless as the tag on a pair of overlaundered pedal pushers

H. J. Heinz Laurel Clot:
(to the film that makes most extensive use of the company's various vegetable derivatives)
Warhol's Frankenstein

Merino Award:
(to that figure who has done the most to enhance the fame and glory of the merino)
Maureen O. McGovern, the curtailment of whose adipose warbling in *The Poseidon Adventure* and now *The Towering Inferno*

excuses in part the effects of the disasters that follow

Best Argument for Vivisection:
Tonto of *Harry and Tonto*

The Victor Mature Award:
(In memory of Victor Mature, who was heard to ask Barabbas in The Robe, "Is this your first crucifixion?," this award is given for the most embarrassing line of dialogue)
George Kennedy's astute remark in *Earthquake*, "Earthquakes bring out the worst in people."

The Ok-Doc-Break-the-Arm-Again Award:
(for the most flagrant example of miscasting)
Dean Martin as an intelligent lawyer in *Mr. Ricco*

The Life-of-the-Party Award:
(to that performer who most thoroughly degrades himself in order to keep the wolf from the door)
Harvey Korman, who showed us in *Blazing Saddles* what seven lean years of being straight man to Carol Burnett can do to a guy

The Remember-You-Saw-It-Here-First Award:
Warren Beatty, that pudgy, self-preening angel of banality, whose—for lack of a better word—performance in an upcoming film biography of John Reed will be —for lack of a worse word —execrable

The Curse-of-the-Living-Corpse Award:
Gloria Swanson, an actress only slightly older than the mountains she is imperiled above in *Airport '75*

The Bosley:
(to that film critic whose work consistently explores the farthest limits of bad taste)
Pat Mitchell, whose televised hysterics can fortunately be shut off at the flick of a dial

The Kill-It-Before-It-Spreads Citation:
(designed to cripple the career of a fledgling performer)
Lee Strasberg, who unfortunately has already infected with bad acting habits more than just his portion of the screen in Godfather Part II

The Dark Fedora:
(this citation reveals the tricky conclusion of a film)
Chinatown, in which Faye Dunaway is shot after confessing that her father actually sired her illegitimate daughter

The Please-Don't-Put-Us-Through-DeMille Award:
That's Entertainment, which wasn't

1975

Ten Worst Movies:
Barry Lyndon
Tommy
At Long Last Love
The Other Side of the Mountain
The Hindenburg
Day of the Locust
Story of O
Mahogany
Shampoo
Once Is Not Enough

Kirk Douglas Award for Worst Actor:
Ryan O'Neal, Barry Lyndon

Natalie Wood Award for Worst Actress:
Diana Ross, Mahogany

Worst Supporting Actor:
Burgess Meredith, Day of the Locust

Worst Supporting Actress:
Madeline Kahn, Sherlock Holmes' Smarter Brother and At Long Last Love

The We-Heard-You-the-First-Time Award:
Daughters, Daughters

The Please-Don't-Put-Us-Through-DeMille Award:
(to the movie which best embodies the pretensions, extravagances and blundering ineffectiveness of the Screen Spectacular)
John Huston, The Man Who Would Be King

The Ayn Rand Award:
(to the writer whose bad books made worse movies)
Jacqueline Susann, Once Is Not Enough

The Tin Pan
(to the most thoroughly obnoxious movie song)
"Do You Know Where You're Going?" Mahogany

Worst Performance by a Cast in Toto:
Let's Do It Again

The Bratwurst Award:
(to that juvenile actor or actress who most convincingly presents a strong argument for compulsory education)
Jodie Foster, Taxi Driver

The Best Argument for Reactivating Ellis Island:
Sweet Movie

The Curse-of-the-Living-Corpse Award:
The limping digits of Arthur Rubinstein for their dis-

tinctly separate perform-
ances in *Love of Life*

The Bosley:
*(to that film critic whose
journalism most consist-
ently challenges the American ideal of a free press)*

John Simon, whose continu-
ance in the critical cult
constitutes the most shocking misuse of trees for
paper pulp since the death
of Hedda Hopper

**The Strongest Argument for
Laxer Divorce Laws:**

Paul Newman and Joanne
Woodward, who made heavy
water of *Drowning Pool*

**The Thanks-for-Nothing
Award:**
*(to that Hollywood person-
ality who has blessedly not
made a motion picture this
year)*

Mel Brooks

**The Wrong-Way Corrigan
Memorial Flight Jacket:**
(for the worst direction)

Stephen Spielberg, *Jaws*, for
turning *Moby Dick* into *King
Kong* and attempting to pass
this fish story off as great
cinematic art

**Cheap-at-Half-the-Price
Award:**
*(for the worst bargain in a
film)*

Roger Corman and anyone
else responsible for *Tidal
Wave*, for splicing fifteen
minutes of Lorne Green into
Japanese footage of model
cities annihilated by whirl-
pool baths

The Handlin Oscar:
*(to the film that has most
distorted the course of
history)*

The Wind and the Lion, which
was actually quite accurate
if you can accept Sean
Connery as a North African
chieftain and Candice
Bergen as having a mental
edge over a five-year-old
sufficient to be a governess

**The Hey-Boswell-Did-You-Get-
That-One-Down Award:**
*(to the film with the worst
dialogue)*

Cooley High which made the
illiterate rumblings in
American Graffiti look like
crackling repartee at the
Algonquin table

**The Women-and-Children-
First-Lt.-Calley Award:**
*(designed to honor violence
above and beyond the call
of duty)*

Sam Peckinpah, *Killer Elite*

The Exhausted Udder:
*(in recognition of attempts
to milk every penny possible
from a marketable idea)*

Once Is Not Enough

**The Not-Tonight-I-Have-a-
Headache Award:**
*(to that movie which gave
us the best excuse to turn
in early)*

Walt Disney Studios, *One of
Our Dinosaurs Is Missing*

**The Charles Manson Memorial
Scalpel:**
*(to the film which shows the
clumsiest job of cutting)*

Shoot It Black, Shoot It Blue

The Lukewarm-Bathos Award:
*(to that scene in a movie
whose stilted sentimentality
succeeds in watering the
eyes only by irritating them)*

Little Bryan's deathbed scene
in *Barry Lyndon*

The Roscoe:
(to that performer who has most unflaggingly exhibited a complete lack of talent, perception, screen presence and intelligence)
Karen Black, who crawls the gamut of human emotions in *Day of the Locust* and *Nashville*

The Arrested-Development Oblation:
(to that adult actor who has displayed the lowest level of maturity on or off the screen)
Jerry Lewis, as always

Best Argument for Vivisection: *Benji*

The Dark Fedora:
(this award serves to save the unsuspecting public from suffering through two hours of cinematic waste for the cheap thrill of uncovering the ingenious conclusion to a contrived and facile story line)
Farewell, My Lovely, which you will enjoy even less now that you know that the long-lost girl has been married to the crooked gangster all along, and gets shot at the end by the pathetic ex-boxer who loved her

The Ok-Doc-Break-the-Arm-Again Award:
(to the most flagrant example of miscasting)
Man Who Would Be King, for casting Sean Connery as anyone but *James Bond*

The Life-of-the-Party Award:
(to that screen performer who most thoroughly demeans himself in order to pull in the paycheck, a hand-somely tooled lampshade goes to)
Julie Christie, that formerly elegant and sophisticated actress, whose understated sensitive appeal to Warren Beatty, "Oh, God, let me suck it," firmly ensconces her in the ranks of the cheap

The Tar Baby:
(in recognition of Hollywood's Second Reconstruction program of employing and exploiting former athletes and would-be welfare recipients)
The producers of *Mandingo*

The Piltdown Mandible:
(to the most obviously and unabashedly spurious scientific phenomenon)
The Land That Time Forgot for its Pleistocene backdrops and plasticene dinosaurs

The If Only Film Were Bio-degradable Citation:
Richard Lester, for recycling the Three Stooges into *The Four Musketeers*

The Victor Mature Memorial Award:
(to the most embarrassing line of dialogue)
Gable and Lombard, for the screen great's insouciant comment following the incendiary demise of his beloved in a plane crash, as he gazes fondly over the twisted wreckage: "She should have taken the train."

The Harvard Independent Award:
(to that film noted for its ignominious failure as both art and politics)
Swept Away

The Merino Award:
(to that figure who has done
the most to enhance the
fame and glory of the
merino)
Marino Berenson, whose name
doesn't even come close to
sounding like merino, for
her threadbare performance
in *Barry Lyndon*

1976

Ten Worst Movies:
A Star Is Born
The Enforcer
Murder By Death
Slapshot
The Omen
Lipstick
Mikey and Nicky
The Missouri Breaks
Carwash
King Kong
Kirk Douglas Award for Worst Actor:
Clint Eastwood in his third
go-round as Dirty Harry
Callahan
Natalie Wood for Worst Actress:
Barbra Streisand, *A Star Is Born* (Her performances
should delight those who
can't tell the difference
between Edie Gormé and
Patti Smith.)
The Burgess Meredith Award for Worst Supporting Actor:
Chris Saradon, *Lipstick*
The Ava Gardner Award for Worst Supporting Actress:
Jodie Foster, *Bugsy Malone*
The Radioactive-Velveeta Award:
(for the most tedious treat-
ment of a tawdry topic)

Survive, the sleazy Mexican
production of the story of a
stranded soccer team that
turns to cannibalism. It's too
bad the scriptwriter wasn't
around when the boys got
hungry.
The Liquid-Paper-Correction-Fluid Award:
Diana Ross for her portrayal
of a fashion model in
Sparkle. We could have
sworn the woman used to
be white.
The Volvo Trophy:
Liv Ullmann in *Face to Face* as
the Swedish import that
always breaks down
The Arrested Development Oblation:
(to that adult actor who has
displayed the lowest level
of maturity on or off the
screen)
Jerry Lewis, as always
The Fertilized Tombstone:
Gable and Lombard and *W. C.
Fields and Me* for making
the wildflowers on their
subjects' graves grow ever
more quickly
The Roscoe Award:
(to that screen performer
who has demonstrated a
complete absence of qualities even resembling talent,
intelligence and appeal)
Margaux Hemingway, *Lipstick*
The Out-to-Pasteur Award:
(to the worst science fiction
movie)
*Jonah, Who Will be 25 in the
Year 2000.* With any luck,
World War III will wipe out
the brat before then
The Bonavena Oscar:
Rocky, for heavyweight box-
officing

The Golden Glob:
(for the pornographic movie that limps along most lamely)
How Funny Can Sex Be?
The You're-Getting-Old-and-Fat-and-Generally-Unappetizing Award:
Elizabeth Taylor

The Merino Award:
(to that figure who has done the most to enhance the fame and glory of the merino)
Shearings, a horror flick about radioactive sheep in the Mojave Desert

12. COMPARISON OF MAJOR AWARDS 1967-76

These charts provide convenient comparisons of the major annual film awards, including the prizes of the British Society of Film and Television Arts, which are England's version of the Oscars. Because the various associations listed below do not confer prizes in exactly the same categories, the following qualifications should be kept in mind. The Best Script Prize for the Academy Awards is divided into Best Adaptation and Best Original. The Best Film Category for the National Board of Review is divided into Best English-Language and Best Foreign-Language categories. The Best Film and Acting awards for the Golden Globes are divided into Dramatic and Musical/Comedy. Because a film may or may not be released in England and the United States during the same year, a movie may be eligible for an Academy Award one year and a British Award the next.

1967	Best Film	Best Director	Best Actor
Academy Awards	*In the Heat of the Night*	Mike Nichols, *The Graduate*	Rod Steiger, *In the Heat of the Night*
National Society of Film Critics	*Persona*	Ingmar Bergman, *Persona*	Rod Steiger, *In the Heat of the Night*
New York Film Critics	*In the Heat of the Night*	Mike Nichols, *The Graduate*	Rod Steiger, *In the Heat of the Night*
National Board of Review	*Far from the Madding Crowd; Elvira Madigan*	Richard Brooks, *In Cold Blood*	Peter Finch, *Far from the Madding Crowd*
Golden Globes	*In the Heat of the Night; The Graduate*	Mike Nichols, *The Graduate*	Rod Steiger, *In the Heat of the Night,* and Richard Harris, *Camelot*
British Academy	*A Man for All Seasons*		British: Paul Scofield, *Man for All Seasons.* Foreign: Rod Steiger, *In the Heat of the Night*

Best Actress	Best Sup. Actor	Best Sup. Actress	Best Script
Katharine Hepburn, *Guess Who's Coming to Dinner*	George Kennedy, *Cool Hand Luke*	Estelle Parsons, *Bonnie and Clyde*	S. Silliphant, *In the Heat of the Night;* William Rose, *Guess Who's Coming to Dinner*
Bibi Andersson, *Persona*	Gene Hackman, *Bonnie and Clyde*	Marjorie Rhodes, *The Family Way*	David Newman and Robert Benton, *Bonnie and Clyde*
Edith Evans, *The Whisperers*	(No award)	(No award)	David Newman and Robert Benton, *Bonnie and Clyde*
Edith Evans, *The Whisperers*	Paul Ford, *The Comedians*	Marjorie Rhodes, *The Family Way*	(No award in this category)
Edith Evans, *The Whisperers,* and Anne Bancroft, *The Graduate*	Richard Attenborough, *Doctor Dolittle*	Carol Channing, *Thoroughly Modern Millie*	Stirling Silliphant, *In the Heat of the Night*
British: Edith Evans, *The Whisperers.* Foreign: Anouk Aimée, *A Man and A Woman*	(No award)	(No award)	British: Robert Bolt, *A Man for All Seasons*

1968	Best Film	Best Director	Best Actor
Academy Awards	*Oliver!*	Carol Reed, *Oliver!*	Cliff Robertson, *Charly*
National Society of Film Critics	*Shame*	Ingmar Bergman, *Shame; Hour of the Wolf*	Per Oscarsson, *Hunger*
New York Film Critics	*The Lion In Winter*	Paul Newman, *Rachel, Rachel*	Alan Arkin, *The Heart is a Lonely Hunter*
National Board of Review	*The Shoes of the Fisherman; War and Peace*	Franco Zeffirelli, *Romeo and Juliet*	Cliff Robertson, *Charly*
Golden Globes	*The Lion In Winter; Oliver!*	Paul Newman, *Rachel, Rachel*	Peter O'Toole, *Lion in Winter;* Ron Moody, *Oliver!*
British Academy	*The Graduate*	Mike Nichols, *The Graduate*	Spencer Tracy, *Guess Who's Coming to Dinner*

Best Actress	Best Sup. Actor	Best Sup. Actress	Best Script
K. Hepburn, *The Lion in Winter*; B. Streisand, *Funny Girl*	Jack Albertson, *The Subject Was Roses*	Ruth Gordon, *Rosemary's Baby*	James Goldman, *Lion in Winter*; Mel Brooks, *The Producers*
Liv Ullmann, *Shame*	Seymour Cassel, *Faces*	Billie Whitelaw, *Charlie Bubbles*	John Cassavetes, *Faces*
Joanne Woodward, *Rachel, Rachel*	*(No award)*	*(No award)*	Lorenzo Semple, Jr., *Pretty Poison*
Liv Ullmann; *Hour of the Wolf*	Leo McKern, *The Shoes of the Fisherman*	Virginia Maskell, *Interlude*	*(No awards in this category)*
J. Woodward, *Rachel, Rachel*; B. Streisand, *Funny Girl*	Daniel Massey, *Star!*	Ruth Gordon, *Rosemary's Baby*	Stirling Silliphant, *Charly*
K. Hepburn, *Guess Who's . . .* and *The Lion in Winter*	Ian Holm, *The Bofors Gun*	Billie Whitelaw, *Charlie Bubbles; Twisted Nerve*	Calder Willingham and Buck Henry, *The Graduate*

1969	Best Film	Best Director	Best Actor
Academy Awards	*Midnight Cowboy*	John Schlesinger, *Midnight Cowboy*	John Wayne, *True Grit*
National Society of Film Critics	*Z*	François Truffaut, *Stolen Kisses*	Jon Voight, *Midnight Cowboy*
New York Film Critics	*Z*	Costa-Gavras, *Z*	Jon Voight, *Midnight Cowboy*
National Board of Review	*They Shoot Horses, Don't They?* and *Shame*	Alfred Hitchcock, *Topaz*	Peter O'Toole, *Goodbye, Mr. Chips*
Golden Globes	*Anne of the 1000 Days; Oh, What a Lovely War!*	Charles Jarrott, *Anne of the 1000 Days*	John Wayne, *True Grit*; Peter O'Toole, *Goodbye, Mr. Chips*
British Academy	*Midnight Cowboy*	John Schlesinger, *Midnight Cowboy*	Dustin Hoffman, *Midnight Cowboy*; *John and Mary*

Best Actress	Best Sup. Actor	Best Sup. Actress	Best Script
Maggie Smith, *The Prime of Miss Jean Brodie*	Gig Young, *They Shoot Horses, Don't They?*	Goldie Hawn, *Cactus Flower*	Waldo Salt, *Midnight Cowboy;* William Goldman, *Butch Cassidy* ...
Vanessa Redgrave, *The Loves of Isadora*	Jack Nicholson, *Easy Rider*	Sian Phillips, *Goodbye, Mr. Chips*	Paul Mazursky and Larry Tucker, *Bob & Carol & Ted & Alice*
Jane Fonda, *They Shoot Horses, Don't They?*	Jack Nicholson, *Easy Rider*	Dyan Cannon, *Bob & Carol & Ted & Alice*	Mazursky and Tucker, *Bob & Carol & Ted & Alice*
Geraldine Page, *Trilogy*	Philippe Noiret, *Topaz*	Pamela Franklin, *The Prime of Miss Jean Brodie*	(No awards in this category)
Genevieve Bujold, *Anne of the 1000 Days;* Patty Duke, *Me Natalie*	Gig Young, *They Shoot Horses, Don't They?*	Goldie Hawn, *Cactus Flower*	Bridget Boland and John Hale, *Anne of the 1000 Days*
Maggie Smith, *The Prime of Miss Jean Brodie*	Laurence Olivier, *Oh, What a Lovely War!*	Celia Johnson, *The Prime of Miss Jean Brodie*	Waldo Salt, *Midnight Cowboy*

1970	Best Film	Best Director	Best Actor
Academy Awards	*Patton*	Franklin J. Schaffner, *Patton*	George C. Scott, *Patton*
National Society of Film Critics	*M*A*S*H*	Ingmar Bergman, *The Passion of Anna*	George C. Scott, *Patton*
New York Film Critics	*Five Easy Pieces*	Bob Rafelson, *Five Easy Pieces*	George C. Scott, *Patton,*
National Board of Review	*Patton; The Wild Child*	François Truffaut, *The Wild Child*	George C. Scott, *Patton*
Golden Globes	*Love Story; M*A*S*H*	Arthur Hiller, *Love Story*	George C. Scott, *Patton;* Albert Finney, *Scrooge*
British Academy	*Butch Cassidy and the Sundance Kid*	George Roy Hill, *Butch Cassidy ...*	R. Redford, *Butch Cassidy; Downhill Racer;* and *Tell Them Willie Boy Is Here*

Best Actress	Best Sup. Actor	Best Sup. Actress	Best Script
Glenda Jackson, *Women in Love*	John Mills, *Ryan's Daughter*	Helen Hayes, *Airport*	Ring Lardner, Jr., *M*A*S*H*; F. F. Coppola and Edmund H. North, *Patton*
Glenda Jackson, *Women in Love*	Chief Dan George, *Little Big Man*	Lois Smith, *Five Easy Pieces*	Eric Rohmer, *My Night at Maud's*
Glenda Jackson, *Women in Love*	Chief Dan George, *Little Big Man*	Karen Black, *Five Easy Pieces*	Eric Rohmer, *My Night at Maud's*
Glenda Jackson, *Women in Love*	Frank Langella, *Diary of a Mad Housewife; and 12 Chairs*	Karen Black, *Five Easy Pieces*	*(No award in this category)*
Ali MacGraw, *Love Story;* Carrie Snodgress, *Diary of a Mad Housewife*	John Mills, *Ryan's Daughter*	Karen Black, *Five Easy Pieces;* Maureen Stapleton, *Airport*	Erich Segal, *Love Story*
Katharine Ross, *Butch Cassidy* and *Tell Them Willie Boy . . .*	Colin Welland, *Kes*	Susannah York, *They Shoot Horses, Don't They?*	William Goldman, *Butch Cassidy*

1971	Best Film	Best Director	Best Actor
Academy Awards	*The French Connection*	William Friedkin, *The French Connection*	Gene Hackman, *The French Connection*
National Society of Film Critics	*Claire's Knee*	Bernardo Bertolucci, *The Conformist*	Peter Finch, *Sunday Bloody Sunday*
New York Film Critics	*A Clockwork Orange*	Stanley Kubrick, *A Clockwork Orange*	Gene Hackman, *The French Connection*.
National Board of Review	*Macbeth; Claire's Knee*	Stanley Kubrick, *A Clockwork Orange*	Gene Hackman, *The French Connection*
Golden Globes	*The French Connection; Fiddler on the Roof*	William Friedkin, *The French Connection*	Gene Hackman, *The French Connection;* Topol, *Fiddler on the Roof*
British Academy	*Sunday Bloody Sunday*	John Schlesinger, *Sunday Bloody Sunday*	Peter Finch, *Sunday Bloody Sunday*

Best Actress	Best Sup. Actor	Best Sup. Actress	Best Script
Jane Fonda, *Klute*	Ben Johnson, *The Last Picture Show*	Cloris Leachman, *The Last Picture Show*	Ernest Tidyman, *The French Connection;* Paddy Chayefsky, *The Hospital*
Jane Fonda, *Klute*	Bruce Dern, *Drive, He Said*	Ellen Burstyn, *The Last Picture Show*	Penelope Gilliatt, *Sunday Bloody Sunday*
Jane Fonda, *Klute*	Ben Johnson, *The Last Picture Show*	Ellen Burstyn, *The Last Picture Show*	tie betw. P. Gilliatt, *Sunday Bloody Sunday* and L. McMurtry, *Last Picture Show*
Irene Papas, *The Trojan Women*	Ben Johnson, *The Last Picture Show*	Cloris Leachman, *The Last Picture Show*	*(No award in this category)*
Jane Fonda, *Klute;* Twiggy, *The Boy Friend*	Ben Johnson, *The Last Picture Show*	Ann-Margret, *Carnal Knowledge*	Paddy Chayefsky, *The Hospital*
Glenda Jackson, *Sunday Bloody Sunday*	Edward Fox, *The Go-Between*	Margaret Leighton, *The Go-Between*	Harold Pinter, *The Go-Between*

1972	Best Film	Best Director	Best Actor
Academy Awards	*The Godfather*	Bob Fosse, *Cabaret*	Marlon Brando, *The Godfather*
National Society of Film Critics	*The Discreet Charm of the Bourgeoisie*	Luis Buñuel, *The Discreet Charm ...*	Al Pacino, *The Godfather*
New York Film Critics	*Cries and Whispers*	Ingmar Bergman, *Cries and Whispers*	Laurence Olivier, *Sleuth*
National Board of Review	*Cabaret; The Sorrow and the Pity*	Bob Fosse, *Cabaret*	Peter O'Toole, *Ruling Class* and *Man of La Mancha*
Golden Globes	*The Godfather; Cabaret*	Francis Ford Coppola, *The Godfather*	Marlon Brando, *The Godfather;* Jack Lemmon, *Avanti!*
British Academy	*Cabaret*	Bob Fosse, *Cabaret*	Gene Hackman, *The French Connection*

Best Actress	Best Sup. Actor	Best Sup. Actress	Best Script
Liza Minnelli, *Cabaret*	Joel Grey, *Cabaret*	Eileen Heckart, *Butterflies Are Free*	Mario Puzo, F. F. Coppola, *The Godfather*; Jeremy Larner, *The Candidate*
Cicely Tyson, *Sounder*	Joel Grey, *Cabaret*, and Eddie Albert, *Heartbreak Kid*	Jeannie Berlin, *Heartbreak Kid*	Ingmar Bergman, *Cries and Whispers*
Liv Ullmann, *Cries and Whispers*	Robert Duvall, *The Godfather*	Jeannie Berlin, *Heartbreak Kid*	Ingmar Bergman, *Cries and Whispers*
Cicely Tyson, *Sounder*	Joel Grey, *Cabaret*, and Al Pacino, *The Godfather*	Marisa Berenson, *Cabaret*	*(No award in this category)*
Liv Ullmann, *The Emigrants*; Liza Minnelli, *Cabaret*	Joel Grey, *Cabaret*	Shelley Winters, *The Poseidon Adventure*	Mario Puzo, F. F. Coppola, *The Godfather*
Liza Minnelli, *Cabaret*	Ben Johnson, *The Last Picture Show*	Cloris Leachman, *The Last Picture Show*	Tie between P. Bogdanovich, L. McMurtry, *The Last Picture Show*, and P. Chayefsky, *The Hosp.*

1973	Best Film	Best Director	Best Actor
Academy Awards	*The Sting*	George Roy Hill, *The Sting*	Jack Lemmon, *Save the Tiger*
National Society of Film Critics	*Day for Night*	François Truffaut, *Day for Night*	Marlon Brando, *Last Tango in Paris*
New York Film Critics	*Day for Night*	François Truffaut, *Day for Night*	Marlon Prando, *Last Tango in Paris*
National Board of Review	*The Sting; Cries and Whispers*	Ingmar Bergman, *Cries and Whispers*	Al Pacino, *Serpico;* Robert Ryan, *The Iceman Cometh*
Golden Globes	*The Exorcist; American Graffiti*	William Friedkin, *The Exorcist*	Al Pacino, *Serpico;* George Segal, *A Touch of Class*
British Academy	*Day for Night*	François Truffaut, *Day for Night*	Walter Matthau, *Pete 'n' Tillie,* and *Charley Varrick*

Best Actress	Best Sup. Actor	Best Sup. Actress	Best Script
Glenda Jackson, *A Touch of Class*	John Houseman, *The Paper Chase*	Tatum O'Neal, *Paper Moon*	William Blatty, *T Exorcist;* David S. Ward, *The Sting*
Liv Ullmann, *The New Land*	Robert De Niro, *Mean Streets*	Valentina Cortese, *Day for Night*	George Lucas, Gloria Katz, William Huyck, *American Graffiti*
Joanne Woodward, *Summer Wishes, Winter Dreams*	Robert De Niro, *Bang the Drum Slowly*	Valentina Cortese, *Day for Night*	George Lucas, Gloria Katz, William Huyck, *American Graffiti*
Liv Ullmann, *The New Land*	John Houseman, *The Paper Chase*	Sylvia Sidney, *Summer Wishes, Winter Dreams*	*(No award in this category)*
Marsha Mason, *Cinderella Liberty;* Glenda Jackson, *A Touch of Class*	John Houseman, *The Paper Chase*	Linda Blair, *The Exorcist*	William Blatty, *The Exorcist*
Stephane Audran, *Discreet Charm . . . ,* and *Juste avant la nuit*	Arthur Lowe, *O Lucky Man!*	Valentina Cortese, *Day for Night*	Luis Buñuel, Jean-Claude Carrière, *The Discreet Charm . . .*

1974	Best Film	Best Director	Best Actor
Academy Awards	*Godfather II*	Francis Ford Coppola, *Godfather II*	Art Carney, *Harry and Tonto*
National Society of Film Critics	*Scenes from a Marriage*	Francis Ford Coppola, *Godfather II*	Jack Nicholson, *Chinatown* and *The Last Detail*
New York Film Critics	*Amarcord*	Federico Fellini, *Amarcord*	Jack Nicholson, *Chinatown*
National Board of Review	*The Conversation; Amarcord*	Francis Ford Coppola, *The Conversation*	Gene Hackman, *The Conversation*
Golden Globes	*Chinatown; The Longest Yard*	Roman Polanski, *Chinatown*	Jack Nicholson, *Chinatown;* Art Carney, *Harry and Tonto*
British Academy	*Lacombe, Lucien*	Roman Polanski, *Chinatown*	Jack Nicholson, *Chinatown* and *The Last Detail*

Best Actress	Best Sup. Actor	Best Sup. Actress	Best Script
Ellen Burstyn, *Alice Doesn't Live Here Anymore*	Robert De Niro, *Godfather II*	Ingrid Bergman, *Murder on the Orient Express*	F. F. Coppola and Mario Puzo, *Godfather II*; Robert Towne, *Chinatown*
Liv Ullmann, *Scenes from a Marriage*	Holger Löwenadler, *Lacombe, Lucien*	Bibi Andersson, *Scenes from a Marriage*	Ingmar Bergman, *Scenes from a Marriage*
Liv Ullmann, *Scenes from a Marriage*	Charles Boyer, *Stavisky*	Valerie Perrine, *Lenny*	Ingmar Bergman, *Scenes from a Marriage*
Gena Rowlands, *A Woman Under the Influence*	Holger Löwenadler, *Lacombe, Lucien*	Valerie Perrine, *Lenny*	*(No awards in this category)*
G. Rowlands, *A Woman Under the Influence*; R. Welch, *The Three Musketeers*	Fred Astaire, *The Towering Inferno*	Karen Black, *The Great Gatsby*	Robert Towne, *Chinatown*
Joanne Woodward, *Summer Wishes, Winter Dreams*	John Gielgud, *Murder on the Orient Express*	Ingrid Bergman, *Murder on the Orient Express*	Robert Towne, *Chinatown*

1975	Best Film	Best Director	Best Actor
Academy Awards	One Flew Over The Cuckoo's Nest	Milos Forman, Cuckoo's Nest	Jack Nicholson, Cuckoo's Nest
National Society of Film Critics	Nashville	Robert Altman, Nashville	Jack Nicholson, Cuckoo's Nest
New York Film Critics	Nashville	Robert Altman, Nashville	Jack Nicholson, Cuckoo's Nest
National Board of Review	Nashville and Barry Lyndon; Story of Adele H.	R. Altman, Nashville, and S. Kubrick, Barry Lyndon	Jack Nicholson, Cuckoo's Nest
Golden Globes	Cuckoo's Nest; The Sunshine Boys	Milos Foreman, Cuckoo's Nest	J. Nicholson, Cuckoo's Nest; W. Matthau, Sunshine Boys
British Academy	Alice Doesn't Live Here Anymore	Stanley Kubrick, Barry Lyndon	Al Pacino, Godfather II and Dog Day Afternoon

Best Actress	Best Sup. Actor	Best Sup. Actress	Best Script
Louise Fletcher, *Cuckoo's Nest*	George Burns, *Sunshine Boys*	Lee Grant, *Shampoo*	L. Hauben, Bo Goldman, *Cuckoo's Nest;* F. Pierson, *Dog Day Afternoon*
Isabelle Adjani, *Story of Adele H.*	Henry Gibson, *Nashville*	Lily Tomlin, *Nashville*	Robert Towne, Warren Beatty, *Shampoo*
Isabelle Adjani, *Story of Adele H.*	Alan Arkin, *Hearts of the West*	Lily Tomlin, *Nashville*	François Truffaut, Jean Gruault, Suzanne Shiffman, *Story of Adele H.*
Isabelle Adjani, *Story of Adele H.*	Charles Durning, *Dog Day Afternoon*	Ronee Blakley, *Nashville*	*(No awards in this category)*
L. Fletcher, *Cuckoo's Nest;* Ann-Margret, *Tommy*	Richard Benjamin, *Sunshine Boys*	Brenda Vaccaro, *Once Is Not Enough*	Laurence Hauben, Bo Goldman, *Cuckoo's Nest*
Ellen Burstyn, *Alice Doesn't Live Here Anymore*	Fred Astaire, *Towering Inferno*	Diane Ladd, *Alice Doesn't Live Here Anymore*	Robert Getchell, *Alice Doesn't Live Here Anymore*

1976	Best Film	Best Director	Best Actor
Academy Awards	*Rocky*	John G. Avildsen, *Rocky*	Peter Finch, *Network*
National Society of Film Critics	*All the President's Men*	Martin Scorsese, *Taxi Driver*	Robert De Niro, *Taxi Driver*
New York Film Critics	*All the President's Men*	Allan Pakula, *All the President's Men*	Robert De Niro, *Taxi Driver*
National Board of Review	*All the President's Men; The Marquise of O*	Alan Pakula, *All the President's Men*	David Carradine, *Bound For Glory*
Golden Globes	*Rocky; A Star Is Born*	Sidney Lumet, *Network*	Peter Finch, *Network*, and Kris Kristoferson, *A Star Is Born*
British Academy	*One Flew Over the Cuckoo's Nest*	Milos Forman, *Cuckoo's Nest*	Jack Nicholson, *Cuckoo's Nest*

Best Actress	Best Sup. Actor	Best Sup. Actress	Best Script
Faye Dunaway, *Network*	Jason Robards, *All the President's Men*	Beatrice Straight, *Network*	William Goldman, *All the President's Men;* Paddy Chayefsky, *Network*
Sissy Spacek, *Carrie*	Jason Robards, *All the President's Men*	Jodie Foster, *Taxi Driver*	Alain Tanner and John Berger, *Jonah, Who Will Be 25 in the Year 2000*
Liv Ullmann, *Face to Face*	Jason Robards, *All the President's Men*	Talia Shire, *Rocky*	Paddy Chayefsky, *Network*
Liv Ullmann, *Face to Face*	Jason Robards, *All the President's Men*	Talia Shire, *Rocky*	*(No awards in this category)*
Faye Dunaway, *Network;* Barbra Streisand, *A Star Is Born*	Laurence Olivier, *Marathon Man*	Katharine Ross, *Voyage of the Damned*	Paddy Chayefsky, *Network*
Louise Fletcher, *Cuckoo's Nest*	Brad Dourif, *Cuckoo's Nest*	Jodie Foster, *Taxi Driver* and *Bugsy Malone*	Alan Parker, *Bugsy Malone*

II. THE "TEN BEST" LISTS

1. DIRECTORS' CHOICES (THE 1952 BELGIAN SURVEY) AND CRITICS' CHOICES (THE 1952, 1962 AND 1972 SIGHT AND SOUND SURVEYS)

In 1952 the committee of the *Festival Mondial du Film et des Beaux Arts de Belgique* asked more than a hundred film personalities (mainly directors) to select the Ten Best films of all time. Sixty-three answers were received: twenty-six from France; ten from England; ten from the United States; seven from Italy; six from Germany; one each from Austria, Denmark, Spain and Brazil; and none from India, Japan, China or Russia. Several directors, like Chaplin, Stroheim, Clair, Cocteau, Hitchcock and Olivier, did not wish to answer the questionnaire.

The committee asked each director to select *his own* favorites and not the films he thought would be preferred by academic orthodoxy. The results are, of course, interesting: who would have thought Dreyer to be so fond of *The Petrified Forest*, or Buñuel of *Portrait of Jennie*? The absence of Renoir's *Rules of the Game* was thought unusual, as were the generally low ratings for Griffith, Vigo and Ford. Many directors voted for their own films: Cecil B. DeMille chose four of his own movies (*The Ten Commandments, King of Kings, The Sign of the Cross, Samson and Delilah*); Buñuel gave his *L'Age d'Or* a ninth-place vote; and Vidor gave his *Big Parade* fourth place.

As a sequel to the 1952 Belgian survey in which approximately a hundred film directors voted for the Ten Best films of all time, *Sight and Sound* (the highly respected magazine published by the British Film Institute) conducted a survey in which critics were given their chance to select the Ten Best films. Eighty-five critics from Britain, France, the United States, Germany, Denmark, Sweden, Belgium, Czechoslovakia and Yugoslavia were asked; sixty-three answered. Surprisingly enough, the directors and the critics agreed on their top four choices, although not on the order of those choices.

Although most of the critics had several reservations about such a poll (their "favorite" films were not always the "best" films; the limitations of only listing ten films were barbarous; the whole concept of the survey was ridiculous, etc.) the survey proved so interesting that it was repeated both in 1962 and 1972.

Between 1952 and 1962, cinema saw the rise of the French New Wave, the discovery of Japanese film, the growth of Italian cinema, as well as growing cinemas in Eastern Europe and Latin America. Some of these changes were reflected in the 1962 survey: only four of the Ten Best films in the 1952 poll remained in the top ten in 1962. The poll revealed several surprises: (1) the rise of *Citizen Kane* to first place—it hadn't even been a runner-up in 1952; (2) the decrease in the number of silent films selected—six in 1952 but only two in 1962; (3) the absence of Ingmar Bergman, who was then one of the most widely talked-about directors; and (4) the disappearance of any Chaplin film from the Ten Best.

The 1962 survey was sent to one hundred critics; seventy answered. Again, *Sight and Sound* asked the critics to select their personal choices, not those they believed others might choose. The majority of critics were British, French and American.

Eighty-nine critics responded to the 1972 poll, and again the results were interesting: (1) Bergman finally entered the list with *Persona,* as did Fellini with *8½;* (2) Buster Keaton had been rediscovered, and Charlie Chaplin was almost forgotten; (3) Jean Vigo's popularity faded; and (4) there was little evidence of the underground's influence.

Only two films have remained on all three lists: *Potemkin* and *La Règle du Jeu (Rules of the Game).*

As the editors of *Sight and Sound* have noted, Top Ten lists are best approached with trepidation or amusement by compilers and with some skepticism by readers. Obviously one doesn't get an "objective" view of the best films ever made from such lists. These lists, however, do provide an important indication of how opinion changes, how international perspective shifts, whether the silent cinema still holds its ground, how cinema looked like in the perspective of 1952, 1962 and 1972. In short, Top Ten lists, despite their obvious limitations, give us vital—not to mention entertaining—information.

Whenever two or more films received the same number of votes in the following surveys, the tied movies are listed under the same numerical placement. The film receiving the next number of votes is then given a numerical placement that takes into account the preceding tie. For example, in the 1972 survey, *L'Avventura* and *Persona* tied for fifth place. *The Passion of Joan of Arc,* which received the next number of votes, is then said to occupy seventh place.

1952
CINEMATHEQUE BELGIQUE SURVEY (CONTINUED)

THE TEN BEST FILMS

1. *Battleship Potemkin*
   (Eisenstein, 1925)
2. *The Gold Rush*
   (Chaplin, 1925)
3. *The Bicycle Thief*
   (De Sica, 1949)
4. *City Lights*
   (Chaplin, 1930)
   La Grande Illusion
   (Renoir, 1937)
   Le Million
   (Clair, 1930)
7. *Greed*
   (Von Stroheim, 1924)
8. *Hallelujah!*
   (Vidor, 1929)
9. *Die Dreigroschenoper*
   (Pabst, 1931)
   Brief Encounter
   (Lean, 1945)
   Intolerance
   (Griffith, 1916)
   Man of Aran
   (Flaherty, 1934)

MAIN RUNNERS-UP

1. *Passion of Joan of Arc*
   (Dreyer, 1928)
2. *Les Enfants du Paradis*
   (Carné, 1944)
   Foolish Wives
   (Von Stroheim, 1921)
   Storm Over Asia
   (Pudovkin, 1928)
5. *L'Age d'Or*
   (Buñuel, 1930)
   Birth of a Nation
   (Griffith, 1915)

1952
SIGHT AND SOUND SURVEY (CONTINUED)

TEN BEST

1. *The Bicycle Thief*
   (De Sica, 1949)
2. *City Lights*
   (Chaplin, 1930)
   The Gold Rush
   (Chaplin, 1925)
4. *Battleship Potemkin*
   (Eisenstein, 1925)
5. *Louisiana Story*
   (Flaherty, 1947)
   Intolerance
   (Griffith, 1916)
7. *Greed*
   (Von Stroheim, 1924)
   Le Jour se lève
   (Carné, 1939)
   The Passion of Joan of Arc
   (Dreyer, 1928)
10. *Brief Encounter*
    (Lean, 1945)
    Le Million
    (Clair, 1930)
    La Règle du Jeu
    (Renoir, 1939)

RUNNERS-UP

1. *Citizen Kane*
   (Welles, 1941)
   La Grande Illusion
   (Renoir, 1937)
   The Grapes of Wrath
   (Ford, 1940)
4. *The Childhood of Maxim Gorki*
   (Donskoi, 1938)
   Monsieur Verdoux
   (Chaplin, 1947)

Continued

Continued

1962
SIGHT AND SOUND
SURVEY (CONTINUED)

TEN BEST

1. *Citizen Kane*
   (Welles, 1941)·
2. *L'Avventura*
   (Antonioni, 1960)
3. *La Règle du Jeu*
   (Renoir, 1939)
4. *Greed*
   (Von Stroheim, 1924)
   Ugetsu Monogatari
   (Mizoguchi, 1953)
6. *Battleship Potemkin*
   (Eisenstein, 1925)
   The Bicycle Thief
   (De Sica, 1949)
   Ivan the Terrible
   (Eisenstein, 1943–46)
9. *La Terra Trema*
   (Visconti, 1948)
10. *L'Atalante*
    (Vigo, 1933)

RUNNERS-UP

1. *Hiroshima Mon Amour*
   (Resnais, 1959)
   Pather Panchali
   (Ray, 1955)
   Zéro de Conduite
   (Vigo, 1933)
4. *City Lights*
   (Chaplin, 1930)
   *The Childhood of Maxim
   Gorki*
   (Donskoi, 1938)

Continued

1972
SIGHT AND SOUND
SURVEY (CONTINUED)

TEN BEST

1. *Citizen Kane*
   (Welles, 1941)
2. *La Règle du Jeu*
   (Renoir, 1939)
3. *Battleship Potemkin*
   (Eisenstein, 1925)
4. *8½*
   (Fellini, 1963)
5. *L'Avventura*
   (Antonioni, 1960)
   Persona
   (Bergman, 1967)
7. *The Passion of Joan of Arc*
   (Dreyer, 1928)
8. *The General*
   (Keaton/Bruckman,
   1926)
   *The Magnificent
   Ambersons*
   (Welles, 1942)
10. *Ugetsu Monogatari*
    (Mizoguchi, 1953)
    Wild Strawberries
    (Bergman, 1957)

RUNNERS-UP

1. *The Gold Rush*
   (Chaplin, 1925)
   Hiroshima Mon Amour
   (Resnais, 1959)
   Ikiru
   (Kurosawa, 1952)
   Ivan the Terrible
   (Eisenstein, 1943–46)
   Pierrot le Fou
   (Godard, 1965)
   Vertigo
   (Hitchcock, 1958)

Continued

1952
CINEMATHEQUE BELGIQUE SURVEY (CONTINUED)

Broken Blossoms
(Griffith, 1919)
Devil in the Flesh
(Autant-Lara, 1946)

1952
SIGHT AND SOUND SURVEY (CONTINUED)

Que Viva Mexico
(Eisenstein, 1931)·
7. Earth
(Dovzhenko, 1929)
Zéro de Conduite
(Vigo, 1933)
9. Broken Blossoms
(Griffith, 1919)
Les Dames du Bois de
Boulogne
(Bresson, 1945)
Hallelujah!
(Vidor, 1929)

VOTING BY DIRECTORS
(not calculated in 1952)

A SELECTION OF LISTS
Robert Bresson:
1. The Gold Rush
2. City Lights
3. Potemkin

Continued

A SELECTION OF LISTS
Lotte H. Eisner (France):
1. Monsieur Verdoux
2. The Gold Rush
3. Birth of a Nation

Continued

1962
SIGHT AND SOUND
SURVEY (CONTINUED)

The Gold Rush
(Chaplin, 1925)
7. *Sunrise*
(Murnau, 1927)
8. *Earth*
(Dovzhenko, 1930)
Monsieur Verdoux
(Chaplin, 1947)
10. *The General*
(Keaton, 1927)
La Grande Illusion
(Renoir, 1937)
Ikiru
(Kurosawa, 1952)
Nazarin
(Buñuel, 1958)
October
(Eisenstein, 1928)
Umberto D.
(De Sica, 1951)

VOTING BY DIRECTORS

1. Sergei Eisenstein
2. Charles Chaplin
3. Jean Renoir
4. Orson Welles
5. Michelangelo Antonioni
6. Vittorio De Sica
7. Alain Resnais
Jean Vigo
9. Kenji Mizoguchi
10. Erich Von Stroheim
11. Luis Buñuel
Luchino Visconti

A SELECTION OF LISTS

Lotte H. Eisner (France):
1. *The Idiot*
(Kurosawa)
2. *Ugetsu Monogatari*

1972
SIGHT AND SOUND
SURVEY (CONTINUED)

7. *La Grande Illusion*
(Renoir, 1937)
Mouchette
(Bresson, 1966)
The Searchers
(Ford, 1956)
Sunrise
(Murnau, 1927)
2001: A Space Odyssey
(Kubrick, 1968)
Viridiana
(Buñuel, 1961)

VOTING BY DIRECTORS

1. Orson Welles
2. Jean Renoir
3. Ingmar Bergman
4. Luis Buñuel
5. Sergei Eisenstein
6. John Ford
Jean-Luc Godard
8. Buster Keaton
9. Federico Fellini
10. Michelangelo Antonioni
Charles Chaplin
Carl Dreyer

A SELECTION OF LISTS

Lotte H. Eisner (France):
1. *Earth*
2. *Greed*

Continued   *Continued*

1952
CINEMATHEQUE BELGIQUE SURVEY (CONTINUED)

4. *Brief Encounter*
5. *The Bicycle Thief*
6. *Man of Aran*
7. *Louisiana Story*

1952
SIGHT AND SOUND SURVEY (CONTINUED)

4. *Potemkin*
5. *Greed*
6. *L'Age d'Or*
7. *Zéro de Conduite*
8. *Earth*
9. *Tabu*
    (Flaherty-Murnau)
10. *Louisiana Story*

Elia Kazan:
1. *Potemkin*
2. *Aerograd*
    (Dovzhenko)
3. *The Gold Rush*
4. *Flesh and the Devil*
    (Brown)
5. *Open City*
6. *The Bicycle Thief*
7. *Shoulder Arms*
    (Chaplin)
8. *Target for Tonight*
    (Watt)
9. *Le Femme du Boulanger*
    (Pagnol)
10. *Marius, Fanny, Cesar*
    (Pagnol)

Penelope Huston (England):
(alphabetical order)
1. *L'Atalante*
2. *Citizen Kane*
3. *City Lights*
4. *Les Dames du Bois de Boulogne*
5. *Earth*
6. *The General*
    (Keaton)
7. *The Grapes of Wrath*
8. *Greed*
9. *October*
10. *La Règle du Jeu*

Carl Dreyer:
1. *Birth of a Nation*
2. *Arne's Treasure*
    (Stiller)
3. *Potemkin*
4. *The Gold Rush*
5. *Sous les Toits de Paris*
    (Clair)
6. *Quai des Brumes*
    (Carné)

Curtis Harrington (USA):
(not in order of preference)
1. *Greed*
2. *Zéro de Conduite*
3. *La Règle du Jeu*
4. *The Devil Is a Woman*
    (Sternberg)
5. *Vampyr*
    (Dreyer)
6. *L'Age d'Or*

Continued

Continued

1962
SIGHT AND SOUND SURVEY (CONTINUED)

3. *Nazarin*
4. *Ivan the Terrible*
   (color sequence, Part II)
5. *Monsieur Verdoux*
6. *Fires on the Plain*
   (Ichikawa)
7. *Greed*
8. *Sunrise*
9. *Partie de Campagne*
   (Renoir)
10. *Zéro de Conduite*

Penelope Houston (England):
   (alphabetical order)
1. *L'Année dernière à
   Marienbad*
2. *L'Atalante*
3. *L'Avventura*
4. *Citizen Kane*
5. *The General*
6. *The Maltese Falcon*
7. *October*
8. *La Règle du Jeu*
9. *La Terra Trema*
10. *Ugetsu Monogatari*

Curtis Harrington (USA):
1. *Greed*
2. *Zéro de Conduite*
3. *La Règle du Jeu*
4. *The Devil Is a Woman*
5. *Dura Lex*
6. *Les Dames du Bois de
   Boulogne*
7. *Rashomon*
8. *I Vitelloni*

1972
SIGHT AND SOUND SURVEY (CONTINUED)

3. *Ivan the Terrible*
   (color sequence, Part II)
4. *The Idiot*
5. *M*
6. *Monsieur Verdoux*
7. *The Passion of Joan of Arc*
8. *La Règle du Jeu*
9. *Senso*
   (Visconti)
10. *Sunrise*

Penelope Houston (England):
   (alphabetical order)
1. *Au Hasard Balthazar*
   (Bresson)
2. *Charulata*
3. *Citizen Kane*
4. *The Eclipse*
5. *The General*
6. *Miracle of Morgan's
   Creek*
7. *Muriel*
8. *La Règle du Jeu*
9. *Silence and Cry*
   (Jancsó)
10. *2001: A Space Odyssey*

Peter Bogdanovich (USA):
   (in chronological order)
1. *Only Angels Have Wings*
2. *Young Mr. Lincoln*
3. *The Magnificent
   Ambersons*
4. *Red River*
5. *She Wore a Yellow Ribbon*
6. *The Searchers*
7. *Rio Bravo*

Continued   *Continued*

1952
CINEMATHEQUE BELGIQUE SURVEY *(CONTINUED)*

7. *Brief Encounter*
8. *Henry V*
9. *The Petrified Forest*
   (Mayo)
10. *Open City*

David Lean:
1. *Intolerance*
2. *Variety*
   (Dupont)
3. *The Crowd*
   (Vidor)
4. *City Lights*
5. *White Shadows In the*
   South Seas
   (Van Dyke)
6. *A Nous la Liberté!*
7. *La Grande Illusion*
8. *Les Enfants du Paradis*
9. *Le Jour se lève*
   (Carné)
10. *Citizen Kane*

Vittorio De Sica:
1. *Man of Aran*
2. *The Kid*
3. *La Chienne*
   (Renoir)
4. *Le Million*
5. *L'Atalante*
6. *Kameradschaft*
   (Pabst)
7. *Storm Over Asia*
8. *Potemkin*
9. *Hallelujah!*
10. *La Kermesse Héroïque*
   (Feyder)

1952
SIGHT AND SOUND SURVEY *(CONTINUED)*

7. *Dura Lex*
   (Kuleshov)
8. *Never Give a Sucker an*
   Even Break
   (Cline)
9. *A Nous la Liberté!*
10. *Les Dames du Bois de*
   Boulogne

Gavin Lambert (England):
1. *Greed*
2. *Earth*
3. *L'Age d'Or*
4. *La Règle du Jeu*
5. *The Kid*
6. *A Diary for Timothy*
   (Jennings)
7. *The Quiet Man*
   (Ford)
8. *Hallelujah!*
9. *Que Viva Mexico*
10. *Les Dames du Bois de*
   Boulogne

André Bazin (France):
1. *Les Vampires*
   (Fouillade)
2. *The Pilgrim*
   (Chaplin)
3. *Broken Blossoms*
4. *Sunrise*
5. *Greed*
6. *La Règle du Jeu*
7. *Le Jour se lève*
8. *The Little Foxes*
9. *Les Dames du Bois de*
   Boulogne
10. *The Bicycle Thief*

Continued

Continued

1962
SIGHT AND SOUND SURVEY (CONTINUED)

9. Citizen Kane
10. L'Avventura

1972
SIGHT AND SOUND SURVEY (CONTINUED)

8. Touch of Evil
9. Vertigo
10. North by Northwest

Gavin Lambert (England/USA):
1. L'Age d'Or
2. El (Buñuel)
3. Nazarin
4. Zéro de Conduite
5. Never Give A Sucker . . .
6. Ivan the Terrible
7. Modern Times
8. Moana
   (Flaherty)
9. Love of Jeanne Ney
   (Pabst)
10. Gone With the Wind

Penelope Gilliatt (England/USA):
1. The Navigator
2. La Règle du Jeu
3. 8½
4. Persona
5. Ikiru
6. Citizen Kane
7. The Apu Trilogy
8. Battleship Potemkin
9. Jules et Jim
10. Weekend

Richard Roud (USA/England):
1. L'Année dernière à
   Marienbad
2. L'Atalante
3. Citizen Kane
4. Cronaca di un Amore
   (Antonioni)
5. Les Dames du Bois de
   Boulogne
6. Hiroshima Mon Amour
7. La Notte
8. Pickpocket
9. La Règle du Jeu
10. Tokyo Story
    (Ozu)

Richard Roud (USA/England):
1. La Règle du Jeu
2. L'Atalante
3. Citizen Kane
4. Tokyo Story
5. Les Dames du Bois . . .
6. Deux ou trois Choses
   que je sais d'elle
   (Godard)
7. Not Reconciled
8. The Spider's Strategy
   (Bertolucci)
9. The Go-Between
   (Losey)
10. Muriel

Continued   Continued

1952
CINEMATHEQUE BELGIQUE SURVEY (CONTINUED)

Carol Reed:
1. *City Lights*
2. *Ninotchka*
   (Lubitsch)
3. *Les Enfants du Paradis*
4. *Gone With the Wind*
5. *La Ronde*
   (Ophuls)
6. *All Quiet on the Western Front*
7. *Le Kermesse Héroïque*
8. *Variety*
9. *La Femme du Boulanger*
10. *Pygmalion*
    (Asquith)

King Vidor:
1. *Intolerance*
2. *Sunrise*
3. *Der letzte Mann*
   (Murnau)
4. *The Big Parade*
   (Vidor)
5. *Brief Encounter*
6. *Red Shoes*
   (Powell-Pressburger)
7. *Open City*
8. *City Lights*
9. *Citizen Kane*
10. *Best Years of Our Lives*

Billy Wilder:
1. *Potemkin*
2. *Greed*

1952
SIGHT AND SOUND SURVEY (CONTINUED)

Lindsay Anderson (England):
1. *Earth*
2. *They Were Expendable*
   (Ford)
3. *Zéro de Conduite*
4. *The Childhood of Maxim Gorki*
5. *The Grapes of Wrath*
   The Bicycle Thief
6. *Louisiana Story*
   The River
7. *Fires Were Started*
   (Jennings)
8. *La Règle du Jeu*
   La Jour se lève
9. *Douce*
   (Autant-Lara)
   Antoine et Antoinette
   (Becker)
   Force of Evil
   (Polonsky)
10. *Meet Me in St. Louis*

Rudolf Arnheim (USA):
1. *The Wedding March*
2. *City Lights*
3. *The General*
4. *Potemkin*
5. *Road to Life*
   (Ekk)
6. *Our Daily Bread*
7. *Sous les Toits de Paris*
   (Clair)
8. *Man of Aran*
9. *The Bicycle Thief*
10. *Rashomon*

Henri Langlois (France):
1. *Chaplin's 1916 films*
2. *The Gold Rush*

Continued   Continued

1962
SIGHT AND SOUND SURVEY (CONTINUED)

Arthur Knight (USA):
1. *The Bicycle Thief*
2. *Citizen Kane*
3. *City Lights*
4. *Hiroshima Mon Amour*
5. *Ikiru*
6. *The Last Laugh* (Murnau)
7. *Moana*
8. *The Apu Trilogy*
9. *Battleship Potemkin*
10. *La Strada*

Dwight MacDonald (USA):
1. *Birth of a Nation*
2. *Intolerance*
3. *October*
4. *Sherlock Jr.* (Keaton)
5. *The Gorki Trilogy*
6. *La Grande Illusion*
7. *Citizen Kane*
8. *Les Enfants du Paradis*
9. *Hiroshima Mon Amour*
10. *L'Avventura*

Jonas Mekas (USA):
(alphabetical order)
1. *Battleship Potemkin*

Continued

1972
SIGHT AND SOUND SURVEY (CONTINUED)

Arthur Knight (USA):
1. *A Nous la Liberté*
2. *The Bicycle Thief*
3. *Citizen Kane*
4. *City Lights*
5. *Ikiru*
6. *La Notte*
7. *The Passion of Joan of Arc*
8. *Persona*
9. *Punishment* (Peter Watkins)
10. *Who's Afraid of Virginia Woolf?*

Richard Corliss (USA):
1. *Sunrise*
2. *La Règle du Jeu*
3. *His Girl Friday*
4. *The Lady Eve*
5. *Citizen Kane*
6. *Casablanca*
7. *Les Enfants du Paradis*
8. *Letter from an Unknown Woman*
9. *The Searchers*
10. *The Seventh Seal*
11. *Psycho*
12. *Chinese Firedrill* (Will Hindle)

Judith Crist (USA):
1. *City Lights*
2. *La Règle du Jeu*

Continued

1952
CINEMATHEQUE BELGIQUE
SURVEY (CONTINUED)

3. *Variety*
4. *The Gold Rush*
5. *The Crowd*
6. *La Grande Illusion*
7. *The Informer*
   (Ford)
8. *Ninotchka*
9. *Best Years of Our Lives*
10. *The Bicycle Thief*

Luchino Visconti:
1. *La Grande Illusion*
2. *Greed*
3. *Potemkin*
4. *Que Viva Mexico*
   (Eisenstein)
5. *Hallelujah!*
6. *Stagecoach*
7. *Monsieur Verdoux*
8. *Tabu*
   (Murnau)
9. *The Lost Weekend*
10. *Les Enfants du Paradis*

Luis Buñuel:
1. *Underworld*
   (Sternberg)
2. *The Gold Rush*
3. *The Bicycle Thief*
4. *Potemkin*
5. *Portrait of Jennie*
   (Dieterle)
6. *Cavalcade*
   (Lloyd)
7. *White Shadows in the*
   South Seas
8. *Dead of Night*
   (Cavalcanti, etc.)
9. *L'Age d'Or*

1952
SIGHT AND SOUND
SURVEY (CONTINUED)

3. *Intolerance*
4. *Birth of a Nation*
5. *Queen Kelly*
   (Von Stroheim)
6. *Potemkin*
7. *Que Viva Mexico*
8. *Monsieur Verdoux*

Siegfried Kracauer (USA):
1. *The Joyless Street*
2. *M*
3. *La Chienne*
4. *Le Million*
5. *Lonesome*
   (Fejos)
6. *Potemkin*
7. *Paisan*
8. *The Gold Rush*
9. *Louisiana Story*
10. *Los Olvidados*

Paul Rotha (England):
1. *Greed*
2. *Potemkin*
3. *The Gold Rush*
4. *The Italian Straw Hat*
5. *Turksib*
   (Turin)
6. *Earth*
7. *Kameradschaft*
8. *L'Atalante*
9. *Open City*
10. *The Bicycle Thief*

Continued   Continued

1962
SIGHT AND SOUND
SURVEY (CONTINUED)

2. Citizen Kane
3. The Gold Rush
4. Greed
5. Intolerance
6. Ivan the Terrible
7. Lola Montès
8. Nanook of the North
9. Le Sang d'un Poète
10. Zéro de Conduite

Jacques Rivette (France):
1. The Life of Oharu
   (Mizoguchi)
2. Germany Year Zero
   (Rossellini)
3. True Heart Susie
   (Griffith)
4. Sunrise
5. The River
6. Ivan the Terrible
7. L'Atalante
8. Day of Wrath
9. Monsieur Verdoux
10. Confidential Report
    (Welles)

Eric Rohmer (France):
   (chronological order)
1. True Heart Susie
2. The General
3. Sunrise
4. La Règle du Jeu
5. Ivan the Terrible
6. Voyage en Italie
7. Red River
8. Vertigo
9. Pickpocket
10. La Pyramide Humaine

1972
SIGHT AND SOUND
SURVEY (CONTINUED)

3. Citizen Kane
4. La Grande Illusion
5. 8½
6. La Guerre est finie
7. Ikiru
8. Winter Light
9. War and Peace
   (Bondarchuk)
10. The Maltese Falcon

Stephen Farber (USA):
1. Citizen Kane
2. 8½
3. Jules et Jim
4. Lawrence of Arabia
5. The Manchurian Candidate
6. Masculin-Féminin
7. The Night of the Hunter
8. Performance
9. Persona
10. La Règle du Jeu

Stanley Kauffmann (USA):
1. The Gold Rush
2. Battleship Potemkin
3. The General
4. The Passion of Joan of Arc
5. La Grande Illusion
6. Citizen Kane
7. Rashomon
8. Tokyo Story
9. L'Avventura
10. Persona

Continued   Continued

1952
CINEMATHEQUE BELGIQUE SURVEY (CONTINUED)

10. *I Am a Fugitive from a Chain Gang*

Orson Welles:
1. *City Lights*
2. *Greed*
3. *Intolerance*
4. *Nanook*
5. *Sciuscia*
   (De Sica)
6. *Potemkin*
7. *La Femme du Boulanger*
8. *La Grande Illusion*
9. *Stagecoach*
10. *Our Daily Bread*
   (Vidor)

1952
SIGHT AND SOUND SURVEY (CONTINUED)

Claude Mauriac (France):
1. *Birth of a Nation*
2. *The Gold Rush*
3. *Que Viva Mexico*
4. *The Magnificent Ambersons*
5. *La Règle du Jeu*
6. *Espoir*
   (Malraux)
7. *The Bicycle Thief*
8. *The Fallen Idol*
   (Reed)
9. *Miss Julie*
   (Sjöberg)
10. *The River*
   (Renoir)

Robin Wood (England):
1. *Sansho Dayu*
2. *Letter from an Unknown Woman*
3. *A Passion*
4. *La Règle du Jeu*
5. *Rio Bravo*
6. *Sunrise*
7. *Vertigo*
8. *Bigger Than Life*
   (Nicholas Ray)
9. *Days and Nights in the Forest*
   (Satyajit Ray)
10. *Viaggio in Italia*

1962
SIGHT AND SOUND SURVEY (CONTINUED)

Colin Young (USA):
1. Citizen Kane
2. The Gold Rush
3. Man of Aran
4. October
5. Song of Ceylon (Wright)
6. L'Avventura
7. Pather Panchali
8. Rashomon
9. The Seventh Seal
10. Umberto D.

1972
SIGHT AND SOUND SURVEY (CONTINUED)

Andrew Sarris (USA):
1. Madame De
2. Lola Montès
3. Ugetsu Monogatari
4. La Règle du Jeu
5. Vertigo
6. The Searchers
7. Sherlock Jr.
8. Francesco Giullare di Dio (Rossellini)
9. The Magnificent Ambersons
10. Belle de Jour

Jay Cocks (USA):
1. The General
2. Jules et Jim
3. The Magnificent Ambersons
4. Persona
5. The Seachers
6. The Seven Samurai
7. The Third Man
8. 2001: A Space Odyssey
9. The Wild Bunch
10. Zéro de Conduite

Paul Schrader (USA):
1. An Autumn Afternoon
2. Journal d'un Curé de Campagne
3. My Darling Clementine
4. The Passion of Joan of Arc
5. Masculin-Féminin
6. La Règle du Jeu
7. Viaggio in Italia
8. Kiss Me Deadly
9. Lolita
10. Performance

Continued

1972
**SIGHT AND SOUND
SURVEY (CONTINUED)**

Paul D. Zimmerman (USA):
1. *A Nous la Liberte*
2. *Les Enfants du Paradis*
3. *Intolerance*
4. *Kind Hearts and Coronets*
5. *Modern Times*
6. *Zéro de Conduite*
7. *Olympic Games 1936*
8. *The Seven Samurai*
9. *The Lady Vanishes*
10. *La Grande Illusion*

2. BRUSSELS WORLD FAIR SURVEY

During the film festival held at the Brussels World Fair in 1958, twelve films were screened as the Best Films of All Time. The selection was made by a jury of 117 film historians from 26 countries and contained few if any individual surprises, consisting largely of conventional "classics." As a group, however, the twelve films surprisingly contained only three sound films. And many people thought it strange that no René Clair or John Ford film got on the list, even though Clair was third and Ford was sixth on a list obtained by combining the number of votes each director received for all of his films mentioned on the ballot.

The list of twelve films was then given to a second jury of young filmmakers to classify the films "acccording to their present-day value." Aften ten hours of debate, the jurors (Robert Aldrich, Alexander Mackendrick, Alexandre Astruc, Juan-Antonio Bardem, Francesco Maselli, Michael Cacoyannis and Satyajit Ray) announced that the films "should not be measured against each other." They also expressed their dismay over the preponderance of silent films and the absence of certain very important schools of filmmaking like the Japanese. Nevertheless, this second jury said that after lengthy discussion, six films emerged as having "a living and lasting value": *The Battleship Potemkin, The Gold Rush, La Grande Illusion, The Bicycle Thief, Mother* and *The Passion of Joan of Arc.* (When this list was read to the audience, several people shouted "And where is *Kane?*")

A third jury, displeased by the decisions of the first two juries, then organized itself to give recognition to the important films that the festival had neglected. This jury's list included: *L'Atalante, L'Age d'Or, La Terra Trema, Sherlock Jr,. Rashomon, Hôtel des Invalides, The Grapes of Wrath, The Childhood of Maxim Gorki, Underworld, Die Dreigroschenoper, Peter Ibbetson* and *Smiles of a Summer Night.*

During this film festival, Eisenstein's *Ivan the Terrible, Part II* had its Western premiere.

BEST FILMS OF ALL TIMES

Rank	Film	Votes
1.	*Battleship Potemkin* (Eisenstein, 1925)	100
2.	*The Gold Rush* (Chaplin, 1925)	85
	The Bicycle Thief (De Sica, 1948)	85
4.	*The Passion of Joan of Arc* (Dreyer, 1928)	78
5.	*La Grande Illusion* (Renoir, 1937)	72
6.	*Greed* (Von Stroheim, 1924)	71
7.	*Intolerance* (Griffith, 1916)	61
8.	*Mother* (Pudovkin, 1926)	54
9.	*Citizen Kane* (Welles, 1941)	50
10.	*Earth* (Dovzhenko, 1930)	47
11.	*The Last Laugh* (Murnau, 1924)	45
12.	*The Cabinet of Dr. Caligari* (Wiene, 1919)	43

By combining the number of votes obtained by each director for all of his films mentioned in the ballot, the following top twelve emerged:

BEST DIRECTORS

Rank	Director	Votes
1.	Chaplin	250
2.	Eisenstein	168
3.	Clair	135
4.	De Sica	125
5.	Griffith	123
6.	Ford	107
7.	Renoir	105
8.	Dreyer	99
9.	Von Stroheim	93
10.	Pudovkin	91
11.	Murnau	90
12.	Flaherty	82

3. BEST FILMS ABOUT WOMEN

The Winter 1975/76 issue of *Film Heritage* was devoted to the study of women and film. For this special issue, Karyn Kay and Gerald Peary asked several leading women film specialists to name the best ten films about women.

The most frequently listed films were Cukor's *Adam's Rib* and Bergman's *Persona*, followed by Cukor's *Pat and Mike*, Rivette's *Céline and Julie Go Boating*, Buñuel's *Belle de Jour*, Godmilow-Collins' *Antonia: Portrait of the Woman*, and De Sica's *Brief Vacation*.

The polltakers noted several interesting results: (1)

films made by men about women were selected much more frequently than those by women about women, a reflection of the obvious fact that there have been many more male directors; (2) television drama deserved "more notice for its women's roles"; and (3) the most highly publicized woman's pictures were not necessarily the most revered: *Alice Doesn't Live Here Anymore* wasn't on a single list, and *Woman Under the Influence* and *Scenes from a Marriage* were mentioned only once each, half as much as *National Velvet*.

List of Contributors

Jan Dawson writes regularly for the British publication *Sight and Sound*.

Sybil Del Gaudio, a member of NOW's Images of Women in Film Committee, teaches film at Brooklyn College.

Patricia Erens, an editor of *The Northwestern Reader,* has written for *The Velvet Light Trap, Jump Cut,* and *Film Comment.*

Ellen Freyer is a filmmaker who has written for *The Velvet Light Trap, The Documentary Tradition* and reviewed films for *Craft Horizons.*

Molly Haskell, critic for *New York* and formerly for the *Village Voice,* is author of *From Reverence to Rape: The Treatment of Women in the Movies.*

Karyn Kay, lecturer in film at Livingston College, Rutgers, has written for *Film Quarterly, Jump Cut, Cinema* and *The Velvet Light Trap.*

Marsha Kinder, contributing editor of *Woman and Film* and co-author of *Close-Up: A Critical Perspective on Film,* is an associate professor of literature and film at Pitzer College. She is a contributor to *Film Heritage* and *Film Quarterly.*

Midge Kovacs, coordinator of the New York chapter of NOW's Images of Women in Film Committee, has been appointed to the International Women's Year Committee on the Media, serving along with Alan Alda and Katharine Hepburn.

Julia Lesage, contributing editor of *Women and Film, Jump*

Cut and *Cinéaste,* teaches film at the University of Illinois, Chicago Circle.

Joan Mellen, associate professor at Temple University, is the author of *Women and their Sexuality in the New Film* and the recent *Voices from the Japanese Cinema.*

Eleanor Perry, screenwriter of *David and Lisa, The Swimmer, Last Summer, Diary of a Mad Housewife* and *The Man Who Loved Cat Dancing,* has completed the screenplay for *Blind Love.*

Amalie Rothschild, filmmaker of *Nana, Mom and Me, It Happens to Us* and *Woo Who, May Wilson,* and one of the founders of the New Day Films, is currently working on a feature script.

Nancy Schwartz, film critic for *The Soho Weekly News,* has written for *Film Comment* and *The Velvet Light Trap.*

Emily Sieger is research librarian for the Museum of Modern Art film division.

Elisabeth Weis, who teaches film at Brooklyn College, has written for *American Film* and the *Village Voice.*

JAN DAWSON
  (listed alphabetically by director)

The Touch (Bergman)
Last Tango in Paris (Bertolucci)
Adam's Rib (Cukor)
India Song (Duras)
Martha (Fassbinder)
Two or Three Things I Know About Her (Godard)
Part-time Work of a Domestic Slave (Kluge)
Muriel (Resnais)
Céline and Julie Go Boating (Rivette)
Sunday Bloody Sunday (Schlesinger)

SYBIL DEL GAUDIO

First Comes Courage (Arzner)
Christopher Strong (Arzner)

Joyce at 34 (Chopra/Weill)
Antonia: Portrait of the Woman (Collins/Godmilow)
A Brief Vacation (De Sica)
Holiday (Cukor)
Adam's Rib (Cukor)
National Velvet (Brown)
Persona (Bergman)
So Proudly We Hail (Sandrich)

PATRICIA ERENS
  (in alphabetical order)

All About Eve (Mankiewicz)
Les Bonnes Femmes (Chabrol)
Charulata (Ray)
Dishonored (Sternberg)
His Girl Friday (Hawks)
Jules and Jim (Truffaut)
Legacy (Arthur)
Persona (,Bergman)
Trouble in Paradise (Lubitsch)
A Very Curious Girl (Kaplan)

ELLEN FREYER

Love and Anarchy
   (Wertmüller)
Bonnie and Clyde (Penn)
Persona (Bergman)
Meshes of the Afternoon
   (Deren/Hammid)
The Blue Angel (Sternberg)
Dance, Girl, Dance (Arzner)
I Am Somebody (Anderson)
Pat and Mike (Cukor)
Lucia (Solas)
Claudine (Berry)

MOLLY HASKELL
   (films listed in no special
   order)

Orphans of the Storm
   (Griffith)
The Sternberg-Dietrich oeuvre
Angel (Lubitsch)
The Major and the Minor
   (Wilder)
Pat and Mike (Cukor)
Gentlemen Prefer Blondes
   (Hawks)
Stromboli (Rossellini)
Belle de Jour (Buñuel)
My Night at Maud's (Rohmer)
The Earrings of Madame de
   (Ophuls)
Gertrud (Dreyer)

KARYN KAY
   (limited to one film per
   director of fictional
   narratives)

Dance, Girl, Dance (Arzner)
Marked Woman (Bacon)
Morocco (Sternberg)
Tarnished Angels (Sirk)
Johnny Guitar (Ray)
Mädchen In Uniform (Sagan)
Bed and Sofa (Room)
Contempt (Godard)
Persona (Bergman)
Zambizanga (Muldorer)

MARSHA KINDER

Scenes from a Marriage
   (Bergman)
Céline and Julie Go Boating
   (Rivette)
August and July (Markowitz)
Old Acquaintance (Sherman)
Legacy (Arthur)
Woman Under the Influence
   (Cassavetes)
Antonia: Portrait of the Woman
   (Collins/Godmilow)
Persona (Bergman)
Woman to Woman (Deitch)
Mosori Monika (Strand)

MIDGE KOVACS
   (exclusively contemporary)

Happy New Year (Lelouch)
Brief Vacation (De Sica)
Middle of the World (Tanner)
My Night at Maud's (Rohmer)
Claudine (Berry)
A Free Woman (Schlondorff)

JULIA LESAGE
   (no special order)

Janie's Janie (Ashur)
Holding (Beesons)
Parthogenesis (Citron)
Women's Happy Time Com-
   mune (Paige/Dougherty)
Self-Health (Allan/Irola/
   Light/Musante)
The Women's Film (San Fran-
   cisco Newsreel Collective)
Home Movie (Oxenberg)
Persona (Bergman)
Adam's Rib (Cukor)
Salt of the Earth (Biberman)

JOAN MELLEN

Belle de Jour (Buñuel)
The Life of Oharu (Mizoguchi)
She and He (Hani)
Untamed (Naruse)
Adam's Rib (Cukor)
Forsaken (Naruse)

Osaka Elegy (Mizoguchi)
Gertrud (Dreyer)
The Story of Adele H.
(Truffaut)
The Effects of Gamma Rays ...
(Newman)

ELEANOR PERRY

Perry answered the survey by
saying there weren't any great
films for women, that most
films—even those with spirited
women like *Ninotchka, Casablanca, All About Eve* and
Sunday Bloody Sunday—perpetuate the myth that a
woman's only fulfillment is in
her reflection in the eyes of a
man. Perhaps, Perry said, only
A Touch of Class is the half-
way great movie for women.

AMALIE ROTHSCHILD
(limited to movies about
women who defy stereo-
types)

The Miracle Worker (Penn)
Rachel, Rachel (Newman)
The Elizabeth Blackwell Story
Pat and Mike (Cukor)
The Elizabeth R Series (BBC
series)
Two Women (De Sica)
Thank You All Very Much
(Hussein)
*The Notorious Woman: The
Life of George Sand*
(Hussein, BBC series)
A Very Curious Girl (Kaplan)
Jenny (BBC series)

NANCY SCHWARTZ

*The Model and the Marriage
Broker* (Cukor)
Les Bonnes Femmes
(Chabrol)
The Earrings of Madame de
(Ophuls)

Annie Oakley (Stevens)
The Scarlet Empress
(Sternberg)
Adam's Rib and *Pat and Mike*
(Cukor)
Antonia: Portrait of the Woman
(Collins/Godmilow)
Belle de Jour (Buñuel)
Persona (Bergman)
Voyage to Italy (Rossellini)
Céline and Julie Go Boating
(Rivette)

EMILY SIEGER
(in chronological order)

The Passion of Joan of Arc
(Dreyer)
Une Partie de Campagne
(Renoir)
Camille (Cukor)
How Green Was My Valley
(Ford)
*Letter from an Unknown
Woman* (Ophuls)
Yokihi (Mizoguchi)
Vertigo (Hitchcock)
Mouchette (Bresson)
Seven Women (Ford)
The Story of Adele H.
(Truffaut)

ELISABETH WEIS

Bed and Sofa (Room)
Adam's Rib (Cukor)
The Battle of Algiers
(Pontecorvo)
Modern Times (Chaplin)
National Velvet (Brown)
To Have and Have Not
(Hawks)
Yudi (Bank)
Dishonored (Sternberg)
Betty Boop for President
(Fleischer)
A Brief Vacation (De Sica)

4. AMERICAN FILM INSTITUTE SURVEY

To celebrate its tenth anniversary, the American Film Institute in 1977 conducted the largest survey in the history of film studies. It asked each of its 35,000 members across the nation and around the world to select the greatest American films of all time.

Each member was asked to list his five choices in order of preference. Although any American movie could be named, a list of 341 films was compiled by the AFI staff to facilitate selection. Films were named by title and year only; directors were not cited.

The auditing firm of Laventhol and Horwath tabulated the balloting on a point system that reflected the order of each members' five choices. The response to the survey was extraordinary: more than 1,100 different film titles were included among the members' selections.

Because of the overwhelming response, a second ballot was compiled by AFI, listing in alphabetical order the fifty films that received the largest point totals. AFI members were then asked to make their final five choices from this list only.

This list of fifty films—reprinted here—is rather strange with regard to historical distribution. There is, I think, a surprising dearth of early films and an unusual excess of recent ones on the list. Almost 25 percent of the films cited have been released since 1970 alone, whereas only 6 percent of the movies chosen were made in the silent era. (It should be noted, however, that two of Chaplin's films on the list—*City Lights* and *Modern Times*—though made after 1930 did not have synchronized dialogue.)

Here is how the fifty films break down into decades:

1910–19:	2	1950–59:	9
1920–29:	1	1960–69:	9
1930–39:	9	1970–77:	12
1940–49:	8		

The preponderance of recent films suggests either that there has indeed been a deluge of good films in recent years (which is doubtful) or that AFI members don't have much sense of history, that they haven't seen or remain unimpressed by early movies. Hollywood has often slighted its own past. Studios, for example, have been reluctant to revise an old film's earnings, in the belief that once a movie has passed its first flush of success it no longer is important. And until quite recently, few theaters in Los Angeles exhibited older movies on a regular basis —classic films have been much more popular in cities like New York and San Francisco than in Los Angeles, where the main interest has been the current film crop.

The abundance of recent films in the second balloting of AFI's survey indicates that Hollywood's disregard for its earlier works is matched, at least to a certain extent, by AFI members. As a group, AFI members are much more impressed by films made in the past few years than those released in any other single period of time. Immediacy and not the "test of time" seems to be the standard in this survey.

It is difficult to discern many trends in the survey regarding directors. Only two directors—John Huston and William Wyler—had three of their films selected on this second ballot. Ten other directors had two of their films cited among the fifty movies: Capra, Chaplin, Coppola, Fleming, Griffith, Hill, Kazan, Kubrick, Lean and Wise. Several popular directors—like Ford, Hitchcock and Welles —had only one of their works chosen. And the films of several important directors—like Lubitsch, Hawks, Cukor, Vidor and Mamoulian—were not mentioned at all. (Cukor did, however, direct portions of *Gone With the Wind*, which is on the list.)

Surprisingly, only two Westerns were selected: *High Noon* and *Butch Cassidy and the Sundance Kid*. Musicals fared better: six were chosen. These included *Cabaret*, *Nashville*, *Singin' in the Rain*, *The Sound of Music*, *West Side Story* and *The Wizard of Oz*. (Although both *Fantasia* and *Snow White* have music in them, I do not consider them musicals.) Fantastic films—including fairy tales, science fiction and horror—were also popular. *Jaws, King Kong, Psycho, Star Wars, 2001: A Space Odyssey, The Wizard of Oz, Fantasia* and *Snow White* all were among the top fifty films. Several epic films like *Ben-Hur, The Birth of a Nation, Gone With the Wind, Intolerance* and *Lawrence of Arabia* were selected. Many of the films on the list belong to that category that's often loosely labeled "social commentary." That is, they are films that either make a political/social statement or depict contemporary manners and morals. Such a category includes everything from *All the President's Men* and *Citizen Kane* to *All About Eve* and *The Graduate.*

The Greatest American Films of All Time selected in AFI second balloting were announced at the Tenth Anniversary celebration at the JFK Center for the Performing Arts in Washington on November 17, 1977. The ceremony, with President Carter in attendance, was televised nationally a few days later.

The Ten Best Films make a surprising list: there is not one silent film among the group. Five of the films were made within two years of 1940. Only one director—Victor Fleming—had two of his films selected. The winner of the poll—*Gold With the Wind*—was a safe, predictable choice.

THE TOP FIFTY

(in alphabetical order)

1. *The African Queen* (1952)
2. *All About Eve* (1950)
3. *All Quiet on the Western Front* (1930)
4. *All the President's Men* (1976)
5. *Ben-Hur* (1959)
6. *The Best Years of Our Lives* (1946)
7. *The Birth of a Nation* (1915)
8. *The Bridge on the River Kwai* (1957)
9. *Butch Cassidy and the Sundance Kid* (1969)
10. *Cabaret* (1972)
11. *Casablanca* (1942)
12. *Chinatown* (1974)
13. *Citizen Kane* (1941)
14. *City Lights* (1931)
15. *Dr. Strangelove* (1964)
16. *Fantasia* (1940)
17. *The General* (1927)
18. *The Godfather* (1972)
19. *The Godfather Part II* (1974)
20. *Gone With the Wind* (1939)
21. *The Graduate* (1967)
22. *The Grapes of Wrath* (1940)
23. *High Noon* (1952)
24. *Intolerance* (1916)
25. *It Happened One Night* (1934)
26. *It's a Wonderful Life* (1946)
27. *Jaws* (1976)
28. *King Kong* (1933)
29. *Lawrence of Arabia* (1962)
30. *The Maltese Falcon* (1941)
31. *Midnight Cowboy* (1969)
32. *Modern Times* (1936)
33. *Nashville* (1975)
34. *On the Waterfront* (1954)
35. *One Flew Over the Cuckoo's Nest* (1975)
36. *Psycho* (1960)
37. *Rocky* (1976)
38. *Singin' in the Rain* (1952)
39. *Snow White and the Seven Dwarfs* (1938)
40. *The Sound of Music* (1965)
41. *Star Wars* (1977)
42. *The Sting* (1973)
43. *A Streetcar Named Desire* (1951)
44. *Sunset Boulevard* (1950)
45. *To Kill a Mockingbird* (1962)
46. *Treasure of Sierra Madre* (1948)
47. *2001: A Space Odyssey* (1968)
48. *West Side Story* (1961)
49. *The Wizard of Oz* (1939)
50. *Wuthering Heights* (1939)

THE TOP TEN

1. *Gone With the Wind* (1939)
2. *Citizen Kane* (1941)
3. *Casablanca* (1942)
4. *The African Queen* (1952)
5. *The Grapes of Wrath* (1940)
6. *One Flew Over the Cuckoo's Nest* (1975)
7. *Singin' In the Rain* (1952)
8. *Star Wars* (1977)
9. *2001: A Space Odyssey* (1968)
10. *The Wizard of Oz* (1939)

5. THE NEW YORK TIMES ANNUAL "TEN BEST" LISTS

The *New York Times* has reviewed a considerable portion of the films released in New York during the past sixty years. In fact, between 1913, when the *Times* decided to cover movies, and 1970, when its reviews were collected and indexed, the *Times* published nearly 19,000 reviews.

Movies were at least fifteen years old by 1913, but the first *Times'* writers did not yet know what quite to make of the new medium. There were no film specialists in those days, just trained journalists trying to come to terms with a new and hybrid art form. But as George Amberg comments in his introduction to the one-volume selection of *The New York Times Film Reviews,* eventually some reviewers went beyond the safe limits of mere reporting into the more perilous arena of critical analysis. This transition from content analysis and performance appraisal to the realization that film is a unique and complicated art in its own right happened not only in the *Times,* of course, but in the art world at large.

The collected *Times* film reviews reflect, then, the writing styles, the moral and cultural stances, and the political and social prejudices—in short, the tastes and attitudes of four generations of moviegoers. And many of those attitudes and tastes can be discerned in the Ten Best Lists printed below.

Mordaunt Hall was the *Times'* principal film reviewer when the newspaper began compiling its annual Ten Best lists in 1924. Andre Sennwald was his successor from 1934 to 1936, and he in turn was replaced by Frank S. Nugent. Bosley Crowther took over in 1940 and retained the position through 1967, proving to be one of America's most durable and influential reviewers. Renata Adler held the post during 1968, and in 1969 Vincent Canby became the *Times'* first-string film critic, a position he still holds.

Through 1968 the films are listed in order of preference.

In 1969 Canby began citing his choices alphabetically. Between 1956 and 1961, foreign-language films are considered separately from English-language films. (Between 1956 and 1961, *Time* also made the same distinction.)

1924

*The Dramatic Life of Abraham
   Lincoln
The Thief of Bagdad
Beau Brummel
Merton of the Movies
The Sea Hawk
He Who Gets Slapped
The Marriage Circle
In Hollywood With Potash and
   Perlmutter
Peter Pan
Isn't Life Wonderful?*

1925

*The Big Parade
The Last Laugh
The Unholy Three
The Gold Rush
The Merry Widow
The Dark Angel
Don Q, Son of Zorro
Ben-Hur
Stella Dallas
A Kiss for Cinderella*

1926

*Variety
Beau Geste
What Price Glory
Potemkin
The Grand Duchess and the
   Waiter
The Black Pirate*

*Old Ironsides
Moana
La Bohème
So This is Paris*

1927

*The King of Kings
Chang
The Way of All Flesh
Wings
Seventh Heaven
Sunrise
Service for Ladies
Quality Street
Underworld
Stark Love*

1928

*The Circus
Street Angel
Czar Ivan the Terrible
The Last Command
White Shadows of the South
   Sea
The Patriot
The End of St. Petersburg
Show People
Homecoming
Four Devils*

1929

*The Love Parade
Disraeli
Hallelujah!*

The Passion of Joan of Arc
The Taming of the Shrew
Bulldog Drummond
They Had to See Paris
The Sky Hawk
The Virginian
Sally

1930

With Byrd at the South Pole
All Quiet on the Western Front
Journey's End
Lightnin'
The Devil to Pay
Outward Bound
Tom Sawyer
Holiday
Abraham Lincoln
Anna Christie

1931

The Guardsman
City Lights
The Smiling Lieutenant
Arrowsmith
Tabu
Bad Girl
Frankenstein
Skippy
Private Lives
A Connecticut Yankee

1932

Mädchen in Uniform
Trouble in Paradise
Der Raub der Mona Lisa
Grand Hotel
Dr. Jekyll and Mr. Hyde
The Mouthpiece
One Hour with You
A Bill of Divorcement

The Doomed Battalion
Reserved for Ladies

1933

Cavalcade
Reunion in Vienna
Morgenrot
State Fair
Dinner at Eight
Berkeley Square
The Private Life of Henry VIII
Little Women
The Invisible Man
His Double Life

1934

It Happened One Night
The House of Rothschild
The Battle
The Thin Man
Catherine the Great
The First World War
One Night of Love
The Lost Patrol
Man of Aran
Our Daily Bread

1935

The Informer
Ruggles of Red Gap
David Copperfield
Lives of a Bengal Lancer
Les Misérables
The Scoundrel
Chapayev
The Man Who Knew Too Much
Sequoia
Love Me Forever

1936

(Eleven films this year)
La Kermesse Héroïque
   (Carnival in Flanders)
Fury
Dodsworth
Mr. Deeds Goes to Town
Winterset
Romeo and Juliet
The Green Pastures
The Ghost Goes West
The Story of Louis Pasteur
These Three
The Great Ziegfeld

1937

The Life of Emile Zola
The Good Earth
Stage Door
Captains Courageous
They Won't Forget"
Make Way for Tomorrow
I Met Him in Paris
A Star Is Born
Camille
Lost Horizon

1938

*Snow White and the Seven
   Dwarfs*
The Citadel
To the Victor
Pygmalion
A Slight Case of Murder
Three Comrades
The Lady Vanishes
The Adventures of Robin Hood
A Man to Remember
Four Daughters

1939

Made for Each Other
Stagecoach
Wuthering Heights
Dark Victory
Juárez
Goodbye, Mr. Chips
The Women
Mr. Smith Goes to Washington
Ninotchka
Gone With the Wind

1940

The Grapes of Wrath
The Baker's Wife
Rebecca
Our Town
The Mortal Storm
Pride and Prejudice
The Great McGinty
The Long Voyage Home
The Great Dictator
Fantasia

1941

The Lady Eve
Citizen Kane
Major Barbara
Sergeant York
The Stars Look Down
Here Comes Mr. Jordan
Target for Tonight
Dumbo
How Green Was My Valley
One Foot in Heaven

1942

In Which We Serve
Journey for Margaret

Casablanca
One of Our Aircraft Is Missing
Wake Island
Mrs. Miniver
Yankee Doodle Dandy
The Gold Rush
Woman of the Year
Sullivan's Travels

1943

Air Force
Desert Victory
The Ox-Bow Incident
The More the Merrier
For Whom the Bell Tolls
Report from the Aleutians
Watch on the Rhine
Corvette K–225
Sahara
Madame Curie

1944

Destination Tokyo
The Miracle of Morgan's Creek
The Purple Heart
Going My Way
Wilson
Hail the Conquering Hero
Thirty Seconds Over Tokyo
None But the Lonely Heart
Meet Me in St. Louis
National Velvet

1945

A Tree Grows in Brooklyn
The Way Ahead
Anchors Aweigh
Pride of the Marines
The House on Ninety-Second
    Street
Story of G.I. Joe
Spellbound

The Last Chance
The Lost Weekend
They Were Expendable

1946

Open City
Road to Utopia
The Green Years
Henry V
Notorious
Brief Encounter
The Well-Digger's Daughter
The Best Years of Our Lives
My Darling Clementine
Stairway to Heaven

1947

The Yearling
Great Expectations
Miracle on 34th Street
Crossfire
Life with Father
Shoe Shine
Gentleman's Agreement
To Live in Peace
The Bishop's Wife
The Fugitive

1948

Treasure of Sierra Madre
The Pearl
The Search
A Foreign Affair
Louisiana Story
Hamlet
Johnny Belinda
Apartment for Peggy
The Red Shoes
The Snake Pit

1949

Command Decision
A Letter to Three Wives
The Quiet One
Lost Boundaries
Pinky
The Heiress
All the King's Men
Battleground
The Fallen Idol
Intruder in the Dust

1950

The Titan—Story of
*   Michelangelo*
Twelve O'Clock High
Father of the Bride
The Asphalt Jungle
Destination Moon
The Men
Sunset Boulevard
Trio
All About Eve
Born Yesterday

1951

Fourteen Hours
The Brave Bulls
Oliver Twist
A Place in the Sun
People Will Talk
A Streetcar Named Desire
An American in Paris
Detective Story
Death of a Salesman
Decision Before Dawn
Best Foreign: *Rashomon*
   (Japan)

1952

The Greatest Show on Earth
Cry, The Beloved Country
Viva Zapata!
Five Fingers
High Noon
Ivanhoe
The Quiet Man
Limelight
Breaking Through the Sound
*   Barrier*
Come Back, Little Sheba

1953

Moulin Rouge
Lili
Shane
Julius Caesar
Man on a Tightrope
Stalag 17
From Here to Eternity
Roman Holiday
Martin Luther
The Conquest of Everest

1954

The Glenn Miller Story
Genevieve
Knock on Wood
Mr. Hulot's Holiday
Seven Brides for Seven
*   Brothers*
On the Waterfront
The Little Kidnappers
Sabrina
The Country Girl
Romeo and Juliet

1955

The Bridges at Toko-Ri
Bad Day at Black Rock
A Man Called Peter
Marty
The Great Adventure
Mister Roberts
The Phoenix City Story
It's Always Fair Weather
Oklahoma!
The Prisoner

1956

Richard III
The King and I
Moby Dick
Bus Stop
Lust for Life
The Silent World
Giant
Around the World in 80 Days
Friendly Persuasion
Anastasia

BEST FOREIGN FILMS

The Proud and the Beautiful
 (France)
Rififi (France)
La Strada (Italy)
The Grand Maneuver (France)
The Magnificent Seven (Japan)

1957

The Great Man
Funny Face
Twelve Angry Men
The Green Man
A Hatful of Rain
Silk Stockings
Love in the Afternoon
Les Girls

Sayonara
The Bridge on the River Kwai

BEST FOREIGN FILMS

We Are All Murderers
 (France)
Gold of Naples (Italy)
The Red Balloon (France)
Torero! (Mexico)
Passionate Summer (France)
The Last Bridge (Germany)
Cabiria (Italy)
Gervaise (France)
Ordet (Denmark)
Smiles of a Summer Night
 (Sweden)

1958

Teacher's Pet
Gigi
The Goddess
God's Little Acre
Cat on a Hot Tin Roof
The Defiant Ones
Damn Yankees
The Horse's Mouth
I Want to Live!
A Night to Remember

BEST FOREIGN FILMS

Gates of Paris (France)
Rouge et Noir (France)
Case of Dr. Laurent (France)
The Captain from Koepenick
 (Germany)
Pather Panchali (India)
Inspector Maigret (France)
The Seventh Seal (Sweden)
My Uncle (France)
Witches of Salem (France)
He Who Must Die (France)

1959

The Diary of Anne Frank
Room at the Top
The Nun's Story
Porgy and Bess
Anatomy of a Murder
A Hole in the Head
North by Northwest
Pillow Talk
Ben-Hur
On the Beach

BEST FOREIGN FILMS

The Devil Strikes at Night
   (Germany)
Forbidden Fruit (France)
Aparajito (India)
The Roof (Italy)
Wild Strawberries (Sweden)
The Magician (Sweden)
The Lovers (France)
The 400 Blows (France)
The Cousins (France)
Black Orpheus (France/Brazil)

1960

I'm All Right, Jack
The Apartment
Psycho
Elmer Gantry
Sunrise at Campobello
The Entertainer
Inherit the Wind
The Angry Silence
Exodus
Tunes of Glory

BEST FOREIGN FILMS

Rosemary (Germany)
Ikiru (Japan)
The Cranes Are Flying
   (Russia)
Hiroshima Mon Amour
   (France)

The World of Apu (India)
Never on Sunday (Greece)
The Virgin Spring (Sweden)
General della Rovere (Italy)
The Big Deal on Madonna
   Street (Italy)
The Ballad of a Soldier
   (Russia)

1961

The Facts of Life
A Raisin in the Sun
Saturday Night and Sunday
   Morning
Fanny
The Hustler
Splendor in the Grass
West Side Story
El Cid
Judgment at Nuremberg
One, Two, Three

BEST FOREIGN FILMS

Don Quixote (Russia)
Breathless (France)
La Dolce Vita (Italy)
The Bridge (Germany)
Two Women (Italy)
Ashes and Diamonds (Poland)
Rocco and His Brothers (Italy)
Purple Noon (France)
Girl with a Suitcase (Italy)
A Summer to Remember
   (Russia)

1962

Lover Come Back
Last Year at Marienbad
Whistle Down the Wind
A Taste of Honey
Divorce—Italian Style
The Longest Day
Long Day's Journey Into Night
Sundays and Cybele

Freud
Electra

1963

Heavens Above!
The L-Shaped Room
Hud
Cleopatra
8½
Tom Jones
Any Number Can Win
The Sound of Trumpets
It's a Mad, Mad, Mad, Mad
    World
America, America

1964

Dr. Strangelove
The Servant
That Man from Rio
One Potato, Two Potato
A Hard Day's Night
Woman in the Dunes
Mary Poppins
My Fair Lady
The Americanization of Emily
Marriage Italian Style

1965

The Pawnbroker
Ship of Fools
Darling
Repulsion
Juliet of the Spirits
The Eleanor Roosevelt Story
Red Desert
Kwaidan
To Die in Madrid
Thunderball

1966

The Shop on Main Street
The Gospel According to St.
    Matthew
Dear John
Morgan!
The Russians Are Coming, The
    Russians Are Coming
Who's Afraid of Virginia
    Woolf?
Georgy Girl
Loves of a Blonde
A Man for All Seasons
Blow-up

1967

La Guerre 'est finie
Ulysses
The Hunt
In the Heat of the Night
Father
Elvira Madigan
Closely Watched Trains
Cool Hand Luke
In Cold Blood
The Graduate

1968

Charlie Bubbles
The Two of Us
Belle de Jour
Faces
Les Carabiniers
The Bride Wore Black
The Fifth Horseman Is Fear
Petulia
Rosemary's Baby
A Report on the Party and the
    Guests

1969

(listed alphabetically)
Alice's Restaurant
The Damned
If . . .
La Femme Infidèle
Midnight Cowboy
Stolen Kisses
Topaz
True Grit
The Wild Bunch
Z

1970

(listed alphabetically)
The Ballad of Cable Hogue
Catch-22
Fellini Satyricon
Little Big Man
Loving
M*A*S*H
My Night at Maud's
The Passion of Anna
Tristana
The Wild Child

1971

(listed alphabetically)
Bed and Board
Carnal Knowledge
Claire's Knee
A Clockwork Orange
The Conformist
Derby
The French Connection
The Last Picture Show
Le Boucher
Sunday Bloody Sunday

1972

(listed alphabetically)
Chloë in the Afternoon
Cries and Whispers
The Discreet Charm of the
   Bourgeoisie
Fat City
Frenzy
The Godfather
The Heartbreak Kid
Tokyo Story
Traffic
Two English Girls

1973

(listed alphabetically)
American Graffiti
Day for Night
Heavy Traffic
Last Tango in Paris
The Long Goodbye
Love
Mean Streets
Memories of Underdevel-
   opment
Playtime
Sleeper

1974

*(eleven films listed alpha-
   betically)*
Amarcord
Badlands
California Split
Claudine
Daisy Miller
Harry and Tonto
Lacombe, Lucien
Man Is Not a Bird
Le Petit Théâtre de Jean Renoir

Phantom of Liberté
Scenes from a Marriage

1975

(listed alphabetically)
Alice Doesn't Live Here
Anymore
Barry Lyndon
Distant Thunder
Hearts and Minds
Love and Death
The Magic Flute
Nashville
Shampoo
The Story of Adele H.
Swept Away ...

1976

*(eight films listed alpha-
betically)*
Seven Beauties

All the President's Men
Face to Face
La Chienne
Network
The Seven-Per-Cent Solution
Memory of Justice
Taxi Driver

1977

(listed alphabetically)
Annie Hall
Close Encounters of the Third
Kind
Effi Briest
The Goalie's Anxiety at the
Penalty Kick
Handle With Care
The Late Show
The Man Who Loved Women
Star Wars
Stroszek
That Obscure Object of Desire

---

6. <u>TIME</u> MAGAZINE'S ANNUAL "TEN BEST" LISTS

1945

(in chronological order)
The Fighting Lady
A Tree Grows in Brooklyn
Colonel Blimp
The Clock
San Pietro
The Southerner
Anchors Aweigh
The True Glory
The House on 92nd Street
The Lost Weekend

1946

(in chronological order)
Open City
Henry V
Anna and the King of Siam
Brief Encounter
The Killers
The Jolson Story
Margie
My Darling Clementine
The Best Years of Our Lives
It's A Wonderful Life

1947

(in chronological order)
Odd Man Out
Boomerang!
Ivan the Terrible
Monsieur Verdoux
Great Expectations
Crossfire
Shoe Shine
Gentleman's Agreement
Man About Town
To Live in Peace

1948

(List not compiled this year)

1949

(List not compiled this year)

1950

(in chronological order)
Tight Little Island
The Titan
The Third Man
The Hasty Heart
Cinderella
Kind Hearts and Coronets
The Men
Sunset Boulevard
The Breaking Point
All About Eve

1951

(in chronological order)
Isle of Sinners
Oliver Twist
A Place in the Sun
A Streetcar Named Desire
An American in Paris
The Red Badge of Courage
The Lavender Hill Mob
La Ronde
Detective Story
Miracle in Milan

1952

(in chronological order)
The African Queen
The Man in the White Suit
The Story of Robin Hood
High Noon
The Strange Ones
Ivanhoe
Flowers of St. Francis
Breaking the Sound Barrier
Forbidden Games
Come Back, Little Sheba
The Member of the Wedding
Moulin Rouge

1953

(twelve films in chronological order)
Lili
Call Me Madam
Shane
Fanfan the Tulip
From Here to Eternity
The Cruel Sea
Roman Holiday
The Captain's Paradise
The Living Desert
The Conquest of Everest

1954

(in chronological order)
Beat the Devil
Genevieve

Seven Brides for Seven
  Brothers
The Earrings of Madame de
On the Waterfront
High and Dry
The Little Kidnappers
Ugetsu
Carmen Jones
Gate of Hell

1955

(eight films in chronological
order)
Game of Love
Wages of Fear
Marty
The Great Adventure
Summertime
The Desperate Hours
Umberto D.
The Man with the Golden Arm

1956

(in chronological order)

AMERICAN

The King and I
Somebody Up There Likes Me
Lust for Life
Giant
Around the World in 80 Days
Secrets of the Reef

FOREIGN

Richard III
The Grand Maneuver
I Vitelloni
Marcelino

1957

(twelve films in chrono-
logical order)

AMERICAN

Full of Life
Twelve Angry Men
Sweet Smell of Success
Love in the Afternoon
A Hatful of Rain
The Pajama Game
Les Girls
Paths of Glory
The Bridge on the River Kwai

FOREIGN

Gold of Naples
The Devil's General
The Last Bridge

1958

(twelve films in chrono-
logical order)

AMERICAN

The Enemy Below
The High Cost of Living
The Hot Spell
The Goddess
The Key
The Defiant Ones
Me and the Colonel
The Big Country
Damn Yankees

FOREIGN

Pather Panchali
The Horse's Mouth
He Who Must Die

1959

*(thirteen films in chrono-
logical order)*

AMERICAN

*Some Like It Hot
The Diary of Anne Frank
Pork Chop Hill
Middle of the Night
Ben-Hur*

FOREIGN

*The Mistress
Aparajito
Room at the Top
The Roof
Wild Strawberries
Black Orpheus
The 400 Blows
Ivan the Terrible, Part II*

1960

*(seventeen films in chrono-
logical order)*

AMERICAN

*The Apartment
Come Back, Africa
Elmer Gantry
Sons and Lovers
Sunrise at Campobello
Spartacus
Weddings and Babies
Exodus*

FOREIGN

*Ikiru
A Lesson in Love
Dreams
The Virgin Spring
I'm All Right, Jack
Hiroshima Mon Amour
The World of Apu
General della Rovere
The Loving Game*

1961

*(nineteen films in chrono-
logical order)*

AMERICAN

*Facts of Life
101 Dalmatians
Shadows
Cold Wind in August
The Honeymoon Machine
Homicidal
The Hustler
The Mark
El Cid*

FOREIGN

*A Midsummer Night's Dream
Ballad of a Soldier
Breathless
Saturday Night and Sunday
    Morning
L'Avventura
La Dolce Vita
Rocco and His Brothers
The Kitchen
The Five-Day Lover
Throne of Blood*

1962–1968

*(Lists not compiled these
    years)*

1969

(Top of the Decade)
Godard's *Breathless* and Fel-
lini's *La Dolce Vita* open in
the U.S., 1961
Dr. No is released, starting
the James Bondwagon, 1963
A Hard Day's Night brings the
Beatles to the screen, 1964

Dr. Strangelove, 1964
The Sound of Music spawns
 endless expensive musicals,
 1974
Bonnie and Clyde, 1967
The Graduate alerts filmmakers to the news that more
 than 60 percent of their
 audience is thirty or under,
 1967
GMRX ratings begin, 1968
Easy Rider establishes a trend
 toward the low-budget, personal movie, 1969
I Am Curious (Yellow) makes
 the X-rated, sex-sated movie
 a nationwide phenomenon,
 1969

1970

 (in alphabetical order)
Catch-22
Husbands
Joe
Little Big Man
A Married Couple
M*A*S*H
The Passion of Anna
Patton
Satyricon
Woodstock

1971

 (in alphabetical order)
A Clockwork Orange
The Clowns
The Conformist
Dirty Harry
The French Connection
Glen and Randa
The Last Picture Show
Minnie and Moskowitz
Straw Dogs
Sunday Bloody Sunday

1972

 *(fourteen films in alpha-
 betical order)*
Chloë in the Afternoon
Cries and Whispers
Deliverance
*The Discreet Charm of the
 Bourgeoisie*
Frenzy
The Godfather
Greaser's Palace
*The Great Northfield, Minne-
 sota Raid*
The Heartbreak Kid
The King of Marvin Gardens
My Uncle Antoine
A Sense of Loss
The Sorrow and the Pity
Why

1973

 *(eleven films in alphabetical
 order)*
American Graffiti
An Autumn Afternoon
Day for Night
Don't Look Now
Last Tango in Paris
Love
Mean Streets
O Lucky Man!
Pat Garrett and Billy the Kid
Pulp
The Spider's Stratagem

1974

 (in alphabetical order)
Amarcord
*Antonia: A Portrait of the
 Woman*
Badlands

Chinatown
The Conversation
The Godfather Part II
The Little Theater of Jean
   Renoir
The Seduction of Mimi
The Phantom of Liberté
The Three Musketeers

1975

   (in alphabetical order)
Alice Doesn't Live Here
   Anymore
Barry Lyndon
Jaws
Just Before Nightfall
The Magic Flute
The Man Who Would Be King
Nashville
The Passenger
Tommy
The Wind and the Lion

1976

   (in alphabetical order)
All the President's Men
Buffalo Bill and the Indians
Carrie
Face to Face
The Marquise of O
Obsession
The Outlaw Josey Wales
Small Change
Seven Beauties
Une Partie de Plaisir

1977

   (in alphabetical order)
Annie Hall
Black and White in Color
Close Encounters of the Third
   Kind
Handle With Care
High Anxiety
1900
That Obscure Object of Desire
The Late Show
Semi-Tough
Star Wars

III. THE MARKETPLACE

1. THE TOP 200 MONEYMAKING FILMS OF ALL TIME

Each year *Variety* publishes its list of All-Time Box-Office Champion Films, one of the most interesting compilations for everyone from the movie producer to the cinema scholar to the film buff. Although *Variety*'s presentation is relatively straightforward, many people don't understand exactly what the list signifies. Here are some important clarifications:

1. The figures indicate rental fees and *not* box-office grosses. The rental fee is the money the theater pays to the distributor to show the movie; the box-office gross is the money the moviegoer pays to the theater to see the film. Box-office grosses would be higher than the rental fees reported here in almost all cases.

2. The figures given here include rentals only for the United States–Canadian market and do not cover foreign-market rentals. According to the industry, the foreign-market rentals usually equal or slightly surpass domestic rentals. Thus, to determine what a film earned in world-wide rentals, simply multiply the figures given here by two.

3. Despite the fact that many old films are often reissued to considerable profit, studios tend not to report such added incomes for old films. Once a movie has passed its first success, a studio is often reluctant to revise a movie's earnings figures. As a result, many of the older films on *Variety*'s list may in fact have made more money than the list would suggest.

4. For years it was said that *Birth of a Nation* made $50 million. After reportedly diligent research, the 1977 Anniversary *Variety* reported that such a figure was more legend than fact. As far as research can show, *Nation* earned $5 million in domestic rentals.

5. This list merely includes the top 200 films on *Variety*'s much longer and more comprehensive compendium.

One thing quickly becomes obvious from this list: most of the top moneymaking films are recent releases. Of the top twenty-five Box-Office Champs, for example, twenty-two have been released since 1960; seventeen since 1970. The rising price of tickets is obviously responsible for this preponderance of recent movies on this list, but other, more complex factors must also be responsible for the greater conformity of recent audience taste. It is thus difficult to determine from this list which films have been seen by the most people.

Note: Film title is followed by name of director; producer or production company; original distributor plus present distributor if different; year of release; and total rentals received to date. Whenever two or more films earned the same rental fees, the tied movies are given the same numerical rank. The film earning the next greatest rental fees is then given a numerical rank which takes into account the preceding tie. For example, *The Dirty Dozen* and *Midway* each earned $20,300,000, giving them both 55th place. *Cabaret,* which earned $20,250,000 is then considered to occupy 57th place.

This list was compiled for the January 5, 1977, issue of *Variety* and hence does not include films released since that time.

Rank	Title (Director; Producer; Distributor; Year)	Total Rentals
1.	*Jaws* (Spielberg; Zanuck/Brown; Universal; 1975)	$118,727,000
2.	*The Godfather* (Coppola; Ruddy; Paramount; 1972)	85,747,184
3.	*The Exorcist* (Friedkin; Blatty; Warner Bros; 1973)	82,015,000
4.	*The Sound of Music* (Wise; 20th C–F; 1965)	78,400,000

Continued

Rank	Title (Director; Producer; Distributor; Year)	Total Rentals
5.	*Gone With the Wind* (Fleming; Selznick; MGM–UA; 1939)	76,700,000
6.	*The Sting* (Hill; Bill/Phillips; Universal; 1973)	72,160,000
7.	*One Flew Over the Cuckoo's Nest* (Forman; Zaentz/Douglas; UA; 1975)	56,500,000
8.	*Towering Inferno* (Guillermin; Allen; 20th C–F; 1975)	55,000,000
9.	*Love Story* (Hiller; Minsky; Paramount; 1970)	50,000,000
10.	*The Graduate* (Nichols; Turman; Avco Embassy; 1968)	49,978,000
11.	*American Graffiti* (Lucas; Coppola; Universal; 1973)	47,308,000
12.	*Doctor Zhivago* (Lean; Ponti; MGM–UA; 1965)	46,550,000
13.	*Butch Cassidy and the Sundance Kid* (Hill; Foreman; 20th C–F; 1969)	45,830,000
14.	*Airport* (Seaton; Hunter; Universal; 1970)	45,300,000
15.	*The Ten Commandments* (DeMille; Paramount; 1956)	43,000,000
16.	*The Poseidon Adventure* (Neame; Allen; 20th C–F; 1972)	42,500,000
17.	*Mary Poppins* (Stevenson; Disney; Buena Vista; 1964)	42,250,000
18.	*M*A*S*H* (Altman; Preminger; 20th C–F; 1970)	40,850,000
19.	*Ben-Hur* (Wyler; Zimbalist; MGM–UA; 1959)	36,650,000
20.	*Earthquake* (Robson; Universal; 1974)	36,094,000
21.	*Blazing Saddles* (Brooks; Hertzberg; Warner; 1974)	35,183,000
22.	*Fiddler on the Roof* (Jewison; UA; 1971)	34,010,000
23.	*Billy Jack* (Frank; Solti; Warner; 1971)	32,500,000
24.	*Young Frankenstein* (Brooks; Gruskoff; 20th C–F; 1975)	30,000,000
25.	*All the President's Men* (Pakula; Coblenz; Warner; 1976)	29,000,000

Continued

Rank	Title (Director; Producer; Distributor; Year)	Total Rentals
26.	*Godfather Part II* (Coppola; Coppola/Fredrickson/Roos; Paramount; 1974)	28,900,000
27.	*Thunderball* (Young; Eon; UA; 1965)	28,530,000
28.	*Trial of Billy Jack* (Laughlin; Cramer; T-1/Warner; 1974)	28,516,000
29.	*Patton* (Schaffner; McCarthy; 20th C–F; 1970)	28,100,000
30.	*What's Up, Doc?* (Bogdanovich; Warner; 1972)	28,000,000
31.	*The Omen* (Donner; Bernhard; 20th C–F; 1976)	27,851,000
32.	*The French Connection* (Friedkin; D'Antoni/Schine/Moore; 20th C–F; 1971)	27,500,000
33.	*Snow White* (animated; Disney; RKO–Buena Vista; 1937)	26,500,000
34.	*Funny Girl* (Wyler; Stark; Columbia; 1968)	26,325,000
35.	*Cleopatra* (Mankiewicz; Wanger; 20th C–F; 1963)	26,000,000
36.	*Airport 1975* (Smight; Fry; Universal; 1974)	25,743,000
37.	*Guess Who's Coming to Dinner* (Kramer; Columbia; 1968)	25,500,000
38.	*The Way We Were* (Pollack; Stark; Columbia; 1973)	25,000,000
39.	*2001: A Space Odyssey* (Kubrick; MGM–UA; 1968)	23,700,000
40.	*Around the World in 80 Days* (Anderson; Todd; UA; 1956)	23,120,000
41.	*Goldfinger* (Hamilton; Eon; UA; 1964)	22,860,000
42.	*Bonnie and Clyde* (Penn; Beatty; Warner; 1967)	22,700,000
43.	*Papillon* (Schaffner; Dorfmann; Allied Artists; 1973)	22,500,000
44.	*Deliverance* (Boorman; Warner; 1972)	22,400,000

Continued

Rank	Title (Director; Producer; Distributor; Year)	Total Rentals
45.	*The Longest Yard* (Aldrich; Ruddy; Paramount; 1974)	22,342,073
46.	*Dog Day Afternoon* (Lumet; Bregman/Elfand; Warner; 1975)	22,300,000
47.	*The Bad News Bears* (Ritchie; Jaffe; Paramount; 1976)	22,266,517
48.	*Shampoo* (Ashby; Beatty; Columbia; 1975)	22,000,000
49.	*Jeremiah Johnson* (Pollack; Wizan; Warner; 1972)	21,600,000
50.	*The Love Bug* (Stevenson; Walsh; Buena Vista; 1969)	21,000,000
51.	*It's a Mad, Mad, Mad, Mad World* (Kramer; UA; 1963)	20,800,000
52.	*Summer of '42* (Mulligan; Roth; Warner; 1971)	20,500,000
53.	*Midnight Cowboy* (Schlesinger; Hellman; UA; 1969)	20,325,000
54.	*Silent Movie* (Brooks; Hertzberg; 20th C–F; 1976)	20,311,000
55.	*The Dirty Dozen* (Aldrich; Hyman; MGM–UA; 1967)	20,300,000
	Midway (Smith; Mirisch; Universal; 1976)	20,300,000
57.	*Cabaret* (Fosse; Feuer; Allied Artists; 1972)	20,250,000
58.	*Magnum Force* (Post; Daley; Warner; 1973)	20,100,000
59.	*The Valley of the Dolls* (Robson; Weisbart; 20th C–F; 1967)	20,000,000
	The Odd Couple (Saks; Koch; Paramount; 1968)	20,000,000
61.	*Diamonds Are Forever* (Hamilton; Eon; UA; 1971)	19,620,000
62.	*West Side Story* (Wise, Robbins; Mirisch/7 Arts; UA; 1961)	19,450,000
63.	*You Only Live Twice* (Gilbert; Eon; UA; 1967)	19,400,000
	Return of the Pink Panther (Edwards; UA; 1975)	19,400,000
65.	*To Sir With Love* (Clavell; Columbia; 1967)	19,100,000

Continued

Rank	Title (Director; Producer; Distributor; Year)	Total Rentals
	Easy Rider (Hopper; Pando/Raybart; Columbia; 1969)	19,100,000
67.	*Three Days of the Condor* Pollack; Schneider; Paramount; 1975)	19,051,501
68.	*Swiss Family Robinson* (Annakin; Disney; Buena Vista; 1960)	19,000,000
	Bullitt (Yates; D'Antoni; Warner; 1969)	19,000,000
	Funny Lady (Ross; Stark; Columbia; 1975)	19,000,000
71.	*Murder by Death* (Moore; Stark; Columbia; 1976)	18,800,000
72.	*Murder on the Orient Express* (Lumet; Brabourne/Goodwin; Paramount; 1974)	18,669,210
73.	*The Getaway* (Peckinpah; Foster/Brower; Warner; 1972)	18,100,000
74.	*Dirty Harry* (Siegel; Warner; 1971)	17,831,000
75.	*Bambi* (animated; Disney; RKO–Buena Vista; 1942)	17,800,000
76.	*The Longest Day* (Annakin/Marton/Wicki; Zanuck; 20th C–F; 1962)	17,600,000
77.	*The Robe* (Koster; Ross; 20th C–F; 1953)	17,500,000
	South Pacific (Logan; Magna/Adler; 20th C–F; 1958)	17,500,000
	Herbie Rides Again (Stevenson; Walsh; Buena Vista; 1974)	17,500,000
80.	*Romeo and Juliet* (Zeffirelli; Havelock-Allan/Brabourne; Paramount; 1968)	17,473,000
81.	*The Bridge on the River Kwai* (Lean; Spiegel; Columbia; 1957)	17,195,000
82.	*Walking Tall* (Karlson; Briskin; CRC–AIP; 1973)	17,000,000
83.	*Tom Jones* (Richardson; UA; 1963)	16,950,000
84.	*Oliver!* (Reed; Woolf; Columbia; 1969)	16,800,000

Continued

Rank	Title (Director; Producer; Distributor; Year)	Total Rentals
85.	*Lawrence of Arabia* (Lean; Spiegel; Columbia; 1962)	16,700,000
86.	*Paper Moon* (Bogdanovich; Paramount; 1973)	16,559,000
87.	*The Other Side of the Mountain* (Peerce; Feldman; Universal; 1975)	16,533,000
88.	*Apple Dumpling Gang* (Tokar; Anderson; Buena Vista; 1975)	16,500,000
89.	*Peter Pan* (animated; Disney; RKO–Buena Vista; 1953)	16,000,000
	Thoroughly Modern Millie (Hill; Hunter; Universal; 1967)	16,000,000
	Tommy (Russell; Stigwood; Columbia; 1975)	16,000,000
92.	*Last Tango in Paris* (Bertolucci; Grimaldi; United Artists; 1973)	15,850,000
	Live and Let Die Hamilton; Eon; UA; 1973)	15,850,000
94.	*Hawaii* (Hill; Mirisch; UA; 1966)	15,550,000
95.	*The Carpetbaggers* (Dmytryk; Levine; Paramount; 1964)	15,500,000
96.	*This Is Cinerama* (Thomas; Cooper; CRC; 1952)	15,400,000
	Woodstock (Wadleigh; Maurice; Warner; 1970)	15,400,000
98.	*Hello, Dolly!* (Kelly; Lehman; 20th C–F; 1970)	15,200,000
99.	*The Bible* (Huston; De Laurentiis; 20th C–F; 1966)	15,000,000
	Planet of the Apes (Schaffner; Jacobs; 20th C–F; 1968)	15,000,000
	Rosemary's Baby (Polanski; Castle; Paramount; 1968)	15,000,000
	Little Big Man (Penn; Millar/Penn; NGP–Warner; 1970)	15,000,000
	A Clockwork Orange (Kubrick; Warner; 1971)	15,000,000
104.	*Dirty Mary, Crazy Larry* (Hough; Herman; 20th C–F; 1974)	14,700,000

Continued

Rank	Title (Director; Producer; Distributor; Year)	Total Rentals
105.	*Ryan's Daughter* (Lean; Havelock-Allan; MGM–UA; 1970)	14,641,000
106.	*Spartacus* (Kubrick; Bryna/Lewis; Universal; 1960)	14,600,000
	Bob & Carol & Ted & Alice (Mazursky; Tucker; Columbia; 1969)	14,600,000
	Serpico (Lumet; Bregman; Paramount; 1974)	14,600,000
109.	*Tora! Tora! Tora!* (Fleischer; Williams; 20th C–F; 1970)	14,530,000
110.	*Who's Afraid of Virginia Woolf?* (Nichols; Lehman; Warner; 1966)	14,500,000
	Paint Your Wagon (Logan; Lerner; Paramount; 1969)	14,500,000
112.	*True Grit* (Hathaway; Wallis; Paramount; 1969)	14,250,000
113.	*The Great Gatsby* (Clayton; Merrick; Paramount; 1974)	14,200,000
114.	*101 Dalmatians* (animated; Disney; Buena Vista; 1961)	14,100,000
115.	*The Greatest Show on Earth* (DeMille; Paramount; 1952)	14,000,000
116.	*Giant* (Stevens; Stevens/Ginsberg; Warner; 1956)	14,000,000
	Those Magnificent Young Men in Their Flying Machines (Annakin; Margulies; 20th C–F; 1965)	14,000,000
	Camelot (Logan; Warner/7 Arts; Warner; 1967)	14,000,000
120.	*The Sand Pebbles* (Wise; 20th C–F; 1967)	13,500,000
121.	*Jesus Christ Superstar* (Jewison; Jewison/Stigwood; Universal; 1973)	13,241,000
122.	*The Last Picture Show* (Bogdanovich; Friedman; Columbia; 1972)	13,110,000
123.	*Pinocchio* (animated; Disney; RKO–Buena Vista; 1940)	13,000,000
	The Guns of Navarone (Thompson; Foreman; Columbia; 1961)	13,000,000

Continued

Rank	Title (Director; Producer; Distributor; Year)	Total Rentals
	The Jungle Book (Reitherman; Disney; Buena Vista; 1967)	13,000,000
	Freebie and the Bean (Rush; Warner; 1974)	13,000,000
127.	Song of the South (Disney; RKO–Buena Vista; 1946)	12,880,000
128.	The Lady and the Tramp (animated; Disney; Buena Vista; 1955)	12,750,000
	A Man for All Seasons (Zinnemann; Columbia; 1966)	12,750,000
130.	Quo Vadis (LeRoy; Zimbalist; MGM/UA; 1951)	12,500,000
	Seven Wonders of the World (Thomas; CRC; 1956)	12,500,000
	That Darn Cat (Stevenson; Disney; Buena Vista; 1965)	12,500,000
133.	Chinatown (Polanski; Evans; Paramount; 1974)	12,400,000
134.	Carnal Knowledge (Nichols; Avemb; 1971)	12,351,000
135.	That Shaggy Dog (Barton; Disney; Buena Vista; 1959)	12,250,000
	Catch-22 (Nichols; Calley; Paramount; 1970)	12,250,000
137.	From Here to Eternity (Zinnemann; Columbia; 1953)	12,200,000
138.	How the West Was Won (Ford/Hathaway/Marshall; Smith/CRC; CRC–MGM–UA; 1962)	12,150,000
139.	Lucky Lady (Donen; Gruskoff; 20th C–F; 1975)	12,107,000
140.	That's Entertainment (Haley; MGM–UA; 1974)	12,020,000
141.	White Christmas (Curtiz; Doland/Berlin; Paramount; 1954)	12,000,000
	Cinerama Holiday (De Rochemont; CRC; 1955)	12,000,000
	El Cid (Mann; Bronston; AA; 1961)	12,000,000
	My Fair Lady (Cukor; Warner; WB; 1964)	12,000,000
	Born Losers (Frank; Henderson; AIP; 1967)	12,000,000

Continued

Rank	Title (Director; Producer; Distributor; Year)	Total Rentals
	Benji (Camp; Mulberry Square; 1974)	12,000,000
147.	*Irma La Douce* (Wilder; Wilder/Mirisch; UA; 1963)	11,910,000
148.	*Cactus Flower* (Saks; Frankovich; Columbia; 1969)	11,850,000
149.	*The Owl and the Pussycat* (Ross; Stark; Columbia; 1970)	11,645,000
150.	*Yours, Mine, and Ours* (Shavelson; Blumofe; UA; 1968)	11,610,000
151.	*The World's Greatest Athlete* (Scheerer; Walsh; Buena Vista; 1973)	11,600,000
	Taxi Driver (Scorsese; M & J Phillips; Columbia; 1976)	11,600,000
153.	*Fantasia* (animated; Disney; RKO–Buena Vista; 1940)	11,500,000
	Samson and Delilah (DeMille; Paramount; 1949)	11,500,000
	Cinderella (Jackson; Disney; RKO–Buena Vista; 1949)	11,500,000
	Peyton Place (Robson; Wald; 20th C–F; 1957)	11,500,000
157.	*Lenny* (Fosse; Worth/Picker; U.A.; 1974)	11,425,000
158.	*The Aristocats* (Reitherman; Hibler; Buena Vista; 1970)	11,400,000
159.	*Duel in the Sun* (Vidor; Selznick; SRO; 1946)	11,300,000
	The Best Years of Our Lives (Wyler; Goldwyn; RKO; 1946)	11,300,000
	The Parent Trap (Swift; Disney; Buena Vista; 1961)	11,300,000
162.	*Psycho* (Hitchcock; Paramount/Universal; 1960)	11,200,000
163.	*The Absent-Minded Professor* (Stevenson; Disney; Buena Vista; 1961)	11,100,000
164.	*20,000 Leagues Under the Sea* (Fleischer; Disney; Buena Vista; 1954)	11,000,000
	Great Race (Edwards; Warner; 1965)	11,000,000

Continued

Rank	Title (Director; Producer; Distributor; Year)	Total Rentals
	For Pete's Sake (Yates; Erlichman/Shapiro; Columbia; 1974)	11,000,000
	Walking Tall Part 2 (Bellamy; Prart; CRC-AIP; 1975)	11,000,000
168.	*In the Heat of the Night* (Jewison; Mirisch, UA; 1967)	10,910,000
169.	*The Three Musketeers* (Lester; Salkind; 20th C–F; 1974)	10,740,000
170.	*The Outlaw Josey Wales* (Eastwood; Daley; Warner; 1976)	10,600,000
	Let's Do It Again Poitier; Tucker; Warner; 1975)	10,600,000
172.	*Goodbye, Columbus* Peerce; Jaffe; Paramount; 1969)	10,500,000
	Sayonara (Logan; Goetz; Warner; 1957)	10,500,000
	No Deposit, No Return (McEveety; Miller; Buena Vista; 1976)	10,500,000
175.	*Ode to Billy Joe* (Baer; Baer/Corman; Warner; 1976)	10,400,000
176.	*Casino Royale* (Huston, Hughes, Guest, Parrish; Mc-Grath; Feldman/Bresler; Columbia; 1967)	10,200,000
	Island at the Top of the World (Stevenson; Hibler; Buena Vista; 1974)	10,200,000
178.	*The Great Waldo Pepper* (Hill; Universal; 1975)	10,050,000
179.	*Lt. Robin Crusoe, USN* (Paul; Disney; Buena Vista; 1966)	10,000,000
	Macon County Line (Compton; Baer; AIP; 1974)	10,000,000
181.	*Hustle* (Aldrich; Paramount; 1976)	9,058,738
182.	*From Russia with Love* (Young; Eon; UA; 1964)	9,820,000
183.	*Mutiny on the Bounty* (Milestone; Rosenberg; MGM–UA; 1962)	9,800,000
184.	*Cat on a Hot Tin Roof* (Brooks; Avon; MGM; 1958)	9,750,000
	The Green Berets (Wayne/Kellogg; Batjac; Warner; 1968)	9,750,000
186.	*Lady Sings the Blues* (Furie; Weston/White; Paramount; 1972)	9,666,000

Continued

Rank	Title (Director; Producer; Distributor; Year)	Total Rentals
187.	*Old Yeller* (Stevenson; Disney; Buena Vista; 1957)	9,600,000
	Robin Hood (Reitherman; Buena Vista; 1973)	9,600,000
189.	*Operation Petticoat* (Edwards; Granart; Universal; 1959)	9,500,000
	Grand Prix (Frankenheimer; Douglas/Lewis; MGM/UA; 1967)	9,500,000
	Blackbeard's Ghost (Stevenson; Walsh; Buena Vista; 1968)	9,500,000
	Joe (Avildsen; Gil; Cannon; 1970)	9,500,000
193.	*Son of Flubber* (Stevenson; Disney; Buena Vista; 1963)	9,350,000
	Man with the Golden Gun (Hamilton; Eon; UA; 1974)	9,310,000
195.	*Auntie Mame* (Da Costa; Warner; Warner; 1958)	9,300,000
	Cat Ballou (Silverstein; Hecht; Columbia; 1965)	9,300,000
	The Valachi Papers (Young; DeLaurentiis; Columbia; 1972)	9,300,000
198.	*Willard* (Mann; Briskin; CRC–AIP; 1971)	9,250,000
199.	*On Her Majesty's Secret Service* (Hunt; Eon; UA; 1969)	9,100,000
	Thunderbolt and Lightfoot (Cimino; Daley; UA; 1974)	9,100,000
	Barry Lyndon (Kubrick; Warner; 1975)	9,100,000

2. ANNUAL TOP MONEYMAKING FILMS

Here are the top moneymaking movies for each year from 1930 to 1977. From 1930 to 1946 the films are listed alphabetically, according to the records of the *Motion Picture Herald*, *Motion Picture Daily* and *Film Daily*. When a film is a top moneymaker for more than one year during these years, only the first year has been listed.

From 1947 to 1977 the movies are listed according to their rental earnings as reported each year in *Variety*. These figures reflect a film's domestic (United States and Canada) and not its foreign earnings. When a picture is released late in the calendar year (October to December), its income is reported in the following year's compendium, unless the film made a particularly fast impact. *Variety*'s lists include reissues.

From 1947 to 1958, the films are listed according to their *total* domestic anticipated earnings; that is, according to the studio's educated guesses as to the film's eventual revenue in the United States and Canada. The figures were based on full market playoff as indicated by the amounts taken in at the time the list was compiled.

Beginning in 1959, however, the films are listed not according to their eventual total domestic earnings, but *only* according to their rental fees up until the end of the calendar year. Thus, the figures in the lists from 1959 are in most cases smaller than a film's eventual domestic earnings.

It is possible for a film released after 1959 to have earned considerable rental fees and yet not appear on one of these annual lists. Let's say, for example, that a film released in September 1959 had earned $2,000,000 by the end of the year, a sum that would not qualify for that year's Top Twenty. That movie, however, could also have earned, let's say, another $2,000,000 during the next year, a sum that would not qualify the film for the following year's Top Twenty either. But between those two calendar years, the film would have made $4,000,000. The film would have earned an impressive sum and yet not have appeared on either the 1959 or 1960 lists of Top Twenty Moneymakers.

Whenever two or more films earned the same rental fees, the tied movies are given the same numerical rank. The film earning the next greatest rental fees is then given a numerical rank which takes into account the preceding tie. For example, in 1969 *Oliver!* and *Goodbye, Columbus* each earned $10,500,000 and thus tied for eighth

place that year. *Chitty Chitty Bang Bang,* which earned
$7,500,000 that year, is then said to occupy tenth place.

1930 / 31

Animal Crackers
Check and Double Check
Cimarron
City Lights
A Connecticut Yankee
Daddy Long Legs
Hell's Angels
Little Caesar
The Man Who Came Back
Min and Bill
Morocco
Politics
Reducing
Strangers May Kiss
Trader Horn

1932

Arrowsmith
Bring 'Em Back Alive
Business and Pleasure
Delicious
Dr. Jekyll and Mr. Hyde
Emma
Frankenstein
Grand Hotel
Hell Divers
The Man Who Played God
Mata Hari
One Hour with You
Shanghai Express
Shopworn
Tarzan the Ape Man

1933

Animal Kingdom
Be Mine Tonight
Cavalcade
42nd Street
Gold Diggers of 1933
I'm No Angel
The Kid from Spain
Little Women
Rasputin and the Empress
State Fair
Tugboat Annie

1934

The Barrets of Wimpole Street
Belle of the Nineties
Chained
It Happened One Night
Judge Priest
Kentucky Kernels
The Lost Patrol
One Night of Love
Queen Christina
Riptide
Roman Scandals
She Loves Me Not
Son of Kong
Sons of the Desert
Wonder Bar

1935

China Seas
David Copperfield
Forsaking All Others
Goin' to Town

Les Misérables
Lives of a Bengal Lancer
A Midsummer Night's Dream
Mutiny on the Bounty
Roberta
She Married Her Boss
Steamboat 'Round the Bend
Top Hat

1935 / 36

Anna Karenina
The Bride Comes Home
Broadway Melody of 1936
Bullets or Ballots
Captain Blood
The Country Doctor
The Crusades
Follow the Fleet
The Great Ziegfeld
Green Pastures
In Old Kentucky
The King Steps Out
The Littlest Rebel
Magnificent Obsession
Modern Times
Mr. Deeds Goes to Town
A Night at the Opera
Rhythm on the Range
Rose Marie
San Francisco
Show Boat
The Story of Louis Pasteur
A Tale of Two Cities
Thanks a Million
These Three

1936 / 37

After the Thin Man
Anthony Adverse
Artists and Models
The Big Broadcast of 1937
Born to Dance
Captains Courageous

The Charge of the Light
  Brigade
College Holiday
Come and Get It
Dodsworth
The Good Earth
The Gorgeous Hussy
Green Light
I Met Him in Paris
The Last of Mrs. Cheyney
Libeled Lady
Lloyds of London
Lost Horizon
Love Is News
Maytime
Mountain Music
My Man Godfrey
One in a Million
On the Avenue
Pigskin Parade
The Plainsman
Rainbow on the River
The Road Back
Romeo and Juliet
Shall We Dance
Slave Ship
A Star Is Born
Swing High, Swing Low
Swing Time
Wake Up and Live
Waikiki Wedding
Wee Willie Winkie
You Can't Have Everything

1937 / 38

The Adventures of Robin Hood
The Adventures of Tom Sawyer
Alexander's Ragtime Band
The Buccaneer
The Firefly
The Girl of the Golden West
The Goldwyn Follies
Happy Landing
Holiday
The Hurricane
In Old Chicago

Rosalie
Snow White and the Seven
  Dwarfs
Test Pilot
Wells Fargo

1938 / 39

Angels with Dirty Faces
Boys Town
Dodge City
Goodbye, Mr. Chips
Gunga Din
The Hardys Ride High
Jesse James
Juárez
Out West with the Hardys
Pygmalion
Stagecoach
Sweethearts
That Certain Age
Three Smart Girls Grow Up
Union Pacific
You Can't Take It With You

1939 / 40

All This, and Heaven Too
Another Thin Man
Babes in Arms
Destry Rides Again
Drums Along the Mohawk
The Fighting 69th
Gone With the Wind
The Grapes of Wrath
Gulliver's Travels
Hollywood Cavalcade
The Hunchback of Notre Dame
Lillian Russell
Mr. Smith Goes to Washington
My Favorite Wife
Ninotchka
Northwest Passage
The Old Maid
The Rains Came
Rebecca

Road to Singapore
The Women

1940 / 41

Aloma of the South Seas
Blood and Sand
Boom Town
The Bride Came C.O.D.
Caught in the Draft
Charley's Aunt
Dive Bomber
The Great Dictator
Hold That Ghost
I Wanted Wings
The Lady Eve
Life Begins for Andy Hardy
Meet John Doe
North West Mounted Police
The Philadelphia Story
Road to Zanzibar
The Sea Wolf
Strawberry Blonde
That Hamilton Woman
This Thing Called Love
The Ziegfeld Girl

1941 / 42

Ball of Fire
Captains of the Clouds
Eagle Squadron
Holiday Inn
Honky Tonk
How Green Was My Valley
In This Our Life
Kings Row
Louisiana Purchase
The Man Who Came to Dinner
Mrs. Miniver
My Favorite Blonde
My Gal Sal
Pride of the Yankees
Reap the Wild Wind
Sergeant York
Somewhere I'll Find You

This Above All
To the Shores of Tripoli
Woman of the Year
Yankee Doodle Dandy

1942 / 43

Air Force
Behind the Rising Sun
Casablanca
Claudia
Commandos Strike at Dawn
Coney Island
Dixie
Heaven Can Wait
Hello, Frisco, Hello
Hers to Hold
Hitler's Children
Immortal Sergeant
In Which We Serve
Keeper of the Flame
Lucky Jordan
Mr. Lucky
The More the Merrier
Now, Voyager
Random Harvest
Road to Morocco
So Proudly We Hail
Stage Door Canteen
Star Spangled Rhythm
This Is the Army

1943 / 44

Arsenic and Old Lace
Cover Girl
Destination Tokyo
Dragon Seed
For Whom the Bell Tolls
The Gang's All Here
Girl Crazy
Going My Way
Guadalcanal Diary
A Guy Named Joe
Lady in the Dark
Let's Face It

Madame Curie
The Miracle of Morgan's Creek
Mr. Skeffington
The North Star
See Here, Private Hargrove
Since You Went Away
The Song of Bernadette
The Story of Dr. Wassell
Sweet Rosie O'Grady
Thank Your Lucky Stars
As Thousands Cheer
White Cliffs of Dover
Wilson

1944 / 45

The Affairs of Susan
Along Came Jones
Anchors Aweigh
And Now Tomorrow
Casanova Brown
Christmas in Connecticut
Diamond Horseshoe
Frenchman's Creek
God Is My Co-Pilot
Here Comes the Waves
Hollywood Canteen
I'll Be Seeing You
Incendiary Blonde
Irish Eyes Are Smiling
The Keys of the Kingdom
Meet Me in St. Louis
Mrs. Parkington
Music for Millions
National Velvet
Nob Hill
The Princess and the Pirate
Rhapsody in Blue
Salty O'Rourke
A Song to Remember
Thirty Seconds Over Tokyo
Thrill of Romance
Thunderhead
Son of Flicka
To Have and Have Not
A Tree Grows in Brooklyn
The Valley of Decision

Winged Victory
Without Love
Wonder Man

1945 / 46

Adventure
Anna and the King of Siam
Bandit of Sherwood Forest
The Bells of St. Mary's
Caesar and Cleopatra
Canyon Passage
The Dolly Sisters
Dragonwyck
Duffy's Tavern
Easy to Wed
Gilda
The Green Years
The Harvey Girls
The House on 92nd Street
Kid From Brooklyn
Kitty
Leave Her to Heaven
The Lost Weekend
Love Letters
Mildred Pierce
Miss Susie Slagle's
Monsieur Beaucaire
My Reputation
Night and Day
Notorious
Road to Utopia
San Antonio
Saratoga Trunk
The Spanish Main
Spellbound
The Stork Club
They Were Expendable
Tomorrow Is Forever
Two Sisters from Boston
Weekend at the Waldorf
Ziegfeld Follies of 1946

1946 / 47

The Bachelor and the Bobby-
   soxer
The Best Years of Our Lives
Blue Skies
California
Dear Ruth
Duel in the Sun
The Farmer's Daughter
The Hucksters
Humoresque
I Wonder Who's Kissing Her
   Now
It's a Wonderful Life
The Jolson Story
Life with Father
Margie
My Favorite Brunette
No Leave, No Love
Nora Prentiss
The Perils of Pauline
Possessed
The Razor's Edge
Till the Clouds Roll By
The Time, the Place and the
   Girl
Two Years Before the Mast
Variety Girl
Welcome Strangers
The Yearling

1947

1.	The Best Years of Our Lives	$11,500,000
2.	Duel in the Sun	10,750,000
3.	The Jolson Story	8,000,000
	Forever Amber	8,000,000
5.	Unconquered	7,500,000
6.	Life with Father	6,250,000
7.	Welcome Stranger	6,100,000
8.	The Egg and I	5,750,000
9.	The Yearling	5,250,000

10.	Green Dolphin	
	Street	5,000,000
	The Razor's Edge	5,000,000
12.	The Hucksters	4,700,000
13.	The Bachelor and the Bobby-soxer	4,500,000
	Till the Clouds Roll By	4,500,000
15.	Mother Wore Tights	4,150,000
16.	California	3,900,000
17.	Dear Ruth	3,800,000
	The Perils of Pauline	3,800,000
19.	The Sea of Grass	3,650,000
	This Time for Keeps	3,650,000

1948

1.	The Road to Rio	$4,500,000
2.	Easter Parade	4,200,000
3.	Red River	4,150,000
4.	The Three Musketeers	4,100,000
	Johnny Belinda	4,100,000
6.	Cass Timberlane	4,050,000
7.	The Emperor Waltz	4,000,000
8.	Gentleman's Agreement	3,900,000
9.	Date with Judy	3,700,000
10.	Captain from Castile	3,650,000
	Homecoming	3,650,000
12.	Sitting Pretty	3,550,000
13.	Paleface	3,500,000
	The State of the Union	3,500,000
15.	My Wild Irish Rose	3,400,000
	When My Baby Smiles at Me	3,400,000
17.	Hamlet	3,250,000
	Key Largo	3,250,000

| 19. | On an Island with You | 3,150,000 |
| 20. | The Fuller Brush Man | 3,100,000 |

1949

1.	Jolson Sings Again	$5,500,000
2.	Pinky	4,200,000
3.	I Was A Male War Bride	4,100,000
	The Snake Pit	4,100,000
	Joan of Arc	4,100,000
6.	The Stratton Story	3,700,000
7.	Mr. Belvedere Goes to College	3,650,000
8.	Little Women	3,600,000
9.	Words and Music	3,500,000
10.	Neptune's Daughter	3,450,000
11.	Gold Old Summertime	3,400,000
	Sorrowful Jones	3,400,000
13.	Take Me Out to the Ballgame	3,350,000
14.	Great Lover	3,300,000
15.	The Barkleys of Broadway	3,200,000
16.	Adam's Rib	3,000,000
	Come to the Stable	3,000,000
	Command Decision	3,000,000
	Conneticut Yankee	3,000,000
20.	Whispering Smith	2,850,000

1950

| 1. | Samson and Delilah | $11,000,000 |
| 2. | Battleground | 4,550,400 |

3. King Solomon's
   Mines   4,400,000
4. Cheaper by the
   Dozen   4,325,000
5. Annie Get Your
   Gun   4,200,000
6. Cinderella   4,150,000
   Father of the
   Bride   4,150,000
8. Sands of Iwo
   Jima   3,900,000
9. Broken Arrow   3,550,000
10. Twelve O'Clock
    High   3,225,000
11. All About Eve   2,900,000
    The Flame and the
    Arrow   2,900,000
    Francis   2,900,000
    On the Town   2,900,000
15. Adam's Rib   2,750,000
16. Three Little
    Words   2,700,000
17. Black Rose   2,650,000
18. The Great Lover   2,625,000
19. The Duchess of
    Idaho   2,600,000
    Fancy Pants   2,600,000

1951

1. David and
   Bathsheba $7,000,000
2. Showboat   5,200,000
3. An American In
   Paris   4,500,000
   The Great Caruso   4,500,000
5. A Streetcar Named
   Desire   4,250,000
6. Born Yesterday   4,150,000
7. That's My Boy   3,800,000
8. A Place in the Sun   3,500,000
9. At War with the
   Army   3,350,000
10. Father's Little
    Dividend   3,100,000
11. Detective Story   2,800,000
    Kim   2,800,000

13. Across the Wide
    Missouri   2,750,000
    Captain Horatio
    Hornblower   2,750,000
15. Halls of
    Montezuma   2,650,000
16. Flying
    Leathernecks   2,600,000
    Harvey   2,600,000
    Royal Wedding   2,600,000
19. Here Comes the
    Groom   2,550,000
20. Go For Broke   2,500,000
    On Moonlight Bay   2,500,000
    On the Riviera   2,500,000

1952

1. The Greatest Show
   on Earth $12,000,000
2. Quo Vadis   10,500,000
3. Ivanhoe   7,000,000
4. The Snows of
   Kilimanjaro   6,500,000
5. Sailor Beware   4,300,000
6. The African
   Queen   4,000,000
   Jumping Jacks   4,000,000
8. High Noon   3,400,000
   Son of Paleface   3,400,000
10. Singin' in the
    Rain   3,300,000
11. With a Song in My
    Heart   3,250,000
12. The Quiet Man   3,200,000
13. The Bend of the
    River   3,000,000
    Plymouth
    Adventure   3,000,000
    Stars and Stripes
    Forever   3,000,000
    World in His
    Arms   3,000,000

17.	I'll See You in My Dreams	2,900,000
	The Iron Mistress	2,900,000
	Just for You	2,900,000
20.	Distant Drums	2,850,000

1953

1.	The Robe	$20–30,000,000
2.	From Here to Eternity	12,500,000
3.	Shane	8,000,000
4.	How to Marry a Millionaire	7,500,000
5.	Peter Pan	7,000,000
6.	Hans Christian Andersen	6,000,000
7.	House of Wax	5,500,000
8.	Mogambo	5,200,000
9.	Gentlemen Prefer Blondes	5,100,000
10.	Moulin Rouge	5,000,000
11.	Salome	4,750,000
12.	Charge at Feather River	3,650,000
13.	Caddy	3,500,000
	Come Back, Little Sheba	3,500,000
	The Moon Is Blue	3,500,000
	Scared Stiff	3,500,000
	Stooge	3,500,000
18.	Stalag 17	3,300,000
19.	Little Boy Lost	3,000,000
	Mississippi Gambler	3,000,000
	The Road to Bali	3,000,000
	Roman Holiday	3,000,000

1954

1.	White Christmas	$12,000,000
2.	The Caine Mutiny	8,700,000
3.	The Glenn Miller Story	7,000,000
4.	The Egyptian	6,000,000

5.	Rear Window	5,300,000
6.	The High and the Mighty	5,200,000
7.	Magnificent Obsession	5,000,000
	Three Coins in the Fountain	5,000,000
9.	Seven Brides for Seven Brothers	4,750,000
10.	Desiree	4,500,000
11.	Knights of the Round Table	4,400,000
12.	Dragnet	4,300,000
13.	Demetrius and the Gladiators	4,250,000
	Living It Up	4,250,000
15.	On the Waterfront	4,200,000
16.	Hondo	4,100,000
17.	The Long, Long Trailer	4,000,000
	Sabrina	4,000,000
19.	River of No Return	3,800,000
	Broken Lance	3,800,000

1955

1.	Cinerama Holiday	$10,000,000
2.	Mister Roberts	8,500,000
3.	Battle Cry	8,000,000
	20,000 Leagues Under the Sea	8,000,000
5.	Not as a Stranger	7,100,000
6.	The Country Girl	6,900,000
7.	The Lady and the Tramp	6,500,000
	Strategic Air Command	6,500,000
9.	To Hell and Back	6,000,000
	Sea Chase	6,000,000
	A Star Is Born	6,000,000
12.	The Blackboard Jungle	5,200,000
13.	East of Eden	5,000,000
	Pete Kelly's Blues	5,000,000

The Seven-Year Itch	5,000,000
16. *The Bridges at Toko-Ri*	4,700,000
17. *A Man Called Peter*	4,500,000
No Business Like Show Business	4,500,000
To Catch a Thief	4,500,000
Vera Cruz	4,500,000

1956

1.	*Guys and Dolls*	$9,000,000
2.	*The King and I*	8,500,000
3.	*Trapeze*	7,500,000
4.	*High Society*	6,500,000
	I'll Cry Tomorrow	6,500,000
6.	*Picnic*	6,300,000
7.	*War and Peace*	6,250,000
8.	*The Eddy Duchin Story*	5,300,000
9.	*Moby Dick*	5,200,000
10.	*The Searchers*	4,800,000
11.	*Conqueror*	4,500,000
	Rebel Without a Cause	4,500,000
13.	*The Man with the Golden Arm*	4,350,000
	The Man in the Grey Flannel Suit	4,350,000
15.	*Bus Stop*	4,250,000
16.	*The Rose Tattoo*	4,200,000
17.	*The Bad Seed*	4,100,000
	The Man Who Knew Too Much	4,100,000
19.	*Friendly Persuasion*	4,000,000
20.	*The Proud and the Profane*	3,900,000

1957

1.	*The Ten Commandments*	$18,500,000
2.	*Around the World in 80 Days*	16,200,000
3.	*Giant*	12,000,000
4.	*Pal Joey*	6,700,000
5.	*Seven Wonders of the World*	6,500,000
6.	*The Teahouse of the August Moon*	5,600,000
7.	*The Pride and the Passion*	5,500,000
8.	*Anastasia*	5,000,000
	Island in the Sun	5,000,000
10.	*Love Me Tender*	4,500,000
11.	*Written on the Wind*	4,400,000
12.	*Gunfight at the O.K. Corral*	4,300,000
13.	*Heaven Knows, Mr. Allison*	4,200,000
14.	*April Love*	4,000,000
	Jailhouse Rock	4,000,000
16.	*Battle Hymn*	3,900,000
17.	*An Affair to Remember*	3,850,000
18.	*Bernadine*	3,700,000
	Loving You	3,700,000
20.	*The Sun Also Rises*	3,500,000

1958

1.	*The Bridge on the River Kwai*	$18,000,000
2.	*Peyton Place*	12,000,000
3.	*Sayonara*	10,500,000
4.	*No Time for Sergeants*	7,200,000
5.	*The Vikings*	7,000,000
6.	*Search for Paradise*	6,500,000
7.	*South Pacific*	6,400,000
8.	*Cat on a Hot Tin Roof*	6,100,000
9.	*Raintree County*	6,000,000
10.	*Old Yeller*	5,900,000

11.	The Big Country	5,000,000
	A Farewell to Arms	5,000,000
	The Young Lions	5,000,000
14.	Don't Go Near the Water	4,500,000
15.	Witness for the Prosecution	3,750,000
16.	Indiscreet	3,600,000
17.	God's Little Acre	3,500,000
	Houseboat	3,500,000
	The Long Hot Summer	3,500,000
	The Sad Sack	3,500,000

1959

1.	Auntie Mame	$8,800,000
2.	Shaggy Dog	7,800,000
3.	Some Like It Hot	7,000,000
4.	Imitation of Life	6,200,000
5.	The Nun's Story	6,000,000
6.	Anatomy of a Murder	5,250,000
	North by Northwest	5,250,000
8.	Rio Bravo	5,200,000
9.	Sleeping Beauty	4,300,000
10.	Some Came Running	4,200,000
11.	Hole in the Head	4,000,000
	Hercules	4,000,000
13.	Inn of the Sixth Happiness	3,600,000
14.	The Horse Soldiers	3,300,000
15.	Don't Give Up the Ship	3,200,000
16.	7 Voyages of Sinbad	3,100,000
17.	The Buccaneer	3,000,000
	The Geisha Boy	3,000,000
	I Want to Live!	3,000,000
20.	Separate Tables	2,700,000
	Big Circus	2,700,000

1960

1.	Ben-Hur	$17,300,000
2.	Psycho	8,500,000
3.	Operation Petticoat	6,800,000
4.	Suddenly, Last Summer	5,500,000
5.	On the Beach	5,300,000
6.	Solomon and Sheba	5,250,000
7.	The Apartment	5,100,000
8.	From the Terrace	5,000,000
	Please Don't Eat the Daisies	5,000,000
10.	Oceans 11	4,900,000
11.	Journey to the Center of the Earth	4,700,000
12.	The Bellboy	3,550,000
13.	Elmer Gantry	3,500,000
14.	The Rat Race	3,400,000
15.	Portrait in Black	3,200,000
16.	Li'l Abner	3,200,000
17.	Visit to a Small Planet	3,200,000
18.	Home from the Hill	3,150,000
19.	Who Was that Lady?	3,000,000
	Toby Tyler	3,000,000
	The Big Fisherman	3,000,000
	Can-Can	

1961

1.	The Guns of Navarone	$8,600,000
2.	The Absent-Minded Professor	8,200,000
3.	The Parent Trap	8,000,000
4.	Swiss Family Robinson	7,500,000
5.	Exodus	7,350,000

6.	The World of Suzie Wong	7,300,000
7.	Alamo	7,250,000
8.	Gone With the Wind (reissue)	6,000,000
9.	101 Dalmatians	5,800,000
10.	Splendor in the Grass	5,100,000
11.	Come September	4,500,000
	North to Alaska	4,500,000
	Fanny	4,500,000
14.	Pepe	4,300,000
	One-Eyed Jacks	4,300,000
16.	Parrish	4,200,000
17.	The Misfits	3,900,000
18.	The Sundowners	3,800,000
19.	Midnight Lace	3,500,000
20.	Never on Sunday	3,300,000
	Where the Boys Are	3,300,000
	The Wackiest Ship in the Army	3,300,000

1962

1.	Spartacus	$13,500,000
2.	West Side Story	11,000,000
3.	Lover Come Back	8,500,000
	That Touch of Mink	8,500,000
5.	El Cid	8,000,000
	The Music Man	8,000,000
7.	King of Kings	7,500,000
8.	Hatari	6,000,000
9.	The Flower Drum Song	5,000,000
	The Interns	5,000,000
11.	Blue Hawaii	4,700,000
12.	Lolita	4,500,000
13.	Babes in Toyland	4,400,000
14.	Bon Voyage	4,100,000
15.	What Ever Happened to Baby Jane?	4,000,000
16.	Sergeants 3	3,955,000
17.	The Man Who Shot Liberty Valance	3,900,000

18.	Judgment at Nuremberg	3,800,000
19.	Moon Pilot	3,500,000
	Splendor in the Grass	3,500,000

1963

1.	Cleopatra	$15,700,000
2.	The Longest Day	12,750,000
3.	Irma La Douce	9,250,000
4.	Lawrence of Arabia	9,000,000
5.	How the West Was Won	8,000,000
6.	Mutiny on the Bounty	7,700,000
7.	Son of Flubber	6,900,000
8.	To Kill a Mockingbird	6,700,000
9.	Bye Bye Birdie	5,600,000
10.	Come Blow Your Horn	5,450,000
11.	Gypsy	5,400,000
12.	The Castaways	4,700,000
13.	The Birds	4,600,000
	The Great Escape	4,600,000
15.	The Brothers Grimm	4,500,000
16.	Diamond Head	4,300,000
17.	The Thrill of It All	4,150,000
18.	Spencer's Mountain	4,000,000
19.	55 Days at Peking	3,900,000
	Hud	3,900,000

1964

1.	The Carpetbaggers	$13,000,000
2.	It's a Mad, Mad, Mad, Mad World	10,000,000
3.	The Unsinkable Molly Brown	7,500,000
4.	Charade	6,150,000
5.	The Cardinal	5,275,000

6.	*Move Over Darling*	5,100,000
7.	*My Fair Lady*	5,000,000
	What a Way to Go	5,000,000
9.	*Good Neighbor Sam*	4,950,000
10.	*The Pink Panther*	4,853,000
11.	*Viva Las Vegas*	4,675,000
12.	*Sword in the Stone*	4,500,000
13.	*Hard Day's Night*	4,473,000
14.	*Dr. Strangelove*	4,148,000
15.	*The Night of the Iguana*	4,000,000
	The Misadventures of Merlin Jones	4,000,000
17.	*From Russia with Love*	3,849,000
18.	*Love with the Proper Stranger*	3,500,000
19.	*Seven Days In May*	3,400,000
	The Prize	3,400,000

1965

1.	*Mary Poppins*	$28,500,000
2.	*The Sound of Music*	20,000,000
3.	*Goldfinger*	19,700,000
4.	*My Fair Lady*	19,000,000
5.	*What's New Pussycat?*	7,150,000
6.	*Shenandoah*	7,000,000
7.	*The Sandpiper*	6,400,000
8.	*Father Goose*	6,000,000
9.	*Von Ryan's Express*	5,600,000
10.	*The Yellow Rolls-Royce*	5,400,000
11.	*How to Murder Your Wife*	5,380,000
12.	*Cat Ballou*	5,150,000
13.	*The Sons of Katie Elder*	5,000,000
14.	*Help*	4,140,000

15.	*Sex and the Single Girl*	4,000,000
16.	*In Harm's Way*	3,900,000
17.	*The Americanization of Emily*	3,600,000
18.	*Monkey's Uncle*	3,500,000
19.	*The Train*	3,450,000
20.	*Goodbye Charlie*	3,400,000
	Operation Crossbow	3,400,000

1966

1.	*Thunderball*	$26,000,000
2.	*Doctor Zhivago*	15,000,000
3.	*Who's Afraid of Virginia Woolf?*	10,300,000
4.	*That Darn Cat*	9,200,000
5.	*The Russians Are Coming, The Russians Are Coming*	7,750,000
6.	*Lt. Robin Crusoe, USN*	7,500,000
7.	*The Silencers*	7,000,000
	Torn Curtain	7,000,000
9.	*Our Man Flint*	6,500,000
10.	*A Patch of Blue*	6,300,000
11.	*The Ugly Dachshund*	6,000,000
12.	*Wild Angels*	5,500,000
13.	*Harper*	5,300,000
14.	*The Blue Max*	5,000,000
	Arabesque	5,000,000
	Nevada Smith	5,000,000
17.	*The Battle of the Bulge*	4,500,000
	Fantastic Voyage	4,500,000
	Texas Across the River	4,500,000
20.	*The Glass Bottom Boat*	4,320,000

1967

1. The Dirty Dozen $18,200,000
2. You Only Live
      Twice   16,300,000
3. Casino Royale   10,200,000
4. A Man for All
      Seasons   9,250,000
5. Thoroughly Modern
      Millie   8,500,000
6. Barefoot in the
      Park   8,250,000
7. Georgy Girl   7,330,000
8. To Sir With Love   7,200,000
9. Grand Prix   7,000,000
10. Hombre   6,500,000
11. Murderers' Row   6,240,000
12. Gone With the
      Wind (reissue)   6,200,000
13. El Dorado   5,950,000
14. Blow-up   5,900,000
15. War Wagon   5,500,000
16. Follow Me, Boys   5,350,000
17. Divorce American
      Style   5,150,000
18. In Like Flint   5,000,000
      Guide for Married
      Man   5,000,000
      Up the Down
      Staircase   5,000,000

1968

1. The Graduate $39,000,000
2. Guess Who's Coming
      to Dinner   25,100,000
3. Gone With
      the Wind
      (reissue)   23,000,000
4. The Valley of the
      Dolls   20,000,000
5. The Odd Couple   18,500,000
6. Planet of the
      Apes   15,000,000
7. Rosemary's Baby   12,300,000

8. The Jungle Book   11,500,000
9. Yours, Mine and
      Ours   11,000,000
10. The Green Berets   8,700,000
11. 2001: A Space
      Odyssey   8,500,000
12. The Fox   8,300,000
13. Wait Until Dark   7,350,000
14. Camelot   6,600,000
15. The Detective   6,500,000
16. The Thomas
      Crown Affair   6,000,000
17. In Cold Blood   5,600,000
18. Bandolero   5,500,000
19. For the Love of
      Ivy   5,075,000
20. Hang 'Em High   5,000,000
      The Happiest
      Millionaire   5,000,000

1969

1. The Love Bug $17,000,000
2. Funny Girl   16,500,000
3. Bullitt   16,400,000
4. Butch Cassidy and the
      Sundance Kid   15,000,000
5. Romeo and
      Juliet   14,500,000
6. True Grit   11,500,000
7. Midnight
      Cowboy   11,000,000
8. Oliver!   10,500,000
      Goodbye,
      Columbus   10,500,000
10. Chitty Chitty
      Bang Bang   7,500,000
11. Easy Rider   7,200,000
12. I Am Curious
      (Yellow)   6,600,000
13. Where Eagles
      Dare   6,560,000
14. The Lion in
      Winter   6,400,000
      Swiss Family
      Robinson
      (reissue)   6,400,000

16.	Winning	6,200,000
17.	The Impossible Years	5,800,000
18.	Three in the Attic	5,200,000
19.	Finian's Rainbow	5,100,000
20.	Support Your Local Sheriff	5,000,000

1970

1.	Airport	$37,650,796
2.	M*A*S*H	22,000,000
3.	Patton	21,000,000
4.	Bob & Carol & Ted & Alice	13,900,000
5.	Woodstock	13,500,000
6.	Hello, Dolly!	13,000,000
7.	Cactus Flower	11,300,000
8.	Catch-22	9,250,000
9.	On Her Majesty's Secret Service	9,000,000
10.	The Reivers	8,000,000
11.	The Adventurers	7,750,000
12.	Beneath the Planet of the Apes	7,250,000
	The Out-of-Towners	7,250,000
14.	Z	6,750,000
15.	They Shoot Horses, Don't They?	6,500,000
16.	Anne of the 1,000 Days	6,134,264
17.	A Boy Named Charlie Brown	6,000,000
	101 Dalmatians (reissue)	6,000,000
	Chisum	6,000,000
	A Man Called Horse	6,000,000

1971

1.	Love Story	$50,000,000
2.	Little Big Man	15,000,000
3.	Summer of '42	14,000,000
4.	Ryan's Daughter	13,400,000

5.	The Owl and the Pussycat	11,500,000
6.	The Aristocats	10,100,000
7.	Carnal Knowledge	9,347,000
8.	Willard	8,200,000
9.	The Andromeda Strain	7,500,000
	Big Jake	7,500,000
11.	The Stewardesses	6,418,170
12.	Shaft	6,100,000
	The French Connection	6,100,000
14.	Klute	6,000,000
15.	Cold Turkey	5,500,000
	Le Mans	5,500,000
	The Anderson Tapes	5,000,000
	A New Leaf	5,000,000
19.	The $1,000,000 Duck	4,700,000
20.	There s a Girl in My Soup	4,500,000

1972

1.	The Godfather	$81,500,000
2.	Fiddler on the Roof	25,100,000
3.	Diamonds are Forever	21,000,000
4.	What's Up, Doc?	17,000,000
5.	Dirty Harry	16,000,000
6.	The Last Picture Show	12,750,000
7.	A Clockwork Orange	12,000,000
8.	Cabaret	10,885,000
9.	The Hospital	9,000,000
10.	Everything You Always Wanted to Know About Sex	8,500,000
11.	Bedknobs and Broomsticks	8,250,000
12.	The Cowboys	7,000,000

13.	Nicholas and Alexandra	6,750,000
14.	Frenzy	6,300,000
15.	Skyjacked	6,001,000
16.	Song of the South (reissue)	5,900,000
17.	Escape from the Planet of the Apes	5,500,000
	Butterflies Are Free	5,500,000
	The New Centurions	5,500,000
20.	2001: A Space Odyssey (reissue)	5,395,000

1973

1.	The Poseidon Adventure	$40,000,000
2.	Deliverance	18,000,000
3.	The Getaway	17,500,000
4.	Live and Let Die	15,500,000
5.	Paper Moon	13,000,000
6.	Last Tango in Paris	12,625,000
7.	The Sound of Music (reissue)	11,000,000
8.	Jesus Christ Superstar	10,800,000
9.	The World's Greatest Athlete	10,600,000
10.	American Graffiti	10,300,000
11.	The Way We Were	10,000,000
12.	Lady Sings the Blues	9,050,000
13.	Mary Poppins (reissue)	9,000,000
	Sounder	9,000,000
15.	Pete 'n' Tillie	8,700,000
16.	The Day of the Jackal	8,525,000
17.	Walking Tall	8,500,000

18.	Jeremiah Johnson	8,350,000
19.	Billy Jack (reissue)	8,275,000
20.	High Plains Drifter	7,125,000

1974

1.	The Sting	$68,450,000
2.	The Exorcist	66,300,000
3.	Papillon	19,750,000
4.	Magnum Force	18,300,000
5.	Herbie Rides Again	17,500,000
6.	Blazing Saddles	16,500,000
7.	Trial of Billy Jack	15,000,000
8.	The Great Gatsby	14,200,000
9.	Serpico	14,100,600
10.	Butch Cassidy and the Sundance Kid (reissue)	13,820,000
11.	Billy Jack (reissue)	13,000,000
12.	Airport 1975	12,310,000
13.	Dirty Mary and Crazy Larry	12,068,000
14.	That's Entertainment	10,800,000
15.	The Three Musketeers	10,115,000
16.	The Longest Yard	10,100,000
17.	Jeremiah Johnson (reissue)	10,000,000
18.	Robin Hood (reissue)	9,600,000
19.	For Pete's Sake	9,500,000
20.	Thunderbolt and Lightfoot	8,500,000

1975

| 1. | Jaws | $102,650,000 |
| 2. | The Towering Inferno | 55,000,000 |

3. *Benji* — 30,800,000
4. *Young Frankenstein* — 30,000,000
5. *The Godfather Part II* — 28,900,000
6. *Shampoo* — 22,000,000
7. *Funny Lady* — 19,000,000
8. *Murder on the Orient Express* — 17,800,000
9. *Return of the Pink Panther* — 17,000,000
10. *Tommy* — 16,000,000
11. *The Apple Dumpling Gang* — 13,500,000
12. *Freebie and the Bean* — 12,500,000
13. *Lenny* — 11,100,000
14. *Island at the Top of the World* — 10,000,000
15. *The Man with the Golden Arm* — 9,500,000
16. *The Great Waldo Pepper* — 9,400,000
17. *Three Days of the Condor* — 8,950,000
18. *Mandingo* — 8,600,000
19. *Escape to Witch Mountain* — 8,500,000
20. *The Other Side of the Mountain* — 8,200,000

1976

1. *One Flew Over the Cuckoo's Nest* — $56,500,000
2. *All the President's Men* — 29,000,000
3. *The Omen* — 27,851,000
4. *The Bad News Bears* — 22,266,517
5. *Silent Movie* — 20,311,000
6. *Midway* — 20,300,000
7. *Dog Day Afternoon* — 19,800,000
8. *Murder by Death* — 18,800,000

9. *Jaws* (reissue) — 16,077,000
10. *Blazing Saddles* (reissue) — 13,850,000
11. *Lucky Lady* — 12,107,000
12. *Taxi Driver* — 11,600,000
13. *Outlaw Josey Wales* — 10,600,000
14. *No Deposit, No Return* — 10,500,000
15. *Ode to Billy Joe* — 10,400,000
16. *The Exorcist* (reissue) — 10,300,000
17. *Hustle* — 9,958,738
18. *Barry Lyndon* — 9,100,000
19. *Gus* — 9,000,000
20. *Marathon Man* — 8,886,753

1977

1. *Star Wars* — $127,000,000
2. *Rocky* — 54,000,000
3. *Smokey and the Bandit* — 39,744,000
4. *A Star Is Born* — 37,100,000
5. *King Kong* — 35,851,283
6. *The Deep* — 31,000,000
7. *Silver Streak* — 27,100,000
8. *The Enforcer* — 24,000,000
9. *Close Encounters of the Third Kind* — 23,000,000
   In Search of Noah's Ark — 23,000,000
11. *The Spy Who Loved Me* — 22,000,000
12. *Oh, God* — 21,200,000
13. *A Bridge Too Far* — 21,000,000
14. *The Pink Panther Strikes Again* — 19,500,000
15. *The Other Side of Midnight* — 17,000,000
    The Rescuers — 17,000,000
17. *Airport 77* — 14,836,000
18. *Network* — 14,500,000
19. *Slap Shot* — 14,497,000
20. *Herbie Goes to Monte Carlo* — 14,000,000

3. MOST POPULAR MOVIES ON TELEVISION

The following chart lists the most popular movies aired on television between September 1961 and December 1976. Because Nielsen ratings were determined according to different standards prior to 1961, comparisons between pre- and post-1960 figures would be useless.

Nielsen ratings are reported in the following format: *Gone With the Wind*, 47.6 rating, 65 share. This means that for this particular showing of *Gone With the Wind*, 47.6 percent of the sets in all the monitored homes were turned on to the film, representing 65 percent of all the television sets turned on during that time period.

This list includes only movies made for theatrical release; it does not cover movies made for TV. It is obvious from this list that the most popular films aired on television do not closely correspond to the All-Time Box-Office Champs, suggesting that television and film audiences have different tastes.

This list is selected from *Variety*'s much longer and more comprehensive compilation that ranks every movie that has earned a national Nielsen rating of 24.0 or better. *Variety*'s list includes both feature movies and made-for-TV films. There are 293 different titles making up the 345 entries on the chart: 189 theatricals and 104 made-for-TV. (Obviously movies made especially for television are quite successful.) *The Wizard of Oz* has chalked up 13 telecasts with rating of 24.0 or better since it was first televised in November 1956, a record no other film can equal. *McLintock* and *The Ten Commandments* have each scored three times on the list. Of the 189 theatricals, 118 are also on *Variety*'s all-time top grossers film chart, but the orders of the two charts are quite different, as mentioned.

Rank	Title	Day	Date	Nielsen Rating	Share
1.	Gone With the Wind (Part 1)	Sun.	11 / 7 / 76	47.6	65
2.	Gone With the Wind (Part 2)	Mon.	11 / 8 / 76	47.4	64
3.	Airport	Sun.	11 / 11 / 73	42.3	63
	Love Story	Sun.	10 / 1 / 72	42.3	62
5.	The Godfather (Part 2)	Mon.	11 / 18 / 74	39.4	57
6.	The Poseidon Adventure	Sun.	10 / 27 / 74	39.0	62
7.	True Grit	Sun.	11 / 12 / 72	38.9	63
	The Birds	Sat.	1 / 6 / 68	38.9	59
9.	Patton	Sun.	11 / 19 / 72	38.5	65
10.	Bridge on the River Kwai	Sun.	9 / 25 / 66	38.3	61
11.	Jeremiah Johnson	Sun.	1 / 18 / 76	37.5	56
12.	Ben-Hur	Sun.	2 / 14 / 71	37.1	56
13.	The Godfather (Part 1)	Sat.	11 / 16 / 74	37.0	61
14.	The Wizard of Oz	Sun.	12 / 13 / 59	36.5	58
15.	The Wizard of Oz	Sun.	1 / 26 / 64	35.9	59
16.	Planet of the Apes	Fri.	9 / 14 / 73	35.2	60
17.	The Wizard of Oz	Sun.	1 / 17 / 65	34.7	49
18.	Born Free	Sun.	2 / 22 / 70	34.2	53
19.	The Wizard of Oz	Sat.	11 / 3 / 56	33.9	53
20.	The Sound of Music	Sun.	2 / 29 / 76	33.6	49
21.	Bonnie and Clyde	Thu.	9 / 20 / 73	33.4	38
22.	The Ten Commandments	Sun.	2 / 18 /.73	33.2	54
23.	The Wizard of Oz	Sun.	12 / 9 / 62	33.0	55
24.	The Wizard of Oz	Sun.	12 / 11 / 60	32.7	52
25.	Beneath the Planet of the Apes	Fri.	10 / 26 / 73	32.6	54
26.	The Wizard of Oz	Sun.	12 / 10 / 61	32.5	53
27.	Cat on a Hot Tin Roof	Thu.	9 / 28 / 67	32.3	50
28.	The Great Escape (Part 2)	Fri.	9 / 15 / 67	31.3	55
29.	McLintock	Fri.	11 / 3 / 67	31.2	54
30.	Ballad of Josie	Tue.	9 / 16 / 69	31.1	56
	The Great Escape (Part 1)	Thu.	9 / 14 / 67	31.1	51

Continued

Rank	Title	Day	Date	Nielsen Rating	Share
	The Wizard of Oz	Sun.	1 / 9 / 66	31.1	49
	Goldfinger	Sun.	9 / 17 / 72	31.1	49
34.	The Robe	Sun.	3 / 26 / 67	31.0	53
35.	The Ten Commandments (Part 2)	Mon.	2 / 18 / 74	30.8	48
36.	The Graduate	Thu.	11 / 8 / 73	30.5	38
37.	The Dirty Dozen	Thu.	9 / 24 / 70	30.4	53
38.	The War Wagon	Sat.	10 / 31 / 70	30.0	53
	Lilies of the Field	Fri.	3 / 24 / 67	30.0	50
	Airport	Sun.	2 / 9 / 75	30.0	42
41.	Your Cheatin' Heart	Fri.	4 / 5 / 68	29.7	50
42.	Gidget Goes Hawaiian	Thu.	3 / 31 / 66	29.6	49
43.	Five Branded Women	Fri.	1 / 6 / 67	29.4	42
44.	PT 109	Fri.	1 / 13 / 67	29.1	50
	Escape From the Planet of the Apes	Fri.	11 / 16 / 73	29.1	50
	Roustabout	Wed.	1 / 3 / 68	29.1	48
	Hombre	Sun.	1 / 25 / 70	29.1	45
48.	The Green Berets	Sat.	11 / 18 / 72	28.9	45
	West Side Story (Part 1)	Tue.	3 / 14 / 72	28.9	41
50.	Cat Ballou	Wed.	10 / 2 / 68	28.8	48

4. MOVIE THEATERS IN THE UNITED STATES

In their earliest days, movies did not have a home of their own. The first movies were not shown on a theater screen, but were viewed by one person at a time through a medium-sized cabinet known as a kinetoscope. Kinetoscopes—which have their modern day equivalent in the peep shows of adult bookstores—could be found in such places as penny arcades and traveling tent shows, where they offered such film fare as a young woman climbing a tree, an ocean wave beating upon the shore or a railroad train speeding directly toward the viewer.

In 1895, however, the Lumière Brothers in Paris projected

film onto a screen for a commercial audience for the first time, and one year later the experiment was successfully repeated by Thomas Edison in New York. Projected films proved so popular that soon many penny arcades, storefronts and music halls were converted into movie theaters, or "nickelodeons" as they came to be called. (The name is usually attributed to John P. Harris, a showman who merged the Greek word for theater with the admission price. The name caught on, although the admission price was soon to rise.)

The interiors of nickelodeons were usually simple: the auditorium was approximately 20 feet wide and 80 feet deep, divided by a central aisle with short straight rows of wooden seats on either side. The piano was located at the front, the projection booth in the back, and the screen was often merely a square of white or silver paint.

The exteriors of nickelodeons, however, were often quite lavish. The façade almost invariably contained an elaborate arch, in the middle of which was the ticket booth. (Above the box office was a small window to provide ventilation and a possible hasty escape for the projectionist, who was handling flammable nitrate film.) The façades could be decorated in various exotic styles—Moorish, Gothic, Oriental—and were embellished with ornamentation, statues, and above all else, with light bulbs. To attract audiences, theater managers hired barkers to announce the programs or even placed a pianist in the arched vestibule to play for passers-by.

By around 1910, film exhibitors began building theaters expressly to show movies rather than continue converting standing structures into nickelodeons. The Columbia Theater in Detroit (1911), the Regent in New York (1913) and the Coliseum in Seattle (1916) were all designed on a lavish scale that had been impossible on the pre-existing storefront sites of the nickelodeons. These new theaters held thousands of people, not hundreds, and an entire symphony replaced the solitary piano of the nickelodeon. Staffs were now uniformed, and mammoth pipe organs entertained audiences before the films. Live shows involving a great number of entertainers, dancers and singers were elaborately and professionally staged during intermissions. If one theater dressed a giant in an outlandish costume to "guard" the box office, another theater would place a midget in its foyer, or would dress its doorman as a Foreign Legionnaire to lure audiences into its splendid lobby. In short, the age of the movie palace had arrived.

Certain architects, in fact, became famous for their elaborate theaters: Thomas W. Lamb, who designed New York's Regent (1913), the Strand (1914) and the Rialto (1916), was one of the first and most prolific theater architects, having designed over three hundred movie palaces by 1921; Rapp and Rapp, whose best work included the Riviera and the Tivoli in Chicago and the famous Paramount Theater (1928) on Times Square, specialized in late-French-court architecture; and John Eberson, designer of the Majestic (1922) in Houston, was known for his "atmospheric" style that made the theater look as if it were outdoors, set in some exotic land.

Exotic styles were, in fact, quite fashionable for movie palaces, the two most famous examples being in Hollywood: Grauman's Egyptian Theater (1922) and Grauman's Chinese (1927), where on opening night Norma Talmadge pressed her hands and feet in wet cement and thereby started a tradition. Both Grauman's theaters were designed by Meyer and Holler.

The movie palace reached its apotheosis in two New York theaters: the Roxy (1927), which called itself the "cathedral of motion pictures" and proudly advertised its $10 million building costs; and Radio City Music Hall (1932), a lasting tribute to the wonders of Art Deco. Each theater seated over 6,000 people, and spared no expense in its luxurious interiors and elaborate equipment. The Roxy, designed by Walter Ahlschlager and decorated by Harold Rambusch, was named after S. L. Rothafel, the famous theater manager who had been nicknamed "Roxy" during his baseball days.

Movie-palace design is now both adamantly praised and criticized, but whether you find its architectural excesses wonderful or merely kitsch, you must admit that the movie-palace style served its function. For one thing, the fantastic décor matched the fantastic narratives of early films—as architect Thomas Lamb wrote when describing his State Theater (1929) in Syracuse, "these exotic ornaments, colors, and scenes are particularly effective in creating an atmosphere in which the mind is free to frolic and becomes receptive to entertainment." Secondly, the resplendent style paradoxically served America's "equalitarian" spirit, for despite our supposed anti-aristocratic sentiments, the American spirit has often been enamored of aristocracy and has secretly wished for everyone to be an aristocrat. The movie palaces afforded that chance: for a small admission fee, anyone could inhabit lush surroundings. As architect George Rapp noted, the movie palaces were "a shrine to democracy where there are no privileged patrons." Thirdly, the grand scale of the movie palaces served to hide the insecurity of an art form that was all too aware of its humble origins. By appropriating the style of legitimate theaters and opera houses—most movie palaces did not really pay much attention to the unique requirements of showing movies but merely imitated dramatic theaters—movies hoped to gain some of the respect conferred on legitimate drama.

But the era of the movie palace did not last very long. Both the Depression and the coming of sound brought an end to the extravagance. Physically, sound required attention to be paid to the acoustics of the theater and not merely to its decoration; and psychologically, sound brought a certain realism to the screen that contradicted the decorative excesses of movie palaces. The Depression, of course, curtailed the extravagant spending, and by the time the country was beginning to recover, World War II had begun and it, too, curtailed theater construction.

After the war, film exhibition in this country met two problems: (1) antitrust actions that forced Hollywood studios to divorce their production/distribution interests from their exhibition facilities, which meant that most theaters no longer had the studios' financial backing; and (2) television. During the early fifties, Hollywood found its audiences decimated by TV. The mammoth theaters, no longer able to draw large audiences, were often demolished or converted into garages, churches and bowling alleys. Hollywood tried to woo back its audiences through the technological curiosities of the wide screen— Cinerama, CinemaScope, VistaVision—but the tricks did not really work. By 1958 there were only 12,000 indoor theaters in the United States, whereas in 1948 there had been nearly 18,000.

Technology did, of course, change the shape of our theater screens. Silent films had been almost square in shape—1.33 feet in width to every 1 foot in height. Early sound films were slightly more rectangular, to accommodate the optical sound track—their ratio was 1.66 to 1. But with the new projection techniques of the early fifties, screens were almost twice as wide as high—18.5 to 1.

One type of theater, however, did thrive after World War II: the drive-in. In 1932 Richard M. Hollingshead, Jr., a chemical manufacturer, had set up a movie screen in front of his New Jersey garage and watched the film from his car. Hollingshead patented the idea, opened a drive-in in nearby Camden the following year and soon had located several drive-ins in other states. The patent was declared illegal and the war put a stop to drive-in construction. But after the war the idea caught on and the country found itself infatuated with drive-ins: in 1948 there were only 820 drive-ins in the United States, but by 1958 the number had increased to over 4,000.

Initially, drive-ins were small rocky lots with few accommodations. But soon they, like the movie palaces before them, turned to grandness. Some drive-ins could handle over 2,000 cars, others featured swimming pools, amusement parks, even laundromats. Complete dinners could be purchased, cars could be serviced, and of course drive-ins grew infamous for the "privacy" they afforded. In their first years, drive-ins were likely to show only B-movies, but with their growing popularity, they soon began to screen first-run films as well.

Today the number of drive-ins has decreased because of stricter zoning regulations and rising costs in land. Now the average drive-in capacity is 550 cars.

In the sixties, indoor theaters moved to the suburbs, and with that move began the rise of the multiple theater. In 1963 Stanley Durwood opened a two-unit complex in a Kansas City shopping center—two small theaters with one projection booth. The arrangement proved successful, and within a few years Durwood opened other "twin" theaters and then the first quad complex. Today, small multiple theaters—particularly in huge suburban shopping centers —are among the most lucrative of theaters. Approximately 10 percent of all indoor theaters in this country are now multiple units.

In recent years, much attention has been paid to the special demands of film exhibition, and several theaters have been constructed to excel in screening diverse kinds of films. The American Film Institute theater in Washington, D.C., the Pacific Film Archives theater in Berkeley, and the American Cinematheque in New York are a few of the well-known theaters which realize that *how* we see films influences *what* we see. Although opinions differ as to what exactly constitutes ideal viewing conditions— whether each viewer should be isolated from all other viewers, whether the theater should be austere so as not to compete with the screen or decorated to enhance the magic of the movie—more and more care is now being given to film exhibition.

Film exhibition represents a considerable segment of the film industry. In 1965 the U.S. Department of Commerce estimated that 94 percent of the total capital invested in the motion picture industry was in theaters; and in 1974 the Department of Commerce reported that of the entire industry employment, 70 percent were employed by theaters.

The money a theater grosses, however, can be deceptive today. To show such popular films as *The Exorcist* or *Star Wars*, for example, a theater might have to pay a huge advance and hand over 90 percent of the box-office take to the distributor. Some theaters even make more money on their concession stands (popcorn, candy, ice cream) than on the ticket price.

Several years ago the Motion Picture Herald Institute of Industry Opinion reported that for every dollar spent on theater expenditures, 24.5 cents went to the House (rent, mortgages, upkeep, etc.); 26.6 cents went to the Staff; 34.4 cents went to the Show (film rentals); 9 cents went to Sales Approach (advertising, publicity); and only 3.5 cents could be counted as operating profit (before state and federal taxes).

Because Hollywood studios are making fewer and fewer pictures these days, the competition among theaters for the best new releases can be quite keen. For a while exhibitors would agree not to bid against one another in order to keep prices down, but the Justice Department has declared "product-splitting" (as this procedure is called) illegal. Because good films are so few in number, a theater will often have to bid for a film without ever having seen it ("blind bidding"), even agreeing to play the film for eight, ten or twelve weeks regardless of the film's success or failure. As a result, towns with a limited number of theaters are showing fewer and fewer films each year. The National Association of Theater Owners is now putting together a model bill outlawing blind bidding in an attempt to ameliorate the current difficulties of film exhibition.

The following figures are only *estimates* of the number of movie theaters in America each year. Through 1966 the statistics are taken from *Film Daily Yearbook*. The Motion Picture Association of America is the source of the figures from 1967 on. Each multi-screen installation is counted as one theater in these figures. (About 80 percent of multiplex units have two screens; 20 percent range from three to seven screens per theater.) The average number of seats in indoor theaters in this country is now 500; in 1950 the average was 750. The estimated capacity of theaters at the end of 1976 was 7,320,000 seats and 1,935,000 cars.

NUMBER OF MOVIE THEATERS IN THE UNITED STATES

Year	Wired for Sound	Silent	Total
1926	—	19,489	19,489
1927	20	21,644	21,664
1928	100	22,204	22,304
1929	800	22,544	23,344
1930	8,860	14,140	23,000
1931	13,128	8,865	21,993
1932	13,880	4,835	18,715
1933	14,405	4,128	18,553
1934	14,381	2,504	16,885
1935	15,273	—	15,273
1936	15,858	—	15,858
1937	18,192	—	18,192
1938	18,182	—	18,192
1939	17,829	—	17,829
1940	19,032	—	19,042
1941	19,645	95	19,750
1942	20,281	99	20,380
1943	20,196	97	20,293
1944	20,277	96	20,375
1945	20,355	102	20,457
1946	18,719	300	19,019
1947	18,059	548	18,607
1948	17,575	820	18,395
1949	17,367	1,203	18,570
1950	16,904	2,202	19,106
1951	16,150	2,830	18,980
1952	15,347	3,276	18,623
1953	14,174	3,791	17,965
1954	15,039	4,062	19,101
1955	14,613	4,587	19,200
1956	14,509	4,494	19,003
1957	14,509	4,494	19,003
1958	11,300	4,700	16,000
1959	11,335	4,768	16,103
1960	12,291	4,700	16,999
1961	15,000	6,000	21,000
1962	15,000	6,000	21,000
1963	9,250	3,550	12,800
1964	9,850	4,100	13,750

Continued

NUMBER OF MOVIE THEATERS IN THE UNITED STATES

Year	Four-Wall Theaters	Drive-Ins	Total
1965	10,150	4,150	14,000
1966	9,330	4,200	14,350
1967	9,500	3,670	13,000
1968	9,650	3,690	13,190
1969	9,750	3,730	13,480
1970	10,000	3,750	13,750
1971	10,300	3,770	14,070
1972	10,580	3,790	14,370
1973	10,850	3,800	14,650
1974	9,645	3,519	13,164
1975	9,857	3,535	13,392
1976	10,044	3,536	13,580

5. THE NUMBER OF FILMS RELEASED IN AMERICA EACH YEAR

Through 1968 the following statistics are taken from the *Film Daily Yearbook.* From 1969 on, the statistics were compiled from various annual reports.

One thing quickly becomes clear from this chart: the fifties and sixties were not a prolific period in Hollywood. For the first time in history, foreign films outnumbered the domestic product as American studios made fewer and fewer films each year.

There has been, however, a slight surge in the seventies, but this recent increase in the annual number of American releases is due both to the large market for porno flicks and to the increase in small, independent production. The major studios are still only making little more than a handful of films each year.

One reason why Hollywood makes fewer pictures these years is the rising cost of filmmaking. In 1941 the average feature cost $400,000. By 1949 the price had risen to more than $1,000,000; by 1961, to $1,500,000; by 1971, to

$1,750,000. And in 1974 the average cost per feature was more than $2,500,000.

According to industry estimates, the typical production budget is divided as follows:

Story costs	5%
Production and direction	5
Sets and props	35
Cast	20
Studio overhead	20
Income taxes	5
Net profit after taxes	10

The statistics printed below do not include re-issues.

DOMESTIC VERSUS FOREIGN

Year	U.S. Produced	Imported	Total
1917	687	—	687
1918	841	—	841
1919	646	—	646
1920	796	—	796
1921	854	—	854
1922	748	—	748
1923	576	—	576
1924	579	—	579
1925	579	—	579
1926	740	—	740
1927	678	65	743
1928	641	193	884
1929	562	145	707
1930	509	86	595
1931	501	121	622
1932	489	196	685
1933	507	137	644
1934	480	182	662
1935	525	241	766
1936	522	213	735
1937	538	240	778
1938	455	314	769
1939	483	278	761

Continued

DOMESTIC VERSUS FOREIGN

Year	U.S. Produced	Imported	Total
1940	477	196	673
1941	492	106	598
1942	488	45	533
1943	397	30	427
1944	401	41	442
1945	350	27	377
1946	378	89	467
1947	369	118	486
1948	366	93	459
1949	356	123	470
1950	383	239	622
1951	391	263	654
1952	324	139	463
1953	344	190	534
1954	253	174	427
1955	254	138	392
1956	272	207	479
1957	300	233	533
1958	241	266	507
1959	187	252	439
1960	154	233	387
1961	131	331	462
1962	147	280	427
1963	121	299	420
1964	141	361	502
1965	153	299	452
1966	156	295	451
1967	178	284	462
1968	180	274	454
1969	232	180	412
1970	186	181	367
1971	233	199	432
1972	229	147	376
1973	295	168	463
1974	280	270	550
1975	362	242	604
1976	353	222	575

6. AVERAGE PRICE OF A MOVIE TICKET IN AMERICA EACH YEAR

Through 1962 the statistics printed below were compiled by *Film Daily Yearbook*. The Research Department of the Motion Picture Association of America is the source of the figures beginning in 1963.

Between 1942 and 1953, there was an amusement tax on movie tickets. In 1942 the tax was 2.7 cents; in 1953, 10 cents. The figures given below for those years include the tax.

Year	Admission Price	Year	Admission Price
1933	23¢	1955	49.8¢
1934	23¢	1956	49.7¢
		1957	50.5¢
1935	24¢	1958	50.5¢
1936	25¢	1959	51¢
1937	23¢		
1938	23¢	1960	69¢
1939	23¢	1961	69¢
		1962	70¢
1940	24.1¢	1963	84.6¢
1941	25.2¢	1964	92.5¢
1942	27.3¢		
1943	29.4¢	1965	$1.010
1944	31.7¢	1966	$1.094
		1967	$1.198
1945	35.2¢	1968	$1.310
1946	40.3¢	1969	$1.419
1947	40.4¢		
1948	40.1¢	1970	$1.552
1949	46¢	1971	$1.645
		1972	$1.695
1950	52.8¢	1973	$1.768
1951	52.8¢	1974	$1.874
1952	60¢		
1953	60¢	1975	$2.048
1954	44.7¢	1976	$2.128

7. AVERAGE WEEKLY MOVIE ATTENDANCE IN AMERICA EACH YEAR

These figures are only *estimates* of the average weekly number of American moviegoers. Industry statistics can never be exact here.

Each year the Opinion Research Corporation of Princeton conducts a study for the Motion Picture Association of America to learn more specific information concerning America's moviegoing habits. According to the 1976 survey, a whopping 76 percent of moviegoers are under 30 years of age, and only 6 percent are 50 years or older. Although teen-agers between the ages of 16 and 20 comprise only 12 percent of the general population, they're 31 percent of the film audience. Here is how America's 1976 moviegoers are divided into age groups:

Age	Percent of Total Yearly Admissions	Percent of Resident Civilian Population
12–15	14	10
16–20	31	12
21–24	15	9
25–29	16	10
30–39	13	15
40–49	5	13
50–59	3	18
60 and over	3	18

The study also showed that there is a tendency toward more frequent attendance among males and that moviegoing increases as income rises. For example:

Family Income	Frequent or Occasional Attendees in Total Public
$15,000 or over	64%
$7,000 to $14,999	29
Under $7,000	49

Frequent moviegoers (those who go to films at least once a month) are 25 percent of the public age 12 and over, and they account for 86 percent of the yearly admissions. Within the age group 16–20, the majority are frequent moviegoers. Within all other age groups up to age 39, the majority are either frequent or occasional (those who go to films once in 2 to 6 months) moviegoers. From age 40 on, the majority are infrequent moviegoers.

The Princeton survey suggested that moviegoing increases with increasing education.

	Some College	High School Completed	Less Than Complete High School
Frequent	29%	25%	12%
Occasional	32	28	11
Infrequent	15	16	14
Never	24	32	64

According to industry estimates, Saturday is the best day for theater business, Friday is second, and Sunday third. Mondays through Thursdays are about equal. July is the best month, with August second and January third. May is the worst month of the year.

Approximately 60 percent of American moviegoers attend a neighborhood theater; 65 percent prefer single to double features; and 39 percent are influenced to some degree by film reviewers. Some 80 percent say the subject matter of a film is important in deciding what movie to see; 30 percent consider a film's stars. A considerable 70 percent like American films over foreign products, and 83 percent prefer color to black-and-white films.

Year	Average Weekly Attendance	Year	Average Weekly Attendance
1926	50,000,000	1952	51,000,000
1927	57,000,000	1953	46,000,000
1928	65,000,000		
1929	95,000,000	1954	49,000,000
		1955	46,000,000
1930	90,000,000	1956	47,000,000
1931	75,000,000	1957	45,000,000
1932	60,000,000	1958	40,000,000
1933	60,000,000	1959	42,000,000
1934	70,000,000	1960	40,000,000
1935	75,000,000	1961	42,000,000
1936	88,000,000	1962	43,000,000
1937	85,000,000	1963	44,000,000
1938	85,000,000	1964	(not reliably reported)
1939	85,000,000		
		1965	44,000,000
1940	80,000,000	1966	38,000,000
1941	85,000,000	1967	17,800,000
1942	85,000,000	1968	18,800,000
1943	85,000,000	1969	17,500,000
1944	85,000,000		
		1970	17,700,000
1945	90,000,000	1971	15,800,000
1946	90,000,000	1972	18,000,000
1947	90,000,000	1973	16,600,000
1948	90,000,000	1974	19,400,000
1949	87,500,000		
		1975	19,900,000
1950	60,000,000	1976	18,400,000
1951	54,000,000		

8. ANNUAL AMERICAN BOX-OFFICE RECEIPTS

These figures chart American box-office receipts in relation to personal consumption expenditures. The source of these statistics is the United States Department of Commerce, Social and Economic Statistics Administration, Bureau of Economic Analysis (Survey of Current Business).

According to these statistics, admissions to American film theaters decreased during the early Depression but began to pick up by 1934. The rise continued throughout the forties. During the fifties and early sixties, however, admissions dropped considerably. The past ten years, particularly the past three, have witnessed another rise in box-office receipts.

Although Americans are now spending more money on movies than ever before, they are spending even greater amounts of money on other forms of recreation. Moviegoing no longer holds the same priority in American lives. In 1943, for example, Americans spent more than 25 percent of their recreation expenditures on the movies. In 1976 that figure had dropped to less than 5 percent.

Year	U.S. Box-office Receipts (in millions $)	% of U.S. Personal Spending	% of U.S. Recreational Spending	% of U.S. Spectator Recreational Spending
1929	720	0.93	16.62	78.86
1930	732	1.05	18.35	82.06
1931	719	1.19	21.77	84.19
1932	527	1.08	21.58	83.52
1933	482	1.05	21.89	84.12
1934	518	1.01	21.22	82.88
1935	556	1.00	21.14	82.74
1936	626	1.01	20.73	82.48
1937	676	1.02	19.99	82.64
1938	663	1.04	20.46	81.25
1939	659	0.99	19.09	80.27
1940	735	1.04	19.54	81.31
1941	809	1.00	19.08	81.31
1942	1,022	1.15	21.85	84.88
1943	1,275	1.28	25.70	87.63
1944	1,341	1.24	24.73	85.80
1945	1,450	1.21	23.62	84.60
1946	1,692	1.18	19.81	81.90
1947	1,594	0.99	17.23	79.58
1948	1,506	0.87	15.54	78.52
1949	1,451	0.82	14.50	77.51

Continued

Year	U.S. Box-office Receipts (in millions $)	% of U.S. Personal Spending	% of U.S. Recreational Spending	% of U.S. Spectator Recreational Spending
1950	1,376	0.72	12.34	77.26
1951	1,310	0.63	11.33	76.34
1952	1,246	0.57	10.30	75.29
1953	1,187	0.52	9.33	73.96
1954	1,228	0.52	9.39	73.44
1955	1,326	0.52	9.42	73.63
1956	1,394	0.52	9.31	73.41
1957	1,126	0.40	7.34	68.04
1958	992	0.34	6.28	64.50
1959	954	0.31	5.59	60.73
1960	956	0.29	5.35	57.87
1961	955	0.29	5.14	56.68
1962	945	0.27	4.72	53.78
1963	942	0.25	4.35	51.76
1964	951	0.24	4.01	49.48
1965	1,067	0.25	4.12	50.26
1966	1,119	0.24	4.03	48.44
1967	1,128	0.23	3.53	46.92
1968	1,294	0.24	3.68	48.77
1969	1,400	0.24	3.67	48.23
1970	1,521	0.25	3.71	48.42
1971	1,626	0.24	3.72	48.41
1972	1,644	0.22	3.35	47.15
1973	1,965	0.24	3.56	50.78
1974	2,495	0.28	4.10	53.99
1975	2,538	0.26	3.84	51.81
1976	2,987	0.27	4.12	53.36

IV. THE STUDIOS

1. HISTORIES OF STUDIOS

COLUMBIA PICTURES

Columbia Pictures had its beginnings in Harry Cohn, a producer of film shorts who in 1920 formed CBC Sales Corporation with his brother Jack and with Harry Brandt, both of whom left Universal to help start the new company. In 1924 CBC (or "Cornbeef and Cabbage," as it was nicknamed) expanded and was incorporated, changing its name to Columbia.

Cohn had unusual power over the studio, for from 1932 he was both its president and its production head, a rare phenomenon in Hollywood. Known for his autocratic personality, Cohn was reportedly the crassest, most demanding and hardest-to-please of all the studio moguls, not to mention the least popular. His unpleasantness was legendary.

Columbia began as a member of Poverty Row, that group of small B-movie studios on Gower Street always in the shadow of Hollywood's Big Five: MGM, RKO, Fox, Warner, and Paramount. But under Cohn's tough dictatorial rule, Columbia grew successful in the 1930s, when it produced most of Frank Capra's popular social comedies—*Mr. Deeds Goes to Town, Mr. Smith Goes to Washington, You Can't Take It With You*, and *It Happened One Night*, the first movie to win the five major Academy Awards. (This feat wasn't repeated until *One Flew Over the Cuckoo's Nest* came along.) During the 1930s Columbia also succeeded with films directed by Howard Hawks and with movies starring Cary Grant.

During the 1940s Columbia produced largely unexceptional films—its main asset during this decade was Rita Hayworth. But the 1950s found the studio on the rebound: (1) in 1951 Columbia established a television division, Screen Gems, to produce television series and thus became one of the first studios to enter the TV industry; and (2) the studio started to back independent producers and directors like Sam Spiegel, David Lean, Elia Kazan, Otto Preminger and Fred Zinnemann who made such films for Columbia as *All the King's Men, Born Yesterday, From Here to Eternity, On the Waterfront, The Caine Mutiny* and *The Bridge on the River Kwai.* By the time Cohn died in 1958, Columbia had become a major studio.

Abe Schneider and Leo Jaffe were Cohn's successors and under their leadership Columbia expanded their range of films, making large movies like *Lawrence of Arabia, A Man For All Seasons, Funny Girl* and *Oliver!* as well as smaller British films like *Georgy Girl, The Pumpkin Eater* and *The Go-Between.* In 1969 Columbia released the then controversial *Easy Rider.*

But in the early 1970s the studio declined rapidly, losing $30 million in 1971, $4 million in 1972, and some $50 million in 1973. In 1972 Columbia was forced to leave its studio and move both its film and television facilities to the Warner Bros. lot. Columbia land is owned 55 percent by Warner and 45 percent by Columbia; and Warner land is owned 65 percent by Warner and 35 percent by Columbia. Columbia and Warner have formed a joint venture to continue for a minimum of seven years from April 1972, known as Burbank Studios. Both studios share in net profits of Burbank Studios in direct proportion to studio usage; net losses are shared in inverse proportion to studio usage.

Under the presidency of Alan Hirschfield, Columbia has begun to recover, particularly with the popular films of Barbra Streisand *(The Way We Were, Funny Lady)* and such recent hits as *Shampoo* and *Tommy.*

As of early 1977, Leo Jaffe was the chairman of the board of Columbia Pictures Industries, and David Begelman was the president of the Pictures Division. Columbia Pictures Industries had some 2,800 employees as of June 1976, and 10,935 stockholders. Columbia's best-known trademark is a woman obviously based on the Statue of Liberty.

METRO-GOLDWYN-MAYER

Metro-Goldwyn-Mayer had its origins in Marcus Loew, a shrewd pioneer during the nickelodeon era. Originally Loew's interest was in the exhibition of motion pictures and not in film production or distribution. Continually expanding his theaters in both their numbers and their locations, Loew organized his enterprises in 1919 as Loew's Inc.

At this time Loew and his associate Nicholas M. Schenck became interested in expanding their interests to include production as well as exhibition. In 1920 they acquired Metro Pictures Corporation and with their new facilities made two highly successful films, *The Four Horsemen of the Apocalypse* and *The Prisoner of Zenda.* Encouraged by success, Loew then purchased the Goldwyn Company in 1924, but Samuel Goldwyn quickly left to establish his own independent organization. Later that same year Loew acquired the assets of Louis B. Mayer Pictures, and the triple merger took the name of Metro-Goldwyn-Mayer. Loew died in 1927.

Under the conservative economic policies of Nicholas Schenck in New York, the dominant force of Mayer as studio head in Hollywood, and the creative ideas of Irving Thalberg as executive producer, MGM developed through the late twenties to become the most successful studio of the thirties. (William Fox's attempt in 1929 to take over the studio had failed.) With "more stars than there are in the heavens," MGM had under contract such illuminaries as Garbo, Crawford, Gable, Harlow, the Barrymores and the Marx Brothers. And the studio's emblematic Leo the Lion could proudly roar with such directors as George Cukor, Mervyn LeRoy, Clarence Brown, Busby Berkeley and Vincente Minnelli. MGM made forty to fifty films a year, with profits as high as $14 million in 1937, a record no other studio could then equal. MGM's films from the decade included such popular movies as *Grand Hotel, Dinner at*

Eight, Mutiny on the Bounty, The Wizard of Oz and *Gone With the Wind.*

The studio continued its success in the early forties, when, having lost many of its male stars to the war effort, it turned to child stars and actresses in films like *Lassie Come Home* and *Meet Me in St. Louis.* Dory Schary, who was the production head of RKO until Howard Hughes took over that studio in 1948, came to MGM in the late forties. But antagonism between Schary and Mayer grew so strong that in 1951 Mayer, once one of Hollywood's most powerful moguls, resigned, and Schenck appointed Schary studio head. During Schary's reign MGM, one of the first studios to use survey research techniques to learn what audiences wanted to see, made several fine musical comedies, most notably *Singin' in the Rain* and *The Band Wagon.*

But even such popular films could do little to fight MGM's two major problems in the early fifties: television and the antitrust actions that forced the studio to divorce its production/distribution interests from its exhibition facilities. Although Schary's style in films was much more economical than the lavish tastes of Mayer, MGM started to decline, and in 1956 both Schary and Schenck lost their positions at the studio.

Under Joseph Vogel, MGM spent $15 million on *Ben-Hur,* which paid back its investment handsomely. But the studio's $27 million remake of *Mutiny on the Bounty* was financially disastrous: in 1963 the studio lost $17 million. In that year Robert O'Brien took over MGM, allowing the studio to invest $12 million in *Doctor Zhivago,* which made more money for the studio than any other film in its history, excepting *Gone With the Wind.* But the studio began to suffer declines again, loosing a whopping $35 million in 1969 alone, and in an attempt to offset such losses, MGM changed management three times in ten months.

In 1969 Kirk Kerkorian took power and within the next few years reduced the studio's film production, auctioned its costumes and properties, and invested the studio's money in a Las Vegas hotel—the MGM Grand, which cost approximately $125 million. In 1973 MGM stopped distributing, and its few current releases are now distributed by United Artists.

As of early 1977, Fred Benninger was chairman of the board of MGM Inc., Kirk Kerkorian was vice chairman, F. E. Rosenfelt was president, and Richard Shepherd was head of production. As of August 1976, MGM Inc. had 6,000 employees and 13,840 stockholders. As mentioned, MGM's famous trademark is a roaring lion.

PARAMOUNT PICTURES

Paramount Pictures is largely the work of Adolph Zukor, whose interests, like those of so many other famous moguls, were initially confined to film exhibition. In 1912 Zukor expanded into distribution as well, acquiring the distributing rights to *La Reine Elizabeth,* a British/French movie starring Sarah Bernhardt. The success of the film—Zukor made $80,000 from it—encouraged Zukor to form his Famous Players Company, which was to feature famous players in famous plays, a policy that helped create the star system. In order to draw Mary Pickford away from Biograph in 1914, for example, Zukor had to offer Pickford a $2,000-a-week contract, and in order to re-sign that contract in 1916, Zukor had to give Pickford a two-year contract that guaranteed her over a million dollars.

In 1914 Famous Players merged with the Jesse Lasky Feature Play organization, which had been established by Lasky, Samuel Goldwyn and Cecil B. DeMille. The films produced by this merger were distributed through W. W. Hodkinson's Paramount Pictures distribution enterprise. Through a complicated series of mergers that included Paramount, Famous Players-Lasky and Artcraft Pictures, Zukor came out on top. Over the following years Zukor concentrated his energies both on acquiring a large number of theater chains and on expanding his stable of stars, which grew to include such players as William S. Hart,

Dorothy Gish, Gloria Swanson, Valentino and John Barrymore. The studio's early successes included *The Sheik* (1921), *The Covered Wagon* (1923) and DeMille's *The Ten Commandments* (1923). B. P. Schulberg was Paramount's general manager from 1925 to 1932.

Throughout the late twenties and early thirties, Paramount excelled in films made by European directors like Stroheim, Lubitsch, Sternberg and Mamoulian that featured European stars like Pola Negri, Marlene Dietrich and Maurice Chevalier.

Although the studio met trouble in the mid-thirties— Paramount Publix (as it was then called) went bankrupt in 1932 but was reorganized in 1935 as Paramount Pictures— it managed to survive. Under the new organization, Barney Balaban ran the studio, with Zukor as chairman of the board in an advisory capacity. During the late thirties and the forties Paramount's players included John Wayne, Bing Crosby, Bob Hope, Dorothy Lamour, Barbara Stanwyck, and Montgomery Clift.

In 1950 the federal government forced Paramount to separate its production/distribution facilities from its extensive exhibition services, resulting in two companies: Paramount Pictures Corporation to make and distribute movies, and United Paramount Theatres to exhibit them.

Although during the early fifties the studio made such successful films as *Sunset Boulevard, A Place in the Sun* and *The Greatest Show on Earth,* it failed to use the wide-screen system developed by Twentieth Century-Fox: CinemaScope. Instead it was determined to develop its own system, called VistaVision, which later proved too expensive to be used. During the late fifties and early sixties many of Paramount's most popular films, like *Gunfight at the O.K. Corral* (1957) and *Becket* (1964), were produced by Hal Wallis.

In 1966 Paramount became a subsidiary of Gulf & Western. Like many of the other studios, Paramount encountered troubles in the late sixties, producing expensive but unsuccessful movies like *Paint Your Wagon* and *Darling Lili.* But under the guidance of such producers as Robert Evans and Frank Yablans, Paramount released some of the most successful films of all time: *Love Story* and *The Godfather*.

As of early 1977, Billy Diller was chairman of the board and David Picker was president of the Motion Picture Division. Paramount's best-known trademark is a snow-capped mountain peak encircled by stars.

TWENTIETH CENTURY-FOX

In the first years of this century William Fox, then in the garment trade, expanded his interests into the movie industry, establishing first a film-distribution branch in 1912 (the Greater New York Film Rental Company), and in 1913 a production facility (Box Office Attractions). Wishing to combine his organizations, Fox founded the Fox Film Company in 1915, moving its headquarters in 1917 from New York to Hollywood.

There the studio produced successful vamp pictures with Theda Bara and popular Westerns with Tom Mix and Buck Jones. In the twenties the studio was among the first to pioneer sound films, using the discoveries of Theodore Case and Earl I. Sponable (whose sound-on-film process the studio renamed Fox Movietone) as well as acquiring the patent rights of the German Tri-Ergon sound process.

In 1929 Fox purchased control of Loew's Inc. (owner of MGM), but the federal government forced him to relinquish its Loew ownership, and in the reorganization Fox himself lost power in 1931. (Spending the rest of his life in retirement, he died in 1952). Sidney R. Kent replaced Fox in 1932, and in 1935 Fox Film merged with Twentieth Century Pictures, then headed by Darryl F. Zanuck and Joseph Schenck, whose brother Nicholas Schenck was one of the powers at Loew's/MGM. With his new merger, Twentieth Century-Fox was born: Darryl Zanuck took charge of production; Schenck became chairman of the board; and Kent remained president until his death in 1942.

Following Kent's death, Spyros Skouras became president, and it was Skouras, along with Zanuck, who

created the Fox image. Under their control the studio—
with one of the largest back lots in Hollywood—made such
films as *My Darling Clementine, The Song of Bernadette,
The Snake Pit, David and Bathsheba* and *Gentleman's
Agreement.* The studio's stars included Shirley Temple,
Alice Faye, Betty Grable, Marilyn Monroe, Tyrone Power
and Gregory Peck; and its roster of directors could boast
of John Ford, Elia Kazan and Joseph L. Mankiewicz.

In an attempt to compete with television in the early
fifties, the studio pioneered the use of the wide-screen
process that had been invented by Henri Chrétien and
which the studio called CinemaScope. The studio's first
wide-screen film was the highly successful *The Robe*
(1953), followed by such films as *There's No Business Like
Show Business* (1954) and *The King and I* (1956).

In 1956 Zanuck left Twentieth Century-Fox to enter
independent production, and he was succeeded first by
Buddy Adler and then by Robert Goldstein and Peter G.
Levathes. During the late fifties and early sixties the
studio returned to spectaculars, disastrously investing
some $40 million in the infamous *Cleopatra.* In an attempt
to offset such losses (deficiencies of $23 million in 1962
and $40 million in 1963), the studio brought back Darryl
Zanuck to take charge of the company. Along with his son,
Richard, Zanuck reversed the company's fortunes: In 1965
the studio released *The Sound of Music,* the biggest hit
in the studio's history and one of the most successful films
of all time.

The studio then invested its gain in such ill-fated movies
as *Doctor Dolittle* (1967) and *Star!* (1968) and began to
lose overwhelming amounts of money: $37 million in
1969 and $77 million in 1970, although that year the studio
did have popular films like *Patton* and *M*A*S*H.* Power
changed hands once again in 1971, as the younger Zanuck
was forced to go. Dennis C. Stanfill replaced Richard
Zanuck as president and was later named chairman of the
board. Several changes took place over the next few years.

In recent years the studio has once again turned to
making large spectacular films like *The Towering Inferno*
(which was made with Warner Bros.) and *The Omen.*

Although the studio does not directly own any American theaters, it does have theaters in Australia, New Zealand, Egypt, Holland and other countries. Like many other studios, Twentieth Century-Fox is also active in television production.

As of early 1977, Dennis C. Stanfill was chairman of the board and Alan Ladd Jr. was president of Production. Twentieth Century-Fox Film Corporation had 5,200 employees and 16,500 stockholders as of December 1976. The company's famous trademark is a large set of futuristic letters spelling the company's name as searchlights scan the sky.

UNITED ARTISTS

In 1919 Mary Pickford, Charles Chaplin, D. W. Griffith and Douglas Fairbanks organized United Artists, the first studio to be established by artists and not by businessmen. The function of United Artists was to finance and distribute movies independently of the Hollywood studio system in the hope of producing quality films.

United Artists owned no studio of its own, but rather rented facilities only when needed for each of its films, a policy that avoided the expensive overhead of the other major studios. Among United's first films were Fairbanks' *His Majesty The American* (1919), Griffith's *Broken Blossoms (1919)* and *Way Down East* (1920), Pickford's *Pollyanna (1920)*, and Chaplin's *A Woman of Paris* (1923) and *The Gold Rush* (1925).

The idea for United Artists came from Oscar Price, who had been assistant to William G. McAdoo when McAdoo was Secretary of the Treasury and Hollywood stars helped sell Liberty Loans. Price was named the first president of United Artists, but was soon succeeded by Hiram Abrahms.

Because Griffith left the company in 1924 and Chaplin made films so slowly, Joseph Schenck was brought in during the mid-twenties to replace Abrahms. Schenck (who later started Twentieth Century Pictures and whose

brother, Nicholas, was a major power at Loew's/MGM)
expanded the studio's talents to include Valentino, Gloria
Swanson, Buster Keaton and Samuel Goldwyn. Howard
Hughes contributed *Hell's Angels* in 1930 *and Scarface* in
1932.

During the early thirties United Artists established
contracts with foreign filmmakers, adding director
Alexander Korda to its roster. Nevertheless, the studio
suffered losses into the early forties, undergoing continual
changes in management: Schenck was replaced by Al
Lichtman, who in turn was succeeded by Atillio H. Giannini
and George Schaefer, who in turn were followed by
Maurice Silverstone.

In 1941 Goldwyn sold his stock to the company, as did
Korda in 1944. By 1950 both Pickford and Chaplin, the two
remaining founders, had sold many of their shares to a
syndicate headed by Paul V. McNutt. The following year
another syndicate acquired the company. This syndicate—
headed by Arthur B. Krim, Robert Benjamin, Matthew Fox,
William J. Heineman, Max E. Youngstein and Arnold Picker
—helped United Artists out of its decline. In 1952 the Krim
syndicate held 50 percent of the company's stock; the
remaining 50 percent was shared by Chaplin and Pickford.
Chaplin sold his 25 percent in 1955, and Pickford followed
in 1956, giving total ownership to the Krim management.
In 1957 United Artists became a public corporation,
offering $17 million in stocks and debentures for sale.

The increase in independent production during the late
fifties and early sixties put United Artists in an
advantageous position. Through a contract with the Mirisch
Brothers, United acquired directors like Billy Wilder, John
Sturges, Robert Wise and Norman Jewison; and later
Stanley Kramer, Fred Zinnemann and Richard Lester made
films under UA. The company's films during these years
included *Marty* (1955), *The Magnificent Seven* (1960), *The
Apartment* (1960), *West Side Story* (1961) and the James
Bond series starting with *Dr. No* (1962).

In 1967 United Artists became a subsidiary of the
Transamerica Corporation, a diversified organization known
largely as a major insurance company. United Artists

bought Warner Bros. pre-1948 films, and currently distributes MGM's films as well as its own.

UNIVERSAL PICTURES

Universal Pictures has its origins in Carl Laemmle, a pioneer in the film industry who, like many other famous producers, started out in the business as a film exhibitor, opening his first theater in Chicago in 1906. Later that year Laemmle expanded into distribution with the Laemmle Film Service, and in 1909 expanded into production with the Independent Motion Pictures Company (IMP). In 1912 Laemmle merged IMP with several other smaller companies, like Nestor and Powers, to form one large organization: Universal.

Laemmle is often credited with launching the star system by hiring Florence Lawrence for $1,000 a week and identifying her by name—an unknown policy at that time. Because of the success of this practice and because of his own independent policies, Laemmle came into considerable conflict with the Motion Pictures Patents Company, which was basically a monopoly formed by most of the major studios. After years of fighting the Patents Company, Laemmle moved Universal to Hollywood, where he could be closer to the Mexican border to avoid prosecution for infringement of patent rights. In 1915 Universal acquired its present site, Universal City (then a chicken farm which Laemmle purchased for a down payment of $3,500), the first incorporated city to consist solely of a film studio.

Universal's first films included the early works of Erich von Stroheim (Blind Husband, The Devil's Passage, Foolish Wives), the exotic films of Valentino, and Westerns featuring popular stars like Ken Maynard and Harry Carey. In 1930 Universal released one of its most highly praised movies, All Quiet on the Western Front. In the following years the studio excelled in horror films, producing all the early classics directed by James Whale and starring Lon Chaney, Boris Karloff and Bela Lugosi.

In 1936 Laemmle lost Universal to J. Cheever Cowdin and Nate J. Blumberg. Under their direction the studio produced the low-budget movies of Abbott and Costello, Deanna Durbin and Frances the Talking Mule, but during these years Universal also made such interesting films as Hitchcock's *Shadow of a Doubt* and George Marshall's *Destry Rides Again,* which included Marlene Dietrich's famous rendition of "See What the Boys in the Back Room Will Have."

In 1946 Universal underwent several changes: the company merged with the International Pictures Corporation of Leo Spitz and William Goetz, both of whom became the studio's production heads; the studio acquired the distribution rights of the prestigious British films produced by the J. Arthur Rank Organisation, which released films like Olivier's *Hamlet* and the Alec Guinness comedies *The Lavender Hill Mob* and *The Man in the White Suit;* and Universal established United World Pictures to produce and distribute nontheatrical films, acquiring the libraries of Bell & Howell and Castle Films.

In 1950 Cowdin resigned, with Blumberg assuming full command. And in 1952 Decca Records—through an extremely complicated arrangement that involved both the open-market sale of the company's stock and the purchase of J. Arthur Rank's holdings—became the controlling stockholders of Universal. The president of Decca, Milton J. Rackmil, became president of Universal later that year. When Decca was consolidated with Music Corporation of America in 1959, MCA, under the leadership of Jules Stein, became the new owner of Universal.

During the late fifties and early sixties the studio's greatest producer was Ross Hunter, who was responsible for the melodramatic films of Douglas Sirk *(Imitation of Life, Written on the Wind, The Tarnished Angels)* and the Rock Hudson/Doris Day comedies. During the mid-sixties Universal, under the guidance of Lew Wasserman, concentrated its energies on television, producing the first movie made for TV in 1966, *Fame is the Name of the Game.* Today Universal is the leading Hollywood studio in the field of television, having made such series as *Kojak, Marcus*

Welby, M.D., Baretta and *The Sunday Night Mystery Movie.* Universal is also known for its conducted tours of the studio.

Today the studio is among the most powerful and wealthiest in Hollywood, having released such blockbusters as *Jaws, The Sting, American Graffiti, Airport, Earthquake* and *Airport 1975.* In recent years MCA has also sponsored development of phonograph records which will allow you to play complete movies on your television set.

WARNER BROS.

In 1917 Harry, Jack, Albert and Sam Warner established a film-distribution company in New York. Five years later they expanded into film production as well, forming Warner Bros. Pictures, Inc. Harry (the company's president) and Albert (its treasurer) managed the New York headquarters, while Jack and Sam ran the studio in Hollywood. Jack Warner was the most powerful of the four, running the studio under tight, economical policies.

Although the studio acquired the Vitagraph Company in 1925, Warner Bros.' first years were nevertheless shaky. Its first great success did not come until the studio's introduction of sound in *The Jazz Singer* (1927). With Western Electric and Bell Laboratories, Sam Warner had invented the sound process, Vitaphone. (Sam died the day before *The Jazz Singer* opened, never knowing what a revolution he had helped to bring about in films.) Almost overnight Warner's rose to pre-eminence in Hollywood because of its early sound films. The company acquired the assets of other film-production firms like First National in 1929, purchased the vast Stanley theater chain in 1932 and established studios in England, acquiring a considerable share of Associated British Pictures Corp. in 1941.

During the thirties and forties Warner's excelled in four types of films: (1) gangster movies (among the best: *Little*

Caesar, Public Enemy, Scarface) that featured performers like Humphrey Bogart, James Cagney and Edward G. Robinson; (2) the Busby Berkeley musicals (the *Gold Diggers* series, *42nd Street, Footlight Parade*) that often starred Dick Powell and Ruby Keeler; (3) social-conscience films *(I Am a Fugitive from a Chain Gang, Confessions of a Nazi Spy* and *Mission to Moscow);* and (4) biographies of famous people like Zola, Pasteur and Reuter.

During these decades Warner's contract players included Bette Davis, Errol Flynn, Paul Muni and Olivia de Havilland. Its roster of directors included Michael Curtiz, Mervyn LeRoy, Raoul Walsh and Elia Kazan.

After unsuccessful ventures into the wide-screen process in the early fifties, Jack Warner lost some control of the studio. During the latter part of the decade the company invested heavily in television series, with some degree of success. Since then the studio has dealt largely with independent producers for its feature films. Hence the studio's releases during the sixties were more variable than they had previously been, ranging from large productions like *My Fair Lady, Camelot* and *The Great Race* to "risky" films like *Who's Afraid of Virginia Woolf?* and *Bonnie and Clyde.*

In 1967 Warner Bros. merged with the television company Seven Arts, and in 1969 was acquired by the conglomerate Kinney National Service. At that time Jack Warner retired from the board and was replaced by Ted Ashley. The studio changed its name to Warner Communications, sold its pre-1948 library to United Artists, and in 1972 started sharing its lot with Columbia. Ashley later resigned, and John Calley became president and production head.

During recent years Warner Bros. has made many popular films, including *The Exorcist, Towering Inferno* (which was made with Twentieth Century-Fox), *All the President's Men, Blazing Saddles, What's Up, Doc?, Deliverance* and *Dog Day Afternoon.*

As of early 1977, Steven J. Ross was chairman of the board and John Calley was vice chairman. Warner's famous trademark is a badge bearing the initials *WB.*

2. THE NUMBER OF FEATURES RELEASED BY MAJOR STUDIOS EACH YEAR

Year	Columbia	MGM	Paramount	RKO–Radio	20th C–Fox	U. Artists	Universal	Warner
1927	25	51	78	—	50	11	66	43
1928	32	52	64	—	49	15	56	26
1929	22	52	68	35	53	17	41	36
1930	29	47	64	32	48	16	36	39
1931	31	46	62	33	48	13	23	24
1932	29	39	65	46	40	14	30	55
1933	32	42	58	48	50	16	37	55
1934	43	43	55	46	52	20	44	58
1935	49	47	63	40	52	19	37	49
1936	52	45	68	39	57	17	28	56
1937	52	51	61	53	61	25	37	68
1938	53	46	50	43	56	16	46	52
1939	55	50	58	49	59	18	46	53
1940	51	48	48	53	49	20	49	45
1941	61	47	45	44	50	26	58	48
1942	59	49	44	39	51	26	56	34
1943	47	33	30	44	33	28	53	21
1944	56	30	32	31	26	20	53	19
1945	38	33	23	33	27	17	46	19
1946	51	25	22	40	32	20	42	20
1947	49	29	29	36	27	26	33	20
1948	39	24	25	31	45	26	35	23
1949	52	30	21	25	31	21	29	25

Year								
1950	59	38	23	32	32	18	33	28
1951	63	41	29	36	39	46	39	27
1952	48	38	24	32	37	34	39	26
1953	47	44	26	25	39	49	43	28
1954	35	24	17	16	29	52	32	20
1955	38	23	20	13	29	35	34	23
1956	40	24	17	20	32	48	33	23
1957	46	29	20	1	50	54	39	29
1958	38	29	25	—	42	44	35	24
1959	36	25	18	—	34	40	18	18
1960	35	18	22	—	49	23	20	17
1961	28	21	15	—	35	33	19	16
1962	30	21	17	—	25	36	18	15
1963	19	35	17	—	18	23	17	13
1964	19	30	16	—	18	18	25	18
1965	29	28	24	—	26	19	26	15
1966	29	24	22	—	21	18	23	12
1967	22	21	30	—	19	19	25	21
1968	20	27	33	—	21	23	30	23
1969	21	16	21	—	18	31	26	21
1970	29	23	15	—	15	39	16	16
1971	32	18	21	—	13	25	17	17
1972	26	24	14	—	25	22	16	18
1973	19	15*	27	—	15	19	16	21
1974	19	*	25	—	20	26	12	22
1975	17	*	12	—	17	23	9	15
1976	15	*	19	—	20	23	12	15

* MGM's movies are now distributed through United Artists. Figures for United Artists include MGM's releases.

Source: Through 1968, *Film Daily Yearbook.* From 1969 on, various annual industry reports.

3. ANNUAL PROFITS OF MAJOR STUDIOS

The July 7, 1977, issue of *The Economist*—the respected British magazine—noted that many of America's film studios were about to celebrate fiftieth anniversaries. In honor of the occasion, *The Economist* compiled the annual profits and losses of the major Hollywood studios since 1932. The statistics were based on Moody's Industrial Manual and annual reports.

As the editors of *The Economist* commented, the only constant in this chart is change: boom and slump is the Hollywood way of life. The most recent slump came between 1969 and 1971, when most of the studios did the one thing that according to *The Economist* has made more businesses bankrupt than any other form of mismanagement: they overstocked. (As too many too-expensive films were being made in the hope of imitating the success of *The Sound of Music,* Hollywood inventory climbed to an astronomical $1.2 billion, although the world market for films was only $750 million.) The real miracle suggested by this chart is that so many of the original companies in this crazy extravagant industry have survived. This chart supplies some fascinating insights into the ups and downs of filmmaking: in 1969, for example, Warner lost $52 million. Yet its profits just the following year exceeded $33 million.

Although the industry throughout its history has attempted to find ways to reduce the horrible risks of spending millions of dollars up front without knowing whether a film will succeed or not, none of those ways have been foolproof. The star system has worked often, but not in a consistent or predictable fashion. Studio ownership of theaters was another way to reduce risk, but that policy was declared illegal almost thirty years ago. Stepping up investment to make films noticeably better than television fare has also failed to work regularly. Movie making remains a risky enterprise.

The Economist in 1973 claimed that diversification was

the answer to filmmaking: the studios in the best shape were those that had been taken over by conglomerates during and after the 1969–71 slump. Many film buffs regret these takeovers: the conglomerates, they say, seem more interested in life insurance than in movies, and much of the unique flavor of the various studios has been lost. Nevertheless, many of the major studios have recovered under conglomerate management and the majors remain a powerful force: in 1972, for example, all but 6 percent of distributors' income was collected by the majors.

In *Gold Diggers of 1933*, Ginger Rogers—along with dozens of women holding giant silver coins—sings: "We're in the money, We're in the money. We've got a lot of what it takes to get along." It could serve as the theme song for any of the studios listed here.

These figures are in millions of dollars. Paramount's profits are not listed until 1936 because for the few years preceding that, the company was in reorganization. United Artists was not a listed corporation until 1950.

Year	Columbia	Loew's/MGM	Paramount	20th–Fox	U. Artists	Universal	Warner	Disney
1932	0.6	8.0		1.7		(1.0)	(14.1)	
1933	0.7	4.3		1.3		(0.2)	(6.3)	
1934	1.0	8.6					(2.5)	
1935	1.8	7.5	4.0	3.1		(0.7)	0.7	[0.8]
1936	1.6	10.6	6.0	7.7		(1.8)	3.2	[0.2]
1937	1.3	14.3	2.8	8.6		(1.1)	5.9	0.4
1938	0.2	9.9	2.8	7.2		(0.5)	1.9	0.5
1939	0	9.5		4.2		1.2	1.7	
1940	0.5	8.7	6.4	(0.5)		2.4	2.7	0.4
1941	0.6	11.0	9.2	4.9		2.7	5.5	0.2
1942	1.6	11.8	13.1	10.6		3.0	8.6	0.3
1943	1.8	13.4	14.6	10.9		3.8	8.3	[0.1]
1944	2.0	14.5	14.7	12.5		3.4	6.9	[0.1]
1945	1.9	12.9	15.4	12.7		4.0	9.9	
1946	3.5	17.9	39.2	22.6	0.3	4.6	19.4	
1947	3.7	10.5	28.2	14.0	0.4	3.2	22.0	
1948	0.5	4.2[a]	22.6	12.5	0.6	[3.2]	11.8	
1949	1.0	6.0	20.8[a]	12.4	0.9	[1.1]	10.5	
1950	1.9	7.6	6.6	9.5		1.4	10.3	0.7
1951	1.5	7.8	5.5	4.3[b]		2.3	9.4	0.4
1952	0.8	4.6	5.9	4.7		2.3	7.2	0.5
1953	0.9	4.5	6.7	4.8		2.6	2.9[a]	0.5
1954	3.6	6.3	8.1	8.0		3.8	3.9	0.7
1955	4.9	5.0	9.4	6.0	2.7	4.0	4.0	1.4
1956	2.6	4.6	4.3	6.2	3.1	4.0	2.1	2.6
1957	2.3	(0.5)	5.4	6.5	3.3	2.8	3.4	3.6

Year								
1958	(5.0)	0.8	4.6	7.6	3.7	(2.0)	(1.0)	3.9
1959	(2.4)	7.7	4.4	2.3	4.1	4.7	9.4	3.4
1960	1.9	9.6	7.0	(2.9)	4.3	6.3	7.1	(1.3)
1961	(1.4)	12.7	5.9	(22.5)	4.0	7.5	7.2	4.5
1962	2.3	2.6	3.4	(39.8)	3.8	12.7	7.6	6.6
1963	2.6	(17.5)	5.9	9.1	(0.8)	13.6	5.7	7.0
1964	3.2	7.4	6.6	10.6	9.3	14.8	(3.9)	7.0
1965	2.0	7.8	6.3	11.7	12.8	16.2	4.7	11.0
1966	2.0	10.2	n.a.	12.5	13.6	16.2	6.5	12.4
1967	6.0	14.0	n.a.	15.4	15.5	16.5	3.0	11.3
1968	10.0	8.5	n.a.	13.7	19.5[c]	13.5	10.0	13.1
1969	6.0	(35.0)	n.a.	(36.8)	16.2	2.5	[52.0][d]	15.8
1970	6.0	(8.2)	(2.0)*	(77.4)	(45.0)	13.3	33.5	22.0
1971	(29.0)	7.8	(22.0)*	6.5	1.0	16.7	41.6	26.7
1972	(4.0)	9.2	31.2*	6.7	10.8	20.8	50.1[g]	40.3
1973	(50.0)	2.1	n.a.	7.7	14.0	25.6	51.2	47.8
1974	(2.3)	26.9	n.a.	10.6	9.9	59.2	48.4	48.5
1975	5.3	31.9	n.a.	17.4	11.5	95.5	9.1[i]	61.4
1976	11.5	31.9	49.6	10.7	16.0	90.2	61.2	74.6

Note: Losses in parentheses. Figures after taxes and write-offs, before special credits.

a. Divorcement: United Paramount Theaters hived off, with profits of $16.7 million in 1948 and $17.6 million in 1949.

b. Divorcement: National Theaters hived off.

c. Divorcement: Loew's Theaters hived off.

d. Warner Bros. bought by Kinney Services, which changed its name to Warner Communications in 1971.

e. Bought by Gulf & Western; figures burned.

f. Bought by Transamerica Corporation.

g. Records & Music $23.8 million. Films $15.8 million. Cable television $1.8 million. Total: $50.1 million.

h. Divorcement, Stanley Warner hived off.

i. $41 million reduction in carrying value of investment in National Kinney Corporation.

• Operating loss or profits.

4. TOP MONEYMAKING FILMS OF EACH MAJOR STUDIO

Film	Rank°

20TH CENTURY-FOX

1. *The Sound of Music* (1965) — 4
2. *Towering Inferno* (1973) (made with Warner Bros.) — 8
3. *Butch Cassidy . . .* (1969) — 13
4. *The Poseidon Adventure* (1972) — 16
5. *M*A*S*H* (1970) — 18
6. *Young Frankenstein* (1975) — 24
7. *Patton* (1970) — 29
8. *The Omen* (1976) — 31
9. *The French Connection* (1971) — 32
10. *Cleopatra* (1963) — 35

MGM

1. *Gone With the Wind* (1939) — 5
2. *Doctor Zhivago* (1965) — 12
3. *Ben-Hur* (1959) — 19
4. *2001: A Space Odyssey* (1968) — 39
5. *The Dirty Dozen* (1967) — 55
6. *Ryan's Daughter* (1970) — 105
7. *Quo Vadis* (1951) — 130
8. *How the West Was Won* (1962) (made with Cinerama) — 138
9. *That's Entertainment* (1974) (released by UA) — 140

Film	Rank°

10. *Mutiny on the Bounty* (1962) — 183

UNITED ARTISTS

1. *One Flew Over the Cuckoo's Nest* (1975) — 7
2. *Fiddler on the Roof* (1971) — 22
3. *Thunderball* (1965) — 27
4. *Around the World in 80 Days* (1956) — 40
5. *Goldfinger* (1964) — 41
6. *It's a Mad, Mad, Mad, Mad World* (1963) — 51
7. *Midnight Cowboy* (1969) — 53
8. *Diamonds Are Forever* (1971) — 61
9. *West Side Story* (1961) — 62
10. *You Only Live Twice* (1967) — 63
    Return of the Pink Panther (1975) — 63

UNIVERSAL

1. *Jaws* (1975) — 1
2. *The Sting* (1973) — 6
3. *American Graffiti* (1973) — 11
4. *Airport* (1970) — 14
5. *Earthquake* (1974) — 20
6. *Airport 1975* (1974) — 36
7. *Midway* (1976) — 55
8. *The Other Side of the Mountain* (1975) — 87

° All-time moneymaking films regardless of studio, as of January 1977.

Film	Rank*	Film	Rank*
9. *Thoroughly Modern Millie* (1967)	89	9. *Deliverance* (1972)	44
10. *Spartacus* (1960)	106	10. *Dog Day Afternoon* (1975)	46

PARAMOUNT

1. *The Godfather* (1972) — 2
2. *Love Story* (1970) — 9
3. *The Ten Commandments* (1956) — 15
4. *The Godfather Part II* (1974) — 26
5. *The Longest Yard* (1974) — 45
6. *The Bad News Bears* (1976) — 47
7. *The Odd Couple* (1968) — 59
8. *Three Days of the Condor* (1976) — 67
9. *Murder on the Orient Express* (1974) — 72
10. *Romeo and Juliet* (1968) — 80

WARNER BROS.

1. *The Exorcist* (1973) — 3
2. *The Towering Inferno* (1975) (made with 20th C–F) — 8
3. *Blazing Saddles* (1974) — 21
4. *Billy Jack* (1971) — 23
5. *All the President's Men* (1976) — 25
6. *Trial of Billy Jack* (1974) — 28
7. *What's Up, Doc?* (1972) — 30
8. *Bonnie and Clyde* (1967) — 42

COLUMBIA

1. *Funny Girl* (1968) — 34
2. *Guess Who's Coming to Dinner* (1968) — 37
3. *The Way We Were* (1973) — 38
4. *Shampoo* (1975) — 48
5. *To Sir With Love* (1967) — 65
   Easy Rider (1969) — 65
7. *Funny Lady* (1975) — 68
8. *Murder by Death* (1976) — 71
9. *The Bridge on the River Kwai* (1957) — 81
10. *Oliver!* (1969) — 84

BUENA VISTA/DISNEY

1. *Mary Poppins* (1964) — 17
2. *Snow White* (1937) (made with RKO) — 33
3. *The Love Bug* (1969) — 50
4. *Swiss Family Robinson* (1960) — 68
5. *Bambi* (1942) (made with RKO) — 75
6. *Herbie Rides Again* (1974) — 77
7. *The Apple Dumpling Gang* (1975) — 88
8. *Peter Pan* (1953) (made with RKO) — 89
9. *101 Dalmatians* (1961) — 114
10. *Pinocchio* (1940) (made with RKO) — 123

V. THE STARS

When movies were young, actors and actresses were not
known by name. Although, as early as 1910, moviegoers
expressed definite preferences for one actor over another
and even wrote letters to the studios asking for the real
names of "Little Mary" or of "The Biograph Girl,"
producers were reluctant to release a performer's name
lest the actor demand a higher salary should he grow
famous.

But in 1910 Carl Laemmle (then the head of Independent
Motion Pictures, which was later to become Universal) had
to promise Florence Lawrence screen credit in order to
make her leave Biograph to work for him. Having acquired
her contract, Laemmle then performed what many people
think was the first publicity stunt; after circulating rumors
that Florence Lawrence had died in a streetcar accident,
Laemmle took out large ads in newspapers announcing that
Lawrence was in fact alive, working for him on some of the
"best movies of her career," and that she would soon start
to make personal appearances to dispel the rumors of her
death. The stunt worked: at Lawrence's first personal
appearances, a joyous mob of fans surrounded her.

Thus was the star system launched.

At first the system was employed only by the
independent companies, but stars proved so popular that
soon the licensed members of the Patents Company
adopted the star policy. By 1911 there was even a dog star,
"Jean," and soon postcards of stars were made available
in theater lobbies.

The first fan magazine, *Motion Picture Story Magazine,*
was published in 1911, and although it was originally
intended only for film exhibitors, it proved so popular that
it had to be sold on newsstands as well. *Photoplay* followed
in 1912, and *Motion Picture Stories* in 1913. Initially these
magazines merely summarized movie plots, but they soon
expanded to include "behind the scenes" glimpses of the

stars' private lives. By 1914 *Motion Picture Story Magazine* had achieved a circulation of 270,000.

Stars, in short, became determining factors in a film's production and publicity, not to mention in its profits. Producers, wishing to safeguard their investments, soon realized that a star was the surest way to guarantee a movie's success. As a result, studios began to organize filmmaking around stars, even tailoring scripts to a particular performer's talents. (Universal even made May McLaren sign a contract with a provision that should she leave the company she was never to use her name with any other studio.)

Studios initially predicted that stars would come from the Broadway stage, but they soon learned that a successful stage actor did not necessarily make an equally successful screen actor. And so the studios started to "create" their own stars, through clever publicity campaigns, type-casting and large salaries.

By the late twenties and early thirties the star system was so closely connected to the studio system that MGM, Hollywood's most successful company, wanted to be known as the studio with "more stars than there are in the heavens." The studios' rigid control of their stars' private lives—their diets, their clothes, their loves—has since become legendary. A few stars like Bette Davis and Olivia De Havilland have become well known for fighting the studios on such issues as contracts and type-casting.

But when the studio system started to collapse in the late forties and early fifties, the star system also suffered. Finding their audiences decimated by television, Hollywood studios could no longer afford to pay their stars thousands of dollars a week regardless of whether they were working or not. As independent production grew more and more prevalent throughout the fifties, it was no longer feasible or profitable for a studio to create a star. (It is often thought that Harry Cohn's grooming of Kim Novak for Columbia was the last example of a studio-created star.)

Free from the restrictions of studio contracts, stars both prospered and declined. Stars found themselves in the position to bargain for incredible salaries for a single picture: Alan Ladd got a reported $290,000 for *Boy on a Dolphin* (1957); Ava Gardner received $400,000+ for *On the Beach;* Elizabeth Taylor was paid $500,000 and 10 percent of the gross for *Suddenly, Last Summer,* after which time her fee was $1 million per picture; and William Holden supposedly received a deferred salary of $2 million for *The Bridge on the River Kwai.* Despite the advantages of such high prices, stars made fewer and fewer pictures each year, and some simply stopped making films altogether.

In recent years certain stars—Barbra Streisand, Paul Newman, Robert Redford, Steve McQueen, Clint Eastwood —can still ensure a movie's success. But many recent blockbusters, like *Jaws, American Graffiti, The Exorcist* and *Star Wars,* have been made without benefit of superstars. *Variety,* in fact, reported that thirteen of the twenty-five top grossers between 1968 and 1972 featured performers of little or no evident box office appeal at the time of release. In comparison, only seven of the twenty–five biggest hits between 1963–67 achieved that success without benefit of stars, while only five of 1958–62's top grossers lacked big names.

But for those moviegoers who believe they don't make stars like they used to, it is tonic to know that as early as 1918, *Motion Picture Magazine* was lamenting: "Where Have All the Stars Gone?" And for those fans who thought a star's death could no longer arouse the mass hysteria caused by Valentino's death in 1926, Elvis Presley's death in 1977 reminded us just how potent a star's attraction still could be.

Perhaps, as Andy Warhol once predicted, future stars shall be famous only for fifteen minutes. Nevertheless, the very concept of fame has played an undeniably important role in the history of modern consciousness and is one of the defining characteristics of modern popular sensibility.

Each year Quigley Publications asks film exhibitors in the United States to name that year's Top Box Office Stars. Although these polls provide only approximate and not exact indices of American tastes—a star who has had three movies released that year has an obvious advantage over an actor with only one film—the polls nevertheless afford some fascinating information. It is interesting, for example, to learn how frequently Abbott and Costello were cited during the forties, or how infrequently Marlon Brando has been mentioned throughout his career.

These polls suggest that during the second half of the thirties, America must have been charmed by children: Shirley Temple was the #1 star from 1935 to 1938, followed by Mickey Rooney from 1939 to 1941. And the lists neatly trace the decline of female stars: whereas women make up 50 percent of the top stars of the thirties, for example, they comprise little over 10 percent during the seventies, and this 10 percent stems from the indomitable presence of Barbra Streisand.

John Wayne has appeared on these lists more often than any other star: between 1949 and 1976, there were only three years Wayne was not cited—1958, 1975 and 1976.

Since 1941, Quigley Publications has also conducted polls for "Stars of Tomorrow," the new talent the exhibitors predicted would achieve major stardom. And from 1936 to 1954, Top Moneymaking Western Stars were compiled. Neither of these polls is listed below.

1. ANNUAL TOP TEN BOX OFFICE STARS

1932

Marie Dressler
Janet Gaynor
Joan Crawford
Charles Farrell
Greta Garbo
Norma Shearer
Wallace Beery
Clark Gable
Will Rogers
Joe E. Brown

1933

Marie Dressler
Will Rogers
Janet Gaynor

Eddie Cantor
Wallace Beery
Jean Harlow
Clark Gable
Mae West
Norma Shearer
Joan Crawford

1934

Will Rogers
Clark Gable
Janet Gaynor
Wallace Beery
Mae West
Joan Crawford
Bing Crosby
Shirley Temple
Marie Dressler
Norma Shearer

1935

Shirley Temple
Will Rogers
Clark Gable
Fred Astaire/
    Ginger Rogers
Joan Crawford
Claudette Colbert
Dick Powell
Wallace Beery
Joe E. Brown
James Cagney

1936

Shirley Temple
Clark Gable
Fred Astaire/
    Ginger Rogers
Robert Taylor
Joe E. Brown
Dick Powell
Joan Crawford

Claudette Colbert
Jeanette Mac-
    Donald
Gary Cooper

1937

Shirley Temple
Clark Gable
Robert Taylor
Bing Crosby
William Powell
Jane Withers
Fred Astaire/
    Ginger Rogers
Sonja Henie
Gary Cooper
Myrna Loy

1938

Shirley Temple
Clark Gable
Sonja Henie
Mickey Rooney
Spencer Tracy
Robert Taylor
Myrna Loy
Jane Withers
Alice Faye
Tyrone Power

1939

Mickey Rooney
Tyrone Power
Spencer Tracy
Clark Gable
Shirley Temple
Bette Davis
Alice Faye
Errol Flynn
James Cagney
Sonja Henie

1940

Mickey Rooney
Spencer Tracy
Clark Gable
Gene Autry
Tyrone Power
James Cagney
Bing Crosby
Wallace Beery
Bette Davis
Judy Garland

1941

Mickey Rooney
Clark Gable
Abbott & Costello
Bob Hope
Spencer Tracy
Gene Autry
Gary Cooper
Bette Davis
James Cagney
Judy Garland

1942

Abbott & Costello
Clark Gable
Gary Cooper
Mickey Rooney
Bob Hope
James Cagney
Gene Autry
Betty Grable
Greer Garson
Spencer Tracy

1943

Betty Grable
Bob Hope

Abbott & Costello
Bing Crosby
Gary Cooper
Greer Garson
Humphrey Bogart
James Cagney
Mickey Rooney
Clark Gable

1944

Bing Crosby
Gary Cooper
Bob Hope
Betty Grable
Spencer Tracy
Greer Garson
Humphrey Bogart
Abbott & Costello
Cary Grant
Bette Davis

1945

Bing Crosby
Van Johnson
Greer Garson
Betty Grable
Spencer Tracy
Humphrey Bogart/
 Gary Cooper
Bob Hope
Judy Garland
Margaret O'Brien
Roy Rogers

1946

Bing Crosby
Ingrid Bergman
Van Johnson
Gary Cooper
Bob Hope
Humphrey Bogart
Greer Garson

Margaret O'Brien
Betty Grable
Roy Rogers

1947

Bing Crosby
Betty Grable
Ingrid Bergman
Gary Cooper
Humphrey Bogart
Bob Hope
Clark Gable
Gregory Peck
Claudette Colbert
Alan Ladd

1948

Bing Crosby
Betty Grable
Abbott & Costello
Gary Cooper
Bob Hope
Humphrey Bogart
Clark Gable
Cary Grant
Spencer Tracy
Ingrid Bergman

1949

Bob Hope
Bing Crosby
Abbott & Costello
John Wayne
Gary Cooper
Cary Grant
Betty Grable
Esther Williams
Humphrey Bogart
Clark Gable

1950

John Wayne
Bob Hope
Bing Crosby
Betty Grable
James Stewart
Abbott & Costello
Clifton Webb
Esther Williams
Spencer Tracy
Randolph Scott

1951

John Wayne
Martin & Lewis
Betty Grable
Abbott & Costello
Bing Crosby
Bob Hope
Randolph Scott
Gary Cooper
Doris Day
Spencer Tracy

1952

Martin & Lewis
Gary Cooper
John Wayne
Bing Crosby
Bob Hope
James Stewart
Doris Day
Gregory Peck
Susan Hayward
Randolph Scott

1953

Gary Cooper
Martin & Lewis

John Wayne
Alan Ladd
Bing Crosby
Marilyn Monroe
James Stewart
Bob Hope
Susan Hayward
Randolph Scott

1954

John Wayne
Martin & Lewis
Gary Cooper
James Stewart
Marilyn Monroe
Alan Ladd
William Holden
Bing Crosby
Jane Wyman
Marlon Brando

1955

James Stewart
Grace Kelly
John Wayne
William Holden
Gary Cooper
Marlon Brando
Martin & Lewis
Humphrey Bogart
June Allyson
Clark Gable

1956

William Holden
John Wayne
James Stewart
Burt Lancaster
Glenn Ford
Martin & Lewis
Gary Cooper
Marilyn Monroe

Kim Novak
Frank Sinatra

1957

Rock Hudson
John Wayne
Pat Boone
Elvis Presley
Frank Sinatra
Gary Cooper
William Holden
James Stewart
Jerry Lewis
Yul Brynner

1958

Glenn Ford
Elizabeth Taylor
Jerry Lewis
Marlon Brando
Rock Hudson
William Holden
Brigitte Bardot
Yul Brynner
James Stewart
Frank Sinatra

1959

Rock Hudson
Cary Grant
James Stewart
Doris Day
Debbie Reynolds
Glenn Ford
Frank Sinatra
John Wayne
Jerry Lewis
Susan Hayward

1960

Doris Day
Rock Hudson
Cary Grant
Elizabeth Taylor
Debbie Reynolds
Tony Curtis
Sandra Dee
Frank Sinatra
Jack Lemmon
John Wayne

1961

Elizabeth Taylor
Rock Hudson
Doris Day
John Wayne
Cary Grant
Sandra Dee
Jerry Lewis
William Holden
Tony Curtis
Elvis Presley

1962

Doris Day
Rock Hudson
Cary Grant
John Wayne
Elvis Presley
Elizabeth Taylor
Jerry Lewis
Frank Sinatra
Sandra Dee
Burt Lancaster

1963

Doris Day
John Wayne

Rock Hudson
Jack Lemmon
Cary Grant
Elizabeth Taylor
Elvis Presley
Sandra Dee
Paul Newman
Jerry Lewis

1964

Doris Day
Jack Lemmon
Rock Hudson
John Wayne
Cary Grant
Elvis Presley
Shirley MacLaine
Ann-Margret
Paul Newman
Richard Burton

1965

Sean Connery
John Wayne
Doris Day
Julie Andrews
Jack Lemmon
Elvis Presley
Cary Grant
James Stewart
Elizabeth Taylor
Richard Burton

1966

Julie Andrews
Sean Connery
Elizabeth Taylor
Jack Lemmon
Richard Burton
Cary Grant
John Wayne
Doris Day

Paul Newman
Elvis Presley

1967

Julie Andrews
Lee Marvin
Paul Newman
Dean Martin
Sean Connery
Elizabeth Taylor
Sidney Poitier
John Wayne
Richard Burton
Steve McQueen

1968

Sidney Poitier
Paul Newman
Julie Andrews
John Wayne
Clint Eastwood
Dean Martin
Steve McQueen
Jack Lemmon
Lee Marvin
Elizabeth Taylor

1969

Paul Newman
John Wayne
Steve McQueen
Dustin Hoffman
Clint Eastwood
Sidney Poitier
Lee Marvin
Jack Lemmon
Katharine Hepburn
Barbra Streisand

1970

Paul Newman
Clint Eastwood
Steve McQueen
John Wayne
Elliott Gould
Dustin Hoffman
Lee Marvin
Jack Lemmon
Barbra Streisand
Walter Matthau

1971

John Wayne
Clint Eastwood
Paul Newman
Steve McQueen
George C. Scott
Dustin Hoffman
Walter Matthau
Ali MacGraw
Sean Connery
Lee Marvin

1972

Clint Eastwood
George C. Scott
Gene Hackman
John Wayne
Barbra Streisand
Marlon Brando
Paul Newman
Steve McQueen
Dustin Hoffman
Goldie Hawn

1973

Clint Eastwood
Ryan O'Neal

Steve McQueen
Burt Reynolds
Robert Redford
Barbra Streisand
Paul Newman
Charles Bronson
John Wayne
Marlon Brando

1974

Robert Redford
Clint Eastwood
Paul Newman
Barbra Streisand
Steve McQueen

Burt Reynolds
Charles Bronson
Jack Nicholson
Al Pacino
John Wayne

1975

Robert Redford
Barbra Streisand
Al Pacino
Charles Bronson
Paul Newman
Clint Eastwood
Burt Reynolds

Woody Allen
Steve McQueen
Gene Hackman

1976

Robert Redford
Jack Nicholson
Dustin Hoffman
Clint Eastwood
Mel Brooks
Burt Reynolds
Al Pacino
Tatum O'Neal
Woody Allen
Charles Bronson

2. STARS' SALARIES

As mentioned, the first film producers did not want to release the names of screen actors for fear an actor would demand a large salary should he grow famous. Those fears were well founded, of course, because actors did obtain exorbitant fees once their popularity became apparent. What those early producers did not realize, however, was that the very fact of large salaries could work for and not against them: large salaries make good news copy.

It would be impossible to deny that our fascination with screen stars stems both from an actor's very real talents and from the magical properties of movies. But it would be similarly foolish to deny that our star craziness does not owe something to our knowledge of their incomes. In a country charmed by rags-to-riches stories, Hollywood's fast money is bound to be paid attention. Stars give truth to American tales of unlimited social and economic mobility.

During the thirties and forties when the Secretary of the Treasury reported major incomes to the Ways and Means Committee, the reports were given wide press coverage: the film industry topped the country for the number of persons earning $75,000 a year or more. A star's income was public knowledge to be debated and discussed, a practice still evident today.

The salaries listed below are taken from trade publications, biographies and government reports. These should not be considered indisputable "facts"; wages have seldom been something about which studios or stars have been especially honest. As early as 1933 an essay in *Literary Digest* commented that "more fiction has been written about the pay envelopes of Hollywood than about the Wild West."

Two other cautions: when a star's salary is listed by the week, it should not be assumed that the salary was paid fifty-two-weeks a year; and inflation has not been taken into account for any of the figures listed below.

Abbot and Costello:
$588,423 in 1941
$789,628 in 1942 (among the
   highest salaries that year)

Julie Andrews:
$125,000 for *Mary Poppins*
   (1964)
$700,000 for *Hawaii* (1966)

Fatty Arbuckle:
$3 a day as a Keystone Cop
   (1913)
$7,000 a week for Famous
   Players in late 1910s

Fred Astaire:
$150,000 per film in mid-1930s
   for RKO

Mary Astor:
$500 per week for Famous
   Players in early 1920s
$1,100 per week for *Beau
   Brummel* (1924)
$3,750 per week for 40 weeks
   for Fox in 1928–29

John Barrymore:
$76,250 per picture plus $7,625
   per week over 7 weeks, plus
   all expenses for Warner
   Bros. in mid-1920s
$100,000 plus % per film for
   United Artists in late 1920s
$30,000 per week plus % for
   Warner Bros. in early 1930s
$150,000 per film at MGM in
   mid-1930s

Constance Bennett:
$30,000 per week for *Bought*
   (1931), one of the highest
   salaries up to that time
$150,000 for 4½ week's work
   in *Two Against the World*
   (1932)
$10,000 for *Law of the Tropics*
   (1941)

Jack Benny:
$125,000 from 20th and
   $125,000 from Warner Bros.
   in 1941

Humphrey Bogart:
$750 per week from Fox in early 1930s
$96,525 from Warner Bros. in 1941
$114,125 from Warner Bros. in 1942

Charles Boyer:
$100,000 from Paramount, $125,000 from Universal, and $125,000 from Warner Bros. in 1941: $350,000 total

Clara Bow:
$50 per week plus fare to Hollywood in 1923
$5,000 per week in 1929
$125,000 for *Call Her Savage* (1932)

Marlon Brando:
$50,000 for *The Men* (1950)
$75,000 for *Streetcar Named Desire* (1951)
$100,000 for *Viva Zapata!* (1952)
$300,000 plus % *Sayonara* (1957)
$1,250,000 for *Mutiny on the Bounty* (1962), including his %
Brando has said he received $250,000 plus % for *Godfather* (1972). *Variety* reported his fee was based entirely on %. Recent accounts have claimed his intake for the film has now passed $1,600,000.
$1,250,000 plus 11.3% of all gross receipts over $8,850,000 for *Missouri Breaks* (1976)

Charles Bronson:
$20,000 to $30,000 per shooting day plus $2,500 daily expenses in mid-1970s

Richard Burton:
$50,000 for *My Cousin Rachel* (1952)
$100,000 per film for Paramount in 1953

$500,000 for *The V.I.P.s* (1963)
$1,000,000 plus % for *Anne of the Thousand Days* (1970)

James Cagney:
$400 per week for Warner Bros. in 1930
$1,250 per week for Warner Bros. in 1932
$3,000 per week for Warner Bros. in 1933
$368,333 from Warner Bros. in 1939

Charlie Chaplin:
$150 per week for Keystone in 1913
$1,250 per week for Essanay plus bonuses in 1915
$10,000 per week plus $150,000 bonus for Mutual in 1916–17
$150,000 per film for First National in 1918–19
$152,000 from the Charlie Chaplin Film Corporation in 1939

Claudette Colbert:
$150,079 from RKO in 1939
$150,000 from RKO and $240,000 from Paramount in 1941
$360,000 in 1942 (among the highest salaries that year)

Sean Connery:
$1,200,000 for *Diamonds Are Forever* (1971)

Gary Cooper:
$311,000 in 1935
$295,106 from Goldwyn and $187,713 from Paramount in 1939
$299,177 from Goldwyn in 1941
$247,397 from Goldwyn in 1942

Joan Crawford:
$195,673 from MGM in 1941
$194,615 from MGM in 1943

Bing Crosby:
$318,907 in 1935
$336,111 in 1942 (among the highest salaries that year)

Bette Davis:

$300 per week at Universal in early 1930s

$129,750 from Warner Bros. in 1939

$252,333 from Warner Bros. in 1941

Goldwyn had to pay $385,000 to Warner Bros. to borrow Davis for *The Little Foxes* (1941)

$365,000 in 1948 (among the highest salaries that year)

$25,000 plus % for *What Ever Happened to Baby Jane?* (1962). Davis is said to have eventually made over $1 million from the film.

Robert De Niro:

$200,000 plus $150,000 when film hits a profit for *The Last Tycoon* (1976)

Marlene Dietrich:

$125,000 per film for Paramount after *Morocco* (1930)

$200,000 for *The Garden of Allah* (1936)

$450,000 for Korda in England for *Knight Without Armour* (1937)

$200,000 from Universal in 1941

Kirk Douglas:

$175,000 for *20,000 Leagues Under the Sea* (1954)

$350,000 for *Paths of Glory* (1957)

$400,000 for *In Harm's Way* (1965)

Marie Dressler:

$1,500 per week for MGM in 1927

$5,000 per week for MGM in 1930

Deanna Durbin:

$3,000 per week plus $10,000 bonus per film for Universal in 1938

$112,125 from Universal in 1941

$282,250 from Universal in 1942–43

Clint Eastwood:

$15,000 for *Fistful of Dollars* (1964)

$50,000 plus % for *For a Few Dollars More* (1965)

$400,000 plus 25% of net for *Hang 'Em High* (1968)

Douglas Fairbanks:

$2,000 per week for Triangle in 1915

$10,000 per week for Triangle in 1916

$300,000 for *Reaching for the Moon* (1931)

Alice Faye:

$140,291 from 20th in 1939

$119,166 from 20th in 1941

W. C Fields:

$5,000 per week for Mack Sennett in 1932

Errol Flynn:

$150 per week for Warner Bros. for *Murder in Monte Carlo* (1934)

$213,333 from Warner Bros. in 1939

$240,000 from Warner Bros. in 1941

Clark Gable:

$350 per week from MGM in 1931

$2,500 per week from MGM in 1933

$298,544 in 1940

$357,000 in 1941

$100,000 for *Soldier of Fortune* (1955)

$750,000 plus $58,000 for each week overtime for *The Misfits* (1961)

Greta Garbo:

$350 per week for MGM in 1926

$5,000 per week for MGM in 1927

$10,000 per week for MGM in 1933

$250,000 for *Anna Karenina* (1935)

$270,000 from MGM in 1938

Judy Garland:

$89,666 from MGM in 1942–43

Janet Gaynor:

$100 per week in 1926 for Fox

$1,500 per week in 1930

$169,750 in 1935

Cary Grant:

$450 per week for Paramount in 1932

$93,750 from RKO in 1939

$150,000 from Warner Bros., $100,000 from Columbia, and $101,562 from RKO in 1941: total $351,562

$150,000 for *Night and Day* (1946)

$300,000 for *People Will Talk* (1951)

Sonja Henie:

$244,166 plus $5,000 bonus from 20th in 1939

Katharine Hepburn:

$221,572 in 1935

$188,916 from MGM in 1941

$110,333 from MGM in 1942–43

$200,000 for *Guess Who's Coming to Dinner* (1967)

Dustin Hoffman:

$17,000 for *The Graduate* (1967)

$250,000 for *Midnight Cowboy* (1969)

$425,000 for *John and Mary* (1969)

William Holden:

10% of gross paid out at $50,000 per year for *The Bridge on the River Kwai* (1957)

$750,000 plus 20% profits for *The Horse Soldiers* (1959)

Bob Hope:

$204,166 from Paramount in 1941

Al Jolson:

$75,000 for *The Jazz Singer* (1927)

Buster Keaton:

$2,000 per week in 1923 plus %

$3,000 per week in 1928

$10,000 bonus from MGM in 1930

$15,000 for *Le Roi de Champs Elysées* in France (1934)

$2,500 per short for Educational (1935–37)

$100 per week as a gag man for MGM in 1940

Ruby Keeler:

$89,583 in 1935

$4,000 per week in 1937

Alan Ladd:

$290,000 for *Boy on a Dolphin* (1957)

Mario Lanza:

$800,000 in 1951

$150,000 for *Serenade* (1956)

Carole Lombard:

$75 per week in *Marriage in Transit* (1925)

$400 per week for *The Swim Princess* (1928)

$156,083 in 1935

$211,111 from RKO in 1939

Sophia Loren:

$25,000 for *Man of La Mancha* (1972)

Jeanette MacDonald:

$300,000 from MGM in 1941

Shirley MacLaine:

$600 per week for Hal Wallis in 1955

$800,000 plus % for *Sweet Charity* (1968)

Steve McQueen:

$19 per day as an extra in *Somebody Up There Likes Me* (1956)

$1,000,000 for *Bullitt* (1968)

Marilyn Monroe:

$125 per week for 20th in 1946

$500 per week for 20th in 1951

$1,200 per week for 20th in 1953

Monroe signed a contract with 20th in 1954 starting with $75,000 per film and going up to $100,000 per film after seven years. Another contract was signed in 1955 for $100,000 per film plus $500 weekly expenses.

Paul Newman:

$1,000 for Warner Bros. in 1954

$17,500 per film for Warner Bros. in late 1950s (at this time, however, Warner Bros. would charge $75,000 per film if another studio wanted him)

$200,000 for *Exodus* (1960)

$350,000 plus % for *Sweet Bird of Youth* (1962)

$750,000 plus 10% of gross and after that profit sharing in mid-1960s

$1,000,000 plus 10% gross (15% after film breaks even) for *The Towering Inferno* (1974)

Jack Nicholson:

$1,250,000 plus 10% of all gross receipts over $12,500,-000 for *Missouri Breaks*

Kim Novak:

$75 per week for Columbia in 1955

Preminger had to pay Columbia $100,000 for Novak's services in *The Man with the Golden Arm* (1956), although her salary at that time was only $100 per week

$13,000 for *Jeanne Eagels* (1957)

Ramon Novarro:

$125 per week for Rex Ingram in 1922–23

$10,000 per week for MGM in 1925

Al Pacino:

$500,000 plus 5% gross for *The Godfather Part II* (1974)

Gregory Peck:

$26,000 in 1944 (after taxes)

$48,000 in 1945 (after taxes)

$60,000 for *Only the Valiant* (1951), although Selznick charged $150,000 for Peck's services

$350,000 for two films: *The Million Pound Note* (1954) and *The Purple Plain* (1955), both made in England

Mary Pickford:

$10 per day for Biograph in 1909

$175 per week for Independent in 1910

$275 per week for Majestic in 1911

$500 per week for Famous Players in 1913

$1,000 per week for Famous Players in 1914

$2,000 per week for Famous Players in 1915

$10,000 per week for Famous Players in late 1915

$1,040,000 for two years plus bonuses starting in 1916

$250,000 for each of three pictures, plus $50,000 for her mother, plus a $100,000 bonus for each of the three films for First National: *Daddy Long Legs, The Hoodlum,* and *Heart o' the Hills*

Tyrone Power:

$151,250 in salary and $15,000 in other compensations from 20th in 1939

$203,125 from 20th in 1941

Ginger Rogers:

$219,500 from RKO in 1939

$215,000 from 20th in 1941

$245,000 from Paramount in 1942

Mickey Rooney:
$158,083 from MGM in 1941
$156,166 from MGM in 1942–43

Rosalind Russell:
$100,000 from Columbia in 1941

George C. Scott:
$1,000,000 plus % of net profit for *Hindenburg* (1975)

Barbara Stanwyck:
$92,500 from Paramount in 1939
$90,000 from Columbia and $100,000 from Warner Bros. in 1941

Barbra Streisand:
$200,000 for *Funny Girl* (1968)
$350,000 for *On a Clear Day* (1970)
$750,000 for *Hello, Dolly!* (1969)

Elizabeth Taylor:
$1,500 per week for MGM in 1951
$5,000 per week for MGM in 1952
$500,000 for *Cat on a Hot Tin Roof* (1958)

$125,000 for sixteen weeks, plus $50,000 for every week overtime, plus $3,000 a week expenses, plus 10% of the gross for *Cleopatra* (1963)

Spencer Tracy:
$233,461 from MGM in 1941
$219,871 from MGM in 1942–43
$165,000 plus % for *Broken Lance* (1954)
$300,000 for *Guess Who's Coming to Dinner* (1967)

Rudolph Valentino:
$5 per day for *Alimony* (1918)
$100 per week for Universal in 1919
$500 per week for Paramount in 1920
$10,000 per week plus % for United Artists in 1925

Mae West:
$5,000 per week for 10 weeks for Paramount in *Night after Night* (1932)
$480,833 in 1935 (highest paid woman in USA that year)
$350,000 for 10 days' work on *Myra Breckinridge* (1969)

Loretta Young:
$85,000 from Columbia in 1941

VI. THE FESTIVALS

1. VENICE FILM FESTIVAL PRIZES

The Venice Film Festival is the oldest of all international cinema festivals. First held in 1932 under the auspices of the Venice Biennial, the first exhibition proved so popular that a second festival was held in 1934. After that time the festival became an annual event in its own right, independent of the Biennial. The goal of those early exhibitions was "to raise the new art of the film to the same level of the other arts," a relatively novel sentiment in those years when film was considered entertainment, not art.

Because of the continued success of the festival, a specially designed building—the Palace of Cinema—was constructed for the 1937 exhibition. At about that time, however, political controversy divided the festival. Many critics, disturbed by the preponderance of German and Italian films that were awarded prizes, claimed that the festival was run by Mussolini and his German allies. (Goebbels had visited the festival in 1936.) In order to counter such criticism, the festival announced that "the object of this Exhibition is to acknowledge and reward with public mention such films as aim at being genuine expressions of art, without any bias regarding nationalities or trends. The hospitality extended by the Exhibition to cinematographic art is such as to exclude political interference in the shows it organizes."

Despite the announcement, controversy continued. In 1937 Jean Renoir's pacifist film, *La Grande Illusion* (which the Italians had ironically translated as *The Impossible Illusion*) aroused considerable friction. And in 1938, when Leni Riefenstahl's *Olympia* won its award, British and American representatives argued that the film was a full-length political propaganda movie that glorified not sports but the Nazi regime.

From 1940 to 1942 the festival continued, although the number of participating countries was of course drastically reduced because of the war. Finally, in 1943, the festival closed and remained closed for the remainder of the war.

Under new regulations, the festival reopened in 1946. Under these new policies, retrospectives were added, short films and documentaries were included, and the artistic merits of movies (as opposed to the commercial standards of Cannes) were again emphasized.

In the sixties the Venice Film Festival once again encountered trouble. Ernesto G. Laura replaced Dr. Luigi Chiarini, and under his direction, the jury and prize systems were abolished in 1969. In 1973 the festival was canceled altogether and was replaced by seven days of an Italian Film Review that did not take place in the Palace of Cinema. In 1975 the exhibition was called the Venice Biennial Cinema and returned to the Palace. The festival's existence has remained complicated ever since. Although the Biennial's budget was tripled in 1977 by an act of parliament, three of its chiefs resigned suddenly, including Giacomo Gambetti, head of the Biennial's cinema-TV section. With these constant changes, Venice no longer holds its former prestige.

The Venice Film Festival is held in late August-early September. In previous years when the festival conferred prizes, its chief prize was the famed Golden Lion of St. Mark. At one time the festival awarded more prizes than any other festival, including awards for scientific, experimental, children's didactic and cultural films. Only the principal awards are listed below.

1932

NO OFFICIAL AWARDS: PUBLIC REFERENDUM

Favorite Actress:
Helen Hayes
Favorite Actor:
Fredric March
Best Director:
Nikolai Ekk, *The Road to Life*
Most Amusing Film:
A Nous la Liberté
Most Touching Film:
The Sin of Madelon Claudet
Most Original Film:
Dr. Jekyll and Mr. Hyde

1934

Best Foreign Film:
Man of Aran, Robert Flaherty
Best Italian Film:
Teresa Confalonieri, Guido Brignone

Best State Entry:
USSR
Largest Industrial Entry:
Motion Picture Producers and
   Distributors of America
Best Direction:
Czech directors (Gustav
   Machaty, *Extase;* J. Roven-
   sky, *Young Love;* Tomas
   Trnka, *Hurricane in the
   Tatras;* and Karel Plicka,
   Zem spleva.)
Best Photography:
Gerard Rutten, *Dood Water*
Best Actor:
Wallace Beery, *Viva Villa*
Best Actress:
Katharine Hepburn, *Little
   Women*
Best Animated Cartoon:
Three Little Pigs, Walt Disney
Best Documentary:
Manovre Navali
Best Story:
Maskerade, Willy Forst
Best First Screening:
Alexander Korda, *The Private
   Life of Don Juan*

1935

Best Foreign Film:
Anna Karenina, Clarence
   Brown
Best Italian Film:
Casta Diva, Carmine Gallone
Best Direction:
King Vidor, *Wedding Night*
Best Actor:
Pierre Blanchar, *Crime and
   Punishment*
Best Actress:
Paula Wessely, *Episode*
Best Screenplay:
The Informer, Dudley Nichols
Best Music:
Bozambo

Best Photography:
The Devil Is a Woman
Best Color Film:
Becky Sharp
Best Animated Cartoon:
Band Concert, Walt Disney

1936

Best Foreign Film:
Der Kaiser von Kalifornien,
   Luis Trenker
Best Italian Film:
Squadrone bianco, Augusto
   Genina
Best Direction:
Jacques Feyder, *La Kermesse
   Héroïque* (Carnival in
   Flanders)
Best Actor:
Paul Muni, *The Story of Louis
   Pasteur*
Best Actress:
Annabella, *Veille d'Armes*
Best Cameraman:
M. Greenbaum, *Tudor Rose*
Best Musical:
Schlussakkord, Detlef Sierck
Best Political / Social Film:
Il cammino degli eroi
Best Documentary:
Jugend der Welt, Hans Weide-
   mann
Best Scientific Film:
Uno sguardo in fondo al mare

1937

Best Foreign Film:
Un Carnet de Bal, Julien
   Duvivier
Best Italian Film:
Scipione l'Africano, Carmine
   Gallone

Best Direction:
Robert Flaherty, Zoltan Korda,
  Elephant Boy
Best Italian Director:
Mario Camerini, *Il Signor Max*
Best Actor:
Emil Jannings, *Der Herrscher*
Best Actress:
Bette Davis, *Marked Woman
  and Kid Galahad*
Best Artistic Ensemble:
La Grande Illusion
**Best Film With Colonial
Subject:**
Sentinelle di Bronzo, Romolo
  Marcellini
Best Screenplay:
Sacha Guitry, *Les Perles de la
  Couronne*
Best Photography:
Peverell Marley, *Winterset*
Best Scientific Film:
Martin Rikli, *Röntgenstrahlen*
Best Animated Cartoon:
Walt Disney, *Hawaiian Holi-
  day; Music Land; Old Mill;
  Alpine Climbers; Country
  Cousin; Mickey's Polo Team*
Best Documentary:
Walter Ruttman, *Mannesmann*
**Best Film Interpreting Natural
and Artistic Beauties:**
Luis Trenker, *Condottieri*
Best First Screening:
Victoria the Great, Herbert
  Wilcox

1938

Best Foreign Film:
  (ex-aequo)
Olympia, Leni Riefenstahl
Best Italian Film:
Lucianno Serra Pilota, Goffredo
  Alessandrini
Great Art Trophy:
Walt Disney, *Snow White and
  the Seven Dwarfs*

Best Actor:
Leslie Howard, *Pygmalion*
Best Actress:
Norma Shearer, *Marie
  Antoinette*

Special Mention Medals:
Artistic Ensemble:
En kvinnas ansikte
Vivacious Lady
Alla en el Rancho Grande
Fahrendes Volk
Jezebel
Acting:
The Rage of Paris
Hanno Rapito Un Uomo
Der Mustergatte
Technique:
Goldwyn Follies
Sotto la Croce del Sud
Story:
Break the News
Geniusz Sceny
Direction:
Karl Ritter, *Urlaub auf
  Ehrenwort*
Marcel Carné, *Le Qual des
  Brumes*

1939

Best Foreign Film:
  (Not awarded this year)
Best Italian Film:
Abuna Messias, Goffredo
  Alessandrini
Best Cameraman:
Ubaldo Arata, *Dernière
  Jeunesse*
Cups of the Biennial:
La Fin du Jour
*Robert Koch, der Bekämpfer
  des Todes*
The Four Feathers
Gläd dig i din ungdom and
  En Handfull Ris
Selection of Swedish films as
  a whole

Special Mention Awards:

Margarita, Armando y su Padre
Tulak Macoun
Jeunes Filles en Détresse
Veertig Jaaren
Bors Istvan
The Golden Harvest of the Wilwatersrand
The Mikado

1940

Best Italian Film:
L'Asseido dell'Alcazar, Augusto Genina
Best Foreign Film:
Der Postmeister, Gustav Ucicky

(Only two prizes awarded this year)

1941

Best Italian Film:
La Corona di Ferro, Alessandro Blasetti
Best Foreign Film:
Ohm Kruger, Hans Steinhoff
Best Actor:
Ermete Zacconi, *Don Buonaparte*
Best Actress:
Luise Ullrich, *Annelie*
Best Direction:
G. W. Pabst, *Komödianten*
Cups of the Biennial:
Lettere d'Amore Smarrite
Alter ego
Marianela
Ich klage an
I Mariti

1942

Best Italian Film:
Bengasi, Augusto Genina
Best Foreign Film:
Der grosse König, Veit Harlan
Best Actor:
Fosco Giachetti, *Un colpo di postola; Bengasi; Noi vivi*
Best Actress:
Kristina Soderbaum, *Der grosse König; Die goldene Stadt*
International Film Chamber Color Prize:
Die goldene Stadt
International Film Chamber Technique Prize:
Alfa Tau
Best Documentaries:
Comacchio (Italy)
Musica nel Tempo (Italy)
Der Seeadler (Germany)
Bunter Reigen (Germany)
La Drapeau de l'Humanité (Switzerland)
Soil of Rome (Rumania)
A Kis Kaku (Hungary)
Rocciatori ed Aquile (Italy)
Erde auf Gewaltmärschen (Germany)
Mounting Guard on the Drina (Croatia)
Life and Death of Istvan Horthy (Hungary)
Best Animated Cartoons:
Anacleto e la Faina
Nel Paese dei Ranocchi

1943

(Festival not held)

1944

(Festival not held)

1945

(Festival not held)

1946

Best Film:
The Southerner (Jean Renoir, USA)
Special Mention:
Children of Paradise (Carné, France)
The Oath (Ciaureli, USSR)
Hangmen Also Die (Lang, USA)
Henry V (Olivier, England)
The Undaunted (Donskoi, USSR)
Paisan (Rossellini, Italy)
Panique (Duvivier, France)
Il Sole Sorge Ancora (Vergano, Italy)
Best Documentary:
In the Sands of Central Asia (Zguridi, USSR)
Best Animated Cartoon:
Le Voleur de Paratonnères (Grimault, France)

1947

Best Film:
International Grand Prize:
Sirena (Stekly, Czechoslovakia)

Best Original Contribution to Film Progress:
La Perla (Fernandez, Mexico)
Dreams That Money Can Buy (Richter, USA)
Best Direction:
Henri-Georges Clouzot, *Quai des Orfèvres*
Most Original Story:
Vesna (Alexandrov, USSR)
Best Actress:
Anna Magnani, *Honorable Angelina*
Best Actor:
Pierre Fresnay, *Monsieur Vincent*
Best Photography:
Gabriel Figueroa, *La Perla* (Mexico)
Best Music:
E. F. Burian, *Sirena*
Best Feature Documentary:
On the Trail of the Animals (Dolin, USSR)
Best Short Documentary:
Piazza San Marco (Pasinetti, Italy)
Special Homage:
Carl Dreyer, *Dies Irae*
Best Italian Film:
Caccia tragica (De Sanctis)

1948

Best Film:
International Grand Prize:
Hamlet (Olivier, England)
Best Direction:
G. W. Pabst, *Der Prozess* (Austria)
Best Actor:
Ernest Deutsch, *Der Prozess*
Best Actress:
Jean Simmons, *Hamlet*
Best Documentary:
Goemons (Bellon, France)

Best Animated Cartoon (ex aequo)
Melody Time (Disney, USA)
Le Petit Soldat (Grimault, France)
Best Story and Screenplay:
Graham Greene, *The Fallen Idol*
Best Music:
Max Steiner, *Treasure of the Sierra Madre*
Best Photography:
Desmond Dickison, *Hamlet*
Best Scenography:
John Bryan, *Oliver Twist*
International Prizes:
John Ford, *The Fugitive* (for its drama)
Robert Flaherty, *Louisiana Story* (for its lyrical beauty)
Luchino Visconti, *La Terra Trema* (for its choral qualities and style)
Best Italian Film:
Sotto il sole di Roma (Castellani)

1949

Best Film: Lion of St. Mark:
Manon (Clouzot, France)
Best Direction:
Augusto Genina, *Cielo sulla Palude* (Italy)
Best Actor:
Joseph Cotten, *Portrait of Jennie*
Best Actress:
Olivia de Havilland, *The Snake Pit*
Best Scenario:
Jacques Tati, *Jour de Fête*
Best Photography:
Gabriel Figueroa, *La Malquerida* (Mexico)
Best Scenography:
William Kellner, *Kind Hearts and Coronets*

Best Music:
John Greenwood, *The Last Days of Dolwyn*
Best Documentary:
L'Equateur aux Cent Visages (Cauvin, Belgium)
International Prizes:
Sydney Meyers, *The Quiet One*
Anatole Litvak, *The Snake Pit*
R. A. Stemmle, *Berliner Ballade*
Best Italian Film:
Cielo sulla (Genina)

1950

Best Film: Lion of St. Mark:
Justice Is Done (Cayatte, France)
Best Direction:
(Not awarded)
Best Actor:
Sam Jaffe, *The Asphalt Jungle*
Best Actress:
Eleanor Parker, *Caged*
Best Scenario:
Jacques Natanson, Max Ophuls, *La Ronde*
Best Photography:
Martin Bodin, *Bara en mor* (Sweden)
Best Music:
Brian Easdale, *Gone to Earth* (England)
Best Scenography:
D'Eaubonne, *La Ronde*
Best Documentary:
Paul Haesaert, *Visite à Picasso* (Belgium)
International Prizes:
Elia Kazan, *Panic in the Streets*
Jean Delannoy, *Dieu a Besoin des Hommes*
Alessandro Blasetti, *Prima Comunione*
Special Jury Prize:
Walt Disney, *Cinderella* and *Beaver Valley*

Best Italian Film:
Domani è troppo tardi
(Moguy)

1951

Best Film: Lion of St. Mark:
Rashomon (Kurosawa, Japan)
Best Direction:
(No longer awarded)
Best Actor:
Jean Gabin, *La Nuit est Mon
Royaume*
Best Actress:
Vivien Leigh, *A Streetcar
Named Desire*
Best Scenario:
T. E. B. Clark, *The Lavender
Hill Mob*
Best Photography:
L. H. Burel, *Le Journal d'un
Curé de Campagne* (France)
Best Music:
Hugo Friedhofer, *Big Carnival*
(USA)
Best Documentary:
Nature's Half Acre (Disney,
USA)
Special Jury Prize:
Elia Kazan, *A Streetcar Named
Desire*
International Prizes
Robert Bresson, *Le Journal
d'un Curé de Campagne*
Billy Wilder, *Big Carnival*
Jean Renoir, *The River*
Best Italian Film:
La Città si difende (Germi)

1952

Best Film: Lion of St. Mark:
Forbidden Games (Clement,
France)

Best Actor:
Fredric March, *Death of a
Salesman*
Best Actress:
(Not awarded this year)
Best Scenario
Jean Negulesco, *Phone Call
from a Stranger* (USA)
Best Music:
George Auric
Best Décor:
Carmen Dillon, *The Importance
of Being Earnest*
Special Jury Prize:
Mendy (England)
International Prizes:
John Ford, *The Quiet Man*
Roberto Rossellini, *Europe 51*
K. Mizoguchi, *Life of Oharu*

1953

Best Film: Lion of St. Mark:
(Not awarded this year)
Best Actor:
Henri Vilbert, *Absolution
Without Confession*
(France)
Best Actress:
Lilli Palmer, *The Fourposter*
(USA)
Silver Prize Winners:
Ugetsu Monogatari (Mizo-
guchi, Japan)
I Vitelloni (Fellini, Italy)
The Little Fugitive (Ashley,
USA)
Moulin Rouge (Huston,
England)
Thérèse Raquin (Carné,
France)
Bronze Prize Winners:
War of God (Spain)
Les Orgueilleux (France)
Sinha Moca (Brazil)

1954

Best Film: Lion of St. Mark:
Romeo and Juliet (Castellani, Italy-England)
Best Actor:
Jean Gabin, *Touchez pas au Grisbi, The Air of Paris* (France)
Best Actress:
(Not awarded this year)
Silver Prize Winners:
On the Waterfront (Kazan, USA)
Seven Samurai (Kurosawa, Japan)
La Strada (Fellini, Italy)
Sansho the Bailiff (Mizoguchi, Japan)
Special Jury Prize for Ensemble Acting:
Executive Suite (with William Holden, June Allyson, Barbara Stanwyck, Fredric March, Walter Pidgeon, Shelley Winters)

1955

Best Film: Lion of St. Mark:
Ordet (Dreyer, Denmark)
Best Actor:
Kenneth More, *The Deep Blue Sea* (England), Curt Jurgens, *The Devil's General* (Germany), and *Les Héros sont Fatigués* (France)
Best Actress:
(Not awarded this year)
Silver Prize Winners:
La Cicala (Samsonov, USSR)
The Big Knife (Aldrich, USA)
Le Amiche (Antonioni, Italy)
Ciske de Rat (Staudte, Holland)

Most Promising New Directors:
Alexandre Astruc (France)
Vaclav Kraka (Czechoslovakia)
William Fairchild (England)
Francesco Maselli (Italy)
Andrejz Munk (Poland)

1956

Best Film: Lion of St. Mark:
(Not awarded this year)
Best Actor:
Bournvil, *La Traverse de Paris*
Best Actress:
Maria Schell, *Gervaise*

Other Awards:

International Catholic Office Award:
Calabuch (Spain)
International Film Critics Award:
Gervaise
Calle Mayor
Italian Critics Award:
Attack! (Aldrich, USA)
San Giorgio Prize:
Burma Harp (Ichikawa, Japan)

1957

Best Film: Lion of St. Mark:
Aparajito (Ray, India)
Best Actor:
Anthony Franciosa, *A Hatful of Rain* (USA)
Best Actress:
Dzidra Ritenberg, *Malva* (USSR)
Silver Prize Winner:
White Nights (Visconti, Italy)

Other Awards:

Catholic Office Award:
A Hatful of Rain (USA)

International Film Critics Award:
A Hatful of Rain (USA)
Most Cooperative Performer at the Festival:
Esther Williams
San Giorgio Prize:
Something of Value (USA)

1958

Best Film: Lion of St. Mark:
Muhomatsu no Issho (Inagaki, Japan)
Best Actor:
Alec Guinness, *The Horse's Mouth* (England)
Best Actress:
Sophia Loren, *The Black Orchid* (USA)
Silver Prize Winner:
Les Amants (Malle, France)
Best Documentary:
The Last Day of Summer (Konwicki & Laskowski, Poland)

1959

Best Film: Lion of St. Mark:
Il Generale della Rovere (Rossellini, Italy)
La Grande Guerre (Laurentiis, Italy)
Best Actor:
James Stewart, *Anatomy of a Murder* (USA)
Best Actress:
Madeline Robinson, *Double Tour* (France)
Silver Prize Winner:
La Grande Guerre (Monicelli, Italy)
Special Jury Prize:
Ingmar Bergman, *The Magician*

Other Awards:

Catholic Film Office:
Il Generale della Rovere
International Film Critics Prize:
Il Generale della Rovere

1960

Best Film: Lion of St. Mark:
Le Passage du Rhine (Cayatte, France)
Best Actor:
John Mills, *Tunes of Glory* (England)
Best Actress:
Shirley MacLaine, *The Apartment* (USA)
Silver Prize Winner:
Rocco and His Brothers (Visconti, Italy)

Other Awards:

Catholic Film Office Award:
Voyage In a Balloon (Lamorisses, France)
International Film Critics Award:
The Motorcart (Spain)
Rocco and His Brothers (Italy)
Best First Feature:
Florestano Vancini, *That Long Night In '43* (Italy)

1961

Best Film: Lion of St. Mark:
Last Year at Marienbad (Resnais, France)
Best Actor:
Toshiro Mifune, *Yojimbo* (Japan)
Best Actress:
Suzanne Flon, *Thou Shall Not Kill* (Yugoslavia)

Special Jury Prize:
Peace to All Who Enter
   (Alexander Alov, USSR)

Other Awards:

Catholic Film Office Award:
Il Posto (Olmi, Italy)
International Film Critics Award:
Il Brigante (Castellani, Italy)
San Giorgio Prize:
Banditti a Orgosolo (de Seta, Italy)

1962

Best Film: Lion of St. Mark:
Childhood of Ivan (Tarkovski, USSR)
Family Diary (Zurlini, Italy)
Best Actor:
Burt Lancaster, *Bird Man of Alcatraz*
Best Actress:
Emmanuelle Riva, *Thérèse Desqueyroux*
Special Jury Prize:
Vivre Sa Vie (Godard, France)

Other Awards:

Best First Film:
David and Lisa (Perry, USA)
Los Innudados (Birri, Argentina)
Catholic Film Office Award:
Term of Trial (England)
International Film Critics Award:
Knife in the Water (Polanski, Poland)
San Giorgio Prize:
Bird Man of Alcatraz

1963

Best Film: Lion of St. Mark:
Le Mani sulla città (Rosi, Italy)
Best Actor:
Albert Finney, *Tom Jones*
Best Actress:
Delphine Seyrig, *Muriel* (France)
Special Jury Prizes:
Le Feu Follet (Malle, France)
Introduction to Life (Talankine, USSR)

Other Awards:

Best First Films:
A Sunday in September (Donner, Sweden)
Le Joli Mai (Marker, France)
Catholic Film Office Award:
Hud (Ritt, USA)
International Film Critics Award:
The Hangman (Berlanga, Spain)

1964

Best Film: Lion of St. Mark:
Red Desert (Antonioni, Italy)
Best Actor:
Tom Courtenay, *King and Country* (England)
Best Actress:
Harriet Andersson, *To Love* (Sweden)
Special Jury Prizes:
Hamlet (Kosintzev, USSR)
Il Vangelo Secondo Matteo (Pasolini, Italy)

Other Awards:

Best First Film:
La Vie à l'Enfers (Jessua, France)

Catholic Film Office Award:
Il Vangelo Secondo Matteo (Italy)
International Film Critics Award:
Red Desert (Italy)
San Giorgio Prize:
Nothing but a Man (USA)

1965

Best Film: Lion of St. Mark:
Of a Thousand Delights (Visconti, Italy)
Vaghe Stelle del 'Orsa
Best Actor:
Toshiro Mifune, *Akahige* (Japan)
Best Actress:
Annie Girardot, *Trois Chambres à Manhattan* (France)
Special Jury Prizes:
Simon of the Desert (Buñuel, Mexico)
I'm Twenty (Koutziev, USSR)

Other Awards:

Best First Film:
Faithfulness (Toderovski, USSR)
Catholic Film Office Award:
Akahige (Kurosawa, Japan)
International Film Critics Award:
Simon of the Desert (Buñuel, Mexico)
Gertrud (Dreyer, Denmark)

1966

Best Film: Lion of St. Mark:
Battle of Algiers (Pontecorvo, Italy)

Best Actor:
Jacques Perrin, *Quest* (Spain) and *Half a Man* (Italy)
Best Actress:
Natalia Arinbasavora, *The First Schoolteacher* (USSR)
Special Jury Prizes:
Au Hasard Balthazar (Bresson, France)
Abschied von Gestern (Kluge, Germany)
Chappaqua (Rooks, USA)

1967

Best Film: Lion of St. Mark:
Belle de Jour (Buñuel, France)
Best Actor:
Ljubisa Samardzic, *Dawn* (Yugoslavia)
Best Actress:
Shirley Knight, *Dutchman* (England)
Special Jury Prizes:
La Chinoise (Godard, France)
China Is Near (Bellocchio, Italy)
Opera Prima Prize:
Edgar Reitz, *Mahlzeiten* (Germany)

Other Awards:

Catholic Office Award:
Silent Voyage (Chalone, France)
International Film Critics Award:
China Is Near (Bellocchio, Italy) for films in competition
Rebellion (Kobayashi, Japan) for films not in competition

1968

Best Film: Lion of St. Mark:
*Die Artisten in der Zirkus-
kuppel* (Kluge, Germany)
Best Actor:
John Morely, *Faces* (USA)
Best Actor:
Laura Betti, *Teorema* (Italy)

Special Jury Prize:
Le Socrate (Lapoujade,
France)
Nostra Signora dei Turchi
(Bene, Italy)

1969

*(Jury and Award System
discontinued)*

2. CANNES FILM FESTIVAL PRIZES

Cannes is the best-known of all the international film
festivals. Originally scheduled for 1939, the first exhibition
at Cannes had to be postponed until 1946 due to the war.
Despite its continued popularity, the festival has been
canceled three times during its history: in 1949 and 1950
owing to insufficient funds and to schisms within the
French film industry, and in 1968 when political
demonstrations led by such respected directors as Truffaut,
Godard and Lelouch forced the festival to close in
mid-progress.

The festival was quick to recover from the 1968
controversy, however, and has since regained its former
prestige and attendant publicity. Cannes is now the largest
of the film festivals: during the festival, as many as six
hundred films can be screened in the town, both at the
festival itself and at the town's many local theaters. It's a
twenty-four-hour-a-day affair, attended by representatives
from all aspects of the film industry—directors, producers,
exhibitors, distributors, actors, writers, publicists and
journalists. As a result, Cannes is famous for its
wheeling-dealing marketplace atmosphere.

Although the structure of the festival continues to
change, the exhibition mainly consists of three parts: (1)
the competition itself, (2) the Critics' Week, and (3) the
Directors' Fortnight. In the past few years, three
noncompetitive segments were added to the festival: (1)

"The Fertile Eyes," for films dealing in theatrical, dance or musical adaptation; (2) "The Air of the Times," with movies exploring important recent events; and (3) "The Composed Past," a look at classic works. Shortly after the 1977 festival, however, Gilles Jacob—the festival's director—announced that these three categories would be deleted from future festivals and that the rest of the festival would likewise be pared down to make it more manageable.

Unlike many of the other festivals that favor shorts and documentaries as well as feature-length films, Cannes concentrates largely on feature-length works.

Through 1950 the festival took place in the fall. But since 1951 it has been held in the spring, usually in May, so as to be the first festival of the calendar year.

Cannes's top prize (for best film) is the famed Golden Palm.

1946

Best Films:
La Bataille du Rail (Clément, France)
Symphonie Pastorale (Delannoy, France)
The Lost Weekend (Wilder, USA)
Brief Encounter (Lean, England)
Open City (Rossellini, Italy)
Maria Candelaria (Fernandez, Mexico)
The Last Chance (Lindtberg, Switzerland)
Best Director:
René Clement, *La Bataille du Rail*
Best Actor:
Ray Milland, *The Lost Weekend*
Best Actress:
Michèle Morgan, *Symphonie Pastorale*

1947

Best Films:
Antoine et Antoinette (Becker, France)
Les Maudits (Clément, France)
Crossfire (Dmytryk, USA)
Dumbo (Disney, USA)
Ziegfeld Follies (Minnelli, USA)
Best Director:
(not awarded)
Best Actor:
(not awarded)
Best Actress:
(not awarded)

1948

(No festival)

1949

Best Film:
The Third Man (Reed, England)
Best Director:
René Clément, *Au Delà des Grilles*
Best Actor:
Edward G. Robinson, *House of Strangers*
Best Actress:
Isa Miranda, *Au Delà des Grilles*

1950

(No festival)

1951

Best Film:
Miracle in Milan (De Sica, Italy) and *Miss Julie* (Sjöberg, Sweden) (tied; awarded *ex aequo*)
Best Director:
Luis Buñuel, *Los Olvidados*
Best Actor:
Michael Redgrave, *The Browning Version*
Best Actress:
Bette Davis, *All About Eve*
Special Jury Prize:
All About Eve (Mankiewicz, USA)

1952

Best Film:
Othello (Welles, Morocco) and *Two Cents Worth of Hope* Castellani, Italy) (tied; awarded *ex aequo*)

Best Director:
Christian-Jaque, *Fanfan la Tulipe*
Best Actor:
Marlon Brando, *Viva Zapata!*
Best Actress:
Lee Grant, *Detective Story*
Special Jury Prize:
Nous Sommes Tous des Assassins (Cayatte, France)

1953

Best Film:
Wages of Fear (Clouzot, France)
Best Director:
Walt Disney, for his work as a whole
Best Actor:
Charles Vanel, *Wages of Fear*
Best Actress:
Shirley Booth, *Come Back, Little Sheba*

1954

Best Film:
Gate of Hell (Kinugasa, Japan)
Best Director:
René Clément, *Monsieur Ripois*
Best Actor:
(Not awarded)
Best Actress:
(Not awarded)
Out of Competition Prize:
From Here to Eternity (Zinnemann, USA)

1955

Best Film:
Marty (Mann, USA)

Best Director:
Jules Dassin, *Rififi*
Serge Vasiliev, *Heroes of
Shipka*
Best Actor:
Spencer Tracy, *Bad Day at
Black Rock*
Ernest Borgnine, *Marty*
Best Actress:
Betsy Blair, *Marty*
Special Prize:
The Lost Continent (Italy)

Other Prizes:

Best Documentary:
Isle of Fire (Italy)

1956

Best Film:
World of Silence (Malle/
Cousteau, France)
Best Director:
Serge Youtkevitch, *Othello*
Best Actor:
(Not awarded)
Best Actress:
Susan Hayward, *I'll Cry
Tomorrow*
Special Prize:
Le Mystère Picasso (Clouzot,
France)

Other Prizes:

Most Poetic Humor:
Ingmar Bergman, *Smiles of a
Summer Night*
Best Human Document:
Satyajit Ray, *Pather Panchali*

1957

Best Film:
Friendly Persuasion (Wyler,
USA)

Best Director:
Robert Bresson, *A Condemned
Man Escapes*
Best Actor:
John Kitzmiller, *Valley of
Peace*
Best Actress:
Guilietta Massina, *Nights of
Cabiria*
Special Prizes:
The Seventh Seal (Bergman,
Sweden)
Kanal (Wajda, Poland)

Other Prizes:

Best Documentary:
The Roof of Japan (Japan) and
Qivitog (Denmark) (tied)

1958

Best Film:
The Cranes Are Flying
(Kalatozov, USSR)
Best Director:
Ingmar Bergman, *Brink of
Life*
Best Actor:
Paul Newman, *The Long Hot
Summer*
Best Actress:
(collective prize)
Eva Dahlbeck, Ingrid Thulin,
Bibi Andersson, Babro
Ornas, *Brink of Life*
Special Prize:
Jacques Tati, *Mon Oncle*

Other Prizes:

Best Documentary:
Bronze Faces (Switzerland)
Best Script:
Mauro Bolognini, *Newlyweds*
International Critics Prize:
Juan Bardem, *Vengeance*

1959

Best Film:
Black Orpheus (Camus, France)
Best Director:
Francois Truffaut, *The 400 Blows*
Best Actor:
(collective prize)
Dean Stockwell, Bradford Dillman, Orson Welles, *Compulsion*
Best Actress:
Simone Signoret, *Room at the Top*
Special Jury Prize:
Stars (Burgaria)
Special Prize:
Luis Buñuel, *Nazarin*

Other Prizes:

International Critics Award:
Hiroshima Mon Amour and *Araya* (tied)
Catholic Film Office Award:
The 400 Blows
Film Writers Award:
Hiroshima Mon Amour

1960

Best Film:
La Dolce Vita (Fellini, Italy) *(Bergman's* The Virgin Spring *and Buñuel's* The Young One *were announced as too good to be judged)*
Best Director:
(Not awarded)
Best Actor:
(Not awarded)
Best Actress:
Melina Mercouri, *Never on Sunday* and; Jeanne Moreau, *Moderato Cantabile*
Special Jury Prize:
Antonioni, *L'Avventura*
Special Prizes:
Ballad of a Soldier (USSR)
Lady with a Pet Dog (USSR)
Kaji (Japan)

Other Prizes:

International Critics Prize:
Bergman, *The Virgin Spring*
Catholic Film Office Award:
Henning-Jensen, *Paw*

1961

Best Film:
Viridiana (Buñuel, Spain) and *Une aussi longue absence* (Colpi, France) (tied)
Best Director:
Yulia Solntzeva, *History of the Flaming Years*
Best Actor:
Anthony Perkins, *Goodbye Again*
Best Actress:
Sophia Loren, *Two Women*
Special Jury Prize:
Jerzy Kawalerowicz, *Mother Joan of the Angels*

Other Prizes:

International Critics Prize:
Hand in the Trap, Torré Nilsson
Chronicle of a Summer, Jean Rouch
Gary Cooper Award for Human Values:
A Raisin in the Sun
Catholic Film Office Award:
Hoodlum Priest, Kershner

1962

Best Film:
The Given Word (Duarte, Brazil)
Best Director:
(Not awarded)
Best Acting:
(given collectively to two films)
Katharine Hepburn, Ralph Richardson, Jason Robards, Jr., Dean Stockwell, *Long Day's Journey Into Night*
Rita Tushingham, Murray Melvin, *A Taste of Honey*
Special Jury Prize:
Robert Bresson, *Le Procès de Jeanne d'Arc*
Michelangelo Antonioni, *L'Eclipse*

Other Prizes:

International Critics Prize:
Buñuel, *The Exterminating Angel*
Catholic Film Office Award:
Antonioni, *L'Eclipse*

1963

Best Picture:
The Leopard (Visconti, Italy)
Best Director:
(Not awarded)
Best Actor:
Richard Harris, *This Sporting Life*
Best Actress:
Marina Vlady, *The Conjugal Bed* (a.k.a. *Queen Bee*)
Special Jury Prizes:
Harakiri, Kobayashi (Japan)
One Day a Cat, Jasny (Czechoslovakia)

Other Prizes:

International Critics Prize:
This Sporting Life, Anderson
Le Joli Mai, Marker
Gary Cooper Award for Human Values:
To Kill a Mockingbird
Catholic Film Office Award:
The Fiancés, Olmi

1964

Best Film:
The Umbrellas of Cherbourg (Demy, France)
Best Director:
(Not awarded)
Best Actor:
Antal Pager, *Pacsirta;* and Saro Urzi, *Seduced and Abandoned* (tied)
Best Actress:
Anne Bancroft, *The Pumpkin Eater;* and, Barbara Barrie, *One Potato, Two Potato* (tied)
Special Jury Prize:
Hiroshi Teshigahara, *Woman of the Dunes*

Other Prizes:

International Critics Award:
The Passenger (Poland)
Catholic Film Office Award:
Umbrellas of Cherbourg (France)
Sterile Lives (Brazil)

1965

Best Film:
The Knack (Lester, England)
Best Director:
L. Ciulei, *The Lost Forest*

Best Acting:
(awarded collectively)
Samantha Eggar and Terence
Stamp, *The Collector*
Special Jury Prize:
Kobayashi, *Kwaidan*

Other Prizes:

International Critics Award:
Tarahumara (Mexico)
Catholic Film Office Award:
Yoyo (France); *Tokyo Olympics* (Japan)

1966

Best Film:
A Man and a Woman (Lelouch,
France) and *Signore e
Signori* (Germi, Italy) (tied)
Best Director:
Serge Youtkevitch, *Lenin in
Poland*
Best Actor:
Per Oscarsson, *Hunger*
Best Actress:
Vanessa Redgrave, *Morgan*
Special Jury Prize:
Gilbert, *Alfie*

Other Awards:

20th Anniversary Tribute:
Orson Welles
International Critics Award:
Young Torless (Germany) and
La Guerre est finie (France)
Catholic Film Office Award:
A Man and a Woman (France)

1967

Best Film:
Blow-Up (Antonioni, England)
Best Director:
Ferenc Kosa, *Ten Thousand
Suns*

Best Actor:
Odded Kotler, *Three Days and
a Child*
Best Actress:
Pia Degermark, *Elvira Madigan*
Special Jury Prize: (tie)
Petrovic, *Happy Gypsies* and;
Losey, *Accident*

Other Prizes:

Jury Homage:
Robert Bresson
International Critics Award:
Losey, *Accident*

1968

(Festival closed)

1969

Best Film:
If (Anderson, England)
Best Director:
Glauber Rocha, *Antonio Das
Mortes* and; Vojtech Jasny,
My Dear (tied)
Best Actor:
Jean-Louis Trintignant, *Z*
Best Actress:
Vanessa Redgrave, *Isadora*
Special Jury Award:
Adalen 31, Widerberg

Other Prizes:

International Critics Award:
Andrei Roublov (USSR)
Best First Film:
Easy Rider, Hopper

1970

Best Film:
M*A*S*H (Altman, USA)

Best Director:
John Boorman, *Leo the Last*
Best Actor:
Marcello Mastroianni, *Drama of Jealousy*
Best Actress:
Ottavio Piccolo, *Metelo*
Special Jury Prize:
Citizen Above Suspicion, Petri
Jury Prizes:
The Balkans (Hungary)
Strawberry Statement (USA)

Other Prizes:

Best First Film:
Raoul Coutard, *Hoa Binh*

1971

Best Film:
The Go-Between (Losey, England)
Best Director:
(Not awarded)
Best Actor:
Ricardo Cucciola, *Sacco and Vanzetti*
Best Actress:
Kitty Winn, *Panic In Needle Park*
Special Jury Prize:
Taking Off, Foreman; and *Johnny Got His Gun* (Trumbo) (tied)

Other Prizes:

Special Prize:
Death in Venice, Visconti
Best First Film:
Nino Manfredi, *By Grace Received*

1972

Best Film:
The Working Class Goes to Paradise (Petri, Italy) and *The Mattei Affair* (Rosi, Italy) (tied)
Best Director:
Miklós Jancsó, *The Red Psalm*
Best Actor:
Jean Yanne, *We Will Not Grow Old Together*
Best Actress: -
Susannah York, *Images*
Special Jury Prize:
Solaris, Tarkovski
Jury Prize:
Slaughterhouse Five, Hill

1973

Best Films:
Scarecrow (Schatzberg, USA) and *The Hireling* (Bridges, England) (tied)
Best Director:
(Not awarded)
Best Actor:
Giancarlo Giannini, *Love and Anarchy*
Best Actress:
Joanne Woodward, *The Effect of Gamma Rays . . .*
Grand Special Jury Prize:
The Mother and the Whore, Eustache
Special Jury Prize:
Wild Planet, Laloux
Jury Prize:
The Invitation, Goretta
Hourglass Sanatorium, Has

Other Prizes:

Best First Film:
Jeremy, Barron

International Critics Award:
La Grande Buffe, Ferreri
The Mother and the Whore,
   Eustache

1974

Best Film:
The Conversation (Coppola,
   USA)
Best Director:
(Not awarded)
Best Actor:
Jack Nicholson, *The Last Detail*
Best Actress:
Marie-Jose Nat, *Les Violons du
Bal*
Special Jury Prize:
Il Fiore delle Mille e una Notte,
   Pasolini
Jury Prize:
La Prima Angelica, Saura

Other Prizes:

International Critics Award:
Lancelot du Lac, Bresson
Fear Eats the Soul, Fassbinder
Best Screenplay:
Hal Barwood, Matthew Rob-
   bins, *Sugarland Express*
Special Tribute:
Charles Boyer, *Stavisky*
**Grand Prix de la Comission
Superieure Technique du
Cinéma Français:**
Russell, *Mahler*

1975

Best Film:
Chronicle of the Burning Years
   (Lakhdar-Hamina, Algeria)
Best Director:
Constantine Costa-Gavras,
   Section Spéciale and; Michel
   Brault, *Les Ordes* (tied)

Best Actor:
Vittorio Gassman, *Scent of
   Woman*
Best Actress:
Valerie Perrine, *Lenny*
Special Jury Prize:
Werner Herzog, *Every Man for
   Himself* and *God Against All*

Other Prizes:

International Critics Award:
Every Man for Himself . . .
   (Herzog, Germany)
The Trip of the Comedians
   (Angelopolous, Greece)
**Ecumenical Prize (Mixed
Catholic and Protestant Jury):**
Every Man for Himself

1976

Best Film:
Taxi Driver (Scorsese, USA)
Best Director:
Ettore Scola, *Brutti, Sporchi,
   Cattivi*
Best Actor:
José-Luis Gómez, *L Familia
   de Pascual Duarte*
Best Actress:
Mari Torocsik, *Deryne, Hol Van*
Dominique Sanda, *L'Eredita
   Ferramonti*
Special Jury Prize:
Cria Cuervos (Saura, Spain)
The Marquise of O (Rohmer,
   W. Germany)

Other Prizes:

International Critics Award:
Ferdinand the Strongman
   (Kluge, W. Germany)
Kings of the Road (Wenders,
   W. Germany)

1977

Best Film:
Padre Padrone (Paolo and
   Vittorio Taviani, Italy)
Best Director:
   (Not awarded this year)
Best Actor:
Fernando Rey, *Elisa My Love*
Best Actress:
Shelley Duvall, *Three Women*
Monique Mercure, *J. A. Martin,
   Photographer*

Other Awards:

Best First Film:
Ridley Scott, *The Duellists*
Best Musical Score:
Norman Whitfield, *Car Wash*
**Ecumenical Prize (mixed
Catholic and Protestant jury):**
The Lacemaker (Goretta,
   Switzerland)
International Critics Prize:
Padre Padrone (Paolo and
   Vittorio Taviani, Italy)

3. BERLIN FILM FESTIVAL PRIZES

The Berlin Film Festival was established in 1951 by Dr.
Alfred Bauer. In its early years the festival, unlike many of
its counterparts, allowed the audience as well as jury to
determine awards. In 1956 the festival received "A"
classification from the International Federation of Film
Producers Association; and the following year, audience
awards were no longer permitted.

It has often been said that the festival initially
succeeded because of its location: it was one of the first
European festivals to be held in a large city instead of in
a small town or resort; and because of the political
importance of Berlin, early festivals received world-wide
attention, including the support of even the U.S. State
Department. The festival has excelled in exhibiting
independent films—unlike Cannes, which leans toward
more commercial entries. Shorts and political cinema have
been especially favored at Berlin. In 1970, political activists
forced the festival to close.

In recent years the festival has been highly praised for
its Forum of Young Films under the direction of Ulrich
Gregor. Each year the forum is a series of films devoted to
the young filmmakers of a specific country, and many
people think the series has the potential of becoming as

important as the Directors' Fortnight in Cannes. Each year the festival also holds highly respected Retrospectives and an International Film Fair. In 1977 Wolf Donner replaced Alfred Bauer as the festival's director and the festival changed. *Variety,* for example, reported that the 1977 festival took a slight turn to the left under Donner's direction: Russian and East German films were numerous; there was a forum dedicated to Lenin and the Soviet Revolution; and jurists included representatives from Russia and Cuba. Donner has also increased the number of sidebar events; some said to undermine Ulrich Gregor's Forum of Young Films.

The Berlin Film Festival takes place in late June-early July. Golden Bears are awarded in the best-film categories; Silver Bears in the directing and acting divisions.

1951

Dramatic Films:
1. *Four in a Jeep* (Switzerland)
2. *The Way of Hope* (Italy)
3. *The Browning Version* (England)

Comedies:
1. *Sans Lasser d'Advance* (France)
2. *Fahrt in Blanc* (Sweden)
3. *The Mating Season* (USA)

Crime and Adventure:
1. *Justice Is Done* (France)
2. Award not given
3. *Destination Moon* (USA)

Musicals:
1. *Cinderella* (USA)
2. *Tales of Hoffmann* (Germany)
3. Award not given

Audience Awards:
1. *Cinderella* (USA)
2. *The Browning Version* (England)
3. *Justice Is Done* (France)

1952

Audience Awards:
1. *She Danced for the Summer* (Sweden)
2. *Fanfan the Tulip* (France)
3. *Cry the Beloved Country* (England)

1953

Audience Awards:
1. *Wages of Fear* (France)
2. *The Green Secret* (Italy)
3. *Sie fanden eine Heimat* (Switzerland)

1954

Audience Awards:
1. *Hobson's Choice* (England)

2. *Bread, Love and Dreams*
   (Italy)
3. *Le Defreque* (France)

1955

Audience Awards:
1. *The Rats* (Germany)
2. *Marcellino* (Italy)
3. *Carmen Jones* (USA)

1956

Best Picture: First Prize:
Invitation to the Dance
   (Kelly)
Best Picture: Second Prize:
Richard III (Olivier, England)
Best Direction:
Robert Aldrich, *Autumn Leaves*
Best Actor:
Burt Lancaster, *Trapeze*
Best Actress:
Elsa Martinelli, *Donatella*

Other Awards:

Best Feature Documentaries:
1. *No Space for Wild Animals*
   (Germany)
2. *The African Lion* (Disney,
   USA)
Best Short Documentaries:
1. *Paris La Nuit* (France)
2. *Spring Comes to Kashmir*
   (India)
   Hitit Gunesi (Turkey)
   Rhythmetic (Canada)
Audience Awards:
1. *Before Sunset* (Germany)
2. *Pepote* (Mexico)
3. *Trapeze* (USA)

1957

Best Picture:
Twelve Angry Men (Lumet,
   USA)
Best Direction:
Mario Monicelli, *Fathers and
   Sons*
Best Actor:
Pedro Infante, *Tizoc*
Best Actress:
Yvonne Mitchell, *Woman in a
   Dressing Gown*

Other Awards:

Best Feature Documentaries:
Secrets of Life (Disney, USA)
Best Short Documentaries:
1. *Far-Off People* (Italy)
2. *The Last Paradise* (Italy)
   *One Thousand Small
      Characters* (Germany)
   Plitvice Lakes (Yugoslavia)
Catholic Film Office Award:
Twelve Angry Men (Lumet,
   USA)

1958

Best Film:
The End of the Day (Sweden)
Best Direction:
Tadashi Ima, *Story of True
   Love*
Best Actor:
Sidney Poitier, *The Defiant
   Ones*
Best Actress:
Anna Magnani, *Wild Is the
   Wind*

Other Awards:

Best Feature Documentary:
Perri (Disney, USA)

Best Short Documentary:
Olive Harvest in Calabria
(Italy)

1959

Best Film:
The Cousins (Chabrol,
France)
Best Direction:
Akira Kurosawa, *The Hidden
Fortress*
Best Actor:
Jean Gabin, *Archimède le
Clochard*
Best Actress:
Shirley MacLaine, *Ask Any Girl*

Other Awards:

Best Feature Documentary:
White Wilderness (Disney,
USA)
Best Culture Film:
1. *Praise the Sea* (Holland)
2. *Hest på ferie* (Denmark)
   Radha and Krishna (India)
   Das Knalleidoskop
   (Germany)
Special Prize:
Hayley Mills, *Tiger Bay*
International Critics Prize:
The Hidden Fortress
(Kurosawa, Japan)

1960

Best Film: First Prize:
Lazarillo de Tormes (Spain)
Best Film: Second Prize:
The Love Game (France)
Best Direction:
Jean-Luc Godard, *Breathless*
Best Actor:
Fredric March, *Inherit the
Wind*

Best Actress:
Juliette Mayniel, *Country Fair*

Other Awards:

Best Feature Documentary:
Faja Lobbi (Holland)
Best Short Documentary:
*Les Songs des Chevaux
Sauvages* (France)
**International Film Critics
Prize:**
Angry Silence (England)

1961

Best Film:
La Notte (Antonioni, Italy)
Best Direction:
Bernhard Wicki, *The Miracle of
Father Malachias*
Best Actor:
Peter Finch, *No Love for
Johnny*
Best Actress:
Anna Karina, *A Woman Is a
Woman*

Other Awards:

Best Documentary:
Description of a Struggle
(Israel)

1962

Best Film:
A Kind of Loving
(Schlesinger, England)
Best Direction:
Francesco Rosi, *Salvatore
Giuliano*
Best Actor:
James Stewart, *Mr. Hobbs
Takes a Vacation*
Best Actress:
Rita Gam and Viveca Lindfors,
No Exit

Other Awards:

Best Documentary:
Galapagos (Germany)
Best Short Subject:
The Painter Karel Appel
   (Holland)
**International Film Critics
Prize:**
Zoo (Holland)
Most Promising Newcomer:
Jon Young Sun, *To the Last
   Day* (Korea)

1963

Best Film:
Oath of Obedience (Germany)
   and *The Devil* (Italy)
Best Director:
Nikos Koundouros, *Little
   Aphrodite*
Best Actor:
Sidney Poitier, *Lilies of the
   Field*
Best Actress:
Bibi Andersson, *The Lovers*

Other Awards:

Best Documentary:
The Great Atlantic (Germany)
Best Short Subject:
Bouwspelement (Holland)
**International Film Critics
Prize:**
The Reunion (Italy)

1964

Best Film:
Dry Summer (Turkey)
Best Direction:
Satyajit Ray, *Mahanager*
Best Actor:
Rod Steiger, *The Pawnbroker*
Best Actress:
Sachiko Hidari, *She and He*

Other Awards:

Best Documentary:
Alleman (Holland)

1965

Best Film:
Alphaville (Godard, France)
Best Direction:
Satyajit Ray, *Charluta*
Best Actor:
Lee Marvin, *Cat Ballou*
Best Actress:
Madhur Jaffrey, *Shakespeare
   Wallah*

1966

Best Film:
Cul de Sac (Polanski, England)
Best Director:
Carlos Sura, *The Chase*
Best Actor:
Jean-Pierre Léaud, *Masculin-
   Féminin*
Best Actress:
Lola Albright, *Lord Love a Duck*

Other Prizes:

Jury Awards:
Off-Season for Foxes
   (Germany)
Manhunt (Sweden)
Jury Tribute:
Satyajit Ray

1967

Best Film:
Le Départ (Skolimowski,
   Belgium)
Best Direction:
Zivojin Pavlovic, *The Rats
   Awaken*

Best Actor:
Michel Simon, *The Old Man
and the Boy*
Best Actress:
Edith Evans, *The Whisperers*

Other Awards:

Special Jury Prize:
La Collectionneuse (Rohmer,
France)
Best Screenplay:
Michael Lentz, *Every Year
Again*
Best Short:
Through the Eyes of a Painter
(India)
International Critics Prize:
Every Year Again (Germany)
Catholic Office Film Award:
The Whisperers (Forbes,
England)

1968

Best Film: First Prize:
Ole Dole Doff (Troell, Sweden)
Best Film: Second Prize:
Innocence Unprotected
(Makavejev, Yugoslavia)
Come l'Amore (Mizui, Italy)
Best Direction:
Carlos Saura, *Peppermint
Frappe*
Best Actor:
Jean-Louis Trintignant,
L'Homme Qui Ment
Best Actress:
Stephane Audran, *Les Biches*

1969

Best Film: First Prize:
Early Years (Zilnik,
Yugoslavia)

Best Film: Second Prize:
Brazil Year 2000 (Lima, Brazil)
Made in Sweden (Bergen-
strähle, Sweden)
I am a Elephant, Madame
(Zadek, Germany)
Greetings (De Palma, USA)
A Quiet Place in the Country
(Petri, Italy)

1970

*(Festival held, but prizes
suspended)*

1971

Best Film: First Prize:
*The Garden of the Finzi-
Continis* (De Sica, Italy)
Best Film: Second Prize:
The Decameron (Pasolini,
Italy)
Best Actor:
Jean Gabin, *Le Chat*
Best Actress:
Shirley MacLaine, *Desperate
Characters*
Simone Signoret, *Le Chat*

Other Awards:

Best Camerawork:
Ragnar Lasse, *Love Is War*
(Norway)
Best Short:
150½ (USA)
International Critics Prize:
Internationale Forum des
jungen Films

1972

Best Film: First Prize:
The Canterbury Tales (Pasolini,
Italy)

Best Film: Second Prize:
The Hospital (Hiller, USA)
Best Direction:
Jean-Pierre Blanc, *The Spinster*
Best Actor:
Albert Sordi, *Detenuto in Attest di Giudizio*
Best Actress:
Elizabeth Taylor, *Hammersmith Is Out*

Other Prizes:

Special Prize:
Peter Ustinov
International Critics Federation Prize:
The Audience (Italy, Ferreri)
Family Life (England, Loach)

1973

Best Film: First Prize:
Distant Thunder (Ray, India)
Best Film: Special Jury Prize:
Where There's Smoke There's Fire (Cayatte, France)
Best Film: Second Prize:
The Revolution of the Seven Madmen (Nilsson, Argentina)
The Tall Blond Man with One Black Shoe (Robert, France)
The Experts (Kückelmann, West Germany)
All Nudity Will be Punished (Jabor, Brazil)
The 14 (Hemming, England)

Other Awards:

International Critics Federation Prize:
Les Noces Rouges (Chabrol, France) and *Lo Stagionale* (Italy)

1974

Best Film: First Prize:
The Apprenticeship of Duddy Kravitz (Kotcheff, Canada)
Best Film: Special Jury Prize:
L Horloger de St. Paul (France)
Best Films: Second Prize:
In the Name of the People (W. Germany)
Little Malcolm (England)
Still Life (Iran)
Bread and Chocolate (Italy)
Rebellion in Patagonia (Argentina)
Best Actor:
Antonio Ferrandiz, *Next of Kin*
Best Actress:
Marta Vancourova, *The Lovers of the Year 1*

1975

Best Film: First Prize:
Orkobefogadas (Meszaros, Hungary)
Best Films: Special Jury Prizes:
Overlord (Cooper, England)
Dupont Lajoie (Boisset, France)
Best Direction:
Sergey Solovyov, *A Hundred Days After Childhood*
Best Actor:
Vlastimil Brodsky, *Jakob der Lügner*
Best Actress:
Kinuyo Tanaka, *Sandakan, House #8*

Other Awards:

Special Award:
Woody Allen
Best Short:
See (Lehman, USA)

1976

Best Film: First Prize:
Buffalo Bill and the Indians (Altman, USA) (award declined)
Best Films: Special Jury Prize:
Canoa (Cazals, Mexico)
Best Director:
Mario Monicelli, *Caro Michele*
Best Actor:
Gerhard Olschewski, *Lost Life*
Best Actress:
Jadwiga Baranska, *Night and Days*

Other Awards:

Best First Film:
Azonositas (Lugossy, Hungary)
Best Short:
Munakata, the Woodcarver (Yanagawa, Japan)
International Critics Prize:
Long Vacations of '36 (Spain)
Ecumenical Award (jury consists of Catholic and Protestant representatives):
Loneliness of Konrad Steiner (Switzerland)

1977

Best Film: First Prize:
The Ascent (Shepitko, USSR)
Best Film: Second Prizes:
The Devil Probably (Bresson, France)
The Bricklayers (Fons, Mexico)
A Strange Role (Sandor, Hungary)
Best Director:
Manuel Gutierrez, *Black Litter*
Best Actor:
Fernando Fernan Gomez, *The Anchorite*
Best Actress:
Lily Tomlin, *The Late Show*

Other Awards:

Best Short:
Not Known at This Address (Sachs, Rinneberg, East Germany)
International Federation of Cinema Press:
The Ascent (Shepitko, USSR). Four members of the jury— Derek Malcolm, Rainer Werner Fassbinder, Basilio Martin Patino and Helene Vager—publicly stated that they had voted against the Russian film.

4. NEW YORK FILM FESTIVAL PROGRAMS

The New York Film Festival is now the most important of the American international festivals, although it is not the oldest. (The San Francisco International Film Festival began in 1957). Established in 1963, the New York Film Festival is presented under the auspices of the Film

Society of Lincoln Center in cooperation with the International Film Importers and Distributors of America, Inc., and the Motion Picture Association of America. Richard Roud, the highly respected film critic, is the festival's director, and members of past program committees include such noted film scholars as Henri Langlois, Andrew Sarris, Susan Sontag and Richard Corliss.

The festival, however, has had its problems, foremost of which has been funding. Despite good attendances in its first years, the festival nevertheless lost money due to the high cost of running any festival in this country: in 1966, for example, the festival deficit ran $95,210. Contributions to the Film Society of Lincoln Center and support from the New York State Council on the Arts now make the festival possible.

The festival's second problem has been severe criticism from the New York film community. Despite its interesting programs, the festival is routinely attacked each year for any of several reasons: for favoring the films of one country over those of another, for slighting this director instead of that director, and even for the dress and life style of the festival's audience.

The most frequent complaint, however, has been the absence of American films. Although such films as *Five Easy Pieces, Bob & Carol & Ted & Alice, Funnyman, Mickey One, Portrait of Jason, Mean Streets, Badlands, Images, The Last Picture Show* and *A Woman Under the Influence* premiered at the festival, many critics have argued that American films have been consistently slighted. Festival directors have answered this argument by reminding the critics that it is after all, an international festival. Richard Roud has pointed out that he wants to avoid concentrating on native products, unlike the practice of Cannes and Venice, which has so frequently led to accusations of chauvinistic favoritism. For a long time, moreover, American studios were reluctant to show their new films to an "art" audience and have only recently begun to realize that it might be worthwhile to hold off the release of a film in order for it to be showcased at the festival.

Because of its location, the New York Film Festival can

expose a film to a wide audience of critics and potential distributors. The festival has introduced to this country such directors as Roman Polanski, Hiroshi Teshigara, Bo Wilderberg, Marco Bellocchio and recently many exciting new directors from West Germany.

It's customary to question the worth—even the function —of film festivals. All film festivals, New York's or Cannes's, are imperfect. It's easy for the circumstances of the festival to take precedence over the content of the films. But the New York Film Festival has served an important function for the American film community. At its best, the festival allows us to remember the magic that attracted us to movies in the first place.

The New York Film Festival is held in the fall, usually in September-October. Short films are often screened before a feature at the festival, but these are not listed below unless several shorts had been grouped to comprise a whole program.

1963

Jàcques Bartier, *Dragées au Poivre*
Robert Bresson, *Le Procès de Jeanne d'Arc*
Luis Buñuel, *The Exterminating Angel*
Robert Enrico, *Au Coeur de la Vie*
Tamás Fejér, *Love in the Suburbs*
Jean-Luc Godard, Ugo Gregoretti, Pier Paolo Pasolini, Roberto Rossellini, *Rogopag*
Takis Kanelopoulos, *The Sky*
Masaki Kobayashi, *Harakiri*
Leacock/Pennebaker, *Crisis & the Chair*
Joseph Losey, *The Servant*
Chris Marker, *Le Joli Mai*

Adolfas Mekas, *Hallelujah the Hills*
Jean-Pierre Melville, *L'Aine des Ferchaux*
Takis Mouzenidis, *Elektra at Epidaurus*
Ermanno Olmi, *The Fiances*
Yasujiro Ozu, *An Autumn Afternoon*
Giuseppe Patroni Griffi, *Il Mare*
Roman Polanski, *Knife in the Water*
Alain Resnais, *Muriel*
Glauber Rocha, *Barravento*
Alex Segal, *All the Way Home*
Leopoldo Torre Nilsson, *The Terrace*

1964

Ricardo Alventosa, *La Herencia*
Bernardo Bertolucci, *Before the Revolution*

Luis Buñuel, *L'Age d'Or*

Luis Buñuel, *Diary of a Chambermaid*

Jörn Donner, *To Love*

Abel Gance, *Cyrano et D'Artagnan*

Jean-Luc Godard, *Bande à Part*

Jean-Luc Godard, *Une Femme est une Femme*

Susumu Hani, *She and He*

Kon Ichikawa, *Conflagration*

Kon Ichikawa, *Alone on the Pacific*

Alain Jessua, *La Vie à l'Envers*

Grigori Kozintsev, *Hamlet*

Joseph Losey, *King and Country*

Sidney Lumet, *Fail Safe*

Adolfas and Jonas Mekas, *The Brig*

Kenji Mizoguchi, *The Taira Clan*

Andrzej Munk, *Passenger*

Don Owen, *Nobody Waved Good-bye*

Satyajit Ray, *The Great City*

Michael Roemer, *Nothing But a Man*

Francesco Rosi, *Le Mani sulla Città*

Francesco Rosi, *Salvatore Giuliano*

Robert Rossen, *Lilith*

Hiroshi Teshigahara, *Woman in the Dunes*

Andrzej Wajda, *Fury Is a Woman*

1965

Michelangelo Antonioni, *La Signora senza Camelie*

Marco Bellocchio, *I Pugni In Tasca*

Kevin Billington, *Twilight of Empire*

Claude Chabrol, Jean Douchet, Jean-Luc Godard, Jean-Daniel Pollet, Eric Rohmer, Jean Rouch, *Paris vu par . . .*

René Clement, *Knave of Hearts*

John Cromwell, *Of Human Bondage*

Carl Dreyer, *Gertrud*

Louis Feuillade, *Les Vampires*

Milos Forman, *Black Peter*

Georges Franju, *Thomas l'Imposteur*

Jean-Luc Godard, *Alphaville*

Jean-Luc Godard, *Le Petit Soldat*

James Ivory, *Shakespeare Wallah*

Jan Kadar, Elmar Klos, *The Shop on Main Street*

Buster Keaton, *Seven Chances*

Laurence L. Kent, *Caressed*

Akira Kurosawa, *Red Beard*

Chris Marker, *Le Mystère Koumiko*

Arthur Penn, *Mickey One*

Gerald Potterton, *The Railrodder*

Satyajit Ray, *Charulata*

Alan Schneider, *Film*

Jerzy Skolimowski, *Identification Marks: None*

Jerzy Skolimowski, *Walkover*

Jean-Marie Straub, *Unreconciled*

Erich von Stroheim, *The Wedding March*

Luchino Visconti, *Vaghe Stelle del'Orsa*

Bo Widerberg, *Raven's End*

1966

René Allio, *The Shameless Old Lady*

Gianni Amico, *Notes for a Film on Jazz*

Vera Chytilova, Jaromil Jires, Jan Nemec, Ewald Schorm, Jiri Menzel, *Pearls on the Ground*

Bernardo Bertolucci, *The Grim Reaper*

Robert Bresson, *Au Hasard, Balthazar*

Clarence Brown, *A Woman of Affairs*

Luis Buñuel, *Simon of the Desert*

Henning Carlsen, *Hunger*

André Delvaux, *The Man with the Shaven Head*

Cecil B. De Mille, *The Cheat*

Vittorio de Seta, *Un Uomo a Meta*

Milos Forman, *Loves of a Blonde*

Jean-Luc Godard, *Masculin-Féminin*

Jean-Luc Godard, *Pierrot le Fou*

Pavel Hobl, *Do You Keep a Lion at Home?*

Kon Ichikawa, *The Burmese Harp*

Miklós Jancsó, *The Roundup*

Robert Machover, Norm Fruchter, *Troublemakers*

Maysles Brothers, *Meet Marlon Brando*

Sergei Paradjhanov, *Shadows of Our Forgotten Ancestors*

Pier Paolo Pasolini, *Accattone*

Pier Paolo Pasolini, *The Hawks and the Sparrows*

Ivan Passer, *Intimate Lightning*

Aleksandar Petrovic, *Three*

Alain Resnais, *La Guerre est finie*

Carlos Saura, *The Hunt*

Leopoldo Torre Nilsson, *The Eavesdropper*

Agnès Varda, *Les Créatures*

Peter Watkins, *The War Game*

Peter Whitehead, *Wholly Communion*

1967

René Allio, *L'Une et l'Autre*

Donald Brittain, John Spotton, *Memorandum*

Shirley Clarke, *Portrait of Jason*

Jonas Cornell, *Hugs and Kisses*

Mark Donskoi, *Sons and Mothers*

Abel Gance, *Napoleon*

Jean-Luc Godard, *Les Carabiniers*

Jean-Luc Godard, Joris Ivens, William Klein, Claude Lelouch, Alain Resnais, Agnès Varda, *Far from Vietnam*

Jean-Luc Godard, *Made in USA*

Alexander Kluge, *Yesterday Girl*

Masaki Kobayashi, *Rebellion*

John Korty, *Funnyman*

Dragoslav Lazic, *The Feverish Years*

Dusan Makavejev, *An Affair of the Heart*

Rouben Mamoulian, *Applause*

Gillo Pontecorvo, *The Battle of Algiers*

Roberto Rossellini, *The Rise of Louis XIV*

Jean Rouch, *La Chasse au Lion a l'Arc*

Volker Schlöndorff, *Young Torless*

Jerzy Skolimowski, *Barbiera*

Jerzy Skolimowski, *Le Départ*

Istvan Szabo, *Father*

King Vidor, *Show People*

Peter Whitehead, *Tonite Let's All Make Love in London*

Peter Whitehead, *The Benefit of the Doubt*

Bo Widerberg, *Elvira Madigan*

1968

Gianna Amico, *Tropics*
Bernardo Bertolucci, *Partner*
Robert Bresson, *Mouchette*
John Cassavetes, *Faces*
Claude Chabrol, *Les Biches*
Dominique Delouche, *24 Heures de la Vie d'une Femme*
Milos Forman, *The Firemen's Ball*
Jean-Luc Godard, *Deux ou trois Choses que je sais d'elle*
Jean-Luc Godard, *Weekend*
Kjell Grede, *Hugo and Josefin*
Werner Herzog, *Signs of Life*
Miklós Jancsó, *The Red and the White*
Alexander Kluge, *Artists Under the Big Top: Perplexed*
Marcel L'Herbier, *L'Argent*
Norman Mailer, *Beyond the Law*
Jiri Menzel, *Capricious Summer*
Vatroslav Mimica, *Kaya*
Jan Nemec, *Report on the Party and the Guests*
Max Ophuls, *Lola Montes*
Maurice Pialat, *L'Enfance Nue*
Jean Renoir, *Toni*
Jacques Rivette, *Suzanne Simonin, La Religieuse de Diderot*
Jean-Marie Straub, *Chronicle of Anna Magdalena Bach*
Orson Welles, *Histoire Immortelle*

1969

René Allio, *Pierre and Paul*
Richard Attenborough, *Oh! What a Lovely War*
Ingmar Bergman, *The Ritual*
Walerian Borowczyk, *Goto, l'Ile d'Amour*
Robert Bresson, *Une Femme Douce*
Bill Duncalf, *The Epic That Never Was (I, Claudius)*
Marguerite Duras, *Détruire, Dit-Elle*
Judit Elek, *The Lady from Constantinople*
Jean-Luc Godard, *Le Gai Savior*
Juro Jakubisko, *The Deserter and the Nomads*
Jaromil Jires, *The Joke*
Paul Mazursky, *Bob & Carol & Ted & Alice*
Ermanno Olmi, *Un Certo Giorno*
Max Ophuls, *La Ronde*
Nagisa Oshima, *Boy*
Paolo Pier Pasolini, *Pigpen*
Eric Rohmer, *My Night at Maud's*
Ousmane Sembène, *Mandabl*
Victor Sjöstrom, *He Who Gets Slapped*
Susan Sontag, *Duet fo. Cannibals*
Erich von Stroheim, *The Merry Widow*
Agnès Varda, *Lions Love*
Bo Widerberg, *Adalen '31*

1970

Bernardo Bertolucci, *The Conformist*
Bernardo Bertolucci, *Strategia del Ragno*

Luis Buñuel, *Tristana*
Liliana Cavani, *I Cannibali*
Claude Chabrol, *Le Boucher*
Carlos Diegues, *The Inheritors*
Marguerite Duras, Paul Seban, *La Musica*
Dick Fontaine, *Double Pisces, Scorpio Rising*
Lasse Forsberg, *Mistreatment*
Hollis Frampton, *Zorns Lemma*
Jean-Luc Godard, *Wind from the East*
Kjell Grede, *Harry Munter*
Marcel Hanoun, *Une Simple Histoire*
Maurice Hatton, *Praise Marx and Pass the Ammunition*
Werner Herzog, *Even Dwarfs Started Small*
Marin Karmitz, *Camarades*
Ken Loach, *Kes*
Kenji Mizoguchi, *Chikamatzu Monogatari*
Ermanno Olmi, *I Recuperanti*
Bob Rafelson, *Five Easy Pieces*
Satyajit Ray, *Days and Nights in the Forest*
Alain Resnais, *Je t'aime, je t'aime*
Carlos Saura, *The Garden of Delights*
Martin Scorsese, *Street Scenes 1970*
Jean-Marie Straub, *Othon*
François Truffaut, *The Wild Child*
French Silent Cinema Program

1971

Marco Bellocchio, *In the Name of the Father*
Peter Bogdanovich, *Directed by John Ford*
Peter Bogdanovich, *The Last Picture Show*

Robert Bresson, *Four Nights of a Dreamer*
Rainer Werner Fassbinder, *Recruits in Ingolstadt*
Abel Gance, *Bonaparte and the Revolution*
Werner Hergoz, *Fata Morgana*
Henry Jaglom, *A Safe Place*
Akira Kurosawa, *Dodes 'Ka-Den*
Dusan Makavejev, *WR-Mysteries of the Orgasm*
Louis Malle, *Murmur of the Heart*
Ermanno Olmi, *In the Summertime*
Marcel Ophuls, *The Sorrow and the Pity*
Gleb Panfilov, *The Debut*
Pier Paolo Pasolini, *Decameron*
Ivan Passer, *Born to Win*
Peter Watkins, *Punishment Park*
Krzysztof Zanussi, *Family Life*

1972

Robert Altman, *Images*
Robert Benton, *Bad Company*
Bernardo Bertolucci, *Last Tango in Paris*
Luis Buñuel, *The Discreet Charm of the Bourgeoisie*
Marguerite Duras, *Nathalie Granger*
Rainer Werner Fassbinder, *Merchant of Four Seasons*
Philippe Garrel, *Inner Scar*
Jean-Luc Godard and Jean-Pierre Gorin, *Tout Va Bien*
Miklós Jancsó, *Red Psalm*
Kenneth Loach, *Wednesday's Child*
Joseph Losey, *The Assassination of Trotsky*
Karoly Makk, *Love*
Adolfas Mekas, *Going Home*

Jonas Mekas, *Reminiscences of a Journey to Lithuania*
Paul Morrissey, *Heat*
Marcel Ophuls, *A Sense of Loss*
Maurice Pialat, *We Won't Grow Old Together*
Bob Rafelson, *The King of Marvin Gardens*
Satyajit Ray, *The Adversary*
Jacques Rivette, *L'Amour Fou*
Eric Rohmer, *Chlöe in the Afternoon*
Hiroshi Teshigahara, *Summer Soldiers*
François Truffaut, *Two English Girls*
Krzysztof Zanussi, *Behind the Wall*

NEW DIRECTORS / NEW FILMS

Tomas Gutterez Alea, *Memories of Underdevelopment*
Bata Cengic, *The Role of My Family in the World Revolution*
Edgardo Cozarinsky, *Dot Dot Dot*
Pal Gabor, *Horizon*
Claude Guillemot, *The Truce*
Barney Platts-Mills, *Private Road*
David Schickele, *Bushman*
Alain Tanner, *La Salamandre*
Christian Braad Thomsen, *Dear Irene*
Wim Wenders, *The Goalie's Anxiety at the Penalty Kick*

1973

Gianni Amico, *Return*
Denys Arcand, *Rejeanne Padovani*
Claude Chabrol, *Just Before Nightfall*
Claude Chabrol, *La Rupture*

Jean Eustache, *The Mother and the Whore*
Rainer Werner Fassbinder, *The Bitter Tears of Petra von Kant*
James Frawley, *Kid Blue*
Fritz Lang, *Doktor Mabuse*
Claude Lanzmann, *Israel Why*
Joseph Losey, *A Doll's House*
Terrence Malick, *Badlands*
Satyajit Ray, *Distant Thunder*
Martin Scorsese, *Mean Streets*
Jean-Marie Straub, *History Lessons*
Andrei Tarkovsky, *Andrei Rublev*
François Truffaut, *Day for Night*
Kyzysztof Zanussi, *Illumination*

NEW DIRECTORS / NEW FILMS

Metodi Andonov, *The Goat Horn*
Niki de St. Phalle, Peter Whitehead, *Daddy*
Claude Faraldo, *Themroc*
Juraj Herz, *The Cremator*
Anthony Korner, *Helen, Queen of the Nautch Girls*
Paul Leduc, *John Reed (Mexican Insurgent)*
Toichiro Narushima, *Time Within Memory*
Shinsuke Ogawa, *Peasants of the Second Fortress*
Ababacar Samb, *Kodou*
Daniel Schmid, *Tonight or Never*
Pascal Thomas, *Les Zozos*

1974

Mirra Bank, *Yudie*
Robert Bresson, *Lancelot of the Lake*

Luis Buñuel, *Le Fantôme de la Liberté*

Luis Buñuel, Homage to Buñuel: *L'Age d'Or, The Exterminating Angel, The Milky Way, The Discreet Charm of the Bourgeoisie*

John Cassavetes, *A Woman Under the Influence*

Martha Coolidge, *An Old Fashioned Woman*

Rainer Werner Fassbinder, *All*

William Greaves, *From These Roots*

Jack Hazan, *A Bigger Splash*

Miklós Jancsó, *Rome Wants Another Caesar*

Alexander Kluge, *Part-Time Work of a Domestic Slave*

Louis Malle, *Lacombe, Lucien*

Jean-Pierre Melville, *Les Enfants Terribles*

Ermanno Olmi, *The Circumstance*

Max Ophuls, *Liebelel*

Alain Resnais, *Stavisky*

Sergio Ricardo, *The Night of the Scarecrow*

Jacques Rivette, *Celine and Julie Go Boating*

Jacques Rivette, *Out One/ Spectre*

Daniel Schmid, *La Paloma*

Martin Scorsese, *Italian-americans*

Alain Tanner, *The Middle of the World*

Pascal Thomas, *Don't Cry with Your Mouth Full*

Wim Wenders, *Alice in the Cities*

1975

Jean-François Davy, *Exhibition*

John Douglas and Robert Kramer, *Milestones*

Marguerite Duras, *India Song*

Rainer Werner Fassbinder, *Fist-Right of Freedom*

Claude Goretta, *The Wonderful Crook*

Werner Herzog, *Every Man for Himself and God Against All*

James Ivory, *Autobiography of a Princess*

Miklós Jancsó, *Elektreia*

Louis Malle, *Black Moon*

Maysles Brothers, *Grey Gardens*

Jean Renoir, *La Chienne*

Michael Ritchie, *Smile*

Volker Schlondorff and Margarethe von Trotta, *The Lost Honor of Katharina Blum*

Ousmane Sembene, *Xala*

Martin Smith, *Companero*

Jean-Marie Straub and Daniele Huillet, *Moses and Aaron*

Andre Techine, *French Provincial*

François Truffaut, *Story of Adele H.*

Luchino Visconti, *Conversation Piece*

Orson Welles, *F for Fake*

Howard Zieff, *Hearts of the West*

1976

Walerian Borowczyk, *Story of a Sin*

Rainer Werner Fassbinder, *Fear of Fear*

Eduardo de Gregorio, *Serail*

King Hu, *Touch of Zen*

Ray Karp, *Sunday Funnies*

Alexander Kluge, *Strongman Ferdinand*

Barbara Kopple, *Harlan County, USA*

Akira Kurosawa, *Dersu Uzala*

Marcel Ophuls, *Memory of Justice*

Nagisa Oshima, *In the Realm of the Senses* (seized by customs, shown after festival)

Satyajit Ray, *The Middleman*

Jean Renoir, *Nana*

Jacques Rivette, *Duelle*

Eric Rohmer, *The Marquise of O*

Francesco Rosi, *Illustrious Corpses*

Joan Micklin Silver, *Bernice Bobs Her Hair*

Alain Tanner, *Jonas Who Will be 25 in the Year 2000*

François Truffaut, *Small Change*

Luchino Visconti, *Ossessione*

Wim Wenders, *King of the Road*

Peter Werner, *In the Region of Ice*

Pereira dos Santos, *Tent of Miracles*

Marguerite Duras, *The Truck*

Claude Goretta, *The Lacemaker*

Werner Herzog, *Heart of Glass*

James Ivory, *Roseland*

Márta Mészáros, *Women*

Kote Mikaberitze, *My Grandmother*

Bill Miles, *Men of Bronze*

Pier Paolo Pasolini, *Salò*

Léonce Perret, *L'Enfant de Paris*

Paolo and Vittorio Taviani, *Padre Padrone*

François Truffaut, *L'Homme Qui Aimait les Femmes*

Agnès Varda, *One Sings, The Other Doesn't*

Robert M. Young, *Short Eyes*

Wim Wenders, *The American Friend*

SAVED (A retrospective of American films)

Clarence Badger, *It*

Monta Bell, *Downstairs*

Monta Bell, *The Letter*

Monta Bell, *The Torrent*

Frank Borzage, *Liliom*

William K. Howard, *Transatlantic*

F. W. Murnau, *City Girl*

Edward Sutherland, *It's the Old Army Game*

King Vidor, *Wild Oranges*

Raoul Walsh, *Regeneration*

Sam Wood, *Paid*

William Wyler, *Dodsworth*

1977

Merzak Allouache, *Omar Gatlato*

Bernardo Bertolucci, *1900*

Robert Bresson, *The Devil Probably*

Martin Brest, *Hot Tomorrows*

Noel Buchner, Mary Dore, Richard Broadman, and Al Gedicks, *Children of Labor*

Luis Buñuel, *That Obscure Object of Desire*

Rafael Corkidi, *Pufnucio Santo*

Jonathan Demme, *Handle With Care* (formerly Citizens Band)

VII. THE CODES AND REGULATIONS

1. THE PRODUCTION CODE

The Production Code was one of the film industry's several attempts to prevent federal censorship. In 1908, for example, key figures in the business had helped establish the National Board of Censorship in order to curb growing criticism over the immorality of movies. And in 1922, after continued public disapproval and the passage of numerous state censorship bills, film producers had created the Motion Picture Producers and Distributors of America (MPPDA) to self-regulate the industry in the hope of curtailing criticism and preventing federal intervention. Will H. Hays, the conservative Postmaster General of the Harding Administration, was the organization's first president, and he grew so powerful that the MPPDA has been generally known, in fact, as "the Hays Office."

Before adopting the Production Code in 1930, the Hays Office tried two other self-regulatory policies. The first of these was the 1924 *Formula*. Faced with the "mature" themes of the jazz era's novelists and playwrights, the MPPDA passed a resolution asking its member studios to submit a summary of each play or novel it proposed to film in order to receive the MPPDA's advice about possible objections. Although there were 125 rejections of submitted material between 1924 and 1930, the *Formula* had limited applicability: for one thing, the MPPDA could only suggest, not enforce its guidelines; and for another, the *Formula* applied only to adapted material and not to original screenplays.

The second code the MPPDA adopted to regulate the subject matter of movies was the 1927 *Don'ts and Be Carefuls*, which listed eleven subjects that should never appear in films and twenty-six themes that should be handled with great care and discretion. Like the *Formula*, the *Don'ts and Be Carefuls* could not be legally enforced and it, too, proved of limited value.

So faced with continued public criticism and repeated calls for federal censorship, the MPPDA adopted the Production Code in 1930. Martin Quigley (the publisher of the influential *Motion Picture Herald)* and Reverend Daniel A. Lord (a St. Louis clergyman who had acted as adviser on many films) collaborated on the new code, which was to become one of the most important social documents in American history. On June 6, 1930, two months after the Code was ratified, an Advertising Code was also adopted.

Despite its length and explicitness, the code was not initially successful. It was not until the Catholic Legion of Decency's overwhelmingly effective campaign against movie immorality in 1934 that the Production Code really took effect. In July 1934 the MPPDA, frightened by the Legion's threats, organized the Production Code Administration Office (PCA), with Joseph Breen as its head. For the first time, the MPPDA had the power to enforce its regulations: if any member studio released a film without the PCA's certificate of approval, that studio would be fined $25,000.

For several years the PCA and the Legion of Decency worked in an unofficial and at times uneasy alliance. Together they managed to control the content of all films shown in this country, both domestic and foreign. The PCA functioned at all stages of production—selecting stories, examining scripts, approving the final cut. The Office even offered its services to nonmember producers to make its powers more complete.

But in 1943 the PCA received its first great challenge: Howard Hughes exhibited *The Outlaw* (starring Jane Russell) without code approval. Although the film was soon withdrawn from distribution, it reappeared in 1946 with an advertising campaign that has since become legendary: "What are the Two Great Reasons for Jane Russell's Rise to Stardom?" ads would coyly ask. (One Baltimore judge claimed that Russell's breasts "hung over the picture like a thunderstorm spread out over a landscape.")

The crowds of people who attended *The Outlaw* demonstrated a change in American morals and hinted at the PCA's increasing obsolescence. In 1945 Warner Bros. even temporarily withdrew from the MPPDA. (In that year Will Hays finally retired as president of the organization. Eric Johnston was his successor and soon after Johnston took over, the MPPDA changed its name to the Motion Picture Association of America—MPAA.)

Although the PCA made slight revisions in the code in 1946 and 1951 to accommodate changes in American morals, the code still came under severe criticism and there were many calls for complete re-examination of the code's usefulness. Even when the Supreme Court, in the famous case over Rossellini's *The Miracle,* decided that movies were an art form (and not an item of commerce, as previously thought) under the protection of the First Amendment, the PCA was still slow to loosen its reigns.

So in 1953 the PCA was once again defied, this time by Otto Preminger when he released *The Moon Is Blue* without the PCA's seal. Like *The Outlaw, The Moon Is Blue* attracted large crowds of moviegoers (although in some small towns police actually took down the names of those people who saw the film), and demonstrated once more that the code was outmoded. When the code refused its seal to Preminger's *The Man with the Golden Arm* in late 1955, United Artists, the film's distributor, pulled out of the MPAA. (Geoffrey Sherlock replaced Joe Breen in 1954.)

In 1956 the code, under continued attack, was considererably revised so that now only two subjects were prohibited: venereal disease and sexual perversion. When the Legion of Decency revised its classification system in 1958, the PCA also began to change. Despite controversies over films like *Suddenly, Last Summer* (1959), the PCA finally altered its attitude toward "sexual perversion" in 1961 when such major studio movies as *The Children's Hour* (1961) and *Advise and Consent* (1962) dealt with the subject.

In 1966 the code was once again revised, this time drastically. Now the PCA merely divided approved films into two categories, those for general audiences and those suggested for mature audiences. These categories were only suggestions—no legal restrictions were involved.

It was becoming increasingly obvious that an entirely new code was necessary. And in 1968 the MPAA initiated the Code of Self-Regulation.

The Don'ts and Be Carefuls

Resolved, That those things which are included in the following list shall not appear in pictures produced by the members of this Association, irrespective of the manner in which they are treated:

1. Pointed profanity—by either title or lip—this includes the words "God," "Lord," "Jesus," "Christ" (unless they be used reverently in connection with proper religious ceremonies), "hell," "damn," "Gawd," and every other profane and vulgar expression however it may be spelled;
2. Any licentious or suggestive nudity—in fact or in silhouette; and any lecherous or licentious notice thereof by other characters in the picture;
3. The illegal traffic in drugs;
4. Any inference of sex perversion;
5. White slavery;
6. Miscegenation (sex relationships between the white and black races);
7. Sex hygiene and venereal diseases;
8. Scenes of actual childbirth—in fact or in silhouette;
9. Children's sex organs;
10. Ridicule of the clergy;
11. Willful offense to any nation, race or creed;

And be it further resolved, That special care be exercised in the manner in which the following subjects are treated, to the end that vulgarity and suggestiveness may be eliminated and that good taste may be emphasized:

1. The use of the flag;
2. International relations (avoiding picturizing in an unfavorable light another country's religion, history, institutions, prominent people, and citizenry);
3. Arson;
4. The use of firearms;
5. Theft, robbery, safe-cracking, and dynamiting of trains, mines, building etc. (having in mind the effect which a too-detailed description of these may have upon the moron);
6. Brutality and possible gruesomeness;
7. Technique of committing murder by whatever method;
8. Methods of smuggling;
9. Third-degree methods;
10. Actual hangings or electrocutions as legal punishment for crime;
11. Sympathy for criminals;
12. Attitude toward public characters and institutions;
13. Sedition;

14. Apparent cruelty to children and animals;
15. Branding of people or animals;
16. The sale of women, or of a woman selling her virtue;
17. Rape or attempted rape;
18. First-night scenes;
19. Man and woman in bed together;
20. Deliberate seduction of girls;
21. The institution of marriage;
22. Surgical operations;
23. The use of drugs;
24. Titles or scenes having to do with law enforcement of law-enforcing officers;
25. Excessive or lustful kissing, particularly when one character or the other is a "heavy."

THE 1930 PRODUCTION CODE

Preamble

Motion picture producers recognize the high trust and confidence which have been placed in them by the people of the world and which have made motion pictures a universal form of entertainment.

They recognize their responsibility to the public because of this trust and because entertainment and art are important influences in the life of a nation.

Hence, though regarding motion pictures primarily as entertainment without any explicit purpose of teaching or propaganda, they know that the motion picture within its own field of entertainment may be directly responsible for spiritual or moral progress, for higher types of social life, and for much correct thinking.

During the rapid transition from silent to talking pictures they realized the necessity and the opportunity of subscribing to a Code to govern the production of talking pictures and of acknowledging this responsibility.

On their part, they ask from the public and from public leaders a sympathetic understanding of their purposes and problems and a spirit of cooperation that will allow them the freedom and opportunity necessary to bring the motion picture to a still higher level of wholesome entertainment for all the people.

GENERAL PRINCIPLES

1. No picture shall be produced which will lower the moral standards of those who see it. Hence the sympathy of the

audience shall never be thrown to the side of crime,
wrong-doing, evil or sin.
2. Correct standards of life, subject only to the requirements of
drama and entertainment, shall be presented.
3. Law, natural or human, shall not be ridiculed, nor shall
sympathy be created for its violation.

I. Crimes Against the Law

These shall never be presented in such a way as to throw
sympathy with the crime as against law and justice or to inspire
others with a desire for imitation.

1. Murder
    (a) The technique of murder must be presented in a way
        that will not inspire imitation.
    (b) Brutal killings are not to be presented in detail.
    (c) Revenge in modern times shall not be justified.
2. Methods of crime should not be explicitly presented.
    (a) Theft, robbery, safe-cracking, and dynamiting of trains,
        mines, buildings, etc., should not be detailed in method.
    (b) Arson must be subject to the same safeguards.
    (c) The use of firearms should be restricted to essentials.
    (d) Methods of smuggling should not be presented.
3. The illegal drug traffic must not be portrayed in such a way
   as to stimulate curiosity concerning the use of, or traffic in,
   such drugs; nor shall scenes be approved which show the
   use of illegal drugs, or their effects, in detail (as amended
   September 11, 1946).
4. The use of liquor in American life, when not required by
   the plot or for proper characterization, will not be shown.

II. Sex

The sanctity of the institution of marriage and the home shall
be upheld. Pictures shall not infer that low forms of sex
relationship are the accepted or common thing.

1. Adultery and illicit sex, sometimes necessary plot material,
   must not be explicitly treated or justified, or presented
   attractively.
2. Scenes of passion
    (a) These should not be introduced except where they are
        definitely essential to the plot.
    (b) Excessive and lustful kissing, lustful embraces,
        suggestive postures and gestures are not to be shown.

(c) In general, passion should be treated in such manner as not to stimulate the lower and baser emotions.
3. Seduction or rape
   (a) These should never be more than suggested, and then only when essential for the plot. They must never be shown by explicit method.
   (b) They are never the proper subject for comedy.
4. Sex perversion or any inference to it is forbidden.[1]
5. White slavery shall not be treated.[2]
6. Miscegenation (sex relationship between the white and black races) is forbidden.
7. Sex hygiene and venereal diseases are not proper subjects for theatrical motion pictures.[3]
8. Scenes of actual childbirth, in fact or in silhouette, are never to be presented.
9. Children's sex organs are never to be exposed.

III. Vulgarity

The treatment of low, disgusting, unpleasant, though not necessarily evil, subjects should be guided always by the dictates of good taste and a proper regard for the sensibilities of the audience.

IV. Obscenity

Obscenity in word, gesture, reference, song, joke or by suggestion (even when likely to be understood only by part of the audience) is forbidden.

V. Profanity[4]

Pointed profanity and every other profane or vulgar expression, however used, is forbidden.

No approval by the Production Code Administration shall be given to the use of words and phrases in motion pictures including, but not limited to, the following:

Alley cat (applied to a woman); bat (applied to a woman); broad (applied to a woman); Bronx cheer (the sound); chippie; cocotte; God, Lord, Jesus, Christ (unless used reverently); cripes; fanny; fairy (in a vulgar sense); finger (the); fire, cries of; Gawd; goose (in a vulgar sense); "hold your hat" or "hats"; hot (applied to a woman); "in your hat"; louse; lousy; Madam (relating to prostitution); nance, nerts; nuts (except when meaning crazy); pansy; razzberry (the sound); slut (applied to a woman); S.O.B.; son-of-a; tart; toilet gags; tom cat (applied to a man); traveling salesman and farmer's daughter jokes;

whore; damn, hell (excepting when the use of said last two words shall be essential and required for portrayal, in proper historical context, of any scene or dialogue based upon historical fact or folklore, or for the presentation in proper literary context of a Biblical, or other religious quotation, or a quotation from a literary work provided that no such use shall be permitted which is intrinsically objectionable or offends good taste).

In the administration of Section V of the Production Code, the Production Code Administration may take cognizance of the fact that the following words and phrases are obviously offensive to the patrons of motion pictures in the United States and more particularly to the patrons of motion pictures in foreign countries:

Chink, Dago, Frog, Greaser, Hunkie, Kike, Nigger, Spic, Wop, Yid.

VI. Costume

1. Complete nudity is never permitted. This includes nudity in fact or in silhouette, or any licentious notice thereof by other characters in the pictures.
2. Undressing scenes should be avoided, and never used save where essential to the plot.
3. Indecent or undue exposure is forbidden.
4. Dancing costumes intended to permit undue exposure or indecent movements in the dance are forbidden.

VII. Dances

1. Dances suggesting or representing sexual actions or indecent passion are forbidden.
2. Dances which emphasize indecent movements are to be regarded as obscene.

VIII. Religion

1. No film or episode may throw ridicule on any religious faith.
2. Ministers of religion in their character as ministers of religion should not be used as comic characters or as villains.
3. Ceremonies of any definite religion should be carefully and respectfully handled.

IX. Locations

The treatment of bedrooms must be governed by good taste and delicacy.

X. National Feelings

1. The use of the flag shall be consistently respectful.
2. The history, institutions, prominent people and citizenry of all nations shall be represented fairly.

XI. Titles[5]

Salacious, indecent, or obscene titles shall not be used.

XII. Repellent Subjects

The following subjects must be treated within the careful limits of good taste.

1. Actual hangings or electrocutions as legal punishments for crime.
2. Third-degree methods.
3. Brutality and possible gruesomeness.
4. Branding of people or animals.
5. Apparent cruelty to children or animals.
6. The sale of women, or a woman selling her virtue.
7. Surgical operations.

Reasons Supporting Preamble of Code

1. Theatrical motion pictures, that is, pictures intended for the theatre as distinct from pictures intended for churches, schools, lecture halls, educational movements, social reform movements, etc., are primarily to be regarded as **entertainment.**

   Mankind has always recognized the importance of entertainment and its value in rebuilding the bodies and souls of human beings.

   But it has always recognized that entertainment can be of a character either HELPFUL or HARMFUL to the human race, and in consequence has clearly distinguished between:

   (a) Entertainment which tends to improve the race, or at least to re-create and rebuild human beings exhausted with the realities of life; and
   (b) Entertainment which tends to degrade human beings, or to lower their standards of life and living.

   Hence the **Moral importance** of entertainment is something which has been universally recognized. It enters intimately into the lives of men and women and affects them closely; it occupies their minds and affections during leisure hours; and ultimately touches the whole of their lives. A man may be judged by his standard of entertainment as easily as by the standard of his work.

So correct entertainment raises the whole standard of a nation.

Wrong entertainment lowers the whole living conditions and moral ideals of a race.

> Note, for example, the healthy reactions to healthful sports, like baseball, golf; the unhealthy reactions to sports like cockfighting, bullfighting, bear baiting, etc.

> Note, too, the effect on ancient nations of gladiatorial combats, the obscene plays of Roman times, etc.

2. Motion pictures are very important as **art**.

Though a new art, possibly a combination art, it has the same object as the other arts, the presentation of human thought, emotion, and experience, in terms of an appeal to the soul through the senses.

Here, as in entertainment,

Art enters intimately into the lives of human beings.

Art can be morally good, lifting men to higher levels. This has been done through good music, great painting, authentic fiction, poetry, drama.

Art can be morally evil in its effects. This is the case clearly enough with unclean art, indecent books, suggestive drama. The effect on the lives of men and women is obvious.

Note: It has often been argued that art in itself is unmoral, neither good nor bad. This is perhaps true of the **thing product** of some person's mind, and the intention of that mind was either good or bad morally when it produced the thing. Besides, the thing has its **effect** upon those who come into contact with it. In both these ways, that is, as a product of a mind and as the cause of definite effects, it has a deep moral significance and an unmistakable moral quality.

Hence: The motion pictures, which are the most popular arts for the masses, have their moral quality from the intention of the minds which produce them and from their effects on the moral lives and reactions of their audiences. This gives them a most important moral quality.

1. They reproduce the morality of the men who use the pictures as a medium for the expression of their idea and ideals.
2. They affect the moral standards of those who, through the screen, take in these ideas and ideals.

In the case of the motion pictures, this effect may be particularly emphasized because no art has so quick and so widespread an appeal to the masses. It has become in an incredibly short period the art of the multitudes.

3. The motion picture, because of its importance as entertainment and because of the trust placed in it by the peoples of the world, has special **moral obligations:**

A. Most arts appeal to the mature. This art appeals at once to every class, mature, immature, developed, underdeveloped, law abiding, criminal. Music has its grades for different classes; so has literature and drama. This art of the motion picture, combining as it does the two fundamental appeals of looking at a picture and listening to a story, at once reached every class of society.

B. By reason of the mobility of a film and the ease of picture distribution, and because of the possibility of duplicating positives in large quantities, this art reaches places unpenetrated by other forms of art.

C. Because of these two facts, it is difficult to produce films intended for only certain classes of people. The exhibitor's theatres are built for the masses, for the cultivated and the rude, the mature and the immature, the self-respecting and the criminal. Films, unlike books and music, can with difficulty be confined to certain selected groups.

D. The latitude given to film material cannot, in consequence, be as wide as the latitude given to book material. In addition:

   (a) A book describes; a film vividly presents. One presents on a cold page; the other by apparently living people.

   (b) A book reaches the mind through words merely; a film reaches the eyes and ears through the reproduction of actual events.

   (c) The reaction of a reader to a book depends largely on the keenness of the reader's imagination; the reaction to a film depends on the vividness of presentation.

   Hence many things which might be described or presented in a book could not possibly be presented in a film.

E. This is also true when comparing the film with the newspaper.

   (a) Newspapers present by description, films by actual presentation.

   (b) Newspapers are after the fact and present things as having taken place, the film gives the events in the process of enactment and with apparent reality of life.

F. Everything possible in a play is not possible in a film:

   (a) Because of the large audience of the film, and its consequential mixed character. Psychologically, the larger the audience, the lower the moral mass resistance to suggestion.

(b) Because through light, enlargement of character, presentation, scenic emphasis, etc., the screen story is brought closer to the audience than the play.

(c) The enthusiasm for and interest in the film actors and actresses, developed beyond anything of the sort in history, makes the audience largely sympathetic toward the characters they portray and the stories in which they figure. Hence the audience is more ready to confuse actor and actress and the characters they portray, and it is more receptive of the emotions and ideals presented by their favorite stars.

G. Small communities, remote from sophistication and from the hardening process which often takes place in the ethical and moral standards of groups in large cities, are easily and readily reached by any sort of film.

H. The grandeur of mass settings, large action, spectacular features, etc., affects and arouses more intensely the emotional side of the audience.

In general, the mobility, popularity, accessibility, emotional appeal, vividness, straightforward presentation of fact in the film make for more intimate contact with a larger audience and for greater emotional appeal.

Hence the larger moral responsibilities of the motion pictures.

Reasons Underlying the General Principles

1. No picture shall be produced which will lower the moral standards of those who see it. Hence the sympathy of the audience should never be thrown to the side of the crime, wrong-doing, evil or sin.

This is done:

(1) When evil is made to appear attractive or alluring, and good is made to appear unattractive.

(2) When the sympathy of the audience is thrown on the side of crime, wrong-doing, evil, sin. The same thing is true of a film that would throw sympathy against goodness, honor, innocence, purity, or honesty.

Note: Sympathy with a person who sins is not the same as sympathy with the sin or crime of which he is guilty. We may feel sorry for the plight of the murderer or even understand the circumstances which led him to his crime. We may not feel sympathy with the wrong which he has done.

The presentation of evil is often essential for art or fiction or drama. This in itself is not wrong provided:

a. That evil is not presented alluringly. Even if later in the film the evil is condemned or punished, it must not be allowed to appear so attractive that the audience's emotions are drawn to desire or approve so strongly that later the condemnation is forgotten and only the apparent joy of the sin remembered.
b. That throughout, the audience feels sure that evil is wrong and good is right.

2. Correct standards of life shall, as far as possible, be presented.

A wide knowledge of life and of living is made possible through the film. When right standards are consistently presented, the motion picture exercises the most powerful influences. It builds character, develops right ideals, inculcates correct principles, and all this in attractive story form.

If motion pictures consistently hold up for admiration high types of characters and present stories that will affect lives for the better, they can become the most powerful natural force for the improvement of mankind.

3. Law, natural or human, shall not be ridiculed, nor shall sympathy be created for its violation.

By natural law is understood the law which is written in the hearts of all mankind, the great underlying principles of right and justice dictated by conscience.

By human law is understood the law written by civilized nations.

1. The presentation of crimes against the law if often necessary for the carrying out of the plot. But the presentation must not throw sympathy with the crime as against the law nor with the criminal as against those who punish him.
2. The courts of the land should not be presented as unjust. This does not mean that a single court may not be represented as unjust, much less than a single court official must not be presented this way. But the court system of the country must not suffer as a result of this presentation.

Reasons Underlying Particular Applications

1. Sin and evil enter into the story of human beings and hence in themselves are valid dramatic material.
2. In the use of this material, it must be distinguished between sin which repels by its very nature, and sins which often attract.

   a. In the first class come murder, most theft, many legal crimes, lying, hypocrisy, cruelty, etc.
   b. In the second class come sex sins, sins and crimes of apparent heroism, such as banditry, daring thefts, leadership in evil, organized crime, revenge, etc.

The first class needs less care in treatment, as sins and crimes of this class are naturally unattractive. The audience instinctively condemns all such and is repelled.

Hence the important objective must be to avoid the hardening of the audience, especially of those who are young and impressionable, to the thought and fact of crime. People can become accustomed even to murder, cruelty, brutality, and repellent crimes, if these are too frequently repeated.

The second class needs great care in handling, as the response of human nature to their appeal is obvious. This is treated more fully below.

3. A careful distinction can be made between films intended for general distribution, and films intended for use in theatres restricted to a limited audience. Themes and plots quite appropriate for the latter would be altogether out of place and dangerous in the former.

Note: The practice of using a general theatre and limiting its patronage during the showing of a certain film to "Adults Only" is not completely satisfactory and is only partially effective.

However, maturer minds may easily understand and accept without harm subject matter in plots which do younger people positive harm.

Hence: If there should be created a special type of theatre, catering exclusively to an adult audience, for plays of this character (plays with problem themes, difficult discussions and maturer treatment) it would seem to afford an outlet, which does not now exist, for pictures unsuitable for general distribution but permissible for exhibitions to a restricted audience.

I. Crimes Against the Law

The treatment of crimes against the law must not:

1. Teach methods of crime.
2. Inspire potential criminals with a desire for imitation.
3. Make criminals seem heroic and justified.

Revenge in modern times shall not be justified. In lands and ages of less developed civilization and moral principles, revenge may sometimes be presented. This would be the case especially in places where no law exists to cover the crime because of which revenge is committed.

Note: When Section I, 3 of The Production Code was amended by resolution of the Board of Directors (September 11, 1946), the following sentence became inapplicable:

Because of its evil consequences, the drug traffic should not be presented in any form. The existence of the trade should not be brought to the attention of audiences.

The use of liquor should never be excessively presented. In scenes from American life, the necessities of plot and proper characterization alone justify its use. And in this case, it should be shown with moderation.

II. Sex

Out of regard for the sanctity of marriage and the home, the triangle, that is, the love of a third party for one already married, needs careful handling. The treatment should not throw sympathy against marriage as an institution.

Scenes of passion must be treated with an honest acknowledgement of human nature and its normal reactions. Many scenes cannot be presented without arousing dangerous emotions on the part of the immature, the young, or the criminal classes.

Even within the limits of pure love, certain facts have been universally regarded by lawmakers as outside the limits of safe presentation. In the case of impure love, the love which society has always regarded as wrong and which has been banned by divine law, the following are important:

1. Impure love must not be presented as attractive and beautiful.
2. It must not be the subject of comedy or farce, or treated as material for laughter.
3. It must not be presented in such a way as to arouse passion or morbid curiosity on the part of the audience.
4. It must be made to seem right and permissible.
5. In general, it must not be detailed in method and manner.

III. Vulgarity; IV. Obscenity; V. Profanity; hardly need further explanation than is contained in the Code.

VI. Costume

General principles:

1. The effect of nudity or semi-nudity upon the normal man or woman, and much more upon the young and upon immature persons, has been honestly recognized by all lawmakers and moralists.
2. Hence the fact that the nude or semi-nude body may be beautiful does not make its use in the films moral. For, in addition to its beauty, the effect of the nude or semi-nude body on the normal individual must be taken into consideration.
3. Nudity or semi-nudity used simply to put a "punch" into a picture comes under the head of immoral actions. It is immoral in its effect on the average audience.
4. Nudity can never be permitted as being necessary for the plot. Semi-nudity must not result in undue or indecent exposures.
5. Transparent or translucent materials and silhouette are frequently more suggestive than actual exposure.

VII. Dances

Dancing in general is recognized as an art and as a beautiful form of expressing human emotions.

But dances which suggest or represent sexual actions, whether performed solo or with two or more; dances intended to excite the emotional reaction of an audience; dances with movement of the breasts, excessive body movements while the feet are stationary, violate decency and are wrong.

VIII. Religion

The reason why ministers of religion may not be comic characters or villains is simply because the attitude taken toward them may easily become the attitude taken toward religion in general. Religion is lowered in the minds of the audience because of the lowering of the audience's respect for a minister.

IX. Locations

Certain places are so closely and thoroughly associated with sexual life or with sexual sin that their use must be carefully limited.

X. National Feelings

The just rights, history, and feelings of any nation are entitled to most careful consideration and respectful treatment.

XI. Titles

As the title of a picture is the brand on that particular type of goods, it must conform to the ethical practices of all such honest business.

XII. Repellent Subjects

Such subjects are occasionally necessary for the plot. Their treatment must never offend good taste nor injure the sensibilities of an audience.

Special Regulations on Crime in Motion Pictures[6]

Resolved, that the Board of Directors of the Motion Picture Association of America, Inc., hereby ratifies, approves, and confirms the interpretations of the Production Code, the practices thereunder, and the resolutions indicating and confirming such interpretations heretofore adopted by the Association of Motion Picture Producers, Inc., all effectuating regulations relative to the treatment of crime in motion pictures, as follows:

1. Details of crime must never be shown and care should be exercised at all times in discussing such details.
2. Actions suggestive of wholesale slaughter of human beings, either by criminals, in conflict with police, or as between warring factions of criminals, or in public disorders of any kind, will not be allowed.
3. There must be no suggestion, at any time, of excessive brutality.
4. Because of the increase in the number of films in which murder is frequently committed, action showing the taking of human life, even in the mystery stories, is to be cut to the minimum. These frequent presentations of murder tend to lessen regard for the sacredness of life.
5. Suicide, as a solution of problems occurring in the development of screen drama, is to be discouraged as morally questionable and as bad theatre—unless absolutely necessary for the development of the plot.
6. There must be no display, at any time, of machine guns, sub-machine guns or other weapons generally classified as illegal weapons in the hands of gangsters, or other criminals, and there are to be no off-stage sounds of the repercussions of these guns.
7. There must be no new, unique or trick methods shown for concealing guns.
8. The flaunting of weapons by gangsters, or other criminals, will not be allowed.
9. All discussions and dialogue on the part of gangsters regarding guns should be cut to the minimum.
10. There must be no scenes, at any time, showing law-enforcement officers dying at the hands of criminals. This includes private detectives and guards for banks, motor trucks, etc.
11. With special reference to the crime of kidnapping—or illegal abduction—such stories are acceptable under the Code only when the kidnapping or abduction is (a) not the main theme of the story; (b) the person kidnapped is not a child; (c) there are no details of the crime of kidnapping; (d) no profit accrues to the abductors or kidnappers; and (e) where the kidnappers are punished.

    It is understood, and agreed, that the word kidnapping, as used in paragraph 11 of these Regulations, is intended to mean abduction, or illegal detention, in modern times, by criminals for ransom.
12. Pictures dealing with criminal activities, in which minors participate, or to which minors are related, shall not be approved if they incite demoralizing imitation on the part of youth.
13. No picture shall be approved dealing with the life of a notorious criminal of current or recent times which uses the name, nickname or alias of such notorious criminal in the film, nor shall a picture

be approved if based upon the life of such a notorious criminal unless the character[7] shown in the film be punished for crimes shown in the film as committed by him.

Special Resolution on Costumes

On October 25, 1939 the Board of Directors of the Motion Picture Association of America, Inc., adopted the following resolution:

Resolved, That the provisions of Paragraphs 1, 3 and 4 of sub-division VI of the Production Code in their application to costumes, nudity, indecent or undue exposure and dancing costumes, shall not be interpreted to exclude authentically photographed scenes photographed in a foreign land, of natives of such foreign land, showing native life, if such scenes are a necessary and integral part of a motion picture depicting exclusively such land and native life, provided that no such scenes shall be intrinsically objectionable nor made a part of any motion picture produced in any studio; and provided further that no emphasis shall be made in any scenes of the customs or garb of such natives or in the exploitation thereof.

Special Regulations on Cruelty to Animals

On December 27, 1940 the Board of Directors of the Motion Picture Association of America, Inc., approved a resolution adopted by the Association of Motion Picture Producers, Inc., reaffirming previous resolutions of the California Association concerning brutality and possible gruesomeness, branding of people and animals, and apparent cruelty to children and animals:

Resolved, by the Board of Directors of the Association of Motion Picture Producers, Inc., that

(1) Hereafter, in the production of motion pictures there shall be no use by the members of the Association of the contrivance or apparatus in connection with animals which is known as the "running W," nor shall any picture submitted to the Production Code Administration be approved if reasonable grounds exist for believing that use of any similar device by the producer of such picture resulted in apparent cruelty to animals; and

(2) Hereafter, in the production of motion pictures by the members of the Association such member shall, as to any picture involving the use of animals, invite on the lot during the shooting and consult with the authorized representative of the American Humane Association; and

(3) Steps shall be taken immediately by the members of the Association and by the Production Code Administration to require compliance with these resolutions which shall bear the same relationship to the sections of the Production Code quoted herein as the Association's special regulations re: Crime in Motion Pictures bear to the sections of the Production Code dealing therewith; and it is

Further Resolved, That the resolutions of Februáry 19, 1925 and all other resolutions of this Board establishing its policy to prevent all cruelty to animals in the production of motion pictures and reflecting its determination to prevent any such cruelty be and the same hereby are in all respects reaffirmed.

Resolutions for Uniform Interpretation

as amended June 13, 1934

1. When requested by production managers, the Motion Picture Association of America, Inc., shall secure any facts, information or suggestions concerning the probable reception of stories or the manner in which in its opinion they may best be treated.
2. That each production manager shall submit in confidence a copy of each or any script to the Production Code Administration of the Motion Picture Association of America, Inc. (and of the Association of Motion Picture Producers, Inc., California). The Production Code Administration will give the production manager for his guidance such confidential advice and suggestions as experience, research, and information indicate, designating wherein in its judgment the script departs from the provisions of the Code, or wherein from experience or knowledge it is believed that exception will be taken to the story or treatment.
3. Each production manager of a company belonging to the Motion Picture Association of America, Inc., and any producer proposing to distribute and/or distributing his picture through the facilities of any member of the Motion Picture Association of America, Inc., shall submit to such Production Code Administration every picture he produces before the negative goes to the laboratory for printing. Said Production Code Administration, having seen the picture, shall inform the production manager in writing whether in its opinion the picture conforms or does not conform to the Code, stating specifically wherein either by theme, treatment, or incident, the picture violates the provisions of the Code. In such latter event, the picture shall not be released until the changes indicated by the Production Code Administration have been made; provided, however, that the production manager may appeal from such opinion of said Production Code Administration, so indicated in writing, to the Board of Directors of the Motion Picture Association of America, Inc., whose finding shall be final, and such production manager and company shall be governed accordingly.

Footnotes

[1] Amended in October 1961 to permit "Sex aberration" when treated with "care, discretion, and restraint."

[2] Later changed to read: "The methods and techniques of prostitution and white slavery shall never be presented in detail, nor shall the subjects be presented unless shown in contrast to right standards of behavior. Brothels in any clear identification as such may not be shown."

[3] Sex hygiene included abortion. In the amended Code of December 1956, the following was specified: "The subject of abortion shall be discouraged, shall never be more than suggested, and when referred to shall be condemned. It must never be treated lightly, or made the subject of comedy. Abortion shall never be shown explicitly or by inference, and a story must not indicate that an abortion has been performed, the word 'abortion' shall not be used."

[4] As amended by resolution of the Board of Directors November 1, 1939, and September 12, 1945.

[5] Amended by resolution of the Board of Directors on December 3, 1947, to include prohibition of (2) Titles which suggest or are currently associated in the public mind with material, characters, or occupations unsuitable for the screen. (3) Titles which are otherwise objectionable.

[6] As adopted by the Board of Directors on December 20, 1938.

[7] As amended by resolution of the Board of Directors, December 3, 1947.

2. THE CODE OF SELF-REGULATION

Throughout the fifties and early sixties, it was obvious that the Production Code was becoming increasingly outmoded. Under the severe restrictions of the Code, American movies could not compete with European films like *La Dolce Vita, Two Women* and *Hiroshima Mon Amour* which were being distributed with greater frequency and popularity at this time. It was also argued that the very premise of the Production Code—that movies had to be carefully regulated because they were the nation's broadest based entertainment—was no longer valid, now that television had usurped much of film's mass audience. And so it was maintained that film, now subject to not one but many audiences, should be granted the freedoms long since conferred to novels and plays, which also had splintered audiences.

Throughout this time there were calls for a classification

system that would recognize moviegoers' various tastes and that would thus allow for enhanced sophistication in American films. Many film scholars maintain that the pros and cons of such a system would have been debated even longer had it not been for two Supreme Court decisions handed down on the same day, April 22, 1968. The first decision, *Ginsberg* v. *New York,* ruled that material which was not obscene for adults might be declared obscene for children. The second decision, *Interstate Circuit* v. *Dallas,* indicated that a classification system for movies could be declared constitutional were the guidelines for the system clearly defined.

Together, these two decisions would allow every city or state to devise its own classification code to protect its children should it desire to do so. Frightened by the chaos of a multitude of contradictory standards, the MPAA was quick to act: on October 7, 1968, just six months after the two Court decisions, the MPAA announced its new self-regulatory code. The new code went into effect November 1. (Jack Valenti had succeeded Eric Johnston as president of the MPAA in 1966.)

According to the new classification system, any film regardless of its theme or treatment could be made, but it would be subject to one of four ratings: G (all ages admitted; general audiences); M (suggested for mature audiences—adults and mature young children); R (restricted; children under sixteen required an accompanying parent or adult); or X (no one under sixteen admitted). These ratings—which the MPAA said did not indicate a film's quality but only its suitability for children —were later modified. In March 1970 the R and X categories raised their age limits to seventeen, and the M category was now labeled GP (all ages admitted; parental guidance suggested), since many people had taken M to mean for mature audiences only. When the GP label also proved confusing—many thought it meant General Public— it was changed in 1972 to PG, to emphasize the parental guidance.

But the new rating system did not do away with the old Production Code entirely: a "Standards for Production" was retained, and many critics have said that this new list was merely a re-wording of the old Code.

Under the new system, the Production Code Administration was replaced by the Code and Rating Administration (CARA). Seven permanent members comprise this board, and they, like their predecessors on the PCA, still examine both scripts and final cuts of films, giving all G, PG and R movies their seal of approval. X-rated films are denied a seal but are still permitted to be shown. Any nonmember company of the MPAA may still use CARA's services.

Although it did ease many obviously anachronistic restrictions, the new classification system was heavily criticized by conservatives (who found the ratings not sufficient) and liberals (who found the ratings not accurate) alike. In 1971, for example, both the National Catholic Office for Motion Pictures and the National Council of Churches' Broadcasting and Film Commission, disturbed by the "clearly unrealistic ratings handed out," refused to support the MPAA any longer. Liberals, on the other hand, argued that the rating system was still a form of censorship and bemoaned the fact that one short scene or phrase could change a movie's overall rating. The fact that sex still seemed to be restricted, while violence was treated much more leniently, was another cause of criticism. And when it was learned that studios were re-editing films to change a film's rating, film critics and scholars were quick to point out the destructive effects the new code could have on a director's artistry.

But the greatest blow to the new code's efficiency came in 1973 when the Supreme Court decided that the question of offensiveness could be judged against "local, not national, community standards," a decision that meant a local community could disregard the MPAA's rating and apply its own standard. The film industry, understandably disturbed, claimed that had the new code been more effective in the first place, the Supreme Court decision would never have been made. The new code, through its R and X ratings, made it easy for self-appointed guardians of public morality to know which films might contain "objectionable" material. And as a result, newspapers could refuse to advertise X-rated films and theaters could decline to show them. A 1969 survey, for example, revealed that 50 percent of theaters in this country would not show an X-rated film. And newspapers representing approximately 11 percent of the national circulation have restrictions or bans on ads for X-rated films, including the *New York Times.*

Many believe that X-rated films should be divided into categories that distinguish run-of-the-mill porno flicks from exceptional erotic films like *In the Realm of the Senses* and *Salò,* but such a distinction would of course be arbitrary at times. Other critics of the code have lamented the disadvantages accrued to G-rated movies: many moviegoers stay away from G films, in the belief that such films would be boring and bland. In fact, *Variety* has reported that while 41 percent of films in 1968 were given G ratings, only 13 percent of the movies in 1977 were so rated. And independent producers have further charged that the code process favors the major studios.

Jack Valenti, however, maintains that the ratings still work, pointing to the annual surveys conducted by the Opinion Research Corporation of Princeton. According to the 1976 survey, 95 percent of the moviegoing public are aware of the ratings. Approximately 25 percent find the ratings "very useful" and about 40 percent believe the rating "fairly useful." Only 30 percent said they thought the ratings "not very useful."

THE CODE OF SELF-REGULATION

The Code of Self-Regulation of the Motion Picture Association of America shall apply to production, to advertising, and to titles of motion pictures.

The Code shall be administered by the Code and Rating Administration, headed by an Administrator.

There shall also be a Director of the Code for Advertising, and a Director of the Code for Titles.

Nonmembers are invited to submit pictures to the Code Administrator on the same basis as members of the Association. After months of examination and debate, the MPAA revised its voluntary rating system on August 1, 1977. Most of the changes were minor and did not take into account many of the system's purported limitations.

Under the new system, the code concept has been eliminated, and the administration—once called the Code and Rating Administration—is now known as the Classification and Rating Administration.

The PG category has also been altered. Whereas the explanation attached to the symbol formerly read "some material may not be suitable for pre-teenagers," it now reads "some material may not be suitable for children." The MPA thought the redefinition of the PG tag "strengthens the PG rating by indicating that parents should exercise guidance concerning PG films for all their children, not just pre-teenagers."

The three principal systems used by the MPAA during its history—the Production Code, the Code of Self-Regulation, and the Classification and Rating System—comprise one of the most important chapters of American social history. The Production Code especially, with its detailed prohibitions and very specific beliefs about film aesthetics, is a fascinating document.

In 1977 the members of the MPAA included: Allied Artists Pictures Corporation, Avco Embassy Pictures Corporation, Bray Studios, Columbia Pictures Industries, Cosmopolitan Corporation, Marten Productions, MGM, Mirisch Productions, Motion Picture Associates, Paramount Pictures Corporation, Hal Roach Studios, Terrytoons, Twentieth Century-Fox Film Corporation, United Artists Corporation, Universal Pictures, Warner Bros. and Warner Bros. Distributing Corporation.

■　　■　　■

**Declaration of Principles
of the Code of Self-Regulation
of the Motion Picture Association**

This Code is designed to keep in close harmony with the mores, the culture, the moral sense and change in our society.

The objectives of the Code are:

(1) To encourage artistic expression by expanding creative freedom;
    and
(2) To assure that the freedom which encourages the artist remains responsible and sensitive to the standards of the larger society.

Censorship is an odious enterprise. We oppose censorship and classification by governments because they are alien to the American tradition of freedom.

Much of this nation's strength and purpose is drawn from the premise that the humblest of citizens has the freedom of his own choice. Censorship destroys this freedom of choice.

It is within this framework that the Motion Picture Association continues to recognize its obligations to the society of which it is an integral part.

In our society parents are the arbiters of family conduct. Parents have the primary responsibility to guide their children in the kind of lives they lead, the character they build, the books they read, and the movies and other entertainment to which they are exposed.

The creators of motion pictures undertake a responsibility to make available pertinent information about their pictures which will assist parents to fulfill their responsibilities.

But this alone is not enough. In further recognition of our obligation to the public, and most especially to parents, we have extended the Code operation to include a nationwide voluntary film rating program which has as its prime objective a sensitive concern for children. Motion pictures will be reviewed by a Code and Rating Administration which, when it reviews a motion picture as to its conformity with the standards of the Code, will issue ratings. It is our intent that all motion pictures exhibited in the United States will carry a rating.

These ratings are:

G **All ages admitted. General audiences.**
This category includes motion pictures that in the opinion of the Code and Rating Administration would be acceptable for all audiences, without consideration of age.

PG **All ages admitted. Parental Guidance suggested. Some material may not be suitable for pre-teenagers.**
This category includes motion pictures that in the opinion of the Code and Rating Administration would be acceptable to all audiences, without consideration of age, as to which because of their theme, content and treatment, parents may wish to obtain more information for their guidance.

R **Restricted. Under 17 requires accompanying parent or adult guardian.**
This category includes motion pictures that in the opinion of the Code and Rating Administration, because of their theme, content or treatment, should not be presented to persons under 17 unless accompanied by a parent or adult guardian.

X **No one under 17 admitted. (Age limit may vary in certain areas.)**
This category includes motion pictures submitted to the Code and Rating Administration which in the opinion of the Code and Rating Administration are rated X because of the treatment of sex, violence, crime, or profanity. Pictures

rated X do not qualify for a Code Seal. Pictures rated X should not be presented to persons under 17.

The program contemplates that any distributors outside the membership of the Association who choose not to submit their motion pictures to the Code and Rating Administration will self-apply the X rating.

The ratings and their meanings will be conveyed by advertising; by displays at the theaters; and in other ways. Thus, audiences, especially parents, will be alerted to the theme, content, and treatment of movies. Therefore, parents can determine whether a particular picture is one which children should see at the discretion of the parent; or only when accompanied by a parent; or should not see.

We believe self-restraint, self-regulation, to be in the American tradition. The results of self-discipline are always imperfect because that is the nature of all things mortal. But this Code, and its administration, will make clear that freedom of expression does not mean toleration of license.

The test of self-restraint—the rule of reason . . . lies in the treatment of a subject for the screen.

All members of the Motion Picture Association, as well as the National Association of Theater Owners, the International Film Importers and Distributors of America, and other independent producer-distributors are co-operating in this endeavor. Most motion pictures exhibited in the United States will be submitted for Code approval and rating, or for rating only, to the Code and Rating Administration. The presence of the Seal indicates to the public that a picture has received Code approval.

We believe in and pledge our support to these deep and fundamental values in a democratic society:

Freedom of choice . . .

The right of creative man to achieve artistic excellence . . .

The importance of the role of the parent as the guide to the family's conduct . . .

Standards for Production

In furtherance of the objectives of the Code to accord with the mores, the culture, and the moral sense of our society, the principles stated above and the following standards shall govern the Administrator in his consideration of motion pictures submitted for Code approval.

The basic dignity and value of human life shall be respected and upheld. Restraint shall be exercised in portraying the taking of life.

Evil, sin, crime and wrong-doing shall not be justified.

Special restraint shall be exercised in portraying criminal or anti-social activities in which minors participate or are involved.

Detailed and protracted acts of brutality, cruelty, physical violence, torture and abuse shall not be presented.

Indecent or undue exposure of the human body shall not be presented.

Illicit sex relationships shall not be justified. Intimate sex scenes violating common standards of decency shall not be portrayed.

Restraint and care shall be exercised in presentations dealing with sex aberrations.

Obscene speech, gestures or movements shall not be presented. Undue profanity shall not be permitted.

Religion shall not be demeaned.

Words or symbols contemptuous of racial, religious, or national groups, shall not be used so as to incite bigotry or hatred.

Excessive cruelty to animals shall not be portrayed and animals shall not be treated inhumanely.

Standards for Advertising

The principles of the Code cover advertising and publicity as well as production. There are times when their specific application to advertising may be different. A motion picture is viewed as a whole and may be judged that way. It is the nature of advertising, however, that it must select and emphasize only isolated portions and aspects of a film. It thus follows that what may be appropriate in a motion picture may not be equally appropriate in advertising. Furthermore, on application to advertising, the principles and standards of the Code are supplemented by the following standards for advertising:

Illustrations and text shall not misrepresent the character of a motion picture.

Illustrations shall not depict any indecent or undue exposure of the human body.

Advertising demeaning religion, race, or national origin shall not be used.

Cumulative overemphasis on sex, crime, violence, and brutality shall not be permitted.

Salacious postures and embraces shall not be shown.

Censorship disputes shall not be exploited or capitalized upon.

Standards for Titles

A salacious, obscene, or profane title shall not be used on motion pictures.

Regulations Governing the Operation of the Motion Picture Code and Rating Administration

1. The Motion Picture Code and Rating Administration (hereinafter referred to as the Administration) is established to be composed of an Administrator and staff members, one of whom shall be experienced in the exhibition of motion pictures to the public.

2 a. All motion pictures produced or distributed by members of the Association and their subsidiaries will be submitted to the Administration for Code and Rating.

b. Non-members of the Association may submit their motion pictures to the Administration for Code approval and rating in the same manner and under the same conditions as members of the Association or may submit their motion pictures to the Administration for rating only.

3. Members and non-members who submit their motion pictures to the Administration should, prior to the commencement of the production of the motion picture, submit a script or other treatment. The administration will inform the producer in confidence whether a motion picture based upon the submitted script appears to conform to the Standards of the Code and indicate its probable rating. The final judgment of the Administration shall be made only upon the reviewing of the completed picture.

4 a. When a completed motion picture is submitted to the Administration and is approved as conforming to the Standards of the Code, it will be rated by the Administration either as G (all ages admitted—general audiences) GP (all ages admitted—parental guidance suggested), or R (restricted), according to the categories described in the **Declaration of Principles.**

b. Completed motion pictures submitted by non-members for rating only will be rated according to the categories described in the **Declaration of Principles** as G, PG, R, or X.

5. Motion pictures of member companies or their subsidiaries which are approved under the Code and rated: G, PG, or R, shall upon public release bear upon an introductory frame of every print distributed in the United States the official seal of the Association with the word "Approved" and the words "Certificate Number," followed by the number of the Certificate of Approval. Each print shall also bear a symbol of the rating assigned to it by the Administration. So far as possible the Seal of the Association and the rating shall be displayed in uniform type, size, and prominence. All prints of an approved motion picture bearing the Code seal shall be identical.

6. Motion pictures of non-member companies submitted for

Code approval and rating or for rating only which receive a G, PG, or R rating shall bear such rating upon every print distributed in the United States, in uniform type, size, and prominence. Prints of such pictures may also display the official Seal of the Association if application is made to the Association for the issuance of a Code Certificate number.

7. If the Administration determines that a motion picture submitted for approval and rating or rating only should be rated X in accordance with the description of that category in the **Declaration of Principles,** the symbol X must appear on all prints of the motion picture distributed in the United States in uniform type, size, and prominence and in all advertising for the picture. Rating or a Rating Certificate shall condition such issuance upon the agreement by the producer or distributor that all advertising and publicity to be used for the picture shall be submitted to and approved by the Director of the Code for Advertising.

9. The producer or distributor applying for a Certificate of Approval for a picture or a Rating Certificate for those pictures receiving a rating only shall advance to the Administration at the time of application a fee in accordance with the uniform schedule of fees approved by the Board of Directors of the Association.

10. The Standards for Titles for motion pictures shall be applied by the Administration in consultation with the Director of the Code for Titles to all motion pictures submitted for approval and rating only and no motion picture for which a Certificate of Approval or Rating Certificate has been issued shall change its title without the prior approval of the Administration.

Advertising Code Regulations

1. These regulations are applicable to all members of the Motion Picture Association of America, to all producers and distributors of motion pictures with respect to each picture for which the Association has granted its Certificate of Approval or Rating Certificate; and to all other producers and distributors who self-apply the X rating to their motion pictures and voluntarily submit their advertising.

2. The term "advertising" as used herein includes all forms of motion picture advertising and exploitation and ideas therefore, including newspaper, magazine and trade paper advertising; publicity copy and art intended for use in pressbooks or otherwise intended for general distribution in printed form or for theatre use; trailers; posters, lobby displays and other outdoor displays; including rear-projection trailers; advertising accessories, including the following: pressbooks, still photo-

graphs, heralds and throw-aways; novelties; copy for exploitation
tieups; and all radio and television copy and spots.

3. All advertising for motion pictures which have been
submitted to the Code and Rating Administration for approval
and rating, or for rating only, shall be submitted to the Director
of the Code for Advertising for approval before use, and shall
not be used in any way until so submitted and approved. All
print advertising shall be submitted in duplicate.

4. The Director of the Code for Advertising shall proceed
promptly to approve or disapprove the advertising submitted.

The director of the Code for Advertising shall stamp
"Approved" on one copy of all advertising approved by him and
return the stamped copy to the company which submitted it.
If the Director of the Code of Advertising disapproves any
advertising, the Director shall stamp the word "Disapproved"
on one copy and return it to the company which submitted it,
together with the reasons for such disapproval; or, if the
Director so desires, he may return the copy with suggestions
for such changes or corrections as will cause it to be approved.

The Director of the Code for Advertising shall send a white
form of approval for teaser and theater trailers. If the Director
disapproves a trailer, a pink form is sent stating the reasons
for disapproval. After the revisions have been made by the
company, the trailers are rescreened and a white form of
approval is sent.

After TV and radio spots are submitted, the Director shall
send a form letter of approval. In cases where material is
questionable, he advises the company and suggests changes.

5. The Director of the Code for Advertising shall require all
approved advertising for pictures submitted to the Code and
Rating Administration by members of the Motion Picture
Association of America and their subsidiaries to carry the
official Code Seal and a designation of the rating assigned to
the picture by the Code and Rating Administration. Uniform
standards as to type, size, and prominence of the display of the
seal and rating as approved by The Advertising Advisory
Council are set forth by the Advertising Code Administrator
as follows:

A. Display Advertising and Posters

1. All display advertising and posters, including trade paper
advertising shall carry the official Code seal, when authorized,
and the rating letter, assigned to the picture.

2. The official Code seal is authorized for pictures rated G,
PG, or R. For pictures rated X, the seal may not be used.

3. In all advertisements of 150 lines or more the definition of
each rating shall be carried in conjunction with the letter
symbol, both in the uniform type face as distributed by the
Association.

4. The lettering size of the symbol should approximate 25 percent of the letter height of the main title.

5. In advertisements less than 150 lines, the rating letter and Code seal should appear next to the main title.

6. In the larger advertisements, the rating and definition shall be given reasonable emphasis in placement and every attempt should be made to avoid burying it in the billings credits. The Director of the Code for Advertising shall have the authority to object to faulty placements.

7. Teaser ads must be submitted for review, but are exempt from the above requirements.

B. Television Spots

60–30–20–10 second spots
>Visual—
>>Show the MPAA Seal
>>Show the Rating Symbol Letter (G, PG, R or X)
>>Show the Full Definition of the Symbol. Full Definition:
>>G—ALL AGES ADMITTED (General Audiences). PG—ALL AGES ADMITTED (Parental Guidance Suggested. Some Material May Not Be Suitable for Pre-Teenagers.)
>>R—RESTRICTED (Under 17 Requires Accompanying Parent or Adult Guardian.) X—NO ONE UNDER 17 ADMITTED (Age limit may vary in certain areas.)
>Audible—
>>State the Rating Symbol Letter: "Rated G," "Rated PG," "Rated R," "Rated X"

Note: The visual Code information (MPAA seal, Rating Symbol and Full Definition) should be included when the title of the film comes on the screen and remain for four seconds.

C. Radio Spots

60–30–20 second spots
>State the Rating Symbol (G, PG, or X)
>State the Abbreviated Definition:
>>"Rated G—General Audiences"
>>"Rated PG—All Ages, Parental Guidance"
>>"Rated R—Under 17, Not Admitted Without Parent"
>>"Rated X—Under 17 Not Admitted"

10 second spots
>"Rated G"
>"Rated PG"
>"Rated R"
>"Rated X"

D. Theater Trailers

1. The complete rating definition and Code seal, as set forth in the attached trailer card Exhibits I, II, and III, for the

appropriate rating, shall conform to the approved new format, screen right with key line of definition in reverse for pictures rated G, PG, or R.

2. For pictures rated X by the Code and Rating Administration, Exhibit IV shall appear as above except the seal may not be used.

3. Trailers are reviewed for two distinct audiences— GENERAL (G, PG) and RESTRICTED (R, X). Trailers for R and X pictures will not be shown during the exhibition of G and PG pictures.

The following exceptions will be applied to the above policy:

(a) The Director of the Code for Advertising will certify that a trailer for an R or X picture is acceptable (as revised) for use with G and PG pictures, if, in his judgment, the contents of the trailer meet the G and PG levels of approval.

or

(b) In lieu of the regular R or X trailer, the distributor will offer exhibitors a special alternate trailer or telop (showing only titles and credits) that has been approved for **Unrestricted** audiences.

(c) In May 1971 the following line was approved for use in trailers approved under (a) and (b) above: "This **Preview** has been approved by the Motion Picture Association of America for General Audiences." This statement should appear on the rating tag for the trailer.

E. Multiple Features

When more than one picture is being exhibited on the same bill, the more restrictive rating will apply to admissions. Advertising shall be governed accordingly.

6. Approved advertising for pictures submitted to the Code and Rating Administration by companies other than members of the Motion Picture Association of America, and their subsidiaries, for Code approval and rating, or for rating only, may bear the official seal at the distributor's option, but all such advertising shall bear the assigned rating.

7. Approved advertising for pictures rated X by the Code and Rating Administration shall bear the X rating but may not bear the official seal.

8. All pressbooks approved by the Director of the Code for Advertising, except for X-rated pictures, shall bear in a prominent place the official seal of the Motion Picture Association of America and a designation of the rating and the full definition assigned to the picture by the Code and Rating administration. Pressbooks shall also carry the following notice:

Approved
(seal)

All advertising in this pressbook, as well as all other advertising and publicity materials referred to herein, has been approved under the Standards for Advertising of the Code of Self-Regulation of the Motion Picture Association of America. All inquiries on this procedure may be addressed to:

Director of Code Advertising
Motion Picture Association of America
522 Fifth Avenue / New York, New York 10036

9. Appeals. Any Company whose advertising has been disapproved may appeal from the decision of the Director of the Code for Advertising, as follows:

It shall serve notice of such appeal on the director of the Code for Advertising and on the President of the Association. The President, or in his absence a Vice-President designated by him, shall thereupon promptly and within a week hold a hearing to pass upon the appeal. Oral and written evidence may be introduced by the Company and by the Director of the Code for Advertising, or their representatives. The appeal shall be decided as expeditiously as possible and the decision shall be final.

On appeals by companies other than members of the Motion Picture Association of America and their subsidiaries, the President shall, if requested, decide the appeal in consultation with a representative of International Film Importers and Distributors of America, as designated by its Governing Board.

10. Any company which has been granted a Certificate of Approval and which uses advertising without securing the prior approval of the Director of the Code for Advertising or if such advertising does not include the assigned rating may be brought up on charges before the Board of Directors by the President of the Association. Within a reasonable time, the Board may hold a hearing, at which time the company and the Director of the Code for Advertising or their representatives, may present oral or written statements. The Board, by a majority vote of those present, shall decide the matter as expeditiously as possible.

If the Board of Directors finds that the company has used advertising for a Code approved and rated picture without securing approval of the Director of the Code for Advertising, or without including the assigned rating, the Board may direct the Code and Rating Administration to void and revoke the Certificate of Approval granted for the picture and require the removal of the Association's seal from all prints of the picture.

11. Each company shall be responsible for compliance by its employees and agents with these regulations.

Code and Rating Appeals Board

1. A Code and Rating Appeals Board is established to be composed as follows:

(a) The President of the Motion Picture Association of America and 12 members designated by the President from the Board of Directors of the Association and executive officers of its member companies;

(b) Eight exhibitors designated by the National Association of Theater Owners from its Board of Directors;

(c) Four distributors designated by the International Film Importers and Distributors of America.

2. A pro tempore member for any particular hearing to act as a substitute for a member unable to attend may be designated in the same manner as the absent member.

3. The President of the Motion Picture Association shall be Chairman of the Appeals Board, and the Association shall provide its secretariat.

4. The presence of 13 members is necessary to constitute a quorum of the Appeals Board for a hearing of any appeal.

5. The Board will hear and determine appeals from:

(a) A decision of the Code and Rating Administration withholding Code approval from a picture submitted for approval and rating and which consequently received an X rating.

(b) A decision by the Code and Rating Administration applying an X rating to a picture submitted for rating only.

On such appeals a vote of two-thirds of the members present shall be required to sustain the decision of the Administration. If the decision of the Administration is not sustained, the Board shall proceed to rate the picture appropriately by majority vote.

6. The Board will also hear and determine appeals from the decision of the Code and Rating Administration applying any rating other than X to a motion picture.

Such appeals shall be decided by majority vote. If the decision of the Administration is not sustained the Board shall proceed to rate the picture appropriately.

7. (a) An Appeal from a decision of the Administration shall be instituted by the filing of a notice of appeal addressed to the Chairman of the Appeals Board by the party which submitted the picture to the Administration.

(b) Provision shall be made for the screening by the members of the Appeals Board at the Hearing or prior thereto of a print of the motion picture identical to the one reviewed and passed upon by the Administration.

(c) The party taking the appeal and the Administration may present oral or written statements to the Board at the hearing.

(d) No member of the Appeals Board shall participate on an appeal involving a picture in which the member or any company with which he is associated has a financial interest.

(e) The appeal shall be heard and decided as expeditiously as possible and the decision shall be final.

(f) The hearing of an appeal shall commence with the screening of the motion picture involved.

(g) If either the party taking the appeal or the Code and Rating Administration desire to present oral or written statements to the Board pursuant to subparagraph (c) of Paragraph 7, any such written statement should be furnished to the Secretary at least two days before the date fixed for the hearing. The Secretary will reproduce such statements and circulate them to the members of the Appeals Board in advance or at the hearing of the appeal. Submission of written statements shall not diminish or alter the right also to present oral statements or arguments on behalf of the party taking the appeal.

(h) The Board will hear oral statements or argument on behalf of the party taking the appeal by not more than two persons, except by special permission. Oral statements or argument on behalf of the Code and Rating Administration shall be made only by the Administrator or his designated representative.

(i) Normally no more than a half hour will be allowed for oral argument to the party taking the appeal, and a like time to the Code and Rating Administration. If a party taking an appeal is of the opinion that statements or more than two persons or that additional time is necessary for the adequate presentation of the appeal, he may make such request by letter addressed to the Secretary stating the reasons why oral statements or more than two persons or more than a half hour is required for the adequate presentation of the appeal.

When such request is made by a party who is a member of the International Film Importers and Distributors of America, Inc., the Secretary shall consult with the Executive Directors or a member of the Governing Committee of that organization. in determining whether and to what extent the request may be granted.

(j) In no circumstances shall the time allowed to any party for the hearing of an appeal extend beyond one hour.

A request for the participation of additional persons or for the allowance of additional time, to the extent that it is not granted, may be renewed to the Appeals Board at the commencement of the hearing of the appeal for disposition by the Appeals Board.

8. The board will also act as an advisory body on Code matters and, upon the call of the Chairman, will discuss the progress of the operation of the Code and Rating Program and review the manner of adherence to the Advertising Code.

3. THE CATHOLIC LEGION OF DECENCY

In October 1933 Monsignor Cicognani spoke to a Catholic Charities Convention in New York. "What a massacre of innocence of youth is taking place hour by hour!" he exclaimed. "How shall the crimes that have their direct source in immoral motion pictures be measured? Catholics are called by God, the Pope, the Bishops, and the priests to a united and vigorous campaign for the purification of the cinema, which has become a deadly menace to morals."

Thus was the Legion of Decency—the most powerful pressure group in the history of film—started.

At the annual American Bishops Convention held the month after Monsignor Cicognani's rousing speech, the bishops heeded the monsignor's advice by appointing an Episcopal Committee on Motion Pictures. After six months of work, the committee in April 1934 announced its plans for a crusade against the immorality and irresponsibility of movies: priests were instructed to preach on the "moral ills" of the movies; the clergy was advised to put pressure on local exhibitors; and millions of Catholics were asked to sign the Legion of Decency Pledge to do all they could to arouse public opinion against the immorality of films. (See Table 1.)

In Philadelphia, Catholics actually boycotted all motion picture theaters, an action that gave national attention to the Legion. Even non-Catholic groups joined the Legion in its attempt to clean up the movies: representatives of the Knights of Columbus, B'nai B'rith, Elks, Masons and Odd Fellows all gave the Legion their support.

The Legion's effort proved so successful, in fact, that three months after it was formed the film industry agreed to establish the Production Code Administration Office to regulate movies. In November 1934 the Legion of Decency was made a permanent institution.

The Legion's main function was to publish lists of films which its staff had morally rated according to prescribed classifications. (See Table 2.) In deciding the ratings, the

Legion ruled that no consideration should be given to artistic, technical or dramatic values. Only moral content was weighed.

The Legion did not consider its activities to be a form of censorship, but rather argued that its aim was to guide public opinion. Many people, however, have claimed that the Legion, in speaking for the movie morality of Catholics, has dictated the tastes of the entire nation.

The Legion continued its fight against immorality in movies even after public morals changed following World War II. In 1956, for example Cardinal Spellman warned Catholics to stay away from *Baby Doll* on "penalty of sin," and bishops even placed a six-month boycott on theaters showing the film. The next year a similar controversy surrounded the Legion's diatribes against *And God Created Woman*, starring Brigitte Bardot.

But in December 1957 the Legion revised its classification system to take into account differences in adolescent and adult sensibilities. (See Table 2.) Even the pledge was revised to reflect the Legion's more lenient attitude toward movies. (See Table 1.) Although in 1966 the Legion created another furor over *The Pawnbroker*, it has in the main eased its standards, giving special classifications to such films as *La Dolce Vita*, *Lolita* and *Suddenly, Last Summer*.

In 1966 the Legion of Decency became the National Catholic Office for Motion Pictures. In 1972 the National Catholic Office for Motion Pictures and the National Catholic Office for Radio and Television were reorganized to form the Office for Film and Broadcasting (OFB). In addition to sponsoring workshops and seminars, the OFB publishes *SHARE*, a twice-monthly packet of film and broadcasting information, and *Film and Broadcasting Review* (formerly the *Catholic Film Newsletter*), which twice a month reviews and classifies current 35mm films. Reviews include artistic as well as moral examinations.

TABLE 1: THE LEGION OF DECENCY PLEDGES

Original Pledge (1934)

"I wish to join the Legion of Decency, which condemns vile and unwholesome moving pictures. I unite with all who protest against them as a grave menace to youth, to home life, to country and to religion.

I condemn absolutely those salacious motion pictures, which, with other degrading agencies, are corrupting public morals and promoting a sex mania in our land.

I shall do all that I can to arouse public opinion against the portrayal of vice as a normal condition of affairs, and against depicting criminals of any class as heroes and heroines, presenting their filthy philosophy of life as something acceptable to decent men and women.

I unite with all who condemn the display of suggestive advertisements on billboards, at theatre entrances, and the favorable notices given to immoral motion pictures.

Considering these evils, I hereby promise to remain away from all motion pictures except those which do not offend decency and Christian morality. I promise further to secure as many members as possible for the Legion of Decency.

I make this protest in a spirit of self-respect and with the conviction that the American public does not demand filthy pictures, but clean entertainment and educational features."

Revised Pledge (1934)

"I condemn indecent and immoral motion pictures, and those which glorify crime or criminals.

I promise to do all that I can to strengthen public opinion against the production of indecent and immoral films, and to unite with all who protest against them.

I acknowledge my obligation to my moral life. As a member of the Legion of Decency, I pledge myself to remain away from them. I promise, further, to stay away altogether from places of amusement which show them as a matter of policy."

Revised Pledge (1965)

"I promise to promote by word and deed what is morally and artistically good in motion picture entertainment. I promise to discourage by my good example and always in a responsible and civic-minded manner."

TABLE 2: THE LEGION OF DECENCY RATINGS

Original Classification (1936)

A-1: **Morally Unobjectionable for General Patronage**
These films are considered to contain no material which would be morally dangerous to the average motion picture audience, adults and children alike.

A-2: **Morally Unobjectionable for Adults**
These are films which in themselves are morally harmless but which, because of subject matter or treatment, require maturity and experience if one is to witness them without danger or moral harm. While no definite age limit can be established for this group, the judgment of parents, pastors and teachers would be helpful in determining the decision in individual cases.

B: **Morally Objectionable in Part for All**
Films in this category are considered to contain elements dangerous to Christian morals or moral standards.

C: **Condemned**
Condemned films are considered to be those which, because of theme or treatment, have been described by the Holy Father as "positively bad."

Separate Classification
This is given to certain films which, while not morally offensive, require some analysis and explanation as a protection to the uninformed against wrong interpretations and false conclusions.

Revised Classification (1957)

A-1: **Morally Unobjectionable for General Patronage**
A-2: **Morally Unobjectionable for Adults and Adolescents**
A-3: **Morally Unobjectionable for Adults**
B: **Morally Objectionable in Part for All**
C: **Condemned**

Reasons for New Classification

(a) The Legion recognizes that in connection with motion picture attendance the average adolescent of our day will not infrequently consider himself more than a child and hence will seek pictures with more adult content and orientation. In keeping with the sound principles of modern Catholic educational psychology, it seems desirable that the Legion aid the adolescent in this quest for more mature movie-subjects

and thereby contribute to his intellectual and emotional maturation. To this end the new A-s classification has been adopted; it is hoped that this classification, while providing the necessary reasonable moral controls upon the adolescent, will at the same time aid him in his "growing up."

(b) The A-3 classification is an attempt on the part of the Legion to provide for truly adult subject matter in entertainment motion pictures, provided that the themes in question and their treatment be consonant with the moral law and with traditionally accepted moral standards.

(c) Although the B and C classifications remain unchanged, it is to be recognized that the new triple A classification is intended also to strengthen the meaning of the B category. Henceforth, there will be no doubt that a B film is one adjudged to contain material which in itself or in its offensive treatment is contrary to traditional morality and constitutes a threat not only to the personal spiritual life of even an adult viewer, but also to the moral behavior-patterns which condition public morality. Catholic people are urged to refrain from attendance at all B pictures, not only for the sake of their own consciences, but also in the interest of promoting the common good.

Current Classification

A–1: Morally Unobjectionable for General Patronage
A–2: Morally Unobjectionable for Adults and Adolescents
A–3: Morally Unobjectionable for Adults
A–4: For adults with reservations
 B: Morally Objectionable in Part for All
 C: Condemned

About the Author

Cobbett Steinberg teaches courses in film, literature, and popular culture at Stanford University, where he is a doctoral candidate. He has written several screenplays, reviews and essays for many San Francisco Bay area publications.